Health Economics and Policy

THIRD EDITION

Health Economics and Policy

THIRD EDITION

JAMES W. HENDERSON
Baylor University

THOMSON

SOUTH-WESTERN

Australia · Canada · Mexico · Singapore · Spain · United Kingdom · United States

THOMSON
™
SOUTH-WESTERN

Health Economics and Policy, 3e
James W. Henderson

VP/Editorial Director:
Jack W. Calhoun

VP/Editor-in-Chief:
Michael P. Roche

Publisher of Economics:
Michael B. Mercier

Acquisitions Editor:
Michael Worls

Developmental Editor:
Jennifer E. Baker

Marketing Manager:
Jennifer Fruechtenicht

Production Editor:
Robert Dreas

Technology Project Editor:
Peggy Buskey

Media Editor:
Pam Wallace

Manufacturing Coordinator:
Sandee Milewski

Production House/Compositor:
DPS Associates, Inc.

Printer:
Thomson/West
Eagan, Minnesota

**Design Project Manager and
Internal Designer:**
Justin Klefeker

Cover Designer:
Justin Klefeker

Cover Images:
© PhotoDisc
© Digital Vision

Leo and Alvadina Henderson
Leo J. and Eunice Potthoff

To the parents who shaped my life
And the parents who blessed me with a wife.

The fear of the Lord is the beginning of knowledge;
Fools despise wisdom and instruction.
Hear, my son, your father's instruction,
And do not forsake you mother's teaching.

Proverbs 1:7-8

Thank you for the way you lived your lives,
For the lessons you tried to teach.
I'd be better off if I'd listened more carefully.

JWH

Preface

The United States stands alone in its reliance on the private sector to finance health care delivery. With spending surpassing $1.5 trillion in 2002, even staunch advocates of the private enterprise system harbor secret doubts about the ability of the private sector to deliver quality medical care at reasonable prices to everyone who has a medical need. Does the future of U.S. health care delivery involve a larger role for government, or will the private market emerge as the primary vehicle for financing medical care delivery? The current health care debate shows no signs of subsiding. The expanding role of government in the provision of care is evident at both ends of the age spectrum. The introduction of a prescription drug benefit for Medicare recipients guarantees that prescription drug spending will be the focus of an ongoing policy dialogue for years to come. Continued pressure to expand the availability of health insurance to children will keep the Children's Health Insurance Program high on the list of policy issues. *Health Economics and Policy* provides important background information, not only on these two important programs affecting the young and the elderly, but addresses the entire spectrum of economic and policy issues that affect the rest of the population.

- This text's primary goals are to enable readers to

- Recognize the relevance of economics to health and medical care and to apply economic reasoning to better understand health-related issues.

- Understand the mechanisms of health care delivery in the United States within broad social, political, and economic contexts.

- Explore the changing nature of health and medical care and its implications for medical practice, medical education and research, and health policy.

- Analyze public policy in health and medical care from an economic perspective.

To accomplish these goals, the book's 18 chapters are organized into five parts.

PART ONE—THE RELEVANCE OF ECONOMICS IN HEALTH AND MEDICAL CARE

The text begins with a basic overview of the health care industry with emphasis on the economic issues that affect medical care delivery and finance. Chapter 1 examines the nature of the economic problem as it pertains to health care. Chapter 2 demonstrates the usefulness of economics in understanding medical care issues—including matters of life, death, disability, and suffering. Chapter 3 examines problems encountered in applying standard economic models to the study of health care markets. Chapter 4 introduces the readers to the tools of economic evaluation as they are applied to medical care with special emphasis on cost-effectiveness analysis, the preferred technique among most health economists.

Technical appendices appear at the end of each of the first three chapters. They are intended for use by more advanced students. Appendix 1A provides an overview of the challenges of measuring medical price inflation using the medical care price index. Appendix 2A serves as a primer on graphing while 2B introduces important statistical tools used in empirical studies. The two appendices at the end of Chapter 3 present the neoclassical models of consumer choice and production.

PART TWO—DEMAND-SIDE CONSIDERATIONS

Part 2 examines the demand side of the market. Chapter 5 identifies and describes various factors that influence the demands for health and health care. It explores and explains observed patterns in the quality and price of medical care. Chapter 6 discusses the market for health insurance, comparing and contrasting the private and social insurance models. Chapter 7 evaluates the efficiency of alternative health care delivery systems, primarily HMOs and PPOs, in containing medical care costs.

PART THREE— SUPPLY-SIDE CONSIDERATIONS

The supply side of the health care market is discussed in Part 3. Chapter 8 looks at the market for health care practitioners and how their behavior is influenced by recent changes in the health care sector, namely managed care. Other sub-sectors are examined through discussion of the markets for nurses and for dentists. Chapter 9 summarizes major theories of hospital behavior and describes the role of not-for-profit hospitals in the U.S. health care industry.

PART FOUR—CONFOUNDING FACTORS—SALT

Part 4 examines the factors that contribute to escalating spending in the U.S. health care system. Think of these chapters using the acronym "SALT"—to flavor the discussion. Chapter 10 is the S, providing a discussion of Socio-cultural concerns that affect health outcomes. Chapter 11 is the A, examining the impact of an Aging population. Chapter 12 is the L, looking into the Legal system and how medical malpractice affects health care costs. The appendix to Chapter 12 presents an economic approach to valuing life in cases involving wrongful death. Finally, Chapter 13 is the T, studying how Technological change serves as a driving force behind spending.

PART FIVE—PUBLIC POLICY IN MEDICAL CARE DELIVERY

The text's final part squarely addresses health policy and its economic implications. Chapter 14 analyzes the roles of government, the family, and religion in improving access to health care. Medicare, Medicaid, and other government programs are introduced and their economic impact examined. The appendix to that chapter addresses some issues of making projections of economic data. Chapter 15 covers recent changes in reimbursement schemes (diagnosis related groups and resource based relative value scales) and their effects on quantity, quality, and accessibility of medical care. Chapter 16 summarizes important characteristics of medical care delivery systems in five major developed nations—Canada, France, Germany, Japan, and the United Kingdom. Chapter 17 describes health care reform initiatives in the United States and summarizes major U.S. policy alternatives. Finally, Chapter 18 restates the major lessons to be learned from the economic approach to public policy.

PEDAGOGICAL FEATURES

This text's ultimate focus is on public policy. The technical tools of economics are important, but they are not treated as ends to themselves. Instead, theory is employed as a way of preparing students to address policy questions.

Each chapter includes a number of special features called "Issues in Medical Care Delivery." They summarize important studies in medical research, epidemiology, public health, and other fields as they relate to the economics of health care delivery. Another feature found in most chapters is the "Profile" of individuals who have made significant contributions to health economics. Many profiled individuals are economists; some are physicians; all have had a profound impact on how we view health, health economics, and health policy.

The "Back of the Envelope" features show the economic way of thinking, using graphs. These and similar graphical presentations are frequently used by economists in informal settings. They might represent scribbles on the back of an old envelope that are used to make a point during lunch with colleagues. Topics include: the valuation of a life, how to calculate a rate of return, the notion of elasticity, the welfare implications of subsidies, the impact of employer mandates, cost-benefit calculations, and the cost effectiveness of disease prevention, among many others. Developing the ability to use models in this way is an important goal of this book.

Chapter 1 introduces 10 key economic concepts that serve as unifying themes throughout the book. As you read you will notice the key icon in the margin reminding you that the adjacent material is related to that key concept. Other marginal notations include definitions of key words and phrases, recommended Web sites where you can go for additional information, and policy issues related to the reading.

NEW IN THE THIRD EDITION

The most obvious change in the third edition is the addition of Chapter 4, "Economic Evaluation in Health Care." In 2003 I had the privilege of attending a 15-day training program on "Health Economics of Pharmaceuticals and Other Medical Interventions" presented by the European School of Health Economics. Organized in three one-week sessions from April to June and set in Sofia Antipole, France, I was introduced to the various techniques of economic evaluation by some of Europe's best health economists, including Tony Culyer and Michael Drummond from England, Claude Le Pen from France, Bengt Jönsson from Sweden, and Matthias vd Schulenburg from Germany. I would like to thank Gisela Kobelt, director of the program, and all of the presenters and participants for their efforts in making it worthwhile. Of course, the final version of the chapter in this book, along with any errors and omissions, is solely my responsibility. That said, I believe that you will find this chapter a good first primer for those interested in actually doing economic evaluation.

Several parts of the book have been extensively rewritten, including the section on the pharmaceutical industry in Chapter 13. The most extensive rewrite is found in Chapter 16 where new developments in France, Germany, and Sweden have been incorporated into the material.

New sections have been added to several chapters. In Chapter 1, the section entitled "Health Economics Defined" illustrates the structure of health economics and provides a historical perspective on the development of the subject. The focus on cost containment has proven a public relations nightmare for the managed care industry. "The Future of Managed Care" has been added to Chapter 7 to examine the prospects for this form of medical care delivery in the wake of the recent turmoil. Chapter 10 includes a new section on "Obesity" addressing this growing problem and its related medical consequences. As the population continues to age, we are being faced with growing concerns on how to deal with chronic illnesses that have no cure. "The Challenge of Treating Chronic Diseases" has been added to Chapter 11 to address those concerns. Finally, a new section in Chapter 17, "Market Response to Uncertainty," addresses employer response to increased risk of providing health plans to workers.

New Issues in Medical Care Delivery features are spread throughout the book. These new issues include "The Lessons from SARS" (Chapter 3), "Population Required to Support a Hospital" (Chapter 9), "Is Addiction Rational?" (Chapter 10), "Who's Got the Best Health Care System?" (Chapter 16), and "Market Response to Uncertainty" (Chapter 17).

Also new profiles have been added detailing the contribution of three prominent health economists. The economists profiled are Bengt Jönsson of the Stockholm School of Economics, Jonathan Gruber from MIT, and Mark McClellan from Stanford and commissioner of the Food and Drug Administration.

Of course, all charts and tables have been updated to include the latest health care cost and outcomes data. These data have been linked to the text's Web site and provided in PDF format to improve access and allow easy transfer to overhead slides.

LEVEL

Health Economics and Policy is written with the non-economics major in mind, but contains enough economic content to challenge economics majors. My class at Baylor University is composed of both economics majors and pre-medical students, most of whom have little or no economics background. There are usually a number of other business majors, many of whom are interested in studying health care administration in the future. I also use this text in a required graduate course for MBA students who are concentrating in health care administration. All these students are good thinkers and most have done well despite having had no previous economics coursework.

The text is appropriate for an introductory health economics course offered in an economics department, in a health care administration graduate program, or in a school of public health, college of medicine, or school of nursing or pharmacy.

SUPPLEMENTARY ITEMS

An Instructor's Manual provides support to instructors who adopt *Health Economics and Policy*, 3rd edition. The manual includes suggested answers to the end-of-chapter questions, lecture suggestions, and additional test questions.

The text's Web site contains resources for both students and instructors. You can access the Web site using either http://business.baylor.edu/Jim_Henderson/ or http://henderson.swlearning.com. In the fast-changing health care arena, information tends to get stale quickly. The Web site will be updated on a regular basis to keep the data in the book fresh. New studies and new teaching ideas will be included as they become available. This site also includes a newsgroup that provides a forum for those who adopt the book to share teaching aids, ask questions, and make suggestions for improvements.

ACKNOWLEDGMENTS

As the sole author of this book, I take full responsibility for its contents. But a single individual could not complete a project of this magnitude. I owe a great deal to my Baylor University colleagues Tom Kelly, Allen Seward, Scott Garner, Earl Grinols, and Beck Taylor, with whom I have spent countless hours discussing economics and health care issues. They were invaluable in the book's development and revision. A number of capable research assistants have contributed to the project over the years, most notably Heather Newsome, Leigh Ann Berry, Jamie Antal Faulkner, and Stephen Cage.

Instructors from across the country have reviewed the manuscript as it was being revised for the second edition. Their comments and suggestions have been important to me, and the book is better because of their efforts. Thanks go to

Stephan F. Gohmann, *University of Louisville*

Don Griffin, *Houston Baptist University*

Deepasriya Sampath Kumar, *Northwestern University*

James Marton, *University of Kentucky*

Stephen T. Mennemeyer, *University of Alabama*

Tiffany Radcliff, *University of Florida*

Nita Stika, *Cardinal Stritch University*

David Torgerson, *Graduate School of the USDA*

Kendra Uhe, *Robert Morris College*

I am also grateful to the hundreds of Baylor University students who used this book in its first two editions and even earlier in manuscript form. Their comments have proven invaluable in developing an integrated framework for discussing health care issues.

Of course, I could never have completed the project without the support of my family. Thank you, Betsy, Luke, and Jesse for your understanding, love, and patience.

James W. Henderson

Brief Contents

Contents

PART 2   DEMAND-SIDE CONSIDERATIONS

PART 5   PUBLIC POLICY IN MEDICAL CARE DELIVERY

Chapter 1

U.S. Medical Care: Crisis or Conundrum

The concern over the future of health care revolves around three broad issues: quality, access, and affordability. As private health insurance coverage gradually declines and the number of uninsured steadily rises, emerging public consensus indicates a system in need of reform. Gaps in coverage, combined with the upward trend in medical care spending over the past several decades, add to the commonly held belief that the United States has a health care crisis. What exactly is the nature of this health care crisis? Is it a crisis in spending? Or is it the way we pay for medical care? Many are concerned over access to care for the uninsured and the prospects for continued access for those currently with insurance. An additional concern is whether quality may deteriorate as medical care is increasingly provided in a **managed care** environment.

Recent polls indicate that most insured Americans are satisfied with the quality of their own health insurance plan. In fact, over 80 percent of Americans said that the medical care that they or their family received during the past year was good-to-excellent. Access, on the other hand, is a real concern. About one-half are concerned that if they become seriously ill they will not be able to afford the medical care they need (Donelan et al., 1999).

Those without insurance coverage who lack the resources to pay out-of-pocket must rely on public assistance and private charity for the care they receive. Even those with health insurance lack the assurance of continued coverage. Because most workers receive their health insurance as an employee benefit, losing a job can mean losing access to medical care, adding to the insecurity of the middle class in an era of slow job growth, corporate downsizing, and intense international competition for jobs. Thus, it is not a contradiction for a survey respondent to be satisfied with the health care received personally and at the same time believe that the system is flawed and needs to be rebuilt.

The "experts" have a completely different perspective of the health care crisis, including the problem, its cause, and preferred solutions (Blendon et al., 1993). They see the health care crisis as one of rising aggregate spending and the government's inability to sustain the growth in the two major programs—**Medicare** and **Medicaid**. Experts themselves are sharply divided on the cause of the crisis. Some consider the unrestrained use of medical technology as the problem. Others believe the culprits are the increased use of health insurance and tax subsidies encouraging individuals to overinsure. Proposed solutions address the perceived causes. If technology is being overused, restrict patient access to expensive procedures. If subsidized insurance is the problem, limit the subsidy.

Although the uninsured receive fewer services and less coordinated care, they do have access to high-quality medical care through public clinics and hospital emergency

Policy Issue

How can we best deal with the trade-off between quality and access on the one hand and affordability on the other?

managed care
A medical care delivery system that integrates the financing and provision of health care into one organization.

Policy Issue

Most privately insured Americans receive health insurance coverage through their employer, while those without insurance rely on public assistance and charity care.

Medicare
Health insurance for the elderly provided under an amendment to the Social Security Act, divided into two parts, mandatory hospital insurance and voluntary physicians insurance.

Medicaid
Health insurance for the poor financed jointly by the federal government and the states.

cost shifting
The practice of charging higher prices to one group of patients, usually those with health insurance, in order to provide free care to the uninsured or discounted care to those served by Medicare and Medicaid.

rooms.[1] Traditionally, indigent care has been financed directly by taxpayers and private charities and indirectly by shifting costs to those with insurance coverage. In 2001 for example, estimates of **cost shifting** were as high as $34.5 billion, amounting to approximately $1,000 for every uninsured person (Hadley and Holohan, 2003). This kind of availability may be undesirable and inefficient, but it is access. In fact, over one-half of the uninsured state that they have no trouble getting or paying for medical care (Donelan et al., 1996). Is it accurate to refer to the circumstances surrounding the delivery and financing of health care in the United States as a crisis, or is it merely a conundrum—a problem that the wealthiest country in the world ought to address?

Historical Developments in the Delivery of Medical Care

premium
A periodic payment required to purchase an insurance policy.

No matter where a health care discussion begins, the topic of conversation soon turns to the issue of affordability. Employees and employers complain about high **premiums**, patients and providers note high treatment costs, and policymakers lament high and rising spending. Each perspective presents a different aspect of the same problem. According to a Kaiser Family Foundation survey (2002), it cost $8,000 to provide a health insurance policy for the typical American family in 2001, the average cost per hospital stay was almost $7,000, and Americans spent $1.4 trillion, or 14.1 percent of the **gross domestic product** (GDP) on health care.

gross domestic product (GDP)
The monetary value of the goods and services produced in a country during a given time period, usually a year.

From 1971 to 2001 the annual growth in nominal health care spending ranged between 4.4 percent and 15.6 percent, increasing at an annual compound rate of over 10 percent for that 30-year time period. Over that same period the Consumer Price Index (CPI), a popular measure of the rate of inflation, increased an average of 5.0 percent per year. With nominal health care spending increasing at twice the overall rate of inflation, real spending (adjusted for inflation) grew approximately 5 percent per year. Figure 1.1 depicts the relative growth rates in nominal and real spending from 1971 to 2001. Many commentators are encouraged by the dramatic slowing of the real rate of growth in health care spending during the 1990s, falling from 9.27 percent in 1990 to 2.15 percent in 1996. History, however, warns against using such short trends as tools for policymaking. The 1972–1974

Policy Issue

How many years does it take to constitute a trend?

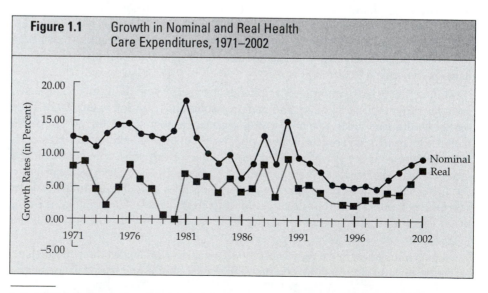

Figure 1.1   Growth in Nominal and Real Health Care Expenditures, 1971–2002

1 Since 1985, federal law (section 9121 of the Comprehensive Omnibus Budget Reconciliation Act) has made it illegal for hospital emergency rooms to deny care to anyone requesting care. Turning away patients because of lack of health insurance is not an option.

time period saw real growth rates fall from 8.7 percent to 2.0 percent only to rise again over the next two years. Beginning in 1976, real growth rates started falling and reached near-zero levels by 1979. This was followed by a steady upward march until 1990. Since 1996, however, growth in real spending has gradually increased each year, reaching 7.61 percent in 2002. The major concern over health care spending is not that it is high but that the steady upward spiral does not seem to have an end to it. Government projections have medical care spending rising to over 16 percent of GDP by the year 2008 (OASDI and Medicare Boards of Trustees' Report, 1999). Although economic theory has yet to determine what the optimal percentage ought to be, the United States spends more on medical care by virtually every measure than any other country in the world. If the optimal percentage is not known, what does it mean to spend 8 percent or 10 percent or 14 percent of a country's GDP on medical care? And more importantly, should the amount spent on medical care be a concern to policymakers?

> *Policy Issue*
>
> What is the optimal percentage of GDP that a country should spend on health care? Is a continuously growing percentage affordable?

Post-War Experience

Medical care spending in the United States over the post-World War II period is summarized in Table 1.1. The four summary measures provide evidence that medical care spending is high and growing. During the decade of the 1950s total spending increased at a rate of 7.7 percent per year. Total spending at the beginning of the decade was $12.7 billion, doubling by its end. Spending as a percent of GDP increased from 4.5 to 5.1 percent, and per capita spending increased from $82 in 1950 to $143 ten years later.

The 1960s was the first of three decades characterized by rapid growth in medical care spending. The annual percentage change in medical care spending averaged over 11 percent between 1960 and 1990. At the beginning of that 30-year period, medical care spending was $26.7 billion, 5.1 percent of GDP, and $142 per capita. By 1990, it stood at $696.0 billion, 12.0 percent of GDP, and $2,738 per capita. Contributing factors included increased federal government involvement in the payment for medical care services for specific groups—Medicare for the elderly and Medicaid for the indigent—and cost shifting by providers to subsidize care for those without any kind of insurance.

| Table 1.1 | United States Health Care Spending Summary Measures, Various Years | | | |

Year	Total Spending (in billions)	Percent Change[a]	Percent of GDP	Per Capita Spending
1950	$ 12.7	—	4.5	$ 82
1960	26.7	7.7	5.1	143
1965	41.1	9.0	5.7	202
1970	73.1	12.2	7.0	348
1975	130.7	12.3	8.0	582
1980	245.8	13.5	8.8	1,067
1985	428.7	11.8	10.3	1,735
1990	696.0	10.2	12.0	2,738
1995	987.0	7.2	13.3	3,686
2000	1,309.4	5.8	13.3	4,670
2001	1,420.7	8.5	14.1	5,021
2002	1,553.0	9.3	14.9	5,440

a Annual rate of change from the previous year listed.

Source: *Health United States, 2000 with Adolescent Health Chartbook*, 2000, Table 114; and Health Care Financing Administration Web site at **http://www.hcfa.gov/stats/nhe-oact/tables/** (March 15, 2002), and Levin et al. (2004).

The National Institutes of Health provides an overview of its programs and activities at **http://www.nih.gov/.**

Employee Retirement Income Security Act (ERISA)
Federal legislation passed in 1974 that sets minimum standards on employee benefit plans, such as pension, health insurance, and disability. The statute protects the interests of employees in matters concerning eligibility for benefits. The law also protects employers from certain state regulations. For example, states are not allowed to regulate self-insured plans and cannot mandate that employers provide health insurance to their employees.

self-insurance
A group practice of not buying health insurance, but setting aside funds in the amount of the combined premiums to cover any losses incurred by members of the group.

entitlement program
Government assistance programs where eligibility is determined by a specified criteria, such as age, health status, and level of income. These programs include Social Security, Medicare, Medicaid, TANF, and many more.

prospective payment
Payment determined prior to the provision of services. A feature of many managed care organizations that base payment on capitation.

capitation
A payment method providing a fixed, per capita payment to providers for a specified medical benefits package. Providers are required to treat a well-defined population for a fixed sum of money paid in advance without regard to the number or nature of the services provided to each person. This payment method is a characteristic of health maintenance organizations and many preferred provider organizations.

Rapid advance in medical technology and the subsequent cost-containment strategies that emphasized regulation and planning characterized the 1970s. The federal government became a major force in biomedical research and development with the expansion of the National Institutes of Health. Technological advances including open-heart surgery, organ transplantation, various types of imaging, and the ability to preserve and prolong life in the intensive care unit increased the public awareness of medicine and served as a major cost driver. While it all seemed justifiable, this emphasis on advanced technologies precipitated a growing concern over cost issues.

Federal legislation, specifically the National Health Planning Act of 1974, created a network of government planning agencies to control medical care costs. In addition, states passed certificate-of-need (CON) laws to limit the growth in hospital investment in capital improvements and technology. Even a brief national experiment with wage and price controls during the Nixon presidency did little to curb the growth in medical care costs and spending.

Possibly the most significant piece of legislation affecting health care was not viewed as particularly significant at the time. The **Employee Retirement Income Security Act of 1974 (ERISA)** was passed to regulate the corporate use of pension funds. One provision of the act exempted self-insured health plans from state-level health insurance regulations. The passage of ERISA provided an incentive for employers to switch to **self-insurance**. Today, more than one-half of all workers who participate in group health insurance plans are employed in companies who self-insure.

The 1980s ushered in a change in direction in health care policy, resulting in a shift away from regulation and planning and toward a greater reliance on market forces. A president who wanted to lower taxes and a Congress that refused to cut spending characterized the era. Federal budget deficits grew dramatically. By the end of the decade, those areas of the budget where spending was mandated—the **entitlement programs** including Medicare and Medicaid—grew seemingly without limit and came under intense pressure to reduce their rate of growth. During this period, the introduction of alternative payment schemes and delivery systems was significant. **Prospective payment, capitation,** the use of **diagnosis-related groups** to pay hospitals, and the introduction of a **relative value scale** to pay physicians are all examples of these changes. Health maintenance organizations, preferred provider organizations, and other systems of managed care became more common.

The 1990s saw a moderation in the growth in spending. Most experts attribute at least part of the slowdown to the movement of patients into managed care. The annual percentage increase in nominal spending fell from 15.2 percent in 1990 to 4.8 percent in 1998; and then increasing to 9.3 percent in 2002. The expansion of medical care spending as a percentage of GDP slowed in recent years, staying between 13.0 and 13.3 percent of GDP until 2001 when it nudged above 14 percent for the first time. The federal government has taken a more activist role in health care policy in the decade. Although an attempt to completely restructure the health care system failed in 1994, important legislation has been enacted that is expected to improve access to care.[2]

The Question of High and Rising Spending

Why do Americans spend so much on medical care? Various researchers have explored this issue and several explanations have been offered. The most-often cited reasons for the rise in spending include the expansion of the third-party payment system, an aging population, the rise in medical malpractice litigation, and the increased use of medical technology (Aaron, 1991).

---

2 At the federal level, Congress established the Health Insurance Portability and Accountability Act (HIPPA) of 1996 providing insurance portability to individuals with health insurance. In 1997 Congress passed the Children's Health Insurance Program (CHIP), the largest expansion of a federal medical program since its original enactment. In late 2003 Congress voted to expand the coverage for out-patient prescription drugs within the Medicare program.

Insurance use has increased dramatically over the past four decades. Out-of-pocket spending has fallen from over one-half of total spending to less than 15 percent. At the same time, per capita spending on health care has increased more than 35 times. Common sense tells us that the demand for medical care increases as the cost to the individual declines. In all societies, the elderly demand more medical care than the nonelderly. As the U.S. population ages, more medical care is demanded. This trend will likely continue as the baby-boom generation reaches retirement age beginning in 2010. Medical malpractice premiums represent costs that are passed on to patients in the form of higher fees. Those costs alone reached $21 billion in 2002 (Tillinghast-Towers Perrin, 2003). Additionally, fear of malpractice litigation changes the way physicians carry out the practice of medicine, resulting in the increased use of **defensive medicine**, practices and procedures whose primary purpose is to reduce the risk of a lawsuit. Estimates of the extent of this practice range from $60 billion to $100 billion per year (ACOG, 2003). The use of expensive technology has become an imperative in most medical practices. If withheld, even in situations where the probability of success is extremely low, the physician will be accused of negligence and likely sued for malpractice.

Many other factors contribute to the increased spending. The imbalance of information between provider and patient is seen by some as a major factor contributing to the increase in spending. The patient is typically uninformed and finds it difficult to get informed. Thus, the medical practitioner, serving as both adviser and provider of care, has the potential to recommend procedures and services with little expected benefit to the patient—a practice known as physician-induced demand.

Others have focused on certain aspects of the U.S. institutional setting as a major reason for the rise in expenditures. In particular, some see the restrictions on competition due to licensing requirements as important. The 125 medical schools in the United States enroll approximately 67,000 students. Not one new school has been accredited since 1985. In contrast, the 15 European countries that comprise the European Union have a combined population that is approximately 1.5 times that of the United States.[3] Their 220 medical schools enroll almost 40,000 new students each year, or 2.3 times the 17,000 new students enrolled in U.S. medical schools annually (Curtoni and Sutnick, 1995). Furthermore, supply constraints are exacerbated by the increased specialization of U.S. physicians. The ratio of specialists to generalists is 70:30, roughly the reverse of that in most other developed countries.

Economic theory suggests that an increase in the number of physicians would decrease the prices they charge for their services. For many years, economists believed that the American Medical Association (AMA), through its control over medical schools via the accreditation process, controlled the number of licensed physicians and thus kept prices high (Friedman and Kuznets, 1945). The evidence presented in Table 1.2 makes it difficult to present a strong case that restrictions in supply have caused prices to increase. Over the past 20 years the number of active physicians has increased by two-thirds while the population has increased less than 20 percent. As a result, the physician population ratio has actually increased by over 35 percent from 18.3 physicians per 10,000 population in 1980 to 25.0 physicians per 10,000 population in 2001. Comparable numbers in the European Union place the number of practicing physicians at 1.2 million, or 33.3 per 10,000 population.

The predominance of **not-for-profit** providers has also been cited as a major factor in the spending increase (Goodman and Musgrave, 1992). Physicians are trained in not-for-profit medical schools, they work in predominantly not-for-profit hospitals, and the majority of their fees are paid by not-for-profit insurance companies (for example, Blue Cross and Blue Shield) or the government. This reliance on not-for-profit institutions creates a dynamic environment where innovation in general is encouraged but where cost-saving innovations are seldom encountered.

diagnosis-related group
A patient classification scheme based on certain demographic, diagnostic, and therapeutic characteristics developed by Medicare and used to compensate hospitals.

relative value scale
An index that assigns weights to various medical services used to determine the relative fees assigned to them.

defensive medicine
Medical services provided that have little or no medical benefit; their provision is simply to reduce the risk of being sued.

not-for-profit
A business classification that is exempt from paying most taxes. In return for this tax-exempt status, the firm is restricted in how any operating surplus is distributed among its stakeholders.

---

3 The 15 countries in the European Union include Austria, Belgium, Denmark, Finland, France, Germany, Greece, Ireland, Italy, Luxembourg, The Netherlands, Portugal, Spain, Sweden, and the United Kingdom.

Table 1.2	Physicians and Physician-Population Ratio United States, Various Years

Year	Number of Active Physicians	Active Physicians per 10,000 Population
1975	340,280	—
1980	414,916	18.3
1985	497,140	20.1
1990	547,310	22.0
1995	625,443	23.8
1996	643,955	24.3
1997	664,556	24.8
1998	667,000	24.7
1999	668,949	24.5
2000	692,368	25.2
2001	713,375	25.0

Source: *Health, United States, 2003 with Chartbook on Trends in the Health of Americans*, Table 102, 2003.

Changes in Medical Care Delivery

The last 30 years have witnessed major changes that have affected medical care delivery and costs. The shift from private to public sector financing, the shift from out-of-pocket spending to third-party payment, the changes in hospital usage and pricing, and deregulation and the growth in managed care have had profound effects on medical care delivery and pricing.

Shift from Private to Public Financing

Quite possibly, the single most important change affecting medical care delivery has been the shift from private-sector to public-sector financing. Referring to Table 1.3, the private sector was responsible for $3 of every $4 spent in the industry in 1960. The government role in financing was modest, standing at less than 25 cents out of every medical care dollar. The introduction of Medicare and Medicaid in the mid-1960s resulted in the government's share of spending increasing to almost 40 percent by the end of the decade. Even though the government's total share has remained at about one-half of total spending, the federal share has nearly tripled from 10.8 percent in 1960 to 32.5 percent in 2002. This translates into a federal budgetary obligation that has grown from $2.9 billion to over $500 billion in four decades. Even as the federal share has exploded, the share of state and local governments has remained relative stable at around 13.5 percent.

Shift to Third-Party Payment

Even as the private share of total spending has fallen, the role of private insurance has expanded. Private insurance paid a little more than 20 percent of the total cost in 1960, with that share rising to over one-third by 1990, where it has remained since that time. The major change in private spending has been the dramatic decline in private out-of-pocket spending. Approximately one-half of total health care expenditures were classified as out-of-pocket spending in 1960. By 2002, that total had fallen to 13.7 percent. With the increased importance of third-party payers (government and private insurers), medical care has been virtually costless to the insured patient at the point of purchase.

Payment by third parties provides little incentive to control spending on the part of provider or patient. As long as insurance companies are willing to pay the bills, physicians will continue to provide all the care that patients request. Patients have no incentive to

Table 1.3 — Financing of Health Care Expenditures, 1960–2002 in Billions of Dollars and Percentage of Total Personal Spending

Category	1960[d] $	%	1970 $	%	1980 $	%	1990[d] $	%	1995[e] $	%	2000 $	%	2001 $	%	2002 $	%
PRIVATE SECTOR																
Out-of-pocket payments	13.1	48.7	25.1	34.3	58.2	23.7	145.0	20.7	146.5	14.8	192.6	14.7	205.5	14.1	212.5	13.7
Private health insurance	5.9	21.9	15.5	21.2	68.2	27.7	239.6	34.3	330.1	33.3	449.3	34.3	495.6	34.9	549.6	35.4
Other private	1.3	4.8	4.8	6.6	14.5	5.9	31.6	4.5	57.4	5.8	72.9	5.6	72.3	5.1	77.5	5.0
PUBLIC SECTOR																
Federal	2.9	10.8	17.6	24.1	72.3	29.0	195.2	27.9	322.0	32.5	416.0	31.8	460.3	32.4	504.7	32.5
State and local	3.7	13.8	10.0	13.7	33.5	13.6	88.5	12.7	134.2	13.6	178.6	13.6	192.0	13.5	208.7	13.4
Medicare[a]	–	–	7.7	10.5	37.4	15.2	111.5	15.9	185.3	18.7	225.1	17.2	246.5	17.4	267.1	17.2
Medicaid[b]	–	–	5.2	7.1	26.0	10.6	75.4	10.8	137.2	13.9	203.4	15.5	224.2	15.8	250.4	16.1
Total health care spending[c]	26.9	100.0	73.1	100.0	245.8	100.0	699.4	100.0	990.3	100.0	1,309.4	100.0	1,420.7	100.0	1,553.0	100.0

a Included in federal spending.

b Included in federal and state and local spending.

c Columns do not add to total due to double-counting for Medicare and Medicaid.

d Katherine R. Levit et al., "National Health Spending Trends in 1996," *Health Affairs* 17(1), January/February 1998.

e Health Care Financing Administration Web site at **http://www.hcfa.gov/stats/nhe-oact/tables/** (March 15, 2002).

Source: Katherine R. Levit et al., "Health Spending Rebound Continues in 2002," *Health Affairs* 23(1), January/February 2004.

ISSUES IN MEDICAL CARE DELIVERY

SPENDING SOMEBODY ELSE'S MONEY

A *Wall Street Journal* article provides an interesting example of how spending someone else's money distorts the decision-making process. A 70-year-old man suffering from a ruptured abdominal aortic aneurysm was brought to the hospital. After several weeks in the intensive care unit with all the modern technology that goes with it and a three-month stay in the hospital, the bill approached $275,000 (none of which would be paid out-of-pocket by the patient). The man's physician determined that his poor eating habits (caused by poorly fitting dentures) were contributing to his slow recovery. He requested that the hospital dentist perform the necessary adjustments. Later, the doctor discovered that the man had not allowed the dentist to adjust the dentures. When asked the reason, the man replied, "$75 is a lot of money." It seems that Medicare would not pay for the adjustment, so it would have been an out-of-pocket expenditure for the patient. When you're spending somebody else's money, $275,000 does not seem like a lot of money. But when you are spending your own money, $75 is a lot. Our reliance on a third-party payment system is the major institutional feature that contributes to rising costs and increased spending. Cost-conscious consumers have little or no role in a system dominated by **third-party payers.**

Source: James P. Weaver, "The Best Care Other People's Money Can Buy," *The Wall Street Journal*, November 19, 1992, A14.

third-party payers
A health insurance arrangement where the individual (or agent of the individual) pays a set premium to a third party (an insurance company, managed care organization, or the government), which in turn pays for health care services.

moral hazard
Insurance coverage increases both the likelihood of making a claim and the actual size of the claim. Insurance reduces the net out-of-pocket price of medical services and thus increases the quantity demanded.

limit their utilization. Even when the expected benefit of a procedure is small, in most cases, it will be demanded because the patient's share of the cost is small.

It should come as no surprise that the cost of services covered by insurance—public and private—has risen at a faster rate than the cost of services that are not covered. Why? When consumers purchase goods and services at discount prices, they tend to purchase more than if they paid the full price. What other reasonable explanation would explain the crowds that flock to clearance sales and enthusiastic consumer acceptance of discount malls? Health economists refer to this phenomenon as **moral hazard**. Between 1970 and 2001, hospital spending (services that are well covered by insurance) increased by over 16 times. Over the same period, spending on eyeglasses (services typically not covered by insurance) increased only 10 times. Insulating patients from the full cost of medical care has had the effect of making them insensitive to the prices that are being charged, and at the same time encouraging greater utilization.

Change in Hospital Usage and Pricing

Hospital usage has also changed dramatically. As seen in Table 1.4, almost every measure of inpatient hospital usage has fallen in the past 30 years, and in some cases quite dramatically. The number of hospital beds is down; admissions are down; average length of hospital stay is down; and occupancy rates have fallen significantly. Some would go so far as to say that hospitals have gone from overcrowded to underused. Another important trend is the shift from inpatient to outpatient care. Per capita outpatient visits have more than doubled since 1970, and outpatient visits per hospital admission have nearly tripled.

Hospital pricing has shifted from cost-plus to competitive. In many cases, payment has shifted from retrospective to prospective, from payment based on services provided to a fixed payment based on the diagnosis determined in advance. As a result the financial risk of treating patients has shifted from the payer to the provider, creating an incentive for providers to limit access to care. Many providers are affiliated with networks of providers that offer discounts to group members. Because all must abide by the fee

Table 1.4	Short-Stay Community Hospital Characteristics, United States						

Category	1970	1980	1990	1995	1998	2000	2001
Beds (per 1,000 population)	4.17	4.38	3.73	3.32	3.11	2.93	2.90
Admissions (per 1,000 population)	144.0	159.6	125.4	117.9	117.7	117.6	118.7
Average length of stay (days)	7.7	7.6	7.2	6.5	6.0	5.8	5.7
Outpatient visits (per 1,000 population)	657.2	893.2	1,211.6	1,578.5	1,754.3	1,882.8	1,890.7
Outpatient visits per admission	4.6	5.6	9.7	13.4	14.9	15.8	15.9
Percent occupancy	78.0	75.4	66.8	62.8	62.5	63.9	64.5

Source: *Health United States*, various years.

limits placed on them by Medicare and Medicaid, actual transaction prices are deeply discounted from the list prices that show up on their bills.

Deregulation and the Growth in Managed Care

Deregulation has resulted in explosion of facilities and practices previously considered unthinkable. The use of outpatient surgicenters has risen, as has the construction of stand-alone clinics. More physicians are advertising, more practices offer evening and weekend hours, and some physicians are even making house calls.

The managed care approach is increasingly popular. By 1999, nine out of ten employees covered by employer-based **group insurance** were enrolled in a managed care plan (either a health maintenance organization, a preferred provider organization, or a point-of-service plan). The remainder were still in the traditional **indemnity insurance** plan. The increased popularity of managed care has begun to change the incentive structure within the industry, forcing providers to consider costs more carefully. Providing all necessary care for a fixed fee changes the nature of the physician-patient relationship. With cost increasingly an issue, the provider has a stake in eliminating all unnecessary care, increasing the risk that potentially beneficial care will be denied in the name of cost savings.[4]

The Nature of Medical Care as a Commodity

Before undertaking the study of medical care using economic techniques, it is important that we understand the differences between medical care and other commodities. If medical care were just like any other commodity, the use of economics to explain pricing and allocation decisions would not be questioned. But if it is substantially different, strict reliance on economic models may lead to inaccurate predictions and ultimately serious policy mistakes.

Just how different is medical care from other commodities? Using the pioneering work of Kenneth Arrow (1963) as a guide, we can identify a number of distinguishing characteristics that contribute to the uniqueness of medical care as a commodity. First, unlike other commodities, the demand for medical care is irregular. Except for the small

group insurance
A plan whereby an entire group receives insurance under a single policy. The insurance is actually issued to the plan holder, usually an employer or association.

indemnity insurance
Insurance based on the principle that someone suffering an economic loss receives a payment approximately equal to the size of the loss. An insured person who suffers a loss merely makes a claim and receives compensation equal to the loss.

4 On June 12, 2000, the U.S. Supreme Court in a unanimous decision ruled that HMOs could not be sued for providing financial incentives to physicians to control costs. The decision applies only to lawsuits brought in federal courts and does not apply to state courts.

Policy Issue

Can medical care be treated like any other commodity for policy purposes, or is it sufficiently different that it must be treated as a special case?

percentage of care that may be defined as preventive, medical care demand follows an accidental injury or the onset of an illness. As a result, medical care is commonly associated with discomfort, pain, and suffering. It may even be an issue of life or death depending on the nature of the accident or illness. Thus, access to medical care often has implications on the patient's ability to return to a state of normal functioning.

Second, the medical care transaction is characterized by information problems that disproportionately affect patients. All consumers are frequently confronted with difficulties in collecting information about a product, but this problem is particularly acute for medical care consumers due to the complexity of medical knowledge. The typical consumer of medical care is poorly informed and finds it difficult to become well informed. Because of this information imbalance, patients rely on their physicians to diagnose their illnesses and prescribe treatments and expect the physician to proceed with no consideration for his or her own personal gain. Thus, the medical transaction carries with it ethical overtones unlike any other transaction. To protect the interests of the uninformed public, government has established licensing requirements and educational standards to ensure a minimum level of quality among providers, and provider organizations have adopted codes of conduct to guard against unethical behavior.

uncertainty
A state in which multiple outcomes are possible but the likelihood of any one outcome is not known.

In addition to the information problem, the medical transaction is characterized by widespread **uncertainty**. The individual finds it difficult to predict the onset of an illness and thus his or her demand for medical care.[5] Physicians are confronted with uncertainty in diagnosis and treatment. Any given medical condition can be taken care of using a number of different treatment alternatives. One physician recommends surgery; another takes a wait-and-see attitude. Both decisions are based on the interpretation of diagnostic tests and the physician's best judgment. But treatment is not always clearly linked to the outcome. Thus, medicine is as much an art as it is a science.

Another interesting feature of the market for medical care is the widespread reliance on not-for-profit providers, especially in the provision of hospital services. Because trust plays such a big role in the patient-provider relationship, restraining the profit motive may be desirable. The conventional wisdom would have us believe that the absence of the profit motive will mean decision making without the influence of **self-interest** on the part of providers. Even with over 85 percent of the nation's hospitals either government owned or otherwise not-for-profit, the profit motive has not been totally eliminated from the medical care sector. Most physicians' practices are for-profit in nature, as are virtually all pharmaceutical companies, retail drug stores, and long-term care facilities.

self-interest
A behavioral assumption of neoclassical economics that individuals are motivated to promote their own interests.

Although it is difficult to predict the onset of illness for any one individual, it is possible to predict the number of people who will suffer from a particular medical condition within a large group of individuals. In order to spread the risk of a financial loss due to an illness, the individual is willing to purchase insurance. Because the probability of a loss is predictable for large groups, insurance companies emerge to underwrite that risk and sell insurance policies. As a result, insurance has become the primary means of payment for medical care. With third parties financing most of the costs of medical care, individuals are insulated from the full cost of the care they receive. Individuals with insurance will demand more medical care than equally healthy individuals who are uninsured. Providers will adjust treatment recommendations depending on the insurance status of their patients and the willingness of third-party payers to cover certain procedures.

Do these characteristics mean that economics is not applicable to medical care markets? A "yes" answer to this question would do away with any reason to proceed any further. Medical care is a unique commodity in many ways, but its uniqueness does not

---

5 Notable exceptions to this observation include the treatment of certain chronic conditions that may be postponed with little risk and the provision of elective procedures, such as cosmetic surgery, pregnancy, and corrective orthopedics.

preclude the use of economic theory to help us understand allocation and pricing decisions in this critical industry. The challenge we face is not whether the theory is applicable but how to apply the theory.

Health Economics Defined

Health economics emerged as a subdiscipline of economics in the 1960s with the publication of two important papers by Kenneth J. Arrow (1963) and Mark V. Pauly (1968), both published in the *American Economic Review*. Arrow's paper is considered by many to be the seminal contribution to the field of health economics and health policy. Recognizing its importance, the *Journal of Health Politics, Policy and Law* (Peterson, 2001) devoted a special issue to the paper's important contributions including a forward written by Pauly.

Health economists examine a wide range of issues extending from the nature and production of health to the market for health and medical care to the microeconomic evaluation of health care interventions and strategies. Figure 1.2 provides a diagrammatic overview of the structure of health economics. Beginning with the box labeled "Nature of Health," we can ask ourselves a number of questions: What does it mean to be healthy? How do we measure health? What is the best possible way to measure quality of life? Because of the nature of the questions being asked, research on this topic is interdisciplinary. Even though economists are not the only ones studying these questions, their contributions have been significant. The development of the quality of life measure called the quality adjusted life year, or QALY, has profited from the participation of economists.

Grossman (1972) developed an economic framework for the study of medical care demand where medical care is simply one of many factors used to produce good health. The "Production of Health" looks at the determinants of health, including income, wealth, education, genetics, and public health. Our ability to maintain a desired level of health depends to a great extent on the lifestyle choices we make. The topic "Confounding Factors" develops the influence of, for example, tobacco, alcohol, drugs, obesity, and sexually transmitted diseases on our ability to produce good health for a given level of medical care spending. The aging population and the introduction of new technology affect the ability of the market to allocate resources in such a way to effectively satisfy consumer demand.

The principle activity of health economists outside the United States is "Microeconomic Evaluation," or the evaluation of alternative ways to treat a specific medical condition. Policymakers within fixed-budget systems find it necessary to conduct studies comparing the costs and consequences of diagnosis and treatment options in order to make informed decisions on the optimal allocation of scarce resources. Cost-benefit analysis with its welfare economics framework provides the foundation for most of the research in economic evaluation, and health economists have adapted that framework in developing cost-effectiveness analysis, the evaluation method of choice in medical care decision making.

The primary focus of U.S. health economists is the market for health care. The boxes in Figure 1.2 numbered 5–7 and the topics covered in them summarize this emphasis. The "Demand for Health Care" is affected by the elements discussed in boxes 1 and 2—the nature and production of health. The early contribution of economics to the study of health care demand considered improved health as a way to increase future productivity (Mushkin, 1962). Thus, the demand for health care is not only influenced by a desire to feel better when ill, but is also viewed as investment in human capital. Factors affecting the demand for medical care include the socioeconomic characteristics of the population, patient demographics, access barriers (including cost-sharing arrangements), and the role of providers in determining the type and level of care prescribed. The "Supply of Health Care" encompasses a broad spectrum of economics on such topics as production theory, input markets, and

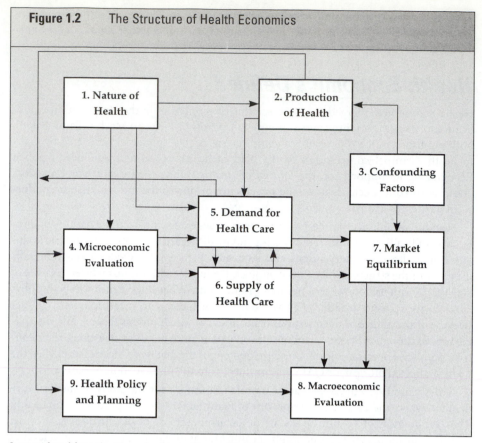

Figure 1.2   The Structure of Health Economics

Source: Adapted from Alan Maynard and Panos Kanavos, "Health Economics: An Evolving Paradigm," *Health Economics 9*, 2000, 183–190.

industrial organization. Specific issues examined include the cost of production, input substitution, and the nature and role of incentives. Demand and supply interact with one another to establish "Market Equilibrium." Markets are able to effectively allocate scarce resources where they are most productive by establishing a price for everything.

Analysis of the overall goals and objectives of the health care system is the subject of "Macroeconomic Evaluation." How well is the system performing? Is it accessible? Is it affordable? Is quality at the desired level? It is here where national and international comparisons are made. How does our system compare to those of our neighbors? Finally, "Health Policy and Planning" involves the interaction of private sector, government, and nongovernmental organizations (NGOs) in setting national goals, determining the strategies for reaching those goals, and establishing the rules of the game that regulate how medical care markets work.

Health care systems are constantly changing. Policymakers and planners are always looking for better ways to produce, deliver, and pay for a growing menu of medical care services demanded by an insatiable public. The goal of this book is to provide you with the tools to better understand the role of economics in this important task.

Ten Key Economic Concepts

Given the complexity of economic theory, it may come as a surprise that economic thought is guided by a relatively small number of key concepts. These concepts will serve as unifying themes throughout the book.

1. *Scarcity and choice* address the problem of limited resources and the need to economize. Not enough resources are available to meet all the desires of all the

people, making rationing in some form unavoidable. We are forced to make choices among competing objectives—an inescapable result of **scarcity**.

2. *Opportunity cost* recognizes that everything and everyone has alternatives. Time and resources used to satisfy one set of desires cannot be used to satisfy another set. The cost of any decision or action is measured in terms of the value placed on the opportunity foregone.

3. *Marginal analysis* is the economic way of thinking about the optimal allocation of resources. Choices are seldom made on an all-or-nothing basis—they are made at "the margin." Decision makers weigh the trade-offs, a little more of one thing and a little less of another. In this environment, consideration is given to the incremental benefits and incremental costs of a decision.

4. *Self-interest* is the primary motivator of economic decision makers. Driven by the power of self-interest, people are motivated to pursue efficiency in the production and consumption decisions they make. According to the well-known eighteenth century economist Adam Smith, this pursuit of self-interest, moderated by market competition, causes each individual to pursue a course of action that promotes the general goals of society.

5. *Markets and pricing* serve as the most efficient way to allocate scarce resources. The market accomplishes its tasks through a system of prices: what Adam Smith called the "invisible hand." The invisible hand can allocate resources because everyone and everything has a price. Prices increase if more is desired and decrease if less is desired. Firms base their production decisions on relative prices and relative price movements. The price mechanism becomes a way to bring a firm's output decisions into balance with consumer desires—something that we refer to as **equilibrium**.

6. *Supply and demand* serve as the foundation for all economic analysis. Pricing and output decisions are based on the forces underlying these two economic concepts. Goods and services are allocated among competing uses by striking a balance (an equilibrium) between the consumers' willingness to pay and the suppliers' willingness to provide—rationing via prices.

7. *Competition* forces resource owners to use their resources to promote the highest possible satisfaction of society: consumers, producers, and investors. If resource owners do this well, they are rewarded. If they are inept or inefficient, they are penalized. Competition takes production out of the hands of the less competent and places it into the hands of the more efficient—constantly promoting more efficient methods of production.

8. *Efficiency* in economics measures how well resources are being used to promote social welfare. Inefficient outcomes waste resources, while the efficient use of scarce resources enhances social welfare. The fascinating aspect of competitive markets is how the more-or-less independent behavior on the part of thousands of decision makers serves to promote social welfare. Consumers attempt to make themselves better off by allocating limited budgets. Producers seek maximum profits by using cost-minimizing methods.

9. *Market failure* arises when the free market fails to promote the efficient use of resources by either producing more or less than the optimal level of output. Sources of market failure include natural monopoly, externalities in production and consumption, and **public goods**. Other market imperfections such as incomplete information and immobile resources also contribute to this problem.

10. *Comparative advantage* explains how people benefit from voluntary exchange when production decisions are based on opportunity cost. The individual or entity that has the lowest opportunity cost of production is said to have a comparative advantage.

scarcity
A situation that exists when the amount of a good or service demanded in the aggregate exceeds the amount available at a zero price.

opportunity cost
The cost of a decision based on the value of the foregone opportunity.

equilibrium
The market-clearing price where every consumer wanting to purchase the good finds a willing seller.

public good
A good that is nonrival in distribution and nonexclusive in consumption.

Summary and Conclusions

The medical care industry in the United States is large and growing in relative size. Medical care is one of the largest industries in the vast U.S. economy. At more than $1.4 trillion, it was three times larger than the domestic auto industry and five times larger than the total defense budget in 2001. In addition, medical care employed more people and exported more goods and services than either defense or automobiles. It may be difficult to imagine, but the economic output of the U.S. medical care industry was almost as large as the entire French economy.

As shown in Figure 1.3, a potpourri of public and private sources finances U.S. medical care. The public sector directly finances 46 percent of total spending. Private health insurance and private philanthropy finance 40 percent, leaving 14 percent coming from direct out-of-pocket payments from individuals.

Most of the money Americans spend on medical care covers either hospital or physicians' services (see Figure 1.4). The percentage of total spending in these two areas has remained relatively stable over time at around 55 to 60 percent. Other professional services, pharmaceuticals, and nursing home care combine for approximately one-fourth of the total spending. The other 6 percent is comprised of home health care and other medical products and services. Even though it represents only 10.5 percent of total spending, pharmaceutical spending is the fastest growing portion of expenditures, doubling since 1995 and increasing over 15 percent in 2001 and 2002.

The U.S. system of medical care delivery is far from perfect. Its weaknesses are easily identified. Critics claim there are too few primary care physicians and too many specialists, leading to a greater reliance on acute and specialty care and underutilization of **primary and preventive care**. The gaps in health insurance coverage limit reliable access for many low-skilled workers and their families. Only recently has federal legislation introduced a modest measure of **portability** in the market for group health insurance. Even with changes in the law, many people are still considered uninsurable because of preexisting conditions.

The system also has its strengths. Defenders argue that quality is unquestionably high. Citing evidence from polls, they note that around 85 percent of Americans are happy with the quality of their own medical care arrangements. It should be noted that the same polls show that one-third feel the system has so much wrong with it that it needs to be completely rebuilt (Donelon et al., 1999). The U.S. system has progressed much faster than its European counterparts in developing quality assessment and output measures. The United States is still the world leader in innovation, research, and the development of new, state-of-the-art technology.

primary and preventive care
Basic medical services that focus on prevention and treatment. Traditionally, primary care physicians have been family practitioners, gynecologists, and pediatricians.

portability
A feature of an insurance policy that allows the individual to maintain coverage in the event of a job change.

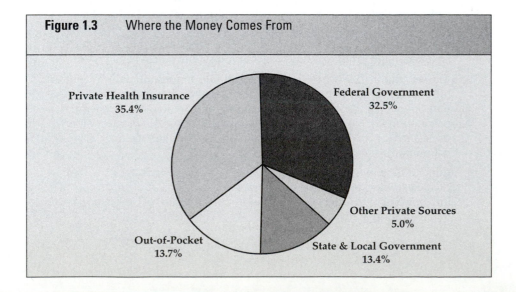

Figure 1.3   Where the Money Comes From

Private Health Insurance
35.4%

Federal Government
32.5%

Other Private Sources
5.0%

Out-of-Pocket
13.7%

State & Local Government
13.4%

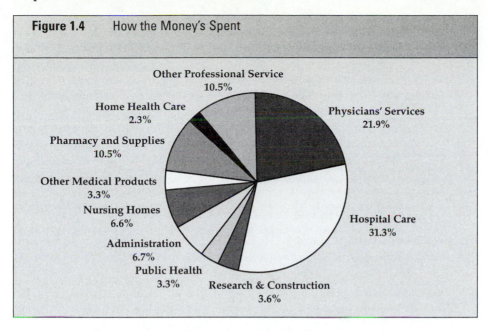

Figure 1.4   How the Money's Spent

Other Professional Service 10.5%
Home Health Care 2.3%
Pharmacy and Supplies 10.5%
Other Medical Products 3.3%
Nursing Homes 6.6%
Administration 6.7%
Public Health 3.3%
Research & Construction 3.6%
Physicians' Services 21.9%
Hospital Care 31.3%

The growth in medical care spending has moderated somewhat since 1990. It could be that the aggressive action by employers and state governments to reverse the escalation in spending is finally paying off. Or possibly, the threat of government intervention at the federal level has served to intimidate providers who now fear public backlash and political reprisals. Whatever the reason, the combined efforts of providers and payers or government jawboning, spending growth has moderated without significant legislative action.

In general, spending growth in the public sector has outpaced spending growth in the private sector. Since 1990, private medical spending has grown at an annual rate of 5.85 percent while public medical spending has risen at an annual rate of 7.78 percent. Over that time Medicare spending has increased 7.29 percent per year and Medicaid 10.41 percent. Spending showed some signs of escalating in 2001, increasing 8.24 percent in the private sector and 9.35 percent in the public sector.

Questions and Problems

1. Thomas Sowell, a senior fellow at the Hoover Institution, has stated that we "have difficulty understanding the strange way words are used by politicians and the media." We often think of a crisis in terms of an emergency, a situation of utmost urgency, maybe even life or death. According to Sowell, politicians use the term differently. They define crisis as any situation they want to change. How do you define the term *crisis*? Does the United States have a health care crisis?

2. Discuss the magnitude of the financing problem in medical care. What are the major reasons that medical spending is absorbing an increasing share of national output?

3. How important is cost containment in establishing a national health care policy? In addition to controlling costs, what are the alternative goals for a national medical care system?

4. What do economists mean by *scarcity*? Why is the concept so important in economic analysis?

Health Economics—Places to Go provides links to sites related to health economics, health policy, managed care, and more:
http://www.medecon. de/HEC.HTM

References

Henry J. Aaron, *Serious and Unstable Condition: Financing America's Health Care*, Washington, DC: The Brookings Institution, 1991.

American College of Obstetricians and Gynecologists, "Who Will Deliver My Baby? Ob-Gyns, Patients Push U.S. Senate for Tort Reform," ACOG News Release, April 28, 2003.

Kenneth J. Arrow, "Uncertainty and the Welfare Economics of Medical Care," *American Economic Review 53*(5), December 1963, 941–973.

Robert J. Blendon, Tracey Stelzer Hyams, and John M. Benson, "Bridging the Gap Between Expert and Public Views on Health Care Reform," *Journal of the American Medical Association 269*(19), May 19, 1993, 2573–2578.

Sergio Curtoni and Alton I. Sutnick, "Numbers of Physicians and Medical Students in Europe and the United States," *Academic Medicine 70*(8), August 1995, 688–691.

Karen Donelan, Robert J. Blendon, Craig A. Hill, Catherine Hoffman, Diane Rowland, Martin Frankel, and Drew Altman, "Whatever Happened to the Health Insurance Crisis in the United States? Voices From a National Survey," *Journal of the American Medical Association 276*(16), October 23/30, 1996, 1346–1350.

Karen Donelan, Robert J. Blendon, Cathy Schoen, Karen Davis and Katherine Binns, "The Cost of Health System Change: Public Discontent in Five Nations," *Health Affairs 18*(3), May/June 1999, 206–216.

Milton Friedman and Simon Kuznets, *Income from Independent Professional Practice*, New York: National Bureau of Economic Research, 1945.

John C. Goodman and Gerald L. Musgrave, *Patient Power: Solving America's Health Care Crisis*, Washington, DC: Cato Institute, 1992.

Michael Grossman, "On the Concept of Health Capital and the Demand for Health," *Journal of Political Economy 80*(2), March/April 1972, 223–255.

Jack Hadley and John Holahan, "Covering the Uninsured: How Much Would It Cost?" *Health Affairs—Web Exclusive* (W3), June 4, 2003, 250–265.

Kaiser Family Foundation and Health Research and Educational Trust, "Employer Health Benefits: 2002 Annual Survey," 2002 [available at **http://www.kff.org/content/2002/3251/**].

Selma J. Mushkin, "Health as an Investment," *Journal of Political Economy 70*(5, part 2), October 1962, 129–157.

OASDI and Medicare Boards of Trustees, *1999 Annual Reports of the OASDI and Medicare Boards of Trustees to Congress*, based on data from the Office of the Actuary, Health Care Financing Administration, 1999.

Mark V. Pauly, "The Economics of Moral Hazard: Comment," *American Economic Review 58*(2), June 1968, 531–538.

_____, "U.S. Health Care Costs: The Untold True Story," *Health Affairs 15*(1), Fall 1993, 152–159.

Mark A. Peterson, ed., "Kenneth Arrow and the Changing Economics of Health Care," *Journal of Health Politics, Policy and Law 26*(5), October 2001.

Tillinghast-Towers Perrin, "U.S. Tort Costs: 2002 Update," Stamford, CT: Tillinghast-Towers Perrin, February 2003.

Appendix 1A

The Medical Care Price Index

The conventional wisdom in many policy circles embraces the notion that medical care inflation is out of control. How much of the increase in medical spending is due to inflation and how much is due to improved services and changing demographic patterns? The way we answer this question will ultimately determine the type of medical care reform we will get. It is important, therefore, to understand how price indexes are used to measure medical care price inflation.

Measuring Price Changes with Index Numbers

The principal measure of inflation used by business and government policymakers is the year-to-year change in the consumer price index (CPI). The index plays an important role in determining cost of living adjustments (COLAs) for everything from union wages to social security and pension benefits to federal income tax brackets. The CPI is a fixed-weight or Laspeyres index that measures price changes for a market basket of items defined for a base time period. In other indexes, such as the gross domestic product (GDP) price deflator, the composition of the market basket changes every year to reflect different spending patterns.

A fixed-weight index has become the index of choice used to measure inflation. Because the weights do not change, movements in a fixed-weight index are due solely to changes in the prices of the goods included in the market basket. In contrast, a movement in a deflator reflects changes in prices of goods and the composition of the market basket. In reality, consumers adjust their spending away from goods whose prices increase making it necessary to change periodically the composition of the fixed-weight market basket to better reflect consumer spending patterns. The weights for the CPI are based on a survey of consumer spending patterns and is changed approximately every ten years. The current CPI weighting scheme was revised in 1988 based on results from the 1993–1995 Consumer Expenditure Survey.

Table A1.1 presents data for the consumer price index from 1970 through 2002. Overall, the index is broken down into seven major spending categories: food (18 percent), housing (42 percent), apparel (6 percent), transportation (18 percent), medical care (6 percent), entertainment (4 percent), and other (6 percent). The index in each case equals 100 for the 1982–1984 time period. When interpreting these indexes note that the inflation rate from one time period to the next can be calculated by dividing the change in the index by its previous value. For example, the CPI changed from 144.5 to 148.2 between 1993 and 1994. This change of 3.7 percentage points divided by 144.5 results in an estimated annual inflation rate of 2.56 percent. Over the time period shown, the medical care component increased at a faster rate than any other component of the CPI, over 700 percent from 1970–2002.

Medical Care Price Index

The major index of medical care prices, the medical care price index (MCPI), is shown in Table A1.2. Medical care is divided into commodities and services. Medical commodities are subdivided into seven categories: prescription drugs, nonprescription drugs, first aid and dressings, general medical equipment, convalescent equipment, hearing aids, and unpriced items. Medical services are divided into nine categories: physician, dental, optometry, other professional, hospital room, other inpatient, outpatient, nursing home, and unpriced. Health insurance is priced using a separate category.

Typically cited as the measure of medical care inflation, the MCPI has steadily increased since 1950. Interpreting the index as a measure of inflation suggests that medical care prices have risen at a compounded rate of over 6.35 percent since 1980, over two-thirds faster than prices in general. If this is true, we have a real problem on our hands. But can we believe what the statistics seem to tell us? Is the MCPI a good measure of medical care price inflation?

Table A1.1	Consumer Price Indexes for Major Expenditure Classes Select Years, 1960–2002 (1982–1984 = 100)

Year	All Items (CPI-U)	All Services	Food	Housing	Apparel and Upkeep	Energy	Medical Care	All Items Excluding Medical Care
1960	29.6	24.1	30.0	—	45.7	22.4	22.3	30.2
1970	38.8	35.0	39.2	36.4	59.2	25.5	34.0	39.2
1980	82.4	77.9	86.8	81.1	90.9	86.0	74.9	82.8
1990	130.7	139.2	132.4	128.5	124.1	102.1	162.8	128.8
1991	136.2	146.3	136.3	133.6	128.7	102.5	177.0	133.8
1992	140.3	152.0	137.9	137.5	131.9	103.0	190.1	137.5
1993	144.5	157.9	140.9	141.2	133.7	104.2	201.4	141.2
1994	148.2	163.1	144.3	144.8	133.4	104.6	211.0	144.7
1995	152.4	168.7	148.4	148.5	132.0	105.2	220.5	148.6
1996	156.9	174.1	153.3	152.8	131.7	110.1	228.2	152.8
1997	160.5	179.4	157.3	156.8	132.9	111.5	234.6	156.3
1998	163.0	184.2	160.7	160.4	133.0	102.9	242.1	158.6
1999	166.6	188.8	164.1	163.9	131.3	106.6	250.6	162.0
2000	172.2	195.3	167.8	169.6	129.6	124.6	260.8	167.3
2001	177.1	203.4	173.1	176.4	127.3	129.3	272.8	171.9
2002	179.9	209.8	176.2	180.3	124.0	121.7	285.6	174.3

Source: *Health United States, 2003: With Chartbook on Trends in the Health of Americans,* 2003, Table 113.

Table A1.2	Medical Care Price Index and Its Major Components Select Years 1950–2002 (1982–1984 = 100)

Year	Total Medical Care	Compound Rate of Change from Previous Year Listed	Medical Care Commodities	Medical Care Services
1950	15.1	—	39.7	12.8
1960	22.3	4.0	46.9	19.5
1970	34.0	4.3	46.5	32.3
1980	74.9	8.2	75.4	74.8
1990	162.8	7.4	163.4	162.7
1991	177.0	8.1	176.8	177.1
1992	190.1	7.4	188.1	190.5
1993	201.4	5.9	195.0	202.9
1994	211.0	4.8	200.7	213.4
1995	220.5	4.5	204.5	224.2
1996	228.2	3.5	210.4	232.4
1997	234.6	2.8	215.3	239.1
1998	242.1	3.2	221.8	246.8
1999	250.6	3.5	230.7	255.1
2000	260.8	4.1	238.1	266.0
2001	272.8	4.6	247.6	278.8
2002	285.6	4.7	256.4	292.9

Source: *Health United States, 2003: With Chartbook on Trends in the Health of Americans,* 2003, Table 113.

Problems with Using a Fixed-Weight Index as a Measure of Inflation

In reality, changes in a fixed-weight index do not accurately reflect changes in the cost of living. Using a fixed-weight index, such as the MCPI, to measure medical care price inflation introduces a substantial upward bias to the estimate. It is important that we understand the problems associated with using indexes to measure inflation and take appropriate steps when interpreting indexes to minimize the bias.

Measuring Inputs Instead of Outcomes

The medical care price index measures the wrong thing. The price index measures the cost of inputs: an office visit, a day in the hospital, a surgical procedure, or a prescription drug. Patients who are ill do not desire the inputs; they are interested in the restoration of their health. But, as we will see in Chapter 5, health is difficult to define, let alone measure.

Given the difficulty in measuring health, one possible solution would be to measure the cost of curing a particular illness. For example, the average length of stay in the hospital has steadily fallen over the course of the past several decades. Reduced stays have dampened the hospital-cost escalation measured in terms of average cost per day (what the CPI measures). Even more dramatic has been the increased use of outpatient procedures to treat illnesses that formerly required extensive hospital stays. Repair of an inguinal hernia (one of the most common surgical procedures) formerly required several days in the hospital and several months of limited activity. Today the procedure, performed on an outpatient basis, requires only a few hours in the surgicenter and minimal rehabilitation time. In fact, most patients are encouraged to resume their normal daily activities as soon as possible.

The shift to outpatient surgery has greatly reduced the cost of treating many common problems, but the cost savings has largely been lost on the medical care price index. As outpatient procedures grow in popularity two things happen. First, the patients who continue to be treated in the hospital are on average sicker than before. They require more resources on average and thus drive up the average cost of their hospital stays. Second, when an outpatient procedure actually replaces a conventional hospital procedure, as is the case with cataract surgery and lens replacement and many orthopedic surgeries, it drops out of the hospital component of the price index and is picked up later in the outpa-

tient component. The end result of both of these factors is an increase in the medical care price index even though the cost of treating the illness has decreased.

Measuring Quality Changes

Technological progress typically results in improvements in the products and services available to consumers. Price increases due to quality improvements are mistakenly identified as inflation in a fixed-weight index. This is not a severe problem in industries where innovation takes place slowly, but technological progress takes place at different rates in different industries. This is especially true in the medical industry where quality of care has improved dramatically over the past 50 years. Treatments for once untreatable diseases now offer hope for those who suffer from them. Inexpensive prevention of diseases such as polio and smallpox has led to near eradication of these once costly illnesses. Improved surgical techniques allow patients to leave the hospital sooner and recuperate faster.

If price indexes are to be an accurate measure of changes in the cost of living, price changes due to quality improvements must have no impact on the value of the index. The Bureau of Labor Statistics (BLS) attempts to factor quality improvements, but once again, infrequent changes in the composition of the index fail to keep up with the rapid advance of technology. As a result, quality improvements are mistakenly interpreted as pure price movements.

Accounting for New Products

The CPI, as a fixed-weight index, relies on the assumption that the product and service mix of the market basket remains unchanged. The use of this assumption makes it difficult to incorporate new products into the calculation. In some industries this poses only minor problems. For gasoline and other components of the energy price index, this assumption works reasonably well. The same cannot be said for the medical care industry. The rapid introduction of new medicines and new technologies over the past several decades poses problems for the fixed-weight medical care price index.

Infrequent revisions in the index mean that the price index fails to account for significant reductions in the price of newly discovered products. Penicillin, for example, did not enter into the index until its price had fallen to about 1 percent of its original level. A more common problem deals with the introduction of generic drugs. Generics are chemically identical to their name-brand alternatives and usually much cheaper. They do not enter into the calculation of the index until weights are periodically revised and only then as an entirely new product. By that time, they may have captured a significant portion of the market and lowered costs to users substantially. Their addition to the index, however, does not reflect the price decline.

The introduction of the laparoscope has revolutionized many forms of surgery, from knee reconstruction for damaged ligaments to the removal of the gall bladder. In most cases, the new surgical method costs considerably less than the traditional alternative because of shorter hospital stays. Gall bladder removal using laparoscopic techniques requires a 1- to 2-day hospital stay compared with 3 to 7 days using traditional surgical techniques. Repairing a damaged anterior cruciate ligament using the new technique costs 75 percent less for the same medical result.

The BLS incorporates new products and procedures into the index by price-linking, replacing the old product with a new one at some arbitrary point in time. This adjustment is made in such a way that the price index remains unchanged. By doing so, price increases are considered an improvement in quality, but price decreases are simply lost to the index.

Other Problems

In addition to the problems already addressed, several other factors play an important role in creating biased indexes. These include the use of list prices instead of transaction prices, the statistical sampling problem, and a substitution bias.

Use of List Prices. All published indexes from the BLS use "list" prices in their calculations rather than "transaction" prices. The list price is the price paid by a full-paying patient. Information on list prices is easier to collect but may bear little resemblance to the payments that providers actually receive. As more and more providers, physicians and hospitals, enter into agreements with managed care networks and other insurers, actual transaction prices represent discounts from normal list prices. In practice, very few patients actually pay list prices for services.

Suppose a hospital that normally charges $2,500 for a hospital stay agrees to accept $2,000 from a private insurer as payment in full. In this case, $2,000 should be the price that enters into the price index. But more often than not, the discounted price differs across payers and is more difficult to determine, so the list price of $2,500 is used.

If list prices and transactions prices change at roughly the same rate, the use of list prices is not particularly glaring. Medical discounting, however, has become an increasingly important phenomenon

in recent years, so the use of list prices produces an upward bias on the medical care price index. In fact, the Centers for Medicare and Medicaid Services (CMS) has developed a transactions price index for hospital services. Since 1978, the transactions price index has increased about 70 percent as fast as the hospital index based on list prices (Tregarthen, 1993).

Sampling. The high cost of collecting price data dictates that only a limited number of transactions are included in the price index. Sampling can introduce several types of biases into the price index. List prices on the day the data are collected may not be totally representative of the prices that consumers actually pay because of routine discounts. Prices paid in the sampled locales may not represent prices paid by most consumers. Discounts for bulk purchases and the increased popularity of generic and store brands is also lost in the sampling procedure used.

Substitution Bias. Economists have observed that when the price of a good increases relative to other goods, consumers tend to buy less of it. So as the prices of goods change relative to one another, spending patterns change. Consumers substitute lower-priced items for higher-priced items. This changing pattern of spending, called the substitution effect, is missed completely by fixed-weight indexes like the CPI. As long as the prices of all items in the index rise at roughly the same rate, this phenomenon causes few measurement problems. Over time, however, small differences can add up and result in the statistical phenomenon called *substitution bias.* This bias does not pose a problem with a deflator since the market basket changes annually to reflect changing spending patterns. In a fixed-weight index, the weights are changed infrequently (every ten years or so with the CPI), placing too much emphasis on goods whose prices rise the fastest.

Alternative Methods to Measure Medical Care Inflation

Researchers have suggested alternative measures that might better reflect changes in the price of medical care. Wilensky and Rossiter (1986) advance the case that a change in the measure of medical output would result in more accurate estimates of price changes in medical care. The most commonly used measure of output is the procedure (e.g., one dose of chemotherapy for the treatment of cancer). Alternatively, output could be defined by the case (e.g., treatment of cancer from diagnosis to final outcome), the episode (e.g., using a particular phase of the illness), or on a per capita basis (e.g., measuring the total cost per patient for all medical care).

Another suggested method involves defining a good by a set of characteristics demanded by consumers. This so-called hedonic approach prices those individual characteristics and recombines them to determine the quality-constant price of the good. Trajtenberg (1990) used the hedonic approach to estimate the change in the cost of computerized tomographic X-rays or CT scanners. Defining a CT scan as a set of characteristics, the hedonic index actually declined from 100 to 27.3 over the time period 1973 to 1982. In contrast, the standard index with no quality adjustment showed an increase from 100 to 259.4.

The use of these alternative approaches, while promising in some cases, is not appropriate in others. Even when appropriate, the cost of data collection rises dramatically. Unfortunately, data collection does not seem to be very high on the list of government priorities.

Summary and Conclusions

Measuring price changes with the indexes we have available is somewhat problematic. Outputs are difficult to measure. New products are included arbitrarily. The methods for dealing with quality improvements are inadequate at best. Depending on how we interpret the evidence, medical care may be the fastest rising component of the consumer price index or, using a quality-adjusted notion, medical care prices may be actually falling.

References

Robert F. Graboyes, "Medical Care Price Indexes," *Federal Reserve Bank of Richmond Economic Quarterly 80*(4), Fall 1994, 69–89.

Joseph P. Newhouse, "Measuring Medical Prices and Understanding Their Effects," *The Journal of Health Administration Education 7*(1), Winter 1989, 19–26.

M. Trajtenberg, "Economic Analysis of Product Innovation: The Case of the CT Scanners," *Harvard Economic Studies 160*, Cambridge, MA: Harvard University Press, 1990.

Suzanne Tregarthen, "Statistics Overstate Health Care Costs," *The Wall Street Journal*, August 18, 1993, A10.

Gail R. Wilensky and Louis F. Rossiter, "Alternative Units of Payment for Physician Services: An Overview of the Issues," *Medical Care Review 43*, Spring 1986, 133–156.

Chapter 2

Using Economics to Study Health Issues

Understanding what economics can and cannot do is the first and possibly most important step in using economics as a tool of public policy. Economics can offer a framework to study the implications of individual decision making and help define the alternative mechanisms available to improve resource allocation. It cannot provide

Policy Issue

Does sound policy making require an understanding of economic principles?

solutions to all the problems of medical care access and delivery. When using economics to study medical care, it is important to avoid extremes. Arguing that economics does not matter (or at least should not matter) when it comes to medical care issues is as ill advised as arguing that economics is all that matters. We cannot avoid the economic implications of our actions in this important arena any more than we can avoid the moral implications.

Sound policy making is based on sound economic principles applied in a sensitive and uniform manner. The premise of this book is that policy making based on sound economics is better than policy making in an economic vacuum. Lessons can be learned from basic economics: lessons about human behavior and the way individuals make decisions and respond to incentives, lessons about the ways that people interact with each other, and lessons about the efficient allocation of scarce resources. Economists do not claim to have the final word about how to organize and run a health care system, but they do have something relevant to add to the discussion.

The goals of this chapter are somewhat ambitious. Those of you who have been exposed to an economics course may be tempted to skip this chapter completely. Avoid the temptation. At a minimum, use the chapter to refresh your memory of the important concepts that will come into play in analyzing medical markets and the policies that affect them. Those of you who have never had the privilege of taking a course in economics will find this chapter useful in setting the tone for the rest of the book. The principle focus of the chapter will be the examination of the basic principles of demand and supply.

The Relevance of Economics in Health Care

Economics is a way of organizing our thinking about problems that confront us in our daily lives. To think like an economist requires a disciplined approach to a problem. Sound reasoning within a systematic framework is essential. The value of economics stems from its usefulness in making sense out of complex economic and social issues, including issues in medical care delivery. Future health care decision makers will need training and knowledge in many areas: not only biology and chemistry but also statistics, epidemiology, behavioral science, ethics, decision analysis, and, of course, economics.

Economics is one of several social sciences that attempts to explain and predict human behavior. It is unique among the social sciences in establishing a context of scarcity and uncertainty. More specifically, economics is concerned with the way scarce resources are allocated among alternative uses to satisfy unlimited human wants.

ISSUES IN MEDICAL CARE DELIVERY

RHETORIC IN ECONOMICS

An important element of economics is conversation. Economists must be persuasive communicators. Economics has its own rhetoric, and those unfamiliar with it have a difficult time understanding economics. Economists use mathematical and statistical tests to make arguments, but when you listen closely to their conversations you hear many literary devices familiar to most freshman English students. They include figures of speech such as metaphors, analogies, and appeals to authority (e.g., Adam Smith's "invisible hand," Milton Friedman and the Chicago School, and John Kenneth Galbraith).

Hundreds of special words comprise the rhetoric of economics (you may like the term *jargon* better), dozens of graphs, and a few mathematical expressions. Words such as *inflation, expenditures, costs, prices, revenues, profits, labor, capital,* and *risk* are just a few examples of economic terminology. Another favorite pastime is the use of diagrams to model a situation and mathematical equations to depict relationships among variables. Diagrams and mathematical expressions are efficient means of representing reality.

Some examples of economic rhetoric include the following:

- The organization of work is represented by a "production function." The economist depicting the delivery of medical care in a hospital environment by a production function is similar to the poet saying, "My love is like a red, red rose."

- Attending medical school is an investment in "human capital." Students who forgo income during medical training expect to reap high returns in the form of pay and prestige in the future.

- Prices serve as an "invisible hand" to guide decision makers in a market economy. High prices direct consumers away from certain products and toward those with relatively lower prices.

The quest for **economic efficiency** stems from the fact that there are never enough resources to provide all the goods and services desired by a society. Economists call this concept *scarcity*. Using resources in one activity precludes the use of those same resources in a different activity. When resources are used in medical care delivery, those same resources are not available for use in other beneficial activities: for example, food distribution, education, housing, and national defense.

The economic concept of cost stems from the notion that resources have alternative uses. The term *opportunity cost* is defined as the potential benefit that could have been received if the resources had been used in their next best alternative. Tax dollars used to purchase medical care for the elderly cannot be used to buy education for the young. Money spent in a rehabilitation program for drug addicts is not available to spend on prenatal care for indigent women. Adopting the concept of economic efficiency implies that choices should be made in a way that maximizes the total benefit from the available resources. In the practice of medical care delivery, this involves the evaluation of health care alternatives by calculating the benefits and costs of each and allocating resources in a way that maximizes the net benefits to the community.

Critical Assumptions in Economics

All scientific models start with assumptions. Economic models start by assuming **rational behavior** on the part of decision makers: Everyone involved in a decision

economic efficiency
Producing at a point where average product is maximized and average variable cost is minimized.

rational behavior
A key behavioral assumption in neoclassical economics that decision makers act in a purposeful manner. In other words, their actions are directed toward achieving an objective.

behaves in a purposeful manner.[1] Economics is different from other social sciences in its emphasis on rational decision making under conditions of scarcity.

microeconomics
The study of individual decision making, pricing behavior, and market organization.

In **microeconomics**, the assumption of rational behavior establishes a consistent framework for individual decision making. We assume that individuals, in an attempt to reach certain objectives, must choose among competing alternatives. The problem becomes one of allocating scarce resources among these competing ends. In other words, we cannot satisfy every desire we have; we must make choices.

Decision makers, motivated by self-interest, respond to incentives. In fact, decision making is dominated by the pursuit of self-interest. Individuals use their resources to advance their own economic well-being. When confronted with alternative actions, they choose the one that makes them better off.[2]

rational ignorance
A situation where consumers stop seeking information on a prospective purchase because the expected cost of the additional search exceeds the expected benefits.

People look for the best way to achieve their goals. This does not rule out impulsive behavior or mistakes. In fact, because information is costly to gather and process, decision makers often practice **rational ignorance**. They decide between alternative actions with incomplete information. From the decision maker's perspective, the information left to be gathered costs more to gather than its perceived worth.

Scarcity is the reason that we study economics. In a world of superabundance, there would be no compelling reason to make choices. All people could have all that they want without concern for alternative uses. Or, if all individuals had the divine nature of saints, our attitude would be one of relative indifference toward material goals and scarcity would not be an issue. But we do not live in a world of superabundance, and the world is not populated by saints, so decision making must take into consideration forgone opportunities.

The Scientific Method

The challenge at hand is to understand economic relationships without the luxury of controlled experiments. Economic inquiry utilizes the scientific method in much the same way that physics or chemistry uses this approach. The five basic steps in the scientific method are as follows:

1. Every scientist starts with a premise or postulate that serves as a foundation for the inquiry. Some may call it an ideology or even a vision. Either way it represents the scientist's understanding of the way the world works. The culture around us, the way our parents raised us, and years of scientific training and inquiry all affect the way we view the world around us. Even the most unbiased among us are affected by some bias; at minimum our biases affect the nature of our inquiry.

2. The world arouses our curiosity. Scientists are careful observers of real-world phenomena and events. These observations concerning the real world are organized and catalogued.

3. A theory is then developed to explain the observed behavior or predict future behavior. Model building captures the essential features of the observed behavior. It is a meaningful abstraction, decomposing the problem into its elemental parts.

4. The scientist then formulates hypotheses to test the predictions of the theory. This requires gathering of facts and data.

5. In the final step, hypothesis testing, we use quantitative techniques to improve our understanding of the issue and promote more accurate predictions.

In practice, an economist might approach a problem using the scientific method as follows. One vision of the way the world works might be that, if people are truly motivated by self-interest, they will respond in measurable ways to changes in incentives. From this vision, a theory is developed that people will respond to higher out-of-pocket

---

1 Note that it is possible to study human behavior without assuming rationality, but that would not be economics.
2 Altruistic behavior is not ruled out; it is merely interpreted as self-interested behavior.

payments by demanding fewer elective procedures. The RAND insurance experiment actually conducted controlled trials, randomly placing individuals into different types of health plans (Manning et al., 1987). By varying the out-of-pocket payments required of individuals, their demand for medical care was analyzed. Empirical results supported the hypothesis that higher out-of-pocket payments would lead to lower utilization measured by fewer physician visits. The RAND experiment has spawned many studies, testing numerous different hypotheses. The way we think about health insurance pricing and payment policies has been significantly affected by this important research.

These are the steps involved in the scientific method: an ideological base, observation of events, development of a theory, hypothesis testing, and, finally, rethinking. Empirical results that run counter to expectations may cause the scientist to rethink the theory or develop different hypotheses.

Model Building

One of the main goals of economics is to understand, explain, and predict the behavior of decision makers. To this end, economists find it necessary to simplify that behavior. Simplification is accomplished through generalization, often through the construction of models.

A model is nothing more than a way of organizing knowledge on a particular issue so that it becomes more than a set of random observations. An economic model explains how the economy or part of the economy works. The terms *model* and *theory* are often used interchangeably. By their very nature models are simplifications of the real-world phenomena they attempt to explain, and model building is an exercise in abstract thinking.

Microeconomic models examine the behavior of individual decision makers—individuals, households, firms, and government agents—or specific markets. We use microeconomic models to study how a patient's demand for a particular diagnostic test varies depending on the out-of-pocket cost of the test. We can examine how a shortage of qualified nurses affects nurses' salaries or how the relative income of specialists affects the demand for residency-training positions in all specialties.

Problem Solving

Economics emerged as a science in the late eighteenth century with the publication of Adam Smith's *The Wealth of Nations.* Since that time a wealth of theory has accumulated to help us understand and describe **economizing behavior**. Most microeconomic theory can be classified under the framework of **neoclassical economics**. Relying heavily on the rationality assumption, the neoclassical framework classifies all decision makers as optimizers—those who attempt to maximize their well-being. **Optimizing behavior**, or optimization, is nothing more than a decision maker seeking to accomplish certain objectives—maximize sales or profit, minimize cost, or maximize income. Economists often talk of decision-making calculus, which refers to the notion that individuals make mental calculations before arriving upon a decision. Optimization fits the calculus model well—evaluating a mathematical function for its maximum or minimum value.

Economic Optimization

When more than one alternative is available, the optimal choice produces an outcome that is most consistent with the decision maker's stated objectives. Optimization is nothing more than discovering the best course of action given the decision maker's goals and objectives. Constrained optimization takes into consideration the cost and availability of resources. Would it be better for the hospital to enter into a contract for housekeeping services with an outside firm or should this activity be performed in-house? Following an increase in patient volume, should physicians in a small group practice hire an office manager, an additional nurse, or both?

economizing behavior
When individuals choose to limit their demand for goods and services voluntarily to save money.

neoclassical economics
A branch of economic thought using microeconomic principles to defend the efficacy of perfectly competitive markets in resource allocation.

optimizing behavior (or optimization)
A technique used to determine the best or most favorable outcome in a particular situation.

positive analysis
A factually based statement whose validity can be tested empirically.

normative analysis
An economic statement based on opinion or ideology.

ISSUES IN MEDICAL CARE DELIVERY

POSITIVE AND NORMATIVE ANALYSIS

To a great extent we will mix positive and normative analysis in our discussions. **Positive analysis** is the testing of hypotheses against facts. It examines the way things are. **Normative analysis** prescribes policies and actions to achieve certain goals. It purports to examine the way things ought to be.

The differences between positive and normative statements are easy to spot. "The United States spends more money per capita on medical care than any other country in the world" is an example of a positive statement. "Congress should guarantee universal insurance coverage by requiring all employers to provide health insurance to their workers" is a normative statement.

Positive statements are either true or false. It is the task of science to determine which they are. Normative statements are matters of opinion. Science is of little help in determining their legitimacy. Fuchs (1996), in a survey of 90 economists concerning issues in health economics and health policy, found that over 90 percent disagreed with the positive statement, "In the long run employers bear the primary burden of their contributions to employees' health insurance." In contrast, opinion was divided almost equally on the normative statement, "National standardized health insurance benefit packages should be established." Disputes over factual information can be settled through careful observation and analysis. Settling disputes over differences of opinion, on the other hand, is almost never easy. In fact, disagreements among economists are typically disputes over normative issues. These disagreements represent differences of opinion based on differences in ideology.

 Key Concept 1
Scarcity and Choice

Key Concept 8
Efficiency

Choices in health care delivery must be made at two levels: (1) individual physicians must decide on a particular course of treatment for a particular patient; and (2) policymakers must decide on a course of action in planning the health services availability for an entire community. The delivery of health care in any form must answer the following questions: whom to treat; when to begin treatment; where to treat; and how much treatment to offer? Of the many ways to go about choosing the best alternatives, economic efficiency will be the criterion examined in this section.

The framework for our analysis is the neoclassical economic model with its assumption of rational behavior on the part of all decision makers. Firms attempt to maximize profit given production technology and the cost of available resources. Consumers attempt to maximize satisfaction subject to limited money income and the prices of goods consumed. Workers supply labor services in an attempt to maximize satisfaction derived from goods and services consumed and leisure time available subject to current wages. Together, this more or less independent behavior results in markets that tend toward equilibrium as represented by the familiar, or soon to be familiar, supply and demand framework.

 Key Concept 3
Marginal Analysis

marginal benefit
The change in total benefits resulting from a one-unit change in the level of output.

marginal cost
The change in total cost resulting from a one-unit change in the level of output.

Within this framework, what does optimal mean? Using the rhetoric of economics, it means that individuals will continue to purchase a good or service as long as the **marginal benefits** from consumption (MB) exceed the **marginal costs** (MC). Given that marginal benefits are declining and marginal costs increasing as more of the good is consumed, eventually the two are equal. As soon as $MB = MC$, equilibrium is reached and the individual will consume no more. In Figure 2.1, the total benefits (TB) received from a medical procedure increase as more care is provided, but at

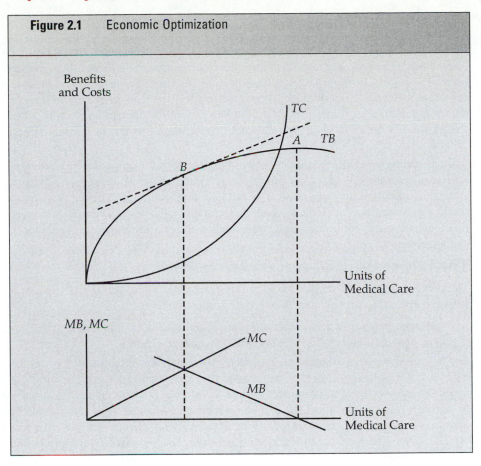

Figure 2.1   Economic Optimization

a decreasing rate. For reasons both ethical and practical, medical practitioners tend to provide additional care as long as the treatment results in positive benefits. Beyond point *A*, additional medical care is considered equivocal or wasteful—the marginal benefits are not worth the medical risk.

From the perspective of economics, exhausting all possible medical benefits wastes scarce resources. In fact, any care provided beyond point *B* is wasteful—the marginal benefits received from the additional care fall short of the marginal costs.[3] Because cost measures forgone opportunities in economics, the resources used up in providing the excess care could be put to better use somewhere else. Money wasted in the provision of unnecessary care cannot be used to further other important goals, such as improving education, repairing the interstate highway system, or cleaning up the environment.

When consumption is being subsidized, as in the case of medical care purchased with insurance, the cost to the consumer is less than the total resource cost. In the case of the insurance subsidy for medical care, the cost of an extra unit of care to the individual is close to zero, providing an incentive to consume medical care with low marginal benefits. When the marginal cost to the consumer is artificially low, resources are treated as if they have little or no value—a prescription for overconsumption. This tendency to overconsume means that medical care consumption is likely to be closer to point *A* (where the marginal benefit is close to zero) than point *B* (where marginal benefit is equal to marginal cost)—a phenomenon called flat-of-the-curve medicine.[4]

Key Concept 2
Opportunity Cost

Key Concept 9
Market Failure

---

3 In this discussion cost is measured in terms of total resource cost, the actual opportunity cost of the resources consumed in the production of medical care and not merely the out-of-pocket cost to the consumer.
4 The phrase "flat-of-the-curve" is attributed to Alain Enthoven (1980).

Supply and Demand

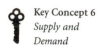

Key Concept 6
*Supply and
Demand*

Many consider supply and demand the two most useful concepts in economics. Regardless of the issue being studied, the analysis often hinges on some aspect of supply and demand. The theory of supply and demand is also a powerful tool in predicting future behavior. How does a change in price affect the consumer's willingness or ability to purchase a commodity? How does a change in the price of a key input affect the producer's decision of the optimal input combination to use in the production process?

In modeling behavior, economists attempt to simplify relationships. The amount of a particular commodity that a consumer plans to purchase depends on several factors. Instead of looking at the large number of variables that would affect demand, we focus on the most important ones: the price of the commodity, the price of related commodities, the number of people desiring the commodity, and consumer income, preferences, and expectations.

The Law of Demand

The theory of demand occupies such an important place in economic analysis that it has been given the status of a law. The law of demand states

There is an inverse relationship between the amount of a commodity that a person will purchase and the sacrifice that must be made to obtain it.

The higher the price of an item, the less is purchased, and the lower the price, the more purchased. It is important to understand that this inverse (negative) relationship holds as long as the circumstances of the consumer do not change materially. Remember, other things affect the demand relationship—prices of related items, the consumer's income, and preferences. As long as there are no changes in these other factors, the inverse relationship holds. When prices rise, less is desired. When prices fall, more is desired.

Changes in price affect the demand relationship in two very important ways. First, consumers have alternative ways to spend their money. If the price of a name-brand drug goes up, an alternative drug or even a generic can be substituted for the name brand. Or if money is tight and no insurance coverage is available, the patient can choose to skip the treatment and let the disease run its course. In any case, when price rises, the quantity demanded goes down. Economists refer to this phenomenon as the substitution effect.

A change in price affects the consumer in another important way. Paying higher prices for a desired commodity reduces the consumer's overall level of satisfaction. Spending more for one item leaves less to spend on everything else. With less money to spend, the consumer is unable to buy as much of everything else as before and thus feels worse off. This aspect of a price change on quantity demanded is called the income effect.

Part (a) of Figure 2.2 illustrates how an increase in price affects quantity demanded. Suppose that the demand for a particular commodity is represented by the demand curve D_1. Assuming no other changes, an increase in the price from P_0 to P_1 will reduce the amount demanded from Q_0 to Q_1. This is depicted by a movement along the stationary demand curve from point A to point B. A change in price, holding everything else constant, changes quantity demanded.

Many factors other than price influence our purchasing decisions. These other factors are sometimes referred to as *ceteris paribus* conditions (remember, economics has a language of its own). The *ceteris paribus* conditions are factors that are held constant when examining the relationship between price and quantity demanded. They include:

- The price of related commodities

- The number and type of people desiring the commodity

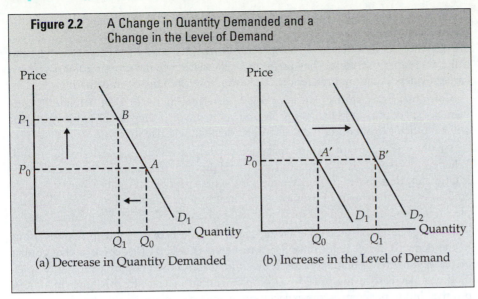

Figure 2.2   A Change in Quantity Demanded and a Change in the Level of Demand

(a) Decrease in Quantity Demanded

(b) Increase in the Level of Demand

- Consumer income
- Consumer preferences
- Consumer expectations about future prices and product availability

A change in the price of a related commodity changes the demand for the commodity in question. Related commodities are either substitutes or complements. An increase in the price of a substitute increases the demand for a commodity. Coronary artery bypass graft surgery (CABGS) and cardiac angioplasty are two procedures used to accomplish the same outcome. If the price of CABGS increases, heart patients (or at least whoever is paying for the procedure) will view cardiac angioplasty as a more viable alternative. The demand for cardiac angioplasty will increase. When the price of a complement goes down, demand goes up. Complementary goods are consumed together. Dentists often recommend that full-mouth X-rays accompany the annual dental exam. X-rays complement the annual exam. If the price of the X-ray goes down, more patients will make appointments for dental exams.

An increase in the size of the population or its composition affects demand. More people means a higher demand for all goods and services—including medical care. The addition of an infant to a family increases the demand for visits to the pediatrician. An increase in the birth rate raises the demand for disposable diapers even if the average baby still uses the same number of diapers per day. An older population has a higher demand for treatments for chronic illnesses such as arthritis and emphysema.[5]

A change in income affects the consumer's ability to purchase goods and services. In situations where higher income leads to increased demand, the good in question is referred to as a normal good. In some cases, an increase in income leads to a decrease in demand. In those situations, the good is called an inferior good. Medical care is usually considered a normal good. For individuals with comparable levels of health, higher income means a higher demand for medical care.

Consumer preferences play a key role in determining an individual's demand for goods and services. Some flu sufferers will consider a visit to the physician only as a last resort. They prefer to treat their ailment with over-the-counter medications.

---

5 The examples point out the importance of distinguishing between the individual demand and market demand. Clearly, the market demand curve is determined by combining the demand curves of all the individuals actively participating in the market.

Some people hold religious beliefs (e.g., Christian Scientists) that strongly discourage the use of medical care. They prefer the power of prayer over the power of medicine. Others are convinced of the efficacy of chiropractors, herbalists, acupuncturists, midwives, and other alternative providers. They prefer these alternatives to the more traditional health care providers. A shift in preferences can have a powerful impact on demand.

Consumer expectations play a key role in determining the level of demand. If consumers expect prices to change steeply and suddenly or if they are afraid the product will be difficult to obtain in the near future, demand will rise sharply.

Finally, it is important to note that the demand for resources is a derived demand. Whenever a resource is used to produce a final product, the demand for that resource is ultimately determined by the demand for the final product. If medical care is considered an essential element in promoting the health of an individual or a group of people, an increase in the demand for health will increase the demand for medical care.

A change in one of these other factors changes the level of demand and causes a shift in the demand curve. Refer once again to Figure 2.2. Part (b) depicts a change that increases the level of demand caused by an increase in the price of a substitute commodity, a decrease in the price of a complement, an increase in consumer income, a positive shift in preferences, the expectation of a price increase, or a decline in availability in the future. Suppose the level of demand is originally D_1 in part (b). At the price P_0, the quantity demanded is Q_0. With the price held constant, an increase in consumer income will cause a rightward shift in the demand curve to D_2. This shift in the demand curve depicts an increased demand for the commodity. The consumer will now desire Q_1 at the price P_0.

To summarize, a change in the price of a commodity or service, holding everything else constant, will result in a change in quantity demanded, shown as a movement along a stationary demand curve. A change in any of the factors that affect the level of demand results in a shift in the demand curve—more or less of the commodity or service is demanded at every price level.

Price Elasticity of Demand

An important corollary to the law of demand is the concept of price elasticity of demand. The law of demand is used to answer the question: When price changes, what is the effect on quantity demanded? Taking this notion one step further, price elasticity of demand is a technical concept used to answer the question: When price changes, how much does quantity demanded change? The inverse relationship between price and quantity is relatively easy to comprehend. In most cases it is important to include not only the direction of the change but the magnitude of the change.

Price elasticity of demand measures consumer responsiveness to a change in price, holding the other variables that affect demand constant. Slope also measures the relationship between quantity demanded and price. But slope is not elasticity. Slope measures the change in quantity demanded that results from a price change in absolute terms; elasticity measures the change in relative terms.

Price elasticity of demand is defined as the percentage change in quantity demanded divided by the percentage change in price. Formally, price elasticity (ε_p) is calculated as

$$\varepsilon_p = \frac{\text{percentage change in } Q}{\text{percentage change in } P}$$

where Q is quantity demanded and P is the unit price.

If consumer demand increases 10 percent because of a 5 percent price decrease, price elasticity of demand is 10 percent divided by 5 percent, or 2.0.[6] Values for the elasticity coefficient range from zero (0) to infinity (∞).

---

6 The actual calculation is $[(+0.10)/(-0.05) = -2.0]$. While the price elasticity coefficient is always negative, for simplicity we usually ignore the negative sign, or more precisely consider its absolute value.

A summary of all possible values for the price elasticity coefficient is provided in Table 2.1. In the case where price elasticity equals zero, consumers are completely unresponsive to changes in price. Their consumption patterns are fixed and a higher price does not affect quantity demanded. Under these circumstances demand is said to be perfectly inelastic, or totally unresponsive. The demand for addictive substances may come about as close to perfectly inelastic demand as anything. The demand for life-saving procedures, such as kidney dialysis and organ transplants, may also fall into this category.

A more likely scenario would be the case where a price change has an impact on quantity demanded, but the consumer response is less than proportional. In other words, we consider consumer demand somewhat unresponsive when the percentage change in quantity demanded is less than the percentage change in price. In this case, the elasticity coefficient is less than one (1) and demand is inelastic. Even addicts and terminally ill patients have their limits on how much they are willing or able to pay for a desired commodity.

An elasticity that is greater than 1 represents a change in quantity demanded that is proportionately greater than the change in price. Consumers are said to be relatively responsive and in this case demand is elastic. In the rare case where the elasticity coefficient is equal to infinity, demand is perfectly elastic. Consumers are intolerant of even small changes in price and refuse to buy the item if its price goes up at all.

An important use of the concept of price elasticity is illustrated in the right-hand column of Table 2.1. When price changes, it is important to know how much quantity demanded changes. It is also important to realize that this same information enables us to predict what will happen to consumer expenditures. With perfectly elastic demand, any price increase causes quantity demanded to fall to zero. In this case it may be obvious that consumer expenditures also fall to zero. The case of unit elasticity may not be so obvious. When price elasticity equals 1, a 10 percent price increase causes quantity demanded to fall by 10 percent, and consumer expenditures do not change. Likewise, price increases cause consumer expenditures to fall when demand is elastic and to increase when demand is inelastic.

What determines the price elasticity of demand? Why are consumers more tolerant of price changes for some items and not others? Price elasticity depends primarily on the consumer's ability to find suitable substitutes for a good or service. The easier it is to substitute, the more elastic the consumer's demand. If the consumer

Table 2.1	Price Elasticity of Demand		
Coefficient Value	Nature of Demand	Impact of a 10 Percent Price Increase on Quantity Demanded	Impact of a 10 Percent Price Increase on Total Expenditures
$\lvert \varepsilon \rvert = \infty$	Perfectly elastic	Falls to 0	Falls to 0
$1 < \lvert \varepsilon \rvert < \infty$	Elastic	Decreases by more than 10 percent	Decreases
$\lvert \varepsilon \rvert = 1$	Unit elastic	Decreases exactly 10 percent	No change
$0 < \lvert \varepsilon \rvert < 1$	Inelastic	Decreases by less than 10 percent	Increases by less than 10 percent
$\lvert \varepsilon \rvert = 0$	Perfectly inelastic	No change	Increases by 10 percent

Back-of-the-Envelope

PRICE ELASTICITY AND HEALTH CARE SPENDING

One suggestion for reducing health care spending is to increase out-of-pocket spending for health services. By making the patient responsible for a larger share of the costs, the amount demanded will decrease. But by how much? Calculating the impact of an increase in the deductible or copayment makes use of estimates of the price elasticity of demand. Suppose the price elasticity of demand for physicians' visits is –0.2. Then:

$$\varepsilon_p = \frac{\text{percentage change in } Q}{\text{percentage change in } P} = -0.2$$

From this we can see that the percentage change in number of physicians' visits in response to a change in the net price to patients is

$$\text{percentage change in } Q = \text{percentage change in } P \times \varepsilon_p$$

Suppose that the insurance copayment increases from 20 percent to 30 percent (a 50 percent increase in the net price to the patient). The resulting change in the number of physicians' visits would be

$$\text{percentage change in } Q = 50\% \times (-0.2) = -10\%$$

If Americans visit their physicians an average of 5.8 times per year, a 10 percent decline in the number of physicians' visits per year would mean that per capita physicians' visits would decrease from 5.8 per year to 5.2.

Source: Joseph P. Newhouse, Charles E. Phelps, and M. S. Marquis, "On Having Your Cake and Eating It Too," *Journal of Econometrics* 13, 1980, 365–390.

perceives a number of good alternatives to the item, demand is likely to be more responsive to changes in price. Patients with no established preference for a general practitioner (GP) might view a 20 percent increase in the price of an office visit as intolerable in light of the number of suitable alternative GPs in practice. However, those individuals who have an established relationship with the GP may be willing to remain a loyal patient in spite of the price increase. In this case, the GP will lose some business but not all of it.

Other factors that influence the degree of consumer responsiveness are the proportion of a person's income spent on the item and the urgency of the purchase. If the cost of the item comprises a substantial portion of a consumer's total income, demand will likely be elastic. Consumers are more sensitive to a price change on the purchase of big-ticket items. Insulin-dependent diabetics are more sensitive to a change in the price of syringes than the typical nondiabetic patient. The diabetic patient buys a lot more syringes per year than the nondiabetic. Finally, demand for nonurgent procedures will be more elastic than demand for emergency procedures. The more time a patient has to make a decision, the more price sensitive he or she will likely be. A patient entering the emergency room with a compound fracture does not have much time to shop around for an orthopedic surgeon. Those patients desiring elective rhinoplasty have the opportunity and the luxury to shop around for the best plastic surgeon, the best price, the best financing, or whatever else they consider important. A patient who shops around is more likely to find suitable alternatives.

Demand curves are typically drawn as straight lines for the sake of simplicity. There are three possibilities, as shown in Figure 2.3. Perfectly inelastic demand curves

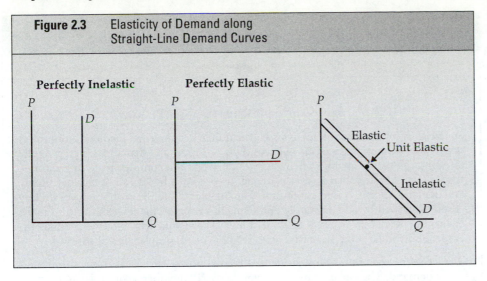

Figure 2.3   Elasticity of Demand along Straight-Line Demand Curves

are drawn as vertical lines indicating zero response, and perfectly elastic demand curves are depicted by horizontal lines. The typical downward-sloping demand curve is shown at the right. Although slope is the same at every point, elasticity is not. The relationship between slope and elasticity at any point on the demand curve can be shown to be

$$\varepsilon = \frac{\Delta Q/Q}{\Delta P/P} = \frac{P\Delta Q}{Q\Delta P} = \frac{P/Q}{slope}$$

where Q is the quantity demanded, P is the unit price, and Δ is used to represent a change in the variable.

A demand curve with a given slope has a constantly declining elasticity. Moving from the upper-left to the lower-right on a downward-sloping demand curve, the P/Q ratio is declining—as price falls, quantity demanded increases. It follows that the demand curve goes from elastic to inelastic as you move down a straight-line demand curve.[7]

The Law of Supply

The theory of supply assumes that decision makers (producers in this case) are faced with scarce resources and must choose among alternative uses. Supply decisions involve the valuation of resources among competing uses. The law of supply states

There is a direct relationship between the amount of a commodity that a producer will make available and the reward that is received.

The higher the price of an item, the greater is its availability. At lower prices, less will be available. Suppliers practice economizing behavior much like consumers do. The market rewards efficiency and punishes wastefulness.

Producers are concerned with cost. This concern is more than an accounting of the value of inputs. It involves establishing the opportunity cost of those inputs. In economics, cost reflects the value of resources in their next-best alternative use. In other words, forgone opportunities are an important element in determining value. Resources used in the production of one commodity are not available to produce another. Economizing behavior guarantees that resources will be used where they have the highest value. Therefore, cost is determined by the value of what is being given up to produce any item.

---

7 Economists sometime refer to an entire demand curve as inelastic if it is generally steep and elastic if generally flat. While technically incorrect, as a matter of convenience we often think in these terms.

ISSUES IN MEDICAL CARE DELIVERY

HOW TO SURVIVE SUPPLY AND DEMAND

Succeeding in any economics course (including a course in medical economics) depends on your mastery of the twin concepts of supply and demand. Listen carefully to economic commentators when they are queried on a complex issue in economic theory or policy and their answer is frequently preceded by "It's all because of supply and demand." The introduction of supply and demand into the economics vocabulary is soon followed by adding supply and demand curves to the lexicon. In this hostile environment survival depends on your ability to keep your wits about you while others around you fail. To ensure your success follow these simple rules of survival.

- *Use common sense.* Most students already know a great deal about supply and demand. The key is to use what you know. Remember, economics is a way of thinking. For the most part, it is intuitive. Think about the market for oatmeal. Scientific evidence has suggested that consuming large quantities of oat products every day reduces the level of cholesterol in the bloodstream and thus the risk of heart attack.* What do you suppose happened to the demand for oatmeal and its price immediately after this information was made public? If you said that demand for oatmeal increased and its price also went up, then you already have some intuitive notion of the workings of supply and demand.

- *Learn the language.* After a few weeks in Econ 101, many students feel they are taking a foreign language. Mastery of economics requires that you learn the language of economists. When it comes to supply and demand, economists speak in graphs. Understand graphs and you understand supply and demand. If freshman literature were taught in Greek, it would be extremely difficult for the typical student. Not that the subject matter is so hard, it's the language. Introductory economics is taught in graphs. Learning to use graphs makes learning economics much easier.

- *Practice, practice, practice.* The rules of graphing are simple. Unlike a foreign language, there are no irregular verbs. But like a foreign language, it takes practice to master the subject matter. Practice whenever you can. Economics is not a spectator sport. Watching your professor manipulate graphs is not enough. You have to do it yourself. Remember, demand curves are downward sloping and supply curves are upward sloping. Economists place price on the vertical axis and quantity on the horizontal axis. Equilibrium price and quantity are determined by the intersection of the supply and demand curves.

- *Shift the appropriate curve.* The discovery that oat products have health benefits affects the market for oats. Does it affect supply or demand or both? Remember what causes shifts in the two curves. For the supply curve to shift, a change in the cost or profitability of making a product available to the market is needed. For the demand curve, it is usually anything that increases the willingness or ability of consumers to buy something. The discovery that oatmeal works like Roto-Rooter to clean out your arteries will affect consumers' willingness to buy the product. So the demand curve will shift. Will it shift to the right or to the left? If in doubt at this step, go back to step one. An increase in demand will increase price. The only way to get this result is to shift the demand curve to the right. Shifting the demand curve to the left or shifting the supply curve is counterintuitive.

It is now time to test your mastery of supply and demand. Consider the market for hospital services. Using a graph similar to the one in Figure 2.5 on page 38, label the vertical axis "Price of Hospital Services" and the horizontal axis "Quantity of Hospital Services." Draw the supply and demand curves and identify the equilibrium price and quantity of hospital services. Now suppose that due to a nursing shortage, the average salary paid to nurses increases 10 percent. What affect will this increased cost have on the market for hospital services?

*See Cynthia M. Ripsin, Joseph M. Keenan, David R. Jacobs, et al., "Oat Products and Lipid Lowering: A Meta-Analysis," *Journal of the American Medical Association* 267(24), June 24, 1992, 3317–3325.

Part (a) of Figure 2.4 illustrates how a change in the price of a commodity affects quantity supplied. Suppose that supply is depicted by the curve S_1. Assuming no other changes, an increase in price from P_0 to P_1 will increase the quantity supplied from Q_0 to Q_1. At higher prices, suppliers will transfer resources to the production of the higher-priced commodity making more of it available to the market. A change in price, holding everything else constant, results in a change in quantity supplied and is depicted by a movement along the stationary supply curve.

Many other factors affect the availability of goods and services in a market. A change in one of these factors, the *ceteris paribus* conditions, will change the level of supply. These other factors that affect the level of supply include:

- The prices of resources used to produce the commodity
- The number of firms supplying the commodity
- The state of technology
- Producer expectations about future prices and availability

In general, anything that changes the costs of producing a commodity will affect the level of supply. Resources have alternative uses. In order to use resources to produce a particular commodity, producers must bid them away from their next best alternative use. An increase in the price of a resource decreases the supply of the commodity that uses the resource as an input in the production process and raises its price. Technicians trained to operate the new magnetic resonance imaging (MRI) machines are in short supply. As competition bids up their wages, the cost of providing MRI services increases, shifting the supply curve for MRIs to the left and raising the price of this service in the market.

Figure 2.4 A Change in Quantity Supplied and a Change in the Level of Supply

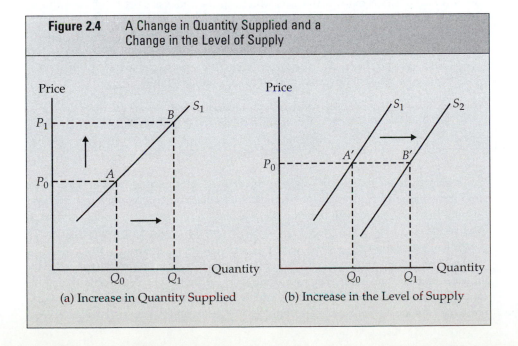

(a) Increase in Quantity Supplied

(b) Increase in the Level of Supply

Back-of-the-Envelope

PRICE FLOORS AND PRICE CEILINGS

In their zeal to control rising medical care prices, policymakers are sometimes tempted to pursue a price fixing strategy. If prices are currently too high, why not roll them back to lower levels? Simply legislate a price that is below the current equilibrium price. In the graph at the left, suppose the legislature sets a maximum price of P_c, below the equilibrium price P_e. This **price ceiling** does two things: (1) it reduces the availability of medical care from Q_e to Q_s and (2) it increases the amount requested to Q_d. The difference between Q_d and Q_s represents a shortage in the medical market. The shortage manifests itself in terms of longer delays in getting appointments, longer waits at physicians' offices, reduced access to high-tech surgical and diagnostic equipment, and lower quality of care.

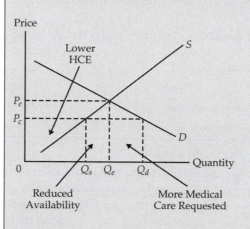

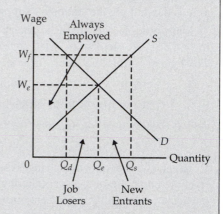

Suppose the market for unskilled labor is depicted by the graph at the right. Without government intervention firms pay workers W_e and employ Q_e. If the government raises the cost of hiring workers by mandating that all firms provide health insurance for their employees, the cost of this new benefit raises the effective wage to W_f. This **price floor** reduces quantity demanded and increases quantity supplied. The job losers, when added to the new entrants, add to the number of unemployed workers in the labor market. Workers who keep their jobs are better off. But those who lose their jobs because of the mandate are noticeably worse off.

Policymakers are desperate to control medical care spending. Many feel that desperate times call for desperate measures. Some even think that their ability to write laws also applies to the laws of supply and demand. Governments have been trying for centuries to rewrite those laws and all have failed miserably.

Note: For a history of government price controls, see Robert L. Schuettinger and Eamonn F. Butler, *Forty Centuries of Wage and Price Controls: How Not to Fight Inflation*, Washington, D.C.: Heritage Foundation, 1978.

price ceiling
The maximum price that can be charged for a good or service, set by law.

price floor
The minimum price that can be charged for a good or service, set by law.

An increase in the number of suppliers increases access to a product or service. More suppliers means that consumers have more choices. The construction of a new 250-bed hospital in a community will increase the availability of inpatient hospital services to local residents. At any given price per day, there are now more beds available to serve the patient population.

New technology that reduces the cost of producing a commodity or service increases the level of supply. The case of medical technology presents certain analytical problems that make it difficult to evaluate the different supply responses of cost-reducing and quality-enhancing technology. Arthroscopic surgery provides a clear

Back-of-the-Envelope

THE IMPACT OF AN EXCISE TAX

The excise tax is becoming an increasingly popular way of imposing user fees on the consumption of specific items, such as gasoline, tobacco, and alcohol. Excise taxes may be set at a fixed dollar amount or a percentage of selling price—called either a *specific tax* or an *ad valorem tax.*

In a competitive market, price and output are determined by the interaction of supply and demand. The commodity will sell for the price P_e, and Q_e will be purchased. An excise tax of a fixed amount will raise the cost of providing the commodity to the market and shift the supply curve leftward to the curve labeled $S + tax$. The dollar magnitude of the shift (measured by the vertical distance between the two supply curves) will be exactly equal to the specific tax.

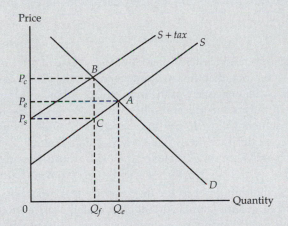

The new equilibrium price will be P_c. Because producers are legally responsible for paying the tax, they only net P_s from the transaction. The difference between the price consumers pay and the price producers receive is the amount of the excise tax. At the higher price, consumers buy less of the commodity, Q_t instead of Q_e. The excise tax generates revenues for the government of P_sP_cBC. The higher price and lower output causes a loss in surplus value—a **deadweight loss** from the tax of ABC.

The impact of this loss is minimized when the lost output is small, that is, when the demand curve is inelastic. It should come as no surprise that excise taxes on cigarettes, alcohol, health insurance, and hospital stays have been proposed as financing alternatives for the various health care reform options. Whenever taxes on alcohol and cigarettes are discussed, the tax is often called a "sin tax."

deadweight loss
The combined loss in consumer and producer surplus resulting from price variations above the competitive equilibrium price due to monopoly or government action.

example of a technological advance that represents both a cost-reducing and quality-enhancing change. The repair of a damaged anterior cruciate ligament was once a major ordeal for both surgeon and patient. Before the introduction of the laparoscope, an athlete who suffered this knee injury was faced with a four-hour surgery requiring a six-inch incision, several days in the hospital, and six weeks on crutches. Today, the same procedure can be performed as outpatient surgery. It requires three small incisions and a much shorter rehabilitation.

If suppliers expect the price of a commodity or service to fall in the future, they have an incentive to make it immediately available. Or if for some reason suppliers expect an increase in future availability, current supply will increase. As the medical marketplace moves systematically toward the managed care model, physicians are scrambling to join provider networks. Expectations create powerful incentives. As more physicians join networks, fueling expectations, others feel an urgency to join them.

An increase in the level of supply is illustrated graphically in part (b) of Figure 2.4. Anything that enhances a producer's ability to bring a product to the market increases the level of supply and results in a rightward shift in the supply curve. A decrease in resource costs, an increase in the number of providers, a technological advance that increases production efficiency, and the expectation of downward-price movements increase the level of supply and cause the supply curve to shift to the right. Suppose that the supply curve shifts from S_1 to S_2. At any given price level, say P_0, providers will be willing to increase the amount supplied from Q_0 to Q_1.

To summarize, a change in the price of a commodity or service, holding everything else constant, will result in a change in the quantity supplied. This change is shown as a movement along a stationary supply curve. A change in any of the factors that affect the level of supply results in a shift in the supply curve and more of the commodity or service available at any given price.

Equilibrium

Price changes affect buyers and sellers differently. An increase in price reduces the consumer's willingness to buy and at the same time increases the producer's willingness to provide. The most fascinating aspect of the marketplace is how this more or less independent behavior of buyers and sellers results in an allocation of resources that guarantees that all consumers willing to pay the market price find willing sellers and all sellers willing to accept the price find willing buyers. Adam Smith observed that it is as if some "invisible hand" were responsible for the price adjustments that promote the best use of resources.

We define the equilibrium price as the market price that exists where the quantity demanded equals the quantity supplied. Suppose that the price of the commodity depicted in Figure 2.5 is P_1. At that price, producers would like to sell more than consumers are willing to buy. There is a surplus because the quantity supplied is greater than the quantity demanded. In the medical marketplace, when prices are too high, hospitals, for example, will have unused capacity. This excess capacity takes the form of idle resources, empty beds, and unused operating rooms. Physicians find their appointment books unfilled and their waiting rooms empty. A surplus serves to increase competition among providers. The competition may manifest itself in many ways, but one sure way to eliminate the surplus and increase quantity demanded is to lower prices.

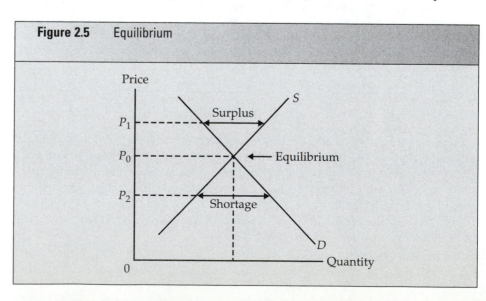

Figure 2.5   Equilibrium

At the price P_2, quantity demanded exceeds quantity supplied, resulting in a shortage. Patients experience significant delays in getting appointments. When they do get an appointment, the waiting room is crowded and delays are frequent. Nonemergency surgeries have to be scheduled far in advance. Access to diagnostic imaging equipment is limited. Under these conditions prices have a tendency to adjust upwards. Competition among consumers bids prices up and reduces quantity demanded. Coupled with an increase in quantity supplied, the shortage is eliminated.

Only one price does not result in either a surplus or a shortage. That price, P_0, the equilibrium price, clears the market. At P_0 the behavior of buyers and sellers coincides. Buyers are willing to pay the price that providers are willing to accept. Everyone who wants to buy at P_0 is able to buy and everyone who wants to sell at that price is able to sell. In a market economy, people are free to make transactions: They are free to bid for goods and services at any price and free to offer those same goods and services at any price. When buyers seek the lowest price that producers are willing to accept and sellers seek the highest price that consumers are willing to pay, the transactions price that clears the market is the equilibrium price.

The Competitive Model

Free markets play a crucial role in the free enterprise system. The market system is grounded in the concept of consumer sovereignty: that what is produced is determined by what people want and are able to buy. No one individual or group dictates what must be produced or purchased. No one limits the range of choice.

The market accomplishes its task of resource allocation through a system of prices: what Adam Smith called the "invisible hand." In a market system, resources can be allocated by this invisible hand because everyone and everything has a price. There is a tendency for prices to increase if more is desired or decrease if less is desired.

Key Concept 5
Markets and Pricing

Firms base their production decisions on relative prices and relative price movements. The price mechanism becomes a way of bringing a firm's output decisions into balance with consumer desires—something that we refer to as equilibrium.

Prices serve not only as a signal to producers but as a means of rewarding popular decisions. Producers who invest in appropriate technology are able to produce goods and services desired by consumers. Their rewards come in the form of profits. Poor decisions are in turn punished by the market and the producer suffers losses. This market discipline, accompanied by the freedom to compete within a system that allows private property ownership, is largely responsible for the efficient use of resources.

Key Concept 7
Competition

The Theory of Firm Behavior

One desirable outcome of a perfectly competitive marketplace is the efficient use of resources. The characteristics of the model of perfect competition are (1) many buyers and sellers, (2) a standardized product, (3) mobile resources, and (4) perfect information. These characteristics guarantee that risk-adjusted rates of return will be equal to the normal rate of return for the economy, that prices are equal to minimum average cost of production, and that all transactions beneficial to both buyer and seller will take place.

Every firm must decide how much to produce and what price to charge. The choice of an output level and a pricing strategy are ultimately determined by the firm's costs. In a perfectly competitive market the pricing decision is easy because the product is standardized and firms must follow the dictates of the market. Firms that charge more than the market price lose customers. At the other extreme, firms have no incentive to charge a lower price because they find willing customers at the market price. Firms are called price takers.

Figure 2.6 provides an illustration of the perfectly competitive market. Market price is determined by the interaction of supply and demand in part (a). At the price P_0, the representative firm can sell all it can produce. A profit maximizer will produce every unit of output where the selling price is greater than the marginal cost of production—as long as P_0 is greater than MC. Because the competitive firm is a price taker, its demand curve is perfectly elastic at the market-determined price. In the case of a horizontal demand curve, the firm's marginal revenue (MR) curve is equal to price. Profit is maximized where $MR = MC$, or at q_0 units of output.

Key Concept 8
Efficiency

Competitive forces will lead to prices equilibrating at minimum average costs. At a price above P_0, price is greater than the average cost of production. Firms enjoy excess profits (higher than normal rates of return), encouraging the entry of new firms into the market. As these new entrants establish their presence, supply increases and prices fall until all excess profits are eliminated.

Welfare Implications

Consider another way to look at demand and supply curves. Instead of viewing the demand curve as the amount demanded at various prices, it can be interpreted as the maximum price that consumers are willing to pay for each unit of a product. Likewise, the supply curve can be interpreted as the minimum price that providers are willing to accept for each unit of a product. From this perspective, demand curves may be viewed as "willingness-to-pay" curves; supply curves viewed as "willingness-to-provide" curves.

Consumer Surplus

Value depends on the consumer's willingness to pay. Items are valued for the utility they provide when purchased and consumed. In free markets consumers do not pay more for a good than the subjective value they place on it. In fact, much of the time the value placed on an item exceeds its price. In those instances, when value exceeds price, consumers enjoy surplus value, or what is called consumer surplus.

In Figure 2.7, the demand curve DD' represents the maximum price that consumers are willing to pay to obtain a good—its subjective value. At the equilibrium price P_0, consumer surplus is depicted as the difference between the value consumers place on the good (shown by the demand curve itself) and the price they must pay (P_0). All Q_0 units of output sold have surplus value. The triangular area between the demand curve and the price, P_0AD, shows total consumer surplus.

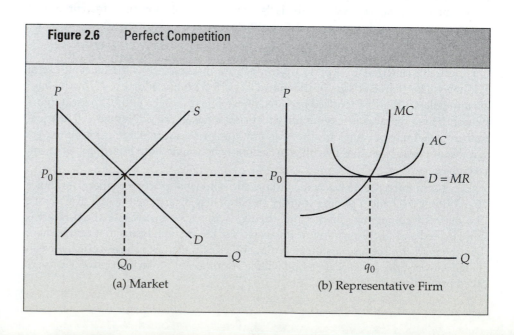

Figure 2.6   Perfect Competition

(a) Market

(b) Representative Firm

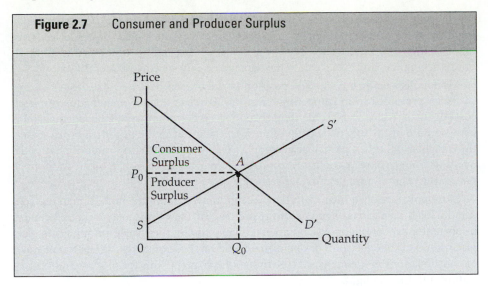

Figure 2.7   Consumer and Producer Surplus

Producer Surplus

In the case of voluntary exchange, surplus value is created for both consumers and producers. A producer's willingness to provide goods and services is determined to a great extent by the opportunity cost of the resources used in production. Supply curves reflect these forgone opportunities. Producer surplus is defined as the difference between the price that is received and the minimum price that producers are willing to accept. Graphically, producer surplus is the area below the equilibrium price (P_0) and above the supply curve (SS').[8] Total producer surplus is the triangular area P_0AS.

Any output level other than Q_0 results in a loss of surplus value, and represents lost social welfare. In other words, given the demand and supply curves, DD' and SS', any price other than the perfectly competitive equilibrium price, P_0, represents an inefficient outcome.

Imperfect Competition

In the case of the medical marketplace, violations of the assumptions of perfect competition are common. Although the incidence of monopoly is rare, the number of providers often falls far short of the perfectly competitive ideal. For example, many communities around the United States are served by a single hospital. Many factors determine the strength of this monopoly status; among them are the relative ease of access to other hospitals and the urgency of the services provided. Monopoly power leads to monopoly returns, or excess payments. In the hospital industry these extra payments are used to cross-subsidize care for the indigent population.

Other violations of the assumptions of the perfectly competitive model include entry restrictions that limit the number of providers that can practice in a particular area. These restrictions come in the form of certification requirements (compulsory licensure for physicians) and limiting hospital privileges to certain providers. Information costs—in particular, unequal distribution of information between patient and provider—also present impediments to the market.

Key Concept 9
Market Failure

Supply-Side Imperfections

Imperfections on the supply side of the market allow providers to enjoy monopoly returns. These imperfections usually deal with the nature of the rivalry or the lack of rivalry among firms. Too few firms, a nonstandardized product, barriers to entry, and information problems manifest themselves in the medical marketplace.

---

8 Remember, the supply curve represents the subjective value providers place on the resources used to produce the good or service—its opportunity cost.

The presence of a single firm in a market is referred to as monopoly. As the sole provider in a market, monopolists have market power—the ability to set a price. This market power is inversely related to the elasticity of demand for whatever the monopolist is selling. The more inelastic is the demand, the greater the market power.

Monopolists enjoy their special position in the market because for various reasons rivals are prevented from competing effectively. Barriers to entry may be the result of cost advantages due to size, something economists call economies of scale. Barriers may exist because of the sole ownership of an essential input in the production process or the franchise rights to a particular geographic region. These barriers can arise naturally or result from legal restrictions on competitors. Whatever the source of the monopoly power, the result is a single provider serving a given market.

Monopoly is really quite rare in the U.S. economy, even in the medical marketplace. A more likely scenario is oligopoly, or the presence of a few firms in a market. The most important aspect of oligopolistic markets is the nature of the rivalry among firms. The pricing and output decisions of one firm depend on those of its rivals. The recent wave of consolidations in the managed care industry is bringing this form of market organization into the spotlight.

A single firm or even a small number of firms does not dominate many local markets, especially those that deal in services. Often, many small firms attempt to differentiate themselves from their competitors by serving these markets by various means. Successful differentiation leads to market power. The degree of market power depends on how different the product is from its alternatives. A market with a large number of suppliers selling a variety of similar products is classified as monopolistic competition.

In all cases of imperfect competition, the firms share a common characteristic: They face downward-sloping demand curves. Firms in perfectly competitive markets, facing horizontal demand curves, have no market power—they are price takers. Whenever a demand curve is downward sloping, the pricing strategy changes. Market power allows firms to set a higher price, one that increases profit. Firms that find themselves in this situation are called price searchers.

Figure 2.8 illustrates the pricing and output strategy of the price searcher.[9] Faced with a downward-sloping demand curve the firm must choose the profit-maximizing price

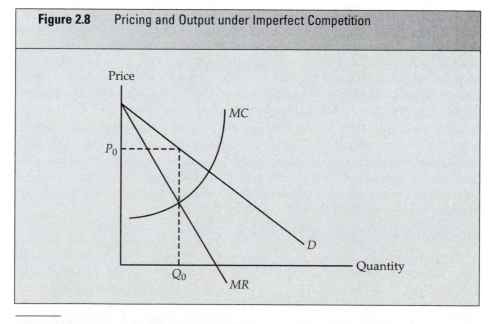

Figure 2.8   Pricing and Output under Imperfect Competition

---

9 The model discussed here is that of the single-priced monopolist, one that sells to each customer at the same price. Other pricing strategies include price discrimination where different consumers are charged different prices depending on their price elasticity of demand.

and quantity. The price searcher is confronted with a marginal revenue curve that is situated below the downward-sloping demand curve. When the demand curve is downward sloping, the firm must lower price to sell more of the product. As a result, the extra revenue from the sale of one more unit of output is less than its price. To sell the extra unit of output, the provider must lower the price on all the output that could have been sold at a higher price. In other words, the marginal revenue curve is below the demand curve. It has the same intercept on the price axis and twice the slope.[10] Although the rule-of-thumb for profit maximization is the same, $MR = MC$, the intersection takes place below the demand curve. So the profit-maximizing output is lower than in the case of perfect competition, and the resulting price is higher.

Whether the price searcher makes a profit depends a great deal on the nature of the entry barriers. A monopolist can expect to maintain profits as long as the level of demand is maintained. In contrast, firms in monopolistic competition will see profits eliminated because profits attract competitors and competition for market share results in lower prices, higher costs, and lower profits.

Demand-Side Imperfections

On the demand side of the market, imperfections manifest themselves in a number of ways—a limited number of buyers and imperfect information are two possibilities. The classic case of demand-side imperfections is called monopsony—a single buyer. This situation emerges in medical care when consumers form into groups to consolidate their purchasing power and get lower prices from insurers and providers. The Canadian single-payer system is an example of a monopsony.

As sole purchaser in the market, the monopsonist faces an upward-sloping supply curve and a marginal cost curve that is above the supply curve. Figure 2.9 illustrates the operation of a market with a single buyer. Faced with an upward-sloping supply curve, the monopsonist must pay increasingly higher prices to obtain more output, even on those items that could have been purchased at lower prices if less had been bought. The relevant purchasing decision takes into consideration the marginal cost of purchasing one more unit of output, not the opportunity cost of that last unit of output. Instead of equilibrium occurring where supply and demand are equal, the monopsonist equates marginal cost with demand.

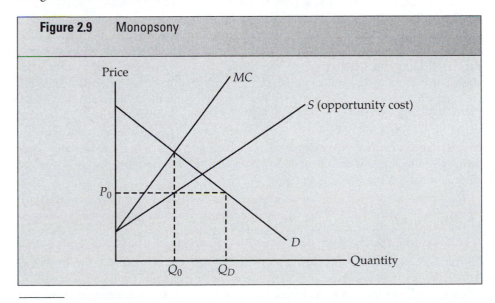

Figure 2.9   Monopsony

---

10 A mathematical proof of this proposition follows:

Demand curve:	$P = a + bQ$
Total revenue:	$TR = P \times Q = (a + bQ) \times Q = aQ + bQ^2$
Marginal revenue:	$MR = \dfrac{dTR}{dQ} = a + 2bQ$

PROFILE

Kenneth J. Arrow

Kenneth J. Arrow, known primarily for his work on general equilibrium and welfare economics, wrote what is considered by many to be one of the classic articles in the field of health economics. "Uncertainty and the Welfare Economics of Medical Care" (*American Economic Review*, 1963) has had as much impact on economic thinking as any single paper written in the modern era. Members of the International Health Economics Association considered his contribution so important that they named their annual award for the outstanding published paper in health economics after him.

Born of immigrant parents in 1921, Arrow spent his early childhood in relatively comfortable surroundings. His father's business, however, fared poorly during the Great Depression, forcing Arrow to attend City College, free at that time to residents of New York. Graduating at the age of 19 and unable to get a job, he decided to pursue graduate studies at Columbia in statistics. Even though his interests were in mathematical statistics, he switched to economics in order to receive financial aid. He soon discovered his interest in economics surpassed his love for statistics.

Arrow's early work completely revolutionized the way economists think about general equilibrium and social choice. Winner of the 1972 Nobel Prize in Economics at the age of 51, he is widely considered one of the most important figures in general economic equilibrium theory and welfare theory.

In his own words, he describes his contribution to health economics as "not so much a specific and well-defined technical accomplishment as a point of view that has served to reorient economic theory" (Breit and Spencer, 1995). Arrow's work to integrate uncertainty into economic models led to his 1963 paper on the economics of medical care. In it he was able to show that the key element in insurance markets was the difference in information between the buyers and sellers of insurance. The very existence of health insurance causes individuals to spend more on medical care than they would otherwise. His emphasis on moral hazard and adverse selection served to focus research in health economics on these important issues.

Arrow joined the U.S. Air Force during the Second World War where he served as a weather officer. His wartime contribution included important work on long-distance flight planning. At the time, the important theoretical work was all based on the assumption of a flat earth. Arrow's reformulation took into consideration the true nature of flight in a spherical world and helped determine optimal flight paths. After almost five years in the military, and still in his mid 20s, he returned to Columbia University to finish his graduate studies. Before receiving his Ph.D., he joined the Cowles Commission at the University of Chicago, but soon moved to Stanford University, where he became a full professor at age 32. By the end of his first decade in academics, he was named president of the Econometric Society and winner of the John Bates Clark medal given by the American Economic Association for the most distinguished work by an economist under the age of 40.

Most of his academic career has been spent at Stanford, except for 11 years at Harvard. He returned to Stanford in 1979 where he is currently emeritus Professor of Economics. In 1981 he was named Senior Fellow at the Hoover Institution. In addition to his many honors and affiliations, he has been President of the American Economic Association, The Institute of Management Sciences, the Western Economic Association, the American Association for the Advancement of Science, and the International Economic Association. Often quoted and frequently criticized, his work has been so far reaching that we may never fully appreciate the extent of his contribution to economic and political thought.

Source: "Kenneth J. Arrow," in *Lives of the Laureates*, 3rd ed., edited by William Breit and Roger W. Spencer, Cambridge, MA: The MIT Press, 1995, pp. 43–58; and "Interview with Kenneth Arrow," *The Region, Review of the Federal Reserve Bank of Minneapolis*, December 1995.

Monopsony equilibrium occurs at a lower level of output and a lower price than in the case of perfect competition. Society is worse off because fewer services are provided. At the lower price, quantity demanded (Q_D) exceeds quantity supplied (Q_0). The monopsonist exercises market power and creates a shortage that is not eliminated by competition with other purchasers, because none exists.

Summary and Conclusions

Economists seldom hesitate in applying economic tools in a variety of circumstances to evaluate individual choice behavior. This tendency should not be misinterpreted. Few members of the economics profession believe that economics provides all the answers. As you progress through this book, it will become obvious that the health care marketplace fails to achieve its theoretical optimum in many cases, making the strict application of the neoclassical model inappropriate. The goal of this book, however, is to show that economics can provide insights into the study of human decision making that few other disciplines offer.

The central message of economics presented in this chapter can be stated briefly:

- Resources are scarce relative to unlimited human wants. Inevitably, we must face the fact that resources used in the delivery of medical care have alternative beneficial uses. To strike a balance between scarce resources and unlimited wants involves making choices. We cannot have everything we want. In the world where most of us live, trade-offs are inevitable.

Key Concept 1
Scarcity and Choice

- Medical care decisions involve costs as well as benefits. For many clinicians, allowing cost considerations into treatment decisions is morally repugnant. To counter this feeling, it is essential that practitioners have a knowledge of the fundamentals of economics to provide a foundation for understanding the issues that affect medical care delivery and policy.

Key Concept 2
Opportunity Cost

- It is important to strike a balance between incremental benefits and incremental costs. Most choices in medical care involve determining the level of an activity, not its very existence. The issue is not whether it is beneficial to perform widespread screenings for colon cancer, but whether it is cost-effective to perform a sixth test when five have already been done (Neuhauser and Lewicki, 1975). Decision making is seldom based on an all-or-nothing proposition. It usually involves a trade-off. If we are to spend a little more on one thing, we must be willing to spend a little less on something else.

Key Concept 3
Marginal Analysis

- Human behavior is responsive to incentives and constraints. If you want people to practice economizing behavior, they must benefit individually from their own economizing. People spending other people's money show little concern for how it is spent. People spending their own money spend it more wisely.

Key Concept 4
Self-Interest

As concern over escalating costs grows, economics takes on a increasingly important role in the study of medical issues. Future clinicians must be well-grounded in economic theory. Only then can they help shape the debate on the future direction of medical care delivery.

Questions and Problems

1. What are the likely consequences on the U.S. market for tobacco products of the events listed below? Does the supply curve or the demand curve shift? In which direction? State whether the equilibrium price and quantity increase, decrease, or stay the same. Show the changes using a standard diagram with an upward-sloping supply curve and a downward-sloping demand curve.

   a. The Food and Drug Administration classifies tobacco an "addictive substance."

    b. The Congress votes to raise the excise tax on all tobacco products.

    c. Hurricane Fran dumps 15 inches of rain on North Carolina and destroys 80 percent of that state's tobacco crop.

    d. Sixteen states sue the major tobacco companies for billions of dollars because of tobacco-related costs in their Medicaid programs.

    e. Medical evidence that more than two cups of coffee a day (considered by many to be a substitute for smoking) greatly increases the risk of stomach cancer.

2. Choices in health care delivery must be made at two levels: (1) the individual physician prescribing a course of treatment for an individual patient and (2) the policy maker determining the availability of medical care to an entire group of patients or a community. One way to choose among alternative treatment regimes and community programs is by using the criterion of economic efficiency. Briefly describe the three types of appraisal that enter into medical economics. Discuss the unique features of each and describe their basic strengths and weaknesses.

3. What is the proper role of economics in the study of health and medical care? What does economics have to offer? What are its limitations?

4. "The laws of supply and demand are immutable. No one, including government, can affect a commodity's demand curve or supply curve." True or false? Comment.

5. Indicate whether the following statements are positive or normative.

    a. Smokers should pay higher health insurance premiums than nonsmokers.

    b. The United States should enact a comprehensive health care plan that provides universal coverage for all Americans regardless of their ability to pay.

    c. The primary reason for the escalation in health care spending over the past 30 years is the rapid development of expensive medical technology.

    d. The high cost of providing health care for their employees is a major reason that U.S. firms are not competitive with their foreign counterparts.

    e. Individuals born with certain genetic defects that predispose them to higher medical care spending over their lifetimes should be charged higher health insurance premiums than people without those defects.

6. (This problem is based on material discussed in Appendix 2B). The relationship between health care spending (E) and per capita national income (Y) was estimated using cross-section data from 24 developed countries. The resulting equation $E = 200 + 0.09\,Y$ relates spending and income in U.S. dollars.

    a. Interpret the coefficient on the national income variable.

    b. Complete the table.

Income	Health Care Spending
$ 5,000	
10,000	
15,000	
20,000	
25,000	

    c. Graph the relationship.

References

Michael Drummond, Greg Stoddart, Roberta LaBelle, and Robert Cushman, "Health Economics: An Introduction for Clinicians," *Annals of Internal Medicine 107*(1), July 1987, 88–92.

Alain Enthoven, *Consumer Choice Health Plan: The Only Practical Solution to the Soaring Cost of Medical Care,* Reading, MA: Addison-Wesley, 1980.

Victor R. Fuchs, "Economics, Values, and Health Care Reform," *American Economic Review 86*(1), March 1996, 1–24.

James W. Henderson, "The Cost Effectiveness of Prenatal Care," *Health Care Financing Review 15*(4), Summer 1994, 21–32.

Michael L. Ile, "When Health Care Payers Have Market Power," *Journal of the American Medical Association 263*(14), April 11, 1990, 1981–1982, 1986.

Willard G. Manning, Joseph P. Newhouse, Naihua Duan, Emmett B. Keeler, Arleen Leibowitz, and M. Susan Marquis, "Health Insurance and the Demand for Medical Care: Evidence from a Randomized Experiment," *American Economic Review 77*(3), June 1987, 251–277.

Duncan Neuhauser and Ann M. Lewicki, "What Do We Gain from the Sixth Stool Guaiac?" *New England Journal of Medicine 293*(5), July 31, 1975, 226–228.

Dorothy P. Rice, Sandler Kelman, Leonard S. Miller, and Sarah Dunmeyer, *The Economic Costs of Alcohol and Drug Abuse and Mental Illness: 1985,* San Francisco, CA: Institute for Health and Aging, University of California at San Francisco, 1990.

Anne A. Scitovsky and Dorothy P. Rice, "Estimates of the Direct and Indirect Costs of Acquired Immunodeficiency Syndrome in the United States, 1985, 1986, and 1991," *Public Health Reports 102*, 1987, 5–17.

Lester C. Thurow, "Medicine Versus Economics," *New England Journal of Medicine 313*(10), September 5, 1985, 611–614.

Appendix 2A

Graphing Data

Someone once said that a picture is worth a thousand words. Economists must take this axiom to heart. Seldom will an economist get far into a discussion without reaching for a pencil and paper. The picture often takes the form of a **graph**—one of several ways that economists use to convey ideas.

Some Basics of Graphing

Most graphs that we use in economics are two-variable graphs. The relationship between the two variables is illustrated by drawing two axes perpendicular to each other. The dependent variable is usually plotted on the vertical axis (or *y*-axis); the independent variable on the horizontal axis (or *x*-axis). Point *a* in Figure 2A.1 represents a combination of the variables *x* and *y* equal to x_0 and y_0, respectively. The *x-y* values for point *a* are called the **coordinates** of point *a*.

Graphs are used to describe relationships between variables. Scatter diagrams are often used for this purpose. The scatter diagram in Figure 2A.1 suggests that variable *x* and variable *y* are associated with one another—as the value of *x* increases the corresponding values of *y* are also larger. Economists use scatter diagrams to get a feel for the relationship between two variables, looking for linkages, a correlation, or simply a random pattern.

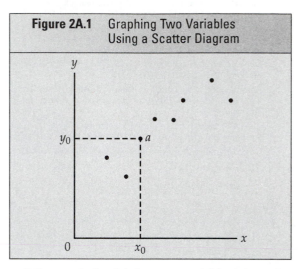

Figure 2A.1 Graphing Two Variables Using a Scatter Diagram

When a relationship between variables is hypothesized, it is often depicted by a linear function or curve. Straight-line relationships can be expressed by the familiar equation $y = mx + b$, where *m* is the slope of the line and *b* is its *y*-intercept. Graphically, this relationship is shown in part (a) of Figure 2A.2. The slope of a straight line is calculated by dividing the change in the variable on the *y*-axis (Δy) by the change in the variable on the *x*-axis (Δx). The slope of the curve in part (b) below is determined by the slope of its tangent (a straight line that touches the curve at only one point).

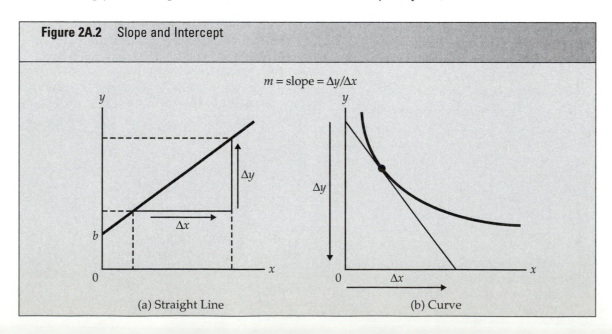

Figure 2A.2 Slope and Intercept

$$m = \text{slope} = \Delta y/\Delta x$$

(a) Straight Line

(b) Curve

The slope of a function or curve is a convenient way to describe the relationship between two variables. A slope of +3.0 indicates that for every one unit increase in the variable measured on the *x*-axis the variable on the *y*-axis increases by 3. The intercept represents the value of the variable measured on the *y*-axis when the variable on the *x*-axis has a value of zero.

Functional Relationships

Graphs are an efficient means of expressing relationships between variables. Often the relationship between two variables is functional in nature, implying dependence or causation. A causal relationship has a **dependent variable** and an **independent variable**. The value of the dependent variable is determined by the value of the independent variable. Suppose that we want to examine the relationship between the amount of money spent on medical care and the health of a person or a group of people. Instead of spending one and one-half pages of valuable paper describing this relationship, I can simply use a graph to convey the main idea.

Figure 2A.3 indicates that there is a direct (positive) relationship between the level of health and the amount spent on medical care. The higher the level of spending the healthier the person or population. The shape of the line indicates that there is a limit to how much health you can buy with increased medical care spending. Additional medical spending buys progressively smaller increments to health. Other variables affect the relationship between health and medical spending, such as genetics and lifestyle choices. Smokers as a group experience more respiratory and circulatory problems than nonsmokers. Figure 2A.4 depicts the relationship between the level of health and medical spending for smokers and nonsmokers. The graph indicates that

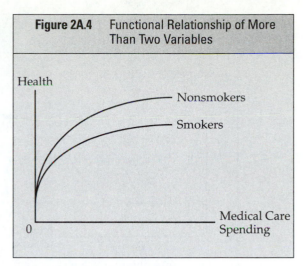

Figure 2A.4 Functional Relationship of More Than Two Variables

at any given level of spending, nonsmokers are on average healthier than smokers.

Sometimes two variables are indirectly (negatively) related to one another. The relationship between infant mortality rates and birthweights is a good example of this phenomenon. Empirical data suggest that as birthweight increases, mortality rates decline. Figure 2A.5 illustrates the negative relationship between infant mortality and birthweight category. Some hypotheses question whether high mortality rates are due to low birthweights or some other factor, such as prematurity (Behrman, 1995). Those issues will be discussed later. For now, focus your attention on the nature of the relationship and how to depict it graphically.

As we discussed earlier, one of the important concepts in economics is optimization. Efficient production techniques promote the goals of average cost minimization. Optimal pricing strategies enable firms to maximize profits. Graphs showing a minimum or a maximum are illustrated in Figure 2A.6.

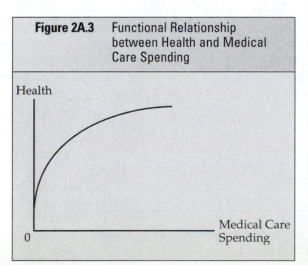

Figure 2A.3 Functional Relationship between Health and Medical Care Spending

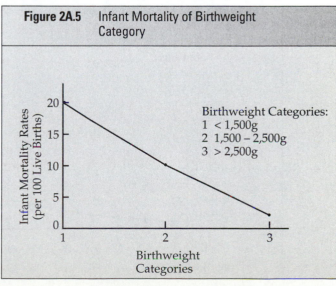

Figure 2A.5 Infant Mortality of Birthweight Category

Birthweight Categories:
1 < 1,500g
2 1,500 – 2,500g
3 > 2,500g

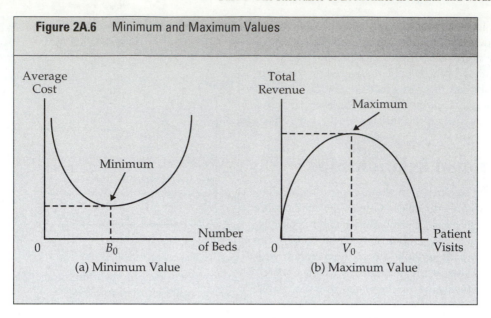

Figure 2A.6   Minimum and Maximum Values

(a) Minimum Value

(b) Maximum Value

Part (a) illustrates the hypothetical relationship between the average cost of services and the number of beds in a typical community hospital. This U-shaped relationship is typical of average costs in producing a product or service. As the size of the operation increases, average costs decrease. If the operation expands beyond a certain level, average costs begin to increase. The most efficient level of operation for the hospital—the optimal level—is B_0.

A functional relationship with a maximum is shown in part (b). Here the relationship between the total revenues of a physician practice and the number of patients visits is illustrated. To generate more patient visits a physician must offer discount prices to some groups—a practice that is typical for physicians who participate in managed care networks.

What is the optimal pricing policy? A physician trying to maximize total revenue will charge a price that will result in a volume of business equal to V_0.

Time-Series Graphs

On occasion it is important to examine how variables change over time. The use of longitudinal (or time-series graphs) often illustrates trends in a data series. Time-series graphs typically use daily, weekly, monthly, quarterly, or annual data to track changes in an economic variable. Figure 2A.7 graphs the changes in U.S. health care spending over the two decades. Health care spending has shown a long-term upward trend since 1970. Starting at less than $100 billion, it has risen dramatically to almost 20 times that amount in just over three decades.

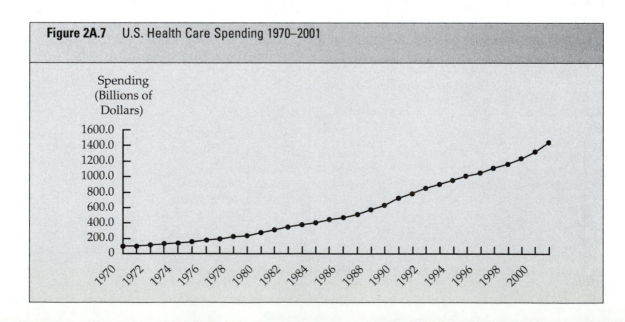

Figure 2A.7   U.S. Health Care Spending 1970–2001

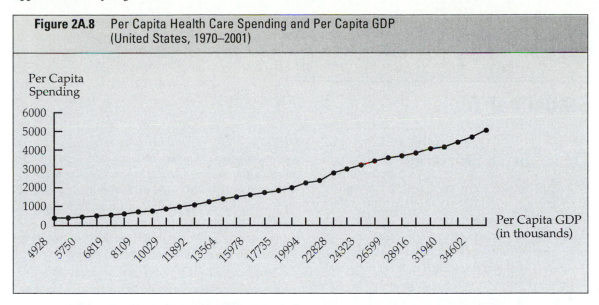

Figure 2A.8 Per Capita Health Care Spending and Per Capita GDP (United States, 1970–2001)

If we were interested in examining the relationship between health care spending and income, we could collect data on spending and income in a single country over a number of years. While a time series on two variables provides insight into the relationship, so many other factors change over time that we may not be sure of our results. Figure 2A.8 illustrates a time-series relationship between per capita health care spending and per capita gross domestic product (GDP) in the United States between 1970 and 2001.

Cross-Section Graphs

Another approach to graphing the same relationship is the use of cross-section data. A cross-section graph provides a number of observations on the two variables at a given point in time across different entities—individuals, firms, states, or countries. Figure 2A.9 illustrates the same relationship for the year 2000 using data from the Organization for Economic Cooperation and Development (OECD). The two graphs depict the relationship between income and spending. Each point on the time-series graph shows U.S. spending compared to income over a number of years. The cross-section graph shows the same two variables for 28 different countries during a single year. Each point represents income and spending (in U.S. dollars) for a given country.

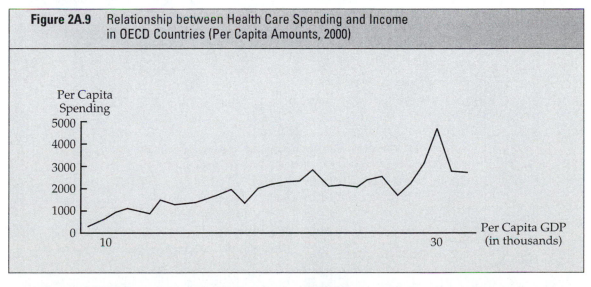

Figure 2A.9 Relationship between Health Care Spending and Income in OECD Countries (Per Capita Amounts, 2000)

References

Richard E. Behrman, ed., *The Future of Children: Low Birth Weight 5*(1), Spring 1995.

Appendix 2B

Statistical Tools

Descriptive Statistics

Whenever we are confronted with a body of data, the challenge is how to summarize the relevant information to make it useful to the reader. Economic researchers are often confronted with large amounts of data, hundreds and sometimes thousands of observations on a number of variables. A useful way of summarizing large amounts of data is by way of a graph, sometimes called a **histogram**.

Figure 2B.1 shows the distribution of maternity patients by age at Hillcrest Baptist Memorial Hospital in Waco, Texas, for 1991. A simple viewing of the histogram tells us a lot about the ages of the 2,476 mothers who delivered that year. The youngest was 12 years old, the oldest 44—a spread of 32 years. The most frequent age was 25 years, the approximate center of the distribution.

Histograms can be summarized by statistical measures. These statistical measures help define the center of the distribution and the spread around the center. These concepts are formally called *central tendency* and *dispersion*.

Measures of Central Tendency

Measures of central tendency are often used to describe the typical value in a data set. The most commonly used measure of central tendency is the **mean**. Often referred to as the average, the mean of a distribution is the sum of the individual values divided by the total number of cases. Summing the ages for the maternity patients comes to 64,137 years. Dividing by the total number of patients, 2,476, gives a mean value of 25.9 years.

Reporting the mean value as the typical value can be misleading since it may place too much weight on extreme values. Suppose five infants were born on a given day and their mothers were 42, 27, 25, 23, and 22 years old. The average age of these five women is

$$\frac{42 + 27 + 25 + 23 + 23}{5} = 28 \text{ years}$$

By weighting the observations equally, the 42-year-old causes the measure of central tendency, or mean in this case, to be inflated and not very "typical" of the rest of the data.

When dealing with data that has a relatively small number of unusually large or small numbers, many researchers use an alternative measure of central tendency known as the **median**. The median is a popular summary statistic for demographic data with extreme values or outliers. To calculate the median, the values of a group of numbers are ranked from largest to

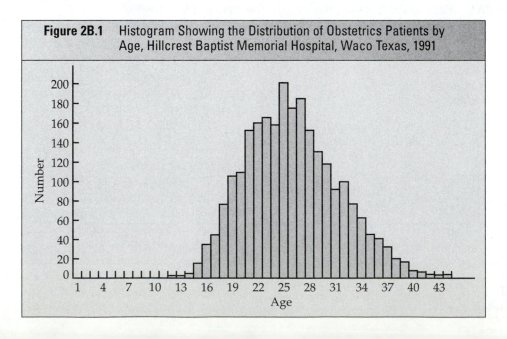

Figure 2B.1 Histogram Showing the Distribution of Obstetrics Patients by Age, Hillcrest Baptist Memorial Hospital, Waco Texas, 1991

smallest. In the case of an odd number of observations, the median is the middle number. In the case of an even number of observations, the median is the average of the middle two values. Its position at the 50th percentile implies that exactly one-half of the distribution is above the median and one-half below it. The median age of the five new mothers listed above is 25 years, a much better indication of the typical age of that sample of patients. The median for all 2,476 maternity patients is 26 years.

Another measure of central tendency is the **mode**. The mode is the value occurring most frequently in the distribution. The most common age of the five maternity patients listed above is 23. For the entire group it is 25. The mode is used primarily on those occasions where the distribution has more than one mode. Under these circumstances, care should be taken to understand what is truly typical of the data values. Confounding factors may cause measures of central tendency to convey quite different results concerning the overall data set. Without controlling for these confounding factors, reliance on a single measure of central tendency may produce spurious results.

Measures of Dispersion

Focusing on the central tendency can obscure other interesting features of a collection of numbers. Concentrating on averages would lead us to conclude that a person standing with one foot in a bucket of scalding hot water and the other foot in a bucket of ice water is, on average, comfortable. Instead of simply looking at the central tendency of the data, it is useful to examine the way the numbers spread out around the center or average. Deviations around the average are typically indexed by statistical measures referred to as variance and/or standard deviation.

The **variance** is a measure of the dispersion of the data around the mean (average) value. It is one way of describing how closely individual observations in a data set cluster around the mean. The sample variance, denoted s^2, is calculated as follows:

$$s^2 = \frac{\sum_{i=1}^{n}(x_i - \overline{X})^2}{N}$$

where X_i is the ith observation on the variable X, $\overline{X}$ is the sample mean, and N is the number of observations in the sample. The deviations from the mean, $X_i - \overline{X}$, are squared to take into consideration all values whether above or below the mean. Otherwise, deviations for those values below the mean would enter the numerator as negative numbers and result in an artificially low measure of dispersion. Whenever the values of a variable are

similar, the variance will be small. Variance, or the variability in the observed values, is a key concept in statistics and plays an important role in the calculation of many statistical tests and procedures. In fact, one of the goals in empirical research is to explain as much of the variance as is practicable.

A related measure of dispersion around the mean is the **standard deviation**. Even though the variance is computed in terms of squared values of the deviations, the standard deviation measures the average deviation. It is an estimate of how far on average the values are from the mean value. Mathematically, the standard deviation is the square root of the variance. This measure of deviation has more intuitive appeal since it is measured in the same units as the original variable. If the variable being considered is years, variance is measured in square years—standard deviation in years. For our sample of maternity patients, the variance is 28.6 square years; the standard deviation 5.3 years.

Another common issue concerning a distribution is its shape. Distributions that are symmetrical are often called **normal distributions**. Those that have long tails are called **skewed distributions** (see Figure 2B.2). A normal distributions is "bell shaped" and can be reconstructed rather well from its summary statistics—mean and standard deviation. For a normal distribution, roughly 70 percent of the observations fall within plus-or-minus one standard deviation of the mean and about 95 percent within two. For our maternity patients, over 72 percent are within one standard deviation ($\pm$ 5.3 years) of the mean (25.9 years). In other words, 1,787 of the 2,476 patients are between the ages of 20 and 31 years. Additionally, over 96 percent (2,386 out of 2,476) are between the ages of 15 and 36 years (two standard deviations from the mean).

Correlation

The descriptive statistics are useful when dealing with one variable at a time. However, a study of the relationship between two or more variables is more interesting and requires other techniques. The scatter diagram described in Appendix 2A is one way of examining the relationship between two variables (see Figure 2A.1). Consider the points on a scatter diagram. A tight clustering around a straight line indicates a strong linear association between the two variables. A loose clustering indicates a weak linear association.

The strength of the association can be measured by a summary statistic commonly called the **correlation coefficient**. The correlation coefficient may be visualized as how two variables are "co-related." It is

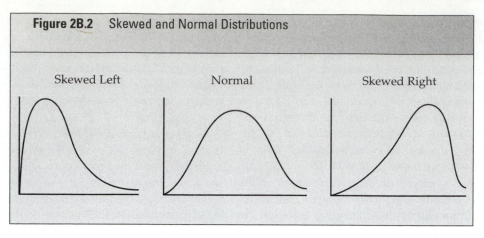

Figure 2B.2 Skewed and Normal Distributions

Skewed Left

Normal

Skewed Right

calculated using the respective means and standard deviations of the variables. Practically speaking, a perfect correlation between two variables indicates that all the observations lie on a straight line—either positively sloped or negatively sloped. In these two cases the correlation coefficient will have the value of either +1 or −1. If the two variables show no tendency to increase or decrease together, the points on a scatter diagram will show no clustering. In such cases, the correlation coefficient will have the value of 0.

It is important to understand that a correlation coefficient indicates an association between two variables. Association, however, does not imply causation. Suppose researchers found a strong negative correlation between the number of cases of influenza and the amount of ice cream consumed. Could we say that eating ice cream reduces the incidence of influenza? As popular as this would be with the children of the world, we cannot honestly make the statement. If it were true, physicians would encourage the consumption of ice cream to reduce the chances of contracting the influenza virus.

Correlation may be telling us that there is a third factor at work in the influenza-ice cream connection; namely, the season of the year. Coincidentally, the flu is most prevalent during the winter months when ice cream sales are low and least prevalent during the summer months when ice cream sales are high. Correlation says nothing about these confounding factors. If it were possible to control for all of these confounding factors, correlation would provide a much stronger argument for causation. What is needed is a way of controlling for these other factors.

Regression

Simple measures of central tendency and dispersion reveal little about the way two or more variables are "co-related." An empirical technique used to determine the nature of the **statistical relationship** among a dependent variable and one or more independent variables is called *regression analysis*. Regression analysis not only allows us to identify systematic relationships among variables, but provides estimates of the relative magnitude of the various relationships. The relationships may be discussed in terms of independent and dependent variables, stimuli and response, explanatory and explained variables, or cause and effect. Because it is one of the most frequently used empirical techniques in economic research, it is important to have a clear understanding of this powerful tool.

Least Squares Methodology

Regression analysis is used to identify a dependent relation of one variable or a set of variables on another. Most regression models use the least-squares method for estimating parameters. The least-squares method provides a means of fitting a curve to a set of data points. This technique is not without its methodological problems. Moving the line closer to some points moves it farther away from other points. Solving the problem is simple. First, find the average distance from the line to all points. Second, minimize the average distance. The least-squares method uses this approach with one difference—instead of using the average distance, it uses the average of the squared distance. This approach avoids the problem of positive and negative differences canceling each other out. Thus, the name *ordinary least squares*.

Suppose we are interested in examining the causes of increased health care spending. The first step in our analysis is to specify the variables to include in the model. The variables that influence health care spending are numerous and may include income, age, and sex among other things. To simplify our discussion, we will specify a simple regression model with one dependent variable and one independent variable. The dependent variable is health care spending and the independent variable is income.

Step 2 in the analysis involves collecting reliable estimates for the two variables. Two approaches are possible—time series and cross-section. A time-series approach would require the collection of data over time—locating data from a published source that looks at spending and income over a number of time periods for a single entity, such as a state, region, or country. A cross-section approach requires data from a number of entities during a single time period.

Data for a cross-section analysis of the effect of income on spending is provided in Table 2B.1. The data comes from the Organization of Economic Cooperation and Development for 28 developed nations. Income is defined as per capita gross domestic product (GDP) and spending is defined in per capita terms. All values are translated into U.S. dollars using purchasing power parity exchange rates.

After collecting the data, the third step is to decide on the functional form of the relationship, or the regression equation. The two standard choices are linear and multiplicative. The linear form can be written as $E = a + bY$, where E is per capita health care expenditures and Y is per capita GDP. The multiplicative form can be written $E = aY^b$. Although the linear model is simpler, the multiplicative form has its advantages. One advantage is the coefficient b in a log transformation of the equation ($\log E = \log a + b \log Y$) has a simple economic interpretation—it is an estimate of "income elasticity."

Choosing the simple linear model, the simple regression model that relates per capita health care spending to per capita gross domestic product for these 28 OECD countries is written

$$E_i = a + bY_i + u_i$$

where i represents the subscript of each observation (countries numbered 1 through 28) and u_i represents the random elements in the relationship.

Figure 2B.3 plots the actual data on spending and income provided in Table 2B.1. The constant term represents the intersection of the regression line with the y-axis and the coefficient on income its slope. Using the least-squares technique, the regression estimate predicts that, on average, for every one-dollar increase in income, health care expenditures increase eight cents.

Often in social science and demographic research, more than one causal variable is identified. The technique used in this situation is called *multiple regression analysis*. Researchers use multiple regression to control for confounding variables, that is, other variables associated with changes in the dependent variable. For example, health care spending may also depend on other factors such as the percentage of population covered by insurance or the number of active physicians per capita. A

| Table 2B.1 | Per Capita GDP and Per Capita Health Care Spending in OECD Countries, 2000 (purchasing power parity U.S. dollars) | | | | |

Country	Per Capita GDP	Per Capita Spending	Country	Per Capita GDP	Per Capita Spending
Mexico	8,845	491	Sweden	26,146	2,195
Slovak Republic	11,279	641	Belgium	26,239	2,293
Hungary	12,204	817	Germany	26,269	2,780
Czech Republic	13,802	987	Australia	26,473	2,350
Korea	15,186	893	Netherlands	27,183	2,348
Greece	16,481	1,556	Austria	28,046	2,233
Portugal	16,857	1,519	Iceland	28,139	2,562
Spain	20,080	1,497	Canada	28,187	2,580
New Zealand	20,214	1,611	Ireland	28,200	1,793
United Kingdom	24,933	1,813	Denmark	28,734	2,398
Italy	25,245	2,060	Switzerland	29,553	3,160
Finland	25,414	1,699	United States	34,602	4,540
France	25,594	2,387	Norway	36,248	2,787
Japan	26,003	1,984	Luxembourg	48,537	2,719

Source: *OECD Health Data 2003: Comparative Analysis of 30 Countries,* Organization for Economic Cooperation and Development, Paris, 2003.

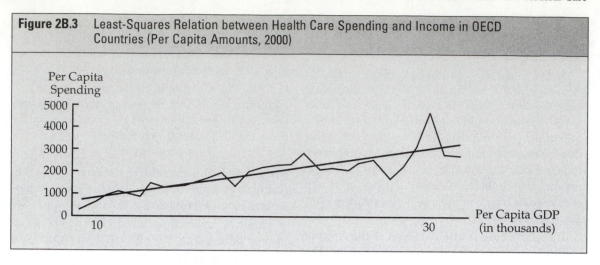

Figure 2B.3   Least-Squares Relation between Health Care Spending and Income in OECD Countries (Per Capita Amounts, 2000)

$$E = -17.29 + 0.084Y$$

Predictor	Coefficient	St. Dev.	t-ratio
Constant	−17.29		
Y	0.084	0.0117	7.15

$F = 51.2$ $R^2 = 66.3\%$

multiple regression equation adding these two regressors would be written in linear form as

$$E = a + bY + cI + dP$$

where I is the percentage of the population with health insurance coverage and P is the number of active physicians per 100 population.[11] The coefficient b on the income variable would now show the independent effect of income on expenditures free from the influence of insurance coverage and the availability of providers.

Measures of Significance

Foremost on the minds of researchers is the reliability of the estimated coefficients. The accuracy of a regression equation can be determined by a number of significance tests. The *standard error of the estimate (S.E.E.)* is the standard deviation of the dependent variable after controlling for the influence of all the independent variables. When data points are widely dispersed about the estimated regression line, standard error is large. If all the data points were to fall on the regression line, the standard error would be zero.

One of the objectives of regression analysis is prediction. Standard error provides an estimate of the accuracy of a prediction based on a particular regression equation. Based on statistical probabilities, when there are roughly 30 or more observa-

tions, there is a 95 percent probability that the dependent variable will lie within two standard errors of its estimated value. The smaller the standard error, the greater is the confidence in the accuracy of the estimate.

Often the standard error of the estimate is used to estimate confidence intervals around a given estimated equation. The 95 percent confidence interval has a range of roughly ± 2 standard errors around the estimate.

A second measure of accuracy is the *coefficient of determination*, or R^2. The coefficient of determination is an estimate of the percentage of variation in the dependent variable explained by the independent variables, sometimes called goodness of fit. R^2 ranges between 0 and 1. The higher its value, the greater is the overall explanatory power of the regression equation.

Standard error and R^2 are both important significance measures, but neither addresses the question of whether the independent variables as a whole explain a significant proportion of the variation of the dependent variable. The *F-statistic* fills this void. Values of F range from 0 upwards. At the extreme, when R^2 equals 0, F equals 0. Whether a particular value of the F statistic indicates a significant set of regressors depends not only on its value, but also on the number of regressors and the

---

11 The multiplicative form of this same question would be $E = aY^bI^cP^d$.

number of observations on which the estimated equation is based. In general, the larger the F-statistic the greater is the likelihood that the set of independent variables explains a significant proportion of the variance in the dependent variable.

Critical values of F are provided in statistical tables that are readily available almost all introductory statistics textbooks. Roughly speaking, with five or fewer independent variables and 25 or more observations, values of F that are greater than 3.0 or 4.0 indicate a statistically significant proportion of the variance explained by the set of independent variables. Smaller sample sizes and a larger number of independent variables require larger values of F for significance.

In addition to the significance of the overall equation, often the researcher is interested in the significance of each independent variable. The standard deviation (or standard error) of the coefficient for each independent variable provides a means of creating a test statistic expressly for this purpose. The most commonly used *t-statistic* in regression analysis is calculated to determine if an individual coefficient is statistically different from zero. The t-statistic is calculated by dividing the coefficient estimate by its standard error. Values of t that are greater than 2.0 are usually associated with coefficients that are statistically different from zero. The critical values of the t-statistic are found in tables in most introductory statistics textbooks.

Summary and Conclusions

With the development of the microcomputer, data analysis is no longer the exclusive purview of statisticians. A standard personal computer equipped with a statistical software package gives the user a powerful set of tools for analyzing information.

The analytical techniques discussed in this appendix are among the most commonly used in the social sciences. Many of the referenced articles use them extensively. A thorough understanding of these tools will go a long way in making the study of health economics more enjoyable and easier.

Chapter 3

Analyzing Medical Care Markets

A compelling argument can be made that medical care delivery is far more complex and dynamic than is typically the case in the standard treatment of the market process. The trade-off between equity and efficiency is quite acute, calling for active government involvement to ensure that the process works. Critics of government involvement offer an equally compelling argument. Even well-meaning government policy has its unintended consequences. Oversight is costly and serves to impede growth and productivity in the private sector.

In this chapter we will examine the competitive market model and its applicability to the medical market. After considering the breakdown in the traditional market model, we will then examine how governments intervene to address the problems that arise. Following a discussion of the causes and consequences of market failure in general will be an examination of **market failure** in medical markets. Government intervention in the form of regulation, public provision, and licensing will then be discussed. Finally, the question of how to deal with government failure is addressed.

market failure
A situation in which a market fails to produce the socially optimal level of output.

The Medical Care Marketplace

As costs have escalated and the number of uninsured individuals has increased, calls for government intervention have mounted. Proponents of more government involvement in medical care claim that medical care is far too complicated to be left to market forces. Because medicine is difficult to understand, patients must rely on their physicians' recommendations. Others add that medical care is a social good and too important to leave to the workings of the impersonal marketplace. Some argue that the externalities involved in medicine, particularly in the area of infectious diseases, require collective action to maximize the benefits to society. Many base their support for government intervention on ethical grounds, claiming that the provision of medical care based on the ability to pay is morally repugnant. Together these arguments are responsible, in varying degrees, for the development of government-financed medical care in most developed countries throughout the world.

Those who oppose more government involvement argue that the U.S. system has remained, for the most part, market based; which is, in part, evidence of the deep American distrust of federal government involvement in health care matters.[1] Experience has taught that government-run programs are costly. For example, when originally proposed in the mid-1960s, Medicaid spending was projected to reach $9 billion in 1990; actual cost in 1990 was $65 billion. The preamble to the original Medicare bill actually prohibited any federal "supervision or control over the practice of medicine or the manner in which medical services are provided." Anyone

---

1 Blendon et al. (1995) note that only 7 percent of Americans express a "great deal of confidence" in federal health care agencies, compared with 19 percent of Canadians and 41 percent of Germans.

familiar with medical care delivery is well aware of how the federal government has violated the original intent of this legislation.

Cost of Care

One of the major factors driving the health care reform debate is spending, including total spending, spending per person, and spending as a share of total economic output. Referring to Table 3.1, national health expenditures rose to $1,553.0 billion in 2002, and 14.9 percent of annual GDP. Of this amount, 86.3 percent, or $1,340.2 billion, was for personal health care expenditures. This category of spending includes the purchase of all goods and services associated with individual health care, such as hospital care, the services of physicians and dentists, prescription drugs, vision care, home health care, and nursing home care.

Hospital Care

Spending on hospital services increased to $486.5 billion in 2002. Hospital costs (valued as actual revenues received) experienced five years of accelerated growth between 1987 and 1991. For much of the decade of the 1990s the growth in hospital spending moderated due primarily to aggressive cost-control efforts on the part of private payers. In 2002, however, hospital-spending growth exceeded 2001 levels by over 9 percent,

http://

National Center for Health Statistics (NCHS) is the principal health statistics agency in the United States. Its goal is to provide accurate, relevant, and timely statistical information that will guide actions and policies to improve the health of the American people.
http://www.cdc.gov/nchs/

Table 3.1	National Health Expenditures, 1960–2002 Billions of dollars (unless otherwise stated)							
Category	1960	1970	1980	1990	1995	2000	2001	2002
Hospital care	$ 9.2	$ 27.6	$101.5	$ 253.9	$ 343.6	$ 413.2	$ 444.3	$ 486.5
Physician and clinical services	5.4	14.0	47.1	157.5	220.5	290.3	315.1	339.5
Dental services	2.0	4.7	13.3	31.5	44.5	60.7	65.6	70.3
Other professional services	0.4	0.7	3.6	18.2	28.5	38.8	42.6	45.9
Home health care	0.1	0.2	2.4	12.6	30.5	31.7	33.7	36.1
Nursing home care	0.8	4.2	17.7	52.7	74.6	93.8	99.1	103.2
Prescription drugs	2.7	5.5	12.0	40.3	60.8	121.5	140.8	162.4
Other medical products	2.3	5.0	13.7	33.1	39.7	48.5	49.2	50.5
Other personal health care	0.6	1.3	3.3	9.6	23.0	38.8	42.6	45.9
Personal health care	$ 23.4	$ 63.2	$214.6	$ 609.4	$ 865.7	$1,135.3	$1,231.4	$1,340.2
Government administration and net cost of private health insurance	1.2	2.8	12.2	40.0	57.2	80.3	90.3	105.0
Public health activities	0.4	1.4	6.7	20.2	31.4	45.8	48.3	51.2
Non-commercial biomedical research	0.7	2.0	5.5	12.7	17.1	28.8	31.5	34.3
New construction	1.0	3.8	6.8	13.7	15.5	19.2	19.2	22.4
National health expenditures	$ 26.7	$ 73.1	$245.8	$ 696.0	$ 987.0	$1,309.4	$1,420.7	$1,553.0
Per capita personal spending (dollars)	$126	$301	$931	$2,397	$3,233	$4,049	$4,353	$4,694
Per capita national spending (dollars)	143	348	1,067	2,738	3,686	4,670	5,021	5,440
National spending as a percent of GDP	5.1%	7.0%	8.8%	12.0%	13.3%	13.3%	14.1%	14.9%

Source: Health Care Financing Administration Web site at **http://www.hcfa.gov/stats/nhe-oact** (Accessed March 26, 2001). And Katharine Levit et al., "Health Spending Rebound Continues in 2002," *Health Affairs 23*(1), January/February 2004, 147–159.

increasing concern that spending will continue to accelerate. Hospital care comprised 36.3 percent of personal health care spending. Patients paid for approximately 3 percent of hospital care out-of-pocket.

Physicians' Services

Spending on physicians' services amounted to 25.3 percent of the total spent on personal health care in 2001. The total of $339.5 billion tends to mask the importance of physicians in the health care sector. Even though only 25 cents of every medical care dollar flows directly to physicians, they are indirectly responsible for most of the rest. Physicians admit patients to hospitals, recommend surgeries, prescribe drugs and eyeglasses, and in general oversee the entire health care delivery system. Roughly 18 percent of physicians' services are financed by patient out-of-pocket payments.

Over-the-Counter and Prescription Drugs

Consumers spent $162.4 billion on pharmaceuticals and another $50.5 billion on other medical products in 2002. Approximately 60 percent of this spending is attributed to prescription drugs, the remainder being spent on over-the-counter drugs and various first-aid and gynecological products. This category accounts for 15.9 percent of personal health care spending and is one of the fastest growing categories of spending. Patients pay over 40 percent of all prescription drugs out-of-pocket.

Other Personal Health Care Spending

Other spending includes payments for dentists' services and other professional services, nursing home care, and home health services. When combined, these categories of care accounted for approximately 20 percent of all personal health care spending. Nursing home care amounted to $103.2 billion and 7.7 percent of total personal health care spending in 2002, making it the fourth largest spending category. Dental services accounted for $70.3 billion and other professional services $45.9 billion. Home health spending at $36.1 billion has almost tripled since 1990.

Prospects for the Future

The average American spent $5,440 on medical care in 2002. At this level, United States per capita spending on medical care is anywhere from 40 to 300 percent higher than in other developed countries. Much of the difference is predictable. Countries with higher living standards (measured by per capita income) spend more on promoting health.

Although high per capita spending paints a dramatic picture of spending disparities, the share of output devoted to medical care is more reflective of shifts in priorities. The percentage of GDP devoted to medical care spending has risen dramatically in the United States since the late 1960s, from less than 6 percent to almost 15 percent. In comparison, in most developed countries worldwide the percentage ranges from 8 to 10 percent. Increasing health care expenditures as a percent of GDP may reflect a conscious choice on the part of the consuming public to spend more for health care. Or, it may reflect an inefficient approach to health care financing and a piecemeal attempt at reform that to date has been concentrated on community hospital inpatient services while virtually ignoring every other aspect of medical care delivery.

> **Policy Issue**
>
> The United States spends significantly more on health care than any other country in the world. Are we getting our money's worth?

Clearly, the United States spends more and devotes a larger percentage of economic output to medical care than any other country in the world. Although interesting, these facts ignore three important questions: What is a reasonable percentage of output to devote to medical care spending? How much can we afford? Are we getting our money's worth?

First of all, no one knows the ideal percentage of GDP that medical care spending should consume. We do know, however, that as income increases, spending on services, including health care, tends to increase. Wealthy countries spend proportionately more on medical care than poor countries. Since the United States is among the leaders in per capita income in the industrialized world, it should come as no surprise that medical care spending is the highest.

Secondly, a growing economy allows more resources to be devoted to those areas of the service sector where productivity may lag (including medical care, education, police protection, and the performing arts). In an economy where productivity is growing in most sectors and declining in none, consumers can have more of everything. It is merely a matter of devoting a different proportion of income to the production of the various sectors (Baumol, 1993). This reapportionment is accomplished by transferring resources from those sectors where productivity is increasing to those where it is stagnant.

Baumol refers to the phenomenon of lagging productivity in the service sector as the "cost disease of personal services." Applying his reasoning to medical care, the lag in productivity may be traced to two main factors. First, medical services are hard to standardize, making it difficult to automate. Before you can cure someone, it is necessary to diagnose the problem. Diagnosis and cure are done on a case-by-case basis. Thus, efficiency and productivity tends to lag behind the rest of the economy. Second, most people perceive that quality of care is positively correlated with the amount of time the physician spends with the patient. Thus, it is difficult to reduce the labor content of medical services. Physicians who speed up the examination process are often accused of short-changing their patients. This same reasoning may also be applied to education, the performing arts, legal services, and insurance.

Finally, empirical evidence indicates that the increase in health care spending witnessed over the past 40 years provides substantial benefits to society that far outweigh the associated costs. Lichtenberg's (2002) analysis strongly supports the hypothesis that medical innovation in the form of new drugs and overall health care spending contributed positively to increased longevity between 1960 and 1997. In fact, he concluded that the most cost-effective way to increase life expectancy is through increased spending on new drug development. Cutler and McClellan (2001) examine the benefits of technological change in five common conditions: heart attacks, low-birthweight infants, depression, breast cancer, and cataracts. They conclude that health care spending on these conditions is worth the cost of care.

Access to Care

According to recent census estimates, more than 42 million Americans were without health insurance in 2002, creating mounting pressure on policymakers to come up with a plan to ensure access to medical care for all Americans (Mills, 2002). It is interesting to note that over 40 percent of the uninsured are between the ages of 18 and 34, age categories where they use relatively less medical care.

Having no health insurance is not the same thing as having no access to medical care. In fact, the uninsured in this country receive about 60 percent of the medical care per capita of those with insurance. In 1990, insured Americans spent $2,683 per capita on medical care compared to $1,640 for the uninsured. In contrast, per capita spending in Canada (ranked second in the world) was $1,610. Uninsured Americans are not going without care. They do, however, receive less care than insured Americans (Stelzer, 1994).

The ideological struggle surrounding medical care reform has focused on two competing visions of universality. One vision argues for **universal coverage** in a system that requires mandatory participation, while the other supports **universal access** in a voluntary system where everyone can buy health insurance if they desire to do so. The debate has not progressed far beyond an argument over the percentage of the population that would have health insurance under the various alternatives. To truly advance the debate we must address the critical issue of individual rights versus social

> ### Policy Issue
> What is the best way to ensure access to medical care for those Americans who do not have health insurance?

universal coverage
A guarantee that all citizens will have health insurance coverage regardless of income or health status. Coverage usually includes a well-defined benefits package and mandatory participation.

universal access
A guarantee that all citizens who desire health insurance will have access to health insurance regardless of income or health status. Those who cannot afford insurance are usually subsidized and participation is voluntary.

Policy Issue

Is access to medicare care an individual right? Does society have a responsibility to provide care to those who cannot afford it?

Policy Issue

Is the U.S. health care system delivering high-qualify medical care to Americans?

responsibility. Is access to medical care an individual right or is it a social responsibility to provide access to those who cannot afford to buy it? How we choose to answer this question will go a long way in determining the future shape of medical care delivery and finance.

Medical Outcomes

The third area of concern is the health of the population. Those critical of the U.S. delivery system will cite the relatively poor health outcomes experienced in this country. The typical indicators used for comparisons are presented in Table 3.2. Male life expectancy at birth, 74.1, is the lowest among the six countries listed. Female life expectancy, also last among the six countries listed, is 79.5 years. Infant mortality rates are the highest in the United States, twice the Japanese rate. Spending, both as a percentage of GDP and on a per capita basis, is much higher in the United States. In fact, per capita spending in Germany, ranked second, is less than 65 percent of U.S. spending. Using these indicators, it appears that we may not be getting value for the money being spent. Is the U.S. system delivering an inferior product, or is there another way to look at the evidence?

The use of health indicators to praise or fault a delivery system ignores the contribution of the underlying demographic and social factors entirely. Health indicators reflect more than health care delivery. Life expectancy and infant mortality say a lot about environment, lifestyle choices, and social problems. The U.S. system must deal with a higher incidence of most of the problems than other industrialized countries—drug abuse, violence, reckless behavior, sexual promiscuity, and obesity. These problems complicate the delivery of medical care and are, in part, responsible for the poor health indicators.

Others argue that other indicators more accurately reflect the effectiveness of a health care system. In particular, how does the system treat people who are critically ill? The story is much different when disease-specific death rates are examined. Data from the OECD in Table 3.3 provide details for death rates per 100,000 for the top ten causes of death in the United States in 1999. Overall, the United States has the highest number of deaths per 100,000 for females and the third highest for males. However, in

| Table 3.2 | Commonly Cited Health Indicators, 2000 |

Country	Life Expectancy at Birth[a] Males	Females	Infant Mortality Rate[b]	Health Care Spending (% of GDP)	Per Capita Health Care Spending[c]
Canada	76.7	82.0	5.3	9.2	$2,397
France	75.2	82.7	4.6	9.3	2,387
Germany	74.7[d]	80.7[d]	4.4	10.6	2,780
Japan	77.7	84.6	3.2	7.6	1,984
Sweden	77.4	82.0	3.4	8.4	2,270
United Kingdom	75.7	80.2	5.6	7.3	1,813
United States	74.1	79.5	6.9	13.1	4,540

Source: *OECD Health Data 2003*, Paris: Organization for Economic Cooperation and Development, 2003.

a In years.
b Perinatal deaths per 1,000 live births.
c In PPP dollars.
d 1999.

Table 3.3	Crude Death Rate per 100,000 Population, 1999 Top Ten Causes of Death, United States

Cause of Death	Canada[a]	France	Germany	Japan	UK	USA
All causes						
Male	789.5	806.8	862.7	699.5	863.6	857.8
Female	485.9	425.6	516.3	361.5	568.9	572.2
Diseases of the circulatory system						
Male	283.2	217.7	371.5	195.4	340.4	320.4
Female	169.6	123.5	237.4	117.7	207.3	213.4
Malignant neoplasms						
Male	222.7	259.4	232.7	224.0	227.8	214.6
Female	144.9	117.9	139.0	105.1	155.9	146.4
Cerebrovascular diseases						
Male	47.7	47.3	70.7	86.8	66.8	45.9
Female	39.2	33.4	54.4	53.5	61.1	42.0
Accidents and adverse effects						
Male	57.4	81.2	49.6	68.8	39.5	76.3
Female	23.1	34.6	19.5	26.2	15.9	28.3
Diseases of the nervous system						
Male	20.2	21.3	16.6	6.9	16.0	24.3
Female	16.7	16.1	10.5	4.5	11.7	20.7
Diabetes mellitus						
Male	19.6	12.7	16.8	8.3	9.1	23.1
Female	13.9	8.9	14.5	5.2	6.3	19.1
Pneumonia and influenza						
Male	26.9	23.0	17.6	67.1	72.1	19.2
Female	16.6	12.4	10.4	30.4	54.3	13.7
Infectious and parasitic diseases						
Male	9.4	11.7	9.7	14.7	6.3	22.6
Female	5.1	6.4	6.0	7.9	4.3	13.9
Mental disorders						
Male	15.8	17.7	12.9	1.9	13.8	11.4
Female	13.6	12.5	4.4	1.5	11.4	9.0
Chronic liver disease and cirrhosis						
Male	8.9	19.3	23.0	12.3	10.3	13.5
Female	4.1	7.3	9.8	4.0	5.8	6.1

Source: *OECD Health Data 2003*, Paris: Organization for Economic Cooperation and Development, 2003.

a 1997.

the specific 20 categories listed, the United States ranks in the top three in 13 of them and fourth in three others. For almost every type of cancer—colon, prostate, cervical, and, breast—death rates in the United States are among the lowest in the world.

Another perspective on the issue is illustrated in Table 3.4. Anderson and Hussey (2000) provide international comparisons of disease-specific mortality and incidence using mortality ratios.[2] Using OECD data they find that there is greater variation in the incidence of diseases than there is in mortality from those diseases. Mortality rates can mask the effectiveness of a health care system in keeping people who suffer from chronic diseases alive. Using mortality ratios, mortality among women diagnosed with breast cancer is lowest in the United States and highest in New Zealand and the United Kingdom. Mortality among men with prostate cancer is lowest in the United States and highest in the United Kingdom. Mortality from AIDS is lowest in the United States and the United Kingdom and highest in Australia.

Favorable disease-specific death rates and favorable disease-specific mortality ratios translate into relatively high life expectancies at later ages. As presented in Table 3.5, U.S. life expectancy at age 65 ranks fourth among the six countries listed, behind Canada, Japan, and France. The other three indicators shown in the table provide a measure of the efficiency of the system in delivering medical care. The United States has the lowest average inpatient length of stay at 6.8 days. Most government-run systems pay a fixed rate per hospital day, resulting in comparatively long average stays in the hospital. Over the course of the typical hospital stay, the later days are usually less costly than the earlier days. Keeping patients in the hospital longer helps to recover the higher costs of the first few days. Longer stays translate into a need for more hospital beds per capita, representing a waste of hospital resources. Predictably, the United States has the fewest number of hospital beds per 1,000 population.

The United States ranks third in terms of the number of physicians per 1,000 population. When physician payments are based on established fee schedules, physicians are able to compensate for low fees by requiring extensive follow-up visits. In France, with one of the highest physician-to-population ratios, patients saw their physicians an average of 6.9 times in 2000. In Japan, with the second fewest physicians per capita, the average was 14.4. In contrast, the typical American had only 8.9 physician's visits that year. In general, patients find it easier to schedule appointments in the United States and spend more time with their physicians during each appointment.

Table 3.4	Mortality Ratios for Selected Countries, 1997 (In percentages)		
Country	**Breast Cancer**	**Prostate Cancer**	**AIDS**
Australia	28[c]	35[c]	14
Canada	28	25	10
France	35[a]	49[b]	9[b]
Germany	31[a]	44	9
New Zealand	46[a]	30[b]	6[b]
United Kingdom	46[b]	57	3
United States	25[b]	19	3

Source: Anderson and Hussey, 2000.

a 1995.
b 1996.
c 1998.

2 Mortality ratios are calculated by dividing the mortality from a disease by the incidence of the disease.

Table 3.5	Other Important Health Indicators, 2000

Country	Life Expectancy at Age 65[a]		Inpatient Length of Hospital Stay	Hospital Beds per 1,000 Population	Physicians per 1,000 Population
	Males	Females			
Canada	16.9	20.5	8.7[b]	3.2	2.1
France	16.5[b]	20.9[b]	13.1	6.7	3.3
Germany	15.5	19.2[b]	11.9	6.4	3.3
Japan	17.5	22.4	39.8[b]	16.5[c]	1.9
United Kingdom	15.6	18.9	10.0[c]	3.9	2.0
United States	16.3	19.2	6.8	2.9	2.7[b]

Source: *OECD Health Data 2003*, Paris: Organization of Economic Cooperation and Development, 2003.

a In years.
b 1999.
c 1998.

The Competitive Market Model

Key Concept 4
Self-Interest

Adam Smith in his famous treatise *The Wealth of Nations* asserted that individual decision making is motivated by self-interest. Guided by the "invisible hand" of the market, this self-serving behavior, in turn, serves to promote the interests of others. In other words, when markets exhibit certain ideal conditions—perfectly competitive conditions—optimizing behavior on the part of individuals and firms leads to efficient outcomes.

Following the traditions established by Smith and the classical school of economics, modern-day economists evaluate markets according to the twin criteria of efficiency and equity. There are two aspects of efficiency—**allocative efficiency** and **technical efficiency.** Allocative efficiency may be viewed as efficiency in the final distribution of consumption. Consumers buy a good until the benefits received from the last unit purchased equals the price.[3] Thus, everyone purchasing a good places a marginal value on the good at least equal to its market price. When everyone pays the same price for the good, there is no way to reallocate consumption from consumers to nonconsumers without lowering overall consumer welfare.

allocative efficiency
The situation in which producers make the goods and services that consumers desire. For every item the marginal cost of production is less than or equal to the marginal benefit received by consumers.

Technical efficiency may be thought of as efficiency in production, or cost efficiency. In perfectly competitive markets, producers must minimize costs to maximize profits. When all producers pay the same input prices, goods and services that are produced will have marginal valuations that are higher than goods and services that could have been produced with the same resources. In summary, perfect competition guarantees both allocative and technical efficiency.

technical efficiency
Efficiency in production, or cost efficiency.

Key Concept 8
Efficiency

Equity considerations are also important when evaluating economic systems. Even though the issue of equity is based on some standard of fairness, ideological differences dictate whether that standard is defined either in terms of outcomes or in terms of opportunities. For example, one economist might define equity in terms of final outcomes. In this case, any differences in infant mortality rates between, say, whites and African Americans would be viewed as inequitable and obviously the result of unequal access to the medical care system. How else could you possibly explain the large gulf between the 6.0 deaths per 1,000 live births among white Americans and 14.2 among African Americans (Hoyert et al., 1999)? Another economist might have a different

Policy Issue
How important is equity in determining the effectiveness of a health care delivery system?

3 Downward sloping demand curves are implied from the law of diminishing returns, indicating that the last unit of a good purchased has a marginal value equal to its market price.

perspective on the same issue. Defining equity in terms of opportunities rather than outcomes, the same differences in mortality rates would be interpreted differently. From this perspective, even in a world of equal opportunities, there will be different outcomes. Blaming the differences on unequal access ignores demographic differences such as age, education, and marital status between the two population cohorts. Additionally, differences in lifestyle choices are also important, including the decision to smoke cigarettes, drink alcohol, or ingest drugs during pregnancy. Whether defined in terms of outcomes or opportunities, equity has become an important component in the evaluation of markets, especially medical markets.

Few people will argue against the importance of an equitable distribution of health care availability. But health care is like any other desirable commodity: It is subject to an equity-efficiency trade-off. Access to medical care differs according to individual circumstances, such as age, sex, income, geographic location, and insurance coverage. No matter how much we may desire equity, it comes at a price. Mandating equity may be desirable, but it is costly.

The formal argument for competitive markets is based on the notions of economic efficiency and social equity, but some favor competition simply because it guards against the concentration of market power and promotes consumer sovereignty. Competition among providers and their desire to satisfy consumer preferences ensures against consumer exploitation. Consumers always have alternative sources of supply in competitive markets. Cost-conscious behavior on the part of consumers increases their sensitivity to price changes. Individual providers face perfectly elastic demand curves when cost-conscious consumers have alternative sources of supply. Consequently, prices of goods and services equal the marginal cost of production.

Key Concept 7
Competition

When markets work, prices reflect the valuation of forgone opportunities. As equilibrium is reached, marginal values and prices converge, and the value of the goods and services that are produced is greater than the value of the goods and services that could have been produced with the same resources. In other words, if individuals in society placed a higher value on the last dollar spent on medical care than on the last dollar spent on, say, education, then they would demand that more be spent on medical care and less on education until the marginal valuations were equal.

Market Failure

Key Concept 9
Market Failure

According to Murphy's Law, if anything can go wrong, it will go wrong. Various imperfections in medical markets make the dual task of delivering a product equitably and efficiently more difficult. When the underlying assumptions of competitive markets are not met, markets fail to deliver the **optimal output levels** (Rice, 1998). Markets fail to allocate resources optimally when firms have market power, when there are externalities in consumption and production, and when the good produced is a public good.

optimal output levels
A market equilibrium where the marginal benefit received from every unit of output is greater or equal to the marginal cost of producing each unit. The social optimum is that output level where the marginal benefit of the last unit produced is equal to its marginal cost.

Key Concept 3
Marginal Analysis

Market Power

Any departure from perfect competition, whether it be monopoly, oligopoly, cartels, monopolistic competition, monopsony, or any other market structure imperfection, violates the optimality considerations discussed earlier. A profit-maximizing firm with market power sets prices at levels that exceed marginal costs. To maintain those prices, the firm must restrict output to levels that are less than optimum. Prices will be too high, costs too high, resources underutilized, and society will suffer an economic loss.

Market power is depicted graphically by any departure from perfectly elastic demand curves. Figure 3.1 points out the differences in pricing and output between firms in perfectly competitive markets and those with market power. When demand curves are perfectly elastic, they are drawn as horizontal lines. Profit maximizers set marginal revenue (*MR*) equal to marginal cost (*MC*). With price equal to marginal revenue, $MR = MC$ at the same output level (Q_0) where $P_0 = MC$ (the condition for allocative efficiency).

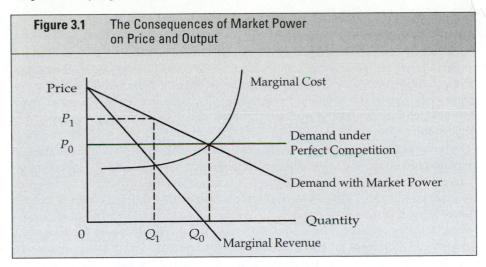

Figure 3.1 The Consequences of Market Power on Price and Output

Market power gives a firm some control over its pricing decisions. Raising price reduces quantity sold without the complete loss of customers. With a downward-sloping demand curve, the firm's marginal revenue is less than the price it charges. Setting $MR = MC$ now results in a lower output level (Q_1) and the ability to charge a higher price (P_1). Higher prices, lower output, and underutilization of resources result in a loss in welfare as measured by the loss in consumer and producer surplus.

In spite of these problems, monopoly may still be the most effective way to organize production in a market. Under conditions where production is subject to economies of scale, the long-run average cost curve declines continuously. Competition will result in the exit of all but one firm. The remaining firm, the **natural monopoly**, will not set price competitively, and since $P > MC$, output is not provided at its optimal level. To correct this misallocation of resources, the most effective option may be regulation.[4]

Using Figure 3.2 to illustrate this point, suppose the firm has a long-run average cost curve that is downward-sloping as it crosses the market demand curve. Under these circumstances, a single firm can supply enough output to satisfy consumer demand and

natural monopoly
A firm becomes a natural monopoly based on its ability to provide a good or service at a lower cost than anyone else and to satisfy consumer demand completely.

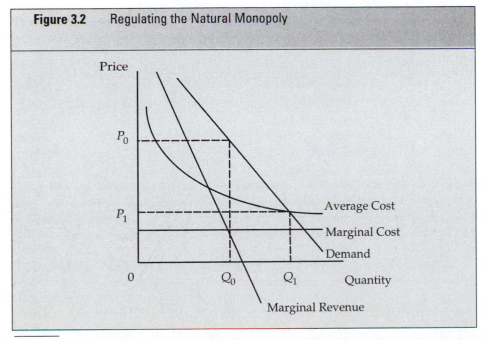

Figure 3.2 Regulating the Natural Monopoly

4 Certain tax and subsidy schemes might actually be more efficient, but discussion of these alternatives is beyond the scope of this presentation.

do so at progressively lower unit costs.[5] Shielded from competition from rival firms, the monopolist has no compelling reason to be efficient. Focusing solely on profit maximization, the firm will produce less than optimal level of output (Q_0) and prices will be higher than if the market were competitive (P_0). To correct this problem, government price controllers often try to establish a maximum price the monopolist can charge that more closely approximates the perfectly competitive solution. Setting a price at P_1, for example, enables the firm to earn a normal return on its investment and produce at higher output levels (Q_1).

Market power in an input market also causes an inefficient allocation of resources. A monopsonist, as the sole buyer of a particular resource, faces an upward-sloping supply curve instead of a perfectly elastic supply curve. As a result, the firm has some discretion over the price it pays for the resource. If more is desired, then the firm must pay a higher price. If less is desired, then prices fall accordingly. The results are shown in Figure 3.3, where the monopsonist faces a situation where the marginal cost of the resource is greater than the price of the resource. Instead of setting demand equal to supply and paying P_0 to employ Q_0 units of the resource, the monopsonist equates demand, its assessment of the marginal value of the resource used in production, with the marginal cost of the resource, and employs Q_1 units of the output. At this level of utilization, the monopsonist has only to pay P_1 to satisfy the firm's demand for resources. Market power in the resource market enables firms to employ fewer resources and pay lower prices for their use than if the market were perfectly competitive. The result of this lost output is lost income to resource owners and fewer goods and services available to consumers. In summary, market power insulates a firm from the competitive forces that ensure allocative and technical efficiency, resulting in a loss to society.

Externalities

externality
A cost or benefit that spills over to parties not directly involved in the actual transaction and thus is ignored by the buyer and seller.

Sometimes the actions taken by individuals in the process of producing or consuming will have an effect on the welfare of others. An **externality** may be either positive or negative, depending on whether it benefits or harms other people. By maintaining her property, a homeowner generates a positive externality for all her neighbors. Not only is it pleasing to look at a freshly painted house and well-kept garden, but the market values of surrounding properties are enhanced at the same time.

Examples of negative externalities abound. Anyone smoking a cigar in a crowded room imposes costs on everyone else in the room. Everyone has less fresh air to breathe than if the smoker were forced to internalize all the costs of his smoking. A factory that

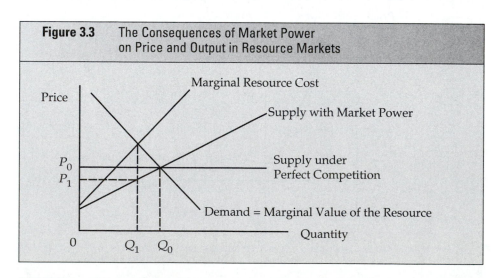

Figure 3.3   The Consequences of Market Power on Price and Output in Resource Markets

---

5 Because price, represented by the demand curve, is above the average cost curve at every point, the firm can increase sales by lowering price and still make an economic profit.

Back-of-the-Envelope

MONOPSONY: WHEN BUYERS HAVE MARKET POWER

Market power on the buyers' side, called monopsony, gives buyers more leverage in determining the prices they pay for goods and services. If buyers have the ability to consolidate their demand under the control of a single collective, they may have market power. In this case, the monopsonist would function as a buyers' union. In today's language, this union would be called an alliance or a cooperative. The larger the cooperative, the more control the group can assert over the prices charged its members. As already discussed, equilibrium for the monopsonist occurs at a price and output level that is below the levels that would exist in perfectly competitive markets, representing lost economic welfare.

Even with the lost productivity, some still argue that monopsony provides a net benefit to society. Proponents of market power for buyers agree that the unilateral exercise of market power should be illegal on either side of the market. They contend, however, that providers in medical markets already exercise a significant degree of market power on the sellers' side of the market. The use of power on the buyers' side represents a countervailing force that encourages competitive behavior among sellers and promotes the efficient use of resources.

The formal explanation of this phenomenon is described in most intermediate microeconomics textbooks under the heading of "**bilateral monopoly.**" A bilateral monopoly exists in a market when there is only one buyer seeking the output of a single seller. In other words, bilateral monopoly is characterized by monopsony on the demand side and monopoly on the supply side. In the following graph, D, MR, and MC are the demand, marginal revenue, and marginal cost curves confronting the monopolist seller. Profit maximizing price and output, P_2 and Q_2, are determined by $MC = MR$ at point A.

A monopsonist with absolute control over demand could force the monopolist to behave like a firm in a perfectly competitive market. Under these conditions, MC is also the firm's supply curve. Likewise, MC_B becomes the relevant marginal cost of buying an additional unit of the output. The monopsonist attempts to equate the marginal cost of buying with its own marginal valuation of the product (MV_P) at point B. At the optimal level of output Q_1, the monopsonist pays the lowest price the provider is willing to accept and still cover marginal cost, P_1.

bilateral monopoly
A situation with monopoly on the seller's side of the market and monopsony on the buyer's side.

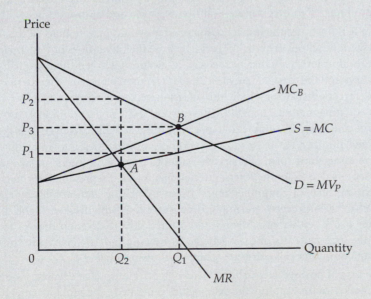

In terms of the final price, the negotiated outcome will fall somewhere between the two extremes, P_1 and P_2. The exact solution depends on the relative bargaining strengths of the two sides. The monopoly provider enters the negotiations wanting a higher price and lower output than the monopsony buyer. To avoid an impasse, the monopolist will likely offer somewhat lower prices and slightly more output. The monopsonist will agree to pay more than P_1 if the monopolist provides more than Q_2. As long as price does not fall below P_3, the final output level will fall between Q_1 and Q_2. Thus, for bilateral monopoly to benefit society, bargaining strengths of buyers and sellers must be approximately equal. If either side has a disproportionate share of the bargaining power, it will be able to tilt the balance in its favor to the detriment of society. (*Technical note:* Relative bargaining strengths and the final outcome will be different if the supply curve is so steeply sloped that $Q_2 > Q_1$. In this case the monopolist wants to provide more output than the monopsonist wants to buy, weakening the monopolist's bargaining position.)

Source: Michael L. Ile, "When Health Care Payers Have Market Power," *Journal of the American Medical Association* 263(14), April 11, 1990, 1981–1982, 1986.

dumps toxic waste into a nearby river shifts some of the cost of production (i.e., waste disposal) onto those people who live downstream from the plant. The same can be said about acid rain, traffic congestion, and the many other examples of negative externalities that could be listed.

Externalities affect economic efficiency. Normal market mechanisms have no way of accounting for externalities. Decision makers are not required to absorb the costs of negative externalities and have no way to capture the benefits of positive externalities. The result is a level of output that is nonoptimal.

Externalities exist as by-products of the decision to produce and consume. Because formal markets do not exist for these by-products, they are produced in nonoptimal quantities. Take, for example, the case of automobile emissions in a crowded metropolitan area. By choosing to drive your own car to work, you impose costs on others in the form of carbon monoxide emissions from the exhaust. A large percentage of the costs of commuting are internalized. You pay for the car, the gasoline, and the insurance. But your fellow commuters pay the costs that cannot be internalized, namely the costs of the by-products of your commute: traffic congestion and air pollution.

Figure 3.4 illustrates the impact of an externality in a private market, the daily commute to work or school. Externalities arise because the driver does not internalize the full cost of the commute. Graphically, the vertical distance between the marginal social cost (*MSC*) curve and the marginal private cost (*MPC*) curve represents the external costs that the driver forces others to pay. Individual decision makers determine their own commuter miles by equating marginal benefit (*MB*) with *MPC*. Given the additional costs that society at large must pay, the number of commuter miles actually driven (Q_m) is greater than the optimal number (Q^*). To incorporate these externalities into individual decision making requires some form of collective action to force commuters to pay the full costs of their actions. For example, voters, through their elected representatives, may decide to reduce the number of commuter miles driven by private automobiles by erecting toll booths on all major freeways or simply forcing everyone who drives into the city to pay a commuter tax. In either case, the goal is to force private decision makers to take into account the external costs of their actions. By moving the *MPC* closer to the *MSC*, the number of commuter miles driven will approach its optimal level, Q^*.

In the case of positive externalities, the competitive output rate will be too small if the decision maker cannot capture the externalities generated. The problem emerges because the marginal private benefit is less than the marginal social benefit. When marginal cost and marginal private benefit are equated, the resulting output is less than optimal.

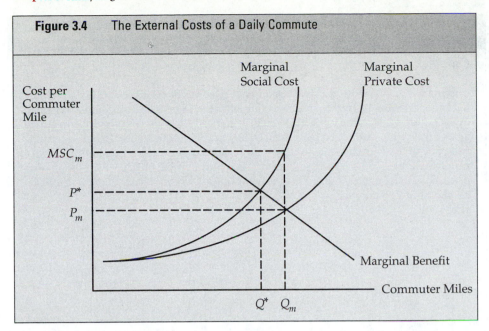

Figure 3.4   The External Costs of a Daily Commute

Public Goods

Markets distribute goods efficiently when people spend their own money in order to enjoy the benefits of consumption. The market for Nike shoes works because those unwilling to pay the price for Nikes do not own Nikes. The market mechanism provides purchasers with the benefits of consumption and excludes nonpurchasers from receiving those benefits. Additionally, the benefits flow to specific individuals. Consumption of a crispy taco by one person does not satisfy the hunger of another.

In certain situations, these two characteristics do not hold. In fact, many important goods, such as national defense and air traffic control, do not exhibit them fully. Nonexcludable and **nonrival goods** are called public goods. Nonexcludability in the distribution of a good results when the costs of preventing nonpayers from consuming are high, making it difficult to impose prices on these individuals. Once a strategic national defense system is operational, there is no way to exclude individuals from its protective umbrella simply because they refuse to pay their share of the costs.

Nonrivalry in consumption means that more than one person can enjoy the benefits of consuming a commodity without affecting the enjoyment of the other. One person's consumption does not reduce the benefit received by someone else. In technical terms, the marginal cost of providing the good to additional consumers is zero. For example, after the Army Corps of Engineers builds a levy, any number of houses may be built in the flood plain without increasing the marginal cost of flood control. If an air traffic control system is in place, the marginal cost of monitoring the flight path of an additional aircraft is zero.

Serious efficiency problems arise when we attempt to provide **nonexcludable goods** through private markets. To understand the problem, note the difference between the provision of excludable and nonexcludable goods. Transactions involving private goods—excludable goods—take place in markets as long as the individual's marginal valuation of that good exceeds its price. Individuals have no incentive to lie about the marginal value placed on a good. Because of excludability, if you understate the marginal value you place on a good, you run the risk of not getting the good and losing out on the marginal benefits of consumption. If you have ever witnessed an auction of any kind, you are familiar with this concept. Marginal valuations are reflected in the prices individuals are willing to pay for items that are being auctioned. You must make those marginal valuations known or you run the risk of finding yourself empty-handed at the end of the auction.

nonrival goods
A situation in which the consumption of a good or service by one individual does not limit the amount available to anyone else.

nonexcludable goods
A situation in which it is difficult to limit access to a good or service to a specific group of consumers. If the item is available to anyone, it becomes available to everyone.

OPTIMAL OUTPUT: PRIVATE VERSUS PUBLIC GOODS

The market demand for a private good is derived by horizontally summing all the individual demands. In this case total output is the sum of the amounts consumed by each individual in the market. When goods are rival goods, the amount consumed by one individual cannot be consumed by anyone else. In the diagram below, assume two consumers with demand curves D_1 and D_2. Equating market demand (ΣD) with supply results in a price of P_0 and an optimal output level of Q^*. Given the market price, each consumer will demand a level of output where price is equal to the marginal cost of production.

Private Good

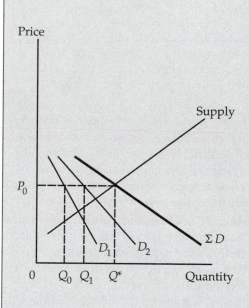

Public Good

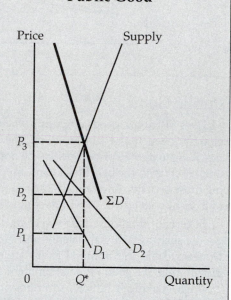

In the case of a public good, the market demand curve is determined by the group's willingness to pay for a given level of output. (In this case, the group consists of two people, 1 and 2.) Since the good is nonrival, the market demand curve is derived by summing the individual demand curves vertically, instead of horizontally as was the case for a private (rival) good. At the optimal level of output (Q^*), the group is willing to pay P_3, the sum of P_1 and P_2. Remember that Q^* is the optimal level for the good because at that level the marginal social benefit is equal to the marginal social cost of production.

In the society at large, identifying the marginal social benefit curve is problematic. No one is required to reveal his or her individual marginal valuations, so determining society's willingness to pay becomes a challenge. Some individuals will find it worthwhile to become **free riders**. The free-rider problem may not be a big issue when there are only two people in the group because of peer pressure. But in a large society no one person places a high enough marginal value on the good to ensure its provision. In other words, the marginal costs are substantially higher than any one person's or small group's demand (Ds in the diagram on the next page). Under these circumstances, the market simply will not ensure the production of the good. Its cost will simply be too high for anyone to absorb without collective action.

free rider
An individual who does not buy insurance knowing that in the event of a serious illness medical care will be provided free of charge.

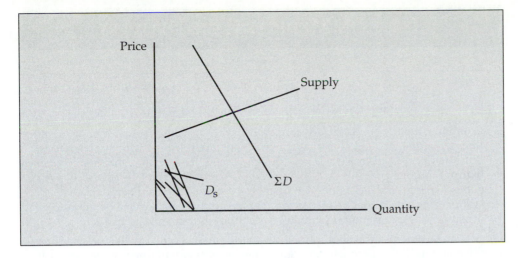

In contrast, when goods are nonexcludable, there is an incentive for individuals to understate their true marginal valuations. If I can enjoy all the benefits of consumption without paying for that privilege, why pay? Those individuals who refuse to pay for a good while still enjoying the benefits of consumption are called free riders (some might even call them free-loaders). Public television provides a good example of the free-rider problem. The number of people who watch public television far exceeds the number who subscribe. Of course, if some ride free, others have to pay or no one rides at all. And that's the point. Private markets tend to undersupply nonexcludable goods.

The case of public goods is simply a special kind of positive externality. So to ensure its availability at optimal levels, public provision of the good may be required. Governments can require individuals to participate in paying for goods through the power to tax. Clearly, all goods publicly provided are not public goods. Whether the good is provided by a government entity is not the issue. Governments often engage in the provision of private goods, for example, by staging concerts in the park and collecting garbage. In both cases, nonpayers may be excluded from consumption at very little cost, eliminating the problem of the free rider.

Even strong defenders of the market admit that private markets do not always provide goods and services at efficient levels. But those critical of market outcomes must address the issue of whether the government can do a better job. Is government provision any more efficient than private provision? Does it result in a more equitable distribution of resources? Is a more equitable distribution of resources worth the cost? We will focus on this question later in the chapter.

> ### Policy Issue
>
> Is government provision of medical care more efficient than provision through the private market?

Market Failure in Medical Markets

The obvious starting point in analyzing market failure in medical markets begins with the three causes of market failure discussed previously. How prevalent are monopolies in medical markets? Are there significant externalities in consumption and production? Is medical care a public good, nonexcludable in distribution and nonrival in consumption?

Traditional Sources of Market Failure

Even though absolute market power in medical markets may be hard to find, lack of competition can still be a significant problem. Most metropolitan areas are served by more than one hospital due to the simple fact that economies of scale in the hospital industry are exhausted at relatively low levels of capacity. Even in communities as

ISSUES IN MEDICAL CARE DELIVERY

MEDICAL CARE AS A "MERIT GOOD"

Economic models predicting consumer behavior usually assume, among other things, that individuals know what they want and are able to rank their preferences. But often people avoid what is good for them and choose items that are actually harmful. Recognizing this fact, Musgrave (1959) classified certain goods as **merit goods** to describe commodities that ought to be provided even if private demand is lacking. Since merit goods have benefits that are not fully appreciated by the average consumer, their consumption should be encouraged through collective action.

Many would place medical care in the merit-good category. Individuals, lacking the ability to fully appreciate the importance of primary and preventive care, will under-consume when it comes to this valuable commodity. Whether this classification is merely a case of imposing preferences on society or whether it is a genuine merit good situation is open to debate.

The usual arguments used to justify government involvement in medical care delivery and finance include market failure, information problems, third-party financing, and even merit goods. These arguments are often compelling, if not always convincing. But when using the merit goods argument we must be careful that we are not merely replacing a personal value judgment that everyone is entitled to medical care with formal terminology in order to justify our personal preferences (Baumol and Baumol, 1981).

Sources: Richard A. Musgrave, *The Theory of Public Finance*, New York: McGraw-Hill, 1959; William J. Baumol and Hilda Baumol, "Book Review," *Journal of Political Economy* 89(2), April 1981, 425–428.

---

merit good
A good whose benefits are not fully appreciated by the average consumer, and thus should be provided collectively.

---

small as 180,000 people, two or three hospitals providing most general services could coexist. In smaller communities, the lack of competition presents a greater challenge for market proponents. In these small markets, some inpatient services must be shared to avoid substantial inefficiencies (Kronick et al., 1993).

Even in larger communities with multiple facilities, some providers may have a degree of market power. There are some services and procedures that exhibit significant economies of scale, such as organ transplantation and various imaging technology that include CT scans (computerized tomographic X-ray device) and MRIs (magnetic resonance imaging).

Although pure monopoly may be difficult to find, firms often engage in interdependent behavior to avoid competition, a form of oligopoly. Recognizing that it is in their collective interest not to engage in price competition, providers differentiate their products to make direct price comparisons difficult. There is competition along the lines of quality and number of services offered, but not price. Differentiation is often accomplished when providers agree to specialize, for example, with one hospital offering cardiac care and another obstetric care. This type of market segmentation is relatively easy because most medical care is provided locally.

Externalities arise in medical care in a number of circumstances. The most obvious type of externality is associated with public health programs. Modern society can be a breeding ground for all sorts of communicable diseases. The ability of the Public Health Service to enforce health regulations and monitor contagious diseases serves to improve public health. Related activities include the provision of clean water, clean air, and adequate sewage disposal, which greatly reduce the incidence of diseases such as cholera and dysentery. In addition, immunization against mumps, measles, small

Back-of-the-Envelope

THE ECONOMICS OF SUBSIDIZING CHILDHOOD IMMUNIZATIONS

Public health officials recommend that children should receive a full round of vaccinations, including polio, measles, mumps, and whooping cough, before the age of two. To the extent that any children are not vaccinated, the entire childhood immunization program is undermined. The children who go unvaccinated are more likely to get sick, which lowers their welfare. They are also more likely to serve as carriers of the disease and infect others, which lowers the welfare of everybody else. This situation describes the classic case of positive externalities in consumption, where the marginal private benefits (*MPB*) fall short of the marginal social benefits (*MSB*).

Consumers, unable to capture the total benefit of their decision to vaccinate, respond only to private benefits. Thus, market demand is the sum of the individual marginal private benefits (*MPB*). The market would equilibrate at point *A* where $MPB = MSC$ with price equal to P_1 and the equilibrium number of vaccinations would be Q_1. Due to the positive externalities associated with vaccinations, the marginal social benefit curve (*MSB*) is above *MPB*. Welfare maximization would equate *MSB* with *MSC* at point *C* and produce Q_2 output at a price P_2. Without a built-in mechanism that enables consumers to capture these external benefits, the relevant demand curve is *MPB* instead of *MSB*. Equating demand with supply, results in equilibrium at P_1 and Q_1. Output falls short of its optimal level and a social loss depicted by the triangle *ABC* occurs.

Policy Issue

Should everyone be required to participate in an immunization program designed to protect the entire population against a communicable disease?

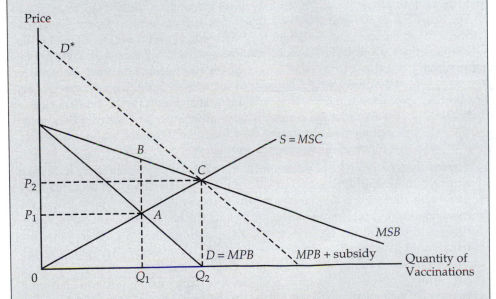

One way to improve social welfare would be to subsidize consumption. A subsidy equal to P_2 would remove the gap between *MPB* and *MSB*. Graphically, this is shown by the dashed line labeled "*MPB* + subsidy." With the subsidy, demand is now D^* and the equilibrium quantity is Q_2. Providers receive a price of P_2 and consumers receive the vaccinations for a net price of zero (P_2 minus the subsidy). Under these circumstances, *MSB* equals *MSC*, output is at its optimal level, and economic welfare is maximized. Economists almost always argue in favor of subsidies for the private provision of goods and services over direct government provision.

Policy Issue

Are subsidies to private providers better than direct government provision when the goal is to improve economic welfare?

in-kind transfer
Welfare subsidies provided in the form of vouchers for specific goods and services, such as food stamps and Medicaid.

Policy Issue
Should medical care subsidies take the form of direct cash payments or in-kind transfers?

pox, polio, and whooping cough offers protection for more than one individual. The benefits extend to the entire population by eliminating potential carriers of the diseases. In other words, the incremental value to society is greater than the value to the individual alone. In a private market, fewer vaccinations would occur than is socially optimal and may call for collective action in the form of mandates or subsidies or both.

Many argue that social or philanthropic externalities are associated with the consumption of medical care. These consumption externalities arise because the healthy and economically well-to-do derive satisfaction from knowing that the sick and indigent also receive medical care—a type of social solidarity. Individuals who share this philanthropic desire can and do join together and fund private foundations and medical organizations. The annual Jerry Lewis telethon provides individuals with the opportunity to unite in the fight against muscular dystrophy. Personal contributions to the United Way, the Ronald McDonald House, the Children's Miracle Network, the American Cancer Society, and numerous other national and local organizations advance the fight against certain diseases and provide access to medical treatments that might otherwise be prohibitively expensive.

Given the nature of the externality, even those who refuse to contribute enjoy the benefits of knowing that medical research is finding cures for certain diseases and that certain medical services are available for those who cannot afford to pay for them. If this consumption externality exists and is significant, then collective action through government can be used to provide medical care to that segment of the population that cannot afford to buy it privately. Those who would not contribute privately now share the responsibility through mandatory taxation. Collective action determines the nature of the subsidy, the level of taxation, and the method of distribution.

The medical subsidy is almost always an **in-kind transfer** rather than a cash payment. Beneficiaries prefer cash rather than services. They almost always find themselves better off with the cash. Donors generally prefer in-kind benefits because of the lack of guarantees that cash would be used for medical care. In fact, Waldo et al. (1989) indicate that a cash transfer to the elderly equivalent to their per capita share of Medicare would do more to improve their welfare than the current subsidy for medical services. It seems that donors (in this case, taxpayers) care about health differently from other aspects of the recipients' well-being, such as whether the food they eat is healthful or the houses they live in are adequately heated and cooled.

Externalities may also be associated with exceptionally large medical expenditures. Frequently, those with no health insurance or incomplete insurance coverage have medical bills that exceed their ability to pay. Faced with this event, they default on their obligation and the community must pick up the tab. In other words, providers are forced to write off the expenses as bad debts and shift the costs of care onto privately insured patients.[6] The fact that we are unable or at least unwilling to exclude anyone from access to medical care for financial reasons gives rise to the problem of the free rider. For this reason, many advocate mandatory health insurance covering catastrophic (high-cost) episodes of illness. In this way, everyone would be forced to participate in the cost of providing medical care and the free-rider problem would be moderated.

Pure medical research that has no easily captured commercial value fits the definition of a public good. This is the type of medical research that is packaged and published primarily in medical journals. Much of the information that is shared in this manner shows other medical practitioners ways of combining activities and procedures into a particular mode of treatment. Unless patentable medical devices are included in

---

6 Medical care providers usually report the delinquent debtor to the appropriate credit bureau. This has become so common that many lenders, such as commercial banks and consumer credit companies, regularly ignore a default on a would-be borrower's credit history if the debt was associated with medical care (private conversation with Bart Cooper, GMAC).

ISSUES IN MEDICAL CARE DELIVERY

THE LESSONS FROM SARS

For those traveling to Canada, Europe, and Asia during the spring of 2003, SARS became a household word. Severe acute respiratory syndrome, or SARS for short, leaped onto the front pages of newspapers from Toronto to Singapore to Tokyo. Reminiscent of the 1995 movie *Outbreak* where a lethal virus spreads from an African monkey, SARS challenged the ability of the public health community to react to the real-life outbreak of a deadly disease.

How easy is it to control a new infectious disease? That depends on how it's transmitted, how hard it is to catch, whether apparently healthy individuals can spread the disease, and whether the organism can find an appropriate host in a non-human species. The SARS challenge was complicated by the fact that the Chinese authorities (where the disease originated) failed to report the existence of SARS for months, and then tried to hide the extent of the spread of the disease.

With no treatment yet available, controlling the disease has been very crude—identifying everyone infected, tracing everyone they have come into contact with, and isolating them all. Tracing everyone may be impossible, so the only option may be mass quarantines, school closures, and cancelled vacations and holidays.

All things considered, SARS was relatively mild as far as epidemics go. As of June 11, 2003, the World Health Organization (WHO) had received reports of 8,435 probable cases from 29 countries, including 70 from the United States. There were 789 deaths, translating into a mortality ratio of 9.4 percent. The world community was lucky this time. We may not be so lucky when the next deadly bug comes along. Designer face masks may not be enough to protect us from a bug that is more contagious than SARS. In the meantime, the public health community must come up with better systems and procedures to effectively enforce large-scale quarantines to give the medical research community time to study the infectious disease agents and come up with the appropriate medical response.

The next time you hear reports of some strange illness in a remote corner of the globe, don't think it will have no impact on your life. Let's hope that the health authorities have learned the lessons from SARS.

Source: Daniel Haydon and Olivia Judson, "A Health Warning to the World," *Financial Times*, May 9, 2003, 13.

the procedures, it is difficult for those responsible for the discovery to capture the benefits of their research. Good examples include radial keratonomy and the use of lasers in ophthalmological surgery.

Many will argue that medical research should be treated as a public good and financed collectively through government. In this way, basic advances financed by the taxpayer would belong in the public domain, freely available to potential users. The other side of the argument recognizes that academicians conduct much of our medical research. Working within the university and medical school setting, they are able to capture the benefits of their discoveries through the rules of promotion and tenure. Thus, at least a portion of the benefits is translated into career enhancement opportunities and personal prestige. Some may choose to keep their findings out of the public domain in order to earn royalties or other payments.

> ### Policy Issue
> Is medical research a public good, thus strengthening the argument in favor of government financing of basic medical research?

To the extent that medical care has characteristics associated with market power among providers, externalities in production and consumption, and public goods, the level of services provided will fall short of the optimal level as defined by competitive markets.

Imperfections in Medical Markets

Other imperfections contribute to the failure of medical markets to provide the socially optimal level of service (see Pauly, 1988). These imperfections include imperfect information, barriers to entry, and the prevalence of third-party payers.

Imperfect Information

Lack of information presents serious problems in a market economy. In medical markets the problems that arise may be even more serious. Most patients are poorly informed about virtually every aspect of the medical transaction. They are usually aware of their symptoms and syndromes, but seldom do they understand the underlying causes of their medical conditions. They have scarcely an opportunity to form a learned opinion about the physician's diagnosis or the prescribed treatment. In most cases, anything other than a complete recovery is not part of the expected outcome.

The overall lack of information available to patients is compounded by the difficulty in securing the information, measured in terms of time and expense. As a result, most patients rely almost exclusively on their providers to keep them informed on matters dealing with their medical conditions, diagnoses, and treatment alternatives. Patients also have little knowledge about price and quality differences among alternative providers. This imbalance of information between patient and provider, referred to as asymmetric information, has led to two important market defects.

First, patients are not able to judge price and quality differences among providers. As a result, providers can charge prices that are higher than the prevailing prices in the market for a given level of quality, or they may choose to offer a lower level of quality for a given price. The impact of this phenomenon can be seen in the variation in prices paid and the quantities of medical care provided to similar groups of patients. Evidence for these variations has been compiled by examining, for example, surgery rates for common procedures. In cases where alternative intervention strategies are not available, such as appendectomy, hernia repair, and hysterectomy, the variation in surgery rates is relatively low. But in cases where alternative treatments are available, such as tonsillectomy, disc surgery, and coronary artery bypass grafts, variation is high, up to four times the rate of the low-variance surgeries (Phelps, 1992).

The second problem may be described as an agency problem. The physician serves as the agent of the patient. The patient delegates most of the decision-making authority to the physician. The expectation, in turn, is that the patient's best interests will be the top priority. The dual role of provider of services on the one hand and the agent in charge of information on the other creates a dilemma. The physician is in a position to induce the patient to purchase more medical care than is actually needed. Physicians can recommend not only medical care with little marginal value, medical care on the flat-of-the-curve, but also medical care that may actually harm the patient. At the other extreme, enrollees in managed-care organizations may find themselves denied care with positive net benefits because it is not in the financial interest of the provider to offer that care.

This information problem does not mean that medical markets are hopelessly non-competitive. Market mechanisms have arisen to minimize the impact of these information differences. The medical community has created licensing, certification, and accreditation requirements for physicians, specialists, hospitals, and medical schools to assure minimum quality standards. Professional organizations establish ethical standards. And if this is not enough, the threat of a malpractice lawsuit is always a reminder of the importance of promoting the best interests of the patient.

Keep in mind that other markets also exhibit this information problem and are relatively competitive. The market for personal computers is a good example. Except for a small segment of the market, the general public is woefully ignorant of the differences

ISSUES IN MEDICAL CARE DELIVERY

ADVERTISING PROFESSIONAL SERVICES: THE CASE OF OPTOMETRY

In most private markets consumers gain access to important information through advertising. The argument against advertising professional services is based on the belief that advertising may mislead consumers, undermine quality, and ultimately raise prices. Professional associations representing medical practitioners have led the battle defending the long-standing restrictions on price advertising in medical markets.

Economic theory argues in favor of advertising in markets characterized by **asymmetric information** between buyers and sellers, where sellers have all the information and buyers have none. For example, advertising provides consumers with information on alternative sources of supply. This will result in lower prices because consumer demand for individual providers becomes more elastic. In addition, one of the goals of advertising is to increase consumer demand. To the extent that advertisers realize this benefit, they can take advantage of economies of scale in production and actually lower prices to consumers.

Although advertising may result in lower prices, its effect on product quality is less certain. In theory, high-quality providers have more to gain by advertising through repeat purchasers. In practice, however, low-quality providers advertise more. Ultimately, the effect of advertising on quality will be determined by consumer demand for quality and provider determination to produce quality; the latter governed in large part by ethical standards established by the specific profession.

Considering all the evidence, a federal appeals court ruled in 1980 that physicians and other medical professionals could advertise prices and services. Kwoka (1984), studying the market of optometric services, was one of the first to examine the impact of advertising on prices and quality. Results indicated that advertisers' prices and quality were lower and that nonadvertisers' prices also fell. However, the quality of the services offered by nonadvertisers actually increased. Given a sufficiently large number of nonadvertisers, overall quality in the market increased. Kwoka estimated that quality-adjusted prices for optometric services fell by 20 percent as a result of advertising. Thus, loosening restrictions on advertising in optometry actually improved economic welfare.

Source: John E. Kwoka, Jr., "Advertising and the Price and Quality of Optometric Services," *American Economic Review* 74(1), March 1984, 211–216.

asymmetric information
A situation in which information is unequally distributed between the individuals in a transaction. The person with more information will have an unfair advantage in determining the terms of any agreement.

Policy Issue
Should physicians and other health care providers be allowed to advertise?

---

between RAM and ROM, the number of meg in a gig, and the merits of the Pentium and Celeron processors. Are there good reasons to buy Mac instead of PC? Do I want a zip drive or a DVD? Do I need an internal fax modem? Even with all this consumer ignorance, the market for personal computers is extremely competitive. Why? Because an informed minority provided the initial market discipline. They wrote the newsletters, contributed to the magazines, and spent endless hours on the Internet participating in forums and posting on bulletin boards. The demand for information fostered by this group created awareness among all consumers.

When consumers perceive that acquiring and using information best serve their own interests, there will be a demand for information. Consumers in medical markets do not perceive that their interests are served by spending time and money to acquire information. The third-party payer—the insurance company or the government—expropriates any savings from the search. Change that aspect of the medical marketplace and consumers will have an incentive to become informed. Virtually all types of medical care, except emergency care, would be purchased in markets with enough informed consumers to ensure economic discipline. The demand for information is evident in the managed care marketplace where many organizations and networks are reporting to their constituencies on how well they perform in certain critical areas, including primary and preventive care, surgical outcomes, and cost (Kenkel, 1994).

Barriers to Entry

An important characteristic found in competitive markets is easy entry and easy exit of suppliers. Profits serve as a signal to prospective providers. If profits are greater than normally expected for a given level of risk, firms will enter the market and drive down prices and profits will adjust to normal levels. Lower-than-normal profits will result in the opposite response, with marginally profitable firms leaving the market and driving up prices and profits for those who remain.

Entry barriers restrict resource movements and result in imperfect competition. Examples of barriers in medical markets are found in numerous restrictions on tasks performed and investments made. The licensing and certification of practitioners are two of the most common ways to restrict entry into the medical profession. The stated purpose of this policy is consumer protection. Its aim is to keep uninformed patients from seeking services from incompetent providers. **Certificate of need** (CON) laws require hospitals to secure approval from government planning agencies before adding new capacity or investing in expensive equipment. CON legislation seeks to eliminate the duplication of costly programs within a service area. Restrictions may sound good in theory, but one of the unintended consequences of any limits placed on a market is the elimination of competition. Reduced competition leads to market power and market power leads to market failure.

Third-Party Payers

In traditional markets, individuals spending their own money provide the discipline that culminates in the efficient provision of goods and services. One of the main reasons medical markets are not efficient is that consumers do not spend their own money. Only about 3 cents of every dollar spent on hospital services and 20 cents out of every dollar spent on physicians' services come directly from patients' out-of-pocket spending. The rest is paid by third parties, primarily health insurance companies and the government. Therein lies the major problem in medical markets. Typically, pricing reflects the interaction of consumers' willingness to pay for goods and services and their ability to buy them. Medical markets regularly ignore the desires of those without insurance or the ability to pay for care out-of-pocket. The desires of those who have insurance are distorted by the subsidy provided by their insurance.

A system financed primarily through retrospective **fee-for-service** insurance reimbursement is open-ended. Providers are able to pass through all their costs, no matter how inefficient the production of services. The system can be described as a **cost-plus pricing** system (Goodman and Musgrave, 1992). In a cost-plus environment, there is no incentive for providers to search for more efficient methods of production, and patients have no incentive to search for providers who offer lower prices. In competitive markets, providers are rewarded for offering quality products at the lowest price. In cost-plus markets, providers are rewarded by offering more services at higher prices, passing on the additional costs to the third-party payers.

Several factors led to the growth and expansion of the cost-plus system from the end of the Second World War through the 1980s. The American Medical Association (AMA) controlled medical licensing. This not-for-profit institution effectively limited competition in the medical profession by requiring that anyone wishing to practice

---

certificate of need
Regulations that attempt to avoid the costly duplication of services in the hospital industry. Providers are required to secure a certificate of need before undertaking a major expansion of facilities or services.

fee-for-service
The traditional payment method for medical care where a provider bills for each episode of care.

cost-plus pricing
A pricing scheme in which a percentage profit is added to average cost.

medicine must graduate from an AMA-approved medical school. Not-for-profit and government-run institutions dominated the hospital sector. Without the economic discipline provided by the profit motive, hospitals competed for physicians. Operating surpluses were directed toward investment in new services and expensive equipment by physician-dominated boards. As a result, excess capacity in beds, nursing staffs, and allied personnel were used to maximize the ability of physicians to generate income for themselves. Finally, Blue Cross/Blue Shield dominated the health insurance industry, and the addition of Medicare and Medicaid in the 1960s meant that not-for-profit payers were financing over one-half of all medical care provided. This dominance created an atmosphere where cost was a secondary consideration. Without a cost constraint, the only thing that mattered was the patient's health. Whether the procedure provided a net benefit was not an issue.

Restraint was not present on the demand side either because insurance was paying the bills. Conventional health insurance distorts the decision-making process by making it appear that medical care is cheap at the point of purchase. Medical care, of course, is not cheap. But cost-plus reimbursement by third-party payers provides an incentive for people to demand interventions that provide little benefit.

> **Policy Issue**
> Conventional health insurance virtually eliminates any cost-conscious behavior on the part of the parties involved in the medical care transaction.

The cost-plus system began to run into problems during the 1980s. No matter how prosperous a nation, each has a limit to how much its people are willing to spend on any single item. As health care spending approached and exceeded 10 percent of gross domestic product, showing no signs of slowing down, policymakers and planners began to address the concerns about the "health care crisis." Thus began the bureaucratic struggle to slow the growth in health care spending.

In its early stages, this struggle focused on reimbursement strategies and restrictions on access to services. Medicare and Medicaid placed restrictions on providers by creating fee schedules and changing the method of reimbursement from **retrospective payment** to prospective payment. Private payers did the same, using the strategy of managed care. In both cases, the focus was not on changing buyer behavior but on limiting unnecessary procedures and services.

retrospective payment
Payment determined after delivery of the good or service. Traditional fee-for-service medicine determines payment retrospectively.

The move to prospective payment creates incentives on the supply side to limit care. The desires of patients become a secondary consideration, subordinated to the desire to control costs. The stage is set for the next phase of the cost-plus cycle. Either the system will evolve into one where individuals are motivated by the economic discipline of the market or one where they are dominated by the bureaucratic discipline of the government.

Government Intervention in Medical Markets

Government involvement in the medical marketplace is extensive. The involvement includes financing, direct provision, regulation, and subsidization. More than 45 percent of all health care spending comes directly from government sources, including Medicare, Medicaid, and the various health plans covering government employees and their dependents, both civilian and military. Government regulators are responsible for licensing, occupational health and safety, the administration of food and drugs, environmental protection, public health, and other oversight functions. Finally, the government uses features of the tax code to subsidize and encourage the provision of group insurance in employer-sponsored plans.

Regulation

The health care industry is one of the most heavily regulated industries in the United States' economy. Price controls, entry restrictions covering both providers and hospitals, and regulations on the development and introduction of new drugs and medical devices are the major areas of regulatory control affecting the health care economy.

Price Controls

The United States has a long history of placing restrictions on markets in the form of wage and price controls. World War II, the Korean War, and the wage-price freeze that was part of the stabilization program enacted during the Nixon Administration are a few of the instances where government has attempted to fight inflation by freezing prices. Since the inception of Medicare and Medicaid, medical markets have been subject to price controls of one variety or another. In the beginning physicians' fees were limited to **usual, customary, and reasonable (UCR) charges**. Under UCR, physicians could charge the minimum of a doctor's usual fee, defined by the median fee during the past year, and the customary fee, defined by the fees charged by other doctors in the area. The use of UCR resulted in a steady escalation of physicians' fees. The formula left no reason for a physician's usual fee to be lower than the customary fee charged in the area. If the usual fee was the minimum in the formula, Medicare paid the usual fee. As individual fees escalated, area fees escalated. The underlying incentive was always to make sure that one's usual fee was not the minimum.

Medical prices continued to rise faster than the rate of overall inflation. As prices increased, spending increased. Efforts to limit spending growth shifted to the hospital sector in the early 1980s with the introduction of prospective payment. The new approach paid hospitals for an episode of treatment instead of the usual cost-plus method. Under prospective payment, hospitals were paid according to the expected cost of treating a particular patient based on the principal diagnosis.[7] If the actual cost of treatment was less than the payment, the hospital kept the surplus. If actual costs were greater, the hospital absorbed the loss or shifted the costs to other patients. Prospective payment changes the incentive structure completely. The hospital is no longer rewarded for providing more services at a higher cost. It is actually in the best interest of the hospital to limit the amount and quality of service offered—to limit admissions and discharge patients as quickly as possible. Although hospital admissions moderated and average length of stay fell dramatically, the use of outpatient services increased dramatically, leading some to question whether the potential for savings has been exhausted (Schwartz, 1987).

Attributing the spending restraint to the method of paying hospitals, the focus shifted back to physicians' fees. The 1990s saw the advent of the relative value scale for determining allowable physician fees. Basing fees on resource use, the relative value scale is an attempt by bureaucrats to mimic markets. If the value scale is set correctly, prices will be set at levels that would exist in a competitive market. The relative value scale has redefined the payment structure, treating evaluation and patient management services to higher relative fees while lowering relative fees paid for invasive procedures.

Entry Restrictions

The government has a long history of licensing, certifying, and accrediting medical care providers. Although the stated purpose of these restrictions is consumer protection, some evidence exists that the self-interest of the providers may be the driving force behind the practice (Kessel, 1958; Moore, 1961). Licensing attempts to limit the likelihood that incompetent providers will treat uninformed patients. Originally, licensing merely placed restrictions on who was allowed to open a medical practice. As time passed, restrictions were expanded to cover a wide range of activities deemed unethical by practicing physicians. These activities included advertising, price cutting, and other conduct considered "unprofessional." Clearly licensing laws serve not only to protect patients but also to limit the number of practitioners, thus protecting physicians from would-be competitors.

usual, customary, and reasonable charges
A price ceiling set to limit fees to the minimum of the billed charge, the price customarily charged by the provider, and the prevailing charge in the geographic region.

---

7 Other factors included in the reimbursement formula are the percentage of free care provided to indigents, whether the institution is a teaching hospital, and whether it is located in an urban area.

Limits on New Product Development

Congress established the **Food and Drug Administration (FDA)** in 1938 to oversee the entry of new drugs and medical devices into the medical market. The FDA does not allow new drugs on the market until they have been thoroughly tested and ultimately proved safe and effective.[8] Even though the FDA has had several major successes in the past (the most notable was keeping the tranquilizer, thalidomide, off the U.S. market), the time from the discovery of a promising chemical compound to drug approval averages 12 years. The cost to the public of a dangerous drug is obvious. The cost of delaying a beneficial drug is hidden.

Food and Drug Administration (FDA)
A public health agency charged with protecting American consumers by enforcing federal public health laws. Food, medicine, medical devices, and cosmetics are under the jurisdiction of the FDA.

Tax Policy

Policymakers and planners often use tax subsidies to encourage certain types of behavior. (Those who do not qualify for them call these subsidies "loopholes.") Federal and state income tax provisions subsidize the purchase of health insurance. A key ruling by the Tax Court after the Second World War exempted certain nonwage benefits from being included in an employee's taxable income. It was during this period of wage and price controls that government policymakers chose to use the power to tax (or in this case, the power not to tax) to encourage employers to offer group health insurance to their workers. Since that time, group health insurance has been a nontaxable benefit for employees and at the same time a tax-deductible expense for employers.

Sheils and Hogan (1999) estimate that the subsidy in terms of forgone tax revenues exceeded $100 billion in 1998. The value of the subsidy to the individual is equal to the annual insurance premium paid by the employer multiplied by the individual's marginal tax bracket. The benefits of the tax subsidy increase as a person's income increases. If the annual premium paid by the employer is $4,000, a person in the 15 percent marginal tax bracket saves $600 a year in taxes by receiving the benefit instead of the income. In contrast, a person in the 42 percent tax bracket saves $1,680 on the same policy.[9]

One of the major consequences of this tax subsidy is that individuals demand more health insurance when it is purchased by their employers than if they had received the income and bought it themselves. Most economists will agree that paying insurance premiums with before-tax dollars leads to overconsumption of medical care. Paying for expensive insurance with before-tax dollars makes more sense than paying for expensive medical care with after-tax dollars. As a result, indemnity insurance policies traditionally have had low deductibles and copayment requirements.

Government Failure

Even markets that work perfectly offer no guarantee that the efficient allocation of resources would satisfy the public's desires for equity in the distribution of goods and services. On the other hand, no credible evidence supports government remedies as the answer for the perceived inequities either. It is debatable whether government solutions will always improve welfare. Markets may fail, but governments may be just as prone to failure. And correcting government failure is inherently more difficult than correcting market failure.

Few will question the intentions of government involvement in medical care. Everyone is in favor of improved access and lower costs. But careful consideration of the unintended consequences of government intervention is equally important. Choosing a health care strategy for yourself and your family is a difficult task. Choosing someone

---

8 In a 1962 amendment to FDA legislation, efficacy was added as a requirement. In other words, the drug had to be safe and work as claimed.

9 The self-employed did not always enjoy the same tax preference. The Tax Reform Act of 1996 allowed the self-employed to deduct only 25 percent of the cost of personal health insurance (up to a maximum of total self-employment income). The percentage increased over time and reached 100 percent in 2003.

ISSUES IN MEDICAL CARE DELIVERY

FDA REGULATION: THE CASE OF THE CARDIOPUMP

How can a patient who has no pulse give an informed consent? Developers of the cardiopump, a cardiopulmonary resuscitation device for heart-attack victims, must find a satisfactory answer to this question before the U.S. Food and Drug Administration (FDA) will allow further testing. Manual CPR exerts downward pressure on the chest, but must rely on the chest to re-expand naturally. The cardiopump, which looks like a modified toilet plunger, exerts pressure in both directions, pulling blood back into the heart and oxygen back into the lungs.

The product is available elsewhere around the world, including England, Germany, Sweden, Canada, Australia, Japan, and Chile. In fact, it is a standard device in ambulances in Austria and France. But the FDA considers it a "significant risk device" that requires informed consent before it can be used on anyone in a medical trial. For the developers of the device, this designation represents a Catch-22. Before the device can be used in a trial, the patient must give informed consent. But how can a patient with no pulse give informed consent?

The FDA is literally protecting patients in the United States to death. Approximately one million Americans have heart attacks every year. Of the 700,000 who are given CPR, only 20,000 survive to leave the hospital. Based on a limited sample in St. Paul, Minnesota, survival rates could increase by as much as 35 percent with the use of the cardiopump. That estimate fits comfortably within the range of a 10 to 50 percent improvement in expected survival rates. Extrapolating that number nationally implies that the device could save 7,000 lives annually.

The caution of the FDA is understandable. Regulators are sensitive to the criticisms that resound in the halls of Congress when a drug or medical device harms a single person during its testing. The agency's success in keeping the tranquilizer thalidomide off the market in the 1960s is an excellent case in point. In contrast, the 7,000 people whose lives could be saved every year with the approval of the cardiopump are silent in their protest. When we are talking about life-or-death situations, would it not be wise to reconsider the requirement for informed consent?

Source: Alexander Volokh, "Feel a Heart Attack Coming On—Go to France," *The Wall Street Journal*, August 2, 1994, A14

---

else to make that decision for you is not only difficult, it can be dangerous. Transferring decision making from the private sector to the public sector substitutes bureaucratic discipline for economic discipline.

The notion of perfect competition in markets is just as rare as the notion of perfect democracy in political science (Becker, 1958). Criticism directed at market failure without at least admitting the possibility of government failure is dishonest, or at minimum naive. Voters face considerable obstacles in getting their collective voices heard. The interval between elections is long, two to six years. The viable choices are limited, usually to the two major-party candidates, and agreement with every aspect of a candidate's platform is highly unlikely. Special interest groups through subsidized lobbying efforts have disproportionate influence on the decision-making process. And at the same time there is a problem in protecting minority desires when government is by majority rule.

These cautions should not discourage us from using government intervention as a strategy to ensure efficient market performance and equitable outcomes. But they should stand as a warning against relying too heavily on government to solve all our problems. Frequently, solutions proposed by well-meaning government policymakers

ISSUES IN MEDICAL CARE DELIVERY

MARKET FORCES: THE BEST WAY TO CONTROL PRICES?

Do prices in medical markets respond to competitive pressures like prices in other markets? As medical care costs continue to rise, some doubt whether competition can be relied upon to rein in medical spending. One medical market where competition is having a major impact is the market for certain pharmaceutical drugs. The industry has seen a major trend in the past decade with the development of "look-alike" drugs. Look-alikes are drugs with different chemical properties but equivalent medical benefits. Vasotec and Capoten are the two industry leaders in the ACE inhibitor class of heart drugs, capturing as much as 80 percent of the market in 1990. The recent introduction of Lotensin, at up to one-half the price of the leaders, has changed the nature of that market completely.

The trend toward look-alike drugs makes sound business sense. The industry leader has already proven the efficacy of the drug, so introducing a similar drug into the class poses less risk to the developer. But with no proven therapeutical advantages, the makers of Lotensin chose a marketing strategy based on deep price discounts and a guarantee to users of a fixed price for life. The potential payoffs can be enormous. For example, in the $2 billion ACE inhibitor market, a 5 percent market share translates into $100 million in annual sales.

Other big markets have experienced this same competitive pressure from look-alikes. Paxil has undercut Prozac and Zoloft, popular antidepressants. Similar stories could be told in the markets for antibiotics, ulcer medications, and cholesterol-reducing drugs. The result has been a dramatic reduction in the rate of increase in pharmaceutical prices in the past several years. Price increases during the 1980s regularly topped 2 to 3 times the rate of inflation in general. During the 1990s, drug inflation has moderated to as low as 5.7 percent in 1992. With the annual rate of inflation stabilizing at just over 3 percent, pharmaceutical companies still have a way to go before their goal of stability in real prices.

Responsibility for price slowdown may be attributed to the buying power of the big institutional purchasers such as Kaiser Permanente, a large West coast **health maintenance organization (HMO)**. Using their monopsony power (see Back-of-the-Envelope earlier in this chapter), the HMOs have been able to negotiate deep price discounts of as much as 40 to 60 percent below list prices and rebates of up to 75 percent of average wholesale prices. In return, the look-alikes are accepted on the HMO **formulary**, or list of drugs covered by the HMO.

Market forces will continue to exert downward pressure on drug prices as long as buyers have reliable alternatives to the established drugs. We may even expect that makers of the established drugs may soon begin discounting their products to discourage competition.

Source: Elyse Tanouye, "Drug Prices Get Dose of Market Pressure," *The Wall Street Journal*, March 11, 1993, B1, B5.

health maintenance organization (HMO)
An insurer and provider of medical care.

formulary
A list of approved pharmaceutical drugs that will be covered under a health plan. Other drugs are typically unavailable to members of the plan.

ignore the realities of the real world. We may not be able to create heaven on earth, but we may be able to improve the circumstances of millions of Americans with the right mix of market discipline and bureaucratic oversight.

The appropriate perspective in this debate is not whether the proposed system is efficient or fair (Pauly, 1997). No matter which alternative is chosen, it will be imperfect in its implementation. The appropriate perspective is whether efficiency and fairness are best addressed by imperfect government or imperfect markets.

Policy Issue
Does imperfect government address the issues of equity and efficiency in health care delivery better than imperfect markets?

Mark V. Pauly

If one journal article can launch a career, Mark Pauly has shown us how it can be done. His 1968 article in the *American Economic Review* entitled "The Economics of Moral Hazard" has become essential reading for anyone desiring to understand the effects of health insurance on health care utilization and cost. After receiving his Ph.D. in 1967, Pauly catapulted himself into the epicenter of health economics with his classic treatise.

After brief academic appointments at Northwestern University and his alma mater the University of Virginia, Pauly moved to the University of Pennsylvania's Wharton School where he became the Executive Director of the Leonard Davis Institute of Health Economics. Founded in 1967, the Leonard Davis Institute (LDI) has maintained a commitment to health services research and education in an interdisciplinary setting. He was named Bendheim Professor in 1990 and is currently chairperson of the Health Care Systems Department.

One article can launch a career, but the reputation of a scholar is based on continuous research output. Continuous may not be the appropriate term to describe Pauly's contribution to the health economics literature—unbelievable is probably better. With over 100 books, articles, and monographs, his research interests encompass medical economics and the role of markets in medical care, national health care policy, and health insurance. In addition, he is a member of the editorial boards of the *Journal of Health Economics*, the *Public Finance Quarterly*, and the *Journal of Risk and Uncertainty*, and an elected member of the Institutes of Medicine of the National Academy of Science.

Pauly is one of a handful of health economists worldwide who argue competition, when appropriately defined and understood, can work effectively in medical markets. Contrast this belief with the mainstream thought that gives little consideration to market solutions for the problems of medical care delivery and finance, and you begin to understand why many of his colleagues consider him an anomaly within the profession.

His belief that the incentive structure can shape both the behavior of patients and providers has resulted in his teaming with John C. Goodman, director of the National Center for Policy Analysis, in publishing the article "Tax Credits for Insurance and **Medical Savings Accounts**" in the Spring 1995 issue of *Health Affairs*. This innovative approach to health care reform recommends the use of tax credits, medical savings accounts, and high-deductible health insurance to improve both efficiency and equity in the health care sector. A colleague who does not share Pauly's faith in market solutions referred to his belief in markets as a "disease." If Pauly's insistence on a place for markets in health care delivery and finance is a disease, he is not likely to accept the "cure" without a struggle; especially when the proposed cure is a government-run system.

On more than one occasion he has stepped to the podium after a previous speaker had stirred the audience into a feeding frenzy on the various evils of the U.S. medical care delivery system only to quiet the crowd with his clear analytical approach and keen insight into the underlying issues, providing balance to a discussion where balance is often lacking. If the essential ingredients for making enlightened choices are knowledge and academic inquiry, Mark Pauly has advanced our ability to make enlightened choices through his outstanding contribution to the field of health economics and the economics of insurance.

Source: Mark V. Pauly, curriculum vitae.

medical savings account
A tax-exempt savings account used in conjunction with high-deductible health insurance. Individuals pay their own medical expenses using funds from the savings account up to the amount of the deductible. Once the deductible is met, the insurance policy pays all or most of the covered expenses.

Summary and Conclusions

Traditional microeconomics views the price mechanism as the invisible hand, leading to economic welfare maximization in a perfectly competitive market. In this chapter we have examined the requirements necessary for competitive markets to result in equitable and efficient outcomes. Sources of market failure, including market power, externalities, and public goods, were described and discussed. Other sources of failure, including information problems, barriers to entry, and third-party payers, were applied to medical markets.

The invisible hand is not able to perform its usual function in a system dominated by government decision makers. When government oversees production and consumption, it is the visible, tangible hand, or its equivalent, that determines prices. With complete knowledge of consumer preferences and producer capabilities, the efficiency problems could be solved. Following the reasoning of Lerner (1944), the planning agency must obtain the prices of all inputs and outputs, publish and distribute a list containing this information, and instruct all decision makers to act as if they were maximizers in a perfectly competitive market. In other words, substitute the superior wisdom of the planners for the collective wisdom of the masses.

Markets sometimes fail to produce the optimal level of output. The challenge facing policymakers is to intervene only in those situations where government action can improve welfare. Substituting government failure for market failure is not welfare enhancing. We need policymakers who understand this important lesson and intervene, not when they see market failure, but whenever government actions will actually take us closer to the social optimum.

If medical markets are to work, that is, if they are to produce acceptable levels of efficiency and equity, the following conditions must be present (Enthoven, 1988).

- Decisions must be made by well-informed, cost-conscious consumers. Motivated by self-interest and adequately informed about treatment alternatives, cost-conscious consumers will economize because they will personally benefit from their own economizing behavior. The patient/buyer must be an active participant in the decision-making process if **cost containment** is to be achieved.

Key Concept 4
Self-Interest

cost containment
Strategies used to control the total spending on health care services.

- Competition among providers is essential. Competition guards against undue concentration because substitutes are readily available. Coupled with the first condition, consumer demand is sensitive to price changes.

Key Concept 7
Competition

- Cost-conscious decisions are possible only if consumers who desire to enter the market have money to spend. Often phrased in terms of equity, the real issue is economic self-sufficiency. As such, medical care markets require either universal insurance coverage or universal access to insurance. The choice depends on whether the majority of the populace is concerned with equal outcomes or equal opportunities. Satisfying this condition ensures that the system is morally acceptable to a majority of the people.

Key Concept 4
Self-Interest

Questions and Problems

1. What is market failure? What are the major reasons that a free, unregulated market in medical care might not be optimal?

2. Proponents of a government-run health care system argue that the market does not work well in the medical care industry. What evidence do they use to support this claim?

3. Explain how market failure can be used to justify government intervention in medical care markets.

4. How do price controls affect the workings of a perfectly competitive market? Use a supply-demand diagram as part of your answer.

5. What assumptions of the perfectly competitive marketplace are violated in medical markets? How does each affect equilibrium price and quantity?

References

Gerard F. Anderson and Peter S. Hussey, *Multinational Comparisons of Health Systems Data*, Commonwealth Fund, October 2000.

William J. Baumol, "Do Health Care Costs Matter?" *The New Republic 209*(21), November 22, 1993, 16–18.

Gary S. Becker, "Competition and Democracy," *Journal of Law and Economics* 1, October 1958, 105–109.

Robert J. Blendon et al., "Who Has the Best Health System? A Second Look," *Health Affairs 14*(4) Winter 1995, 220–230.

David M. Cutler and Mark McClellan, "Is Technological Change in Medicine Worth It?" *Health Affairs 20*(5), September/October 2001, 11–29.

Alain C. Enthoven, "Managed Competition: An Agenda for Action," *Health Affairs 7*(3), Summer 1988, 25–47.

John C. Goodman and Gerald L. Musgrave, *Patient Power: Solving America's Health Care Crisis*, Washington, DC: Cato Institute, 1992.

D. L. Hoyert, K. D. Kochanek, and S. L. Murphy, "Deaths: Final Data for 1997," *National Vital Statistics Reports 47*(19), Hyattsville, MD: National Center for Health Statistics, 1999.

Paul J. Kenkel, "Health Plans Face Pressure to Find 'Report Card' Criteria That Will Make the Grade," *Modern Healthcare*, January 10, 1994, 41.

Reuben A. Kessel, "Price Discrimination in Medicine," *Journal of Law and Economics* 1, October 1958, 20–53.

Richard Kronick, David C. Goodman, John Wennberg, and Edward Wagner, "The Marketplace in Health Care Reform: The Demographic Limitations of Managed Competition," *The New England Journal of Medicine 328*(2), January 14, 1993, 148–152.

Abba Lerner, *The Economics of Control*, New York: Macmillan, 1944.

Frank R. Lichtenberg, "Sources of U.S. Longevity Increase, 1960–1997," NBER Working Paper No. 8755, Cambridge, MA: National Bureau of Economic Research, February 2002.

Robert J. Mills and Shailesh Shandari, "Health Insurance Coverage in the United States: 2002," *Current Population Reports*, P60–223, September 2003, 1–21.

Thomas G. Moore, "The Purpose of Licensing," *Journal of Law and Economics* 4, October 1961, 93–117.

Mark V. Pauly, "A Primer on Competition in Medical Markets," in *Health Care in America: The Political Economy of Hospitals and Health Insurance*, edited by H.E. Frech III, San Francisco: Pacific Research Institute for Public Policy, 1988, 27–71.

_____, "Is Medical Care Different? Old Questions, New Answers," *Journal of Health Politics, Policy and Law 13*(2), Summer 1988, 227–237.

_____, "Who was that Straw Man Anyway? A Comment on Evans and Rice," *Journal of Health Politics, Policy, and Law*, April 1997, 467–473.

Charles E. Phelps, "Diffusion of Information in Medical Care," *Journal of Economic Perspectives 6*(3), Summer 1992, 23–42.

Thomas Rice, *The Economics of Health Reconsidered*, Chicago, IL: Health Administration Press, 1998.

William B. Schwartz, "The Inevitable Failure of Current Cost-Containment Strategies: Why They Can Provide Only Temporary Relief," *Journal of the American Medical Association 257*(2), January 9, 1987, 220–224.

John Sheils and Paul Hogan, "Cost of Tax-Exempt Health Benefits in 1998," *Health Affairs 18*(2), March/April 1999, 176–181.

Irwin M. Stelzer, "There is No Health Care Crisis," *The Wall Street Journal*, January 25, 1994, A12.

Daniel Waldo, et al., "Health Expenditures by Age Group, 1977–1987," *Health Care Financing Review 10*(4), Summer 1989, 111–120.

Appendix 3A

The Economics of Consumer Choice

To explain consumer behavior economists use a simple model based on the concept of utility. The theory posits that individuals derive satisfaction, or utility, from consuming goods and services. The more goods and services consumed the higher the level of satisfaction achieved. A consumer's ability to satisfy his or her desire for goods is limited by the amount of money income to spend and the prices of the goods available for purchase. The three prerequisites for the development of a theory of consumer choice are: (1) there must be goods to buy, (2) consumers must have money to spend, and (3) they must be able to rank their preferences.[10]

As in all neoclassical economics, consumers are assumed to be maximizers. In the case where there are two goods available for consumption, consumers are interested in maximizing utility subject to a budget constraint, or

$$\text{Maximize } U = U(X, Y)$$
$$\text{subject to } M = P_X X + P_Y Y$$

where U is the level of utility, X and Y are the two goods in question, M is the money income available for spending on the two goods, and P_X and P_Y are their respective prices.

Consumer Preferences: Indifference Curves

Economists depict consumer preferences graphically with indifference curves. An indifference curve illustrates the various combinations of goods that are equally satisfying to the consumer. In Figure 3A.1, having X_0 of good X and Y_0 of good Y places the consumer at point R on the indifference curve labeled U_0. Points S (X_1 and Y_1) and T (X_2 and Y_2) are likewise on U_0, indicating that these three combinations of X and Y provide the same level of satisfaction. The consumer is said to be indifferent as far as these three alternatives are concerned.

Higher levels of satisfaction are depicted by higher indifference curves. A combination of goods on indif-

ference curve U_1 such as V is preferred to R, S, and T. Similarly, W on indifference curve U_2 is preferred to V. Because W is preferred to V and V is preferred to R, S, and T, the transitive nature of preferences implies that W is also preferred to R, S, and T.

When the consumer is able to rank all available alternatives, the set of indifference curves represents a preference map. Indifference curves serve the same purpose on this preference map that contour lines serve on a topographical map. As you move along an indifference curve, the level of utility stays the same. As you move along a contour line, the elevation stays the same. Move from one indifference curve to another and the level of utility changes. Move from one contour line to another and you move to a different elevation.

Indifference curves have certain properties that are important in the development of the theory of consumer choice. They are all negatively sloped, indicating that combinations of goods that have more of one good and the same or more of the other good are preferred. This property indicates that the goods in question are desirable. The consumer prefers more to less.

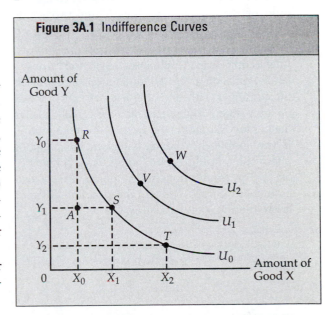

Figure 3A.1 Indifference Curves

---

10 The model does not require that consumers have the ability to attach numerical values to the utility levels. The requirement is that they be able to rank their preferences in an ordinal sense; e.g., most preferred to least preferred.

Indifference curves are typically drawn convex to the origin (they bow in, as shown in Figure 3A.1). Convexity implies that consumers are more willing to give up good Y for some amount of X when Y is plentiful. If the consumer has only a small amount of Y, it will take more X in the exchange to keep the consumer at the same level of satisfaction. The marginal rate of substitution (MRS) is defined as the amount of Y that the consumer would be willing to give up for a small increase in X and maintain the same level of utility. In other words, MRS is the importance attached to an additional unit of good X in terms of the amount of Y given up.

Movement from R to S on indifference curve U_0 results in a different combination of X and Y. Point S has more X, but less Y than point R. The slope of U_0, defined as the change in the amount of Y relative to the change in the amount of X, is also the marginal rate of substitution. The movement from R to S may be broken down into two distinct moves. A move from R to A lowers the level of utility by reducing the amount of good Y. For small movements along U_0, this change in utility is equal to the marginal utility of Y (the change in utility resulting from a unit change in Y) multiplied by the total change in Y, or $(MU_Y) \times (\Delta Y)$. Similarly, a move from A to S restores utility to its previous level due to the increase in the amount of good X. Using the same logic, that change is equal to $(MU_X) \times (\Delta X)$. These two changes offset each other and are thus equal in magnitude, so $\Delta Y/\Delta X = MU_X/MU_Y$. In other words, the slope of the indifference curve ($\Delta Y/\Delta X$), the MRS good X for good Y, equals the ratio of the marginal utilities of the two goods (MU_X/MU_Y).[11]

Indifference curves do not intersect one another. Intersecting curves would present a logical inconsistency. Points on any one indifference curve provide the consumer with the same level of utility. Points on a separate indifference curve are equally satisfying to the consumer but at a different level of utility. If two indifference curves intersect, the point of intersection would be on both curves simultaneously. The implication is that points on the two indifference curves represent the same and different levels of utility simultaneously.

Consumer Constraints: The Budget Line

Consumers have a limited capacity to satisfy their preferences. Because of limited money income and positive prices for the goods and services, the ability to achieve the desired level of consumption is constrained. The consumer's money income constraint may be written $M = P_X X + P_Y Y$. By rearranging terms, the constraint may be written in the form of an equation, or budget line, as follows

$$Y = (M/P_Y) - (P_X/P_Y)X$$

M/P_Y is the value of Y when $X = 0$ and is equal to the Y intercept. The corresponding X intercept, M/P_X, is the value of X when $Y = 0$. The slope of the budget line, P_X/P_Y, is the relative prices of the two goods. The budget line represents all combinations of goods X and Y the consumer is able to buy. Any combination of X and Y that is on or below the budget line is attainable. Given the prices of the two goods, the consumer does not have enough money to reach points above the budget line. In our model, we assume the consumer spends all budgeted money for the two goods, and thus ends up on the budget line, not below it.

Holding prices constant, changes in income will shift the budget line. Using Figure 3A.2, it can be seen that increases in income shift the curve to the right and decreases in income shift it to the left. Changes in relative prices will cause the curve to rotate. Holding P_Y constant, if P_X increases, the curve will rotate to the left. If P_X decreases, it will rotate to the right.

Consumer Choice: The Concept of Equilibrium

Consumer preferences, graphically depicted by indifference curves, represent what the consumer is willing to buy. The money income constraint, depicted by the budget line, represents what the consumer is able to buy. Determining consumer choice is a matter of bringing together these two concepts—willingness to buy and ability to buy. The consumer's decision on

---

11 This derivation may be shown more formally using the Lagrangian multiplier method. The consumer's effort to maximize utility $U = U(X, Y)$ is constrained by limited money income, $M = P_X X + P_Y Y$. The problem becomes one of maximizing $L = U(X, Y) + \lambda(M - P_X X - P_Y Y)$. Setting the partial derivatives of L with respect to X, Y, and λ equal to zero gives

$$\partial L/\partial X = \partial U/\partial X - \lambda P_X = 0$$
$$\partial L/\partial Y = \partial U/\partial Y - \lambda P_Y = 0$$
$$\partial L/\partial \lambda = M - P_X X - P_Y Y = 0$$

Solving the first two equations for λ and setting them equal to each other yields

$$\lambda = (\partial U/\partial X)/P_X = (\partial U/\partial Y)/P_Y$$

In other words,

$$\lambda = MU_X/P_X = MU_Y/P_Y$$

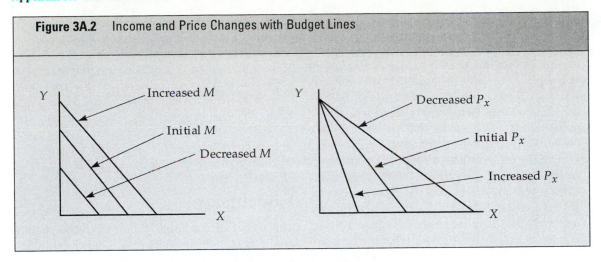

Figure 3A.2 Income and Price Changes with Budget Lines

how to allocate scarce money income between the two goods is an attempt to match preferences with spending power—wants with affordability, willingness to buy with ability to buy—and in the process attain maximum satisfaction.

Individuals adjust their consumption behavior to the point where they cannot increase total utility without increasing their budget. Graphically, the choice may be shown as one of finding a point of tangency between the consumer's budget line and the highest attainable indifference curve. This point is identified by superimposing the preference map over the budget line and determining the unique point of tangency. This point of tangency represents an equilibrium because it is the only point where the slope of the indifference curve equals the slope of the budget line.

The consumer maximizes utility at point B in Figure 3A.3. Points like A do not represent equilibrium since the consumer can reach a higher level of utility simply by moving down the budget line toward point B, spending the same amount of money, purchasing a different combination of X and Y, and reaching a higher level of utility. Likewise, the consumer could move down indifference curve U_1, maintain a constant level of utility, and spend less money.

At point B, the slope of the indifference curve, MU_X/MU_Y, is equal to the slope of the budget line, P_X/P_Y. Thus, the equilibrium condition as already stated is satisfied. In equilibrium, $MU_X/MU_Y = P_X/P_Y$. This condition may be rewritten $MU_X/P_X = MU_Y/P_Y$. In the case where the number of goods the

consumer may choose from is equal to n instead of two, this condition may be written

$$MU_X/P_X = MU_Y/P_Y = \ldots = MU_n/P_n$$

It may be said the consumer maximizes utility when the last dollar spent on each good consumed provides the same increment to utility as the last dollar spent on every other good.[12]

This equilibrium condition provides one point on the individual's demand curve for each good consumed, X_0 at price P_X. Changing the price of the good and finding the new level of consumption identifies additional points on the demand curve. Connecting all these price-quantity pairs in a separate graph traces out the actual demand curve.

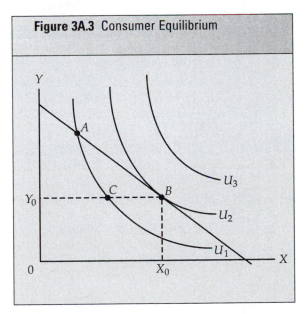

Figure 3A.3 Consumer Equilibrium

---

12 The marginal utility of the last dollar spent on every good is equal to the λ in the previous footnote.

Implications of the Model

The shapes of indifference curves depend on the consumer's own assessment of the desirability of the available alternatives. Consumers with a strong preference for X will have relatively steep indifference curves. Those with strong preferences for Y will have indifference curves that are relatively flat. One possible extension of the model might be to examine the consequences of preference switching. The left-hand side of Figure 3A.4 shows the equilibrium between physicians' office visits (V) and other uses of income (Y). The healthy consumer will have a relatively flat preference map, indicating a strong desire to spend money on goods other than visits to the physician. With equilibrium at point A, this consumer will spend Y_1 income on all other goods and visit the physician V_1 times per year, resulting in a utility level of U_1.

The onset of an illness results in a preference switch, depicted by a steeper preference map on the right. The consumer now places more importance on visits to the physician relative to other spending. The result is a new equilibrium at point B, spending Y_2 on other goods, V_2 visits to the physician, and utility on indifference curve U_1. If the consumer cannot afford to reduce spending on other goods below Y_1, the preferred equilibrium cannot be attained. Instead the consumer will remain at point A, spending Y_1 on other goods, visiting the physician V_1 times, and attaining a lower level of utility, U_0.

Conclusion

The model of consumer choice discussed in this appendix is used to explain and predict consumer behavior. Even though consumers may not consciously apply this decision calculus in each and every situation, this does not mean that the model serves no useful purpose. Remember the model was developed to explain and predict. If it helps us accomplish these tasks, it serves us well.

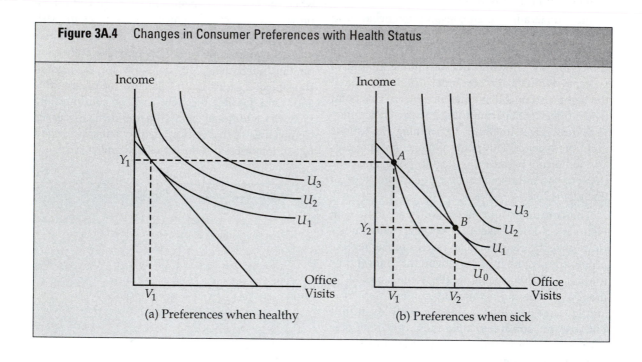

Figure 3A.4   Changes in Consumer Preferences with Health Status

(a) Preferences when healthy

(b) Preferences when sick

Appendix 3B

Production and Cost in the For-Profit Sector

In a world of competitive markets, firms that are successful in minimizing costs will earn a normal profit. Cost minimization is accomplished by the efficient use of resources. In this appendix, we will examine production and cost in a competitive market where firms attempt to maximize profits.

Production with Two Variable Inputs

Economists describe the production process as a functional relationship between inputs and outputs. The so-called **production function** shows the maximum output that can be produced from a given level of inputs using the available technology. Unlike utility, output is a measurable concept—bushels of grain, tons of steel, barrels of oil, or number of appendectomies performed. The inputs include land, natural resources, machinery, labor, and the entrepreneurial energies used to combine them and produce a product

or service that people wish to buy. The production process with two variable inputs, labor (L) and capital (K), may be depicted in its generalized form

$$Q = Q(L, K)$$

where Q represents the amount of the good produced and $Q(\dots)$ the mathematical relationship describing the production process. Production functions are usually presented in one of three forms: a table, an equation, or a graph.

Figure 3B.1 summarizes the output levels that may be attained when labor and capital are combined according to the production function $Q = 100\sqrt{LK}$. The amount of labor used in the production process is listed across the bottom of the table, and the amount of capital is listed along the left-hand side. Interpreting the data in the table is straightforward. For example, when five units of capital are combined with six workers, the firm is able to produce 548 units of output. Different combinations of labor and capital

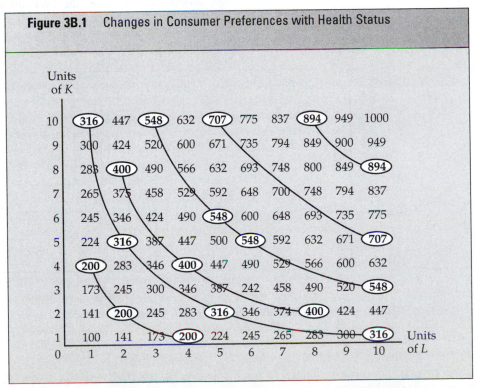

Figure 3B.1 Changes in Consumer Preferences with Health Status

Units of K

10	316	447	548	632	707	775	837	894	949	1000
9	300	424	520	600	671	735	794	849	900	949
8	283	400	490	566	632	693	748	800	849	894
7	265	375	458	529	592	648	700	748	794	837
6	245	346	424	490	548	600	648	693	735	775
5	224	316	387	447	500	548	592	632	671	707
4	200	283	346	400	447	490	529	566	600	632
3	173	245	300	346	387	242	458	490	520	548
2	141	200	245	283	316	346	374	400	424	447
1	100	141	173	200	224	245	265	283	300	316
0	1	2	3	4	5	6	7	8	9	10

Units of L

Note : Above table produced from a Cobb-Douglas production function of the form $Q = 100\sqrt{LK} = 100\, L^{0.5}\, K^{0.5}$.

will result in different levels of output. As long as the inputs are used efficiently, the firm will produce exactly the level of output shown in the table.

Production Isoquants

It is possible to produce the same level of output using different combinations of the two inputs. For example, the firm may produce 316 units of output using ten units of capital and one unit of labor. The same level of output can be produced using five units of capital and two units of labor, two units of capital and five units of labor, or one unit of capital and ten units of labor. A similar observation may be made about 200 units of output, or 400 units, or any one of many different levels of output. The curves drawn in the body of the table represent the different combinations of L and K that produce the same level of output. These equal quantity curves are called **isoquants**, and serve the same purpose in production theory as indifference curves in consumer theory.

Plotting the isoquants in Figure 3B.2 provides a clear picture of the production levels that are attainable using the various combinations of labor and capital. The firm may use a number of different combinations of labor and capital to produce Q_1 units of output. Although only three are shown below, an infinite number of isoquants exist, one for every possible level of output. Because isoquants farther from the origin represent higher levels of output, $Q_3 > Q_2 > Q_1$.

Isoquants are usually drawn convex to the origin. The slope of the isoquant measures the ability to substitute one input for the other while maintaining the same level of output. As the firm adjusts its input mix, the ability to substitute, called the **marginal rate of technical substitution (MRTS)**, changes. When the production process uses a large amount of capital relative to labor, the marginal productivity of labor is high relative to that of capital. One additional worker can easily make up for the reduction of capital. Substitution of labor for capital is relatively easy and the marginal rate of technical substitution labor for capital ($MRTS_{LK}$) is relatively high.

When the amount of capital employed is low relative to the number of workers, the marginal productivity of labor is low relative to that of capital. It takes many more workers to make up for a reduction in capital. In other words, substitution of labor for capital is more difficult when capital is scarce relative to the number of workers competing for its use. Thus, as we move down an isoquant, using more labor and less capital, the $MRTS_{LK}$ declines.

All along the isoquant, the marginal rate of technical substitution is the slope of the isoquant. It can be shown that $MRTS_{LK}$ is the ratio of the marginal product of labor to the marginal product of capital (MP_L/MP_K).[13] If labor and capital are perfect substitutes, $MRTS_{LK}$ will be the same regardless of the amount of labor and capital used in the production process. In this case, the isoquant will be a

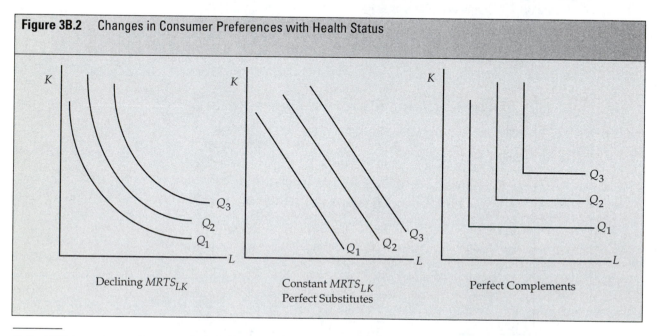

Figure 3B.2   Changes in Consumer Preferences with Health Status

Declining $MRTS_{LK}$ Constant $MRTS_{LK}$ Perfect Complements
                              Perfect Substitutes

---

13 The *MRTS* at any point on an isoquant may be derived by taking the total differential of the production function $Q = Q(L, K)$, and setting it equal to zero.
$$dQ = (\partial Q/\partial L)dL + (\partial Q/\partial K)dK = 0$$
As the amount of L and K change along an isoquant, the level of output does not change, or $dQ = 0$. Solving this equality for the slope of the isoquant, $dK/dL = (\partial Q/\partial L)/(\partial Q/\partial K)$. Since $(\partial Q/\partial L)$ equals MP_L and $(\partial Q/\partial K)$ equals MP_K,
$$dK/dL = MP_L/MP_K = MRTS_{LK}$$

downward-sloping straight line. If instead labor and capital are perfect complements, always used in fixed proportions, the isoquants are L-shaped.

Production in the Short Run

When a firm uses its resources efficiently, the only way to increase output is to increase the amount of inputs used. In most cases, it is easier to increase the workforce than it is to add capital equipment. Inputs whose levels can be adjusted quickly, such as labor, are called **variable inputs**. Inputs that take more time to increase, such as machinery, are called **fixed inputs**. The time lags required for these adjustments further define the production process as either short run or long run. In the case of a two-input production function, the **long run** is defined as the time period where both inputs are variable. The **short run** is the time period where one of the inputs, usually capital, is fixed.

In the short run, the only way to change output is to change the amount of the variable input used. The amount of the fixed input cannot be changed. In other words, the size or scale of the operation is fixed in the short run. From Figure 3B.1, short-run production may be shown by fixing the capital input at, say, five units and varying the amount of labor used from one to ten units. Presented in tabular form that information is shown in Table 3B.1.

From the first two columns, production increases as the number of workers hired increases. The **average product** of labor (AP_L) and the **marginal product** of labor (MP_L) may also be derived from the data on the **total product** of labor (TP_L). The average product, a measure of technical efficiency, is calculated by dividing the total product of labor by the

number of workers, or $AP_L = TP_L/L$. The marginal product is the change in total product when one additional worker is hired. It is calculated by dividing the change in the total product by the change in the number of workers used in the production process, or $MP_L = \Delta TP_L/\Delta L$.

The production function utilized in this discussion illustrates an important empirical observation in short-run production, the **law of diminishing returns**. Holding the amount of capital constant, each added worker has less capital on average to work with, as evidenced by a constantly declining capital-labor ratio (K/L). So each additional worker contributes less to output than the previous worker. The law of diminishing returns is not based on an economic theory, it is physical law that holds true for production in general.

Although the law of diminishing returns characterizes every short-run production process, marginal product and average do not always decline from the outset. Some production processes display increasing marginal and average product initially due to the benefits derived from specialization and the division of labor. Figure 3B.3 presents a generalized short-run production function. As the number of workers increases, total product increases at an increasing rate up to point A. Beyond point A, production continues to increase as more workers are used, but at a decreasing rate. The rate of increase in output slows until a maximum output is reached at point B. Beyond point B, given the amount of capital available per worker, further increases in output are not possible. Adding workers actually decreases output.

Firms do not operate where the marginal product of an input is negative. Doing so would imply the

Table 3B.1   Short-Run Production with $K = 5$

Units of Labor	Total Product	Capital-Labor Ratio	Average Product	Marginal Product
0	0	∞	—	—
1	224	5.00	224	224
2	316	2.50	158	92
3	387	1.67	129	71
4	447	1.25	112	60
5	500	1.00	100	83
6	548	0.83	91	48
7	592	0.72	85	44
8	632	0.63	79	40
9	671	0.56	75	39
10	707	0.50	71	36

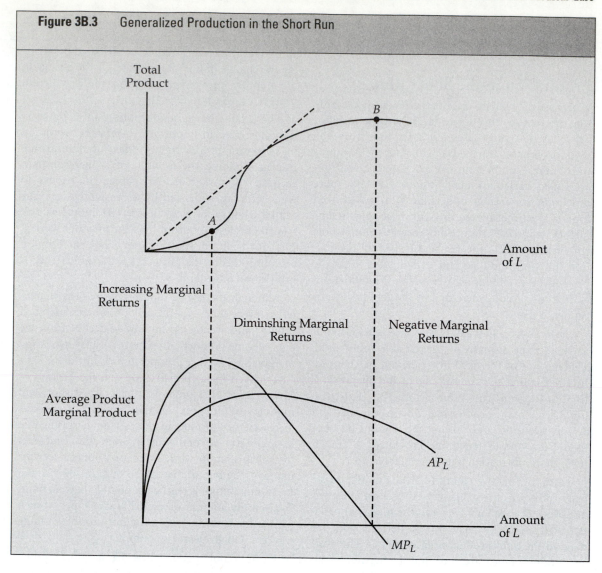

Figure 3B.3   Generalized Production in the Short Run

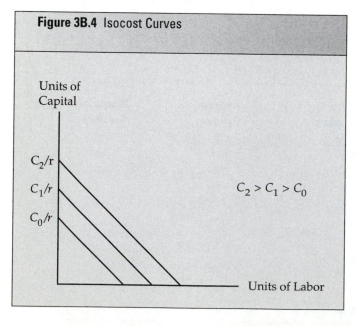

Figure 3B.4 Isocost Curves

firm could increase its output by decreasing the amount of the input used, increasing revenue and lowering cost. Thus, efficient production occurs when the marginal products of all inputs are positive.

Optimal Input Use

The profit-maximizing firm will attempt to maximize output from the resources committed to production. The firm faces a resource constraint determined by the cost of inputs and the amount of money it is willing to spend. When two inputs, labor (L) and capital (K), are used in production, the constraint may be written $C = wL + rK$, where C is the total cost, w is the wage rate paid labor, and r is the unit cost of capital. This cost constraint may be rewritten as an **isocost curve**, or $K = (C/r) - (w/r)L$. The isocost curve is shown in Figure 3B.4, and may be interpreted as all possible combinations of L and K that can be hired for a total cost equal to C_i when

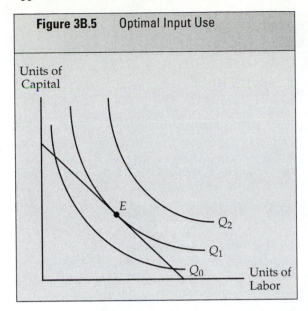

Figure 3B.5   Optimal Input Use

Units of
Capital

E

Q_2

Q_1

Q_0

Units of
Labor

input prices equal w and r. The more money the firm is willing to commit to production, the farther the isocost curve is from the origin and the greater the output that can be produced.

The slope of the isocost curve is the relative price of the inputs, or $-(w/r)$. Combining the isoquant map with the relevant isocost curve allows us to determine the combination of inputs the profit-maximizing firm will choose. Maximizing output at a given level of cost requires that the firm use the optimal or least-cost combination of the inputs. This is shown in Figure 3B.5 at point E where the isocost curve is just tangent to the isoquant Q_1. At the point where the isoquant is tangent to the isocost curve, their slopes are equal. In other words, the slope of the isoquant, or the $MRTS_{LK}$ $(= MP_L/MP_K)$, equals the slope of the isocost curve, or w/r, when the firm is using the least-cost combination of inputs L and K. Formally, this equilibrium condition may be written $MRTS_{LK} = MP_L/MP_K = w/r$.[14]

The equilibrium condition may also be written $MP_L/w = MP_K/r$. In this form it is easily seen that firms adjust the amounts of labor and capital used until the marginal product from the last dollar spent on labor is equal to the marginal product from the last dollar spent on capital.

Extensions of the Model

The optimal input mix for producing a given level of output will change as the relative prices of the inputs change. Figure 3B.6 illustrates the least-cost method of producing Q^* medical care at two different prices for physicians' services. When the price of physicians' services is high (P_H), equilibrium will be at point H, using S_H. If physicians are paid less, holding the price of other medical inputs (P_O) constant, the same level of medical care will be provided using a different mix of physicians' services and other medical inputs. At low physicians' prices (P_L), equilibrium will be at point L, using S_L physicians' services.

The model provides several interesting implications. When the fees paid physicians are relatively high, the physician-population ratio will be relatively low and patients will visit their doctors less often. Additionally, higher physicians' prices encourage the use of other medical inputs. Thus, when physicians' prices are higher, we expect medical care to be produced using more capital per patient.

Estimating Production Functions

The simplest and most widely used production function in empirical work is of the Cobb-Douglas variety. The Cobb-Douglas production function may be written as $Q = AL^\alpha K^\beta$ where α and β are positive parameters estimated from the empirical data. Using this functional form, the exponents represent output elasticities, or the percentage change in output for every 1 percent change in the quantity of the input used. In the case of the labor input, a 1 percent increase in L will result in an α percent increase in Q. Likewise for capital, a 1 percent increase in K will result in a β percent increase in Q.[15] If $\alpha + \beta = 1$, the production

---

14 The mathematical derivation of the equilibrium condition in production mirrors that of the equilibrium condition in consumer theory. Using the Lagrangian multiplier method, it can be shown that the firm's effort to maximize output $Q = Q(L, K)$ is limited by a total cost constraint, $C = wL + rK$. The problem becomes one of maximizing $L = Q(L, K) + \lambda(C - wL - rK)$. Setting the partial derivatives of L with respect to L, K, and λ equal to zero gives

$$\partial L/\partial L = \partial U/\partial L - \lambda w = 0$$
$$\partial L/\partial K = \partial U/\partial K - \lambda r = 0$$
$$\partial L/\partial \lambda = C - wL - rK = 0$$

Solving the first two equations for λ and setting them equal to each other yields

$$\lambda = (\partial Q/\partial L)/w = (\partial Q/\partial K)/r$$

In other words,

$$\lambda = MP_L/w = MP_K/r.$$

15 The marginal products of labor and capital for a Cobb-Douglas production function are determined as follows:

$$MP_L = \partial Q/\partial L = \alpha AL^{\alpha-1}K^\beta = \alpha(Q/L)$$
$$MP_K = \partial Q/\partial K = \beta AL^\alpha K^{\beta-1} = \beta(Q/K)$$

The output elasticities E_K and E_L are

$$E_L = (L/\partial Q)/(Q/\partial L) = (L/Q)(\alpha Q/L) = \alpha$$
$$E_K = (K/\partial Q)/(Q/\partial K) = (K/Q)(\beta Q/K) = \beta$$

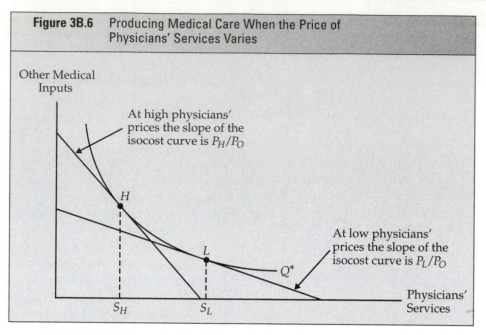

Figure 3B.6   Producing Medical Care When the Price of Physicians' Services Varies

function exhibits const'ant returns to scale. In this case a 1 percent increase in the amount of both inputs used yields a 1 percent increase in output. If $\alpha + \beta > 1$, say 1.2, then a 1 percent increase in L and K results in a 1.2 percent increase in Q and the production function exhibits increasing returns to scale.

The Cobb-Douglas production function is estimated empirically by first taking the logarithm of both sides, resulting in

$$\log Q = \log A + \alpha \log L + \beta \log K$$

Regressing $\log Q$ on $\log L$ and $\log K$ provides estimates of the output elasticities from the estimated coefficients (refer back to the statistical appendix to Chapter 2 for the discussion on regression analysis).

Production to Cost

Cost may be divided into two categories: fixed and variable. Costs associated with the fixed inputs, costs that do not change as the level of production changes, are **fixed costs**. Costs associated with the variable inputs, costs that change as the level of production changes, are **variable costs**. Using the two-input production function introduced above with capital representing the fixed input and labor the variable input, capital costs are fixed costs and labor costs are variable costs.

Total cost is the amount that must be spent on all inputs to produce a given level of output, including all applicable opportunity costs.[16] Total cost is comprised of fixed costs and variable costs, all the costs associated with the capital inputs and all the costs associated with the variable inputs. Using the same notation developed earlier, the total cost function may be written $C = rK + wL$. In other words, the production function and the prices of inputs determine the firm's total cost function. The production function determines how much capital and labor are used in the production process, and the respective input prices determine the total amount spent on each input.

In practice, the short-run total cost curve may be derived from the short-run production function. With the amount of capital available fixed in the short run, rK is constant and represents fixed costs. In order to increase the level of output, the amount of labor used must increase. The production function determines the amount of labor needed to produce any given level of output. The short-run variable cost associated with each level of output (Q) is determined by the amount of labor required (L) multiplied by the cost of labor (w). Figure 3B.7 depicts the short-run total cost function associated with the production function shown in Figure 3B.3. Note the symmetry. In the range of output where production increases at an increasing rate (up to point A in Figure 3B.3), cost increases at a decreasing rate. When production increases at a decreasing rate, cost increases at an increasing rate.

---

16 Opportunity costs include both the explicit costs associated with actual payments to resources used in production and the implicit costs associated with the owners' time and investment. Explicit costs are all those costs recorded by the firm for accounting purposes, including rent paid on buildings, salaries paid to workers, and interest paid on loans. Implicit costs are the opportunity costs of using resources owned by the firm, including forgone earnings on money invested in the business.

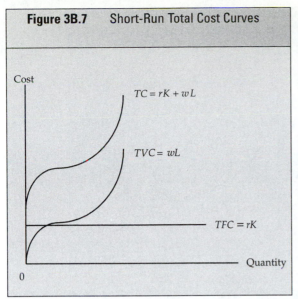

Figure 3B.7 Short-Run Total Cost Curves

$TC = rK + wL$

$TVC = wL$

$TFC = rK$

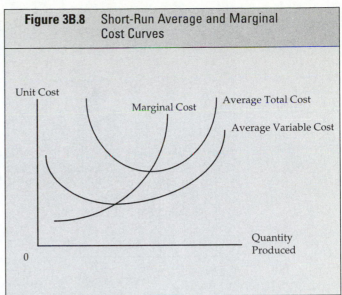

Figure 3B.8 Short-Run Average and Marginal Cost Curves

Marginal Cost

Average Total Cost

Average Variable Cost

This relationship is much clearer when viewed from the perspective of the short-run average and marginal cost curves. By definition, average variable cost (AVC) is the total variable cost (TVC) divided by the level of output produced (Q), or $AVC = TVC/Q$. Since $TVC = wL$, $AVC = wL/Q$ or $w(L/Q)$. Remembering that Q/L is the average product of labor (AP_L), we note $AVC = w/AP_L$. As the average product of labor increases, average variable cost decreases. When AP_L reaches its maximum AVC reaches its minimum. As AP_L decreases, AVC increases.

Likewise, the relationship between marginal cost (MC) and the marginal product of labor (MP_L) can be determined: $MC = \Delta TVC/\Delta Q$. Substituting wL for TVC yields $MC = \Delta wL/DQ$. In competitive labor markets, the firm is a price taker, so the only way to change wL is to change L, implying $MC = w(\Delta L/\Delta Q)$. Because $\Delta Q/\Delta L$ is the marginal product of labor, $MC = w/MP_L$. As marginal product increases, marginal cost decreases. When MP_L reaches its maximum, MC reaches its minimum. As MP_L decreases, MC increases. Thus, we expect short-run average costs and short-run marginal costs to be

U-shaped, initially decreasing, then reaching a minimum, and finally increasing.

The relationship between average costs and marginal costs is shown in Figure 3B.8. Average total cost is the sum of average fixed cost and average variable cost. As long as marginal cost is below average cost, notice that average cost decreases. When marginal cost rises above average cost, average cost begins to increase. Thus, marginal cost intersects each average cost curve at its respective minimum.[17]

Long-Run Costs

Long-run costs are also U-shaped, but for different reasons. In the long run the firm has the option of increasing the size of its physical plant. Doing so often means the use of more efficient equipment, specialized labor, and lower average costs. The economic principle is called economies of scale. The long-run average cost curve may be thought of as an envelope curve, depicting the least-cost option for producing each level of output. Figure 3B.9 shows the long-run average costs associated with three different plant

---

17 For those with a little knowledge of calculus, the intersection of average and marginal cost at minimum average cost may be shown by noting that the slope of the average cost curve is equal to zero at its minimum; that is, its first derivative is equal to zero at its minimum. For the average variable cost curve

$$\frac{dAVC}{dQ} = \frac{d(TVC/Q)}{dQ} = 0$$
$$= \frac{Q(dTVC/dQ) - TVC(dQ/dQ)}{Q^2} = 0$$

Dividing both terms in the numerator and factoring out $1/Q$ results in

$$\frac{1}{Q}[MC - AVC] = 0$$

For the right side of the expression to equal zero, $MC = AVC$, or marginal cost equals average variable cost when the slope of average variable cost equals zero (when AVC has reached its minimum).

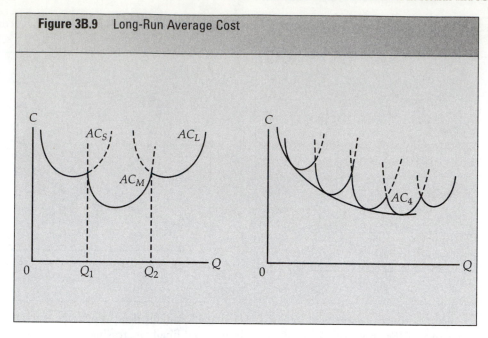

Figure 3B.9   Long-Run Average Cost

sizes: small (AC_S), medium (AC_M), and large (AC_L). The minimum cost of producing each level of output depends on the size of the physical plant. If the desired level of output is less than Q_1, the firm will minimize cost if it uses the small plant. For output levels between Q_1 and Q_2, costs are minimized using the medium-sized plant. For output levels greater than Q_2, the large plant minimizes costs.

The envelope curve in the diagram on the right-hand side depicts all possible plant sizes. Competition will force the firm to use the plant whose costs are given by AC_4, the optimal plant.

Firms that do not use this sized plant will find themselves with higher costs than their competitors, and they will lose money.

Conclusion

The theory discussed in this appendix provides a summary of the economic theory of the firm. The material is not intended to cover the full range of topics presented in a microeconomics course, but it should be sufficient to give the reader a broad overview of the standard neoclassical theory of the firm.

Chapter 4

Economic Evaluation in Health Care[1]

As we have seen, the existence of trade-offs is an inevitable fact of life that we all must come to grips with sooner or later. Eventually every physician must decide if the improvement in a patient's health is worth the additional spending for a particular intervention. In society at large, health insurers and health plans must decide whether to cover a specific intervention or treatment. The formulary committee for a health maintenance organization must decide which drugs in a particular category will be available to HMO members. The administrator of a hospital must decide where to invest the hospital's capital budget. Government agencies must determine which drugs will be eligible for reimbursement through public programs. By considering costs and benefits, these decision makers are actually applying economic analysis to their particular situations. In other words, they are looking for ways to improve how resources are used in pursuit of better health for individual patients, for groups of patients, or for society as a whole.

Key Concept 3
*Marginal
Analysis*

This chapter discusses the use of economic evaluation in health care decision-making. In the first two sections we explore the importance and meaning of economic evaluation. The third section provides a detailed discussion of the types of economic evaluation, including cost-of-illness studies, cost-benefit analysis, and cost-effectiveness analysis. Because cost-effectiveness analysis is currently the preferred method in analyzing treatment options in health care, this technique is the focus of the chapter. Details are provided on calculating the incremental cost-effectiveness ratio, issues in measuring costs and benefits (including a discussion of the quality adjusted life year), and the steps in performing a cost-effectiveness analysis. Section four is a discussion on the use of modeling in economic evaluation, looking specifically at decision analysis and Markov modeling. Section five looks at the trend toward standardization of economic evaluation techniques, particularly in Europe. Section six summarizes several case studies using the techniques discussed in the chapter. The final section provides a summary and conclusions.

Importance of Economic Evaluation

Because we live in a world of scarce resources, we do not have the ability to satisfy the desires of all the people all of the time. Different people have different objectives. We must make choices and often the choices are difficult, if not downright unpleasant. Beneficial projects compete for the same resources. Investing in a new mammography-screening program may preclude the local hospital from expanding its prenatal care program. Paying for the newest and most expensive drugs to treat asthma, high blood pressure, and diabetes may mean that the health plan requires physicians to perform sigmoidoscopy instead of colonoscopy for routine colon cancer screening.

Key Concept 2
*Opportunity
Cost*

---

1 Much of the content and examples used in the presentation of this chapter can be traced, either directly or indirectly, to the 2003 training program "Health Economics of Pharmaceuticals and Other Medical Interventions." I would like to thank Gisela Kobelt, director of the European School of Health Economics, and all the presenters and participants for their efforts in making the program worthwhile.

ISSUES IN MEDICAL CARE DELIVERY

MEDICARE RATIONING UNDER THE NAME OF "FUNCTIONAL EQUIVALENCE"

Without the benefit of an act of Congress, much less a Congressional debate, Medicare officials have adopted policies that limit what the program will pay for new drugs and medical procedures. Using what Thomas Scully, director of the Centers for Medicare and Medicaid Services (CMS), calls "functional equivalence," agency officials are making decisions on whether Medicare will cover certain drug treatments and what prices it will pay.

Functional equivalence is virtually identical to reference pricing, a favorite method of price controls used by many European health care systems to control the price of prescription drugs. It works something like this. The appropriate government agency negotiates the price of every new prescription drug and then, using the best scientific evidence available, pegs the price at the same level of the low-price drug that treats the same disease or condition.

Medicare already controls the prices of every physician's visit and the hospital stay for the nation's 33 million senior citizens covered by the program. Under the guise of spending tax dollars prudently, the agency is making medical decisions about the efficacy of new drug treatments without the necessary expertise. Two recent decisions illustrate the approach:

- The new biotech drug Aranesp was developed to treat anemia in cancer patients. Not only is it faster acting and longer lasting than the existing drug Procrit, but Aranesp can be administered less often, making it a less-invasive treatment. But CMS determined that there was not enough evidence to justify the difference in price between the two drugs and set reimbursement rates for Aranesp at one-third of its market price.

- Medicare patients cannot receive Nexium, a new drug developed to treat ulcers caused by acid reflux and the resulting oesophagitis. Even though medical trials indicate that patients treated with Nexium had fewer physician's visits, faster healing, and fewer hospitalizations, agency officials determined that the drug was identical to Prilosec, which became available in a cheaper generic form in December 2002.

Federal efforts to hold down spending are not new. In fact, a federal advisory committee in early 2003 urged CMS to weigh costs and benefits in its drug coverage decisions. Under Medicare law, the agency has broad powers to set payments at any level. The question to consider is not whether costs should be compared to benefits, but who should make those comparisons. Is this the task of lawyers, lobbyists, and politicians? Or should physicians, scientists (including economists), and patients make these decisions?

Source: Robert Goldberg, "Medicare Reform, French Style; Tom Scully Can't Wait to Put Price Controls on Drugs," *Washington Times*, April 30, 2003, A23.

Key Concept 1
Scarcity and Choice

Every day we are forced to make choices among competing alternatives. We do not have unlimited resources, so programs compete for the same funds and some worthwhile programs go unfunded. How we make these decisions is critically important. In most cases the way we address these issues is a matter of quality of life. In many cases it is a matter of life and death. In either case, it is important that we approach resource allocation decisions in health care in a clear and systematic way.

Meaning of Economic Evaluation

Before we get too far into our discussion, it may be helpful if we define what we mean by economic evaluation. Drummond et al. (1997) use the term to mean "the comparative analysis of alternative courses of action in terms of both their costs and consequences" (pp. 8–9). Economic evaluation is a comparative analysis. There must be at least two alternatives or interventions under consideration to perform a comparative analysis. We typically do not compare an intervention or procedure to "do nothing" unless doing nothing is a reasonable option. "What about clinical trials?" you may ask. Human testing is often done in a clinical setting where one group of patients (called the experimental group) is given the treatment under consideration (often a drug being tested) and a second group (called the control group) is given a placebo (a sugar pill). Remember, this is a clinical setting. It is a test and at the end of the test no one suggests that the sugar pill, the do nothing strategy, is a reasonable option.

As stated above, an economic evaluation examines alternative courses of action. We do not examine a treatment option in isolation from all other treatment options. Economic evaluation compares alternative treatment options that are reasonable alternatives to treating a well-defined medical condition. Mandelblatt et al. (2002) study the most effective use of resources associated with a general-population screening program for cervical cancer. The study examines the cost effectiveness of Pap testing alone, HPV testing alone, or a joint use of the two tests at two screening intervals (two and three years) beginning at age 20 and continuing until age 65 or 75 years, or until death. The analysis compares costs and consequences for eighteen different screening strategies.

The comparisons in an economic evaluation are made in terms of costs and consequences. The specific costs to be included in the analysis are largely determined by the perspective taken—the individual patient, a health insurance company, a health plan, a government agency, or society as a whole. They include direct and indirect costs, both tangible and intangible. The consequences of an action are the benefits that accrue primarily to individuals, unless, of course, significant externalities are associated with the treatment, such as a vaccination program. The primary tasks required to successfully conduct an economic evaluation will be to identify, measure, value, and compare all the relevant costs and consequences. All of these issues will be explored in more detail later.

Types of Economic Evaluation

Three types of economic evaluation are frequently used in health care decision making: cost-of-illness studies, cost-benefit analysis, and cost-effectiveness analysis (Garber, 2001). Each in its own unique way is really nothing more than an attempt to logically weigh the costs and consequences of alternative medical actions.

Cost-of-Illness Studies

Cost-of-illness studies merely look at the question, "What is the cost?" The quantification of the economic burden of a specific disease provides information on the cost structure related to that disease for a specific population in a well-defined geographic area. Because there is no outcome measure, per se, a cost-of-illness study is not an economic evaluation in the strictest sense of the term. It does provide important information to policy makers and health economists on the burden of a disease. In that sense a cost-of-illness study may be a first important step in cost identification leading to an economic evaluation.

Providers can use this type of analysis to guide medical decision making when the clinical effectiveness of treatment options is equivalent. Under these circumstances a better description might be cost-minimization analysis—a study to determine the low-cost treatment option to bring about a defined health outcome; e.g., the low-cost option to treat acute otitis media (middle ear infection).

Druss et al. (2001) examine the economic burden of five chronic conditions affecting the U.S. population in 1996—mood disorders, diabetes, heart disease, asthma, and hypertension. Medical care costs to treat these five conditions amounted to $62.3 billion with heart disease and hypertension making up over one-half of the total. Additionally, the cost of treating coexisting medical conditions totaled $207.7 billion. Adding to the total health costs of $270 billion, the estimated $36.2 billion in lost earnings due to missed work days brings the total societal costs for persons suffering from these five conditions to over $306 billion. Finkelstein et al. (2003) estimate the national medical spending attributable to overweight and obesity to be $92.6 billion (in 2002 dollars). Even though the estimate in obesity-related expenditures is less than 6 percent of total health care spending, the research indicates that over one-third of the annual increase in health care spending is associated

Policy Issue

A large percentage of health care spending is attributable to life-style factors.

with the conditions attributable to obesity—type 2 diabetes, cardiovascular disease, muscleoskeletal disorders, sleep apnea, gallbladder disease, and several types of cancer (including endometrial, post menopausal breast, kidney, and colon). Other cost-of-illness studies have examined the societal costs of AIDS (Scitovsky and Rice, 1987), alcohol, drug abuse, and mental illness (Rice et al., 1990), and cocaine-exposed infants (Henderson, 1991).

Even though the results of cost-of-illness studies are interesting, they do not answer questions related to the most effective options for treating the disorders. To answer questions concerning optimal resource allocation we must try a different approach to economic evaluation—either cost-benefit analysis or cost-effectiveness analysis.

Cost-Benefit Analysis

Managers of for-profit firms must make decisions on how to allocate their firms' scarce resources among alternative investment projects. If a firm is to maximize profits and remain competitive in the marketplace, the net gain from a project (benefits minus costs) should also be maximized. The financial analysis of alternative investment projects is known as capital budgeting.[2] But managers are not the only decision makers who have to make these capital budgeting decisions. Public sector managers must make decisions on how to spend scarce tax dollars to maximize the public welfare. But capital budgeting is a technique developed for and applied to decision making in a market environment. Public sector managers make these decisions in most cases insulated from the full discipline of the market that directs private sector managers.

A simple extension of the capital budgeting process is cost-benefit analysis. First developed to assist government agencies in making decisions about the provision of public goods, cost-benefit analysis is an analytical technique comparing all the costs and all the benefits arising from a program or project. Thus, cost-benefit analysis is to the public, not-for-profit sector what capital budgeting is to the private, for-profit sector.

Key Concept 3
Marginal Analysis

As we saw in Chapter 2, the optimal use of resources requires that every program or project undertaken by the public sector has a marginal social benefit (MSB) that exceeds its marginal social cost (MSC). The problem for public sector decision makers is that the information required to construct MSB and MSC curves is not readily known, making it difficult to determine the social optimum. Cost-benefit analysis is a practical attempt to ensure optimal choice in the absence of markets while remaining true to the traditional welfare economics approach (Sen, 1977).

Elements of a Cost-Benefit Analysis

Given the budgetary constraints on most public policy decisions, cost-benefit analysis is often used to justify expenditures on specific public sector projects. By forcing decision makers to determine whether the benefits from the project are worth the associated costs, measuring both in monetary terms, only those projects that show a positive net benefit are warranted on economic grounds. Alternatively, the ratio of benefits to costs can be calculated and only those projects with a benefit-cost ratio greater than or equal to 1.0 are accepted.

In practice, benefits and costs accumulate over time, requiring that they be adjusted for the time value of money through the use of present value discounting. The concept

2 Any good managerial economics textbook will have a chapter analyzing long-term investment decisions and many will have a chapter on public sector decision-making. See for example, McGuigan, Moyer, and Harris (2002).

of time preference simply recognizes that a dollar today is worth more than a dollar in the future. The inherent uncertainty of the future and the forgone opportunities of not having the dollar today are the two biggest reasons that people place a higher value on today's dollar. Because most people have a positive time preference, future costs and benefits must be discounted to make them comparable with current costs and benefits.

Key Concept 2
Opportunity Cost

Most people are familiar with the concept of compounding—earning interest on interest. Suppose that you could invest \$1,000 in a 12-month certificate of deposit (CD) with a guaranteed 10 percent annual return. One year from now that initial \$1,000 investment would be worth \$1,100. The general formula may be stated as follows:

$$FV_1 = PV \times (1 + r)$$

Where

FV_1 = the future value of the initial investment in one year

PV = the present value of the initial investment

r = the annual return on the initial investment or interest rate

Compounding would require that you expand the number of time periods that you left the money in the CD. At the end of the second year, you would have \$1,210.[3] Continuing this logic through n periods, the formula for compounding is:

$$FV_n = PV(1 + r)^n$$

In other words, an investment of PV today will grow to FV_n in n years at an annual interest rate of r percent.

Discounting takes the opposite perspective. If an individual wishes to have FV_n in n years, then PV would have to be invested at an interest rate of r percent. To solve this problem, we simply solve the above equation for PV and get:

$$PV = FV_n / (1 + r)^n$$

This same fundamental relationship may be used to estimate the present value of a stream of earnings, let's say Y_i, per year for n years. This may be written:

$$PV = \frac{Y_1}{(1+r)^1} + \frac{Y_2}{(1+r)^2} + \ldots + \frac{Y_n}{(1+r)^n}$$

Assuming a constant discount rate (r) over time, this expression may be written more simply as:

$$PV = \sum_{t=1}^{n} \frac{Y_t}{(1+r)^t}$$

This relationship may be adapted to depict the present value of a net benefits stream over time (NB) by defining the stream of earnings (Y_t) in the above equation as the difference between the annual benefits (B_t) and the annual costs (C_t) of the project:

$$NB = \sum_{t=1}^{n} \frac{B_t - C_t}{(1+r)^t}$$

Projects are accepted only if the present value of the net benefits stream is positive. Alternatively, the relationship may be presented as a benefit-cost ratio. In this case, the ratio of benefits-to-costs must be greater one before a project is accepted.

$$B/C = \sum_{t=1}^{n} \frac{B_t}{(1+r)^t} \bigg/ \sum_{t=1}^{n} \frac{C_t}{(1+r)^t}$$

Valuing Benefits

Cost-benefit analysis requires that all benefits and costs be valued in monetary terms. Valuing benefits is usually not a cause of concern when the project involves the construction

3 This calculation would be [\$1,000 × (1 + 0.1)] × (1 + 0.1).

of a dam or an interstate highway. However, when the technique is applied to medical care, the practice is equivalent to placing a monetary value on human life.

Placing a dollar value on life may be unsettling to many. But the monetization of benefits is necessary to calculate a benefit-cost ratio. The technique rests entirely on the premise that the values used in social decision making are simply the sum of all individual values. As we saw earlier, the values individuals place on things are based on the prices they are willing to pay for them. Benefits are typically valued using the willingness-to-pay approach. An individual's willingness to pay for an improvement in health depends on four factors: wealth, life expectancy, current health status, and the possibility of substituting current consumption for future consumption (Bleichrodt and Quiggin, 1999). To the extent that the results of a cost-benefit analysis applied to a medical care decision reflect the willingness and ability to pay of the individuals who stand to benefit, the subsequent allocation of medical resources based on that analysis may be viewed suspiciously because it will likely favor certain groups—the wealthy, the young, and those with serious health problems.

It is the task of decision makers to ensure that spending and investment decisions reflect stakeholder values. Individual providers make decisions with values of their patients as the primary consideration and those of the hospital, health plan, and community of secondary importance. On the other hand, government policy makers are more likely to take the perspective of society as a whole and be as concerned with equity and other welfare considerations as they are with economic efficiency.

Choosing a Discount Rate

The choice of the discount rate is one of the most critical factors in determining the net present value of a project or program. In fact, the net present value of a net benefits stream is inversely related to the discount rate. Higher discount rates place more importance on costs and benefits realized early in the life of the program. Costs and benefits realized far into the future are discounted substantially.

In theory the appropriate discount rate used to evaluate an investment depends on the opportunity cost of funds, or to be more specific, the risk-adjusted rate of return on the next best investment alternative. For many private investment opportunities, the appropriate discount rate is the interest rate that must be paid on funds borrowed to undertake the project.

In the final analysis, the choice of discount rate depends critically on the perspective taken in the analysis. From the perspective of society, the appropriate discount rate should be reflective of society's collective time preference, or the rate at which future consumption is collectively discounted. In practice, there are a number of interest rates that might be used, ranging from the prime lending rate charged by large money-center banks to their best customers to the interest rate on U.S. government treasury bonds. In those countries that require an economic evaluation before a medical device or new drug is approved for reimbursement, the typical discount rate is between 1.5 and 6.0 percent.[4]

Applying Cost-Benefit Analysis

A number of studies have used the cost-benefit approach to examine the effectiveness of medical care programs. One of the early applications of cost-benefit analysis in medical care is the classic study of poliomyelitis by Weisbrod (1971). The study compared the costs and benefits of the medical research program that led to the development of the Salk and Sabin vaccines used against polio. The analysis included only a subset of benefits, focusing on reduced treatment costs and increased productivity. Per capita benefits were estimated as the sum of market value of work lost due to premature mortality, market value of work lost to morbidity, and the savings from resources used to treat and rehabilitate. Work-loss estimates were defined as the present value of expected

---

4 Australian and Canadian guidelines require a mandatory 5 percent discount rate, the UK calls for costs to be discounted at 6 percent and benefits at 1.5 percent, and The Netherlands mandates 4 percent (Hjelmgren et al., 2001)

future earnings lost due to the effects of the disease. Research costs were estimated as the sum of the awards for polio research. Weisbrod used several estimates for the vaccination costs to determine rates of return on the research. Rates of return on the basic research program ranged from four percent for the high-cost estimate to 14 percent for the low-cost estimate with the most likely rate of return about 11–12 percent. Even though Weisbrod's study focused on polio research, the analysis showed that the methodology could be applied to wide range of programs in the medical research field.

The use of cost-benefit analysis in medical care prior to 1980 is reviewed in Hellinger (1980). More recent examples include the study by Goddeeris and Bronken (1985) on gonorrheal screening in asymptomatic women and the examination of a vaccination program by Jackson et al. (1995). Clarke (1998) examines the costs and benefits of a mobile mammographic screening program for rural Australia. Ginzberg and Lev (1997) study the treatment of amyotrophic lateral sclerosis.

Cost-Effectiveness Analysis

If improving the health of a given population is the primary goal of health policy, then the preferred measure of health benefits may be the health outcomes themselves and not their dollar value. Cost-effectiveness (CE) analysis, developed outside the welfare economics framework, is a way to quantify trade-offs between resources used and health outcomes achieved without having to value health outcomes in monetary terms—a prospect that appeals to many policy makers.

The intuitive appeal of cost-effectiveness analysis is based on its pragmatic approach to resource allocation, sometimes referred to as a decision makers' approach. The entire framework of CE analysis sounds like an economic problem—maximize the level of health for a given population subject to a budget constraint. Thus, CE analysis provides a practical guide for choosing between programs when limited budgets do not allow decision makers to implement every program that might improve the health of the population.

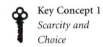

Key Concept 1
Scarcity and Choice

Elements of a Cost-Effectiveness Analysis

Cost-effectiveness analysis relates the cost of two or more treatment options to a single, common consequence that differs among options (e.g., blood pressure reduction, hip fractures avoided, or increased life expectancy). The treatment options may be different treatments for the same condition (e.g., kidney dialysis compared with kidney transplantation) or unrelated treatments with a common effect (e.g., life-saving treatment for heart disease compared to end stage renal failure). The usefulness of CE analysis is more limited when the effectiveness of treatment options is measured differently or when there are multiple measures of effectiveness. If one treatment option prevents premature death and the other reduces disability days, comparing the two is more problematic. One way around this dilemma (other than placing monetary values on outcomes and using cost-benefit analysis) is to use utility measures for health outcomes—actually measures of health preferences. Cost-utility analysis, a special case of CE analysis, addresses quality of life concerns through the use of quality-adjusted life-years (QALYs), determined by the presence of intangibles such as pain, suffering, and disability. More will be said about QALYs later.

Incremental Cost-Effectiveness Ratio (ICER)

When decision makers are faced with limited budgets, CE analysis provides a systematic methodology to achieve the best overall health benefit for a given population. When the most effective treatment option for a medical condition is also the least expensive, the choice is easy. The difficulty arises when the most effective treatment option is also more expensive. Policy makers need an objective measure to help determine the preferred treatment option.

The measure provided by CE analysis is the incremental cost-effectiveness ratio (ICER). The incremental cost-effectiveness ratio provides a way to compare the differences in costs and effectiveness of two treatment options using the following formula:

$$ICER = \frac{C_B - C_A}{E_B - E_A}$$

where $C_{A,B}$ = costs of treatment options A and B
          $E_{A,B}$ = clinical effectiveness of treatment options A and B

When CE analysis is used in clinical decision making, the usual approach is to define the treatment option being studied (treatment B) and the alternative treatment option it is being compared with (treatment A). If $C_A > C_B$ and $E_A < E_B$, option A is both more costly and less effective. In this case we say that treatment option B dominates. If $C_A < C_B$ and $E_A > E_B$, option B is both more costly and less effective. In this case we say that treatment option A dominates. In both of these cases, further analysis is unnecessary, the most effective treatment option is also cheaper, and the choice is simple. If, however, $C_B > C_A$ and $E_B > E_A$, the choice is not as obvious, and a CE analysis is in order.

The ICER may be clearly depicted graphically as seen in Figure 4.1. The gain in effectiveness is plotted on the y-axis and the net present value of the total costs on the x-axis. With each treatment option represented by a point on the graph, it is easy to see that the higher the point, the more effective the treatment; and the farther to the right, the more expensive the treatment.

Using this graphical presentation, the ICER comparing the two treatment options is the inverse of the slope of the line between the two points A and B. A steeply sloped line indicates a low ICER, or in other words, a substantial improvement in health effects for a relatively small cost. As the slope gets flatter, the ICER increases, indicative of higher cost interventions relative to their effectiveness.

If a number of treatment options are being considered for the same medical problem, the graphical presentation clearly depicts the preferred strategies (Mark, 2002). Points A through G in Figure 4.2 represent the costs and effects of seven options for the screening or treatment of a disease. The options that form the solid line ($ABDFG$) represent the economically rational subset of treatment options. Points that lie below the line, such as point C and E, represent treatment options that are dominated by those that are on the line.[5] As the slope of the line gets flatter, the ICER increases, providing a clear depiction of the theoretical construct called the flat-of-the-curve (Enthoven, 1980).

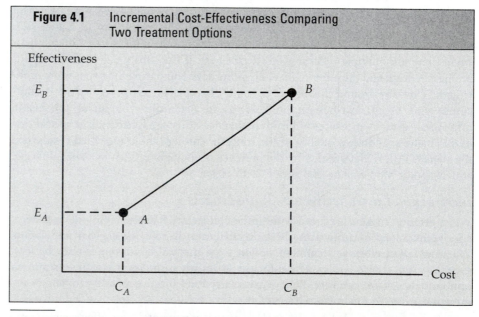

| **Figure 4.1** | Incremental Cost-Effectiveness Comparing Two Treatment Options |

---

5 Note that the treatment option represented by point E is not only less effective than the one represented by point D, but it is more expensive. Thus, treatment option E is strictly dominated by treatment option D. The treatment option represented by point C is dominated due to the logic of extended dominance. Because there are points on the line between B and D that represent combinations of options B and D that are more effective and cheaper, C is dominated by a combination of treatment options B and D.

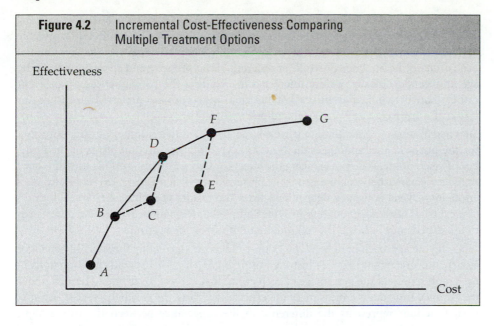

Figure 4.2   Incremental Cost-Effectiveness Comparing Multiple Treatment Options

Measuring Costs and Effects

All types of economic evaluation require the measurement of costs and effects, inputs and outputs associated with the treatment. The costs of the treatment are the opportunity cost of the resources used in providing the treatment minus the value of any resources saved due to the treatment. Costs may be classified as direct, indirect, or intangible. Direct costs are typically divided into direct medical and direct nonmedical costs. Direct medical costs include the cost associated with the use of medical resources. This includes hospitalization, outpatient visits, medical procedures, laboratory testing, pharmaceutical drugs, medical devices, and other medical services such as home care and nursing care. Direct nonmedical costs are those costs typically borne by the patients themselves and their families. These costs include transportation expenses, home services such as cleaning, cooking, shopping, and other personal maintenance services, and other nonmedical investments such as home remodeling to accommodate a physical handicap.

Indirect costs are the costs related to lost productivity. This includes sick leave, reduced productivity at work, and other productivity losses due to early retirement or premature death. Intangible costs are those costs associated with a diminished quality of life. These costs include pain and suffering, grief and anxiety, and disfigurement. Because these costs are difficult to measure, they are often ignored.[6]

The effectiveness of a treatment is measured in terms of the improvement in health associated with it and may be expressed in terms of surrogate, intermediate, or final measures. Surrogate measures examine the clinical effect of a treatment option, or its clinical efficacy, and may be stated in terms of blood pressure, cholesterol level, bone-mass density (BMD), or tumor size. Intermediate measures include clinical effectiveness, or outcome, measures and may be stated in terms of events, such as heart attack, stroke, hip fracture, remission/recurrence of cancer, or death. Scores on standard evaluative exams, such as the EuroQol, SF-36, or MMSE, are also intermediate measures. Final outcomes measure economic effectiveness and may be stated in terms of events avoided, infections cured, disease-free days, life years saved, or quality adjusted life years gained.

Generally speaking, the clinical endpoints, both the surrogate and intermediate measures, should be linked to final economic outcomes or endpoints in order to calculate the cost effectiveness of the various treatment options. Representing these linkages

Key Concept 2
Opportunity Cost

---

6 One line of economic research, highlighted by the work of Kip Viscusi, attempts to develop a measure of utility in monetary terms. This approach, when used to value health benefits, values an individual's or society's willingness to pay for improvements in health. See Viscusi and Aldy (2003) for an extensive literature review on the topic.

usually requires some type of modeling using epidemiological data to estimate the transition probabilities from one stage in the course of a treatment to another. It is possible to determine the probability of a hip fracture using BMD scores at various ages and the probability of heart attack or stroke at different blood pressure and cholesterol levels by age and gender. Ideally, we are interested in avoiding the consequences of an event rather than the clinical event itself. Thus, final outcomes are preferably measured in terms of improvements in survival and quality of life.

Survival Measures. Even though survival may be stated in a number of different ways, for the purpose of economic evaluation, it is typically measured in terms of the number of years of life. When comparing the effects of two treatment options the difference in life expectancy between the two is the preferred survival measure. Evidence of differences in survival is usually determined from the results of a clinical trial. Seldom do clinical trials last long enough to provide complete information to calculate differences in life expectancy between the treatment and nontreatment groups.[7]

Using the approach in Kobelt (2002), the problem in calculating the survival benefit of a particular treatment may be illustrated using Figure 4.3. The two survival functions in the graph represent the percentage of each group that survives over time. The area under the survival function is a measure of life expectancy. Thus, the area between the two survival functions represents the difference in life expectancy between the two groups. Suppose that the two groups have been chosen to test the effects of a new pharmaceutical drug for the treatment of heart disease. At the end of the 18-month trial, 90 percent of the treatment group is still alive while only 77 percent of the control group is alive. For simplicity, assume that 20 percent of each group dies each year after the trial, implying that all are dead five years after the trial is over.[8]

The gain in life expectancy during the trial due to the treatment is the area of the triangle *ABC*. The calculation is ½ (0.90 − 0.77) (1.5) or 0.0975 years.[9] Even if the treatment does not increase the overall longevity of the group receiving the drug, there is still a gain in life expectancy after the trial ends, represented in the graph by the triangle *BCD*. The post-trial gain in life expectancy for the treatment group is ½ (0.90 − 0.77) (5) or 0.325 years. Thus, the total gain in life expectancy for the group receiving

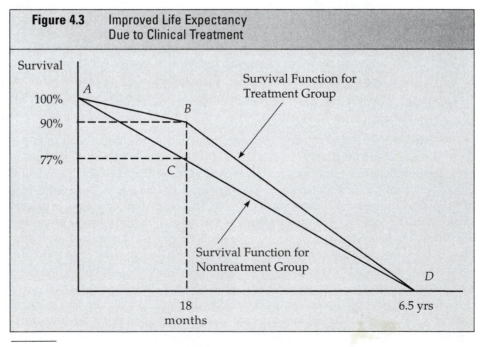

Figure 4.3   Improved Life Expectancy Due to Clinical Treatment

---

7 Clinical trials usually last 1–3 years, much less than the life expectancy of the typical participant.

8 The typical survival function is not linear, but is drawn convex to the origin, or decreasing at a decreasing rate. The usual function may be written S(t) = e–lt. In this functional form, life expectancy is 1/λ.

9 Remember that the area of a triangle is ½ base times height.

the new drug is 0.4225 years, with over three-fourths coming after the trial is over. At the beginning of the trial, life expectancy without the treatment is 3.25 years. As a result of the treatment, life expectancy increases to 3.6725 years, or 13 percent.

Quality-of-Life Measures. Quite often improvements in life expectancy do not fully capture the benefits of a medical intervention. Extending life can result in a decrease in the quality of life. Furthermore, an intervention may result in quality-of-life improvements without actually extending life. What is needed is a measure of effectiveness that captures improvements in the quality of life as well as extensions in the length of life. The quality adjusted life year, or QALY (pronounced *kwa-lee*), serves such a purpose.

The concept of the QALY was first introduced in the study of chronic renal failure (Klarman et al., 1968). The actual term was used for the first time a decade later (Weinstein and Stason, 1977) and has since become the quality-of-life measure of choice in CE analysis. The measure simultaneously captures the value of reduced morbidity (improved quality of life) and reduced mortality (increased quantity of life).

The QALY may be viewed as life expectancy with a preference weight or quality weight attached to each year. Life is affected by functional limitations, pain and suffering, and the daily burden of a disease—all having an impact on the utility attached to each additional year of living. Normally, an additional year of life while suffering the effects of a particular disease will have less weight associated with it than an additional year of life in a healthy state. To use the QALY concept to represent quality of life for the health states under consideration, quality weights must be attached to the various health states. These quality weights are based on individual preferences for the various health states, measured on an interval scale anchored by death (equal to 0) and perfect health (equal to 1).

A QALY is a probability-weighted average of the expected quality of life estimates associated with each possible health state. QALY converts the number of years spent in a given health state to a smaller number of years spent in perfect health, which, according to the individual's preferences, is equally satisfying.

Consider a 55-year-old male with type 2 (non-insulin-dependent) diabetes. Complications from type 2 diabetes include kidney disease, retinopathy, and damage to the nervous system that results in over one-half of all lower limb amputations in the United States. The risk of heart disease and stroke are two to four times greater for someone with diabetes. Normally a 55-year-old male could expect to live an additional 25 years; however, diabetes shortens life expectancy by an average of 10 years. Thus, a 55-year-old male can expect to live to age 70. Based on individual preferences, suppose our subject places a utility value on each of his 15 remaining years at 0.4. His 15 remaining years have a QALY value of 6 (15 × 0.4). Based on individual preferences, the total utility of living an additional 15 years with type 2 diabetes is the same as the total utility of living an additional 6 years in perfect health. Thus, this man would be indifferent between living 15 years with diabetes and 6 years in perfect health.

Using Figure 4.4, the utility of living one year with diabetes, $U(h_i)$, is 40 percent of the utility of living one year in perfect health, $U(h_1)$. The total utility over the 15 remaining years of life, $15U(h_i)$, is equal to the total utility of living 6 years in perfect health, $6U(h_1)$.

There is some disagreement on whose preferences should be measured in determining QALY weights—people currently in the health state or the general population. If people in the health state were surveyed, they would be asked to compare the current health state to their ideal health state. If the general population were surveyed, they would be asked to rate a described hypothetical health state. A second major issue is how to measure quality of life. The World Health Organization (WHO) defines quality of life along three dimensions: physical, mental, and social well-being. Using a quality of well-being (QWB) approach, Kaplan et al. (1998) develop a classification system using four patient attributes: mobility, physical activity, social activity, and a symptom-problem complex. Dolan et al. (1996) use a time trade-off technique to measure preferences. This so-called EuroQol includes five health state attributes—mobility, self-care, usual activities, pain-discomfort, and anxiety-depression—to define 245 possible health states. Both

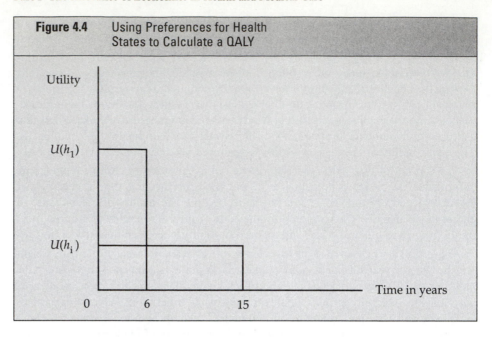

Figure 4.4   Using Preferences for Health States to Calculate a QALY

approaches have been linked with the QALY to serve as a measure of the level of utility associated with the various health states.

The QALY may be calculated using the standard time trade-off method where the individual is offered two alternatives:

- The chronic health state i for t years, followed immediately by death.

- Perfect health for x years (where x is less than t), followed immediately by death.

Time x is varied until the individual is indifferent between the two alternatives. The utility of the chronic health state is determined by the individual's preferences for perfect health. Thus, the value of one year in the chronic health state (h_i) is x/t.

An alternative approach to calculating a QALY uses the standard gamble. Used to measure the utility that a person attaches to a particular health state, the standard gamble is a direct application of one of the fundamental axioms of classical utility theory (von Neumann and Morgenstern, 1944). Intuitively, the premise behind the standard gamble is simple:

- A treatment is available for individuals in chronic disease state.

- When it works, the treatment provides a permanent cure. When it does not work, the result is immediate death.

- How high does the risk of dying have to be before the patient refuses treatment?

- The utility value of each year in the chronic disease state is equal to the associated probability that the treatment works.

More formally, the axiom is based on the continuity of preferences, and states that if there are three outcomes (x_1, x_2, and x_3), some probability (p) exists whereby the individual is indifferent between the certain outcome x_1 and the risky prospect comprised of outcome x_2 with probability equal to p and outcome x_3 with probability equal to $1 - p$.

Consider a situation where an individual in the chronic disease state x_1 (preferred to death) has a choice of rejecting treatment and remaining in x_1 for the remainder of her life (t years) or accepting a treatment that has two possible outcomes: perfect health, x_2, for t years with a probability equal to p or sudden death, x_3, with a probability equal to $1 - p$. Based on the continuity of preferences axiom, the probability p can be adjusted until the individual is indifferent between the two alternatives: either rejecting treatment and living in the chronic disease state for t years or accepting the risk of treatment and living t years in perfect health with a probability equal to p, or dying immediately. Under these conditions the health preference weight for each year living in chronic disease state x_1 is equal to p.

Steps in Performing a Cost-effectiveness Analysis

The pieces involved in actually conducting a CE analysis are all in place. All that is left now is to actually set one up. The following steps summarize the process.

1. Rank the alternative treatment options by health benefit (beginning with the one with the lowest benefit).
2. Eliminate treatment alternatives that are strictly dominated.
3. Calculate the ICER between each treatment option and the next most expensive option.
4. Eliminate treatment options that display extended dominance.
5. Determine which treatment options have an ICER that is below the cut-off ICER.

Nothing in the exercise provides information on what society is willing to pay for a particular health benefit; in other words, what the optimal ICER should be. This step is somewhat problematic for those wanting to avoid valuing health benefits, implicit in choosing a cut-off value. One approach has been to construct league tables.

The concept of the league table originated from European football rankings (soccer to Americans). These so-called league tables compare the ICER for various interventions. The usual practice is to compile ICERs for a number of common medical interventions from a literature search and to place the intervention under study in the mix. In this context, a case for or against a particular intervention can be made through comparison with other interventions. Garber and Phelps (1997) provide a good example of a league table listing the cost per life year gained for a number of commonly used medical interventions. The usual practice is to discard interventions with high ICERs indicative of poor value in favor of interventions with low ICERs indicative of good value. A commonly used rule-of-thumb places the cut-off at $50,000 per QALY (or roughly twice annual per capita income).

Approaches to Modeling in Economic Evaluation

The biggest challenge in conducting a cost-effectiveness analysis is the availability of quality data. The proverbial gold standard for data on the costs and effectiveness of various treatment options is the randomized trial. In practice, however, randomized trial data is not always available. As we have discussed earlier, trial periods are typically too short to capture all the costs and consequences of the treatment options. Additionally, randomized trials are costly to undertake and are driven by the requirements to prove safety and efficacy. Under the controlled conditions of randomized trials, many of the variables that would determine effectiveness and efficiency in the course of normal clinical practice are not present, limiting the researchers' ability to generalize from the trial results. These limitations highlight the importance of using sound modeling techniques as a framework for economic evaluations. The two modeling frameworks frequently used in economic evaluation are decision trees and Markov models (Kuntz and Weinstein, 2001).[10]

Decision Trees

Decision trees provide a logical framework for decision analysis, clearly illustrating the sequential nature of the decision-making process and capturing the uncertain nature of

---

10 TreeAge Software, Inc. developed the decision analysis software used in developing the figures in this section. TreeAge has been producing decision analysis tools used in the medical care industry since 1988. In addition to cost-effectiveness analysis and Markov modeling, the software can be used for Monte Carlo simulation in clinical decision making, epidemiological modeling, and pharmaceutical outcomes research. A student version of their DATA™ software is available on their Web site http://www.treeage.com/.

the environment in which decisions are made. Decision trees are designed to analyze problems that involve a series of choices that are in turn constrained by previous decisions. They provide a convenient way to show the effects of decision choices and the impact of the probabilities of subsequent events on final outcomes.

The elements of a decision tree flow logically from an initial decision point, or decision node. Branches from a decision node represent courses of action taken by the decision maker. Chance events, shown as chance nodes in the decision tree, are all possible outcomes that stem from each decision. Branches from chance nodes represent the events that result from each decision and their associated probabilities. Final outcomes are shown by terminal nodes and represent the stopping point in the decision analysis.

Figure 4.5 represents the elements of a simple decision tree with one decision node, whether to choose treatment A or treatment B. The decision to choose either treatment is followed by a chance node, live or die. In this simple decision tree the only difference in the sequence of events is the probabilities associated with life or death after the choice of treatments is made. The probabilities of life and death are p and $1 - p$ if treatment A is chosen and q and $1 - q$ if treatment B is chosen. This simple model has four possible terminal nodes, each with an associated cost (C_i) and effect (E_i).

When decision trees are used in the economic evaluation of health care decisions, the model is solved using a technique called "roll back." In other words, the tree is solved working from right to left, as if there were no uncertainty involved in the process. The expected cost of each possible action is calculated by summing the costs of each branch multiplied by the probability of reaching the terminal point of that branch. Each treatment option is ranked by expected cost and then incremental cost-effectiveness ratios are calculated.

The data required to evaluate treatment options using decision analysis is typically gathered from different sources. Because clinical trials are usually protocol driven, they seldom collect all the information required to complete an economic evaluation. The usual practice in gathering data for the analysis involves integrating information from different sources including disease data from epidemiological studies, patient management data based on clinical practice, and resource utilization data from accounting sources.

	Treatment A	Treatment B
Mortality rate	5%	10%
Life expectancy for survivors	20 years	10 years
Initial treatment cost	$50,000	$20,000
Follow up costs, year 1	$20,000	$10,000
Annual follow up costs, all subsequent years	$2,000	$2,000

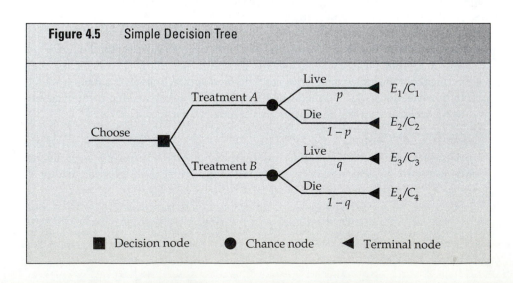

Figure 4.5   Simple Decision Tree

Choose

Treatment A — Live p — E_1/C_1
Treatment A — Die $1 - p$ — E_2/C_2
Treatment B — Live q — E_3/C_3
Treatment B — Die $1 - q$ — E_4/C_4

■ Decision node   ● Chance node   ◀ Terminal node

Suppose the previous information above has been gathered on the costs and effectiveness of the two treatments described above.[11] Total cost for survivors receiving treatment A is $108,000; for decedents it is $50,000. Survivors live an additional 20 years; decedents experience sudden death. For the group receiving treatment B, cost for survivors is $68,000; for decedents it is $20,000. Survivors of treatment B live an additional 10 years.

At each decision node, the expected cost and consequences of each treatment option is calculated. For treatment A, the expected cost is $105,100 [0.95($108,000) + 0.05($50,000)] and the expected benefit is 19 life years saved [0.95(20 years) + 0.05(0 years)].[12] For treatment B, the expected cost is $63,200 [0.90($68,000) + 0.10($20,000)] and the expected benefit is 9 life years saved [0.90(10 years) + 0.10(0 years)].

Treatment	Expected Cost	Expected Benefit	Incremental Cost	Incremental Benefit	ICER
B	$63,200	9 years	—	—	—
A	$105,100	19 years	$41,900	10 years	$4,190

The treatment options are then ranked by expected cost (lowest to highest). After calculating the incremental cost and incremental benefit of the treatment options, the ICER is calculated. In this example, treatment A results in an additional 10 years of life expectancy at a cost of $41,900, or $4,190 per life year gained.

Key Concept 3
Marginal Analysis

Markov Models

Decision trees can be as simple or as complex as the decisions they model. But when there are numerous health states, and including the possibility of transitions from one health state to another and back to the original health state, the decision tree may become far too complex to handle the problem efficiently. This problem of complex and recurring disease states is particularly challenging when modeling the progression of a chronic condition such as loss of bone density, breast cancer, and the many forms of dementia. In these situations a Markov model is the appropriate choice for modeling these type of recurring health states.

Disease states and disease transitions may be modeled effectively with a Markov cycle tree as depicted in Figure 4.6.[13] This simple model shows two mutually exclusive health states, or Markov states, corresponding to all possible health states. The health states, alive or dead in this example, are shown at the Markov node. Transition subtrees, constructed at the transition node, depict the progression of the disease from one state

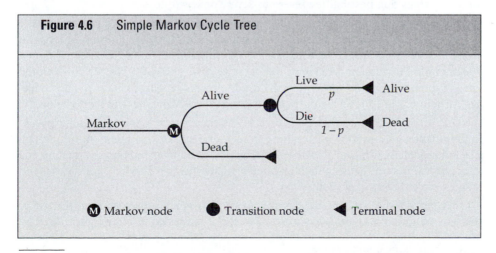

Figure 4.6　Simple Markov Cycle Tree

M Markov node　● Transition node　◀ Terminal node

---

11 In this simple example, costs and consequences are not discounted.
12 The calculation for expected cost for either treatment is the sum of the cost for survivors multiplied by the probability of surviving and the cost for decedents multiplied by the probability of dying.
13 The simple Markov model described in Figure 4.6 is actually a life-expectancy model. Age memory can be programmed into the Markov process, changing the transition probabilities from cycle to cycle.

to another. Transitions between disease states are based on probabilities that certain events occur—probabilities determined using data from epidemiological studies or clinical trials. In this example, there are only two events, live and die. The probability of living is p, while the probability of dying is $1 - p$.

The branches of the transition subtree end with a terminal node, indicating the end of a cycle, not the termination of the process. Transition subtrees are recursive and continue for a predetermined number of time periods, called Markov cycles, or until everyone who began the process ends up in the absorbing state, in this case, dead.[14] The length of each Markov cycle is fixed and should represent an interval that has clinical meaning for the disease being studied. If cycles are too short, disease transitions are infrequent. If they are too long, individuals transition from one health state to another and back again during the same cycle and the explanatory power of the model is diminished.

Markov Decision Models

One of the most practical ways to take advantage of the power of the decision tree and the Markov model is to combine the two, creating a Markov decision model. In this format the model starts at the initial decision node of a decision tree, where two treatment options are available. But instead of attaching a chance node to each option, a Markov node is attached. Now the decision model has two Markov processes, each associated with a treatment option, and we have a valuable tool for economic evaluation.

Each Markov process has costs and utilities associated with it. As the Markov process proceeds and participants transition from one health state to another, costs and utilities accumulate for each treatment group. The economic evaluation must keep track of these costs and utilities so expected costs and expected utilities (usually QALYs) can be calculated. The expected values are calculated on a per capita basis and compared across treatment options to determine incremental cost-effectiveness ratios.

The Markov decision model depicted in Figure 4.7 may be used to estimate the cost effectiveness of a new drug treatment for Alzheimer's disease, a form of dementia. In this example, data on the clinical effectiveness of the new drug, call it treatment A, is collected from a clinical trial where the control group is given a placebo (no treatment). There are three health states for patients suffering from the disease—mild, moderate, and severe—and one absorbing state, death. The underlying disease progression is shown by transitions from one health state to another. For example, there are three possible transitions for someone beginning a cycle with a diagnosis of mild Alzheimer's: mild-to-mild, mild-to-moderate, or mild-to-dead. Those with severe Alzheimer's have only two transition possibilities: severe-to-severe or severe-to-dead.

The development of Alzheimer's is slow and difficult to confirm. Even though the actual diagnosis of Alzheimer's is not possible without a post-mortem analysis of brain tissue, several cognitive tests are used to measure the patient's mental ability. One popular instrument is the mini-mental state exam (MMSE). The MMSE is scored on a 30-point scale. Mild Alzheimer's is linked to scores ranging from 21 to 26, moderate Alzheimer's to scores between 10 and 20, and severe Alzheimer's to scores below 10.

This Markov decision model was used to estimate the expected costs and expected utilities (measured in QALYs) resulting from four years of treatment with donezepil (Neumann, Hermann, and Kuntz, 1999). The data used in estimating the incremental cost effectiveness of the drug therapy came primarily from a 24-week clinical trial and other sources (Clegg et al., 2000).

It is beyond the scope of this chapter to go into much more detail on the use of Markov models in economic evaluation. For those interested in more information on the subject, there is a rich literature on the process. The interested reader might begin with Briggs and Sculpher (1998).

---

14 Transition states are temporary, tunnel, or absorbing. Individuals move in and out of temporary states. The progression through a tunnel state follows a predetermined path; e.g., the progression of a pregnancy. No one escapes an absorbing state once entered.

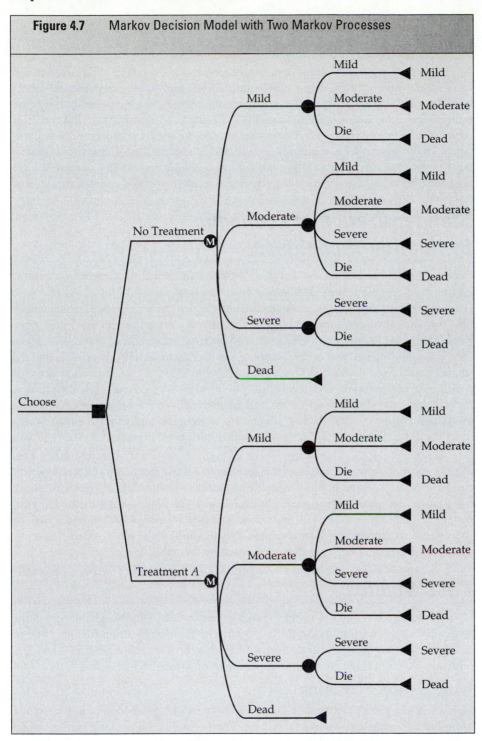

Figure 4.7   Markov Decision Model with Two Markov Processes

Sensitivity Analysis

The reliability of the results of any economic evaluation depends on the quality of the data used in the study. Due to uncertainty, economic evaluations may be sensitive to changes in key assumptions and parameters. One way to determine whether the results are influenced by this uncertainty is to conduct a sensitivity analysis. A sensitivity analysis is a way of systematically exploring the variability of the results due to uncertainty. A basic sensitivity analysis entails changing one of the model's parameters or assumptions at a time. A one-way sensitivity analysis might test the variability of the results to a change in the transition probability from one health state to another, or the initial cost of a treatment option, or the utility associated with a particular health state. Two-way or multi-way sensitivity analyses are also quite common.

The typical sensitivity analysis described previously is called a cohort analysis. Conducted with one of the decision models described previously, a hypothetical cohort of individuals is followed through every event and cycle, expected costs and utilities are estimated, and treatment options are compared using calculated ICERs. This process is repeated for every parameter/assumption change and the impact on final results are compared. Other approaches to sensitivity analyses include Monte Carlo simulations where a large patient cohort is tracked through the model individually. The simulations are repeated over and over to estimate the variance in results associated with the parameters.

Standardization of Economic Evaluation Techniques

Health care systems around the world are setting standards for economic evaluations and making reimbursement decisions for various treatment options based on those economic evaluations. In 1992 Australia became the first country to issue formal guidelines for mandatory economic evaluation of all pharmaceutical products prior to reimbursement (Commonwealth, 1992). The National Institute for Clinical Excellence (NICE), established as part of the National Health Service (NHS) in 1999, is making similar decisions in the United Kingdom. Its mission is to provide individual patients, health care professionals, and the British public with clear guidance on the efficacy, clinical, and cost effectiveness of both individual health technologies (including pharmaceutical drugs, medical devices, diagnostic techniques, and other medical procedures) and the clinical management of specific health conditions (NICE, 2001).

Hjelmgren et al. (2001) provides a detailed study of the similarities and differences of the health economics guidelines that have been issued in Europe, North America, and Australia. Presented in table format, the authors classified the 25 guidelines into three categories: seven formal, eight informal, and ten dealing with methodological issues. Most countries in the European Union already require or will soon require the submission and approval of formal economic evaluations for all new and existing medical technologies before they can be reimbursed by the public sector.

Case Studies

Literally hundreds of studies using the techniques discussed in this chapter are published in journals around the world each year. The following section highlights three recent studies that clearly illustrate the use of these techniques in lung cancer screening, cervical cancer screening, and the drug treatment of Alzheimer's disease.

Lung Cancer Screening

Mahadevia et al. (2003) examine the cost effectiveness of regular lung cancer screening using helical Computed Tomography (CT). The prevalence of smoking in the United States and the deadly nature of the disease make population-based screening an important policy issue. Approximately 50 million adult Americans between the ages of 45 and 75 are current, quitting, or former heavy smokers. Over 170,000 Americans are diagnosed annually with lung cancer—and over 80 percent die within one to two years. The study began with three hypothetical cohorts of 100,000 adults in each of the three smoking categories. If annual screening began at age 60, the program would prevent 553 lung cancer deaths (for every 100,000 screened) over a 20-year period—a 13 percent reduction in the death rate from lung cancer. The program would also result in 1,186 unnecessary biopsies (per 100,000 screenings). At a cost of $500 per CT scan, if one half of all adult smokers received an annual screening, the program cost, discounted over 20 years, would be over $115

Back-of-the-Envelope

CHECKLIST FOR ASSESSING ECONOMIC EVALUATIONS

As the interest in the economic evaluation of health care interventions has grown, so too has the interest in publishing the results of those studies in peer-reviewed journals. In an attempt to promote the quality of the economic evaluations published in the *British Medical Journal*, the editors established a working group to clarify the components of an acceptable article. The guidelines are grouped under three major headings: study design, data collection, and analysis and interpretation of results.

I.   Study design addresses seven issues:

   1.   Is the research question clearly stated?
   2.   Is the economic importance of the research question clearly stated?
   3.   Is the perspective of the analysis clearly stated and justified?
   4.   Is the rationale for the choice of comparison alternatives stated?
   5.   Are alternative treatment options clearly described?
   6.   Is the type of economic evaluation clearly stated?
   7.   Is the type of economic evaluation justified given the question addressed?

II. Data collection addresses 14 issues:

   8.   Are the sources of the effectiveness data clearly stated?
   9.   Is a systematic overview of the studies used as data sources provided?
   10. If based on several studies, are details on the method of data synthesis provided?
   11. Are the outcome (utility) measures clearly stated?
   12. Are valuation methods clearly stated?
   13. Are details provided identifying the individuals making the valuations?
   14. Are productivity changes (indirect) reported separately?
   15. Is the relevance of productivity changes discussed?
   16. Are resource prices and quantities reported separately?
   17. Is the methodology for estimating prices and quantities described?
   18. Are all currency and pricing data clearly recorded?
   19. Are all inflation adjustments and currency conversions clearly stated?
   20. Is the model clearly explained?
   21. Is the choice of model and key parameters justified?

III. Analysis and interpretation of results addresses 14 issues:

   22. Is the time horizon for costs and benefits stated?
   23. Is the discount rate used stated?
   24. Is the choice of discount rate justified?
   25. If costs and benefits are not discounted, is rationale stated?
   26. If stochastic data is used, are confidence intervals and statistical tests discussed?
   27. Is the sensitivity analysis explained?
   28. Is the choice of variables for the sensitivity analysis justified?
   29. Is the range over which the parameters are varied stated?
   30. Are all relevant alternatives compared?
   31. Is the incremental analysis reported?
   32. Are all major outcomes presented in both disaggregated and aggregated forms?
   33. Is the original study question answered?
   34. Does the reported data support the conclusions?
   35. Are conclusions accompanied by the appropriate caveats?

continued

Even though the guidelines are not intended to stifle innovative approaches, they are meant to improve the quality of economic evaluations that are eventually published in the *BMJ*. Many of you who read these guidelines may never submit an economic evaluation to the *BMJ*, but knowing what goes into a publishable economic evaluation will help you read, understand, and critique those you read from other sources.

Source: Michael F. Drummond, T.O. Jefferson, et al., "Guidelines for authors and peer reviewers of economic submissions to the *BMJ*," *British Medical Journal 313*, August 3, 1969, 275–283.

billion. The risk profile of the screened population affects the cost effectiveness of the program. If only former smokers are screened, the cost per QALY is $2.3 million. If screening is limited to current smokers, the cost per QALY is $116,300. Even with the prospective life-saving consequences of CT screening, age and smoking status may not represent high enough risk factors to make population-based screening cost effective.

Cervical Cancer Screening

Mandelblatt et al. (2002) examine the social costs and quality-adjusted life expectancy of a number of different testing strategies for cervical cancer. With a model simulating the natural progression of the disease, they compare 18 different screening strategies using a combination of testing for the human papillomavirus (HPV), the traditional Papanicolaou (Pap) test, and a combination of the two at two to three year intervals beginning at age 20 and continuing to 65 years, 75 years, or death. Direct costs for screening, diagnosis, and treatment were included in the analysis, along with the indirect costs of the patients' time associated with the process. Eliminating the screening options that were dominated, either strictly or via extended dominance, the six strategies listed below comprised the frontier of economically rational strategies.

Screening Strategy	Expected Cost	Expected QALYs Saved	ICER
No screening	$5,018	26.8666	
Pap every 3 years to age 75	6,833	27.0200	$11,830
Pap every 2 years to age 75	7,280	27.0350	29,781
Pap every 2 years to death	7,308	27.0355	56,440
Pap plus HPV every 2 years to age 75	7,934	27.0444	70,347
Pap plus HPV every 2 years to death	7,980	27.0450	76,183

The following QALY adjustments for each year in the various health states were used: 0.97 for healthy and diagnosed with a low-grade squamous intraepithelial lesion (LSIL), 0.93 for having a high-grade lesion, 0.9 for having local invasive cancer, 0.7 for regional invasive cancer, and 0.5 for distant invasive cancer. Of course, 1.0 represents perfect health and 0 is death. Maximum benefit in terms of QALYs saved results from Pap plus HPV testing every two years until death with an incremental cost of $76,183. Stopping the screening at age 75 captures approximately 98 percent of the benefits of lifetime screening at an incremental cost that is about $6,000 lower. Combining Pap plus HPV testing in a population screening program consistently saves more lives but at higher costs. Sensitivity analysis revealed that if the cost of the HPV test fell from $30 to $5, the use of the HPV test every two years (to death) would become the cost-effective strategy with an ICER of $50,100.

Drug Treatment for Alzheimer's Disease

Wimo et al. (2003) examine the costs and consequences of donepezil treatment in patients with mild to moderate Alzheimer's disease. Patients were evaluated as part of a one-year clinical trial where patients were randomized into a treatment group receiving the therapy and a placebo control group. Mean annual health care costs were $16,438 for the treatment group, including $1,280 for the donepezil, and $16,147 for the control group. Average caregiver costs, both direct and indirect, were $8,531 for the treatment

PROFILE

Bengt Jönsson

Bengt Jönsson is part of what could arguably be called Sweden's first family of health economics. He and his wife, Gisela Kobelt, regularly collaborate on research projects and are assisted by Bengt's son, Linus, when additional analytical brainpower is needed. Born into a family without academic traditions, Jönsson managed to challenge the Swedish academic system that rewards a pedigree and became one of the most respected health economists in all of Europe.

Jönsson was born in the port city of Helsingborg, located at the narrowest point of the Oresund (one of the world's most frequented sounds and gateway to the North Sea), and raised in the small industrial town of Höganäs 10 miles to the north. He received his academic training at nearby Lund University, just across the sound from Copenhagen. His undergraduate degree in economics and statistics allowed him to combine his interest in social issues with his training in math and science. His interest in health economics was driven in part by Swedish national politics. Given the significant growth in Sweden's welfare state at the time, surprisingly there was little academic interest in the subject. His masters' thesis in 1972 was a study of the rationale for subsidized child care. Although these services were interesting and important, the study of the child care industry did not lend itself to his vast technical expertise. While visiting a bookstore at the University of York that summer, Jönsson came across a book on health economics coauthored by A. J. Culyer and M. H. Cooper. Subsequent conversations with Culyer and Alan Williams provided the inspiration for the dissertation that followed.

While a lecturer in the economics department at Lund, Jönsson completed his Ph.D. in 1976. After a short tenure as director of the Swedish Institute for Health Economics at Lund, he became professor of health economics in Sweden and director of the Center for Medical Technology Assessment at Linköping University. In 1991, he moved to the Stockholm School of Economics where he is currently Professor of Health Economics. Jönsson also serves as a member of the Scientific Advisory Board of the National Board of Health and Welfare, and is a member of the board of the Swedish Institute for Health Economics. He is associate editor of the *Journal of Health Economics* and a member of the editorial boards of both *PharmacoEconomics* and the *European Journal of Health Economics*.

Being one of the pioneers of a field and living in a small country has its advantages. Jönsson has had a stimulating research agenda with interests in technological change, health care financing and organization, and health care policy. But his most important contribution to the field has been his application of the methods of economic evaluation in health care. He has served as a consultant and policy adviser, not only in Sweden but also for the World Health Organization, the World Bank, and the Organization of Economic Cooperation and Development. These opportunities have "taught [him] modesty in terms of what you can expect to achieve in the short term" and a greater appreciation for the long-term impact of economic fundamentals. Agreeing with his younger colleagues that an academician can have only limited influence in policy making, Jönsson, with the perspective of 30 years in the discipline, "is more surprised about what has been achieved than disappointed about what is left to do."

Jönsson is an excellent cook, something you would expect from a person who lives in southern France part of the year. A better gardener than golfer, one might question how he finds the time for any of his extra-scholarly pursuits. But if you're around him long enough, you realize that he won't let his work get in the way of what is really important. His wife, Gisela, summarizes it best: "He is unique and best in motivating, forming, and coaching bright, young people. I never met a teacher like him: rough, challenging, provocative—yet patient, indulgent, and kind."

Source: Bengt Jönsson curriculum vitae and personal correspondence.

group and $9,919 for the control group. Average total costs for the treatment group were $24,969 and those for the control group were $26,066. Patients receiving the treatment showed cognitive and functional benefits as evidenced by scores on two cognitive tests.

Jönsson et al. (2000) review several studies on the effectiveness of donepezil (including Neumann, Hermann, and Kuntz, 1999) and find that patients receiving the drug have better outcomes in terms of both less time spent in more severe states and improved quality of life. In three of the five studies reviewed donepezil was the dominant strategy (better outcome with a slight cost saving), and it was only slightly more costly in the other two. Jönsson et al. conclude that donepezil is a cost-effective treatment when prescribed to patients with mild to moderate Alzheimer's disease.

Summary and Conclusions

This chapter provided an overview of economic evaluation in health care decision making. Techniques that have become standard practice in Europe over the past decade are not as well integrated in the decision-making process in the United States. Of the three types of economic evaluation discussed, cost-effectiveness analysis is by far the most widely used technique for evaluating the economic efficiency of medical treatment options. The use of modeling in economic evaluation was also emphasized, highlighting the importance of strong quantitative skills for anyone interested in using this valuable analytical tool.

> **Policy Issue**
>
> To what extent should economic evaluation be incorporated into medical decision making?

Even though economic evaluation as a tool has the potential to bring cost-conscious behavior back into the decision-making process, it is not the only thing that matters when judging health care alternatives. Equity in the distribution of care and the quality of care are also important considerations. The quantitative value of an incremental cost-effectiveness ratio should never be the sole consideration in the decision to fund or not to fund a treatment program. The fact that one treatment option has a higher or a lower ICER means very little by itself. The number of patients who are affected by the program, the number and quality of treatment alternatives, and the final impact on overall spending is also critically important.

Cost-effectiveness considerations are more formally integrated into health policy making in Canada, Australia, and Europe. Health economists abroad are more familiar with the methodology and receive substantially more formal training in the concepts and techniques that define the discipline. In fact, if you use the term "health economics" in Europe, it is assumed you mean "economic evaluation."

With only a few minor exceptions, economic evaluation has yet to be used extensively in the appraisal of medical technology in the United States (Eddy, 1991). Ignoring cost-effectiveness issues may no longer be an option for U.S. policy makers. U.S. citizens want comprehensive coverage. They are concerned with issues of affordability and accessibility, and are obsessed with freedom of choice. Federal officials in charge of Medicare and Medicaid, the medical programs for the elderly and indigent, are looking carefully at cost as a factor in deciding whether to pay for certain pharmaceutical drugs. Federal efforts to hold down drug spending will only increase now that Congress has expanded the Medicare program to include a pharmaceutical benefit for the 33 million senior citizens eligible for the program. It may be just a matter of time before these government-run programs begin to ask for formal cost-effectiveness studies to accompany all applications for approval of new medical technologies, creating what the Europeans call the fourth hurdle in the medical technology approval process.

Questions and Problems

1. The health authorities are considering the treatment alternatives for three types of diseases: heart disease, cancer, and infectious disease. Each year there are 10,000 new cases of heart disease, 10,000 new cases of cancer, and 5,000 new cases of infectious disease. For each diagnosis there are a number of mutually independent treatment alternatives (including no treatment) as shown in the following table.

Treatment	Cost per Treatment	QALYs Gained
Heart Disease		
A	0	0
B	100	2
C	300	8
D	400	8
E	600	12
F	800	15
Cancer		
G	0	0
H	200	8
I	400	10
J	500	12
K	600	9
L	700	14
M	800	15
Infectious Disease		
N	0	0
O	100	2
P	350	4
R	650	6

a. Identify all dominated treatment alternatives. Explain why each is dominated.

b. Calculate the incremental cost, incremental QALYs, and incremental cost-effectiveness ratios (ICERs) for all economically rational strategies (ICER = incremental cost/incremental QALYs). Why are these considered economically rational?

c. Using separate graphs for heart disease, cancer, and infectious disease, show the alternative treatment options, label the dominated options, and show the economically feasible alternatives. (Place QALYs on the vertical axis and cost per treatment on the horizontal axis.)

d. The local health district has asked your opinion on the "best" strategy from a public health perspective (disease covered, treatment strategy). What do you tell them? How much will it cost?

2. A recent article in *JAMA* by Mandelblatt et al (2002) compared the societal costs and benefits of human papillomavirus (HPV) testing, Pap testing, and their combination to screen for cervical cancer. The paper studied 18 different population screening strategies—Pap testing alone, HPV testing alone, and Pap plus HPV testing—every 2 or 3 years for women beginning at age 20 and continuing to 65 years, 75 years, and death. The following table summarizes some of the results (low cost to high cost). Costs include screening and treatment costs, discounted over the individual's expected lifetime.

Strategy	Cost ($)	QALYs Saved	Incremental Cost	Incremental QALY	Incremental CE ratio
0. No screening	5,000	26.87	—	—	—
1. Pap every 3 years to age 75	6,825	27.02			
2. HPV every 3 years to age 75	6,950	27.02			
3. Pap every 2 years to age 75	7,275	27.04			
4. Pap + HPV every 3 years to age 75	7,400	27.04			
5. HPV every 2 years to age 75	7,450	27.04			
6. Pap + HPV every 2 years to age 75	7,925	27.05			

    a. Identify all dominated screening strategies. Explain why each is dominated.

    b. Calculate the incremental cost, incremental QALYs, and incremental CE ratios for all economical rational strategies (Incremental CE = incremental cost/incremental QALYs). Why are these considered economical rational?

    c. The local health district has asked your opinion on the "best" strategy from a public health perspective. What do you tell them?

3. The following information has been gathered on the costs and effectiveness of two treatments, A and B. In this problem, costs and consequences are not discounted.

	Treatment A	Treatment B
Mortality rate	2%	5%
Life expectancy for survivors	20 years	10 years
Initial treatment cost	$10,000	$3,000
Follow up costs, year 1	$5,000	$1,000
Annual follow up costs, all subsequent years	$1,000	$500

    a. What is the total cost for the survivors receiving treatment A? For decedents (assuming sudden death)?

    b. What is the total cost for survivors receiving treatment B? For decedents?

    c. What is the expected cost for those patients receiving treatment A? Treatment B?

    d. Draw a simple decision tree showing the costs and consequences of each treatment option.

    e. Calculate the incremental cost and incremental benefit of the treatment alternatives.

    f. What is the ICER?

4. A new treatment is discovered that improves survival probability from 85 percent to 95 percent. Discuss the different ways a researcher might look at these results versus the way that the marketing department might discuss them. What is the difference in the way you would view a new treatment that improves survival probability by the same absolute magnitude, say, from 5 percent to 15 percent?

5. How does cost-benefit analysis differ from cost-effectiveness analysis? Why has cost-effectiveness analysis become the method of choice for health economists around the world?

6. In what sense is a cost-of-illness study a technique of economic evaluation? In what sense is it not? What is the primary motivation for doing a cost-of-illness study?

7. Calculating costs in an economic evaluation is very important. Classify the following costs as direct (D), indirect (ID), or intangible (IT).

Cost	Classification
Transportation (ambulance or personal auto)	
Sick leave	
Informal care performed by spouse	
Visit to private practitioner	
Inpatient hospital stay	
Nursing home stay	
Reduced productivity at work	
Pain and suffering	
Home health care services	
Diagnostic test	
Surgical intervention	
Grief and anxiety	

8. How would you explain the concept of a QALY? When is it appropriate to use QALYs instead of simply improved life expectancy as the outcome measure in an economic evaluation?

9. The following table represents the costs and benefits of four alternative clinical programs designed to treat a single disease. Benefits are measured in terms of the number of lives saved.

Program	Cost ($)	Lives Saved	ICER
A	100,000	10	
B	100,000	12	
C	200,000	12	
D	200,000	15	

a. Finish the table. Which is the best program in terms of the number of lives saved? In terms of the ICER per life saved?

b. How does the cost-effectiveness ratio defined as the average cost per life saved differ from the ICER?

c. Which program would an economist favor? What would your argument be?

10. A controversial new device, the implantable cardiac defibrillator (ICD), was used in a clinical trial to determine if it improved survival for heart attack patients over the standard drug treatment. The trial provided the following information. Two years after the first heart attack, 85 percent of the ICD patients were still alive, compared to 70 percent of the drug treatment group. No additional data is available after the 24-month trial.

a. What is your best guess on survival probability after the trial is over?

b. Calculate the improvement in life expectancy during the trial. What is your best estimate of improved life expectancy after the trial?

c. Graph the mortality function for both the ICD group and the drug therapy group.

d. What is the difference in life expectancy between the two groups?

References

H. Bleichrodt and J. Quiggin, "Life-cycle preferences over consumption and health: when is cost-effectiveness analysis equivalent to cost-benefit analysis?" *Journal of Health Economics 18*, 1999, 681–708.

Andrew Briggs and M. J. Sculpher, "An Introduction to Markov Modelling for Economic Evaluation," *PharmacoEconomics 13*(4), April 1998, 397–409.

Philip M. Clarke, "Cost–benefit analysis and mammographic screening: a travel cost approach," *Journal of Health Economics 17*(6), December 1998, 767–787.

A. Clegg et al., "Clinical and cost-effectiveness of donepezil, rivastigmine, and galantamine for Alzheimer's disease: a rapid and systematic review," *Health Technology Assessment* 5, 2000, 1–137.

Commonwealth Department of Health, Housing, and Community Services, *Guidelines for the Pharmaceutical Industry on Preparation of Submissions to the Pharmaceutical Benefits Advisory Committee,* Canberra: Australian Government Publishing Service; 1992.

Paul Dolan et al., "The Time Trade-off Method: Results from a General Population Study," *Health Economics* 5(2), March 1996, 141–154.

Michael F. Drummond et al., *Methods of Economic Evaluation of Health Care Programmes,* Second Edition, Oxford: Oxford University Press, 1997.

Benjamin G. Druss et al., "Comparing the National Economic Burden of Five Chronic Conditions," *Health Affairs* 20(6), November/December 2001, 233–241.

D. M. Eddy, "Oregon methods: did cost-effectiveness analysis fail?" *Journal of the American Medical Association* 266(15), October 16, 1991, 2135–2141.

Alain Enthoven, *Consumer Choice Health Plan: The Only Practical Solution to the Soaring Cost of Medical Care* (Reading, MA: Addison-Wesley, 1980).

Eric A. Finkelstein, Ian C. Fiebelkorn, and Guijing Wang, "National Medical Spending Attributable to Overweight and Obesity: How Much, And Who's Paying?" *Health Affairs—Web Exclusive* W3, May 14, 2003, 219–226.

Alan M. Garber, "Recent Developments in CBA/CEA," in *Handbook of Health Economics,* Volume 1A, edited by Anthony J. Culyer and Joseph Newhouse, Amsterdam: North Holland, 2001.

Alan M. Garber and Charles E. Phelps, "Economic Foundations of Cost-effectiveness Analysis," *Journal of Health Economics* 16(1), 1997, 1–31.

Gary M Ginsberg and Boaz Lev, "Cost-Benefit Analysis of Riluzole for the Treatment of Amyotrophic Lateral Sclerosis," *PharmacoEconomics* 12(5), November 1997, 578–584.

John H. Goddeeris and Thomas P. Bronken, "Benefit-Cost Analysis of Screening," *Medical Care* 23, 1985, 1242–1255.

James W. Henderson, "Economic Impact of Cocaine and Crack Abuse: Private and Social Issues," in Glen E. Lich, ed., *Doing Drugs and Dropping Out: Assessing the Costs to Society of Substance Abuse and Dropping Out of School.* A Report prepared for the Subcommittee on Economic Growth, Trade, and Taxes of the Joint Economic Committee, Congress of the United States, Washington, DC: U.S. Government Printing Office, August 1991.

Fred J. Hellinger, "Cost-Benefit Analysis of Health Care: Past Applications and Future Prospects," *Inquiry* 17(3), Fall 1980, 204–215.

Jonas Hjelmgren, et al., "Health Economic Guidelines—Similarities, Differences, and Some Implications," *Value in Health* 4(3), May 2001, 225–250.

Lisa A. Jackson et al., "Should College Students Be Vaccinated against Meningococcal Disease? A Cost-Benefit Analysis," *American Journal of Public Health* 85, June 1995, 843–846.

Bengt Jönsson, Linus Jönsson, and Anders Wimo, "Cost of dementia: a review," in *Dementia,* edited by Mario Maj and Norman Sartorius, John Wiley and Sons Ltd., 2000, 335–363.

Robert M. Kaplan et al., "The Quality of Well-Being Scale: Critical Similarities and Differences with SF-36," *International Journal for Quality in Health Care* 10(6), December 1998, 509–520.

H. Klarman, J. Francis, and G. Rosenthal, " Cost-Effectiveness Analysis Applied to the Treatment of Chronic Renal Disease," *Medical Care* 6(1), 1968, 48–54.

Gisela Kobelt, *Health Economics: An Introduction to Economic Evaluation,* London: Office of Health Economics, 2002.

Karen M. Kuntz and Milton C. Weinstein, "Modelling in Economic Evaluation," in *Economic Evaluation in Health Care: Merging Theory with Practice,* Michael Drummond and Alistair McGuire, eds., Oxford: Oxford University Press, 2001.

Parthiv J. Mahadevia, et al., "Lung Cancer Screening with Helical Computed Tomography in Older Adult Smokers: A Decision and Cost-effectiveness Analysis," *Journal of the American Medical Association* 289(3), January 15, 2003, 313–322.

Jeanne S. Mandelblatt, et al., "Benefits and Costs of Using HPV Testing to Screen for Cervical Cancer," *Journal of the American Medical Association* 287(18), May 8, 2002, 2372–2381.

David H. Mark, "Visualizing Cost-effectiveness Analysis," *Journal of the American Medical Association* 287(18), May 8, 2002, 2428–2429.

James R. McGuigan, R. Charles Moyer, and Frederick H. deB. Harris, *Managerial Economics: Applications, Strategy, and Tactics,* Ninth Edition, South-Western College Publishing, 2002.

P. J. Neumann, R. C. Hermann, and K. M. Kuntz, "Cost-effectiveness of donepezil in the treatment of mild or moderate Alzheimer's disease," *Neurology* 52, 1999, 1138–1145.

NICE, *Guidance for Manufacturers and Sponsors,* London: National Institute for Clinical Excellence, June 2001, available from **http://www.nice.org.uk**.

Dorothy P. Rice, Sandler Kelman, Leonard S. Miller, and Sarah Dunmeyer, *The Economic Costs of Alcohol and Drug Abuse and Mental Illness: 1985,* San Francisco, CA: Institute for Health and Aging, University of California at San Francisco, 1990.

Anne A. Scitovsky and Dorothy P. Rice, "Estimates of the Direct and Indirect Costs of Acquired Immunodeficiency Syndrome in the United States, 1985, 1986, and 1991," *Public Health Reports* 102, 1987, 5–17.

Amartya Sen, "Social Choice Theory: A Re-examination," *Econometrica* 45(1), January 1977, 53–89.

W. Kip Viscusi and Joseph E. Aldy, "The Value of a Statistical Life: A Critical Review of Market Estimates throughout the World," NBER Working Paper No. 9487, February 2003.

John von Neumann and Oskar Morgenstern, *Theory of Games and Economic Behavior,* Princeton University Press, 1944.

M. Weinstein and W. Stason, "Foundations of Cost-effectiveness Analysis for Health and Medical Practices," *New England Journal of Medicine* 296(13), March 31, 1977, 716–721.

Burton A. Weisbrod, "Costs and Benefits of Medical Research: A Case Study of Poliomyelitis," *Journal of Political Economy* 79(3), May/June 1971, 527–544.

Anders Wimo et al., "An Economic Evaluation of Donepezil in Mild to Moderate Alzheimer's Disease: Results of a 1-Year, Double-Blind, Randomized Trial," *Dementia and Geriatric Cognitive Disorders* 15, 2003, 44–54.

Chapter 5

Demand for Health and Medical Care

Michael Grossman (1972) first introduced economic researchers to the notion that the demand for medical care is derived from the more fundamental demand for good health. Creating the economic framework for the formal study of the demand for medical care, Grossman's work established two approaches for consideration. In the first, medical care is viewed as an input in the production function for health, and in the second, as an output produced by medical care providers.

Using the first approach, medical care is one of several factors that may be used to improve the health status of an individual or population. Other factors may be even more important in producing good health, including improvements in living standards, advances in medical research, changes in lifestyle, reductions in environmental pollution, and better nutrition. The production of health with medical care as an input is the subject of the first section of this chapter.

Alternatively, the process may be viewed as one where various inputs are combined to produce the final product we call medical care. These inputs include the provider services of physicians, dentists, and others; hospital services, prescription drugs, medical equipment, and other components. In the second section of this chapter, we see how this approach enables us to evaluate the performance of the medical services industry from the perspective of production efficiency.

The Demand for Health

Americans place a high value on health, evidenced by the fact that the pursuit of good health is a multibillion dollar business. In addition to the money spent on medical care, countless dollars are spent on health foods, fitness videos, and weight-loss programs. As important as good health is to our overall well-being, it would be a mistake to conclude that every person considers good health as the primary goal in life. Our day-to-day behavior undermines this notion. Otherwise, how do you explain our overconsumption of food, alcohol, and drugs?[1] How can you explain the popularity of such risky behavior as motocross, skydiving, and bungee jumping? Why do many people refuse to wear their seat belts? Why all the fuss about motorcycle helmets? Why do so many people still smoke cigarettes?

As we begin to think about the demand for health, our starting point will be the relationship between health and the factors that contribute to health. Within this framework, medical care is but one of many inputs that contribute to enhancing the health of the population. Two important questions will be addressed. What is the most efficient way to produce and distribute health? What is the incremental contribution of medical care to the production of health?

---

1 According to the government's technical definition of obesity, over 60 percent of American males and 50 percent of American females are either overweight or obese (Cutler et al., 2003). Almost 30 percent of Americans are classified as obese, or at least 35 pounds overweight (Wessel, 2003) and an estimated 300,000 to 582,000 deaths annually are associated with the diseases of obesity (Allison et al., 1999).

The Production of Health

In economics, production is depicted as a functional relationship showing how inputs are combined to produce output. Specifically, the health production function summarizes the relationship between health status and the various factors that may be used to produce good health. The relationship may be written as follows:

Health = H (medical care, other inputs, time)

Simply stated, people use medical care in combination with other inputs and their own time to produce good health.[2] In much the same way, teachers' services, books, and an individual's own time are used to produce knowledge. Similarly, baseball, hot dogs, apple pie, and the family Chevy are used to produce an enjoyable afternoon at the ballpark.

The hypothesized relationship between health status and medical care spending is shown in Figure 5.1. Stated in terms of the health status of an individual or a population, graphically, it is drawn as a positively sloped function that increases at a decreasing rate. As the amount of medical care spending increases, health status improves. The incremental change in health status declines, however, as more is spent on medical care. In other words, at low levels of overall medical spending, additional spending improves health status substantially. At higher levels of medical spending, the same increase in spending buys a smaller improvement in health status. The economic principle is the law of eventually diminishing marginal returns, or more simply, the law of diminishing returns.[3] Graphically, the law of diminishing returns may be depicted in the top half of the diagram by a total product curve flattening out as medical care spending increases.

The relationship between the change in medical care spending and the change in health status is shown in the lower diagram. The marginal product of medical spending decreases as spending increases, clearly depicting the law of diminishing returns.

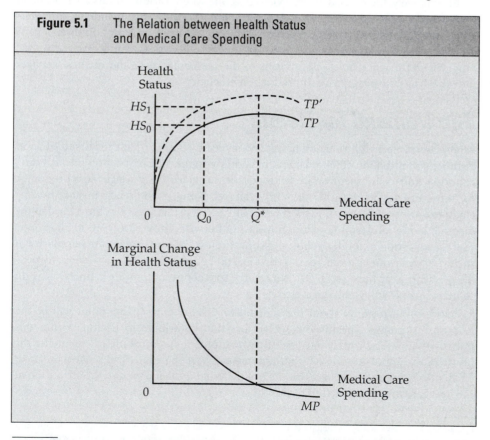

Figure 5.1   The Relation between Health Status and Medical Care Spending

---

2 Formally, H(. . .) is the shorthand way of describing the process whereby inputs are combined to produce health.
3 The production function in Figure 5.1 has the parabolic form $HS = a + bM - cM^2$, where HS denotes health status and M medical care spending. The constant term, a, represents the level of health realized with no medical care spending.

In economics, decisions are seldom made on an all-or-none basis. It is almost always an issue of adjusting priorities, a little more of this and a little less of that. The use of the marginal product graph shows how much extra health status can be purchased with increased outlay on medical care.[4] Understanding this relationship is critical because most issues in health care relate to changes in the level of medical care provided. The relevant issues deal with marginal changes in utilization and spending, not overall utilization and spending.

Economists and policymakers use the information provided by the marginal product curve to make decisions on the allocation of scarce resources among competing alternatives, such as education, police protection, and economic infrastructure projects. The marginal product curve makes a clear distinction between the impact of medical care on total health status and its marginal contribution to health status.

Medical care spending is not the only thing that improves health. Other factors affecting health status, such as lifestyle, environmental pollution, and technological developments, will shift the total product curve. For example, the presence and severity of respiratory problems are associated with high levels of air pollution. In many major metropolitan areas, automobile emissions are the single largest contributor to air pollution. The incidence of these health conditions will likely fall with reductions in automotive emissions. Also, better eating habits and increased exercise will also improve health status. These improvements are depicted graphically by shifting the health status production function from TP to TP'. At every level of medical care spending, improving these other factors will result in better health.

Another way to look at the relationship is to view the production function as the maximum health status that can be achieved at a given level of medical care spending. If an individual is spending Q_0 on medical care, holding the other factors that affect health status constant, the maximum health status achievable is HS_0. There are two obvious ways to improve health status: spend more on medical care and move to a higher point on a stationary health production function (TP), or make better lifestyle decisions and shift the entire curve upward (TP'). At high levels of spending, even more spending on medical care does not buy much of an improvement in health status. The curve has already flattened out. Without spending any more money on medical care, however, HS_1 can be achieved with changes in lifestyle, such as losing weight, getting more exercise, and reducing stress.

One additional clarification may be in order before proceeding further. The health status production function is drawn with a negative slope at spending levels greater than Q^*. Beyond that point, more spending does not result in improvements in health. While it may be unlikely that we will ever reach that point as a society, in individual cases it may be a possibility. The graphical depiction recognizes the existence of **iatrogenic disease**, net harm caused to a patient because of overuse of medical care.

Every year thousands of patients are harmed, some permanently, by unnecessary procedures and overmedication. After comparing the results of a Harvard Medical School Study of New York hospital records and a similar study from California, Brennan (1992) concluded that adverse events occurred in approximately 4 percent of all hospitalizations. In addition, more than one-fourth of the adverse events can be attributed to substandard care, often the result of overtreatment or improper treatment. A 1999 study conducted by the Institute of Medicine estimated that medical errors are responsible for the deaths of at least 44,000 Americans annually and possibly as many as 98,000 (Kohn, Corrigan, and Donaldson, 1999).

A given level of health may be achieved using different combinations of the inputs. Of interest to economists and policy analysts is the most efficient way to combine the inputs to generate the maximum output possible. In this context, efficiency refers to economic efficiency, or that combination of inputs that minimizes the cost of producing a

Key Concept 4
Marginal Analysis

The Institute of Medicine chartered as a component of the National Academy of Sciences provides information related to health and welfare issues. Recently released reports on such issues as schools and medicine, telemedicine, and medical outcomes research may be found at **http://www.iom.edu/**

> **Policy Issue**
> In addition to increases in medical care spending, other factors affect the health of the population, including lifestyle choices, environmental factors, and developments in technology.

iatrogenic disease
An injury or illness resulting from medical treatment.

Key Concept 8
Efficiency

---

4 The difficulty in measuring health status makes the practical application of this relationship somewhat tenuous.

mortality
The probability of death at different ages, usually expressed
as the number of deaths for a
given population, either 1,000 or
100,000, or the expected number of years of life remaining at
a given age.

morbidity
The incidence and probability
of illness or disability.

given level of health. To determine the efficiency of resource allocation in health care, we begin by estimating the production function for health. Before we can estimate the production function for health, we must first agree on a measure of health status.

Measures of Health Status

Everyone has his or her own opinion on what constitutes good health. If we are to give our discussion on the relationship between health status and medical spending practical importance, it is critical that we develop a quantifiable measure of health status. No single measure can capture all of the aspects relating to life and the quality of life that are considered important. Studies in the production of health have used such quantifiable measures of health as life expectancy and **mortality** rates. Disability statistics, lost days due to illness, the incidence of high blood pressure, and other measures of **morbidity** have also been used as measures of health status including the quality-adjusted life-year discussed in Chapter 4.

Mortality

One of the most common aggregate measures of health status is crude death rate for a given population, measured as the number of deaths per 100,000 population. Often this measure is adjusted for age, sex, and race to make comparisons among subgroups (across geographic regions or countries) more meaningful. Table 5.1 ranks the top ten causes of death in the United States in 1980 and 2000. Heart disease and cancer are responsible for over one-half of the deaths in this country annually and have been for the past 20 years. Add to that strokes and the number increases to roughly two-thirds. After these three, no single cause is responsible for more than 5 percent of the total deaths. In fact, after the top ten, no single cause is responsible for more than 1 percent of the total.[5] Not shown by the table is the fact that the leading causes of death vary

Table 5.1	Top Ten Causes of Death, 1980 and 2000					

| **Cause of Death** | 1980 | | **Cause of Death** | 2000 | |
	Number (in thousands)	**Percent**		**Number** (in thousands)	**Percent**
All Causes	1,989.8	100.0	All Causes	2,403.4	100.0
1. Diseases of the heart	761.1	38.3	1. Diseases of the heart	710.8	29.6
2. Malignant neoplasms	416.5	20.9	2. Malignant neoplasms	553.1	23.0
3 Cerebrovascular diseases	170.2	8.6	3. Cerebrovascular diseases	167.7	7.0
4. Unintended injuries	105.7	5.3	4. Chronic obstructive pulmonary diseases	122.0	5.1
5. Chronic obstructive Pulmonary diseases	56.1	2.8	5. Unintended injuries	97.9	4.1
6. Pneumonia and influenza	54.6	2.7	6. Pneumonia and influenza	65.3	2.9
7. Diabetes mellitus	34.9	1.8	7. Diabetes mellitus	69.3	2.7
8. Chronic liver disease and cirrhosis	30.6	1.5	8. Alzheimer's disease	49.6	2.1
9. Atherosclerosis	29.4	1.5	9. Nephritis, nephritic syndromes, and nephrosis	37.3	1.6
10. Suicide	26.9	1.4	10. Septicemia	31.2	1.3

Source: *Health, United States, 2002 with Chartbook on Trends in the Health of Americans,* Table 32.

5 Only three of the top ten causes of death in the United States make the worldwide top ten list. In addition to diseases of the heart, cerebrovascular disease, and chronic obstructive pulmonary disease, the top ten killers worldwide include tuberculosis, malaria, measles, and lower respiratory infections and diarrhea in children under five years of age (World Health Organization, *World Health Report* 110(4), July–August 1995, 509).

considerably by age. Overall, unintended injuries were the leading cause of death for all age groups from 1 to 44 years. HIV infection, once the leading cause of death for those between the ages of 25 to 44 years, was the fifth leading cause of death for that age group in 2000. Cancer was the leading cause for those between 45 to 64 years of age, and for those over age 65 heart disease was the leading cause.

Other commonly used measures include male and female life expectancies at birth and infant mortality rates. At least two problems arise from using mortality rates to measure health status. First, when studying the health status of individuals, aggregate mortality rates have little meaning. Secondly, mortality rates tend to be poor indicators of the quality of life. A low crude death rate does not always indicate a healthy population.

Morbidity

An alternative way to measure health status is to consider the prevalence of certain diseases or medical conditions. Typical morbidity measures include restricted-activity days due to illness, the incidence rate of certain chronic conditions, and a self-assessment of health status. Table 5.2 ranks the top 15 health conditions in terms of work days lost and activity impairments.

Although the rank ordering differs, the number of work days lost and the number of activity impairments have the same causes. Arthropathies or other orthopedic impairments are responsible for the most activity impairments, and more specifically back problems result in the most work days lost. Chronic conditions with the highest overall prevalence (but not necessarily the highest number of activity impairments) include chronic sinusitis, arthritis, asthma, chronic bronchitis, and diabetes.

Newhouse and Friedlander (1980) use six physiological measures to analyze the health status in a particular geographic region in relation to the level of medical resources available. The measures they used were diastolic blood pressure, serum cholesterol concentration, electrocardiogram abnormalities, abnormal chest X-rays, presence of varicose veins, and a periodontal index. The first three measures were chosen because

Table 5.2	Selected Conditions with the Highest Number of Work Days Lost and Activity Impairments, 1996			
Condition	**Work Days Lost (Millions)**	**Rank**	**Activity Impairments (Thousands)**	**Rank**
Acute respiratory infection	69.2	4	1,949.6	3
Arthropathies	67.2	5	3,070.5	1
Asthma	31.4	7	690.4	9
Back problems	83.0	1	1,380.9	5
Cardiac dysrythmias	7.2	12	528.7	13
Cerebrovascular disease	8.2	13	1,084.1	6
Chronic obstructive pulmonary disease	57.5	6	889.3	7
Congestive heart failure	1.1	15	494.6	14
Diabetes	27.5	8	1,954.0	2
Hypertension	12.0	11	544.3	12
Ischemic heart disease	21.8	9	638.3	10
Mood disorders	78.2	2	1,400.9	4
Motor vehicle accidents	70.0	3	808.6	8
Peripheral vascular disorders	12.8	10	591.4	11
Respiratory malignancies	2.5	14	121.5	15

Source: Druss et al., 2002.

of their association with cardiovascular disease, the number one cause of death. The latter three were included for the following reasons: abnormal chest X-rays are associated with cancer, the presence of varicose veins reflects the general status of the body's connective tissues, and periodontal disease reflects overall preventive-care practices.

Using morbidity measures has one serious drawback. Since the observed relationship between medical care spending and the incidence of high blood pressure, for example, is negative, more medical care reduces the incidence of hypertension. Care should be taken when graphing the relationship as we did in Figure 5.1. Because of the negative relationship, health status must be defined as the absence of the specific condition.

Quality of Life

Some may view measuring health status as a nice academic exercise, but it is a deadly serious proposition for health policy planners. In a world of scarce resources, some means of resource allocation is inevitable. Responsible planning requires that the actual scheme should be clearly stated and easily understood, and those responsible for its implementation should be accountable for their decisions. Effective resource allocation requires establishing a measurable output. Otherwise, it is based on intuition without regard to explicit information on costs and benefits.

Key Concept 4
*Marginal
Analysis*

Recall from the previous chapter a measure of quality of life popular among European policymakers called the quality-adjusted life-year, or QALY. This measure of health status combines quality of life and survival duration into an index that is frequently used to evaluate programs and analyze clinical decisions especially in countries with government-run systems on fixed budgets. The QALY provides a common unit of measurement that allows valid comparisons across alternative programs.

Possibly the most appropriate use of QALY analysis is the consideration of resource allocation within a single program. Setting priorities within the waiting list for kidney transplants provides a useful example. Members of the relevant population suffer from the same disease, end-stage renal disease (ESRD), and share the same disease-specific outcome measure. The use of the QALY approach arouses strong opinions among both supporters and critics. Those interested in more information about QALYs are directed to the vast British literature on the subject (see Broome, 1988; Culyer, 1990; Lockwood, 1988; and Loomes and McKenzie, 1990).

Determinants of Health Status

Medical care is not the only factor that contributes to the production of health. Others include income and education, environmental and lifestyle factors, and genetics. Research on the relationship between health status and medical care frequently has found that the marginal contribution of medical care to health status is rather small. Some argue that at the current level of overall medical care spending, we are at the flat-of-the-curve (Enthoven, 1980). Referring back to Figure 5.1, the flat-of-the-curve would correspond to a level of medical care utilization where spending approaches the point where *TP* is maximized. As spending approaches Q^* the marginal productivity of additional spending approaches zero, and we are on the flat-of-the-curve. Further spending will buy only small improvements in health. Even though this generalization may be true for overall spending, it is obvious that we are not on the flat-of-the-curve for some services, including primary, prenatal, and preventive care. In either case, any significant improvements in health status are more likely to originate from factors other than medical care. The easiest way to improve health may be to shift the production function for health.

Income and Education

The link between an individual's state of health and socioeconomic status may not be direct, but the theoretical underpinnings are obvious. Income, education, and employment represent a level of social advancement that, to a large extent, determines access to medical care. (In the U.S. system employment determines insurance coverage to a great degree.) In turn, improved access to care improves health.[6]

This association does not prove that low socioeconomic status causes poor health. It may be that low status is merely associated with the actual determinants of poor health. Other factors associated with socioeconomic status that may provide a more direct link include nutrition, housing, environment, and even individual time preference. Although the issue provides a wealth of data to examine, no real consensus has emerged.

Pappas et al. (1993) have examined mortality rates for Americans at various income levels. Their research shows that the 1986 death rates for Americans with incomes less than $9,000 were significantly higher than those for Americans earning more than $25,000. More importantly, these differences have widened since 1960. They concluded that socioeconomic status is a strong indicator of health status.

Guralnik et al. (1993) have shown that one of the most important factors influencing good health and life expectancy is education (independent of income levels). The research still begs the relevant question: Does more schooling result in better health, or are the two variables related in some other way?

> **Policy Issue**
> Does additional medical care spending on the poor significantly improve their health status?

Research represented by Grossman (1972) and others assumes that individuals with more education are more efficient producers of good health. Education increases the ability to understand the importance of avoiding unhealthy behavior, the ability to communicate with health practitioners and understand instructions, and the ability to take advantage of the services available in the medical marketplace. By improving long-term opportunities, education increases the return on investing in health improvements.

Examining the relationship between income and health at the national level requires a completely different perspective. In comparisons of modern industrial nations, little correlation emerges between the level of national income and the various measures of health. When countries from the less developed world are included, however, a connection between income and health can be made. This connection is probably due to better **public health** measures as the level of development increases, including sanitary water and sewage systems, and immunization programs that reduce the spread of disease.

> **public health**
> Collective action undertaken by government agencies to ensure the health of the community. These efforts include the prevention of disease, identification of health problems, and the assurance of sanitary conditions, especially in the areas of water treatment and waste disposal.

Environmental and Lifestyle Factors

Our discussion on market failure due to externalities in Chapter 3 emphasized the economic costs associated with environmental problems such as air and water pollution. In addition to the high economic costs, the toll on human life and the quality of life is also significant. For example, the American Cancer Society estimates that 65 percent of all cancer in the United States can be linked to lifestyle and environmental factors, including the air we breathe and the food we eat. Exposure to environmental toxins, especially during infancy and childhood, can be linked to illness in children. Harmful chemicals, such as lead, mercury, and PCBs (polychlorinated biphenyls), are associated with poor fetal growth, poor growth during childhood, reduced intelligence (measured by IQ), small head circumference (associated with mental retardation), and decreased lung capacity (Shannon and Graef, 1992; Rogan et al., 1986; Needleman and Bellinger, 1990).

Regardless of the level of income and education, health status depends to a large degree on personal behavior. Lifestyle factors including diet, exercise, sexual behavior, cigarette smoking, substance abuse, and brushes

> **Policy Issue**
> Much of the illness experienced by residents of industrialized countries is due to lifestyle and environmental factors, including the food we eat and the air we breathe.

---

6 There is a glaring weakness with this line of reasoning. Countries with universal medical coverage experience the same correlation between socioeconomic status and health. For example, age-standardized mortality rates in the United Kingdom are twice as high for men in the lowest occupational classification. England's lowest socioeconomic group has infant mortality rates that are double those of the highest socioeconomic group, a difference that has persisted since the late 1940s. In Scandinavia with its relatively homogeneous population, age-standardized mortality rates vary significantly across occupational categories. Certain low-income occupations, such as restaurant workers, have mortality rates that are twice as high as some high-income occupations, such as school teachers.

necessity
A good or service with an income elasticity between 0 and 1.

Key Concept 9
Market Failure

ISSUES IN MEDICAL CARE DELIVERY

HEALTH COSTS OF OZONE ALERTS

Americans love their automobiles. Given the distances traveled and the relative lack of mass-transit alternatives, the availability of a private vehicle is more a **necessity** than an option. Our reliance on our cars produces an important by-product: air pollution. Automobile exhaust provides one of the most vivid examples of negative externalities in private markets. This by-product of urban living is largely responsible for the outdoor air pollution that exists today. Sulfur dioxide, ozone, and particulate matter, especially from diesel engines, act as irritants and are thought to be causal factors in the prevalence and severity of many respiratory problems.

Children, and adults for that matter, who suffer from asthma are increasingly at risk when exposed to higher levels of ozone. Even those with no underlying pulmonary disease are more likely to suffer from respiratory distress in areas with higher air pollution levels. Chronic bronchitis, frequent sinus infections, wheezing, and breathlessness are all more frequent in large cities or along major thoroughfares.

Ozone, the principle element in summer smog, is the most pervasive air pollutant in the United States. Cities across the country regularly report ozone levels and post "ozone-alerts" when levels are dangerously high. It is no longer sufficient to measure the cost of our daily commute to work by the cost of gasoline and parking. Only when we factor in the increased medical care costs associated with pollution-induced respiratory disease can we fully reflect the marginal social cost of our love affair with our cars.

Source: "Children at Risk from Ozone Air Pollution—United States, 1991-1993," *Morbidity and Mortality Weekly Report* 44(16), April 28, 1995, 309–315.

---

with violence are important determinants of health status. The observed relationship between health status and socioeconomic status is interesting. But insufficient evidence prevents a determination of whether we are actually witnessing a link between socioeconomic status and health, or lifestyle behavior and health.

Genetic Factors

Two factors play a critical role in determining the health of an individual: the risk of exposure to a particular disease and the ability of the individual to resist the disease (and recover from its consequences) once exposed. The former is the purview of public health, the latter is determined largely by genetics. Thinking about the etiology of certain inherited diseases, sickle cell anemia for example, differs from thinking about causation in infectious diseases. If a critical number of bacteria enter the system, you get sick. If the bacteria is Salmonella typhi, you get salmonellosis. With certain cancers, the process is different. Cells mutate and multiply, and sometimes a single cell can become cancerous through a series of events. Inherited traits may predispose individuals to certain diseases.

Your genetic makeup is determined directly by your parents. You receive 50 percent of your genes from your father and 50 percent from your mother. You share 50 percent of your genes with your siblings, or 100 percent if you happen to be an identical twin. These are all referred to as your first-degree relatives. You get 25 percent of your genes from each grandparent, and you share that same percentage with each aunt and uncle. These are called second-degree relatives. You also get 12.5 percent of your genes from each great-grandparent, so there is a chance that their genetic defects could surface in you.

ISSUES IN MEDICAL CARE DELIVERY

GENETIC DISCRIMINATION

When is a person considered sick? In California, a person cannot be considered sick until he or she exhibits symptoms of an illness. This issue is not as silly as it may seem on the surface. It is a serious legal matter. We are already becoming extremely sophisticated in our ability to diagnose ailments at very early stages. In fact, hundreds of tests are currently available to identify a person's genetic predisposition to a number of inherited diseases.

From a medical perspective, the availability of genetic information can be life-saving. Genetic testing can provide valuable information to medical providers on the probability that a person might contract a specific disease. Better predictability improves the chance of prevention. From an insurance perspective, this same information can be used to determine eligibility for health insurance coverage or even the level of premiums.

Otherwise healthy individuals may be unable to secure health insurance coverage because of information about their genetic makeup. Entire families could be denied insurance coverage, even infants before they are born, because someone in the family carries a recessive gene for a disease, such as sickle cell anemia or Tay Sachs disease. (Carriers of a disease possess a recessive gene, but will never contract the disease.)

The growing trend toward preventive medicine will increasingly use genetic analysis to forecast an individual's likelihood to contract a particular disease. Who should have access to this genetic information? How should it be used? Given the expensive nature of disease treatment, if genetic tests are performed, it is understandable that health insurance firms would want access to the information. Individuals who have information about their potential health problems are likely to desire additional health insurance coverage. Is it fair to deny this information to insurance companies who are being asked to underwrite the future costs? It is illegal to discriminate against a person on the basis of sex or race. Should it also be illegal to discriminate against someone on the basis of his or her DNA?

Policy Issue

Should the results of genetic tests be made available to all stakeholders: patients and their families, medical providers, and health insurance payers?

Source: Seth Shulman, "Preventing Genetic Discrimination: California Law Prohibits Discriminating Against People Genetically Predisposed to Rare Diseases," *Technology Review* 98(5), Massachusetts Institute of Technology Alumni Association, July 1995, 16.

Attempts to understand the hereditary factor in determining the predisposition to certain diseases have received a great deal of attention. Genetic research has focused on the mapping of the 100,000 plus genes in the human body with one of the goals being to determine the genes responsible for certain forms of inherited diseases. The inheritance of a particular gene greatly increases the risk of acquiring certain diseases. For example, women with a family history of ovarian cancer have a lifetime risk of developing the disease of about 40 percent compared with population risk of about 7 percent. Other genes are associated with an increased incidence of colon, breast, uterine, and prostate cancers. Genetic factors may account for as much as 10 to 15 percent of all colorectal cancers and 5 to 10 percent of breast cancers (Marra and Boland, 1995).

A hereditary component is suspect in many different disorders. A strong family predisposition is a significant factor in allergies, hypertension, obesity, cystic fibrosis, sickle cell anemia, and even snoring. Heredity may also be linked to pancreatic cancer, certain melanomas, and even kidney and lung cancer. But scientists are still trying to understand the biological basis for many diseases. A mere clustering of a common disease in certain families is not enough to prove a genetic link. The cause may be environmental or it may be lifestyle related instead of genetic. But as the genetic components of many diseases are being discovered, a complete family medical history is becoming an important tool in the early diagnosis and treatment of certain diseases. Until more is known, choose your parents well.

The Role of Public Health and Nutrition

Research by Thomas McKeown (1976) serves as the basis of most of our understanding concerning the improvement in mortality. Ranked in order of importance, McKeown attributed the secular decline in mortality rates in Europe and North America to four major sources.

- Living standards, primarily better nutrition and housing, advanced dramatically.

- Intervention of public health authorities improved sanitary conditions in the growing urban centers. Water purification and the treatment and disposal of sewage vastly improved the water supplies.

- Certain diseases declined in importance because of reduced exposure and increased natural immunity.

- Advances in medical science increased the ability to treat certain conditions. Improvements in surgery enabled physicians to treat accidents and digestive disorders, especially appendicitis; obstetric and pediatric care improved treatment of pregnant women and infants; and immunizations contributed to the control of certain diseases.

The result was a decline in waterborne diseases responsible for intestinal infections, including cholera, dysentery, diphtheria, and other diarrheal diseases. Food hygiene, especially with respect to milk, improved significantly leading to a reduction in the number of infant deaths. The spread of airborne diseases resulting in upper-respiratory problems, such as bronchitis, pneumonia, influenza, and smallpox, became less of a problem because of reduced exposure due, in part, to the diligence of health officials in controlling their spread.

Policy Issue

Improvements in public health programs are responsible for much of the improvement in human life span experienced over the past century.

Most of the reduction in mortality occurred before effective medical interventions were discovered. When considering the reasons for increased longevity, the role of public health intervention should not be overlooked. The U.S. Public Health Service was formed in 1912, emerging from the Marine Hospital Service. The purview of public health includes the control of communicable diseases, epidemics, and environmental hazards. Public health activities promote health through immunization programs, quarantines, and standards for clean air, clean water, sewage disposal, and the safe handling of food.

Although few critics argue with McKeown's list of reasons for the decline in mortality and morbidity, they do question his rankings and the relative importance he places on each. In particular, Woods and Hinde (1987) question McKeown's conclusion that up to one-half of the decrease in mortality was due to improved nutrition. They agree that nutrition played a significant role in determining the health of a population by increasing the resistance to disease. Obviously, the overt types of malnutrition, including rickets and beriberi, contribute to poor health. More importantly, an undernourished population lends itself to more frequent infections and more serious infections. Woods and Hinde, however, placed more weight on the importance of improvements in environmental conditions and less on nutrition. Neither attributed much of the decline in the incidence of disease to improvements in medical care.

The relationship between nutrition, mortality, and morbidity is complicated. Better nutrition played a significant role in the reduction in mortality from infectious disease, in particular, childhood diseases related to respiratory and intestinal infections. But

McKeown's (1976) research, based on national data, did not include data on infant mortality, an important cause of death until well into the twentieth century. The debate rages on among demographers and is likely to continue for some time. It is important to note that the increased availability of medical care is only one way to improve the health status of an individual or population. In the developed world at least, better lifestyle decisions and a cleaner environment may do more to improve health than increased availability of medical care.

Policy Issue

Improvements in public health may do as much to improve life expectancy in the less developed world than increases in medical care spending.

The Demand for Medical Care

As medical care spending continues to escalate, the search for alternatives to slow its growth has focused on the supply side of the market. Modifying provider behavior is seen by some as the only way to control runaway spending. By ignoring the demand side of the market, we may be forgoing one of the most powerful forces available for cost-control, individual self interest. A basic understanding of the demand side of the market is an important step toward fiscal responsibility in medical care. In this section we will identify and examine the factors that determine the demand for medical care.

Key Concept 4
Self-Interest

Medical Care as an Investment

One demand-side approach treats medical care like any other investment that enhances future productivity. Stated in economic terms, medical care increases human capital (Fuchs, 1982; Mushkin, 1962). Resources used to improve health reduce current consumption with the expectation that future consumption will be increased. Individual willingness to invest in human capital improvements is determined by several factors, including the current cost, the size of the future payoff, the time span over which the payoff is realized, and individual time preference. It is irrelevant whether the human capital investment is spending on medical care or the spending for a college education. Individuals who are willing to invest in a college education are the same individuals who are willing to spend time and money on improving their health.

Policy Issue

The most powerful force for controlling medical spending is the cost-conscious consumer.

Demand for medical care is not based solely on the desire to feel better, but also on the desire to increase productivity. Within this framework, the demand for medical care has a consumption component and an investment component. People who invest in their health desire to have more healthy days available to produce income and leisure. This view incorporates the concept of the depreciation of health capital as one ages and the use of medical care to slow the process.

Key Concept 2
Opportunity Cost

The model of derived demand provides the basis for our study of the determinants of medical care demand. The demand for medical care is derived from the demand for good health. Using this framework, the demand for medical care is inversely related to its price. Other relevant factors affecting the level of demand will now be examined.[7]

Factors Influencing Demand

The demand for medical care is determined to a great extent by patient need. Admittedly, need is a difficult concept to define, but one thing is certain, need and demand are not synonymous. Needs tend to be self-defined and thus represent unconstrained desires. Defining medical care demand in terms of self-defined need is a prescription for wasting medical care resources. As a society we can never fully satisfy unconstrained desires. In economics, demand is defined in terms of the sacrifice an individual is willing to make in order to obtain a given amount of a particular good or service. In this context, to restrain medical care spending, we simply modify the incentive structure.

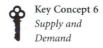

Key Concept 6
Supply and Demand

---

[7] Further discussion of the human capital model may be found in Chapter 8.

ISSUES IN MEDICAL CARE DELIVERY

FIFTY YEARS AT THE CDC

Centers for Disease Control
Established in 1946, this agency of the U.S. Department of Health and Human Services is charged with promoting the public health of Americans around the world.

For years, the control of the spread of infectious diseases has been tightly linked to the **Centers for Disease Control (CDC)**. When public health officials were faced with problems of immunization or eradication, they turned to the CDC. July 1, 2003, marked the 57th anniversary of the establishment of the Atlanta-based operation. But the task of the CDC is much more complex than its mission statement would indicate: To promote health and quality of life by preventing and controlling disease, injury, and disability. The issues are no longer merely epidemiological. The world of public health is now more complicated than studying and stopping chains of infection. The challenge has become less scientific and more behavioral.

- How do we promote healthy lifestyles?

- Should nicotine be classified as an addictive substance and kept out of the hands of minors?

- Can we reduce the homicide rate by requiring the registration of hand guns?

- What is the best way to break the chain of HIV infection, condoms or quarantine?

Much of the work of the CDC is still related to the original mission. The CDC had representatives in Zaire in 1995 to study the outbreak of the deadly Ebola virus. The world looked to the CDC for reassurance that this was an isolated occurrence and not the first of many exotic viruses to emerge from the wilderness to infect modern civilization. Similar stories can be told about Legionnaires' disease, toxic shock syndrome, and severe acute respiratory syndrome (SARS).

Even critics of the organization view the study of infectious diseases an important element in prevention and cure. Their concern deals with the controversial issues, such as a recommended ban on all cigarette advertising to reduce teenage smoking, the promotion of condom use to control the spread of HIV, and mandatory licensing of hand guns to reduce the rate of homicides.

The very nature of the operation places the CDC in contact with the unloved populations of the world and opens it up to criticism. Promiscuous gay men, drug addicts, violent teenagers, and the homeless receive a great deal of attention. Critics contend that too much money and too much effort are spent on medical issues affecting these groups. Instead, they argue, attention should be focused on keeping healthy people from getting sick. Even though AIDS accounts for less than one percent of the deaths annually, the HIV/AIDS budget is almost one-third of the total CDC budget. In comparison, cancer accounts for 25 percent of the annual deaths and cardiovascular disease over 40 percent.

The twenty-first century task of the CDC is even more complicated. With over 70 percent of the deaths in the United States the result of chronic diseases, the future of the medical care delivery system lies in disease prevention. Not only is prevention difficult to sell, but prevention research is complicated and costly. It is much easier to study the effectiveness of a drug treatment or how to cure a disease than it is to demonstrate a pattern of disease prevention. Chronic illness lacks immediacy. Lung cancer materializes as a result of a lifetime of poor decisions about smoking. It is difficult to convince someone that their decision to smoke today will affect their quality of life 40 years from now. For many young smokers, their chance of dying violently at a young age far surpasses the perceived risk of a few cigarettes. With a combined budget of a little over $2 billion and about 6,000 employees, the Centers for Disease Control has set out to find practical uses for basic medical research. It is not nearly as easy as it sounds.

Source: Anne Rochell, "Turning 50: The CDC's Mid-Life Crisis," *Dallas Morning News,* January 28, 1996, 12J.

Following Intriligator (1981), an individual's demand for medical care may be depicted by the demand curves in Figure 5.2. Q_M represents some minimum level of medical care required to maintain health. This minimum level will vary depending on the individual's current health status. Individuals with acute or chronic health problems will require more medical care. The demand curve D_0 represents the level of care established by the medical community as the clinical standard. It is the level of care that should be provided without consideration for cost. Medical planners often use D_0 to determine future requirements for medical facilities and personnel. Planning based solely on clinical standards (medically defined need) ignores the price of medical care completely. Under these circumstances, demand is treated as if it were perfectly inelastic. Consumers desire the same level of services (Q_1) regardless of the price they pay.

Demand based on willingness to pay does not ignore need completely. Clinical need is merely considered one of several determinants of demand. In this case, demand is shown by the downward-sloping demand curve D_1. As the price of care changes, quantity demanded changes. When medical care is free to the patient ($P = 0$), the quantity demanded will be Q_1. As patients are required to pay more out-of-pocket, they demand less. When price rises to P_0, quantity demanded falls to Q_0. In this framework, health status becomes a demand shifter. A change in an individual's health status will change the level of demand and shift the demand curve, to the right to D_2 if health deteriorates and to the left if it improves. Note that when demand shifts to D_2, clinical need also increases to Q_2.

The following discussion examines the major factors that influence medical care demand. Factors can be categorized as patient factors and physician factors. Patient factors include health status, demographic characteristics, and economic standing. Physicians affect demand through their standing as both providers of medical services and advisers to (or agents for) their patients. Because physicians also serve as agents, they are in a unique position to create demand for their own services. Medical care demand may be viewed as a functional relationship between medical care and its determinants.

$$\text{Medical Care} = M(HS, DC, ES, PF)$$

where patient factors include health status (HS), demographic characteristics (DC), and economic standing (ES). Physician factors are denoted by PF. $M(\dots)$ is a shorthand depiction of how these factors interact to generate a demand for medical care.

Figure 5.2 Demand Based on Need versus Willingness to Pay

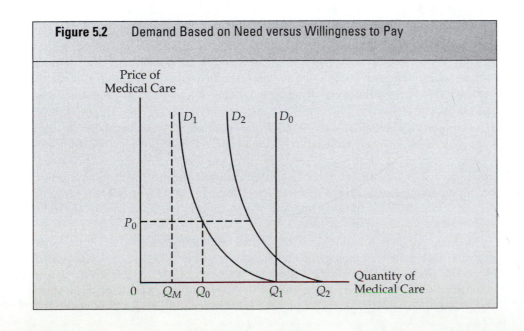

Patient Factors

With medical care, as with any other commodity or service, consumers must decide among the available alternatives designed to satisfy their desires. For the demand relationship to have any economic meaning, patients must have money to spend on treatment alternatives and the ability to rank them in order of preference. Otherwise, patients are merely pawns in the game of medical resource allocation.

Substitutes in medical care are the alternative methods of treatment that lead to the same outcome. Natural childbirth results in a newborn infant; so does cesarean delivery. Balloon angioplasty, along with stainless-steel stents, is one way to treat blocked coronary arteries; bypass graft surgery is another. Tennis elbow will improve in time with RICE (rest, ice, compression, and elevation); for those less patient, cortisone injections will also do the trick. Other examples include surgery performed on an outpatient instead of an inpatient basis; the use of the laparoscope for abdominal and knee surgeries; and lithotripsy instead of abdominal surgery to treat kidney stones. In most cases, the choice of treatment alternative is not solely a physician decision. The desires of patients are also taken into consideration.

Health Status. A patient seeking treatment for a medical condition typically initiates medical treatment. The patient's desire for treatment is often a response to an accident, injury, or other episode of illness. Thus, an individual's demand for medical treatment is usually triggered by the onset of an episode of illness. The desire to remain healthy will increase the demand for preventive care. For example, many people visit the local clinic annually for a flu shot to avoid the onset of an illness, women are encouraged to visit their gynecologists regularly for preventive tests, and some people see their dentists twice a year for check-ups and cleanings.

The acute care model of medical treatment follows an expected pattern: a patient develops a medical condition (illness, injury, pregnancy, etc.), seeks out a physician, receives treatment, and either recovers or dies. Increasingly, a significant minority of patients does not fit the pattern. Their medical conditions do not go away. Instead of recovering or dying, they simply live on with a chronic medical problem.

Chronic illness, defined as a condition where a complete cure is not possible, has become a major factor in U.S. health care spending. In fact, chronic conditions begin to dominate medical care demand as a person ages. The incidence of Parkinson's, Alzheimer's, and other dementias increases as we age. Individuals who once died of heart attack or stroke in their 60s are living into their 80s only to experience the effects of a chronic illness. Arthritis, diabetes, asthma, and emphysema are growing problems among the elderly.

Chronic conditions are not solely a feature of the elderly population. An increase in the number of HIV infections and the cost of treating AIDS is a growing concern. Other sexually transmitted diseases, especially chlamydia and HPV, and respiratory diseases such as tuberculosis and pneumonia, are increasingly resistant to traditional methods of treatment. These realities are all subtle reminders that we have not won the battle against infectious disease.

Demographic Characteristics. Individual and population demographics are also important determinants of medical care demand. First of all, a growing population will increase the demand for medical care. Even as the population grows, the family structure is changing dramatically, increasing the demands on the medical care sector. More single parents, more women in the labor force, later marriages, fewer children per family, and greater mobility translate into fewer opportunities for direct family care and a greater reliance on medical providers.

An aging population is another factor contributing to increased demand for medical care. Using the terminology of the Grossman model (1972), as a person grows older, the stock of health capital begins to depreciate. Over the life cycle, people attempt to offset their depreciating stocks by increasing their spending on medical care. In addition to the increased frequency of chronic conditions discussed above, the

ISSUES IN MEDICAL CARE DELIVERY

TREATMENT ALTERNATIVES FOR PEPTIC ULCERS

What is the best way to treat duodenal ulcers? Until recently, most members of the medical profession felt that the overproduction of stomach acid due to stress, diet, or environmental factors was the major cause of this common peptic ulcer. If excess acid is the source, then the best treatment is the use of an acid blocker such as Tagamet, Zantac, Prilosec, or the little purple pill Nexium. Recent information made available by the National Institutes of Health indicate that a common bacterium causes most of the duodenal ulcers, opening up a new treatment pattern including acid blockers and antibiotics.

Research by Imperiale et al. (1995) examined the costs of three different treatments: (1) treat with acid blockers initially, and if the problem recurs, verify the presence of bacteria by endoscopy and treat with antibiotics; (2) prescribe routine endoscopy followed by acid blockers and antibiotics if bacteria is present; otherwise use acid blockers alone; and (3) use acid blockers and antibiotics and resort to endoscopy only if the problem recurs within a year.

All three methods are proven means of treating this common form of peptic ulcers. But recurrence rates are extremely high with acid blockers alone, and endoscopy is an expensive diagnostic test, costing as much as $3,000. Because research confirms that a high percentage of ulcer patients are also infected with the bacterium, avoiding the invasive test can save money. Thus, the most cost-effective treatment may be an aggressive regimen of acid blockers and antibiotics without the expensive diagnostic testing.

Source: Thomas F. Imperiale, Theodore Speroff, Randall D. Cebul, and Arthur J. McCullough, "A Cost Analysis of Alternative Treatments of Duodenal Ulcers," *Annals of Internal Medicine* 123(9), November 1, 1995, 665–672.

---

elderly are more likely to suffer from cancer, heart attack, stroke, osteoporosis, poor eyesight, and hearing loss. All of these conditions are costly and contribute to the increased per capita spending for medical care.

Substantial differences are noted in medical care demand by sex (Sindelar, 1982). Early in the life cycle men and women spend approximately the same amounts on medical care. Later in life, especially during the childbearing years, women spend approximately 50 percent more than men. Women are hospitalized more often (primarily due to 1.9 child births per fertile female), but when men are hospitalized, they remain hospitalized 50 percent longer. Men are more able to substitute home health care for hospital care, especially older men because they typically have a wife at home to take care of them. Older women, because they live longer than their husbands, are more likely to be living alone with no one at home to take care of them. Single individuals, regardless of age, are hospitalized more often than married persons.

Men suffer more frequent health losses due to lifestyle choices, such as drinking, smoking, and overeating. With more women in the labor force, patterning themselves after their male counterparts, these differences in lifestyle factors are beginning to narrow. As women continue to act more like men, with higher rates of smoking, drinking, and stress, some medical experts suggest that they may one day start dying like men.

Economic Standing. In the United States, education, income, and medical care spending have always been closely associated. Historically, individuals with higher incomes have demanded more medical care. More recently, the importance of income in determining medical care demand has diminished with the increase in third-party insurance

Links to over 100 sites with health information for women are provided in an annotated guide by the New York Times: Women's Health Resources at **http://www.nytimes.com/specials/women/whome/resources.html.**

coverage.[8] The availability of insurance increases demand for medical care by lowering direct out-of-pocket payment requirements. When someone else is paying the bills, there is no incentive to limit demand. Beginning in the early 1980s, individuals with higher incomes actually had fewer physicians' visits than those with lower incomes (reported in Somers, 1986). In spite of the importance of third-party coverage, direct out-of-pocket payments still account for about 20 percent of all personal health care expenditures, keeping income high on the list of important economic factors.

> **Policy Issue**
>
> When spending someone else's money, consumers have little incentive to limit their demand.

Income levels are highly correlated with educational levels. The association between income and education has fostered a huge body of economic research on the economic rewards of education called human capital theory. Formal recognition of human capital research as a legitimate area of study may be attributed to the work of Nobel laureate Gary Becker (1964) and Jacob Mincer (1974).[9]

The role of education as a determinant in the demand for medical care goes beyond its association with higher incomes. It is hypothesized that higher levels of education make a person a better consumer of medical care services. Education improves a person's ability to recognize early symptoms of medical problems when treatment is less expensive. Those with more education have healthier occupations; they eat better and are more efficient users of medical care.

financial risk
The risk associated with contractual obligations that require fixed monetary outlays.

With its complex system of private and public insurance programs, the United States has developed a system of third-party insurance to spread the **financial risk** associated with sickness and injury. Third-party payers cover 80 percent of all medical care spending. Patients who are not directly responsible for their spending decisions tend to demand more medical care than they would otherwise purchase with their own money. Medical care that carries no out-of-pocket cost is treated as if it had no underlying resource cost. The result is moral hazard, demanding more than the social optimum. (See Chapter 6 for a more complete discussion of moral hazard.)

deductible
The amount of money that an insured person must pay before a health plan begins paying for all or part of the covered expenses.

Recognizing that health insurance acts to rotate the demand for medical care to the right, health insurance providers offer policies with features that serve to reduce moral hazard. The features typically include **deductibles**, **coinsurance**, and **copayments**. The deductible is the initial amount the policyholder must pay before the insurance coverage begins paying. Coinsurance is the percentage of the total spending (beyond the deductible) the policyholder pays. A copayment is a fixed dollar amount charged directly to the patient at the time of treatment.

coinsurance
A standard feature of health insurance policies that requires the insured person to pay a certain percentage of a medical bill, usually 10 to 30 percent per physician visit or hospital stay.

The impact of health insurance on medical care demand is depicted in Figure 5.3. D_{100} represents the demand for medical care for a person with no insurance (100 percent coinsurance). D_{50} is that same individual's demand curve with a 50 percent coinsurance. With a 50 percent coinsurance, where the insurance company pays one-half and the policyholder pays one-half, the policyholder demands Q_1 at price P_0. Without insurance the individual would pay the full price for the medical care, P_0, and demand only Q_0. Thus, the availability of insurance, or more generally reducing the coinsurance rate, increases the demand for medical care by rotating the demand curve upward.[10] In the case of complete coinsurance (coinsurance rate equal to zero), the demand curve would rotate to the vertical and become D_0 and quantity demanded would be equal to Q_2 at a zero price to the patient.

copayment
A standard feature of many managed care plans that require the insured person to pay a fixed sum for each office visit, hospital stay, or prescription drug.

Even as insurance coverage has expanded, approximately 15 percent of the population is without medical insurance at any one point in time. This situation presents an

---

8 With no adjustment for health status, individuals with less than $14,000 in income had 7.3 physicians' visits on average in 1993. Individuals with over $50,000 had 5.8 (Health United States, 1994, Table 75, p. 169). The differential narrows when health status is considered. The poor and near poor still see the doctor more often than the nonpoor, with 5.7, 5.3, and 5.1 annual visits for each group (Health United States Chartbook, 1993, Figure 26, p. 36).

9 See the human capital discussion in Chapter 8.

10 More technically, the availability of insurance also makes the policyholder less sensitive to changes in the price of medical care. Demand is more inelastic when consumers spend a smaller percentage of their budgets on an item. Remember, as you move downward and to the right on a straight-line demand curve, price elasticity falls.

Figure 5.3   The Effect of Insurance on Medical Care Demand

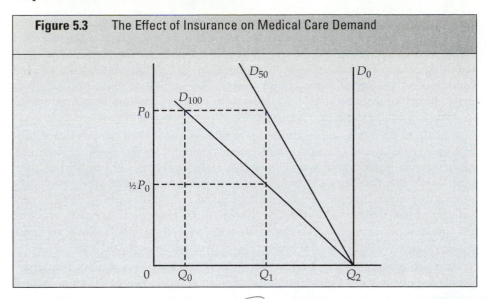

interesting dilemma for policymakers. Those who are fully insured are probably using more medical care than they really need. At the same time those who have no insurance are probably using less.

The presence of insurance has changed the nature of medicine over the past half century by changing the incentive structure pertinent to the purchase of medical care. Insurance, to a degree, has distorted the medical market by creating a bias toward acute care instead of preventive care, specialty care instead of primary care, and hospital care instead of home care (Weisbrod, 1991). The direction of research and development is determined by what insurance will buy. As new technology and procedures become available, pressure mounts to include them under covered services. Efforts to restrain demand by deductibles and coinsurance, managed care networks, and alternative delivery mechanisms result from a growing awareness of the distortions caused by the third-party payment mechanism.

Of all the factors that affect the demand for medical care, the economic factors are more important for policy considerations since they are more readily affected by public policy. Demographic factors change gradually. The population grows older, more couples divorce, and fewer children are born, but these factors are not easily manipulated by public policy.

In addition to the personal factors, changing attitudes and preferences of the population have a tremendous impact on demand. Over the last 50 years the public attitude toward medicine has become increasingly positive. Once viewed with a certain amount of distrust, the medical profession today is highly respected. Part of that increased respect is due to the increased ability to actually cure patients of their ailments. With each new drug, with each new procedure, faith in medicine continues to grow.

As quickly as attitudes toward the medical profession have improved, there is a new movement toward patient autonomy. Terminally ill patients are increasingly demanding the "right to die." Patients suffering poor outcomes are questioning the quality of their care and turning to the tort system to rule on claims of malpractice. All these economic factors have contributed to a growing demand for medical care and are at least partly responsible for increased medical spending.

> **Policy Issue**
> The availability of health insurance has changed the incentive structure within the medical care market.

> **Policy Issue**
> The movement for more patient autonomy has created added pressures to increase medical care spending.

Physician Factors

Even though only 20 percent of all medical spending goes for physicians' services, physicians determine the vast majority of total spending. Physicians prescribe the drugs, admit patients into hospitals, and order the tests. Their influence on demand stems from the physician's dual role as adviser to the patient and provider of services.

principal-agent relationship

A relationship in which one person (the principal) gives another person (the agent) authority to make decisions on his or her behalf.

A vast economic literature has been developed examining the **principal-agent relationship**. An agency relationship exists where an individual (the principal) gives someone else (the agent) authority to make decisions on his or her behalf. Problems arise when the interests of the principal and the agent diverge. In medicine patients are relatively uninformed concerning alternative diagnoses and treatments. They are willing to trust physicians to make choices for them because of the difficulty in gathering and understanding medical information. But the physician's role as supplier can create a conflict of interest.

A physician's ability to induce demand is greatly enhanced when patients have a difficult time gathering and processing information. Given this unique position, physicians can serve as imperfect agents, serving their own interests over those of their patients. In other words, they have the ability to influence their patients' demand for the services they personally provide. In theory, efficacy and cost guide a physician when faced with alternative treatment options for a particular disorder. If two treatments are equally effective, the physician can choose the cheaper alternative and save the patient money, or the more expensive alternative and buy a new flat screen plasma television for the den.

Standard economic analysis assumes that the demand and supply curves are independent of one another. A given increase in supply results in a new equilibrium reached by moving down a stationary demand curve. The equilibrium price falls and more output is purchased and supplied. Demand inducement posits, however, that a given exogenous shift in supply causes a shift in demand as providers advise their patients to buy more medical care.

Beginning with demand curve D_0 in Figure 5.4, when the supply curve is S_0, equilibrium is at point a and price and quantity are P_0 and Q_0. An increase in supply to S_1 should result in a new equilibrium at point b with P_2 and Q_2. If the demand curve is inelastic, as it is expected to be, the new price/quantity equilibrium will be at a lower level of total spending.[11] In other words, P_2 times Q_2 will be less than P_0 times Q_0. More

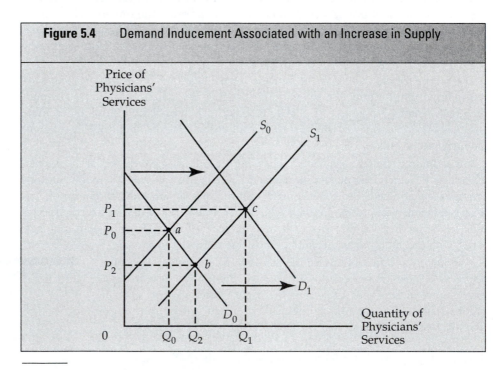

Figure 5.4   Demand Inducement Associated with an Increase in Supply

---

11 Proof of this assertion follows. Total revenue (*TR*) is calculated by multiplying the price of a good (*P*) times the quantity purchased (*Q*).

$$TR = P \times Q$$

Taking the total differential $$dTR = QdP + PdQ$$

Factoring QdP $$dTR = Qdp\,[1 + (PdQ)/(QdP)]$$

Or $$dTR = QdP\,[1 + \varepsilon_p]$$ where ε_p is the price elasticity of demand

When price falls (when *dP* is negative) and demand is inelastic ($\varepsilon_p < 1$), then total revenue falls (*dTR* is negative).

ISSUES IN MEDICAL CARE DELIVERY

SELF-REFERRAL: THE REAL CULPRIT IN HIGH SPENDING?

One of the most important ethical issues confronting the medical community is the practice of self-referral. With increasing frequency, physicians in most communities are supplementing their incomes with profits from ownership interests in medical facilities. Holding interest in a diagnostic laboratory, imaging center, physical therapy center, or mammography center is not a conflict of interest per se; however, the potential for abuse is substantial.

These facilities actually seek out physicians as investors and often refuse to offer ownership interest to nonphysicians. The reason is obvious: physicians refer patients. Information problems abound in medical markets, and are particularly troublesome in the market for referral services. Patients requiring the specialized services of a diagnostic testing center are particularly vulnerable to the provision of unnecessary services. Lacking the expertise to evaluate treatment alternatives, the patient expects the physician to act as a well-meaning agent in recommending treatment. But physicians who have financial interests in these outside facilities tend to order more tests, charge higher fees for them, and have higher total bills. Hillman et al. (1992) found that self-referring physicians ordered two to eight times more lab tests and charged up to six times more for them. Mitchell and Scott (1992) found that physicians who owned interest in physical therapy centers referred 39 to 45 percent more patients and generated 30 to 40 percent higher net revenues.

The AMA's official position considers self-referral an ethical practice as long as the patient is informed of the physician's interest in the outside facility. Most states have enacted legislation to force disclosure of any financial interest in a testing facility and a few have gone as far as to prohibit ownership. Recognizing self-referral as a potential problem, Congress has enacted legislation to eliminate the practice where Medicare and Medicaid patients are involved.

Self-referral is emerging as an important economic issue. When the physician is largely responsible for both sides of a transaction, clearly potential for abuse exists. Developing a workable policy on ownership of facilities and balancing it against the rights of the individual to invest in such facilities will challenge reformers intent on reigning in the escalating costs of medical care.

Sources: Bruce J. Hillman, George T. Olson, Patricia E. Griffith, Jonathan H. Sunshine, Catherine A. Joseph, Stephen D. Kennedy, William R. Nelson, and Lee B. Bernhardt, "Physicians' Utilization and Charges for Outpatient Diagnostic Imaging in a Medicare Population," *Journal of the American Medical Association* 268(15), October 21, 1992, 2050–2054; and Jean M. Mitchell and Elton Scott, "Physician Ownership of Physical Therapy Services," *Journal of the American Medical Association* 268(15), October 21, 1992, 2055–2059.

physicians and lower overall spending translate into lower average incomes unless demand shifts at the same time.

The demand inducement hypothesis recognizes that physicians, rather than allow their incomes to fall, may recommend additional procedures, perform more surgeries, and schedule more follow-up visits—all increasing the demand for their services. This shift in the demand curve to D_1 results in a new equilibrium at point c with P_1 and Q_1 and an increase in total spending. Mechanisms that serve to support demand inducement include fee splitting and referral fees that provide a means for a referring physician to share in the service charges by specialists and hospitals (Waldholz and Bogidanich, 1989). Another common practice is self-referral, where physicians have patients tested and treated in facilities where they have a financial interest. Physician ownership is prevalent in diagnostic imaging and testing laboratories.

The potential for demand inducement is naturally limited. Patients will eventually detect a practice style that consistently overtreats and change providers if they do not agree with the practice. The potential for inducement is greatest in those areas where the procedure is a one-time event, such as surgery.

The important issue is not whether physicians have the capability to induce demand, but whether they actually practice demand inducement. Studies examining the demand inducement hypothesis show mixed results. Early research focused on the association between the physician-population ratio and physician fees. Fuchs and Kramer (1986) concluded that the most important factor influencing the demand for physicians' services was the number of physicians. Reinhardt (1985) provided an alternative explanation for the observed positive association between the supply of physicians and the fees they charge. Physicians may simply be migrating into areas where the demand for their services is higher.

physician-induced demand
A situation in which providers take advantage of uninformed consumers to purchase services that are largely unnecessary.

The confusing body of research on the subject of **physician-induced demand** represented by these two studies has several implications. First, the phenomenon is probably not as widespread as it was once thought to be. Physicians may have the ability to induce demand, but the extent to which they use this ability is difficult to estimate empirically. In any event, recent changes in the payment structure in medical care delivery, including capitation and diagnosis-related fees, have reduced the incentive to practice demand inducement. Second, because we are dealing with a complex phenomenon in an environment of imperfect information, we may never know empirically the full extent of physicians' ability to induce demand for their services (Pauly, 1988). As patients, payers, and lawmakers become more knowledgeable about medical practices and procedures, the phenomenon of demand inducement will likely become less of a concern.

Measuring Demand

Literally hundreds of studies have attempted to measure the impact of the various factors influencing the demand for medical care. Early research focused on the differences in utilization between individuals who had health insurance and those who did not.[12] Newhouse (1978) has provided an excellent review of later research attempting to quantify the relationship between out-of-pocket payments and the amount of medical care demanded. Even individuals with comprehensive insurance coverage have different out-of-pocket payment requirements due to differences in deductibles and copayments. Deductibles and copayments may be treated analytically as subsidies to the unit price of medical care. As the subsidy varies, the effective unit price to the individual patient varies. The research focus is on the impact of these price variations on the quantity of medical care demanded, alternatively defined as physicians' services, hospital services, dental services, and pharmaceutical services in the various studies.

In addition to price variations, differences in income, insurance coverage, and time-costs measured by the hourly wage also affect the demand for medical care. You should recall from our discussion of price elasticity of demand in Chapter 2 that elasticity measures the responsiveness of quantity demanded to a change in the price. Empirical studies measuring medical care demand have focused on the calculation of the various elasticities. In addition to price elasticity, the medical care studies have also estimated income elasticity, insurance elasticity, time-cost elasticity, and **cross-price elasticity** between different types of medical care.

cross-price elasticity
The sensitivity of consumer demand for good *A* as the price of good *B* changes.

Estimating Demand Functions

Demand is typically estimated using regression analysis. The process is not nearly as straightforward as it may seem. The subject of the analysis can be the individual, the household, or an entire population. The unit of measurement may be the number of physicians' visits, the number of hospital admissions, the length of hospital stay, or total medical care spending, and variations in quality of services and intensity of services

---

12 See Donabedian (1976) for a comprehensive review of this literature.

come into play. When studies include different countries, whether the currency translations are made using market exchange rates or purchasing power parity, exchange rates affect the results. It should come as no surprise then that estimates of demand elasticities vary considerably across studies.

Calculating Elasticities

The literature contains considerable disagreement on the magnitude of the various elasticity estimates. Table 5.3 provides a summary of the elasticity estimates from a number of representative studies. Mean estimates of price elasticity usually range from a low of –0.1 to a high of –1.5, depending on study design and dependent variable. Clearly, estimates indicate that demand for medical care is in most cases inelastic with respect to price. Additionally, the higher the patient's out-of-pocket spending, the greater the price elasticity of demand. The demand for outpatient visits is more elastic than the demand for hospital care (Davis and Russell, 1972). Increase the coinsurance rate and demand becomes more elastic (Rosett and Huang, 1973). Demand for preventive care is more price elastic than demand for hospital services (Manning et al., 1987).

Taking the empirical evidence as a whole, consumer demand seems to be relatively unresponsive to changes in the price of medical care. That does not mean that quantity demanded does not change when price changes, only that the percentage change in quantity demanded will be less than the percentage change in price. Based on the cited studies, a 10 percent increase in price will lead to small decrease in quantity demanded, anywhere from 1 to 7 percent. When dealing with levels of expenditure that total in the billions of dollars, every one percent change in quantity demanded translates into a $10–15 billion change in expenditures.

Estimates of the **income elasticity of demand** for medical care vary considerably depending on whether the relationship being studied is the impact of individual income on personal medical expenditures or national income on aggregate medical expenditures. Research by Newhouse (1977) represents the conventional wisdom on income elasticities using national income and expenditure data. Using data from 13 developed countries, Newhouse found income elasticities to be greater than 1. If this is true, medical care is, at least on the margin, a **luxury or superior good**.[13] When income increases, demand increases and the percentage of income spent on luxury goods also increases.[14]

income elasticity of demand
The sensitivity of demand to changes in consumer income, determined by the percentage change in quantity demanded relative to the percentage change in consumer income.

luxury or superior good
Goods are considered superior if an increase in consumer income causes the percentage of the consumer's income spent on the good to increase, and vice versa.

---

13 Income elasticity, defined as $e_M = \dfrac{\text{Percentage change in quantity demanded}}{\text{Percentage change in income}}$, is used to classify goods as inferior or normal, depending on whether it is negative or positive. Economists often classify goods as necessities if $e_M \geq 1$ and luxuries if $e_M \leq 1$.

14 Define the percentage of income (M) spent on good X as $P_X Q_X / M$. The issue being addressed is what happens to this percentage when there is a change in income (ΔM). If the percentage increases, the following ratio will be greater than one.

$$\frac{\text{Percentage after } \Delta M}{\text{Percentage before } \Delta M} = \frac{P_x(Q_x + \Delta Q_x)}{M + \Delta M} \div \frac{P_x Q_x}{M}$$

$$= \frac{P_x(Q_x + \Delta Q_x)}{P_x Q_x} \times \frac{M}{M + \Delta M} \qquad \text{multiply 2nd term by } \frac{\frac{1}{M}}{\frac{1}{M}}$$

$$= \left[1 + (\Delta Q_x / Q_x)\right] \times \left[\frac{1}{1 + \Delta M / M}\right]$$

$$= \frac{1 + (\Delta Q_x / Q_x)}{1 + \Delta M / M} \qquad \text{multiply by } \frac{\frac{M}{\Delta M}}{\frac{M}{\Delta M}}$$

$$= \frac{\dfrac{M}{\Delta M} + \left[\dfrac{\Delta Q_x}{Q_x} \times \dfrac{M}{\Delta M}\right]}{\dfrac{M}{\Delta M} + 1} \qquad e_M = \frac{\Delta Q_x}{Q_x} \times \frac{M}{\Delta M}$$

$$= \frac{\dfrac{M}{\Delta M} + e_M}{\dfrac{M}{\Delta M} + 1}$$

The value of the ratio depends on the relationship between e_M and one. If $e_M > 1$, the percentage of income spent on good X increases when income increases. If $e_M < 1$, the percentage of income spent on good X decreases when income increases.

Table 5.3	Price and Income Elasticities from Selected Studies

Study	Dependent Variable	Elasticity
PRICE ELASTICITIES		
Davis and Russell (1972)	Outpatient visits	−1.00
	Hospital admissions	−0.32 to −0.46
Rosett and Huang (1973)	Hospital and physician spending	−0.35 to −1.50
Newhouse and Phelps (1976)	Hospital length of stay	−0.06 to −0.29
	Physicians' office visits	−0.08 to −0.10
Manning et al. (1987)	Overall spending	−0.22
	Hospital care	−0.14
	Preventive care	−0.43
Wedig (1988)	Level of care	−0.16 to −0.23
Newhouse et al. (1993)	Medical care	−0.22
Eichner (1998)	Medical care	−0.62 to −0.75
INCOME ELASTICITIES		
Rossett and Huang (1973)	Household medical spending	0.25 to 0.45
Newhouse (1977)	Per capita medical spending	1.15 to 1.31
Parkin, McGuire, and Yule (1987)	Per capita medical spending	0.80 to 1.57
Gerdtham and Jonsson (1991)	Per capita medical spending	1.24 to 1.43
Moore, Newman, and Fheili (1992)	Short-run per capita spending	0.31 to 0.86
	Long-run per capita spending	1.12 to 3.22
Murray, Govindaraj, and Musgrove (1994)	Total health expenditures	1.43

The policy implications are far reaching. If medical care is a luxury good, countries with higher per capita incomes will spend a greater percentage of income on medical care. Since there is no corroborating evidence that countries that spend more on medical care have healthier populations, this additional spending on medical care may not improve physiological health status much at all.

Work by Parkin, McGuire, and Yule (1987) cast doubt on these earlier findings and concluded that when estimated correctly, the income elasticity of demand for medical care is less than 1, making it a necessity rather than a luxury good. Their work does, however, support the conclusion that income elasticities are greater when estimated across countries than when they are estimated across individuals within the same country. Gerdtham and Jonsson (1991) and Moore, Newman, and Fheili (1992) responded to the criticisms of Parkin, McGuire, and Yule. Using alternative models with different functional forms and alternative ways of converting currencies to dollars, they concluded that the income elasticity of demand for medical care is greater than 1, at least in the long run. More recently, Murray, Govindaraj, and Musgrove (1994) calculated a GDP-health expenditure elasticity of 1.43, indicating that when GDP increases by 1 percent, health expenditures increase by 1.43 percent, implying that medical care is a luxury good.

Policy Issue

Defining medical care as a necessity or a luxury may depend on whether the issue is being addressed to an individual or a nation.

What conclusion should we draw from this seemingly contradictory evidence? Is medical care a luxury or a necessity? The answer may be that medical care is a necessity at the individual level and a luxury at the national level. In other words, when individuals receive an increase in income, their demand for medical care changes little. Increases in aggregate income, on the other hand, may result in significant increases in medical care spending at the national level.

The RAND Health Insurance Study

Most of the empirical research on the demand for medical care is based on nonexperimental data. Typical of most social science research, nonexperimental data may be either longitudinal or cross-section in nature, but it is always based on the actual historical experience of a sample of individuals or geographic regions. In contrast, experimental data is used in the physical sciences, such as chemistry, biology, and physics, where controlled experiments are possible. In a controlled experiment, individuals are randomly assigned to different groups, sometimes referred to as the control group and the experimental group. The use of data from a controlled experiment eliminates the self-selection bias inherent in nonexperimental data. When individuals are free to choose their groups, at least part of the differences in outcomes is due to differences in tastes for different programs. Those individuals who expect to have higher medical care costs will usually select more generous health insurance policies.

The RAND Corporation conducted the most extensive controlled experiment in health insurance from 1974 to 1982.[15] Over that period, approximately 7,000 individuals were randomly placed into one of 14 separate insurance plans and one health maintenance organization. Some plans had deductibles and others did not. Copayments ranged from zero to 95 percent with up to a maximum out-of-pocket outlay of $1,000 per participant. A number of studies have used data from the RAND Health Insurance Study, most notably, Manning et al. (1987). Overall the results indicate that individual demand responds to cost sharing. Manning's price elasticity estimate was approximately –0.17 when comparing free care with a 25 percent coinsurance requirement. Over the coinsurance range of 25 percent to 95 percent, the overall price elasticity of demand was estimated at –0.22, ranging from –0.14 for hospital care to –0.43 for preventive care. Demand for those provided with free medical care was about 50 percent higher than demand for those who had to pay 95 percent of the total cost. Finally, once admitted to the hospital, the type of plan had little effect on the level of spending.

From these results it may be concluded that changes in out-of-pocket spending explain a small, but significant, portion of the overall change in medical care spending. Changes in deductibles and coinsurance can have an effect on the overall quantity of medical services demanded. Increasing the out-of-pocket spending required from individuals will have a dampening effect on demand for medical care, with the notable exception of hospital spending once a person is admitted to the hospital.

Summary and Conclusions

The demand for medical care is derived from the individual's desire for good health. Access to medical care is only one of a number of ways that individuals can improve their health. In fact, when the other factors are taken into consideration, the marginal contribution of medical care is relatively small. The contribution of environmental, lifestyle, and genetic factors weigh heavily in determining overall health status.

Individual patient factors play a key role in determining the demand for medical care. These patient factors include health status and demographic characteristics. Seldom do individuals seek medical care unless there is at least a perceived illness.[16] Age, race, and gender are also important contributors to medical care demand. Even though these patient factors are important, policymakers are more interested in economic factors that affect demand. Individual incomes, the level of out-of-pocket spending, and the availability of medical insurance are more easily manipulated and thus studied more intensively.

http://

RAND is a nonprofit institution established to improve public policy through research and publications. Interdisciplinary in nature, the organization has a health sciences program that can be accessed at **http://www.rand.org/health/**.

---

15 Even though Rand did not totally eliminate self-selection in its experimental design, it reduced it by making it economically costly for individuals to choose alternate plans.

16 The case of preventive care is of course the major exception to this statement. Even with preventive care, however, the patient is attempting to avoid a perceived illness.

Paul J. Feldstein

"Health legislation arises from individuals, groups, and legislators acting in their own self-interest—usually economic self-interest." This statement by Paul J. Feldstein on the jacket of his book *The Politics of Health Legislation: An Economic Perspective* (Health Administration Press, 1996) stands in sharp contrast to the common notion that altruism and concern for the indigent are the driving forces behind the health care reform movement. It should come as no surprise that Feldstein would make this statement. It is a sentiment he shares with hundreds of other graduates of one of the most prestigious economics departments in the country—the University of Chicago.

After finishing his Ph.D. in 1961, Feldstein spent the first three years of his professional career as director of research for the American Hospital Association. He then joined the faculty at the University of Michigan. In 1987, he moved to the University of California at Irvine, where he is currently Professor and Robert Gumbiner Chair in Health Care Management.

Feldstein has served as principal investigator on 17 research grants, five of which were funded by the Robert Wood Johnson Foundation. During several academic leaves of absence he has served as a consultant with the Office of Management and Budget, the Social Security Administration, the World Health Organization, and the National Bureau of Economic Research. He regularly serves as an expert witness in legal cases involving health care antitrust issues.

Author of nine books and over 75 journal articles and book chapters on health care issues, Feldstein's current research interests focus on the cost-containment strategies used by insurance companies. He has had a profound influence on thousands of students in health economics worldwide, primarily through his book *Health Care Economics* (Delmar Publishers Inc., 1998). First published in 1973 and now in its fifth edition (and translated into Chinese in 1999), this book has been required reading for three decades for an entire generation of health economics students.

The physician-patient relationship is also the subject of a great volume of literature. The dual role of the physician as adviser to the patient and provider of services places physicians in a unique position to create demand for their services. Despite literally dozens of studies on the subject, it is difficult to know the extent of physician-induced demand.

Empirical research on the demand for medical care has taught us a great deal.

- Using the economic standards established by the concept of price elasticity, demand seems to be relatively insensitive to price changes (usually the result of changes in coinsurance rates). Even modest coinsurance requirements of 20 to 30 percent reduce demand by 10 to 15 percent compared with totally free care.

- While individual income elasticities are low (probably less than one), at the aggregate level they tend to be higher (somewhat greater than one). In other words, medical care may be treated as a necessity good at the individual level and at the same time as a luxury good at the national level.

The most important lesson of this chapter may be that economic incentives do matter in determining the demand for medical care. Therefore, we must be careful how we use incentives. In all fairness we do not want to exclude the sick and poor from medically necessary care simply because they cannot afford to pay for it.

Questions and Problems

1. According to studies undertaken by the U.S. Department of Agriculture, the price elasticity of demand for cigarettes is between –0.3 and –0.4 and the income elasticity is about +0.5.

   a. Suppose the Congress, influenced by studies linking cigarette smoking to cancer, plans to raise the excise tax on cigarettes so the price rises by 10 percent. Estimate the effect the price increase will have on cigarette consumption and consumer spending on cigarettes (both in percentage terms).

   b. Suppose a major brokerage firm advised its clients to buy cigarette stocks under the assumption that, if consumer incomes rise by 50 percent as expected over the next decade, cigarette sales will double. What is your reaction to this investment advice?

2. In what ways is medical care different from other commodities? In what ways is it the same?

3. If a wealthy person chooses to spend large sums of money to increase the probability of surviving an ordinarily fatal disease, should the rest of society object? Explain.

4. It is difficult to argue against the scientific merit of medical discoveries such as treatments for cancer or AIDS. Is scientific merit alone sufficient to determine the rational allocation of medical funds in such high-cost cases? What other kinds of information are relevant?

5. What does it mean to be on the "flat-of-the-curve" in health care provision? Why do some argue that the United States is on the "flat-of-the-curve"? Why is this phenomenon not an issue in the typical developing country?

6. "Estimating a model of health care demand by the individual patient is a futile exercise since physicians determine what their patients use." Comment. Does the model of a utility-maximizing consumer have any application in medicine?

7. In what sense is health care an investment? In what sense is it pure consumption?

8. Some argue that the price elasticity of demand can be used to determine whether a good or service is a luxury or a necessity. In medical care a procedure with an elastic demand would be considered optional or elective and a procedure with an inelastic demand would be a medical necessity. Should planners use price elasticity of demand as a guide to defining services that are medically necessary? What are the advantages of such a classification scheme? What are the drawbacks?

9. What has been the role of public health measures in improving the health status of the population?

10. Visit the Web site of the National Center for Health Statistics. Spend some time studying the leading causes of death for different age groups at **http://www.cdc.gov/nchs/data/hus/tables/2003/03hus031.pdf**. What are the three leading causes of death for each age cohort listed? What are some of the policy implications?

References

David B. Allison, Kevin R. Fontaine, JoAnn E. Manson, June Stevens, and Theodore B. Van Itallie, "Annual Deaths Attributable to Obesity in the United States," *Journal of the American Medical Association 282*(16), October 27, 1999, 1530–1538.

Gary S. Becker, *Human Capital: A Theoretical and Empirical Analysis, with Special Reference to Education*, New York: Columbia University Press, 1964.

Troyen A. Brennan, "An Empirical Analysis of Accidents and Accident Law: The Case of Medical Malpractice Law," *St. Louis University Law Journal* 36, Summer 1992, 823–878.

John Broome, "Good, Fairness, and QALYS," in J. M. Bell and S. Mendus, eds., *Philosophy and Medical Welfare*, New York: Cambridge University Press, 1988, 57–73.

Anthony J. Culyer, "Commodities, Characteristics of Commodities, Characteristics of People, Utilities, and the Quality of Life," in S. Baldwin, C. Godfrey, and C. Propper, eds., *Quality of Life: Perspectives and Policy*, London and New York: Routledge, 1990, 9–27.

David M. Cutler et al., "Why Have Americans Become More Obese?" NBER Working Paper No. 9446, Cambridge, MA: National Bureau of Economic Research, January 2003.

Karen Davis and Louise B. Russell, "The Substitution of Hospital Outpatient Care for Inpatient Care," *Review of Economics and Statistics 54*(2), May 1972, 109–120.

A. Donabedian, *Benefits in Medical Care Programs*, Cambridge, MA: Harvard University Press, 1976.

Benjamin G. Druss et al., "The Most Expensive Medical Conditions in America," *Health Affairs 21*(4), July/August 2002, 105–111.

Matthew J. Eichner, "The Demand for Medical Care: What People Pay Does Matter," *American Economic Review Papers and Proceedings 88*(2), May 1998, 117–121.

Alain C. Enthoven, *Health Plan*, Reading, MA: Addison-Wesley, 1980.

Victor R. Fuchs, "Time Preference and Health: An Exploratory Study," in Victor R. Fuchs, ed., *Economics Aspects of Health*, Chicago: University of Chicago Press, 1982, 93–120.

——— and Marcia J. Kramer, "Determinants of Expenditures for Physicians' Services," in Victor R. Fuchs, ed., *The Health Economy*, Cambridge, MA: Harvard University Press, 1986, 67–107.

Ulf-G. Gerdtham and Bengt Jönsson, "Conversion Factor Instability in International Comparisons of Health Care Expenditure," *Journal of Health Economics 10*(2), July 1991, 227–234.

Michael Grossman, "On the Concept of Health Capital and the Demand for Health," *Journal of Political Economy 80*(2), March/April 1972, 223–255.

Jack M. Guralnik, Kenneth C. Land, Dan Blazer, Gerda G. Fillenbaum, and Laurence G. Branch, "Educational Status and Active Life Expectancy Among Older Blacks and Whites," *The New England Journal of Medicine 329*(2), July 8, 1993, 110–116.

Michael D. Intriligator, "Major Policy Issues in the Economics of Health Care in the United States," in J. van der Gaag and M. Perlman, eds., *Health, Economics, and Health Economics,* Amsterdam: North-Holland Publishing, 1981.

Linda T. Kohn, Janet M. Corrigan, and Molla S. Donaldson, *To Err Is Human: Building a Safer Health System*, Washington, DC: National Academy Press, 1999.

Katherine R. Levit, Arthur L. Sensenig, Cathy A. Cowan, et al., "National Health Expenditures, 1993," *Health Care Financing Review 16*(1), Fall 1994, 247–294.

M. Lockwood, "Quality of Life and Resource Allocation," in J. M. Bell and S. Mendus, eds., *Philosophy and Medical Welfare*, New York: Cambridge University Press, 1988, 33–56.

G. Loomes and L. McKenzie, "The Scope and Limitations of QALY Measures," in S. Baldwin, C. Godfrey, and C. Propper, eds., *Quality of Life: Perspectives and Policy*, London and New York: Routledge, 1990, 84–102.

Willard G. Manning, Howard L. Bailit, Bernadette Benjamin, and Joseph P. Newhouse, "The Demand for Dental Care: Evidence from a Randomized Controlled Trial in Health Insurance," *Journal of the American Dental Association 110*(6), June 1987, 895–902.

Thomas McKeown, *The Rise of Modern Population*, New York: Academic Press, 1976.

John B. McKinlay, Sonja M. McKinlay, and Robert Beaglehole, "A Review of the Evidence Concerning the Impact of Medical Measures on Recent Mortality and Morbidity in the United States," *International Journal of Health Services 19*(2), 1989, 181–208.

Jacob Mincer, *Schooling, Experience, and Earnings*, New York: National Bureau of Economic Research, 1974.

William J. Moore, Robert J. Newman, and Mohammad Fheili, "Measuring the Relationship Between Income and NHEs," *Health Care Financing Review 14*(1), Fall 1992, 133–139.

C. J. L. Murray, R. Govindaraj, and P. Musgrove, "National Health Expenditures: A Global Analysis," *Bulletin of the World Health Organization 72*(4), 1994, 533–692.

Selma J. Mushkin, "Health as an Investment," *Journal of Political Economy 70* (5, part 2), October 1962, 129–157.

H. L. Needleman and D. Bellinger, "Low-Level Lead Exposure and the IQ of Children: A Meta-Analysis of Modern Studies," *Journal of the American Medical Association 263*(5), February 2, 1990, 673–678.

Joseph P. Newhouse, "Insurance Benefits, Out-of-Pocket Payments, and the Demand for Medical Care: A Review of the Recent Literature," *Health and Medical Care Services Review 1*(4), July/August 1978, 1–15.

———, "Medical Care Expenditure: A Cross-National Survey," *Journal of Human Resources 12*(1), Winter 1977, 115–125.

——— and Lindy J. Friedlander, "The Relationship Between Medical Resources and Measures of Health: Some Additional Evidence," *Journal of Human Resources 15*(2), Spring 1980, 200–218.

——— and Charles E. Phelps, "New Estimates of Price and Income Elasticities of Medical Care Services," in R. N. Rosett, ed., *The Role of Health Insurance in the Health Services Sector*, New York: National Bureau of Economic Research, 1976, 261–312.

—— and the Insurance Experiment Group, *Free for All? Lessons from the RAND Health Insurance Experiment*, Cambridge MA: Harvard University Press, 1993.

Gregory Pappas, Susan Queen, Wilbur Hadden, and Gail Fisher, "The Increasing Disparity in Mortality Between Socioeconomic Groups in the United States, 1960 and 1986," *The New England Journal of Medicine 329*(2), July 8, 1993, 103–109.

David Parkin, Alistair McGuire, and Brian Yule, "Aggregate Health Care Expenditures and National Income," *Journal of Health Economics 6*(2), June 1987, 109–127.

Mark V. Pauly, "Is Medical Care Different? Old Questions, New Answers," *Journal of Health Politics, Policy and Law 13*(2), Summer 1988, 227–237.

Uwe Reinhardt, "The Theory of Physician-Induced Demand: Reflections After a Decade," *Journal of Health Economics 4*(2), June 1985, 190–193.

W. J. Rogan, B. C. Gladen, J. D. McKinney, Beth C. Gladen, James D. McKinney, Nancy Carreras, Pam Hardy, James Thullen, Jon Tingelstad, and Mary Tully, "Polychlorinated Biphenyls (PCBs) and Dichlorodiphenyl Dichlorethene (DDE) in Human Milk: Effects of Maternal Factors and Previous Lactation," *American Journal of Public Health 76*(2), February 1986, 172–177.

Richard N. Rosett and Lien-fu Huang, "The Effect of Health Insurance on the Demand for Medical Care," *Journal of Political Economy 81*(2), March/April 1973, 281–305.

M. W. Shannon and J. W. Graef, "Lead Intoxication in Infancy," *Pediatrics 89*(1), January 1992, 87–90.

Jody L. Sindelar, "Differential Use of Medical Care by Sex," *Journal of Political Economy 90*(5), October 1982, 1003–1009.

Anne R. Somers, "The Changing Demand for Health Services: A Historical Perspective and Some Thoughts for the Future," *Inquiry 23*(1), Winter 1986, 395–402.

Michael Waldholz and Walt Bogidanich, "Patients for Sale," 2-part series in *The Wall Street Journal*, February 28 and March 1, 1989, A1, A12.

Gerald J. Wedig, "Health Status and the Demand for Health: Results on Price Elasticities," *Journal of Health Economics 7*(2), June 1988, 151–163.

Burton A. Weisbrod, "The Health Care Quadrilemma: An Essay on Technological Change, Insurance, Quality of Care, and Cost Containment," *Journal of Economic Literature 29*(2), June 1991, 523–552.

Bruce L. Welch, J. Hay, D. Miller, R. Oisen, R. Rippey, and A. Welch, "The RAND Health Insurance Study: A Summary Critique," *Medical Care 25*(2), February 1987, 148–156.

David Wessel, "We're Not Too Fat, It's Technology's Fault," *The Wall Street Journal*, February 12, 2003, A2.

Robert Woods and P. R. Andrew Hinde, "Mortality in Victorian England: Models and Patterns," *Journal of Interdisciplinary History 18*(1), Summer 1987, 27–54.

Chapter 6

The Market for Health Insurance

Many who argue that the United States has a medical care crisis point to the large number of Americans who are uninsured. Census estimates place the size of this group at around 43 million in 2002. Not only has the number of uninsured grown significantly over the last decade, but also the percentage of the population without insurance has grown from 13 percent in 1987 to 15.2 percent in 2002 (Mills and Shandari, 2003). As this group grows in size, the pressure to reform the system of financing medical care intensifies. To address this problem rationally, we must understand the principles that govern the provision of insurance.

Because a firm understanding of our historical roots is necessary to understand how we can effectively reform our system of medical care financing, this chapter will examine the development of employer-based insurance in the United States. A discussion of the theory of risk and insurance will serve as the basis for understanding the demand for private health insurance. We will then address the issue of market failure in the provision of medical care, focusing on the institutional features in the U.S. setting. Finally, we will examine the primary concern of reformers—the uninsured. Who are they? How are they affected by lack of insurance coverage? How do they pay for medical care?

Historical Setting

Insurance coverage for health services in the United States was first made available in 1798 (refer to Table 6.1). Funded by mandatory payroll deductions, the U.S. Marine Hospital services provided prepaid hospital care for eligible seamen. While the first company to offer sickness insurance was organized in 1847, most of the early insurance policies covered loss of income due to accidents or disability rather than health services due to illness.

http://

The Health Insurance Association of America (HIAA) is a trade association whose members are insurance companies and managed care companies. Visit this site at **http://www.hiaa.org/**.

Plans offering medical benefits became more prevalent in the 1870s and 1880s. Many of these policies offered coverage to employees in certain industries and individuals who suffered from certain diseases. By the turn of the century, forty-seven insurance companies were actively writing policies covering accidental injury. Collectively, they had written over 463,000 individual policies. Most early plans offered protection against the loss of income due to illness or disability. Until the 1920s, loss of income was the largest single cost associated with an accident or illness. In 1899, the Aetna Life Insurance Company began offering disability coverage for all diseases except tuberculosis, venereal disease, insanity, and alcohol or drug-related problems.

Group health insurance was first offered in 1910 to the employees of Montgomery Ward and Company. The policy, written by the London Guarantee and Accident Company in New York, provided cash benefits in the event of disability or illness. The rest of the world moved toward mandatory insurance coverage after the First World War, but the movement never gained acceptance in the United States.

During the 1920s, hospitals began offering prepaid plans to individuals covering hospital benefits. This practice was expanded in 1929 by Baylor Hospital in Dallas,

Table 6.1	Important Dates in the Development of the U.S. Health Insurance Industry

Date	Event
1798	Congress established U.S. Marine Hospital services for seamen. Funded by compulsory deductions from salaries.
1847	The first insurer to issue sickness insurance was organized: The Massachusetts Health Insurance Company of Boston.
1849	New York state passed first general insurance law.
1850	Individual accident insurance became available with the chartering of the Franklin Health Assurance Company of Massachusetts. For a 15 cent premium the insured could receive $200 in the event of injury due to a railway or steamboat accident; payment of $400 in the event of total disability.
1870	Companies in several industries, including mining, lumber, and railroads, begin developing plans to cover medical services.
1890	Policies providing benefits for disability from specified diseases were first offered.
1899	Aetna Life Insurance Co. offers insurance covering disabilities caused by most diseases.
1910	Montgomery Ward and Co. offers employees an insured plan regarded as the first group health insurance policy.
1920s	Individual hospitals began offering hospital expense benefits on an individual prepaid basis.
1929	First health maintenance organization, the Ross-Loos Clinic, was established in Los Angeles.
1929	A group of Dallas teachers arranged with Baylor Hospital to provide room and board and specified ancillary services at a predetermined monthly cost—considered the forerunner of what later became known as Blue Cross.
1932	First citywide Blue Cross plan offered by a group of Sacramento hospitals.
1935	Social Security Act provided for the first time grant-in-aid to states for public health activities.
1937	The Blue Cross Commission was organized.
1939	The first Blue Shield plan (surgical-medical), called California Physicians' Service, developed.
1940s	During W.W. II, due to the freezing of wages, group health insurance became an important component of collective bargaining for employees.
1949	Major medical expense benefits were introduced by Liberty Mutual to supplement basic medical care expenses.
1956	Disability insurance added to the Social Security System.
1959	Continental Casualty Company issued the first comprehensive group dental plan written by an insurance company.
1964	Prescription drug expense benefits were introduced.
1966	Medicare and Medicaid become law.
1972	Medicare extended to disabled and end-stage renal disease patients.
1973	Health Maintenance Organization Act passed by Congress.
1974	ERISA passed regulating provision of employee benefit plans—encouragement for firms to self-insure.
1988	Medicare Catastrophic Care Act passed.
1989	Medicare Catastrophic Care Act repealed.
1996	Congress passes the Health Insurance Portability and Accountability Act.
1997	State Children's Health Insurance Program (SCHIP)

Source: *Source Book of Health Insurance Data, 1990*, Health Insurance Association of America.

Texas. In what is considered the forerunner of the Blue Cross plans, the hospital agreed to provide a group of Dallas teachers twenty-one days of hospital care and related services annually for a fixed monthly premium. In the same year, one of the first health maintenance organizations (HMOs) was formed, the Ross-Loos Clinic in Los Angeles. Another important HMO, Kaiser Permanente, can trace its origin back to the 1930s.[1]

The Great Depression challenged the hospital sector to maintain its solvency. With people unable to afford hospital care, hospital occupancy rates fell to 50 percent. In 1932, a group of Sacramento, California, hospitals combined resources to offer the first area-wide plan supported by more than one hospital. Within three years, similar plans in 13 states provided a guaranteed cash flow to financially strapped hospitals. The California Physicians Service first introduced prepayment for physicians' services in 1939. Later known as Blue Shield, the plan provided medical and surgical benefits for a fixed monthly fee for members of employee groups earning less than $3,000 annually.

In the aftermath of the Second World War, group health insurance became a major component of the collective bargaining process. A wage-price freeze forced firms to offer nonwage benefits to attract and keep employees. A 1954 ruling by the Internal Revenue Service exempted employer contributions to health insurance benefits from employee taxable income. Today the tax exemption is a significant feature of the health insurance market in the United States and is responsible for the predominance of employment-based group insurance (Thomasson, 2000). The next two decades witnessed improvements in insurance coverage. **Major medical** benefits were introduced in 1949. Dental care, prescription drugs, and vision care were added to many plans in the 1950s.

In 1965, after repeated failures to pass a nationwide universal insurance plan, Congress passed comprehensive coverage for the elderly and indigent—known as Medicare and Medicaid. A new era of government involvement in medical care financing saw its beginnings. Much of the upward pressure on health care spending can be traced to this legislation. As spending increased, so did pressure to control the cost spiral. The Health Maintenance Organization Act in 1973, the Employee Retirement Income Security Act (ERISA) in 1974, and the Medicare Catastrophic Care Act in 1988 were all attempts to curb runaway costs and improve access to those without insurance.

Reformers and would-be reformers must understand the development of the employer-based insurance system and its place in the business culture. Anyone ignoring this rich history runs the risk of misreading public sentiments concerning health care reform.

Types of Insurance

The current policy debate over health care reform is based on two conflicting approaches to health care financing: the indemnity (or casualty) insurance approach and the **social insurance** approach. Indemnity insurance is the type of insurance that provides reimbursement for certain expenditures or direct payments due to loss of income. This category of insurance includes fire, theft, casualty, life, and in the United States, health insurance. It is based on the premise that the premium should reflect the expected loss. Those individuals who have higher risks should pay higher premiums. Social insurance is the basis of all assistance programs associated with the welfare state: cash assistance, public education, and health care for the elderly. This model ignores expected losses in calculating premiums and instead attempts to allocate costs based on ability to pay. Subsidies are used extensively across risk categories.

The United States uses a combination of the indemnity insurance approach and the social insurance approach. Everyone covered by private insurance sees his or her premiums determined by the indemnity insurance approach. Most policies are written as group policies and premiums are uniform within groups, varying only by size of family. Premiums reflect expected use and vary across groups, depending on past claims experience. So policies are community rated within groups and experience rated across

major medical
Health insurance to provide coverage for major illnesses requiring large financial outlays, characterized by payment for all expenses above a specified maximum out-of-pocket amount paid by the insured (often $1,000 to $5,000).

social insurance
Serves as the basis of all government redistribution programs. An insurance plan supported by tax revenues and available to everyone regardless of age, health status, and ability to pay.

---

1 Kaiser actually celebrates 1947 as its founding year, when it opened its enrollment to the public.

groups, which means that everyone within the group pays the same premium but premiums across groups differ. Groups with higher health care spending pay higher premiums. Proponents of this approach argue that not only is it more efficient, it is more equitable. To the extent that medical costs are based on lifestyle choices, individuals should pay for the choices they make. Individuals and groups who practice a healthy lifestyle and are more cost-conscious should be rewarded with lower premiums. Those who choose to indulge in unhealthy behavior should pay higher premiums.

The elderly, the disabled, the indigent, and those suffering from certain diseases, such as kidney failure, have their medical coverage provided by social insurance. Medicare and Medicaid are the two major social insurance programs in the United States. Proponents of this approach argue from the premise of individual rights and social responsibility. Some argue that justice dictates that all individuals be provided with medical care as an individual right. Medical care is not only an individual right; its provision is the socially responsible thing to do. Because participation is mandatory, the savings in administrative costs offset any loss in efficiency caused by a departure from the indemnity approach.

Policy Issue

Is access to medical care an individual right? Should it be?

In general, health insurance may be classified into two broad categories: medical expense insurance providing reimbursement for actual expenditures and disability income insurance providing periodic payments when the insured individual is unable to work. Although the combination of policies is virtually endless, all contain certain basic health insurance benefits that may be offered separately or in combination with other benefits.

- Hospitalization provides daily room and board and the usual hospital services and supplies required during a normal hospital stay. Coverage includes lab fees, nursing care, use of the operating and recovery rooms, outpatient services, and certain medicines and supplies. Hospitalization policies are usually sold in combination with a surgical expense policy and/or a major medical policy.

- Physicians' or surgical expense policies provide set allowances for surgical procedures performed by licensed physicians and physicians' inpatient hospital visits.

- Regular medical benefits cover physicians' services and other surgical procedures and are usually written in conjunction with other types of insurance.

- Major medical expense insurance, introduced in 1951, is designed to cover large medical bills on a blanket basis with few limitations imposed on specific items. Major medical is typically offered in one of two ways: as a supplement to hospitalization, physicians', and surgical insurance; or as part of a comprehensive package integrating basic and extended coverage. This type of insurance is often issued with substantial deductibles, coinsurance, and a maximum limit on out-of-pocket spending.

- Dental expense insurance has been developed mainly under group plans since 1968. It usually covers fillings, extractions, bridgework, dentures, root canals, inlays, and orthodontics. There is also an emphasis on preventive dentistry with coverage on examinations, X-rays, and cleanings. Most dental insurance includes a substantial copayment, usually up to 50 percent. According to the Centers for Disease Control, more than 108 million Americans do not have dental insurance (CDC, 2000).

- Disability income protection provides periodic payments when the insured is unable to work as a result of illness, accident, or injury. Policies are provided on both a group and an individual basis. When available on a group basis, benefits are usually integrated with Social Security disability benefits and provide up to 60 percent of the individual's predisability income. Individual disability insurance is written for fixed dollar amounts to fit the needs of the policyholder. Policies usually contain a waiting period and limit on the maximum number of years that benefits are received. The disability must be one that prevents the insured from his or her usual occupation. The employer provides most disability insurance through group policies. In 2000, 70 percent of all full-time employees had long-term disability insurance and 61 percent had short-term disability insurance (U.S. Chamber of Commerce, 2000).

- Long-term care insurance has only recently gained much popular support in the insurance market. This insurance provides long-term nursing home care for individuals with chronic illnesses and disabilities, both physical and mental. The first policies were written in 1985. By 2001 over 8.3 million policies had been issued, a number that grew an average of 18 percent annually since 1987 (HIAA, 2003).

Health Insurance Providers

Providers are generally classified as commercial insurance carriers, Blue Cross and Blue Shield associations, and managed care organizations. More than 1,200 commercial insurance companies sell health insurance in the United States today, covering over 100 million Americans with hospital and surgical benefits. Most of them operate nationally. Some offer only health insurance, but many also offer property and casualty insurance, liability coverage, and life insurance. Typically premiums are based on **experience rating**; that is, based on the loss experience of the insured. Employers with better records of loss control can receive better rates from commercial insurers.

The Blue Cross and Blue Shield System is actually a network of 42 independent associations operating regionally around the United States. The Blue Cross plans provided health benefits for 85.2 million Americans by the end of 2002. Under most state laws the Blues receive preferential treatment as nonprofit associations.[2] They are taxed at lower rates and typically have lower overhead expenses. Originally the Blue Cross and Blue Shield plans offered insurance at premiums based on **community rating**. This practice is all but extinct as competition has increased pressure on all insurance providers to lower premiums.

Managed care organizations, in particular health maintenance organizations and **preferred provider organizations (PPOs)**, offer comprehensive health care coverage where the provider is responsible for the health care services of enrollees for a fixed fee. More will be said about this arrangement in Chapter 7.

In addition, an increasing number of health insurance plans are handled directly by the sponsoring employers through self-insurance. By 1985 over one-half of the company-sponsored group insurance plans were operated under Administrative Service Only (ASO) arrangements and Minimum Premium Plans (MPPs). Under ASO arrangements, third-party administrators (TPAs) process claims and handle paperwork for a set fee. MPPs offer insurance against large, unpredictable claims.

Approximately 83 percent of the civilian population under age 65 has hospital or surgical health insurance, or both. Of the population over 65 covered by Medicare, approximately 60 percent carry private supplemental coverage (Medigap insurance). Thus, about 15 percent of the civilian population is without health insurance protection.

Private Insurance Demand

Insurance serves an important function in medical care. Having insurance does not protect a person against illness, but it can provide a measure of protection against the financial consequences of an illness. Formally, insurance is defined as a means of protecting against risk. Because we live in an uncertain world, demand for insurance has emerged in modern markets.

---

2 There are obvious exceptions to this statement in states where Blue Cross and Blue Shield have converted to for-profit entities—most notably in California.

ISSUES IN MEDICAL CARE DELIVERY

IMPORTANT CONCEPTS IN HEALTH INSURANCE

Adverse selection is a situation in which a high-risk individual is able to conceal his or her true risk level and purchase insurance for the average premium. A disproportionate number of these high-risk individuals in any risk pool will threaten the pool's solvency.

Expected value of an outcome is the weighted average of all possible outcomes, with the probabilities of those outcomes used as weights. In other words, $E(x) = \Sigma\, x_i p_i$, where $E(x)$ is the expected value, x_i is the ith outcome, and p_i is its associated probability. The expected value is summed over all possible outcomes.

"Free rider" refers to an individual who does not buy insurance, knowing that in the event of a serious illness medical care will be provided free of charge.

Moral hazard arises because the fact that a person has insurance coverage increases both the likelihood of making a claim and the actual size of the claim. Insurance reduces the net out-of-pocket price of medical services and thus increases the quantity demanded.

Probability of an event is the likelihood or chance that the event will occur. Probability is measured as a ratio that ranges in value from 0 to 1. A probability of 1 means that an event is certain to happen—it happens every time. A probability of 0.25 means that the event happens one-fourth of the time.

Risk is a state in which multiple outcomes are possible and the likelihood of each possible outcome is known or can be estimated.

Uncertainty is a state in which multiple outcomes are possible but the likelihood of any one outcome is not known.

The Theory of Risk and Insurance

The theory of risk and insurance is based on the pioneering work of Friedman and Savage (1948). Individuals enter into insurance contracts to shift the uncertainty of financial risk to others. It is impossible to determine whether one particular individual will suffer from a medical condition, such as a heart attack or stroke. When individuals are combined into large enough groups, or risk pools, the probability that someone in the group will suffer from heart attack or stroke can be estimated. The estimated probability of an event is based on the historical frequency of the event occurring in the past. The larger the group, the greater the accuracy of the prediction. Tracing health care spending back to 1928, Berk and Monheit (2001) show a remarkable stability in distribution of health care expenditures over time. Using national survey data they estimate that in 1996 five percent of the population was responsible for 55 percent of the aggregate spending on health care. Additionally, the top 10 percent of the users accounted for 69 percent of the spending, the top 30 percent accounted for 90 percent, and the top one-half accounted for 97 percent of the total spending.

Some individuals are more willing to take chances than others. But even people who willingly take chances generally prefer less risky situations. Most people try to avoid risk. The dominant attitude among the population is risk aversion. Attitudes toward risk are depicted by the marginal utility of income. When evaluating two alternatives with the same expected value, a risk-averse individual will choose a certain prospect over the uncertain prospect. Risk aversion is shown by a diminishing marginal utility of income, measuring the rate of change of the total utility of income.

expected value of an outcome
The weighted average of all possible outcomes, with the probabilities of those outcomes used as weights. In other words, $E(x) = \Sigma\, x_i p_i$, where $E(x)$ is the expected value, x_i is the ith outcome, and p_i is its associated probability. The expected value is summed over all possible outcomes.

probability
The likelihood or chance that the event will occur. Probability is measured as a ratio that ranges in value from 0 to 1. A probability of 1 means that an event is certain to happen—it happens every time. A probability of 0.25 means that the event happens one-fourth of the time.

risk
A state in which multiple outcomes are possible and the likelihood of each possible outcome is known or can be estimated.

uncertainty
A state in which multiple outcomes are possible but the likelihood of any one outcome is not known.

Key Concept 3
*Marginal
Analysis*

The more income a person has, the higher that person's level of utility. In addition, each additional increment to income increases utility by an amount smaller than the previous increment. Figure 6.1 depicts the total utility of income curve for a risk-averse person. Total utility is drawn concave from below, that is, increasing at a decreasing rate. As income increases from w_0 to w_1, total utility increases from u_0 to u_1. As the level of income increases, each increment to income increases utility by a smaller amount. In other words, as income increases from w_1 to w_2, the change in utility is less than it was when income increased from w_0 to w_1, an equal increment.

When actual outcomes are uncertain, individuals do not know where they will end up on their utility of income curve. Even though individuals cannot know with certainty the actual income they will receive in a given time period, their expected income can be estimated. Expected utility is the average of all possible utilities weighted by their respective probabilities. When making a choice under conditions of uncertainty, individuals attempt to maximize expected utility. Assume there are two possible health states: sick and healthy. A probability of being sick equal to 5 percent means a 95 percent probability of being healthy. (The sum of the probabilities of all possible health states must equal 100 percent.) If the cost of treating the illness is equal to $20,000, a person with an annual income of $50,000 has an expected income of $49,000.[3]

Risk is costly and a risk-averse person will pay to avoid the consequences of the risk. To illustrate this principle, take the case of health insurance. An individual facing the uncertainty of an illness has two choices: (1) purchase insurance and voluntarily reduce wealth by the amount of the premium, or (2) self-insure facing the small probability of a financial loss should an illness occur. It is impossible to know the actual probability that any one person will suffer from an illness. With a large population, the proportion of the population that suffered from the illness in a previous time period can be used to estimate the probability.

The goal of insurance is to spread or pool the risk over a large group of people within the population. Risk pooling works as long as the group purchasing insurance has the same probability of illness as the entire population. In that case they are able to share the costs of treating the illness by collecting premiums from everyone and paying benefits to those who become ill. For this arrangement to work, the insurance company must collect enough in premiums to pay out all claims, cover all operating and administrative costs, and have a reasonable profit left over for the owners of the company.

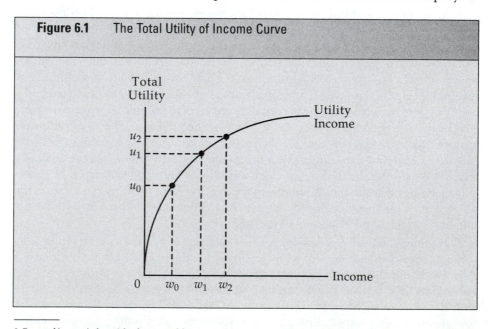

Figure 6.1   The Total Utility of Income Curve

---

3 Expected income is the weighted average of the two possible outcomes. The calculation is the sum of the income at each health state weighed by the probability that state will occur, or $E(Y) = (\$50{,}000 \times 0.95) + (\$30{,}000 \times 0.05) = \$47{,}500 + \$1{,}500 = \$49{,}000$.

To illustrate how this works consider the following example. Suppose our prospective insurance customer faces a 4 percent probability of suffering from an illness that would result in a catastrophic financial loss equal to an entire year's income of $50,000. Under these circumstances the range of uncertainty extends from a net income (after the financial loss due to the illness) of 0 to $50,000. The expected utility of income is depicted by a straight line from the origin to the point on the actual utility of income curve corresponding to $50,000.[4] The concave utility of income depicts the level of utility associated with a guaranteed income (i.e., no uncertainty). The straight-line expected utility of income curve is the utility adjusted for the different probabilities (ranging from 0 to 1) of illness. In other words, this straight line represents the expected utility of the $50,000 loss associated with the illness at all the probabilities between 0 and 1. The difference between the two curves represents the reduction in utility associated with the risk of illness.

Choice under conditions of uncertainty means that a person tries to maximize expected utility. Because the probability of illness is 4 percent, the probability of not being ill is 96 percent. Referring to Figure 6.2, expected wealth in this case is $48,000 and expected utility is $96U$.[5]

Given the utility of income curve shown in the figure, our prospective insurance customer has the same level of utility (equal to $96U$) with a guaranteed income of $45,000 or an expected income of $48,000. In other words, this person's actual level of utility is the same when he has a 100 percent probability of an income level of $45,000 or a 96 percent chance of $50,000 coupled with a 4.0 percent chance of zero income. The difference between $48,000 and $45,000 (or $3,000) is the price of uncertainty. In this case, if insurance can be purchased for less than $5,000, the individual will be better off; that is, at a higher level of utility.

Obviously, a lot of people have similar utility of income curves—all risk averse—otherwise insurance companies would not sell millions of insurance policies annually. If 1,000 people in a group seek insurance, an insurer can expect that 40 will make claims totaling $2 million. The insurer must charge a minimum of $2,000 per person to cover the expected payout, but can charge up to $5,000 (the expected payout plus the price of

Figure 6.2   The Choice of Insurance

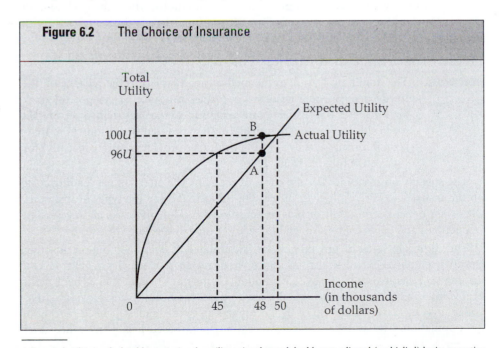

---

4 Expected utility is calculated by summing the utility enjoyed at each health state adjusted (multiplied) by its respective probability. The expected utility curve is derived by varying the probability of each health state from 0 to 1 and plotting the results.

5 $E(y) = (0.96 \times \$50,000) + (0.04 \times \$0) = \$48,000$. $E(U) = (0.96 \times 100U) + (0.04 \times 0U) = 96U$.

uncertainty). Remember, the difference between the maximum value of the insurance and the minimum cost of the insurance is the value of the risk reduction, the price of uncertainty. As long as the administrative costs and profit of the insurance company are less than the price of uncertainty, insurance can be successfully marketed to this group. With no insurance each individual in the group has an expected utility of $96U$. With insurance costing less than \$5,000, utility is higher. The person is better off insured, depicted by point B, than uninsured, depicted by point A.

Several factors affect the decision to buy insurance. The shape of the utility of income curve is important. Obviously, individuals who are risk seekers or risk neutral will not buy insurance.[6] The magnitude of the loss also plays a key role in the decision. When the range of uncertainty is large (i.e., when the potential financial loss is large relative to the actual level of income), the distance between the actual utility curve and the expected utility curve is greater than when the range of uncertainty is small. The greater the expected loss, the greater the maximum value of the insurance and the higher the likelihood that the individual will purchase insurance. As the probability of the loss changes, the likelihood of buying insurance changes. Even those who are risk averse do not buy insurance when the probability of a loss is at one of the extremes. The perceived cost of the risk is too low to stimulate demand at low probabilities and minimum cost of the insurance too high as the probability of illness approaches certainty. As with the demand for any product, it goes without saying that the price of the insurance and the level of income also play important roles in determining whether or not insurance will be purchased.

In summary, the theory implies that under indemnity insurance arrangements, risk-averse individuals will insure against low-probability, high-loss events. Hospitalization falls into this category and insurance pays 97 percent of all hospital spending. Coverage for high probability, low loss events such as dental care, eyeglasses, and prescription drugs is not as generous. Insurance covers less than one-half of the overall spending in each of these categories (Levit et al., 1994). The premium paid by the policyholder is equal to the insurer's expected payout plus a markup to cover administrative overhead and a profit. For an individual to purchase insurance the markup must be less than the perceived value of risk of self-insurance.[7] In these situations, where the likelihood of use is high and the costs are relatively low, the markup exceeds the value of the risk reduction, and the customer chooses not to buy insurance.

Health Insurance and Market Failure

Key Concept 9
Market Failure

net loading costs
The difference between the actual premium and the minimum cost of the insurance based on actuarial principles.

The dominant feature in the medical marketplace is the reliance on the third-party payment mechanism. Just as insurance has shaped the market for medical care, the tax subsidy to insurance has shaped the market for health insurance. Thus, in addition to the traditional sources of market failure, this subsidy to health insurance provides a strong incentive for over consumption (Pauly, 1986).

The subsidy on insurance has the effect of reducing the after-tax **net loading costs** on the insurance. The result is an increase in the demand for the types of insurance where net benefits are small, such as prescription drugs, dental care, and eyeglasses. Deductibles and copayments also tend to be lower on average with the subsidy.

The aggregate value of this tax subsidy is estimated at over \$100 billion. In other words, if employer-based health insurance were treated as a taxable benefit, federal income tax receipts would rise by that amount (Gruber and Levitt, 2000). The benefits of this tax subsidy flow primarily to those with generous health plans providing first-dollar coverage. Over 60 percent of the tax savings go to the highest-paid 20 percent of the population. The average worker with employment-based health insurance saves

---

6 For the risk seeker, risk contributes to utility. The actual utility function falls below the expected utility function, implying that risk adds to the level of utility. The risk-neutral person is indifferent to uncertainty. Risk has neither benefit nor cost associated with it.

7 This statement assumes that the insurer and the policyholder place the same value on the expected payout.

about $800 per year in taxes. At the extremes, the uninsured and low-income workers get no tax benefits while those earning between $100,000 and $200,000 save $1,710 (Goodgame, 1994).

There is widespread agreement among economists that this favorable tax treatment distorts the composition of the typical employee compensation package. The theoretical argument is strong. For a person in the 28 percent tax bracket, it takes $1.39 in gross income to provide $1.00 in after-tax income. With this tax treatment it only takes $1.00 to provide $1.00 in health benefits. This kind of subsidy provides a strong incentive to accept a compensation package disproportionately weighted in favor of nontaxable health benefits. Although it is clear that the tax subsidy matters, the empirical estimates of the impact are less precise.

Information Problems

Although the medical care sector in the United States has many problems, it is difficult to say how many can be traced directly to the traditional reliance on markets. The perceived failure of the medical marketplace to efficiently allocate resources and control spending has led most developed nations worldwide to adopt a system of extensive collective involvement through social insurance. One of the most promising routes to understanding the functioning of the medical marketplace is by tracing the implications of widespread information problems in that market. Information costs are a central factor in economic decision making. The most challenging problems that arise because of costly information are due to unequal access to information. One party to an economic transaction has more and better information than all other parties. Two issues arise when access to information is not equal, or, more formally, when information is asymmetrically distributed: imperfect consumer information on price and quality, moral hazard, and adverse selection.

Consumer Information Problems

Rational or purposeful choice is based on the decision making ability of consumers with disposable income who know their own preferences. When consumers have trouble gathering and understanding information, the ability to make informed decisions is compromised (Rice, 1998). Health care markets are seriously deficient in this regard. The quality of information tends to be poor with most information passed from consumer to consumer by word-of-mouth with little formal advertising. Not only is medical information difficult to gather, it is also difficult to understand. A great deal of medical decision making is based on highly technical information. Physicians spend a great deal of time in medical school to learn how to interpret the technical data on which they base diagnosis and treatment. Patients are usually not equipped to make the same decisions. It is this dual role as provider and adviser that can potentially lead to abuse. Finally, the cost of poor decision making is often quite high.

The Economics of Moral Hazard

Information about the present and future is costly. Economic modeling no longer utilizes the assumption of perfect and costless information exclusively, but has attempted to recognize information costs as a central factor in decision making. Nobel laureate George Stigler (1961) wrote "information occupies the slum dwelling in the town of economics." Now it seems that all of the interesting problems in economics are due to the fact that information is costly.

Information costs present problems during economic transactions. All contracts involve expectations of future behavior. The moral hazard problem arises when one party to a contract cannot monitor the other party's performance. After reaching an agreement on terms, one or both parties may engage in post-contractual opportunistic behavior because private actions are hidden from view. If people were perfectly honest, writing contracts would be easy. But people are often opportunistic. People who are moral in most ways may still take advantage of situations when their behavior cannot be monitored. By exploiting the imbalance of information existing between the two parties to the contract a person is engaging in economic opportunism—attempting to secure more utility than would be permitted or anticipated by a particular contract.

Key Concept 4
Self-Interest

The fact that a person has insurance coverage increases expected medical care spending. Two aspects to moral hazard affect both patient and provider. Having insurance (1) increases the likelihood of purchasing medical services and (2) induces higher spending in the event of an illness.[8]

These information problems affect the structure of insurance contracts. The person with insurance recognizes that the service is "sale priced." Patients experience net prices as low as 10 to 20 cents on the dollar, especially for hospital and physicians' services. It naturally follows that people pursue the rational tendency of purchasing more services than they would under full-invoice pricing. Lowering the cost of medical care to the individual through the availability of insurance increases the amount purchased.

It is easy to understand how this happens. A person visiting a physician for a battery of diagnostic tests will behave differently if he has insurance coverage. A patient with full insurance coverage will ask about the benefits of the tests, the nature of the complications, and the amount of time required for the entire procedure. A physician with a fully insured patient will provide the tests knowing that the insurance company will pay the bill. Seldom will cost enter the discussion. On the other hand, the uninsured patient will ask about the cost of the tests, the cost of alternative tests, whether the tests are absolutely necessary, and the likely consequences if they are postponed or skipped completely. And the physician of a patient without insurance will take the patient's financial situation into consideration when choosing which tests to run.

Studies by the RAND Corporation and others have shown that individuals who receive free care use more medical services than those who are required to pay a portion of the cost. It is widely understood that health insurance, by lowering the out-of-pocket cost of medical care to the individual, may increase the amount demanded. In other words, people demand more medical care when it is covered by insurance.

From a strictly economic perspective we can argue that the response of seeking more medical care when one has insurance than when one does not is a result of rational economic behavior, not moral turpitude. The quantity of medical care demanded by an individual is a function of (1) tastes and preferences for medical care, (2) income, (3) the extent of the illness, and (4) the price charged for medical services. The effect of insurance against medical care expenditures is to reduce the price paid by the individual from its positive market price to some lower price. Even if illness is a perfectly random event, the presence of medical insurance will alter the randomness of medical expenditures unless the demand for medical care is perfectly inelastic.

Pauly (1968) presented these ideas more formally. Consider that there are three health events that can take place during a particular time period:

$$I_1 = \text{ person will not be sick (with probability } p_1 = 0.5)$$
$$I_2 = \text{ person will be moderately ill (with probability } p_2 = 0.25)$$
$$I_3 = \text{ person will be seriously ill (with probability } p_3 = 0.25)$$

Using Figure 6.3, the position of the individual's demand curve for medical care during any time period depends on which health event occurs. Assume perfectly inelastic demand curves D_1, D_2, and D_3 corresponding to the events. With no medical insurance the individual faces the probability p_1 that he will incur no medical expenses, p_2 that he will need 50 units of medical care at a cost of $50 \times MC$, and p_3 that he will require 200 units of medical care at a cost of $200 \times MC$ (where MC is the cost of one unit of medical care).

---

8 In practice, economists view moral hazard as one aspect of the law of demand. Patients respond to lower net prices by purchasing more. Providers recognize that demand for their services is price inelastic and thus charge higher prices and prescribe more services.

Figure 6.3   The Effect of Moral Hazard on Medical Care Demand

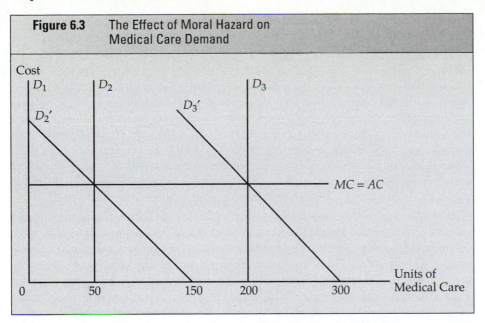

The expected value of the individual's medical care expenses, equals $62.5 \times MC$. The calculation is $(0.5 \times 0) + (0.25 \times 50 \times MC) + (0.25 \times 200 \times MC)$. Arrow's (1963) welfare proposition indicates that the risk-averse individual will prefer paying a premium of $62.5 \times MC$ for medical insurance to risking the probability distribution with the mean equal to $62.5 \times MC$.

Suppose, however, that the individual's demand curves are not perfectly inelastic. If, instead, they are as D_2' and D_3', the individual without insurance faces the probability distribution as above with mean $62.5 \times MC$. However, in order to indemnify against medical costs, the actuarially necessary insurance premium will be equal to $112.5 \times MC$, which is equal to $(0.5 \times 0) + (0.25 \times 150 \times MC) + (0.25 \times 300 \times MC)$. In such a case the individual may prefer taking the risk to purchasing the insurance.

The presence of demand curves that are not perfectly inelastic implies that the individual will alter his or her desired expenditures for medical care when insurance is present. The individual who has insurance that covers all cost demands medical care as though it had a 0 price. If the demand for medical care has a price elasticity greater than 0, forcing individuals to purchase insurance will create inefficiencies. For an efficient solution, some form of price rationing at the point of service may be necessary; that is, deductibles and coinsurance.

Adverse Selection

Adverse selection arises because individuals have more information about expected medical expenditures than insurance companies. The ability of prospective insurance customers to conceal their true risks can result in some insurance groups having a disproportionate number of high users. This will lead to higher than average premiums for the group and create an incentive for low-risk individuals to drop out of the group in search of lower-cost coverage elsewhere.

Adverse selection may be illustrated using the following example. Assume that there are 1,000 individuals, each with a 4 percent chance of $50,000 loss. The insurer expects 40 claims, or $2,000,000 in losses, and requires a premium of $2,000 plus loading costs. Suppose the original pool is merged with one that has 1,000 new people each with a 30 percent chance of making a $50,000 claim. There will be 300 additional claims and an additional $15,000,000 in medical spending. If the insurer cannot distinguish between the two groups, the premium must rise for everyone because the minimum cost of insuring each of the 2,000 people is $8,500. If members of the high-risk segment were pooled separately, their premium would be $15,000, so $8,500 is a bargain for them. For members of the low-risk segment of the pool, the premium increase is staggering.

The problem is shown using Figure 6.4. Assuming that risk preferences are the same for individuals in each group, we can use the same utility function to illustrate their situations. Low-risk individuals can self-insure, ending up at point A with the 4 percent risk of a $50,000 loss, or when pooled separately purchase insurance for $2,000 plus loading costs as long as they end up no lower than point B on their (income certain) utility curve. They enjoy a utility level equal to U_2 in either case. High-risk individuals may choose to self-insure and end up at point E with a 30 percent risk of the catastrophic loss, or when pooled separately purchase insurance for $15,000 plus loading costs as long as they end up no lower than point F on their (income certain) utility curve. The utility level of the high-risk group can be no lower than U_0.

When the two groups are pooled together, a premium of $8,500 plus loading allows all members of the two groups to end up at point D and enjoy a utility level of U_1 with certainty. High-risk group members may choose to go without insurance and end up at point E with utility of U_0, or buy pooled insurance and end up at point D with utility of U_1. Low-risk users may buy pooled insurance and end up at point D with utility of U_1, or choose not buy insurance at all and end up at point A with utility level U_2. In this example, low-risk users will forgo the purchase and self-insure, leaving high-risk users in a separate pool with the higher premium of $15,000 plus loading costs. The only way to guarantee the solvency of the insurance pool is to force members of the low-risk group to remain in the pool.

Insurers' Response to Information Problems

Moral hazard and adverse selection are information problems. Both arise due to the inability of insurers to monitor customer use and identify prospective risk. Insurers respond to the overspending associated with moral hazard by charging deductibles and coinsurance. The insurance deductible is a set amount of medical expense that must be paid by the insured patient before the insurance pays any part of the claim. In the traditional fee-for-service indemnity plan, the typical deductible is anywhere between $100 and $300. Whether the deductible works to discourage spending depends on the prospects of total spending exceeding the deductible. In practice deductibles seem to have some depressing effect on spending when prospective expenses are below the deductible. Otherwise, they have little impact. Obviously, one way to increase the impact of the deductible is to increase its size. Deductibles of $2,500 will reduce spending more than deductibles of $250.

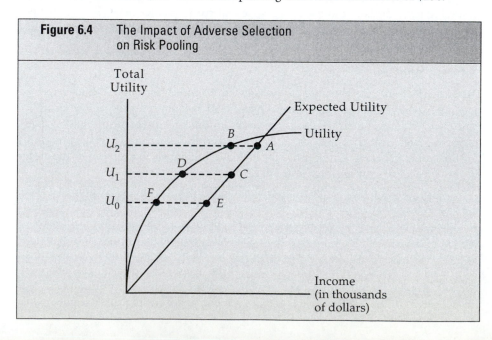

Figure 6.4   The Impact of Adverse Selection on Risk Pooling

In most cases, the insured patient pays a fixed percentage of every claim. The typical coinsurance rate of 10 to 20 percent provides a measure of discipline to the cost-conscious patient. Higher coinsurance rates raise the marginal cost to the insured and serve to restrain use to some degree. This cost sharing usually stops after total out-of-pocket spending reaches some limit, anywhere from $2,000 to $5,000.

The insurer's response to adverse selection is twofold. Insurance companies will only underwrite prospective risk. The insurer will try to determine the expected level of usage prior to entering into the contract. This risk rating of prospective customers is done either through the use of a questionnaire or a physical exam or a combination of the two. In addition, insurance companies will not provide insurance for known ailments. A **preexisting condition** is associated with an extremely high probability of use (approaching unity). Without the ability to spread risk, the insurance premium would likely exceed the expected loss. Consumers experience no gain from joining such a risk pool and thus have little demand for this high-cost insurance.[9]

preexisting condition
A medical condition caused by an injury or disease that exists prior to the application for health insurance. Policies often exclude them from individual coverage or at minimum include them only after a waiting period (usually 6–12 months).

The failure of the market to provide opportunities for the chronically and congenitally ill to purchase insurance at average premiums should come as no surprise. The purpose of insurance is to share risk, not wealth. Policymakers, even those not interested in wealth redistribution, have used market failure to justify the provision of social insurance as a safety net. Since the private insurance market cannot provide adequate insurance for those with preexisting conditions, it seems reasonable that the government take on this responsibility by operating and subsidizing high-risk insurance pools.

Policy Issue
Should the government provide insurance for high-risk individuals with preexisting conditions?

Other policymakers justify the provision of social insurance because of the external costs associated with the uninsured (e.g., high-cost emergency room use, cost-shifting, social unrest). Social insurance makes a pooling solution possible. Low risks are required to support the risk pool through compulsory taxation or higher insurance premiums. This approach to insurance is used in the United States in both a means-tested (Medicaid) and an age-tested (Medicare) program. It is used less effectively in state-sponsored, high-risk pools for those with preexisting conditions.

The Provision of Health Insurance in the United States

Health insurance is sold primarily to groups that are formed for reasons other than the purchase of insurance. Most nonelderly Americans with private insurance (about 68 percent in 2000) are covered under group policies sold to employers or employee associations. The implications of this feature are important for policy purposes. Group insurance means that individuals do not own their own insurance policies. Without individual ownership, portability among employer groups has been a chronic problem, especially if a preexisting medical condition affects the person's eligibility across plans.

Policy Issue
Most Americans receive their health insurance through employer-sponsored plans.

The practice of exempting employees from income taxation on the value of health insurance benefits has contributed to the growth of group insurance. Employers treat the outlay as a tax-deductible expense, reducing their own income-tax liability. Employees receive the insurance coverage tax-free, providing a strong incentive to demand excess coverage.

Traditionally, health care premiums were set according to community ratings. Under community rating, premiums are based on the average risk for everyone residing in a

---

9 The Health Insurance Portability and Accountability Act passed in 1996 modified the provision of insurance to those with preexisting conditions somewhat. An individual who has insurance and subsequently becomes ill may not be denied continued coverage under any circumstances. The policy is portable across plans. Individuals without insurance coverage who are sick may still be denied coverage.

specific community. Given the tax advantages of a nonprofit organization, Blue Cross-Blue Shield was able to price policies below those of the typical commercial insurer. In order to compete with the Blue Cross-Blue Shield plans, commercial insurers were forced to look for ways to offer specific groups better rates. The only way to accomplish this feat was to find groups with lower-than-average risks and offer them insurance at lower premiums based on the actual experience of the group.

The extensive use of experience rating in setting insurance premiums has given rise to claims of **cream skimming** by insurers. Cream skimming can occur when insurers are able to identify subgroups of the population with different expected medical costs. When the low-risk subgroup is paying the same premium as everyone else, there is an incentive to seek out these preferred risks and sell insurance to them at reduced premiums.

Many policymakers mistakenly believe that insurance companies make money by denying coverage to those identified as high risks. If insurance companies were free to set premiums according to strict actuarial principles, then high-risk individuals would pay higher premiums, and there would be no incentive to cream skim. Cream skimming is the result of regulation in the insurance industry, not competition (Pauly, 1984). Without an efficient mechanism of risk-adjusted premium differentials, the likelihood of cream skimming exists.

The Practice of Self-Insurance

As insurance premiums rise, private-sector employers have increasingly looked to self-insurance as a means of reducing the cost of providing health insurance to their workers. Currently, over one half of all private insurance is provided in plans where the employer of the group assumes all or a significant part of the financial risk. The growth of self-insurance is easy to understand. Most private insurance **underwriting** is based on experience rating in the first place. After experiencing a large number of medical episodes, an employer may be able to predict medical expenses from year to year. Thus, it is practical for large employers to self-insure. The predictability of expenses and the ability to spread risk over a large group makes self-insurance feasible.

Firms that self-insure do not actually contract with an insurance company to assume the financial risk. Instead, they accept this responsibility internally by simply placing funds previously paid in insurance premiums into a reserve account to pay medical claims directly. Many self-insured firms arrange for commercial insurance companies to administer their plans. This includes claims processing, actuarial services, and utilization review. A large percentage of the plans limit risk through **reinsurance**—a liability cap at some stop-loss threshold.

Government regulation provides a strong incentive for firms to self-insure. Most states levy a tax on premiums that insurers must pass onto their customers. This extra premium expense does not apply to self-insured plans. Firms that self-insure are also exempted from providing state-mandated benefits that apply to all private insurance plans. Specifically, the provisions of the Employee Retirement Income Security Act of 1974 (ERISA) superseded state laws and prohibited the application of state mandates to self-insured plans. Finally, states that sponsor high-risk insurance pools will require commercial insurance carriers to participate in providing insurance to those individuals with pre-existing conditions. Usually self-insured plans are not required to participate.

The increased popularity of self-insurance has changed the nature of risk rating. Firms that are large enough to self-insure do so. Community rating is no longer a viable way to determine premiums for groups with below-average levels of risk. Even Blue Cross-Blue Shield, traditionally a proponent of community rating, has been forced to abandon the practice in favor of experience rating for large firms that have the option of self-insuring.

cream skimming
A practice of pricing insurance policies so that healthy (low-risk) individuals will purchase coverage and those with a history of costly medical problems (high-risk) will not.

 Key Concept 6
Supply and Demand

underwriting
The insurance practice of determining whether or not an application for insurance will be accepted. In the process, premiums are also determined. Factors considered may include age, sex, health status, and prior use of health care services.

reinsurance
Stop-loss insurance purchased by a health plan to protect itself against losses that exceed a specific dollar amount per claim, per individual, or per year.

Policy Issue
State regulations create incentives for firms to set up self-insured plans.

ISSUES IN MEDICAL CARE DELIVERY

WHAT DOES AN ARM AND A LEG COST?

Although there is little argument that industrialization has benefited society, with it came many problems that dramatically changed family and work life. Cottage industries became large manufacturing organizations, thus increasing the concerns for worker safety. In many respects, workers' rights with respect to injury and death were largely ignored until the last half of the nineteenth century. Common law liability rules made it difficult for injured workers to collect benefits from their employers.

Gradually the courts began to recognize the employer's responsibility to provide a safe workplace, and by the early 1900s states began the slow process of drafting legislation to formally establish the responsibility. In 1911 Wisconsin passed the first **workers' compensation** law to be declared constitutional. By the end of that decade, all but six states and the District of Columbia had such legislation. It was not until 1948 that the last state, Mississippi, adopted its own workers' compensation law.

Workers' compensation establishes a **no-fault** approach to addressing worker safety and health issues in the employment setting. Workers' compensation laws cover virtually all types of injuries "arising out of and in the course of employment." The laws provide medical, disability income, death, and rehabilitation benefits. Perhaps the most controversial category of benefits compensates injured workers for permanent partial disabilities. Each state establishes a schedule of benefits for certain types of injuries. In Rhode Island the loss of an arm at the shoulder results in a maximum payment to the injured worker of $28,080. In nearby New Hampshire that same loss would be worth $132,930. Illinois values the arm at $196,719. A worker who loses a leg at the hip receives $28,080 in Rhode Island, $88,620 in New Hampshire, and $180,325 in Illinois. A worker losing an arm and a leg would receive $24,000 in Puerto Rico and $373,100 in Pennsylvania. That same worker, if engaged in interstate commerce working for the railroad, would receive $722,616 regardless of where the injury occurred.

In 1993, the nationwide cost of workers' compensation benefits was estimated at over $60 billion. Given its costs, it is not surprising that state legislators are constantly under pressure to tinker with the system.

Source: State Workers' Compensation Laws, U.S. Department of Labor, Employment Standards Administration, Office of Workers' Compensation Programs, January 1992.

workers' compensation
Insurance to protect employees against financial loss caused by work-related injury or illness.

no-fault
A method of compensating for injury where no attempt is made to determine fault. The magnitude of injury becomes the basis of the compensation and is the only issue in the legal proceedings.

Medical Care for the Uninsured

It is important to understand the nature and extent of the problems associated with being uninsured. The most recent estimates from the Census Bureau place the number of uninsured at 43.6 million Americans, roughly 15 percent of the total population (Mills and Shandari, 2003). As the numbers grow, the pressure mounts to provide some relief to the situation. Providing coverage for the uninsured is a formidable task. Understanding who the uninsured are and the reasons they lack insurance coverage are critical in developing policy to deal with the problem. Fuchs (1991) has suggested a useful classification schema that will serve as a basis for our discussion. The uninsured fall into six categories: (1) the poor, (2) the sick and disabled, (3) the difficult, (4) low users, (5) gamblers, and (6) free riders. Although we have no means of determining the exact numbers that fall into each category, the exercise will aid in policy discussions that follow in subsequent chapters.

Policy Issue

Over 43 million Americans do not have health insurance.

http://

Health insurance statistics are available from the U.S. Census Bureau Web site at **http://www.census.gov/ftp/pub/ hhes/www/hlthins.html.**

The majority of the uninsured can be categorized as working poor. These are individuals who earn too much to qualify for cash assistance and are therefore ineligible for Medicaid. They usually work for small businesses where health insurance is not part of the employee benefit package. Forced to purchase insurance at individual rates, they do not consider the purchase of health insurance a very good buy for the money.

Almost one-half of the uninsured have incomes at least two times the official poverty level. While the number of uninsured poor has remained fairly stable in recent years, this group has seen the most dramatic increase in numbers. Not everyone without health insurance is poor. Approximately one-third of all uninsured Americans live in households with incomes over $50,000 (Mills and Shandari, 2003). In fact, households in this income category have experienced the greatest percentage increase in the number of uninsured of all income groups.

Individuals with preexisting health conditions represent a substantial number of the uninsured. Insurers will try to avoid offering coverage at average premiums to individuals with diabetes, cancer, AIDS, heart disease, or other special health problems. If insurance is available at all, the premiums will be high. The size of this group has been estimated at less than 1 percent of the population or less than 10 percent of the uninsured.

Many individuals who are not poor and who do not have preexisting health problems still find it difficult to obtain insurance at average premiums. Most of these "difficult to insure" are self-employed, employees of small businesses, or temporarily unemployed. Without access to group insurance, the premiums paid are anywhere from 10 to 40 percent higher than average, due to additional sales and administrative costs.

Other reasons explain why some people fail to purchase insurance. They may have no intentions of using medical care at all. Low users may be very healthy, have an extreme dislike for formal medical services, or simply not believe in medical care. Some people are gamblers. In other words, they are not as risk averse as the typical buyer of health insurance. No doubt a significant portion of the uninsured can be classified as free riders. They do not buy insurance because they feel that if they become seriously ill, medical care will be provided and someone else will pay for it.

How Many Americans Are Uninsured?

There is a lot of confusion about the actual number of uninsured in the country. Most of the 43.6 million Americans who find themselves without health insurance experience short spells without insurance, often the result of a job change. Analysis of health insurance coverage for the twelve months ending September 1995 shows that over two thirds of all spells without health insurance last less than one year; over half ended in five to six months (Swartz et al., 1993a; Bennefield, 1998; CBO, 2003). Applying this figure to the number of uninsured in 2001 indicates that approximately 14 million Americans are chronically uninsured (spells without insurance lasting more than one year). This group of chronically uninsured presents the challenging policy consideration. Going without insurance even for short spells is a problem. But the longer the duration of time a person goes without insurance, the lower the probability of getting reinsured (Copeland, 1998).

Policy Issue
Approximately 14 million uninsured Americans are without insurance for over one year.

An even larger issue may be the trend in the number and percentage of the population who go without insurance. Between 1989 and 2001, the percentage of the population without insurance has fluctuated from year to year but has remained essentially unchanged. Up until 1993, a rising percentage of the population without insurance could be attributable to a decrease in the portion of the population covered by employer-based insurance. But since 1993, employment-based coverage has increased from 60.5 percent of the nonelderly to 68.3 percent. At the same time the number of Americans with public insurance, notably Medicaid and CHAMPUS, and private nongroup coverage has fallen slightly. The overall impact of these changes is a fall in the percentage of uninsured since 1993 (Holahan and Kim, 2000; Holahan and Pohl, 2002).

ISSUES IN MEDICAL CARE DELIVERY

MEASURING THE NUMBER OF UNINSURED

The most commonly cited estimate of the number of uninsured in the United States originates from the Census Bureau's Current Population Survey (CPS). Based on a nationally representative sample, the survey has been conducted annually since 1980. The CPS estimate is intended to measure the number of Americans uninsured for the entire year. Based on evidence available from other surveys, the CPS estimate more likely measures the number of Americans uninsured on a specific date during the year.

There are at least 6 national surveys that gather information on the characteristics of the uninsured. In addition to the CPS, other surveys, including the Survey of Income and Programs Participation (SIPP), the National Health Interview Survey (NHIS), and the Medical Expenditure Panel Survey (MEPS) address many of the same issues. Short (2001) tackles the methodological problems associated with estimating the number of uninsured to show how different survey techniques can result in different estimates. One of the major differences across the surveys is the frequency of data collection. CPS data comes from a survey conducted in March of each year, and asks questions about insurance status for the previous year. CPS asks for insurance status over the previous year and calculates the uninsured as the residual. Many analysts argue that individuals underreport their insurance status, especially those covered by Medicaid. SIPP interviews every four months asking questions about insurance status for each month since the previous interview. The MEPS survey is conducted every 3 to 5 months, so the reference period varies across participants.

A study by the Congressional Budget Office analyzed data from the four surveys estimating the number of uninsured in 1998. In that year, CPS estimated that 43.9 million Americans were uninsured for the entire year, or 18.4 percent of the population. Using the data available in MEPS, the estimate was 31.1 million, or 13.3 percent of the population. If SIPP data is used, the number of uninsured is 21.1 million, or 9.1 percent of the population. When these latter two surveys are used to estimate the number of uninsured on a certain date, SIPP estimates the number at 40.5 million; using MEPS the number is 42.6—both very close to the CPS estimates for the number uninsured the entire year. Although Census estimates are used throughout this section, keep in mind there is a minority report on this important issue.

Sources: Pamela Farley Short, "Counting and Characterizing the Uninsured," *ERIU Working Paper* 2, University of Michigan, Economic Research Institute on the Uninsured, December 2001; and Congressional Budget Office, "How Many People Lack Health Insurance and for How Long?" A CBO Paper, Washington, DC: Congress of the United States, May 2003.

After almost a decade of uninterrupted economic growth, the percentage of Americans who are uninsured has remained virtually unchanged.

Who Are the Uninsured?

Many people have the mistaken impression that most people without insurance are unemployed. On the contrary, 58.8 percent of all uninsured Americans were employed in full-time or part-time jobs in 2001. Approximately one in five (19.9 percent) were nonworking adults, meaning that 21.3 percent were dependent children (Mills, 2002). If dependent children are distributed proportionately according to employment status, it is a fair approximation to say that over 75 percent of the uninsured has some labor force connection—through their own employment or that of a family member.

> **Policy Issue**
>
> The economic growth of the 1990s had little effect on the rate of uninsurance.

Table 6.2 provides information on individuals without insurance. Of the estimated 43.6 million Americans who are uninsured, 23.3 million are male and 20.2 million are female. Of those under 18 years of age, 11.7 percent are uninsured. For 18 to 24 year olds, the percentage of uninsured jumps to 28.1. The percentage without insurance steadily falls in older cohorts since older individuals have a higher demand for medical care and more money to spend on items such as health insurance.

Insurance is closely associated with level of income. One fourth of the population with incomes below $25,000 does not have coverage. Less than 10 percent of those with incomes over $50,000 go without insurance. Individuals with annual incomes between one and two times the official poverty income level are more likely to be uninsured than those making more than that amount. Given the close association between income and education, it is not surprising that the risk of being without insurance increases for those with less education. Individuals who have never been married have a higher risk of being uninsured. The same is true for those living outside the Northeast. Hispanics and African Americans have a higher incidence of uninsurance than whites. Individuals between the ages of 18 and 24 are also more likely to be without insurance than any other age cohort. The uninsured change jobs frequently and are more likely to work part time (see Swartz, Marcotte, McBride, 1993a; Mills, 2002).

Table 6.2	**Individuals Without Health Insurance by Selected Characteristics, 2001 and 2002**					
		2002			**2001**	
Group	**Uninsured (000)**	**Percentage of Group**	**Percentage of Total**	**Uninsured (000)**	**Percentage of Group**	**Percentage of Total**
All Persons	43,574	15.2	100.0	41,207	14.6	100.0
Sex:						
Male	23,327	16.7	53.5	21,722	15.8	52.7
Female	20,246	13.9	46.5	19,485	13.5	47.3
Age:						
Under 18 years	8,531	11.6	19.6	8,509	11.7	20.6
18 to 24 years	8,128	29.6	18.7	7,673	28.1	18.6
25 to 34 years	9,769	24.9	22.4	9,051	23.4	22.0
35 to 44 years	7,781	17.7	17.9	7,131	16.1	17.3
45 to 64 years	9,106	13.5	20.9	8,571	13.1	20.8
65 years and over	258	0.8	0.6	272	0.8	0.7
Income:						
Less than $25,000	14,776	23.5	33.9	14,474	23.3	35.1
$25,000 to $49,999	14,638	19.3	33.6	13,516	17.7	32.8
$50,000 to $74,999	6,904	11.8	15.8	6,595	11.3	16.0
Over $75,000	7,256	8.2	16.7	6,623	7.7	16.1
Race:						
White, Non-Hispanic	20,782	10.7	47.7	19,409	10.0	47.1
Black	7,228	20.2	16.6	6,833	19.0	16.6
Asian and Pacific Islander	2,132	18.4	4.9	2,278	18.2	5.5
Hispanic origin	12,756	32.4	29.3	12,417	33.2	30.1

Source: United States Census Bureau, *Health Insurance Coverage in the United States: 2002*, P60–223, September 2003.

Why Are They Uninsured?

The fact that over 75 percent of the uninsured have some sort of labor force attachment is both troubling and reassuring. It is troubling in the sense that most people who are uninsured have a job, and at the same time reassuring since they are already connected to the primary mechanism used in this country to provide health insurance—private-sector employment.

Why is it that so many workers lack coverage? Broadly speaking, there are three primary reasons that a worker does not have health insurance (Kronic and Gilmer, 1999; Holahan and Kim, 2000):

- The employer does not offer a health plan;
- The employer offers a health plan, but the employee is not eligible for the plan because of part-time status or some other rule;
- The employer offers a plan and the employee is eligible for that plan but chooses not to participate because the plan is either too expensive, the employee can get a better plan elsewhere (usually through a spouse's employment), or the employee does not perceive a need for a health plan.

Many of the uninsured work for small firms that typically do not provide health benefits as part of the standard compensation package. Small firms are at a distinct disadvantage when buying health insurance. It simply costs too much. In setting premiums for group plans, insurers usually charge small firms more per employee than they charge large firms. The estimated administrative costs for small-group plans (those with fewer than five employees) are about 40 percent of claims. For large-group plans (those with more than 10,000 employees), the comparable number is about 5.5 percent of claims. General and administrative expenses are higher for small-group plans, along with selling expenses and commission costs (Helms, Gauthier, and Campion, 1992).

Insurers perceive a higher level of risk in the small-group setting. The private insurance market is fragmented in nature. Instead of the concept of community rating, where everyone in a particular geographic area pays the same premium, groups pay different premiums based on perceived risk. Perceived risk is higher the smaller the group. One large claim can have a catastrophic impact on the calculated premium for a small group—effectively pricing the group out of the market or resulting in making insurance unavailable at any price.

For the same reason, small firms are not able to take advantage of self-insuring. According to a 1992 survey by Foster Higgins, a nationwide consulting firm, over 80 percent of all private-sector companies with more than 1,000 workers self-insure. Even smaller firms see the benefits offered by this practice. One half of all self-insured companies have fewer than 100 employees (Thompson, 1993). With so many firms self-insuring, up to one-half of all private sector employees are now in self-insured pools. Self-insurance carries with it a substantial risk of adverse selection for small firms. Sound underwriting principles would suggest a minimum of 100 to 300 employees before self-insurance is recommended.

Taking all the relevant small-group factors into consideration, it is not surprising that small firms do not offer health benefits to their employees. In addition, small firms usually pay comparatively low wages.

The other reasons that workers go without insurance are equally important. Many part-time workers are uninsured because they do not work enough to qualify for the health plan that is offered. Many eligible workers choose not to participate in the health plan because it is too expensive or they are eligible through another plan, typically through a spouse. Bundorf and Pauly (2002) present an alternative explanation. They present evidence that as many as 75 percent of the uninsured can actually afford insurance coverage by two different standard definitions of affordability, but choose spend their money on other things.

Does Lack of Insurance Mean Poor Health?

The connection between lack of insurance and poor health may be decomposed into two parts. First, how does the lack of health insurance affect access to medical care? Second, does poor access result in poor health outcomes? Significant differences of opinion weigh in on whether the lack of insurance contributes to poor health. Evidence from the RAND Health Insurance Experiment suggests that more generous health insurance benefits have little effect on health outcomes (Newhouse, 1993). Brook (1991) provides additional evidence that the absence of insurance does not reduce the

> ### Policy Issue
> Poor access to medical care often results in poor health, especially for the chronically ill poor.

health status of the average American. While the uninsured have only about two-thirds the number of physicians' visits per year as those with insurance and about one-half the number of hospital days per year, these differences in utilization do not translate into significant differences in health status. With the exception of those who were poor and sick, there seems to be no relationship between health status and insurance status.

These differences could be due to the fact that up to one third of the care provided to the insured is considered inappropriate or equivocal. In other words, the medical benefit does not exceed the medical risk. Because of the questionable nature of such a large percentage of the medical care provided to the insured, differences in the amount of care may not be responsible for differences in health status.

Other research suggests that those without insurance have trouble in accessing the medical care system, resulting in poorer health outcomes. The access problem manifests itself in a lower likelihood of having a regular source of care (Berk, Schur, and Cantor, 1995; Bindman et al., 1995; Zuvekas and Weinick, 1999), delays in seeking care (Burstin et al., 1998; Weissman et al., 1991), and receiving fewer services than those with health insurance (Berk and Schur, 1998; Brown, Bindman, and Lurie, 1998). Even those individuals with health problems find that a lack of insurance significantly affects their access to the system (Berk, Schur, and Cantor, 1995).

Lack of insurance may lead to lower levels of utilization, but establishing a connection between reduced access and poor health outcomes is a more difficult task. The literature supporting the connection generally fails to overcome several important empirical problems.[10] Results from the RAND Health Insurance Experiment cited previously (Manning et al., 1987) show that those individuals who receive free care have better control of their blood pressure and have better vision. Other studies indicate that those without insurance delay seeking needed medical care, resulting in avoidable hospitalizations (Billings, Anderson, and Newman, 1996; Bindman et al., 1995), higher than expected mortality rates (Hadley, Steinberg, and Feder, 1991; Franks, Clancy, and Gold, 1993), and poor birth outcomes (Currie and Gruber, 1996). Even though the empirical evidence is inconclusive, the argument that individuals without insurance experience poorer health outcomes is powerful. As the number of uninsured continues to grow, policymakers will find it increasingly difficult to ignore the apparent health consequences of poor access.

The Safety Net for the Uninsured

Since 1985, with the passage of Section 9121 of the Comprehensive Omnibus Budget Reconciliation Act, it has been illegal for hospital emergency rooms—public or private—to deny care to anyone requesting care. Private hospitals have been systematically reducing their free care in nonacute cases, forcing the public hospitals to absorb the burden of the responsibility of providing care to the uninsured. Estimates indicate that fewer than 10 percent of the nation's public hospitals provide almost one half of all hospital care for the uninsured. Much of this uncompensated care is

---

10 The most notable problem is endogenity bias where the empirical data is unable to determine whether lack of insurance leads to poor health or whether poor health decreases the probability of being insured. Additionally, the research suffers from selection bias where omitted variables that jointly determine the availability of insurance and health status are not included in the analysis.

provided in the hospital emergency room or as a result of a hospital admission from the emergency room.

The Congressional Budget Office estimated that the uninsured received over $15 billion in "free" hospital care in 1991. In addition to the free care provided by hospitals, physicians provided another $10.2 billion in uncompensated care. After adjustments the CBO estimated that this resulted in over $20.3 billion in costs shifted to insured patients. By 1995 this figure would grow to $27.6 billion (NCPA, 1994).

Most of this "free" care is financed from municipal budgets, Medicaid subsidies for the treatment of the indigent poor, or through cost shifting. As the number of uninsured increase and medical costs continue to climb, government budgets at all levels are coming under closer scrutiny. Competitive pressures are making it more difficult for hospitals to pass the cost of care for the uninsured onto private patients. Private insurers, employers, and payers of all kinds are increasingly unwilling to pay for the treatment of the uninsured. Payers are refusing to accept cost shifting and are negotiating discounts in return for guaranteed patient volume.

> ### Policy Issue
> Competitive pressures are jeopardizing the ability of hospitals and physicians to provide free care to the uninsured. Budget pressures are forcing state and local governments to rethink how they will pay for indigent care.

Universal insurance coverage requires accepting the principles of subsidization and compulsion. The chronically ill cannot afford risk-rated insurance premiums. If the insurance market is to provide a solution, the healthy must subsidize the sick through community rating. And even if insurance is provided at community rates, in many cases the poor simply do not have enough resources to buy health insurance without subsidies. But the solution is not as simple as mandating that all insurance premiums be based on community rating. Under community rating, the healthy may face premiums that exceed the maximum value of the insurance. If the purchase of insurance is based on voluntary choice, many of the healthy will choose not to buy. Under these circumstances, mandatory participation may be the best way to provide the subsidies that ensure universal insurance coverage.

Key Concept 10
Voluntary Exchange

The market has found it increasingly difficult to subsidize care for the elderly, the indigent, and the uninsured. One of the main casualties of increased competition in the health insurance market is the complex system of cross subsidies for experimental treatment, care for the elderly and indigent, and medical education and research. As market pressures mount, insurance providers, along with Medicare and Medicaid, will find it increasingly difficult to remain competitive if they do not restrict payments for these services. And if no one wants to pay for medical education or research and development, the quality of care will suffer.

Key Concept 5
Competition

The search for solutions to the problem of providing medical care for the uninsured has resulted in numerous options but few tangible results. Whether the suggestion involves tax increases to pay for insurance coverage for the poor, hospital surcharges on every insurance claim, or **employer mandates**, the general approach is the same—providing a subsidy, either public or private, for those who cannot afford to buy insurance on their own. The alternative is to continue to rely on the hospital industry and private-practice physicians to provide free care.

employer mandate
A feature of certain health care reform proposals requiring employers to provide health insurance for their employees.

Summary and Conclusions

Medical care in the United States, predominantly a private out-of-pocket expense as recently as 1965, is now overwhelmingly financed by third parties (government and private insurers). Government at all levels directly finances over 40 percent of all medical care. Coupled with the tax subsidy provided to purchasers of private insurance, the taxpayers finance over one-half of all medical care spending in this country.

The private sector insures over 178 million Americans, not including the 20 million Medicare recipients who buy private supplementary insurance. Commercial insurance companies, the Blue Cross-Blue Shield plans, self-funded employer plans, and prepaid health plans provide the vast majority of this coverage. The two primary government

PROFILE

Uwe E. Reinhardt

Once introduced at a conference by Representative Pete Stark (D-Calif.) as an "expert on contrariness," Uwe (pronounced *oo-vuh*) Reinhardt is regarded by many as the "bad boy" of the health care reform debate. Born in 1937, Reinhardt's formative years were spent in war-torn Germany, where his family literally lived in a tool shed. During these years of abject poverty Reinhardt grew to appreciate universal health care financed primarily through taxation. "I grew up in countries where health care was treated as a social good, where the rich paid significantly more than their health-care costs to subsidize the poor," he says. "I found that a civilized environment."

Reinhardt migrated to Canada in 1956, where he attended the University of Saskatchewan. After graduation in 1964, he came to the United States to study at Yale University, where he received his Ph.D. in economics in 1970. He also holds an honorary doctorate from the Medical College of Pennsylvania. As an academic, Reinhardt is a bit unusual, in that he has taught at Princeton his entire career. His title is currently the James Madison Professor of Political Economy.

Most of his scholarly work has been in health care economics. He is on the editorial board of several journals, including *Health Affairs, The New England Journal of Medicine,* and *Health Management Quarterly*. He has also served as associate editor of the *Journal of Health Economics*. This is quite a contrast for someone who was considering a Ph.D. dissertation topic on optimal tolls on the Connecticut Turnpike. Fortunately, one of Reinhardt's Yale professors suggested the economics of health care and the rest is history.

His fascination for the topic has continued to grow over the last three decades. Over this time he has become a devout advocate for the uninsured. Prone to black humor about many health-related issues, Reinhardt never jokes about the plight of the uninsured. Although Reinhardt does not see, nor does he want to see, health care defined as a constitutional right, he firmly believes that health care plays a social role. It is a right "implied in the social contract. . . . It's not a consumer good. It's a quasi-religious commodity. . . . It's the cement that makes a nation out of people."

Ever controversial, Reinhardt has earned the respect of individuals on both sides of the health care debate. Equally comfortable in front of a class or a Congressional committee, he leaves little doubt about where he stands on the important issues surrounding health care reform.

Source: Julie Rovner, "MM Interview: Uwe Reinhardt," *Modern Maturity* 37(6), November–December 1994, 64–72.

---

health programs, Medicare and Medicaid, provide health care coverage to almost 70 million Americans. Medicare enrollment topped 38 million elderly and disabled in 2001 while Medicaid served more than 31 million nonelderly.

This patchwork coverage provides health insurance to approximately 85 percent of the American population but still leaves more than 40 million without insurance at any one point in time. Considering that over three fourths of the uninsured have some labor-force connection, it should come as no surprise that reform proposals have focused on employment-related solutions.

Those favoring more government involvement support either the expansion of the Medicaid program or the use of employer mandates. Expanding Medicaid will require both the liberalization of eligibility criterion for specific groups and the subsidization of premiums for the working poor who would buy into the system voluntarily. Employer mandates would require that all employers provide and pay for a basic benefits package determined by the government.

Back-of-the-Envelope

THE WELFARE LOSS FROM A SUBSIDY

Insured customers compare benefits of services with the out-of-pocket costs incurred directly (where true costs are the total of out-of-pocket costs plus charges covered by insurance). By not considering total cost, the decision calculus results in overuse of resources (that is to say, using more than the socially desirable amount). This may be the single most important factor in the escalation of total medical care expenditures.

Key Concept 9
Market Failure

The economics of an insurance subsidy can be shown graphically. Initial demand for medical care is shown by the demand curve D_0E. Access to insurance (and the subsidy it provides) causes the demand curve to become more inelastic (D_1E). Without insurance consumer surplus is P_0AD_0. Since insurance does not change the value of medical care to the individual, only its price, consumer surplus with insurance is evaluated using D_0E and will be P_2D_0C. Likewise, producer surplus increases with insurance from P_0AS to P_1BS.

Economic Concept	Before Insurance	After Insurance
Consumer surplus	P_0AD_0	P_2CD_0
Producer surplus	P_0AS	P_1BS
Cost of insurance	—	P_1BCP_2
Net gain to society	D_0AS	$D_0AS - ABC$
Deadweight loss	—	ABC

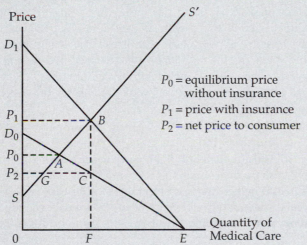

P_0 = equilibrium price without insurance
P_1 = price with insurance
P_2 = net price to consumer

Note the overlap of surpluses with insurance, the area D_0AGP_2. However, the cost of the insurance P_1BCP_2 erases the overlap and part of both consumer surplus (ACG) and producer surplus (P_1BAD_0). Is society better off with the subsidy? Actually, the insurance subsidy reduces surplus by ABC. Instead of D_0AS, surplus is now $D_0AS - ABC$.

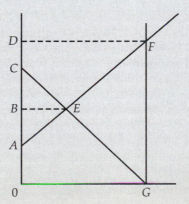

If the government provides insurance that covers 100 percent of the cost of medical care with no coinsurance requirement, the demand curve for medical care becomes perfectly inelastic. This is shown in the diagram above where the new demand curve is now *FG* (instead of *CG*). The price of medical care becomes 0*D* and the quantity demanded becomes 0*G*. Total cost to the taxpayers is 0*DFG*, consumer surplus 0*CG*, and producer surplus *ADF*. Expenditures exceed the combined surplus by *FEG − ACE*, representing a net welfare loss to society when *FEG* is greater than *ACE* and a net gain if the opposite is true.

In both the case of insurance with copayments and taxpayer-financed insurance with no copayments, the loss to society is caused by the consumption of medical care where the cost of care to society exceeds the net benefit to the patient.

Advocates of a private-sector solution contend that public-sector solutions are largely responsible for pricing many of the working poor out of the insurance market completely. Their response focuses on reducing the cost of private insurance to make it more affordable. Establishing high-risk insurance pools is one measure typically considered as a means of providing insurance for those with preexisting medical conditions. Although not a complete solution, it would offer coverage to 20 percent of the chronically uninsured and go a long way in providing access to this medically deserving group.

Small employers find themselves at a distinct disadvantage in the purchase of private insurance for their workers. Small size means two things: they lack the bargaining power to negotiate favorable rates with large insurers, and they have too few employees to adequately share the risk of catastrophic illness. The goal of increasing the bargaining power and spreading the risk can be accomplished by allowing firms to combine into purchasing cooperatives. Coupled with the elimination of state insurance mandates for small firms, these cooperatives would likely bring the cost of insurance down by 15 to 20 percent.

Proponents of more government involvement and proponents of the more pluralistic approach agree on very little. How big is the problem? What approach should be taken to solve it? And although little if any agreement can be found on these two issues, the two sides do share the common goal of improving access for those who are currently uninsured. Whether this is accomplished within the framework of the current private insurance system or whether the United States will go the route of the rest of the world and allow more government involvement is yet to be determined.

Questions and Problems

1. In what way is insuring for a medical loss different from insuring for any other loss?

2. Define the following concepts. How important are they in determining the efficient functioning of medical markets?

    a. moral hazard

    b. adverse selection

    c. asymmetric information

    d. third-party payer

    e. cream skimming

3. What are the major reasons that health insurance policies have deductibles and coinsurance features? Are they really necessary?

4. What are the four types of medical insurance? Briefly describe the coverage available with each one.

5. Should insurers be allowed to refuse health insurance policies to individuals who are genetically predisposed to certain diseases? To those whose lifestyles place them in high-risk categories for certain diseases? Support your answers.

6. One of the major issues driving the health care reform debate is the number of uninsured Americans and their limited access to medical care. Describe the typical person in the United States without insurance. Does lack of insurance mean the uninsured have no access to medical care?

7. What is asymmetric information? How does it present a problem to medical providers and health insurers?

8. Why do firms self-insure?

9. Does the availability of free health care improve health status? Explain.

10. What is the purpose of deductibles and coinsurance? To what problem are insurers responding?

References

Kenneth J. Arrow, "Uncertainty and the Welfare Economics of Medical Care," *American Economic Review 53*(5), December 1963, 941–973.

Robert L. Bennefield, "Dynamics of Economic Well-Being: Health Insurance 1993 to 1995, Who Loses Coverage and for How Long?" U.S. Census Bureau, *Current Population Reports*, P70–64, August 1998, 1–6.

Mark L. Berk and Alan C. Monheit, "The Concentration of Health Care Expenditures, Revisited," *Health Affairs 20*(2), March/April 2001, 9–18.

Mark L. Berk and Claudia L. Schur, "Access to Care: How Much Difference Does Medicaid Make?" *Health Affairs 17*(1), January/February 1998, 169–180.

Mark L. Berk, Claudia L. Schur, and Joel C. Cantor, "Ability to Obtain Health Care: Recent Estimates from the Robert Wood Johnson Foundation National Access to Care Survey," *Health Affairs 14*(3), Fall 1995, 139–146.

John Billings, Geoffrey M. Anderson, and Laurie S. Newman, "Recent Findings on Preventable Hospitalizations," *Health Affairs 15*(3), Fall 1996, 239–249.

A. B. Bindman, K. Grumbach, D. Osmond, et al., "Preventable Hospitalizations and Access to Care," *Journal of the American Medical Association 274*, 1995, 305–311.

Robert H. Brook, "Health, Health Insurance, and the Uninsured," *Journal of the American Medical Association 265*(22), June 12, 1991, 2998–3002.

M. E. Brown, A. B. Bindman, and N. Lurie, "Monitoring the Consequences of Uninsurance: A Review of Methodologies," *Medical Care Research and Review 55*, 1998, 177–210.

M. Kate Bundorf and Mark V. Pauly, "Is Health Insurance Affordable for the Uninsured?" NBER Working Paper No. 9281, Cambridge, MA: National Bureau of Economic Research, October 2002.

H. R. Burstin, K. Swartz, A. C. O'Neil, E. J. Orav, and T. A. Brennan, "The Effect of Change of Health Insurance on Access to Care," *Inquiry 35*(4), 1998, 389–397.

Centers for Disease Control, "Oral Health 2000: Facts and Figures," available at **http://www.cdc.gov/OralHealth/factsheets/sgr2000-fs1.htm**, May 2000.

Congressional Budget Office, "How Many People Lack Health Insurance and for How Long?" A CBO Paper, Washington, DC: Congress of the United States, May 2003.

Craig Copeland, "Characteristics of the Nonelderly with Selected Sources of Health Insurance and Lengths of Uninsured Spells," *EBRI Issue Brief* No. 198, June 1998.

Janet Currie and Jonathan Gruber, "Saving Babies: The Efficacy and Cost of Recent Expansions of Medicaid Eligibility for Pregnant Women," *Journal of Political Economy 104*(6), December 1996, 1263–1296.

P. Franks, C. M. Clancy, and M. R. Gold, "Health Insurance and Mortality: Evidence from a National Cohort," *Journal of the American Medical Association 270*, 1993, 737–741.

Milton Friedman and Leonard J. Savage, "The Utility Analysis of Choices Involving Risk," *Journal of Political Economy 56*(4), August 1948, 279–304.

Victor R. Fuchs, "National Health Insurance Revisited," *Health Affairs 10*(4), Winter 1991, 7–17.

Dan Goodgame, "This May Hurt a Bit," *Time 143*(20), May 16, 1994, 50.

Jonathan Gruber and Larry Levitt, "Tax Subsidies for Health Insurance: Costs and Benefits," *Health Affairs 19*(1), January/February 2000, 72–85.

Jack Hadley, Earl P. Steinberg, and Judith Feder, "Comparison of Uninsured and Privately Insured Hospital Patients: Conditions on Admission, Resource Use, and Outcome," *Journal of the American Medical Association 265*(3), January 16, 1991, 374–379.

Health Insurance Association of America, *Long-Term Care Insurance in 2000-2001*, Washington, DC: HIAA, January 2003.

———, *Source Book of Health Insurance Data 1996*, Washington, DC: HIAA, 1997.

W. David Helms, Anne K. Gauthier, and Daniel M. Campion, "Mending the Flaws in the Small-Group Market," *Health Affairs 11*(2), Summer 1992, 7–27.

John Holahan and Johnny Kim, "Why Does the Number of Uninsured Americans Continue to Grow?" *Health Affairs 19*(4), July/August 2000, 188–196.

———— and Mary Beth Pohl, "Changes in Insurance Coverage: 1994–2000 and Beyond," *Health Affairs—Web Exclusive*, April 3, 2002, W162–171.

Richard Kronik and Todd Gilmer, "Explaining the Decline in Health Insurance Coverage, 1979–1995," *Health Affairs 18*(2), March/April 1999, 30–47.

Katharine Levit et al. "National Health Expenditures, 1993," *Health Care Financing Review 16*(1), Fall 1994, 247–281.

Willard G. Manning, Joseph P. Newhouse, Naihua Duan, Emmett B. Keeler, Arleen Leibowitz, and M. Susan Marquis, "Health Insurance and the Demand for Medical Care: Evidence from a Randomized Experiment," *American Economic Review 77*(3), June 1987, 251–277.

Robert J. Mills, "Health Insurance Coverage: 2001," U.S. Census Bureau, *Current Population Reports*, P60–220, September 2002, 1–23.

National Center for Policy Analysis (NCPA), "Are the Uninsured Freeloaders?" *Brief Analysis* No. 120, August 10, 1994.

Joseph Newhouse, *Free for All? Lessons from the RAND Health Insurance Experiment*, Santa Monica, CA: RAND Corporation, 1993.

Mark V. Pauly, "Is Cream Skimming a Problem for the Competitive Medical Market?" *Journal of Health Economics 3*(1), April 1984, 87–95.

————, "The Economics of Moral Hazard: Comment," *American Economic Review 58*(2), June 1968, 531–538.

————, "Taxation, Health Insurance, and Market Failure in the Medical Economy," *Journal of Economic Literature 24*(2), June 1986, 629–675.

Thomas Rice, *The Economics of Health Reconsidered*, Chicago, IL: Health Administration Press, 1998.

George Stigler, "The Economics of Information," *Journal of Political Economy 69*(3), June 1961.

Katherine Swartz, John Marcotte, and Timothy D. McBride, "Personal Characteristics and Spells without Health Insurance, *Inquiry 30*(1), Spring 1993a, 64–76.

————, "Spells without Health Insurance: The Distribution of Durations when Left-Censored Spells Are Included," *Inquiry 30*(1), Spring 1993b, 77–83.

Melissa A. Thomasson, "The Importance of Group Coverage: How Tax Policy Shaped U.S. Health Insurance," NBER Working Paper 7543, Cambridge, MA: National Bureau of Economic Research, February 2000.

Roger Thompson, "Going, Going, . . . Gone?" *Nation's Business 81*(7), July 1993, 24.

U.S. Chamber of Commerce, *2000 Employee Benefits Study*, Washington, D.C.: U.S. Chamber of Commerce, 2000.

J. S. Weissman, R. Stern, S. L. Fielding, and A. M. Epstein, "Delayed Access to Health Care: Risk Factors, Reasons, and Consequences," *Annals of Internal Medicine* 114, 1991, 325–331.

S. H. Zuvekas and R. M. Weinick, "Changes in Access to Care, 1977–1996: The Role of Health Insurance," *Health Services Research 34*(1 Pt 2), 1999, 271–279.

Chapter 7

Managed Care

As recently as 1975, almost the entire insured population in the United States received medical care services financed under traditional indemnity insurance arrangements. With favorable legislation in place, the decade of the 1980s witnessed major growth in managed care along with other related changes in medical care financing and delivery. These changes were, in part, a response to the high and rising cost of medical care and the increase in the number of Americans receiving their health insurance coverage from self-insured group plans.

Managed care is a term used to describe any number of contractual arrangements that integrate the financing and delivery of medical care. Purchasers (usually employers) contract with a select group of providers to deliver a specific package of medical benefits at a predetermined price. The wide variety of financing and delivery arrangements in the market today makes it difficult to classify managed care organizations precisely, thus complicating the attempts to evaluate the efficiency and effectiveness of managed care.

The initial popularity of managed care was due to the perception that it could provide significant cost savings over the more traditional fee-for-service delivery mechanism. Between 1984 and 1991 the average health insurance premium per employee increased 119 percent. At the same time, the overall increase in the price level, as measured by the change in the consumer price index, was 31 percent. With insurance premiums outpacing inflation by almost four to one, the pressure to control costs mounted accordingly.

The traditional managed care arrangement has been the health maintenance organization (HMO). Table 7.1 shows that there were only 37 HMOs nationwide in 1970 with 3 million enrollees. By 2002, enrollment in the nation's 500 HMOs was more than 76 million.

Numerous differences mark the way managed care is organized—how physicians are paid, how financial risk is shared, whether physicians see only managed care patients, or whether they also see fee-for-service patients. This chapter will focus on the historical development of managed care and its emergence as an important element of the health care delivery system in the United States and worldwide.

We begin our discussion with a brief history of the emergence of managed care as an alternative to traditional fee-for-service delivery, and then turn to the basic categories of managed care. We will also look at the cost-saving features of managed care and the practical evidence that this form of delivery actually saves money. Finally, the future of managed care will be discussed.

History of Managed Care

Although the concept of the prepaid medical plan can be traced back to the nineteenth century, the first health plans with the organizational structure of today's health maintenance organization were formed in the 1920s (Friedman, 1996). Industrialist Henry J. Kaiser organized one of the first managed care plans. Kaiser-Permanente, the largest

Table 7.1	Health Maintenance Organizations, 1970–2002	

Year	Number	Enrollment (in millions)
1970	37	3.0
1975	174	6.0
1980	235	9.1
1985[a]	478	21.0
1990	572	33.0
1995	562	50.9
1996	630	59.1
1997	652	66.8
1998	651	76.6
1999	643	81.3
2000	568	80.9
2001	541	79.5
2002	500	76.1

Source: *Health United States, 2003: With Chartbook on Trends in the Health of Americans*, 2003.

[a]Increases due in part to changes in reporting methods.

http://

Kaiser-Permanente is the largest not-for-profit health maintenance organization in the country with 8.1 million members. Visit its Web site at **http://www.kaiserpermanente. org/.**
Group Health Cooperative of Puget Sound, the nation's sixth largest not-for-profit HMO, serves over 700,000 members in the northwestern United States. Their Web address is **http://www.ghc.org/.**

managed care organization in the country today, was created to provide medical care in geographically isolated areas of northern California. Physicians working on a fixed salary provided medical care for employees of Kaiser's steel mill and shipyards, a group of relatively high-risk workers, in Kaiser-owned clinics and hospitals. The idea of using HMOs for cost containment purposes was not an issue at the time and would not become one until the 1970s.

When Kaiser opened the plan to other patient groups in 1947, the HMO concept was still untested in the greater community. Today, Kaiser-Permanente is the nation's largest not-for-profit HMO, serving 8.1 million members in nine states and the District of Columbia. The pioneering efforts of Kaiser and others on the West Coast served as a model for prepaid medical care.

Many physicians were opposed to the concept of prepaid medical care, calling it "contract medicine," and they organized to ban the practice entirely. Their efforts were successful in slowing the growth of managed care, keeping the number of HMOs nationally to fewer than 40 throughout the 1960s (Gruber, Shadle, and Polich, 1988). By 1970 only 37 HMOs were operating with a combined enrollment of 3 million. As recently as 1980 fewer than 10 million Americans were enrolled in managed care plans, less than 5 percent of the population.

Passage of Medicare and Medicaid in 1965 led to more direct federal involvement in the provision of medical care and a growing political concern for escalating costs. Research by InterStudy proposed a health maintenance strategy based on the health maintenance organization as an alternative to traditional fee-for-service medicine.[1] Despite strong opposition from provider groups including the American Medical Association, the Nixon administration embraced the concept of the **prepaid group practice** to control medical care costs.

Working with Congressional leaders, primarily from the Democratic party, Richard Nixon was successful in passing legislation that defined the health maintenance

prepaid group practice
An arrangement through which a group contracts with a number of providers who agree to provide medical services to members of the group for a fixed, capitated payment.

1 InterStudy is a research and policy institute headed by Paul M. Ellwood. For years, Ellwood invited a group of individuals interested in health policy to his Jackson Hole, Wyoming, retreat to discuss medical care reform. Out of this gathering, details of Alain Enthoven's proposal for managed competition emerged. Collectively, the group is referred to as the Jackson Hole group.

organization, including a list of covered benefits, pricing and enrollment practices, physician organization, and requirements regarding financial risk. The Health Maintenance Organization Act of 1973 provided over $364 million in subsidies to nonprofit groups to establish HMOs. Even with this funding, the government fell far short of its goal of establishing 1,700 HMOs and enrolling 40 million participants by 1976. The episode sent a clear message to the medical industry: The federal government was concerned with the high cost of medical care and was willing to intervene through the legislative process. But the real lesson was that government action alone (short of overt coercion through mandatory participation) is not sufficient to push people into prepaid health plans. That task was not accomplished until corporate America began its move to managed care as a cost-control measure in the late 1980s. It took another decade of rising costs to emphasize the role of cost-effective behavior and spur the development and expansion of managed care arrangements through the private sector.

Types of Managed Care Plans

Managed care has many of the aspects of the familiar all-you-can-eat buffet—a single price, paid in advance, good for everything on the menu. Just as the buffet must price its product based on the expected behavior of would-be diners, managed care must be sure that its pricing is sufficient to cover all the medical needs of its enrollees. One way the buffet can guarantee the "right" price is by offering plenty of the low-cost basics and limiting the availability of expensive entrees. Similarly, a successful pricing strategy in managed care must provide easy access to low-cost primary and preventive care as a way to discourage the use of expensive services including specialty care and hospitalization.

Enlisting the services of a buffet supervisor (a gatekeeper) to steer diners to the cheaper alternatives and limit access to expensive entrees may not be harmful to most consumers. In the case of the buffet, a diet of soup and salad may be healthier than red meat and potatoes in the long run. But those diners accustomed to meat and potatoes will find the transition painful. And those with special dietary needs may actually end up worse off if their choices are limited.

Most diners understand the rules of the all-you-can-eat buffet. They do not pay $6.95 at the local eatery expecting steak and lobster. But expectations are much different in the U.S. medical care sector. Therein lies the challenge to managed care. Americans have developed a taste for unlimited access to expensive treatments. Traditional fee-for-service medicine financed through indemnity insurance is like dining with a group of coworkers on a business trip. Instead of ordering from the menu and paying separately, one member of the group agrees to pay the bill using her expense account. In other words, the boss is now paying for the meal and individual accountability is virtually nonexistent. In this situation, the incentive structure encourages overeating. We tend to be more extravagant when someone else pays the bill. In other words, we seldom practice economizing behavior when someone else will benefit from our prudent actions.

Typical managed care arrangements include health maintenance organizations (HMOs), preferred provider organizations (PPOs), **point-of-service (POS)** plans, and managed indemnity plans. Traditional managed care restricts patient choice and controls utilization of medical services more closely than managed indemnity plans. Some plans, including closed-panel HMOs, pay only for care received through an established network of providers. Others, including most PPOs and POS plans, offer options for enrollees to obtain medical care outside the established network (although at higher out-of-pocket costs to enrollees).

Although precise definitions are difficult, all managed care plans are designed to limit the high levels of utilization frequently found in traditional indemnity insurance

http://

The American Association of Health Plans (AAHP) represents more than 1,000 HMOs and other network based plans, serving over 100 million Americans nationwide. Their Web site is found at **http://www.aahp.org/**.

 Key Concept 4
Self-Interest

 Key Concept 7
Competition

 Key Concept 4
Self-Interest

point-of-service plan (POS)
A hybrid managed care plan that combines the features of a pre-paid plan and a fee-for-service plan. Enrollees use network physicians with minimal out-of-pocket expense and may choose to go out of the network by paying a higher coinsurance rate.

plans. In the strictest sense of the term, managed care refers to any health plan that directs its enrollees to a panel of providers who have agreed to follow established guidelines to control utilization and cost. In the broadest sense of the term, it attempts to monitor and direct the use of health services, thereby reducing health care costs. In either case, the goal is to manage utilization to varying degrees by controlling both the patient and provider sides of the market.

Health Maintenance Organizations (HMOs)

The five recognized types of HMOs are: (1) group model, (2) staff model, (3) network model, (4) Independent Practice Association (IPA), and (5) direct contract.[2] In the **group-model HMO,** the health benefit intermediary (usually a private-sector corporation) contracts with a large multispecialty group practice to provide medical care to a defined patient population (usually the employees of the corporation). In the staff-model HMO, physicians are employees of the HMO. Their incomes are usually paid in the form of a fixed salary but may include supplemental payments based on some measure of performance. The **network-model HMO** utilizes contracts with several different providers, including physicians' practices and hospitals, in order to make a full range of medical services available to its enrollees.

The **Independent Practice Association (IPA)** contracts with individual physicians or small group practices to provide care to enrolled members. Among all variants of the managed care model, the IPA has been the fastest growing over the past decade. Payment for treating enrolled members is based on a negotiated fee-for-service schedule or a capitated payment (a fixed amount paid in advance). IPA plans select providers for various reasons including practice location, practice style, quality of care, and willingness to comply with established **practice guidelines.** Many physicians participating in IPAs contract with one or more managed care plans and, at the same time, maintain their own private practice where they treat non-HMO patients on a fee-for-service basis. Finally, the **direct contract model HMO** establishes contractual relationships with individual physicians to provide care for a specific group of patients.

Preferred Provider Organizations (PPOs)

The preferred provider organization (PPO) is emerging as one of the more popular types of managed care plans. The PPO is a health care organization that serves as intermediary or broker between the purchaser of medical care and the provider. The PPO establishes a network of providers (physicians, hospitals, dentists, pharmacies, rehabilitative services, home health care, etc.) who agree to provide medical services to a specific group of enrollees at discounted rates. In most cases, providers must agree to a set of utilization controls (that is, practice guidelines) in order to be included on the preferred list. Despite the lower fees and utilization controls, participating providers view the arrangement as a means of securing a steady volume of patients. Even though enrollees are free to use any provider, incentives and disincentives are used to encourage them to choose from the preferred list. Enrollees find their out-of-pocket costs higher (in the form of higher deductibles and copayments) when they receive care from providers who are not on the preferred list.

The typical arrangement provides 5 to 30 percent discounts from normal charges for physicians' services and 10 to 15 percent discounts on hospital services. The patient is usually required to make a modest copayment when using preferred physicians. When using nonpreferred physicians, however, the patient is subject to a deductible and a 20 to 40 percent coinsurance payment. Often a small copayment is required when using a preferred hospital and a much larger one when not.

The PPO typically lacks the strict cost control features of the closed-panel HMO. With no risk sharing, providers have no direct incentives to control utilization in the

group-model HMO
A group of physicians, often a large multispecialty group practice, that agrees to provide medical care to a defined patient group (usually the employees of the corporation) in return for a fixed per capita fee or for discounted fees. The physicians often provide medical care to several different groups concurrently.

network-model HMO
A managed care organization that contracts with several different providers, including physicians' practices and hospitals, in order to make a full range of medical services available to its enrollees.

Independent Practice Association (IPA)
An organized group of health care providers that offers medical services to a specified group of enrollees of a health plan. Providers typically maintain their private practices and at the same time agree to the practice guidelines established by the health plan.

practice guideline
A specific statement about the appropriate course of treatment that should be taken for patients with given medical conditions.

direct contract model HMO
A managed care organization that establishes contractual relationships with individual physicians to provide care for a specific group of patients.

---

2 Those interested in a more comprehensive discussion of the types of HMOs are directed to Kongstvedt (1997) and Glied (1999).

ISSUES IN MEDICAL CARE DELIVERY

VIVAHEALTH: MARKETING HMOS TO ETHNIC COMMUNITIES

It is a common practice for the makers of consumer products to tailor their marketing efforts to specific demographic and ethnic groups. Virginia Slims cigarettes' marketing to women and Colt 45 Malt Liquor's efforts in the African-American community are just two examples that come to mind. Now it seems that the health care industry is using the same approach to market its services directly to distinct groups in the various ethnic communities.

The Latino community has been the target of an all-out effort by two Southern California HMOs. It took the founders of VivaHealth seven years to convince providers, investors, and regulators that the concept of medical care tailored for a particular ethnic group was viable. Beginning its marketing campaign in May 1994, VivaHealth became one of the first HMOs nationwide to exclusively target the Latino community.

VivaHealth has assembled a network of providers, many of whom are Latino and almost all are Spanish-speaking. VivaHealth is relying on its physicians' experience in treating members of the Latino community. An understanding of the culture and an ability to communicate are seen as major marketing advantages.

Another California HMO, FHP Health Care, has established a network of providers serving ethnic communities in East Los Angeles, including Vietnamese, Korean, Cambodian, and Chinese. Ethnic marketing is rapidly becoming a way to distinguish among providers in a market that is becoming increasingly competitive. Increased competition among providers is forcing everyone to consider more cost-effective ways of delivering medical care.

Ethnic patients present problems for providers who do not understand the culture or the language. Patients cannot follow instructions they do not understand; providers tend to overtreat when they do not understand what the patient is trying to tell them.

Understanding the language is not the only advantage offered by these niche players. An appreciation for the unique culture is also important. Therefore, providers in other states with a large foreign-born population—including Colorado, New Mexico, Texas, and Florida—are getting into the act.

With more than 8 percent of the U.S. population foreign-born, these ethnic communities are becoming an important niche market in the medical industry. Many of these ethnic groups, including Latinos, Vietnamese, Cambodian, Korean, and Chinese, are good health risks. They are younger, healthier, and more stable than the general population. By setting uniform premiums according to ethnic group, the HMOs will be able to charge about 10 percent less than the lowest premiums currently in the market. The lesson is simple: Specialization leads to cost savings through a more efficient allocation of resources. But success in the marketplace will depend on the continued ability to use this blended risk rating (experience rating within a defined ethnic community) which in turn will depend on what kind of health care reform emerges from Congress.

Source: Mary Chris Jaklevic, "Programs, Ad Campaigns Reach Out to Members of Ethnic Communities," *Modern Healthcare*, August 1, 1994, 32; and Tim W. Ferguson, "An Ethnic-Flavored HMO vs. Clinton's Cookie-Cutter," *The Wall Street Journal*, February 8, 1994, A17.

Key Concept 7
Efficiency

Key Concept 8
Market Failure

short run. The key to controlling costs is not the discounts offered by providers, but the selection of cost-conscious providers and the threat of dropping any physician who refuses to follow the practice guidelines established by the plan.

Point-of-Service (POS) Plans

The most recent ingredient in the managed care alphabet soup is the point-of-service (POS) plan. The POS plan is a mixed-model health plan. It incorporates many of the cost-control features of HMOs along with the provider-choice features of PPOs. Enrollees are given the option of choosing among various types of plans: HMO, PPO, or managed indemnity. The choice of plan, however, does not have to be made at the time of enrollment. It is made each time the enrollee seeks medical treatment—at the point of service. POS enrollees choose a primary care "gatekeeper" to coordinate all network-based care. Offering incentives in the form of better benefits and lower copayments encourages use of the network providers.

Hybrid Varieties

The competitive response to the high cost of medical care has resulted in a blurring of the distinctions among the different types of medical care arrangements. Traditional indemnity insurance plans have taken on the characteristics of managed care plans, including features intended to limit physician autonomy and patient choice. Health maintenance organizations have added out-of-plan options for patients who want to consult providers who are not on the **closed panel**, or preferred list. As time passes, it is becoming more and more difficult to distinguish among the various types of arrangements. Indemnity insurance plans are incorporating utilization management methods to control costs, and HMOs are offering out-of-plan options to increase flexibility.

Network-based managed care (including HMOs, PPOs, and POS plans) is beginning to dominate health care delivery in the United States. Managed care networks are similar to group model HMOs but with one major difference. Instead of contracting with one multispecialty group practice, the network plan contracts with several. Therein lies the primary challenge to network-based care. The very success of the network depends on the ability to control costs. Without rigorous policies to control utilization, including provider risk sharing, **utilization review**, and limiting access to nonpreferred providers, such organizations will have a difficult time surviving.

Most private sector employees who have group health insurance coverage are enrolled in some type of managed care plan. Table 7.2 provides dramatic evidence of the popularity of managed care for private-sector employees. In 1979, over 98 percent of all group insurance policies were written under traditional indemnity insurance arrangements with few restrictions on choice of provider or service option. As medical care costs escalated in the 1980s, employers sought to reduce costs by moving away from traditional fee-for-service care to managed care. William M. Mercer, Inc., estimated that by 2002, only 6 percent of the private sector was covered by traditional indemnity plans. Employees seem to be moving into the less restrictive managed care

closed panel
A designated network of providers that serve the recipients of a health care plan. Patients are not allowed to choose a provider outside the network.

utilization review
Evaluating the appropriateness and efficiency of prescribed medical services and procedures, including hospital admissions, lengths of stay, and discharge procedures. Utilization review may be conducted concurrently or retrospectively.

Table 7.2	Health Care Coverage for Private Employees with Group Insurance Percentages by Type of Plan							
Type of Plan	**1979**	**1988**	**1990**	**1993**	**1995**	**1998**	**2001**	**2002**
Traditional Indemnity	98	71	62	48	29	13	6	6
Managed Care	2	29	38	52	71	87	94	94
HMO	2	18	20	19	27	32	35	31
PPO	*	11	13	27	29	36	44	49
POS	*	*	5	7	15	19	15	14

Source: John K. Iglehart, "The American Health Care System: Managed Care," *New England Journal of Medicine 327*(10), September 3, 1992, Table 1; and Blaine Bos, "National Survey of Employer-Sponsored Plans—2002," Mercer Human Resource Consulting, 2002.

*No data available.

option, the PPO. Since 1993 the percentage of employees enrolled in PPOs has risen from 27 percent to 49 percent. After steady growth throughout the past decade, HMO enrollment dropped in 2002 to 31 percent of all covered employees. POS membership has fallen from 1998 levels to 14 percent. The effect of managed care becomes even more evident by the fact that over 85 percent of all private-practice physicians and virtually all community hospitals belong to at least one managed care network.

The Theory of Managed Care Cost Saving

The theoretical underpinnings of managed care suggest that medical care costs and spending may be affected by changing patient utilization, physicians' practice styles, and the introduction of new technology. Managed care arrangements are similar to traditional indemnity health insurance in many ways. A premium is charged to cover a prescribed set of medical benefits. Both use demand-side cost-sharing provisions, such as deductibles and coinsurance, to reduce moral hazard. In addition, managed care utilizes a combination of provider-side provisions to control moral hazard and the spending associated with it. These provider-side provisions include (1) selection of providers, (2) cost-sharing arrangements, and (3) practice guidelines and utilization review.

Key Concept 9
Market Failure

Selection of Providers

To varying degrees, managed care limits the patient's choice of provider for a given medical service. The limits include the use of gatekeepers, closed panels, and preferred providers. A gatekeeper is a physician responsible for providing all primary medical care and coordinating access to high-cost hospital and specialty care. Patients who wish to see a specialist must first get a referral from their primary care gatekeeper. A closed panel further limits a patient's choice of physician to a list of participating providers. To be part of a panel, physicians must agree to a set of standards established by the sponsoring organization. Networks that contract with **"any willing provider"** ensure enrollees a wide choice of physicians, but exclusive networks result in better cost controls. The criteria for inclusion vary depending on the selectivity of the plan. At minimum, providers are usually board certified, professionally accredited, and meet medical liability standards. More selective networks consider practice styles and use only those providers who meet established goals for cost-effective use of resources. The preferred provider organization allows the patient to choose a provider who is not a part of the panel. Patients who use physicians who are not part of the panel usually pay higher coinsurance rates, further discouraging off-panel utilization.

any willing provider
A situation in which a managed care organization allows any medical provider to become part of the network of providers for the covered group. Often, state law will require this practice.

Cost-Sharing Arrangements

The method of reimbursement is an important mechanism in controlling costs. Managed care utilizes various reimbursement schemes with the common goal of shifting some of the financial risk to providers. Shifting risk discourages overutilization of services, primarily the use of expensive technology, prescription drugs, referrals to specialists, and in-patient hospital procedures.

Many HMOs and some PPOs contract with primary care physicians using prospective payment or capitation—lump-sum payments per enrollee determined in advance. Prepayment shifts the financial risk to the providers. Instead of being paid on a per-service basis, primary care physicians receive a fixed payment determined in advance to provide all the medically necessary primary care for a specific group of patients. Some managed care plans withhold a percentage of the authorized payment to ensure that providers control utilization and cost.[3] Primary care physicians serve as gatekeepers and are subject to strict budgets for hospital services, specialty referrals, and prescription drugs for their covered patients. Physicians who provide care within the predetermined

Key Concept 4
Self-Interest

---

3 In the past these withholds have been as high as 50 percent of the capitated payment. Recently, more aggressive regulations have brought the amount of capitated payment at risk to more manageable levels.

budgets receive bonuses. Those who do not are penalized by forfeiting part or all of their withholdings to the plan. This risk-sharing arrangement provides strong incentives to physicians to control utilization.

Figure 7.1 provides a schematic depiction of the allocation of premiums for a typical managed care arrangement. In this example, the primary care physicians are paid on a capitated basis and serve as gatekeepers to more advanced services. Enrollees (most likely employees working at the same firm) are charged a premium of $100 per member per month (PMPM) for a defined package of medical benefits. The HMO uses $13 of the PMPM payment to cover operating expenses, administrative overhead, and profit. The remainder goes into four separate categories: primary care, pharmaceuticals, specialty care, and hospital care. The general practitioner serving as gatekeeper receives a capitated payment of $14 PMPM for each enrollee who designates him or her as their primary care physician. Some plans withhold a percentage

---

Policy Issue

Do risk-sharing contracts affect the quality of care provided? What percentage of a physician's income should be at risk?

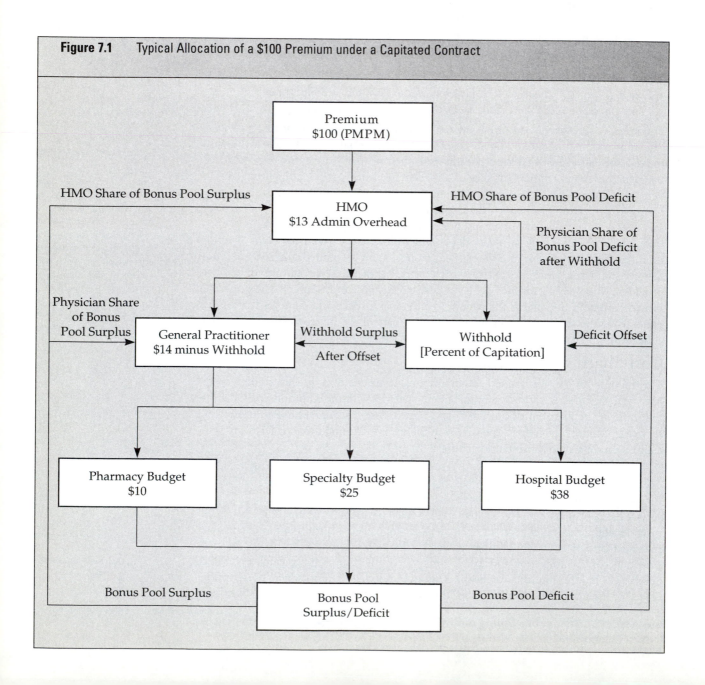

Figure 7.1   Typical Allocation of a $100 Premium under a Capitated Contract

of this capitated payment as insurance against expense overruns in the other three budgetary categories. The pharmacy budget receives $10 PMPM, the specialty budget receives $25 PMPM, and the hospital budget receives $38 PMPM.[4] A bonus pool is created with the surpluses or deficits in each expense category. The providers and HMO share surpluses and deficits according to a specified formula, often on a 50/50 basis. Bonus pool deficits are covered by the physician's withholding account. Any surplus in the withholding account is paid to the physician directly. If the physician's share of the bonus pool deficit is greater than the funds in the physician's withholding account, he or she is responsible for reimbursing the HMO the difference. Recent changes in the bonus arrangement have added positive inducements for physicians to modify their practice patterns. These inducements include a target percentage of the enrolled children receiving their inoculations in a timely manner, a target percentage of enrolled women receiving appropriately timed cancer screenings, and specific scores on patient satisfaction surveys. Mixed bonus arrangements are much more popular than those based solely on cost considerations.

Providers paid according to the traditional fee-for-service arrangement are more likely to recommend and perform services that are reimbursed. When given an option, providers are more likely to perform services that are reimbursed more generously relative to their resource cost. Because an insured patient's share of the total cost of care is relatively small, some services are provided that have little marginal value.

> **Policy Issue**
>
> When patients are fully insured, the therapeutic benefit of some covered services may be relatively small compared to the cost.

In contrast, the managed care organization structures the financial arrangements to shift some of the financial risk onto physicians. Providers are given incentives to practice in a more cost-effective manner. When a cheaper care option exists, providers are rewarded for choosing it. Such an arrangement changes the incentive structure completely. Instead of encouraging the provision of too many services, as is the case with fee-for-service payment, this type of risk sharing arrangement can, if not properly monitored, create pressures to do just the opposite—provide too few services.

Practice Guidelines and Utilization Review

Selection of providers based on conservative practice patterns and the sharing of financial risk is often insufficient to control medical care expenditures. Most medical plans find it necessary to establish practice guidelines to directly control clinical decisions. Practice guidelines are clinical rules developed to encourage providers to evaluate the marginal benefit of prescribed care more carefully. Through "evidence-based" medicine—the systematic monitoring and evaluation of treatment methods—managed care plans try to determine the relative efficacy of treatment options and in turn their cost effectiveness. Managed care is quick to adopt cost-saving innovations and slow to adopt those that increase costs (Baker and Phibbs, 2000).

More than 90 percent of all health plans, whether indemnity insurance or managed care, utilize some form of utilization review. The most popular technique for controlling utilization is requiring some type of authorization for the use of hospital services—preadmission review, concurrent review, or retrospective review. In addition, second surgical opinions and **case management** are used to control costs associated with surgeries.

case management
A method of coordinating the provision of medical care for patients with specific high-cost diagnoses such as cancer and heart disease.

Utilization management focuses primarily on services provided in the hospital sector. Preadmission review establishes the appropriateness of a procedure. Either the admitting physician or the patient must receive approval prior to the hospital admission. Often a maximum length of stay is specified at the same time. Concurrent review utilizes established guidelines to determine whether a hospital stay should be continued. Retrospective review examines the appropriateness of care after it has been completed.

---

4 The numbers used in this example are representative of the typical allocation of a $100 premium. If the premium is higher, $150 for example, the appropriate adjustment would be to multiply each number by 1.5.

Inappropriate care is recognized and providers who deviate from the established standards are identified.

Many managed care plans require second surgical opinions before recommended surgeries are performed. This method of utilization control forces the physician who recommends the surgery to seek the opinion of a second physician before authorization is granted. Another commonly used utilization review technique is case management. In situations where costs and risks are high, case management is used to monitor resource use and thus lower the overall cost of the treatment. A case manager, usually a member of the hospital nursing staff, often coordinates hospital care for costly conditions such as coronary artery bypass surgery and organ transplantation.

Overall, managed care plans use these three mechanisms to varying degrees and with different rates of success. The ability to control moral hazard depends on the combination of features utilized and how strictly they are applied. These mechanisms can also affect the choice of technology by encouraging less technology-intensive practice styles. When patients and providers are required to share in the costs of care, the use of expensive technologies is discouraged (Cutler and Sheiner, 1998).

Evidence of Managed Care Cost Savings

Some evidence suggests that managed care offers employers cost savings over the traditional indemnity option. A survey by William M. Mercer, Inc., estimated the average annual premium for an active employee with traditional indemnity insurance was $5,642 in 2002. All forms of managed care had lower average premiums than traditional indemnity insurance. The typical HMO had an average premium of $4,803, over 17 percent lower. PPO premiums were $5,227, or 8 percent less than indemnity, and POS premiums were $5,219, also 8 percent less than indemnity (Mercer, 2002).

The story is similar when comparing single and family coverage. A survey by the Kaiser Family Foundation (2002) estimated the average annual premium across all plans for a single person to be $3,060, and for a family $7,954. The traditional indemnity insurance premium for a single person was $3,582, and for a family was $8,479. Managed care premiums were lower for families, with HMO premiums estimated at $7,541, PPO premiums at $8,037, and POS premiums at $8,137. Family HMO premiums were 12.4 percent lower than traditional indemnity, PPO premiums 5.5 percent lower, and POS premiums 3.7 percent lower. Premium differences were even more dramatic for single coverage. HMO premiums estimated at $2,764 were 29.6 percent lower than traditional indemnity. PPO premiums at $3,119 were 14.8 percent lower, and POS premiums at $3,175 were 12.8 percent lower.

Empirical evidence supporting managed care's cost savings is complicated by the difficulty in classifying plans according to their cost-saving features. The extensive combination of features utilized by the various plans makes it difficult to control for the differences, making comparisons tricky. By designing benefit packages that appeal to low users, plans can successfully segment their market and avoid high users. Thus, cost differences across plans may be a phenomenon due in part to patient selection.

Empirical research on the effectiveness of managed care has examined several important issues: selection bias, utilization of services, quality of care, and ability to control costs (Glied, 1999). Hellinger (1995) examined the differences between the characteristics of managed care and traditional indemnity insurance enrollees. Overall, the research suggests that managed care plans attract a healthier group of enrollees than indemnity plans do. However, the evidence is mixed. It is difficult to determine how health differences affect utilization and cost because of differences in group characteristics (Newhouse, 1996).

A number of studies have attempted to estimate the difference in medical care utilization between managed care and traditional indemnity insurance. Luft (1981) conducted one of the earliest studies on HMO utilization. Using data from 1959–1975, he concluded

http://

The National Committee for Quality Assurance (NCQA), is an independent, not-for-profit organization that serves as the accrediting agency for the nation's managed care plans. Visit its site at **http://www.ncqa.org/.** NCQA maintains HEDIS 3.0, the standard report card used to rate and compare managed care plans. Links to HEDIS 3.0 may be found at the NCQA Web site.

ISSUES IN MEDICAL CARE DELIVERY

EVALUATING THE EFFECTIVENESS OF HMOS

The use of report cards to measure performance and ensure accountability is not new. Students receive grades from their teachers, employees get performance reviews from their supervisors, and publicly held corporations are evaluated daily by the stock market. One of the most interesting trends in managed care is the movement to direct accountability through the use of a report card.

Evaluating the quality of a health plan is not simple. Not only do health experts disagree on what to measure and how to measure it, but also many question the usefulness of nationwide standardized reporting. A key element of President Clinton's 1994 health care reform proposal called for a federal regulatory committee to specify quality indicators that every health plan would have to measure. The demise of the Clinton plan and the emergence of a Republican majority in the Congress made the creation of a federal agency to regulate quality unlikely in the near future. But this has not stopped private organizations from developing and using their own performance measures.

Notable among efforts to develop quality score cards is the Health Plan Employer Data Information Set (HEDIS) project developed by the National Committee for Quality Assurance (NCQA), an independent organization based in Washington, DC, that accredits health maintenance organizations. HEDIS 3.0 is a 70-item survey measuring health plan quality and performance. The instrument is an attempt to develop a standard reporting format for the nation's managed care organizations.

The elements of the typical report card include quality of service, patient access and satisfaction, membership and utilization of services, financial stability, and descriptive information on the plan's management. The quality of service category measures the health plan's performance in delivering specific services. The categories include (1) preventive services, such as childhood immunizations, cholesterol screening, mammography screening, and cervical cancer screening, (2) prenatal care, including first trimester care, incidence of low-birth-weight babies, and cesarean-section rate, (3) treatment for chronic illness, such as hospital admission rate for asthma patients and diabetic patients receiving yearly eye exams, (4) mental health, and (5) substance abuse.

Membership and utilization data include length of hospital stay, outpatient visits, and enrollment turnover. Financial stability is assessed by such characteristics as performance, liquidity, efficiency, and statutory compliance. Access is measured by the ease of getting appointments.

As the report card movement grows, dozens of HMOs and PPOs nationwide are scrambling to develop and issue their own report cards. Employers are forming alliances to produce regional report cards (most notable among these coalitions are the North Central Texas HEDIS coalition and the New England HEDIS coalition). The HMOs serving the Federal Employees Health Benefits Program regularly survey employee satisfaction. Even national magazines such as *Newsweek* and *Consumer Reports* have contributed with surveys of their own.

Still many problems are yet to be overcome in collecting reliable data and interpreting its results. Survey techniques can be manipulated to improve a plan's scores. The phrasing of a question can skew survey results. "How do you rate your health plan?" gets more critical responses than "How satisfied are you with your health plan?" Phone surveys yield more favorable responses than mail-in surveys. Information collected in the middle of the year tends to be more favorable than end-of-year responses.

As more groups get into the survey business, the need for standard definitions and processes becomes more critical if meaningful comparisons are to emerge. Even while HEDIS is gaining widespread acceptance because of its standardized definitions and reporting standards, many plans are balking at the thought of an independent group administering surveys to members chosen at random.

Source: Norma Harris, "Are Health Plans Making the Grade?" *Business and Health 12*(6), June 1994, 22; Paul J. Kenkel, "Health Plans Face Pressure to Find 'Report Card' Criteria that Will Make the Grade," *Modern Healthcare*, January 10, 1994, 41; and George Anders, "Polling Quirks Give HMOs Healthy Ratings," *The Wall Street Journal*, August 27, 1996, B1.

Policy Issue

Managed care has been shown to be cost saving. But is there a quality trade-off?

http://

The accounting firm PricewaterhouseCoopers maintains an active consulting practice in the managed care industry. Access survey and research information through their Web site at **http://www.pwcglobal.com/**.

that managed care plans had 10 to 40 percent lower costs per enrollee than conventional health plans such as Blue Cross. Although HMO enrollees experienced as many ambulatory visits, they had 25 to 45 percent fewer hospital days per capita. The reason was not shorter hospital stays but fewer admissions.

The most extensive study of the cost-saving potential of health maintenance organizations was the RAND Health Insurance Experiment (see Manning et al., 1984). This study avoided selection bias by randomly assigning individuals to a staff-model HMO or to one of several indemnity plans. The results of this study confirm the cost-savings potential of managed care. The HMO had per capita costs that were 28 percent lower than the indemnity plan without cost sharing. This difference was due largely to 40 percent fewer hospital admissions and shorter hospital stays.

Miller and Luft (1994, 1997) analyzed the most recent literature comparing HMO and fee-for-service costs. Their findings suggest that HMOs provide care comparable to traditional fee-for-service care at costs that are 10 to 15 percent lower. Cost savings are due to shorter hospital stays, fewer tests, and the use of less costly medical procedures. HMOs are able to accomplish these savings in spite of higher rates of physician office visits and more comprehensive benefits packages than fee-for-service plans.

A few studies have attempted to explain the cost-saving features of the newer forms of managed care, especially the network-based PPOs and POS plans. The results of these studies are mixed. Using data from the Medical Outcomes Study of 20,000 adult patients, Greenfield et al. (1992) found no statistically significant difference in four treatment categories between three types of managed care organizations and two fee-for-service arrangements.[5] Murray et al. (1992) examined two small private group practices that treated both HMO and fee-for-service patients diagnosed with hypertension and found that HMO patients had fewer laboratory tests and consequently lower spending. Smith (1997) found that preferred provider plans reduced costs and Hosek, Marquis, and Wells (1990) found that they increased costs.

Overall, the evidence suggests that managed care can reduce health care spending, even after controlling for enrollee characteristics and type of plan. In most cases, these cost savings have been accomplished primarily through the initial reduction in hospital use. A great deal of resource savings was possible at first by simply reducing the rate of hospitalization. As summarized in Glied (1999), the evidence is far from conclusive and the long-run cost-saving potential of managed care is still open to debate.

Evidence of Quality Differences Between Managed Care and Fee-for-Service Care

Another issue explored by the empirical literature is whether there are quality differences between managed care and traditional fee-for-service care. Building on their earlier

---

5 The four treatment categories were the percent of enrollees hospitalized, the use of office visits, the number of prescription drugs utilized, and the number of tests per patient per year.

research, Miller and Luft (1997) summarized the research on the relationship between the type of plan and quality of care. In their review of 15 studies comparing quality of care, they found equal numbers of statistically significant positive and negative effects of managed care on quality. Four studies found significantly better quality in managed care and four found worse. The others found insignificant differences or were inconclusive.

Robinson (2000) reviewed 24 studies, mostly from the 1988–1995 period. The overall patterns identified by these studies suggested lower levels of utilization for managed care plans. In most cases managed care had fewer hospitalizations, shorter hospital stays, and lower levels of discretionary services. Another important difference was the relative emphasis on preventive care as evidenced by more diagnostic screening and testing among managed care plans. Once again Robinson found little conclusive evidence that managed care quality was lower than that found in fee-for-service.

Even though managed care has not decreased the overall effectiveness of care, certain vulnerable subpopulations, including older and sicker patients and those with low incomes, may have less favorable outcomes under managed care (Ware et al., 1996). Robinson (2000) identified five studies comparing quality of care for Medicare enrollees under fee-for-service and managed care. He found some evidence that managed care fared worse than fee-for-service, but most of the studies were inconclusive. Hellinger (1998) reported that managed care enrollees are less satisfied with their health plans than fee-for-service enrollees. Their lower levels of satisfaction resulted from difficulties in accessing specialized care, leaving enrollees with the perception that the overall quality of care was somewhat lower.

The strongest disincentive for providing quality care is for the sickest and most expensive patients. Plans that provide quality care for their sickest patients will attract the sickest patients. At average premiums this strategy leads to losses. If premiums are increased to cover higher costs, the plans lose enrollment.

To summarize, the empirical research does not provide definitive evidence about the overall effect of managed care on quality of care.

Managed Care and Its Public Image

Accustomed to the lack of restrictions in fee-for-service medicine, the American consumer has found it difficult to adjust to the limitations of managed care delivery. Everyone has a favorite HMO story they like to tell. The anecdotes abound. Helen Hunt, in the movie *As Good as It Gets,* treats the viewing audience to a diatribe against a fictitious HMO that has denied care to her asthmatic son. The fee-for-service physician who finally diagnoses and treats him is viewed sympathetically. In light of the lack of evidence suggesting poor quality of care, why does managed care have such a poor public image?

Miller and Luft (1997) offer one possible answer to this question. They note the inevitable time lag for published research to get into print. The result of the delay is that the most recent research findings are not published in a timely manner. As a result, available research results do not relate well to current market conditions.

A second possible explanation relates to the diversity of managed care arrangements. Few studies to date have taken into consideration the newer types of managed care plans and the preponderance of cost-cutting rules and financial incentives affecting providers since the early 1990s. Anecdotal evidence abounds, but lack of empirical research makes generalizations difficult. Additionally, many of the newer managed care organizations are for-profit in nature and thus place a greater emphasis on cost-saving strategies, which eventually may affect managed care quality. To the extent that they exist, these differences will not show up in the research for several years.

Finally, the role of medical providers in influencing public perception about managed care should not be ignored. Managed care is unpopular among health care professionals.

Their clinical autonomy is challenged and their incomes are lower as a result of certain managed care strategies. When physicians complain loudly about the restrictions of managed care, their patients are likely to pick up on the discontent and mimic the criticism. This combination has resulted in a powerful force that has found a sympathetic hearing among policymakers at all levels of government.

The Future of Managed Care

In many ways the future of medical care financing and delivery and the future of managed care are intimately connected. Patient dissatisfaction with managed care has led Congress to consider legislation to protect patients' rights and increase patient choice. Regardless of future legislative measures, however, some form of managed care will likely remain an important feature in the landscape of the medical care marketplace.

Policy Issue

A health care system that focuses on cost containment will tend to shortchange other important goals, including quality and access.

The nature of health care delivery has changed. As it became more competitive, the shift to more restrictive managed care gained momentum. With that shift came increased utilization management, increased use of capitation, and an expanding role for general practitioners. Ironically, the United States, in seeking market alternatives, has turned to a private version of the government-run systems that prevail in the rest of the world. Problems are inherent in any system that emphasizes cost containment over quality and access. All fixed-budget systems, whether government run or privately run, are learning this lesson and finding that rationing becomes a necessary part of any system that does not give both patient and provider incentives to control costs.

Whether the new forms of managed care that have emerged in the market actually lower costs system wide is a question that has yet to be answered. Plans that are more restrictive in terms of patient choice and physician practice seem to have more cost-saving potential than those that allow extensive out-of-plan options. To make managed care more attractive, many of the more restrictive plans have had to increase flexibility by including more patient options, which translates directly into higher costs.

Despite the public relations problems that managed care has suffered in the United States, policymakers in many European countries are seriously considering adopting elements of managed care for their systems. Automated record keeping systems, clinical guidelines, and the gatekeeper system are just a few of the features of U.S.-style managed care that are being adopted in other countries. In fact, countries such as Israel, the Philippines, and Switzerland already have well-established managed care sectors. Other nations, such as Germany, New Zealand, and the United Kingdom, are using features of managed care to control costs and improve the quality of care. Even though it may not yet be called a movement, managed care giants such as Cigna and Aetna have significant investments in the world health market (Gentry, 1999).

The retreat from managed care in the United States will likely improve access, but it will also remove many of the constraints on spending that existed. With the supply side constraints relaxed, the consumer may be left as the last defense against excess spending. The consumer is uniquely equipped to take on the role of the cost-conscious decision maker, provided that the appropriate incentives are in place. An exclusively consumer-driven health care system is unlikely. Other stakeholders—payers, providers, politicians, and employers—will continue to influence decision-making. It is difficult to predict what the future system will look like. One thing is certain: If the trend of escalating costs continues, another consumer backlash will occur and with it an increased willingness to support more structure in the way we make medical care decisions.

As the focus of health care delivery has shifted, there have been casualties. Open-ended fee-for-service financed by traditional indemnity insurance is well down the road to extinction. The wealthy will always have access to fee-for-service care, but maintaining that option for all Americans will be difficult, if not impossible.

ISSUES IN MEDICAL CARE DELIVERY

THE MANAGED CARE "BLUES"

For over 70 years, Blue Cross and Blue Shield were virtually synonymous with health insurance. A network of 42 independent, community-based plans nationwide, they have dominated the industry, covering 85 million people, or about 30 percent of the total U.S. population. Their nationwide dominance does not accurately reflect their importance. In many states a single Blue Cross entity covers over one-half of the population.

These nonprofit companies, once considered the insurer of last resort for many, are rapidly changing their operating practices and drawing sharp criticism from some circles. Over the first half of the 1990s, the market has witnessed the private, for-profit health insurers transforming themselves into managed care companies. While the "Blues" have not reacted as quickly as many of the commercial insurers, such as Prudential, CIGNA, and Aetna, many have adopted an aggressive strategy in setting up managed care networks.

Simply by virtue of their size, the Blues are the largest providers of managed care in the country. The various Blues plans own 84 HMOs, 72 PPOs, and 66 POS plans, with over 52 million enrollees, or over two thirds of the total number of enrollees in managed care plans nationwide. The system is also the largest provider of managed care to Medicare and Medicaid, enrolling 2.7 million in the two programs combined.

The most controversial step by plan administrators was the approval in July 1994 of a change in organizational status. Traditionally nonprofit in nature, the plans can now become for-profit entities or establish for-profit subsidiaries. This will affect more than their tax-exempt status. It will also allow the Blues greater access to the private capital market and increase their ability to expand, which is essential if they are to be competitive with the commercial carriers.

No one is quite sure what the new health care environment will look like. But one thing is certain. The Blues, once dominant players in the health insurance market, are not sitting around, waiting to be swallowed up by the system. They are merging, partnering, and integrating; in general, preparing for the new managed care environment of the twenty-first century.

Source: Steven Findlay, "The Remaking of the Blues; Blue Cross and Blue Shield Association; Company Profile," *Business and Health* 12(8), August 1994, 37ff.

Summary and Conclusions

In this chapter we have examined how managed care emerged as the alternative payment and delivery mechanism to traditional fee-for-service indemnity insurance. What began as an experiment expanded in the 1990s until more than 90 percent of all Americans with insurance are now covered under a managed care plan.

Legitimately viewed as an economic success, managed care, for all practical purposes, can be considered a sociopolitical failure. Promising comprehensive benefits at lower premiums, managed care delivered on the premium promise, but at the expense of consumer choice. Lower costs were accomplished by limiting patient choice of provider and provider choice of treatment. Stakeholders learned valuable lessons from the experience of the past decade.

- *Patients* learned that a one-size-fits-all solution to medical care is too restrictive. As medical technology provides more treatment options, the definition

PROFILE

William B. Schwartz

Trained as an internist, William B. Schwartz had invested a lifetime in academic medicine and became a respected biomedical researcher and national authority on kidney disease. So when this distinguished scholar announced his plans for a mid-career change from clinical medicine to health policy, it raised more than a few eyebrows. Many of his colleagues probably thought he was taking the mid-life crisis thing a bit too far. They could understand gold chains and a red sports car, but giving up a medical career to study economics seemed a bit extreme.

His medical career reads like a Who's Who in academic medicine. Schwartz graduated from Duke medical school in 1945. After five years he settled at Tufts University where he became head of the Nephrology Division at the New England Medical Center. In 1971 he was appointed chair of the Department of Medicine and Physician-in-Chief at the medical center. That same year he spent the first of several summers working with health economists Charles Phelps and Joseph Newhouse at the RAND Corporation. Under their tutelage, Schwartz was introduced to the economic concepts of scarcity and opportunity cost and his professional career as a health policy analyst began to bud.

Because his administrative and clinical duties at Tufts required most of his energies, he had little time left to devote to his research interests. Lack of research opportunities and a newly acquired interest in health care policy analysis provided enough incentive to convince him to resign as department chair and pursue an alternative career path.

Since shifting to health policy, his research interests have focused on applying economics to problems in medical care delivery. His first article on health policy was published in *Science* in 1972. Since that time, he has devoted his efforts to explaining the role of market forces and competition in promoting efficiency in medical care delivery.

One of his most widely read works was coauthored in 1984 with Brookings economist Henry J. Aaron. Entitled *The Painful Prescription: Rationing Health Care*, the publication examined nonprice rationing of hospital services in the United Kingdom. His book is not a criticism of the National Health Service, but an honest attempt to understand resource allocation within that system and learn from the British experience. The consummate iconoclast, Schwartz has also challenged the conventional wisdom on physician supply in the United States. Instead of forecasting a surplus of 150,000 physicians by the year 2000, he made a solid case for a balance between supply and demand.

Currently the Vannevar Bush University Professor at Tufts University, Schwartz has distinguished himself as a clinician and health policy analyst. Most scholars work a lifetime to make a contribution in a single preferred field of study. William Schwartz has had the good fortune of contributing in two areas. His accomplishments stand as an inspiration to clinicians and economists everywhere.

Source: John K. Iglehart, "From Research to Rationing: A Conversation with William B. Schwartz," *Health Affairs 8*(3), Fall 1989, 60–75; and William B. Schwartz, Frank A. Sloan, and David N. Mendelson, "Why There Will Be Little or No Physician Surplus Between Now and the Year 2000," *New England Journal of Medicine 318*(14), April 1988, 892–897.

of what constitutes medical care also expands. Rising expectations against a backdrop of access restrictions creates tension.

- *Providers* learned that risk sharing presents a challenge to their clinical autonomy and financial security. Forced into a double-agent role (as agent for both patient and plan), providers dislike the restrictions as much as patients do.

- *Payers* learned that cost control is unpopular. The backlash against managed care presented not only an image problem, but was dangerous for corporate survival.

- *Employers* learned that there is no magic pill to solve the health care cost problem. Overly aggressive measures to control costs are not only unpopular among employees, but they can lead to litigation problems as plaintiffs search for deep pockets.

- *Politicians* learned that restrictions on access and limits to spending are unpopular and cost votes. They also learned that expansions of treatment options and increases in spending are popular and win votes.

It may be a bit too early to talk about the demise of managed care. But the dynamics of change are at work. Medical consumers like choice, and they are also concerned about cost. The desire for more patient autonomy is not likely to disappear soon, and cost concerns are always an issue, especially with premiums rising at annual rates exceeding 8 percent (except for one year, true every year since 1998). To control costs, patients must be involved in medical decision-making. Without cost-conscious consumers and providers, the goal is unattainable.

Questions and Problems

1. Define each of the following terms used regularly by the major third-party payers.

   a. fee-for-service

   b. assignment

   c. capitation

   Explain how they are supposed to affect providers' incentives, fees, and overall utilization.

2. "As the health care delivery system becomes increasingly cost conscious, physicians are no longer able to serve as advocates for their patients' medical needs." In light of this concern, discuss the changing role of the physician in the managed care environment.

3. What are the distinguishing characteristics of a health maintenance organization? How do HMOs differ from other insurers operating in the health insurance industry?

4. What are the primary cost-saving features of managed care?

5. How will the expansion of managed care produce competitive effects throughout the health care system?

6. In theory, how is managed care expected to affect patient and provider incentives, and hence, the cost and use of medical care? What is the evidence?

7. In a series of articles in the February 10, 1993, issue of the *Journal of the American Medical Association*, researchers estimate that 2.4 percent of all bypass surgeries are inappropriate and 7 percent are clearly unnecessary—roughly one fourth as much as previously estimated. Similar results were found for coronary angioplasty and coronary angiography. Some analysts are using these results to claim the problem is now underuse instead of overuse. How do you define terms such as "inappropriate" and "unnecessary"? What are the lessons to be learned about the use of outcomes research?

References

Laurence C. Baker and Ciaran S. Phibbs, "Managed Care, Technology Adoption, and Health Care: The Adoption of Neonatal Intensive Care," Working Paper No. 7883, Cambridge, MA: National Bureau of Economic Research, September 2000.

David M. Cutler and Louise Sheiner, "Managed Care and the Growth in Medical Expenditures," in A. M. Garber, ed., *Frontiers of Health Policy Research*, Volume 1, Cambridge, MA: MIT Press, 1998.

E. S. Friedman, "Capitation, Integration, and Managed Care: Lessons from Early Experiments," *Journal of the American Medical Association* 275(12), 1996, 957–962.

Carol Gentry, "A Surprisingly Popular U.S. Export: Managed Care," *The Wall Street Journal*, December 20, 1999, B1, B4.

Sherry Glied, "Managed Care," *NBER Working Paper Series No. 7205*, Cambridge, MA: National Bureau of Economic Research, July 1999.

Sheldon Greenfield, Eugene C. Nelson, Michael Zubkoff, Willard Manning, William Rogers, Richard L. Kravitz, Adam Keller, Alvin R. Tarlov, and John E. Ware, Jr., "Variations in Resource Utilization among Medical Specialties and Systems of Care," *Journal of the American Medical Association 267*(12), March 25, 1992, 1624–1630.

L. R. Gruber, M. Shadle, and C. L. Polich, "From Movement to Industry: The Growth of HMOs," *Health Affairs 7*(3), Summer 1988, 197–208.

Fred J. Hellinger, "The Effect of Managed Care on Quality: A Review of Recent Evidence," *Archives of Internal Medicine* 158, April 27, 1998, 833–841.

———, "Selection Bias in HMOs and PPOs: A Review of the Evidence," *Inquiry* 32, Summer 1995, 135–143.

S. D. Hosek, M. S. Marquis, and K. B. Wells, *Health Care Utilization in Employer Plans with Preferred Provider Organizations*, RAND Corporation, February 1990.

Kaiser Family Foundation and Health Research and Educational Trust, "Employer Health Benefits: 2002 Annual Survey," 2002 [available at **http://www.kff.org/content/2002/3251/**].

Peter R. Kongstvedt, *Essentials of Managed Health Care*, Gaithersburg, MD: Aspen Publishers, 1997.

Harold S. Luft, *Health Maintenance Organizations: Dimensions of Performance*, New York: Wiley, 1981.

Willard Manning, Arleen Leibowitz, George Goldberg, William Rogers, and Joseph Newhouse, "A Controlled Trial of the Effect of a Prepaid Group Practice on Use of Services," *New England Journal of Medicine 310*(23), June 7, 1984, 1505–1510.

Mercer Human Resource Consulting, "Rate hikes pushed employers to drop health plans, cut benefits in 2002—but average cost still rose," December 8, 2002 [available at **http://www.mercerhr.com/pressrelease/details.jhtml?idContent =1076975**].

Robert H. Miller and Harold S. Luft, "Does Managed Care Lead to Better or Worse Quality of Care?" *Health Affairs 16*(5), September/October 1997, 7–25.

———, "Managed Care Plan Performance Since 1980: A Literature Analysis," *Journal of the American Medical Association 271*(19), May 18, 1994, 1512–1519.

J. Murray, Sheldon Greenfield, S. Kaplan, and E. Yano, "Ambulatory Testing for Capitation and Fee-for-Service Patients in the Same Practice Setting: Relationship to Outcome," *Medical Care 30*(2), March 1992, 252–261.

Joseph Newhouse, "Reimbursing Health Plans and Health Providers: Selection versus Efficiency in Production," *Journal of Economic Literature 34*(3), September 1996, 1236–1263.

Ray Robinson, "Managed Care in the United States" A Dilemma for Evidence-Based Policy?" *Health Economics 9*(1), January 2000, 1–7.

D. G. Smith, "The Effects of Preferred Provider Organizations on Health Care Use and Cost," *Inquiry* 34, Winter 1997, 278–287.

J. E. Ware, M. S. Bayliss, W. H. Rogers, M. Kosinski et al., "Differences in Four-Year Health Outcomes for Elderly and Poor, Chronically-Ill Patients Treated in HMO and Fee-for-Service Systems: Results from the Medial Outcomes Study," *Journal of the American Medical Association* 13, 1996, 1039–1047.

Chapter 8

The Market for Health Care Professionals

Physicians occupy the central role in the provision of medical services. Even though physicians receive less than one-fourth of total medical spending, they determine how much money is spent on medical care. Physicians are responsible for admitting patients to the hospital, recommending treatment, writing prescriptions, and scheduling and performing surgeries. In addition to the details of patient care, physicians also control other important aspects of the decision-making process in medical care delivery, including the acquisition of medical equipment in hospitals, the direction of biomedical research, and medical school curricula.

The 1990s were an unsettling period for both active physicians and those hoping to some day practice the healing arts. Major changes in the market include a movement away from fee-for-service practice toward managed care, shifts from retrospective to prospective payment, and more intrusion into medical practice from both public and private payers. We begin our analysis with a brief discussion of the theory of labor markets. In the second section, we will focus our analysis on the physicians' services market. The final two sections will explore briefly the markets for nursing services and dental services.

The Theory of Labor Markets

The standard economic theory of labor markets views individual marginal productivity as one of the main determinants of wage levels. Because wages are determined by productivity, higher productivity is translated into greater demand for labor services, and, in turn, higher wages.

Input Pricing

Broadly speaking, the theory of input pricing is no different from the theory of pricing of goods and services presented in Chapter 2. Both are based on the interaction of demand and supply. However, several important differences arise. First, demand for an input is determined by its marginal contribution in the production process. The second important difference between input demand and product demand is related to the first. Inputs are not consumed directly; therefore, the quantity of the input demanded will depend on the amount of the final product desired for consumption. Thus, input demand is derived from the demand for the final product and affected by the prevailing conditions in the market for the final product.[1]

The economic model of input pricing is based on a firm's decisions concerning the input combination used to produce a given level of output (or in the case of physicians' services, an individual's decisions concerning the combination of medical services used to produce a given level of health). Once the firm (individual) decides on a level of production (health), the level of input demand is simultaneously determined. The process

---

1 When examining the demand for physicians' services, keep in mind that the final product is a desired level of health.

involves determining the optimal, or least-cost combination of inputs required to produce the profit-maximizing (utility-maximizing) level of output (health). Generalizing from the discussion in Appendix 3B, the least cost combination of inputs in the production process $Q = Q(X, Y, \ldots, Z)$ may be written as the following equilibrium condition

$$\frac{MP_X}{P_X} = \frac{MP_Y}{P_Y} = \cdots = \frac{MP_Z}{P_Z}$$

where MP_i is the marginal product of the ith input ($i = X, Y, \ldots, Z$) and P_i is its price.

It can also be shown that the reciprocal of each of the ratios is equal to the marginal cost of production (MC), or

$$\frac{P_X}{MP_X} = \frac{P_Y}{MP_Y} = \cdots = \frac{P_Z}{MP_Z} = MC$$

To prove this equality consider that the use of one more unit of input X, holding the other inputs constant, will increase output by MP_X units. Thus, using an additional $1/MP_X$ units of input X will increase output by one unit. If one unit of input X costs P_X, then $1/MP_X$ units of X costs P_X/MP_X, which is the cost of producing an additional unit of output, or marginal cost.

If firms are maximizing profit, they are producing an output level where marginal revenue (MR) equals marginal cost. Thus, it follows that

$$\frac{P_X}{MP_X} = \frac{P_Y}{MP_Y} = \cdots = \frac{P_Z}{MP_Z} = MR$$

By rearranging terms and writing a separate equation for each input, it follows that

$$P_X = MP_X \cdot MR$$
$$P_Y = MP_Y \cdot MR$$
$$\cdot$$
$$\cdot$$
$$\cdot$$
$$P_Z = MP_Z \cdot MR$$

Interpreting these results, we see that in a world where buyers are profit (utility) maximizers, inputs used in a production process are paid an amount (P_X, P_Y, and P_Z in this case) equal to each input's marginal product multiplied by the marginal revenue generated by the production and sale of an additional unit of the final product. This result serves as the underlying principle for deriving the demand curve for an input.

Demand for Inputs

In order to derive the demand curve for an input, we must first determine the maximum price buyers are willing to pay to obtain the desired amount of the input. The maximum price that buyers are willing to pay is determined by incremental value placed on an additional unit of the input in the production process. As already demonstrated, price is determined by the value of the input's marginal productivity ($MP_i \cdot MR$), or what is called **marginal revenue product (MRP)**.

marginal revenue product
The change in total revenue resulting from the sale of the output produced by an additional unit of a resource.

Figure 8.1 represents the marginal revenue product for any given input. It is downward sloping for the same reason that the marginal product curve is downward sloping, the law of diminishing returns. If the input is labor, the market wage rate determines the number of workers hired. At wage rate W_0, L_0 workers will be hired. If the wage rate falls to W_1, more will be hired (L_1). Thus, the marginal revenue product curve is the input demand curve, reflecting the two important concepts that determine input demand: the level of product demand and the marginal productivity of the input.

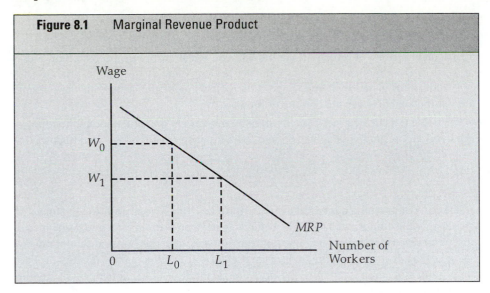

Figure 8.1   Marginal Revenue Product

Generally speaking, more productive inputs command higher prices in the market, as do inputs that are used in the production of highly valued commodities. It is no wonder that most medical inputs carry such high price tags. They are very effective in improving health status, something consumers value highly.

Human Capital Investment

One of the most popular ways for an individual to improve his or her marginal productivity is to attend school. Presumably school attendance enables a person to learn a set of skills that enhances productivity. Schooling affects income in two important ways. First, while a person is attending school, income is lower due to forgone earnings. The time spent in school could have been used in gainful employment. In other words, the opportunity cost of attending school is the income that could have been earned if the individual had chosen to work. Second, after completing school the individual's income will be higher. Individuals who attend school make more money than those who do not. The time spent in school valued by the opportunity cost of the income forgone is called *human capital investment*.

Investment in Medical Education

Medical education is a time consuming process—four years of undergraduate study followed by four years of medical school. And that's only the beginning. After eight years of formal education, the medical school graduate must complete a clinical residency program that lasts a minimum of three years before beginning a medical practice. The forgone income is obviously a major expense of attending medical school. Even though tuition and fees comprise less than five percent of overall medical school revenues, the typical medical school student graduates with an average educational debt of over $75,000 (*AAMC Data Book*, 1997).

No one undertakes such a course of action without at least considering the payoff. The potential earnings must be enough to overcome the huge cost of the investment. As is the case with many investments, the costs are borne early in a person's life and the returns are realized later on. Is attending medical school a good economic investment? To answer this question we must compare the value of the forgone earnings early in a person's life with the value of the extra earnings later in life. One major complication comes into play: Most individuals exhibit a positive rate of time preference, meaning that one dollar invested today has a higher value than one dollar earned tomorrow.

The Rate of Return to Investment

To determine whether medical school attendance is a good economic investment, we can calculate the **rate of return** on that investment. Recall from our discussion on present value discounting from Chapter 4, the net present value of a human capital investment can be calculated by comparing the present value of the costs with the present value of the benefits over the lifetime of the investor.

The present value of a net benefits stream over time (NB) is defined by the difference between the annual benefits (B_t) and the annual costs (C_t) of the investment.

$$NB = \sum_{t=1}^{n} \frac{B_t - C_t}{(1+r)^t}$$

The costs of pursuing a medical degree tend to be front-loaded and take the form of forgone income, tuition, and fees. The benefits tend to be realized later and come in the form of increased earnings. The value of the investment depends on the discount rate—the higher the discount rate, the smaller the present value of the net benefit stream. The rate of return on an investment is the discount rate that results in a net benefit stream summing to zero.

How does the income physicians receive compare to that of other professionals? Higher rates of return to a medical education will encourage more students to pursue medicine as a career. Is the investment a good one from the individual's perspective? Even with the high salaries of physicians, the forgone income during the long investment period may discourage many from pursuing medicine and instead attend business or law school. Should society encourage more students to pursue medicine as a career? Greater subsidies in the form of grants to medical schools and loan forgiveness programs lower the cost of attending medical school and increase the rate of return to the investment.

What is the rate of return to a medical education? Weeks et al. (1994) compared the rate of return on the investment made by the typical physician (both primary care and specialist) with those of college graduates entering business, law, and dentistry. Estimated returns were adjusted for the amount of time required to train for the chosen profession and the average number of hours worked.

Empirical results indicate that the annual rate of return on the educational investment made by primary care physicians was 15.9 percent. Dentists and medical specialists fared substantially better, enjoying a 20.7 and 20.9 percent return, respectively. However, attorneys and those entering business fared much better with 25.4 and 29.0 percent rates of return. Even though these are crude estimates for the respective rates of return, it is clear that despite their high incomes, individuals who choose medical careers receive lower economic returns on their educational investments than many other professionals. The lower returns are due to much higher training costs, especially 7 to 12 years of forgone income, and the resulting shorter payoff periods.

The perception that high physicians' salaries are a contributing factor in the high cost of medical care is widely shared by the public and policymakers. To better address this issue, we need to strive for a better understanding of the market for physicians' services.

The Market for Physicians' Services

The changing demographics of the population have played an important role in determining demand and supply in the physicians' services market. Since 1970 the population in the United States has increased from 214 million to 284 million by 2001, or approximately 25 percent. At the same time the number of active physicians has doubled from 310,845 to 713,375. The result, clearly shown in Table 8.1, is a doubling of the ratio of physicians per 100,000 population from 122 to 250. No matter which measure we use, the figures indicate a greater supply of physicians today than 30 years ago.

Back-of-the-Envelope

ESTIMATING RATES OF RETURN TO SCHOOLING

For the past two decades economists have used an approach popularized by Jacob Mincer (1974) to estimate rates of return to education. The returns to schooling can be calculated by comparing the age-earnings profiles of individuals with different levels of schooling. In the following diagram, Y_0 represents the earnings profile of an individual with no schooling and Y_1 represents that of someone with one year of schooling.

Ignoring the direct costs of training (which are usually small relative to forgone income), an additional year of schooling will cost the individual Y_0 income for one year. In return the individual will receive an increment $Y_1 - Y_0$ for the remainder of his work life.

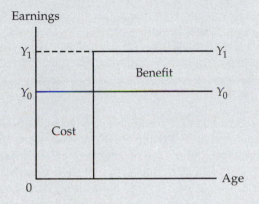

The rate of return to the additional year of schooling can be estimated by

$$r_1 = \frac{Y_1 - Y_0}{Y_0}$$

Solving for Y_1, we get
$$Y_1 = Y_0(1 + r_1).$$
Similarly, the return to the second year of schooling, r_2, would be

$$r_2 = \frac{Y_2 - Y_1}{Y_1}$$

Likewise, $\qquad\qquad Y_2 = Y_1(1 + r_2)$
Substituting from above $\qquad Y_2 = Y_0(1 + r_1)(1 + r_2)$
After s years of schooling $\qquad Y_s = Y_0(1 + r_1)(1 + r_2) \dots (1 + r_s)$

If the returns to schooling are small (i.e., less than 100%) and similar in size, then:
$$Y_s = Y_0 e^{rs}$$

The estimated rate of return is calculated by taking the natural logarithm of both sides of the equation, resulting in:
$$\ln Y_s = \ln Y_0 + rs$$

Empirical tests are conducted by gathering data on earnings and schooling for a cross-section of individuals. Regressing the logarithm of income on the number of years of schooling results in a coefficient estimate for the schooling variable, r, that is interpreted as the estimated rate of return to additional schooling.

Source: Jacob Mincer, *Schooling, Experience, and Earnings*, (New York: National Bureau of Economic Research, 1974).

Key Concept 2
Opportunity Cost

Table 8.1	Active Physicians in the United States			
Year	Active Physicians	Rate per 100,000 Residents	Primary Care Physicians	Primary Care as a Percent of Active
1960	247,257	—	125,359	50.7
1970	310,845	122	115,822	37.3
1980	414,916	183	146,093	35.2
1990	547,310	221	183,294	33.5
1995	625,443	238	207,810	33.2
1996	643,955	243	216,446	33.6
1997	664,556	248	216,598	32.6
1998	667,000	247	218,421	32.7
1999	669,949	245	221,206	33.0
2000	692,368	246	227,992	32.9
2001	713,375	250	246,714	34.6

Source: *Health, United States, 2003 with Chartbook on Trends in the Health of Americans*, U.S. Department of Health and Human Services, Table 101, 2003.

In 2000 the United States had 125 medical schools, enrolling 66,444 students. These same schools graduate between 15,000 and 16,000 per year and are expected to remain at that level for the foreseeable future. Approximately one fourth of the physicians practicing in the United States graduated from foreign medical schools. Reliance on graduates of foreign medical schools has increased dramatically over the past 30 years from less than 15 percent of the total number of practicing physicians in the mid-1960s to almost 25 percent today. By the mid-1990s, international medical graduates (IMGs) filled about 20 percent of all residency positions. Much of the attraction of the U.S. medical market may be attributable to higher relative salaries and fewer practice restrictions than in other countries.

> **Policy Issue**
>
> International medical graduates make up 25 percent of the physician workforce in the United States.

Another important aspect of physician supply has been the number of U.S. citizens attending foreign medical schools. As the ratio of applicants per opening in U.S. medical schools rose to 2.8 in the mid-1970s, many Americans were attracted to the option of studying in foreign countries. Some schools in Mexico and the Caribbean began accepting large numbers of American citizens, causing concern about the future quality of medical school graduates to fill residency positions in academic health centers.

Anyone trained in a foreign medical school and seeking admission to a residency-training program in the United States must pass an examination and be certified by the Educational Commission for Foreign Medical Graduates. The number of U.S. citizens receiving certification increased steadily until 1984 when a more rigorous exam was administered. The number certified for residency programs has fallen dramatically from over 1,500 per year in the mid-1980s to less than 500 in recent years.

Given the long training period for physicians, one would expect the supply of physicians to be fairly inelastic in the short run. The slow supply response means that changes in physicians' incomes do not translate into immediate adjustments in the number of physicians practicing medicine. U.S. immigration laws, however, currently place relatively few restrictions on the entry of foreign-trained physicians, especially during times of perceived shortages. This allows physician supply to remain fairly responsive to market conditions. The importance of foreign-trained physicians in staffing many rural and inner city facilities highlights the potential impact of changes in U.S. immigration policy on physician supply.

> **Policy Issue**
>
> Many rural and inner-city hospitals rely on foreign trained physicians to staff their facilities.

ISSUES IN MEDICAL CARE DELIVERY

DEFENDING THE BORDERS FROM FOREIGN COMPETITION

The 1996 election brought the legislative and media spotlight on the intense nationalistic tendencies of the American electorate at the time. Proposition 187 in California was the first political move to tap into this anti-immigrant sentiment. The aborted presidential bid by Republican Pat Buchannan and the strong populist rhetoric of on-again, off-again presidential candidate Ross Perot fed on this anti-NAFTA, antiforeigner, antifree-trade mindset. But it is a long way from campaign rhetoric to actual practice—or is it?

The 104th Congress considered legislation that would have enacted some of the most restrictive policies regarding both legal and illegal immigration in recent history. Sponsored by retiring Republican Senator Alan Simpson, the bill would have done three things:

- Limit the flow of immigrants into the United States by increasing border enforcement.

- Install a verification system that would make it feasible to require employers to check the legal status of all foreign workers.

- Require employers to pay a fee for every foreigner hired equal to the greater of 10 percent of the first-year salary or $10,000.

Even though the legislation did not pass, its potential impact on U.S. industry, especially those who recruit specially trained technical and professional workers in the global marketplace, highlights the predicament of many employers in areas of labor shortage. Falling into this category, the medical care industry would be seriously affected by similar legislation should it ever become law. Nationwide, international medical graduates (IMGs) occupy almost one fourth of all residency positions. Many rural and inner-city areas, facing severe physician shortages, have relied heavily on foreign-trained physicians to staff their facilities. More than one half of the hospital residents in New York City alone are IMGs. Similarly, medical facilities in the remote areas of North Dakota and inner-city New Jersey recruit graduates of foreign medical schools to staff their operations. Foreign-trained physicians have been more inclined to accept positions in unpopular places. Many from India and even Canada can earn more and have fewer restrictions placed on them, even in rural and inner-city settings.

Hospitals, under pressure to cut costs, could see personnel costs escalate significantly if such restrictive legislation ever passes. In New York City some estimate that costs could rise by $60 million annually by restricting the pool of foreign-trained physicians. For patients in underserved areas, this could mean longer waits to see a physician and in some cases fewer specialty services available.

Source: Almar Larour, "How Curbing Immigration Could Hurt Health Care in Inner Cities, Rural Areas," *The Wall Street Journal*, March 5, 1996, B1, B6.

Key Concept 6
Supply and Demand

Increases in relative supply do not tell the entire story. Policymakers have voiced concern over certain aspects of the supply side of the market, including the distribution of physicians across specialty areas and regions of the country, the relative salaries of physicians, the pricing of their services, and the organizational structure of physicians' practices.

Key Concept 6
Supply and Demand

Specialty Distribution

Many policy analysts and health maintenance organizations have established a goal to increase the number of physicians in the primary care specialties to 50 percent of the physician workforce. In the rest of the developed world, this percentage is not unusual. In fact, primary care physicians comprise 50 to 70 percent of the total active physicians in most developed countries (Schroeder and Sandy, 1993). In the United States, however, only about one third of all active physicians are in primary care.[2]

The percentage of generalists has been on a downward trend since 1970 when the figure was almost 40 percent. Referring again to Table 8.1, the number of primary care physicians has increased from 115,822 to 246,714, or 130 percent. Over the same time period, the number of specialists has increased from 195,023 to 466,661, or 139 percent.

At least a dozen large, national organizations, including the Accreditation Council for Graduate Medical Education (ACGME), the American Medical Association (AMA), the National Governors Association, and the Robert Wood Johnson Foundation have voiced concern over the falling percentage of generalists and advocated a reversal of the trend. With only 15 percent of the recent medical graduates pursuing a generalist career, the prospects for reaching the goal of 50 percent generalists appears bleak at best (Levinsky, 1993).

The appropriate percentage of primary care physicians is not easy to determine. Policy concerns are based on the projected number of patients compared to the number of physicians required to provide for their primary care needs. Several studies have examined this physicians' services market and identified a mismatch between supply and demand. Analyzing the results of five different projection methods, Politzer et al. (1996) predict a substantial shortage of primary care physicians and a surplus of specialists by the year 2020. Other studies have reached the same general conclusions, pointing to some challenging policy issues. Since specialists use more expensive technology, the obvious concern is that more specialists will lead to higher spending. With government at all levels playing such a large role in financing medical education, what role if any should it play in determining specialty mix?[3] Or should we simply rely on market forces to drive down fees in the surplus specialty market and raise them in the shortage primary care market?

Geographic Distribution

Even as the concern for the falling percentage of generalists grows, so does the concern for the declining number of physicians willing to practice in rural and inner-city areas. The problem of providing medical care in many rural areas has reached near critical stages. Overall, almost 30 percent of the U.S. population lives in market areas with fewer than 180,000 inhabitants, where the physician-population ratios are substantially lower. The majority of the population in 19 states lives in these small market areas and over 20 percent of the population in 42 states lives in such areas (Kronick et al., 1993).

The nation's inner cities face the same challenge in attracting and keeping qualified physicians. With a large minority and indigent population, inner cities depend heavily on hospital emergency rooms and public clinics, staffed by international medical graduates, for a substantial portion of their medical care.

Pennsylvania provides a good example of the problem of attracting physicians to rural areas. According to the most recent census of population, the state has the largest rural population in the country (with rural defined as areas with fewer than 2,500 population). The three counties surrounding the state's two major urban centers, Pittsburgh and Philadelphia, have approximately 25 percent of the state's population

---

2 For purposes of this discussion, primary care is defined as family practice, general internists, and pediatricians.

3 By the time a physician finishes residency, he or she will have received an average federal subsidy of $70,000.

ISSUES IN MEDICAL CARE DELIVERY

AN ENDANGERED SPECIES: THE MALE GYNECOLOGIST

Obstetrics was once a field dominated by women. At one time the local midwife delivered most of the babies. Modern medicine has changed that relationship in most urban areas. Over the course of the twentieth century, childbirth became an integral part of a medical practice, and midwifery lost much of its clientele.

Obstetricians deliver most of the babies born in the United States today. Obstetrics and gynecology (OB/GYN) has become a popular specialty, primarily because it is one of only a few that combines primary care with surgery. But women today are deserting their male gynecologists in increasing numbers and turning to female OB/GYNs. Just as men prefer a same-sex physician almost two-to-one, an increasing number of women are beginning to voice a similar preference. As recently as 1980, women filled less than 30 percent of the residency positions in obstetrics and gynecology. Today, that number has doubled to more than 60 percent.

The increase in supply of female OB/GYNs may be in part a response to the rapidly expanding demand for their services, especially among health maintenance organizations and previously all-male OB/GYN practices. This shift in preferences has several major implications, all indicative of a shortage of female OB/GYNs in the market:

- Initial salaries for women within the specialty are $20,000 a year more than for men.

- While the median salary for female physicians is about 70 percent of the male median, female OB/GYNs enjoy pay parity with their male counterparts.

- Patients have shown a willingness to wait for appointments with their female OB/GYNs who are booked months in advance.

For women this preference shift may not be solely an issue of seeing a same-sex physician. There seems to be a significant difference in practice styles between the sexes. Male gynecologists are more likely to perform hysterectomies, and patients of female gynecologists are more likely to be current on their Pap tests and mammograms. Whether female gynecologists are more sensitive to their patients' needs or whether the practice styles of more recent graduates (male and female) are simply different is an unanswered question.

For whatever reason, many newly trained female gynecologists are opening all-female practices and marketing them as such. This trend has opened up a completely different set of questions dealing with reverse discrimination. Can an obstetrical practice seeking to fill a vacancy on its staff advertise for females only? When patients are voicing a preference for female physicians, is it legal for employers to discriminate against male applicants? Under what circumstances is gender a legitimate qualification? When it comes to performing a gynecological exam, is patient preference an appropriate concern? It is only a matter of time, given our litigious society, before this issue will be addressed by our judicial system. How will the courts respond? Is the desire for a same-sex provider of a gynecological exam different from wanting a same-sex stockbroker or sales clerk in a shoe store? Reason is not always a good indicator. No matter how the courts respond, it is unlikely that the male gynecologist will vanish anytime soon. With over 70 percent of the practicing OB/GYNs still male, even if the trend toward female residencies continues unabated, it will take several decades before we see a female-dominated specialty.

Source: Andrea Gerlin, "The Male Gynecologist: Soon to Be Extinct?" *The Wall Street Journal,* February 7, 1996, B1, B5.

and over one half of its physicians (Rabinowitz, 1993). The remaining 64 counties with over 75 percent of the state's population are severely underserved.

Nationwide, individuals living in the smaller market areas have fewer physicians per 100,000 than those living in more populated markets. The physician-population ratio in the 700 counties with fewer than 10,000 inhabitants is one third that of the rest of the country. Nurse practitioners and physicians' assistants are filling some of these gaps. A number of physicians operate satellite offices in rural areas, some at permanent sites and others using mobile units. Providing medical care to these low-density, remote areas will be a continuing challenge for the medical care delivery system.

Physician Compensation

To a large degree the strength of the U.S. health care system may be attributed to the dominance of specialty care. The increasing number of specialists has been accompanied by a more frequent use of the latest diagnostic, therapeutic, and surgical procedures. This approach has contributed to improving the quality of care, but it has also consumed large quantities of resources and served as a primary cost driver (Schroeder and Sandy, 1993).

Many critics of the U.S. system have focused on physicians' incomes as the primary cause of high and rising health care spending, even though physicians' compensation consumes less than 20–25 percent of total spending. Mean income of physicians in 1998 was $194,400 (net of practice costs and before taxes). Mean values, with their tendencies to mask variations, do not provide a clear picture of physician compensation. Self-employed physicians earn an average of $228,200 while physician employees earn an average of $154,000.

Using data from Table 8.2, the average physician's income increased over 98 percent between 1982 and 1998. Incomes of general practitioners increased 100 percent from $71,400 to $142,500. At the other extreme, physicians specializing in internal medicine saw their incomes increase 110 percent on average from $86,900 to $182,100. The two highest paid specialties were radiology and surgery, with mean incomes in 1997 of $261,400 and $273,400.

Since the implementation of Medicare's prospective payment for physicians in 1993, the various specialties have fared far differently from one another. The mean income of

Table 8.2	Medical Practice Incomes of Physicians

Mean Values, Net of Practice Expenses

	All Physicians	General/ Family Practice	Internal Medicine	Surgery	Pediatrics	OB/GYN	Radiology
1982	$ 97.7	$ 71.4	$ 86.9	$128.6	$ 70.5	112.3	$133.3
1985	112.2	77.9	102.0	155.0	76.2	124.3	144.3
1990	164.3	102.7	152.5	236.4	106.5	207.3	219.4
1991	170.6	111.5	149.6	233.8	119.3	221.8	229.8
1992	181.7	114.4	162.1	250.5	123.9	220.7	257.3
1993	189.3	116.8	180.8	262.7	135.4	221.9	259.8
1994	182.6	121.4	175.1	255.3	126.2	200.7	237.5
1995	195.5	131.2	185.7	269.4	140.5	244.3	244.4
1996	199.0	139.1	185.7	275.2	140.6	231.0	275.1
1997	199.6	140.9	193.9	261.4	143.5	228.7	273.4
1998	194.4	142.5	182.1	268.2	139.6	214.4	—

Source: *Socioeconomic Characteristics of Medical Practice, 2000,* Chicago: American Medical Association, 2002.

Back-of-the-Envelope

IS THERE AN OPTIMAL PHYSICIAN-POPULATION RATIO?

How many physicians do we need? In theory, an optimal physician-population ratio can be determined. In practice, however, determining that ratio is not so easy. Even though other inputs in the medical care process must be considered, most medical services require at least one physician input. Some inputs complement physicians; others are substitutes. The list of other labor inputs includes nurses, physicians' assistants, receptionists, bookkeepers, lawyers, medical technicians, and therapists. Nonlabor inputs include the office and its equipment, computers, supplies, electricity, and, of course, medical malpractice insurance. Medical care can be provided using different combinations of physicians' services and these other inputs. The optimal combination depends on the relative price of the inputs and the preferences of the decision makers responsible for combining the inputs and making the medical care available.

Using the production isoquants developed in the appendix to Chapter 3, we can show how prices and preferences affect the optimal number of physicians used in the production of medical care. The isoquant mapping in the following diagram depicts the preferences of a managed care organization (with a greater willingness to substitute other inputs for physicians' services). Increases in the price of physicians' services (relative to the prices of the other inputs) create an incentive to use fewer physicians' services. The isocost curve rotates inward due to the increase in price and the equilibrium number of physicians used falls from S_1 to S_0.

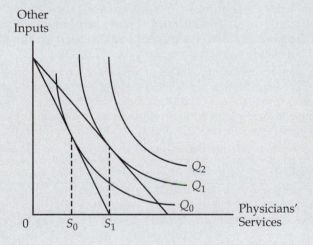

Decision makers with a strong preference for using physicians in the production process will have steeper isoquants. Other things equal, any given increase in the price of physicians will have much less of an impact on the use of physicians' services than indicated in the diagram. The following diagram depicts the preference mapping of a physicians' group practice. Using the same starting point, S_1, defined as the equilibrium quantity of physicians' services, the same increase in the price of physicians' services (as shown in the previous diagram) has less of an impact on the use of physicians' services, lowering utilization to S_0'. The obvious implication deals with the use of physicians in the tightly controlled managed care environment. A good example is the **staff-model HMO**, where substitution for high-cost physicians' services is more widely practiced, resulting in a flatter isoquant mapping (as shown in the first diagram) and a demand for physicians' services that is relatively price elastic. A difference in staffing patterns between the staff-model HMO and traditional fee-for-service physicians' practice (as shown in the second diagram) supports this view. Based on a nationwide survey of HMOs, Dial et al. (1995) estimate that the staff-model HMO will use about

staff-model HMO
An HMO in which physicians are employees of the HMO. Their incomes are usually paid in the form of a fixed salary, but may include supplemental payments based on some measure of performance.

140 physicians per 100,000 enrollees with 40 percent of those being involved in primary care. HMOs are also more likely to utilize nonphysician providers, advanced practice nurses (APNs) and physicians' assistants (PAs) to supplement their clinical staffing needs. The median number of APNs per 100,000 of the responding HMOs was 19.7. Overall, the median number of PAs was 8.1.

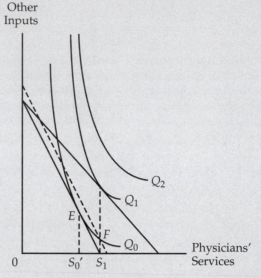

In contrast, the overall physician-population ratio stood at 230 per 100,000 in 1992 with only about one-third of those practicing primary care. Additionally, Kronick et al. (1993) report that the ratio of physicians-to-population is anywhere from 10 to 200 percent higher in the fee-for-service sector when compared with the classic HMO, depending on specialty examined.

Restrictions on the minimum number of physicians used to produce a given level of care generally lead to higher costs. Suppose S_1 physicians' services are required by law to provide Q_0 medical care. Precluded from using the least-cost combination of inputs at point E, providers must use a minimum of S_1 at point F, resulting in equilibrium on a higher isocost curve.

Sources: Thomas H. Dial et. al, "Clinical Staffing in Staff- and Group-Model HMOs," *Health Affairs 14*(2), Summer 1995, 169–180; and Richard Kronick et al., "The Marketplace in Health Care Reform—The Demographic Limitations of Managed Competition," *New England Journal of Medicine 328*(2), January 14, 1993, 148–152.

all physicians has increased only 2.7 percent between 1993 and 1998, a rate of increase that is down substantially from the previous five-year period. General practitioners' incomes increased 22.0 percent, internists' 0.7 percent, and pediatricians' 3.1 percent. The higher paid specialties fared much worse. Surgeons had a 2.1 percent increase in their incomes, radiologists a 5.2 percent increase, and OB/GYNs actually saw their incomes fall 3.5 percent.

Pricing of Physicians' Services

A lot has been written about the escalation of medical care prices. Between 1990 and 2001 the overall consumer price index (CPI) rose 36 percent and the CPI for physicians' services increased 58 percent. Using the CPI for physicians' services for support, many observers argue that medical inflation is the primary reason that health care spending is a growing problem. As discussed in the appendix to Chapter 1, several problems are inherent in using the CPI as a measure of inflation. These same arguments may be applied to the use of the CPI for physicians' services as a measure of inflation in the physicians' services market.

Another measure of the rising cost of physicians' services is the actual fees charged for office visits. In addition to the CPI measure, Table 8.3 provides data collected by the

| Table 8.3 | Pricing Physicians' Services |

Price Index and Mean Fees, Various Years

Year	CPI for Physicians' Services	Percent Change	Mean Fee for an Office Visit with an Established Patient	Percent Change	Mean Fee for an Office Vist with a New Patient	Percent Change
1985	113.3	—	28.05	—	51.87	—
1990	160.8	7.3	39.87	7.3	74.84	7.6
1995	208.8	5.4	59.39	8.3	102.75	6.5
1996	216.4	3.6	58.57	−1.4	97.32	−5.3
1997	222.9	3.0	60.63	9.8	102.46	5.3
1998	229.5	3.0	65.60	8.2	111.12	8.5

Source: Bureau of Labor Statistics, *CPI Detailed Report*, various issues, and *Socioeconomic Characteristics of Medical Practice*, Chicago: American Medical Association, various years.

American Medical Association on the average fees charged for established and new patients. The mean charge for an office visit with an established patient rose from $28.05 in 1985 to $65.60 in 1998, or 134 percent. Physicians tend to spend more time with new patients and thus charge them more than established patients. The mean charge for a new patient increased from $51.87 in 1985 to $111.12 in 1998, or 114 percent. Variously measured, the price of physicians' services seems to be increasing twice as fast as the overall price level.

> **Policy Issue**
> Medical care costs are increasing at approximately twice the rate of overall inflation.

Explaining the reasons for this trend is not as easy. Intuitively, the higher rate of increase in physicians' fees is either the result of increased practice costs, more extensive use of advanced technologies, increased physician compensation, or some combination of the three. Even with answers to this question, the entire story is not evident. As fees for office visits have increased, the desire to spend less on medical care has forced fees for certain procedures, especially those purchased by Medicare, to fall dramatically. In Central Texas, for example, the reimbursement for cataract removal and lens replacement, a very common ophthalmologic procedure, fell from $1,393 in 1990 to $693 in 2000. Between 1997 and 1999, the Medicare payment for total hip replacement surgery fell from $1,813 to $1,543. In fact, the allowable fees for many common Medicare procedures have fallen so dramatically that physicians have begun exploring options such as the **unbundling** of services to increase reimbursements for certain procedures.

unbundling
Separating a number of related procedures and treating them as individual services for payment purposes.

Organization of Physicians' Practices

One possible explanation for rising prices in the physicians' services market may be rising expenses. Practice expenses for self-employed physicians increased 57 percent between 1982 and 1992, with almost two thirds of the increase coming in the first half of the decade. Responding to higher practice costs, physicians are increasingly forming group practices to take advantage of economies of scale. In 1965, only one in ten physicians were involved in group practice. The figure had increased to one in four by 1980 and one in three by 1991. Approximately 45 percent of the physicians who practice in groups are organized in single-specialty practices. Another 50 percent have formed multispecialty practices. The remaining physicians have formed into general and family practice groups.

Most of the group practices are relatively small. The mean number of physicians in group practices in 1991 was 11.5, with a median of five. Almost one half of the group practices had from three to four physicians in the group and only one percent had over 100. Organizing into group practices not only lowers the overhead costs per physician

http://

Agency for Research & Quality (AHRQ), established in 1989 as a part of the Department of Health and Human Services, is the lead agency supporting research designed to improve the quality of health care, reduce its cost, and broaden access to essential services. Part of the agency's mission is to support outcomes research with the goal of developing practice guidelines. Check it out at
http://www.ahrq.gov.

but it increases the range of services offered within the practice. Almost 5 percent own or lease a pharmacy, 30 percent have a clinical laboratory, 33 percent have their own radiology lab, 23 percent have their own ultrasound equipment, 28 percent have ECG equipment, and almost 4 percent have MRIs. The shift to group practice has enhanced the full-service capabilities of physicians' practices and contributed to the shift in services from the hospital to the ambulatory setting.

The potential benefits of taking advantage of economies of scale in a medical practice are clearly shown in Figure 8.2. *LAC* depicts the long-run average cost of a typical medical practice. The small-group practice is able to carry a patient load equal to Q_S. At this service level, SAC_S represents the short-run average cost of the practice and AC_S the actual average cost per patient. Larger practices can combine activities and spread administrative overhead over a larger number of patients. The larger practice is able to move down the *LAC*, utilizing a larger physical plant (larger office, more equipment, on-site laboratory). The short-run average cost of the larger operation is depicted by SAC_L and represents, in this case, the optimal plant size. Average cost per patient is lower at AC_L.

Patients will benefit from the lower operating costs when there is competition in the market. Competition forces providers to charge prices reflecting these lower costs. If, however, these consolidations lead to the concentration of market power, providers will be able to act more like monopolists, restrict the availability of services, and charge higher prices. Evidence provided by Noether (1986) indicates that the physician services market has become more competitive since 1965, resulting in an increased supply of physicians and a subsequent fall in their incomes.

Key Concept 7
Competition

Variations in Practice Patterns

It is a well-documented phenomenon that physicians have very different practice styles depending on the geographic region in which they work (Phelps, 1992). Small area variations (SAV) refer to the wide dispersion in per capita utilization rates for many common medical procedures found among otherwise similar health care markets across the country. These cross-regional differences do not seem to be the product of demographic differences in education, income, and insurance coverage, or the underlying pattern of diseases. Physicians, faced with symptoms and syndromes, are expected to make decisions on the appropriateness of care with the scientific accuracy of *Star Trek's* Doctor McCoy. Patients do not always come to their physicians with readily identifiable diseases. Even if they did, the outcome of a particular treatment is not always predictable.

Policy Issue

Variations in practice patterns across geographic regions result in patients with similar health condition being treated differently.

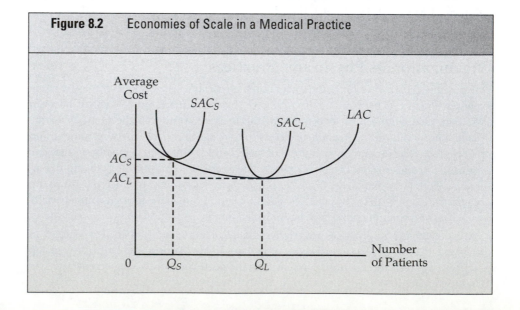

Figure 8.2   Economies of Scale in a Medical Practice

McPherson et al. (1982) compared the utilization rates for several common surgical procedures within New England and observed wide variations even after adjusting for differences in the age and sex composition of the population. Procedures showing the most variation included hysterectomy, prostatectomy, and tonsillectomy. Additionally, they found significant differences in utilization rates when comparing New England with Norway and England.

The reasons for SAV are not well understood. Wennberg (1984) speculated that the observed variations in practice styles across regions could be explained by uncertainty associated with diagnosis and treatment. A lack of consensus on the efficacy of a medical procedure will lead to a substantial variation in treatment. The important public policy issue deals with the costs and consequences of these variations. Do regional variations mean that some physicians overtreat and others undertreat? Do different treatment patterns indicate inappropriate and unnecessary care? From the individual's perspective appropriate care is a level of care that the fully informed patient would demand comparing the marginal benefit of the care being considered with the out-of-pocket marginal cost of the care. Therein lies the problem. From society's perspective the level of care demanded by the individual patient may be an inefficient use of scarce resources, since the fully insured patient bears only a small fraction of the total cost.

Key Concept 3
Marginal
Analysis

Eddy (1990) explored the role of patient preferences in explaining the variations in treatment across regions. Figure 8.3 provides a framework for examining the role of patient preferences in determining the level of care provided in treating certain medical conditions. In the diagram, D_1 and S_1 represent the demand and supply conditions in Region 1; P_1 and Q_1 the equilibrium price and quantity. Suppose there is a second region with the same physician supply but where consumers have a different demand for the same medical procedure, represented by D_2. The different level of demand may be due to differences in income, insurance coverage, or other demographics, or it may be due to different health preferences or attitudes toward risk, pain, and discomfort. Information about these different demand preferences is communicated to providers specializing in this procedure. They, in turn, increase the quantity supplied to Q_2, receiving higher prices for their services, P_2. Assuming easy mobility between the two regions, there is an incentive for physicians to relocate to Region 2. Under these circumstances, utilization rates are even higher than Q_2.

Key Concept 6
Supply and
Demand

Over time the dissemination of medical knowledge through the widespread introduction and use of practice guidelines should serve to reduce the variations in practice patterns across the country attributable to physician practice styles. That part of the difference attributable to differences in patient preferences will be harder to change. In

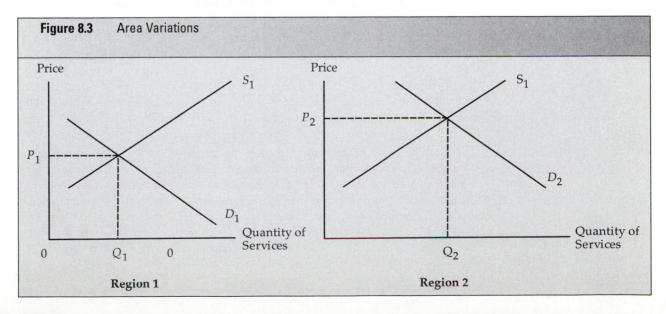

Figure 8.3   Area Variations

Region 1

Region 2

general, old habits are difficult to change, and no reason would indicate that changing medical practice patterns would be any easier. With few exceptions, medical services are highly localized in their delivery. As a result, the usual market forces that serve to eliminate inefficiencies in manufacturing, for example, are not as active in medical care markets.

Whether any gains are to be made by a more standardized approach to treatment remains to be seen. In a sense, patient welfare may actually be enhanced by the variations because of the treatment alternatives available across regions. It will be the goal of medical outcomes research to determine whether the gains in the efficacy and efficiency of medical care delivery outweigh the losses to patients by limiting the choice of treatment that will likely follow from the standardization of services.

Models of Physician Behavior

To adequately model physician behavior we must take into consideration the characteristics of the market for physicians' services. Many urban markets have a substantial number of physicians practicing in the same specialty area; however, a large percentage of Americans live in geographic areas that are considered underserved. Rice (1998) in his reexamination of the economics of health care points out that this market is also characterized by widespread uncertainty on the part of both the patient and the practitioner. A lack of readily available information makes it difficult for patients to make informed choices. Third-party insurance coverage makes moral hazard a dominant feature of both sides of the market. Barriers to entry in the form of strict licensing and a professional code of conduct that discourages direct-to-consumer-advertising make it difficult for patients to price shop. These imperfections, as economists call them, seem to point to a market where providers have a certain degree of market power.

The Physician as Monopolistic Competitor

The physicians' services market shares many of the characteristics of the standard model of monopolistic competition with many sellers, each providing a slightly different product or service. Physicians strive to differentiate their practices by various means—location of their practice, hospital affiliations, and quality of the care provided. At the same time patients have little information to judge physicians, relying mainly on the recommendations of friends and family. As a result, physicians are imperfect substitutes for one another.

The major implication of market power is downward-sloping demand curves. Physicians with market power are not price takers, instead they vary the prices they charge and patients respond to those price variations. In other words, demand is less than perfectly elastic.

The large percentage of patients with health insurance complicates the development of the model to explain physician pricing. Ignoring for the moment the impact of health insurance on the demand for physicians' services, Figure 8.4 depicts the pricing strategy of a physician with a degree of market power.[4] If the physician is a profit-maximizer, the optimal strategy will be to provide services as long as marginal revenue is greater than marginal cost. Profit is maximized where $MR = MC$ with the physician providing Q^* services and charging the maximum price that patients will pay to get those services, or P^*.

The availability of health insurance affects the patients' responsiveness to changes in price. Less concerned about the prices they are charged, patients with insurance have demand curves that are more price inelastic. Inelastic demand, however, does not change the basic implications of the standard model. It merely provides the physician with the opportunity to charge patients different prices for the same services based on the extent of their insurance coverage. Patients with more elastic demand are charged lower prices and patients with more inelastic demand are charged higher prices.

---

4 Refer to Figure 5.3 and the related discussion on the impact of insurance on the demand for medical care.

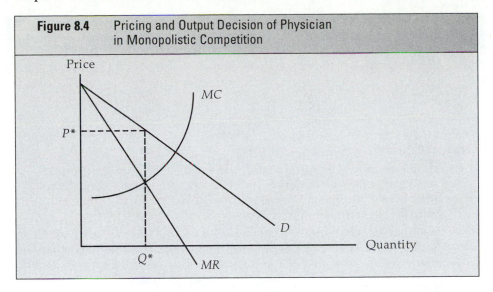

Figure 8.4   Pricing and Output Decision of Physician in Monopolistic Competition

The Physician as Imperfect Agent

Another key assumption when using standard economic theory to model physicians' behavior is that supply and demand are independently determined. As we discussed in Chapter 5, the relationship between the patient and the physician can be described using a principal-agent model. The patient/principal seeks out the physician/agent for advice on a medical problem. The perfect agent will recommend only the treatment that a fully informed patient would demand. The problem arises because the physician not only serves as an adviser to the patient, but is also the provider of the recommended services. This dual role as adviser and provider creates a potential conflict of interest between what is best for the patient in terms of clinical efficacy and what is best for the physician in terms of financial reward. By law the physician must act in the best interests of the patient. Due to the uncertainty of diagnosis and the question of best treatment alternative, the best interests of the patient are not always clear.

> **Policy Issue**
>
> The physician's dual role as agent and provider creates a potential conflict of interest. The choice is whether to serve the patient's medical interest or the physician's own financial interest.

Physicians acting as imperfect agents will recommend unnecessary procedures, especially if they pose little clinical risk to the patient and the patient is fully insured. When prices fall, physicians may see their incomes fall due to inelastic demand for their services. To compensate for falling incomes physicians may practice demand inducement, using their role as advisers to enhance their personal incomes. Reinhardt (1999) presents a model of physician behavior that incorporates the potential for demand inducement as one of the factors that affects a physician's well-being or utility. In this model a physician's utility depends on three factors: income, hours worked, and the extent of demand inducement. Income and leisure time increase a physician's utility. The practice of demand inducement reduces utility, presumably because of guilt feelings due to a professional code of ethics, or the stigma associated with the behavior should it become public knowledge. Physicians are faced with a trade-off among income, leisure, and conscience. Depending on individual circumstances, the trade-off can affect the quality of care provided to patients.

Controlling Physician Behavior

Patients delegate medical decisions to their physicians because physicians have better information about the causes and consequences of medical conditions. However, physicians' motives are unobserved and may not correspond perfectly with those of the patient and the payer. The problem with the arrangement is that there are two incentive regimes at work that generally interfere with one another. One is the financial

Back-of-the-Envelope

PRICE DISCRIMINATION IN MEDICAL CARE

When suppliers have market power, they are faced with downward-sloping demand curves. The price searcher will frequently discover that in searching for the profit-maximizing price, the opportunity arises to charge customers different prices for the same product. In order to be a successful price discriminator, two important conditions must be met:

- Customers must be classified according to willingness-to-pay and providers must have some way to distinguish which ones are willing to pay higher prices. Conceptually, the provider attempts to determine each group's price elasticity of demand for the product.

- **Arbitrage** must be difficult. Those customers who are able to buy at the low price must have no easy way to resell the product to those charged the higher price.

Medical care delivery provides a classic case where the conditions exist that allow providers to practice **price discrimination**. Patients approach providers with certain identifiable characteristics that help determine their willingness to pay, most notably, whether they have insurance. As with any service, it is difficult for a low-pay patient to resell a medical procedure to a high-pay patient.

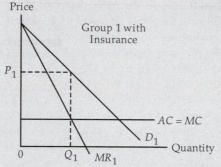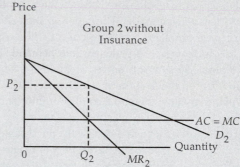

The preceding diagram provides a graphical depiction of how a supplier with market power becomes a price discriminator. Suppose that the medical provider identifies two distinct groups of patients—one with insurance and one without. Those patients with insurance (Group 1) are less price-sensitive than those paying out-of-pocket (Group 2) and thus have a steeper demand curve. To simplify the analysis assume that marginal cost (MC) is constant and equal to average cost (AC). The profit-maximizing level of output for each group is determined by equating marginal revenue (MR) with marginal cost. For Group 1, $MR_1 = MC$ at Q_1. For Group 2, $MR_2 = MC$ at Q_2. At these respective output levels, the provider charges the highest price that the groups are willing to pay, P_1 for Group 1 and P_2 for Group 2.

Clearly, Group 2 pays a lower price for the same medical care, $P_2 < P_1$. Why? Without insurance, their demand is more elastic. Recognizing this, providers charge them less for the same services. Does this really happen in medical care delivery? Four decades ago Kessel (1958) showed how the model of price discrimination applied to medical care. One of the more interesting conclusions of Kessel's research was the implication that the growing popularity of pre-paid medical plans will reduce the ability of providers to practice price discrimination. More competition will mean less price discrimination.

Source: Reuben A. Kessel, "Price Discrimination in Medicine," *The Journal of Law and Economics* 1, 1958, 20–53.

Key Concept 5
Markets and Pricing

arbitrage
The practice of simultaneously buying a commodity at one price and selling it at a higher price.

price discrimination
The practice of selling the same good or service to two different consumers for different prices. The price differential is not based on differences in cost.

Key Concept 7
Competition

arrangement between the payer and the provider designed to control for moral hazard. The other is the moral obligation between patient and provider designed to guarantee the provision of all medically necessary care. Both payer and patient compete for the providers' loyalty to advance their competing goals.

In search of ways to influence provider behavior, health plans have designed incentive regimes to influence the way physicians practice medicine. These regimes include capitation, withholds and bonuses, diagnosis-related groups, clinical rules, and utilization review. To encourage cost-conscious practice patterns, some health plans pay primary care physicians on a capitation basis and make them responsible for referring patients to approved specialists. Under capitation physicians are responsible for the management of care within a fixed budget. In other words, they accept some of the financial risk in making clinical decisions. When the managed care plan establishes a risk-sharing plan, using withholdings and bonuses, the end result curtails the independence of participating physicians. Management tends to focus on costs and with few exceptions, the trade-off is between controlling costs and improving the quality of care.

Do Physicians Respond to Incentives?

Efforts to control costs have led many health plans to adjust the way physicians are paid. One popular approach establishes reduced fee-for-service rates for all covered procedures. When physicians are paid in this manner, many increase the dollar volume of services by changing the way they bill (e.g., unbundling of services and/or upcoding) and by providing more services (Lee, Bumbach, and Jameson, 1990; Wedig, Mitchell, and Cromwell, 1989; Holahan, Dor, and Zuckerman, 1990). Canada has learned that controlling physician fees does not lower expenditures on physicians' services. Fee schedules lead to changed patterns of medical care delivery, including an increased number of follow-up visits (Lomas et al., 1989; Hughes, 1991).

When financial incentives exert pressures, no matter how subtle, clinical decisions may be influenced (Hillman, 1990). Managed care places the physician's clinical judgment on a collision course with his or her pecuniary interests. Theoretically, physicians, well schooled in economic principles, will consider the costs to society when making clinical decisions. But in practice, the payment scheme used by many managed care plans induces physicians to take into consideration the impact of their clinical decisions on their own income. Since physicians share financial risk with managed care plans, they share the same incentives with insurance companies to avoid sick patients (Stone, 1997).

Strong financial incentives essentially turn a physician into an insurance company, usually without the patient base to adequately spread actuarial risk. In a fixed-budget environment, the care that a physician withholds is closely correlated with the income that he or she earns. The current trend of placing physicians at financial risk mixes two types of risk: probability risk and efficiency risk. Probability risk measures the likelihood that patients will utilize medical care based on the characteristics of the patient pool, including age, sex, and health status. Efficiency risk measures how effectively the physician treats the patient. Although physicians control their own efficiency risk, they have no control over probability risk. It is appropriate to hold physicians responsible for efficiency risk; it is inappropriate to hold them responsible for probability risk.

If compensation is adjusted for population characteristics, at least part of the probability risk is transferred back to the insurer. But most plans adjust for only two variables, age and sex, even though age and sex account for less than 20 percent of the annual costs of medical care among patients (Goldfield et al., 1996).

Managed care attempts to shape physician behavior through either clinical rules or financial incentives. Clinical rules establish guidelines that encourage physicians to adopt a particular practice style.[5] The effectiveness of clinical rules depends on the ability of managed care plans to educate physicians about the appropriate practice style, to

---

5 A clinical rule is a specific practice required of all participating physicians, such as a policy to refer patients only to a specific panel of specialists.

use peer pressure to ensure compliance, and to select the physicians who
may participate in the provision of care. In contrast, financial incentives
leave the treatment choice to the physician. But financial incentives create a conflict of interest by compromising the physician's fiduciary
responsibility or exercise of independent clinical judgment. Both
approaches share the goal of encouraging less expensive care.

Less expensive care, however, does not necessarily mean poor-quality
care. Hellinger (1998) cites evidence that the cost-cutting measures practiced by managed care may adversely affect the health of certain vulnerable subpopulations, including older and sicker patients, and that managed care enrollees may suffer because of
problems accessing certain specialized services. In fact, the strongest disincentive for
quality care is for the sickest and most expensive patients. Physicians who provide quality care for their sickest patients will find their practices attracting the sickest patients.
Because most capitation rates are adjusted only for age and sex and not health status,
this strategy results in lost income for the provider. The alternative strategy is to offer a
level of care that encourages sick patients to change providers. This strategy, sometimes
called "patient dumping," does not have to be overt. It may be accomplished in more
subtle ways, including delays in scheduling appointments for certain types of procedures, refusal to refer sick patients to specialists, and failure to meet patient expectations on treatments prescribed and provided.

In other research, Hellinger (1996) examines the impact of financial incentives on
physician behavior, specifically capitation and the use of withholds and bonuses, and
concludes that financial incentives are a key element in explaining lower levels of
spending and utilization in managed care plans. It is important to recognize that all of
the studies comparing utilization rates in managed care with those in fee-for-service
care are unable to differentiate between the impacts of financial incentives and those of
clinical rules. To the extent that plans with strong financial incentives also include stringent clinical rules, it is difficult to separate the impact of the two. However, it is possible to conclude that plans with strong financial incentives and strong clinical rules have
lower utilization rates compared to plans that do not.

Empirical Evidence on the Impact of Financial Incentives

The empirical literature examining the impact of financial incentives on physician
behavior may be divided into three categories: randomized trials, same-disease studies,
and same-physician studies. The largest and most widely cited randomized trial is the
RAND Health Insurance Experiment (Manning et al., 1984). Results of this study concluded that participants in a group model HMO had fewer in-patient hospital days and
lower overall medical expenditures than did participants in a traditional fee-for-service
plan. Martin et al. (1989) examined the impact of a **gatekeeper** operating under a risk-
sharing contract and concluded that physicians at risk for budget deficits had lower
spending per enrollee, attributable to lower specialist referral costs.

gatekeeper
A primary care physician who
directs health care delivery and
determines whether patients
are allowed access to specialty
care.

A limited number of same-disease studies have examined the treatment decisions of
physicians facing different financial incentives. These studies look at the treatment and
diagnostic services provided patients with a variety of diseases, including heart disease,
colorectal cancer, childbirth, and acute myocardial infarction. These studies conclude
that patients treated by HMO physicians receive fewer procedures, diagnostic tests, and
treatments than do patients who use physicians paid under traditional indemnity
insurance arrangements. Epstein, Begg, and McNeil (1986) studied the practices of 27
physicians certified in internal medicine, 10 with fee-for-service practices and 17 in prepaid group practices. They conclude that patients treated in fee-for-service practices
receive 50 percent more electrocardiograms than patients treated in prepaid practices.

Finally, the same-physician studies avoid some of the potential biases inherent in other
approaches. Because practice styles may differ substantially across physicians, by contrasting an individual physician's practices with fee-for-service patients and managed care

patients, same physician studies control for many of the sources of variation that incorrectly affect results. Using this approach, Welch, Pauly, and Hillman (1990) and Murray et al. (1992) conclude that physicians used more services in treating patients enrolled in fee-for-service plans than patients enrolled in prepaid plans.

Not all studies conclude that financial incentives systematically affect physician behavior. Cangialose et al. (1997) and Conrad, Maynard, Cheadle et al. (1998) are two of the most often cited studies that reach the opposite conclusion. However, these studies have methodological problems that bring their results into question. Cangialose et al. (1997) was published in a managed care industry journal bringing into question the objectivity of the peer-review process. Conrad, Maynard, Cheadle et al. (1998) chose health plans where 96 percent of the enrollees were being treated by primary care physicians who shared in the financial risk of treatment. In their own words, this choice "eliminated the influence of health plan payment in this sample" (p. 857).

All of the studies on incentives are potentially subject to certain biases. It may be that patients self-select physicians who practice the style of medicine they prefer. Healthy patients may cluster in prepaid practices. But virtually every study that adjusted for the available information on differences in type of enrollee, physician, and plan concluded that physicians facing financial incentives provided fewer services, diagnostic tests, and procedures than did physicians who are not faced with them. The robustness of these findings suggests that when faced with financial incentives, specifically capitation and the use of withholds and bonuses, physicians alter their practice style to provide fewer services, diagnostic tests, and procedures. This practice may not affect the health status of healthy patients; however, certain vulnerable patients—those who are sick or suffer from chronic conditions—may receive lower quality care.

Most physicians practice in a setting where a variety of insurance arrangements exist simultaneously, variations of both managed care and indemnity insurance. Theory suggests that managed care patients will receive less intensive care than fee-for-service patients. However, a physician may find it difficult to modify his or her practice style based on the type of plan covering the patient. Empirical findings by Glied and Zivin (2002) indicate that financial incentives in fact do affect treatment intensity across patients according to method of payment. Additionally, and more importantly, variations in treatment intensity depend on the relative mix of managed care and fee-for-service patients in the physician's practice. Physicians with a large percentage of their patients covered by HMOs change their practice styles across the board, treating all patients with the lower managed care intensity.

The Market for Nursing Services

Nursing services may be provided by a number of different occupational groups. The two that have specific educational and licensing requirements are registered nurses (RNs) and licensed practical nurses (LPNs). Registered nurses make up the largest component of the nursing workforce. To qualify for the basic RN license, one of three educational programs must be completed—a two-year associate degree, a three-year hospital diploma, or a four-year baccalaureate degree. None of the attempts to raise the minimum educational requirement for the RN license to a baccalaureate degree have gone very far. Licensed practical nurses generally have only 12 to 14 months of training and earn about two-thirds of the $36,000 average annual income of a registered nurse.

As indicated in Table 8.4 on page 221, registered nurses held over 2.3 million jobs in 1999, an increase of almost 27 percent over the decade. Approximately 70 percent of those jobs were in hospitals and one fourth were part time. In 1996 there were 1,508 programs nationwide training registered nurses. First-year nursing enrollment numbered near 120,000 in 1996 with almost 95,000 graduating that same year.

Efforts to curb the growth of health care costs are likely to have significant effects on the market for nursing services. By redesigning the medical work place, hospitals will

NurseWeek.com is the online magazine for nursing professionals. The site offers information about the nursing industry, including continuing education opportunities, seminars and events of interest, and employment opportunities for nursing professionals. The site can be found at **http://www.nursingexcellence. com/.**

ISSUES IN MEDICAL CARE DELIVERY

Do We Really Want Low-Cost Primary Care?

The shortage of primary care physicians and the increased popularity of managed care, with its emphasis on cutting costs, has provided momentum to those who advocate greater autonomy for nurses in treating patients. By allowing advanced-practice nurses to take over some of the more routine duties now reserved for physicians, the United States could save billions of dollars in medical care costs annually. Advanced-practice nurses, comprised of nurse practitioners, nurse anesthetists, and nurse midwives, usually have two years of clinical training beyond the four-year baccalaureate degree. As such, even without experience, they have more training than first-year residents who provide a great deal of the primary care in the nation's teaching hospitals.

Legislation dating back to the 1930s restricts nurses in two important ways. First, nurse practitioners do not have prescriptive authority in many states, which means they are unable to write prescriptions unless they are in a collaborative practice with a licensed physician. Second, not all payment sources, including many private insurance companies and the government, recognize nurse practitioners as qualified providers and thus will not directly reimburse them for their services.

Still, more than 100,000 advanced-practice nurses nationwide offer physical exams, immunizations, preventive screening, and treatment for minor illnesses such as ear infection, sore throat, and the flu. Many see nurse practitioners, who offer their services at a 30 to 70 percent cost-saving compared to general practitioners, as a way to lower costs and improve access to primary care in many underserved areas. Critics, however, feel that lowering the barriers to nurse practitioners will only drive more physicians from general practice into the higher-paying specialties and in the long run will do little to lower costs and improve access.

How many of the restrictions on nursing are based on concerns over quality of care and how many are merely a cultural artifact of an era when female nurses assisted male physicians? One thing is certain: As concern over cost cutting grows, the barriers to an expanded role for nurses will gradually disappear. It is simply a matter of time until economics once again promotes a more effective use of scarce resources.

Source: Adrienne Perry, "Nurse Practitioners Fight Job Restrictions," *The Wall Street Journal*, September 3, 1993, B1, B8.

Key Concept 4
Scarcity and Choice

be able to use more nursing aides to provide much of the low-skill, routine care. Using lower-paid aides can save as much as $25,000 for each job converted from a registered nurse to an aide. In addition, demand will increase for advanced-practice nurses to help providers cut costs for routine primary and preventive care.

The Market for Dental Services

Most of the 168,000 dentists actively practicing in the United States are general practitioners. The remainder practice as specialists in one of eight areas. Orthodontists, comprising the largest group of specialists, straighten teeth. The next largest group is oral and maxillofacial surgeons who specialize in surgery of the mouth and jaw. Other specialties include pediatric dentistry, periodontics, prosthodontics, endodontics, dental public health, and oral pathology.[6]

---

6 Dentists in these areas specialize in the practice of children's dentistry, the treatment of diseases of the gums and supporting bone structure, making dentures and artificial teeth, root canal therapy, epidemiology, and the study of diseases of the mouth.

Table 8.4	Registered Nurses (RNs) in the United States

	Active RNs (thousands)	RNs per 100,000 Population	Nursing Programs	First-Year Enrollment	Nursing Graduates
1950	na	na	1,170	na	25,790
1960	na	na	1,137	na	30,113
1970	750	368	1,340	na	43,103
1980	1,273	560	1,385	105,952	75,523
1985	1,538	641	1,473	118,224	82,075
1990	1,790	714	1,470	108,580	66,088
1995	2,116	798	1,516	127,184	97,052
1996	2,162	815	1,508	119,205	94,757
1997	2,203	823	na	na	76,523
1998	2,239	821	na	na	71,392
1999	2,271	833	na	na	68,709

Source: *Statistical Abstracts of the United States 1999*, Table No. 196; U.S. Department of Health and Human Services, *Health, United States, 2003 with Chartbook on Trends in the Health of Americans*, Table 103, 2003.

More than 90 percent of the dentists practice privately as "solo practitioners." They own their own businesses and employ a small staff of assistants to complement their work effort. Some dentists practice in partnership with others and a small percentage are employed as associates in a larger group practice.

As summarized in Table 8.5, there are 55 dental schools enrolling over 4,300 new students each year in four-year programs. Most dental schools require a minimum of two years of predental education at an accredited undergraduate institution. Most dental students, however, have at least a four-year baccalaureate degree in one of the physical sciences. The course work in dental school is similar to the medical school curriculum. The first two years are spent in learning the basic sciences through classroom instruction and laboratory training. The final two years are spent in clinical work, treating patients under the supervision of licensed dental professors.

Table 8.5	Dentists in the United States

	Active Dentists (thousands)	Dentists per 100,000 Population	Dental Schools	First-Year Enrollment	Dental Graduates
1970	96.0	47	53	na	3,749
1980	121.9	54	60	6,132	5,256
1985	133.5	57	60	5,047	5,353
1990	147.5	59	58	3,979	4,233
1995	153.3	61	54	4,121	3,908
1997	156.5	58	54	4,255	3,930
1998	157.9	58	55	4,347	4,041
1999	164.7	60	55	4,268	4,095
2000	168.0	61	55	4,314	4,171

Source: *Statistical Abstracts of the United States 1999*, Table No. 196; U.S. Department of Health and Human Services, *Health, United States, 2003 with Chartbook on Trends in the Health of Americans*, Table 103, 2003.

Back-of-the-Envelope

MONOPSONY POWER IN THE MARKET FOR REGISTERED NURSES

Chronic shortages have often plagued the labor market for nurses. Public policy has traditionally focused on the supply side of the market offering recommendations to increase the number of nursing graduates. Economists examine the problem from a different perspective. Chronic and persistent shortages may be an indicator of monopsony power. In competitive markets, a shortage results when wages are set below their equilibrium level. Employers compete to attract and retain workers by bidding up the wage until demand and supply are back in balance.

The market for registered nurses may not work this way. Several aspects of the market contribute to the development of monopsony power among employers. The hospital industry is the largest employer of nursing services. Over 70 percent of all nurses in the United States are employed in this setting. This institutional feature establishes a single-buyer model in the local labor market for nursing services with the hospital as the dominant purchaser. Mobile workers can overcome local market monopsony. If enough nurses were willing to move to other communities where wages are higher or transferred their skills and experience to other types of work within the local labor market, competition would raise local wages.

Historically, these normal checks and balances on monopsony power are relatively inoperative in the nursing market. Nursing skills are very job-specific and do not readily transfer to other occupations. The wholesale exodus of nurses leaving the profession for jobs in some other industry poses little threat to the local hospital employer. Additionally, geographic mobility among nurses is also low. Most nurses are married females and often earn less than their spouses. As the secondary income earner within the family, the typical nurse is restricted to the geographic location chosen by the higher-paid spouse.

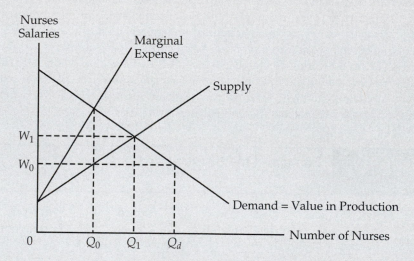

What do these factors mean for nurses in general? Using the diagram, we can see that the monopsonistic employer equates the workers' value in production with their marginal expense, and therefore only Q_0 are hired. To hire that number, the monopsonist pays a wage equal to W_0, substantially less than the competitive wage of W_1 determined by the intersection of supply and demand. With wages below the competitive equilibrium, a shortage of $(Q_d - Q_0)$ exists. Normally, competitive pressures bid wages back up to W_1, but in this case without competitive pressures, wages remain at W_0 and the shortage persists. Nursing unions and the increased mobility of professional women over the past decade have served to improve salaries and

Key Concept 6
Supply and Demand

> muffle the cry of shortages in the profession. In fact, by demanding the competitive wage W_1, the union actually increases the quantity of nurses demanded to Q_1.
>
> **Source**: Lavonne A. Booten and Julia I. Lane, "Hospital Market Structure and the Return to Nursing Education," *Journal of Human Resources 20*(2), 1985, 184–196. Julia Lane and Stephan Gohmann, "Shortage or Surplus: Economic and Noneconomic Approaches to the Analysis of Nursing Labor Markets," *Southern Economic Journal 61*(3), January 1995, 644–653.

The net median income for dentists in private practice was $130,000 per year in 1995. For those in specialty practice the median was $196,000, for generalists it stood at $125,000. First-year dental school enrollment was 6,132 in the 1980–1981 academic year. By 2000, the size of the first-year class had fallen to 4,314. Total student enrollments fell from 22,482 in 1980 to 16,926 in 1998. This decline seems to be the market's response to a surplus of dentists and increased competition for patients. The job outlook for the dental profession looks relatively good. Demand for dental services will grow as the baby-boom generation ages. On average, this group has retained more of its teeth than previous generations and has more disposable income. Thus, the demand for preventive care will remain solid.

Summary and Conclusions

In this chapter we have examined the market for health care professionals, focusing on the market for physicians. Policymakers speak with near unanimity in their claim that residency programs in the United States are turning out too few generalists and too many specialists. The imbalance, if one actually exists, may be corrected by imposing more regulations on the medical education establishment or relying on market forces. Those who would rely on regulation do not believe that the current system will respond to market incentives and change the proportion of residents entering general practice. Advocates of the market approach argue that regulators do not have enough information to correctly predict the needs of the medical care delivery system, and probably would not get it right if they tried. They argue that the proper specialty mix and geographic distribution are better determined through market incentives. In any event, managed care is already bidding up the salaries of primary care physicians, a phenomenon that many believe is the beginning of the adjustment process.

Another important topic in this chapter is the changing incentive structure of the physicians' services market. In a fee-for-service environment the most valuable patient in the physician's practice is the sickest patient. More office visits, more services, and more procedures all translate directly into more income for the physician. In a capitated environment the most valuable patient is the healthiest patient. Sick patients consume costly medical resources without contributing any additional income. Healthy patients generate the same income, and do not consume valuable resources.

Physician behavior is affected when more than 20 percent of patient revenue originates from managed care. If more than one-half originated from a single HMO, we can expect a complete adjustment to the HMO's approach (Kongstvedt and Stanford, 1997). Godbey (1997) states that no doctor wants more than 20 percent of his or her patients from a managed care organization. More than 20 percent "would be a controlling interest."

PROFILE

Gary S. Becker

Considered an imaginative, original thinker by his supporters and accused of intellectual imperialism by his detractors, Gary S. Becker, more than any other scholar, has inspired a revolution in economic thought, extending the boundaries of economic inquiry and ultimately redefining what economists do. Beginning with his dissertation research published in 1957 under the title *The Economics of Discrimination*, Becker's theoretical work has opened to economists the fertile research fields of the other social sciences. An entire generation of economists challenged by his insights has used his theories as a springboard for their own policy-oriented research.

In addition to his early work on discrimination, Becker is responsible for path-breaking research on important social issues such as fertility and demographics, education, crime and punishment, and marriage and divorce—all aspects of human behavior once considered outside the scope of economics. He is best known for his contribution to a symposium on Investment in Human Beings published in a special issue of the *Journal of Political Economy* in 1962. This work, expanded into a book in 1964 entitled *Human Capital*, is recognized as a classic piece of research by economists and serves as the theoretical foundation for a field of study under that same title. Within this framework individuals spend and invest in themselves and their children with the future in mind. Education and training, job search, migration, and medical care are all viewed as investments in human capital. The decision to spend is based on a comparison of the present value of the expected benefits with the present value of the costs.

His innovative thought did not end there. Later research into crime and punishment and the economics of the family has been equally revolutionary, affecting not only economics but also criminology and sociology. In 1992, he became the third straight University of Chicago economist to be awarded the Nobel Prize in Economic Science for extending "the domain of microeconomic analysis to a wide range of human behavior and interaction including nonmarket behavior."

Born in Pottstown, Pennsylvania, Becker graduated from Princeton in 1951. He completed his doctoral training at the University of Chicago in 1955 and was asked to remain there as a member of the faculty. Except for 12 years at Columbia University and the National Bureau of Economic Research, Becker has maintained his Chicago affiliation throughout his professional career. Probably more than any other proponent of the Chicago School of Economics, he has developed and applied the ideas of classic free-market economics in ways his predecessors never considered.[*]

Becker appeared on the academic scene in the 1960s when neoclassical economics was under attack from all fronts. The resurgence of the Marxist critique of capitalism challenged the orthodoxy from the outside, and a subtle movement toward a less rigorous analysis (as exemplified by the work of John K. Galbraith) challenged it from within. But Becker's unrivaled imagination saved the discipline from irrelevancy. For that we are all deeply thankful.

Source: J. R. Shackleton, "Gary S. Becker: the Economist as Empire-builder," in J. R. Shackleton and G. Locksley, eds., *Twelve Contemporary Economists*, Macmillan, 1981; Jonathan Peterson, "Chicago's Lock on the Nobel; Economics Professor is University's Third Winner in Three Years," *Los Angeles Times*, Home Edition, October 14, 1992, D1; and Peter Passell, "New Nobel Laureate Takes Economics Far Afield," *The New York Times*, Late Edition, October 14, 1992, D1.

[*]The Chicago School is more than a geographic location. It is a school of thought based on a methodology rooted in the microeconomic foundations of all of economics. Its theoretical basis is one of self-interested decision makers, market equilibrium, the universal application of the concept of capital, and a healthy skepticism for government-based solutions to economic problems.

ISSUES IN MEDICAL CARE DELIVERY

THE DEMAND FOR DENTAL CARE

Dental care, hospital care, physicians' services, pharmaceuticals—they are all medical care, so they must be the same. Right? If all these medical services are the same, why are they treated so differently in most health insurance plans? Out-of-pocket payments for medical care averaged roughly 20 percent of total spending in 1995. That percentage differs significantly when viewed by category of spending. It stands at 3 percent of hospital spending, 18 percent of physicians' services, 48 percent of dental services, and 60 percent of pharmaceuticals. Why do these percentages vary so dramatically?

The demand for dental care is associated with the same variables that affect the demand for the other types of medical care—prices, income, tastes and preferences, and health status. But there are elements of dental care that are different from other types of medical care. A large portion of dental services is preventive in nature; some might even be considered elective. Since teeth may be thought of as a durable good, much of the normal demand for dental care is for maintenance or repair. Roughly 85 percent of the services performed are comprised of fillings, extractions, cleanings, and examinations. Much of the rest is performed for cosmetic reasons. We want good teeth so we can chew our food free from pain and look good at the same time.

Insurance coverage for dental services has been slow in developing because of the individual's ability to postpone care, plus the fact that it is sometimes difficult to delineate the difference between maintenance and repair on the one hand and pure cosmetics on the other. Because of these characteristics, even partial insurance coverage results in a substantial increase in demand for services. The insured population spends roughly 1.8 times more on dental services than the population at large.

In terms of economics, the demand for dental care is more price elastic than the demand for other forms of medical care. Elasticity estimates vary by type of service and type of person. It is estimated that white females have the price elasticities of demand that range from –0.5 to –0.7. In general, demand of white males and children is more elastic than that of females. This means that adults of both sexes with free dental care will spend two times more than adults with no insurance, and fully insured children will spend three times more than children with no insurance.

Any improvement in dental insurance coverage must be carefully coordinated with policies to increase the supply of dentists. Improved insurance coverage will mean increased demand for dental care. Increased demand coupled with an inelastic supply of dentists will mean increased prices, increased queues, and higher quasi-rents for dentists. Markets will ration scarce resources. That rationing will take the form of higher prices or longer waiting times for office visits.

Source: Willard G. Manning and Charles E. Phelps, "The Demand for Dental Care," *The Bell Journal of Economics* 10, Autumn 1979, 503–525.

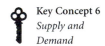

Key Concept 6
Supply and Demand

Questions and Problems

1. If surgeons really have the ability to increase the demand for operations, which kinds of operations will be most affected? Can you think of a way to determine which operations are unnecessary? Provide several examples from your own readings or experience.

2. If the theory of supplier-induced demand is valid, what are the implications for public policy?

3. How does the dual nature of the physician's role—adviser and provider—support the demand-inducement hypothesis? What institutional mechanisms support the possibility of demand inducement? How is this effect reinforced by health insurance? What are the natural limits to the alleged problem?

4. Why is the supply of physicians a major cause of concern? In theory, how would you expect the supply of physicians to affect the price and quantity of medical services provided and physicians' incomes? What is the actual evidence?

5. The American Medical Association (AMA) has been actively involved in shaping the regulation of nursing and other health care practitioners. What are the arguments for and against the AMA determining the scope of legitimate activities for other health care practitioners?

6. "High salaries are essential if we are to have the most capable students pursuing medical careers." Comment.

References

AAMC Data Book: Statistical Information Related to Medical Education, Washington, DC: Association of American Medical Colleges, January 1997.

Charles B. Cangialose, S. J. Cary, L. H. Hoffman, and D. J. Ballard, "Impact of Managed Care Arrangements on Quality of Care: Theory and Evidence," *American Journal of Managed Care 3*(8), August 1997, 1153–1170.

Douglas A. Conrad, et al., "Primary Care Physician Compensation Method in Medical Groups: Does It Influence the Use and Cost of Health Services for Enrollees in Managed Care Organizations?" *Journal of the American Medical Association* 278, March 18, 1998, 853–858.

David M. Eddy, "Clinical Decision Making: From Theory to Practice," *Journal of the American Medical Association 263*(3), January 19, 1990, 441–443.

A. M. Epstein, C. B. Begg, and B. J. McNeil, "The Use of Ambulatory Testing in Prepaid and Fee-For-Service Group Practices: Relation to Perceived Profitability," *The New England Journal of Medicine* 314, April 24, 1986, 1089–1094.

Sherry Glied and Joshua Graff Zivin, "How Do Doctors Behave When Some (But Not All) of Their Patients Are in Managed Care?" *Journal of Health Economics 21*(2), March 2002, 337–353.

Neil A. Godbey, "How Capitation Turned Red Ink to Black at Harris Methodist Health System," *Managed Care 6*(8), August 1997, 88–114.

N. Goldfield, et al., "Methods of Compensating Managed Care Physicians and Hospitals," in N. Goldfield and P. Boland, eds., *Physician Profiling and Risk Adjustment*, Gaithersburg, MD: Aspen Publishers, 1996.

Fred J. Hellinger, "The Effect of Managed Care on Quality: A Review of Recent Evidence," *Archives of Internal Medicine* 158, April 27, 1998, 833–841.

———, "The Impact of Financial Incentives on Physician Behavior in Managed Care Plans: A Review of the Evidence," *Medical Care Research and Review* 53, September 1996, 294–314.

A. L. Hillman, "Health Maintenance Organizations, Financial Incentives, and Physicians' Judgements," *Annals of Internal Medicine 112*(12), June 15, 1990, 891–893.

J. Holahan, A. Dor, and S. Zuckerman, "Understanding the Recent Growth in Medicare Physician Expenditures," *Journal of the American Medical Association 263*(12), March 23–30,1990, 1658–1661.

J. S. Hughes, "How Well Has Canada Contained the Costs of Doctoring?" *Journal of the American Medical Association 265*(18), May 8, 1991, 2347–2351.

Peter R. Kongstvedt and Jean Stanford, "Managed Care Maturity: A New Multidimensional Model," *Future Health: New Dimensions in Strategic Thought*, Washington, DC: Ernst & Young, March 1997.

Richard Kronick, David C. Goodman, John Wennberg, and Edward Wagner, "The Marketplace in Health Care Reform—The Demographic Limitations of Managed Competition," *New England Journal of Medicine 328*(2), January 14, 1993, 148–152.

P. Lee, K. Grumbach, and W. Jameson, "Physician Payment in the 1990s: Factors That Will Shape the Future," *Annual Review of Public Health* 11, 1990, 297–318.

Norman G. Levinsky, "Recruiting for Primary Care," *New England Journal of Medicine 328*(9), March 4, 1993, 656–660.

J. Lomas, C. Fooks, T. Rice, and R. Labelle, "Paying Physicians in Canada: Minding our P's and Q's," *Health Affairs 8*(1), Spring 1989, 80–102.

W. F. Manning, A. Leibowitz, G. A. Goldberg, W. H. Rogers, and J. P. Rogers, "A Controlled Trial of the Effects of a Prepaid Group Practice on Use of Services," *New England Journal of Medicine 310*(23), June 7, 1984, 1505–1510.

D. P. Martin, P. Diehr, K. F. Price, and W. C. Richardson, "Effect of a Gatekeeper Plan on Health Services Use and Charges: A Randomized Trial," *American Journal of Public Health 79*(12), December 1989, 1628–1632.

Klim McPherson, John E. Wennberg, Ole B. Hovind, and Peter Gifford, "Small-Area Variations in the Use of Common Surgical Procedures: An International Comparison of New England, England, and Norway," *New England Journal of Medicine 307*(21), November 18, 1982, 1310–1313.

J. P. Murray, S. Greenfield, S. H. Kaplan, and E. M. Yano, "Ambulatory Testing for Capitation and Fee-For-Service Patients in the Same Practice Setting: Relationships to Outcomes," *Medical Care 30*(3), March 1992, 252–261.

Monica Noether, "The Growing Supply of Physicians: Has the Market Become More Competitive?" *Journal of Labor Economics 4*(4), October 1986, 503–537.

Charles E. Phelps, "Diffusion of Information in Medical Care," *Journal of Economic Perspectives 6*(3), Summer 1992, 23–42.

Robert M. Politzer; Sandra R. Gamliel, James M. Cultice, Carol M. Bazell, Marc L. Rivo, and Fitzhugh Mullan, "Matching Physician Supply and Requirements: Testing Policy Recommendations," *Inquiry 33*(2), Summer 1996, 181–194.

Howard K. Rabinowitz, "Recruitment, Retention, and Follow-Up of Graduates of a Program to Increase the Number of Family Physicians in Rural and Underserved Areas," *New England Journal of Medicine 328*(13), April 1, 1993, 934–939.

Uwe E. Reinhardt, "The Economist's Model of Physician Behavior," *Journal of the American Medical Association 281*(5), February 3, 1999, 462–465.

D. K. Remler et al., "What Do Managed Care Plans Do to Affect Care? Results from a Survey of Physicians," *Inquiry* 34, 1997, 196–204.

Thomas Rice, *The Economics of Health Reconsidered* (Chicago, IL: Health Administration Press, 1998).

Steven A. Schroeder and Lewis G. Sandy, "Specialty Distribution of U.S. Physicians—The Invisible Driver of Health Care Costs," *New England Journal of Medicine 328*(13), April 1, 1993, 961–963.

D. A. Stone, "The Doctor as Businessman: The Changing Politics of a Cultural Icon," *Journal of Health Politics, Policy and Law 22*(2), April 1997, 533–556.

G. Wedig, J. B. Mitchell, and J. Cromwell, "Can Price Controls Induce Optimal Physician Behavior?" *Journal of Health Politics, Policy, and Law 14*(3), Fall 1989, 601–620.

William B. Weeks, Amy E. Wallace, Myron M. Wallace, and H. Gilbert Welch, "A Comparison of the Educational Costs and Incomes of Physicians and Other Professionals," *New England Journal of Medicine 330*(18), May 5, 1994, 1280–1286.

W. P. Welch, Mark V. Pauly, and Alan L. Hillman, "Toward New Topologies for HMOs," *Milbank Quarterly 68*(2), 1990, 221–230.

John E. Wennberg, "Dealing with Medical Practice Variations: A Proposal for Action," *Health Affairs 3*(2), Summer 1984, 6–32.

Chapter 9

The Market for Hospital Services

The publication of the **Flexner Report** in 1910 served as a catalyst for general reform in medical care delivery. Nowhere are the effects more noticeable than in the hospital services industry. Hospitals, once notorious places more likely to spread diseases than cure them, have since been transformed into the focal point of the medical care delivery system.

This chapter examines the market for hospital services. The first two sections provide a brief history of hospitals and an examination of the institutional setting in the United States. Following this is a discussion of the role of the private, not-for-profit hospital as the dominant organization in the industry. The chapter also examines several popular theories of hospital behavior, and finally, recent developments in the industry, in particular the trend toward multi-hospital systems.

A Brief History of American Hospitals[1]

Three important factors served to transform hospitals into the modern medical institutions they have become today: the germ theory of disease, advances in medical technology, and increased urbanization. These changes have been accompanied by a dramatic change in patient expectations. No longer do patients seek a caring environment exclusively; they have come to expect a cure.

The development of the germ theory of disease, first articulated by Louis Pasteur in 1870, revolutionized the treatment of patients. Diseases were seen as having specific causes, rather than being viewed as disequilibria or the result of moral turpitude. The search for causal factors required more elaborate testing and diagnostic services. Centralized medical care, bringing the patient to the practitioner, became a necessity.

New hospital technology, especially advances in surgical and diagnostic imaging, provided physicians with the tools that would revolutionize medical intervention. Anesthesia was first used in surgery in 1846. But it was not until the adoption of antiseptic procedures beginning in 1867 that the high rates of death from infection following surgery began to fall. The introduction of X-ray technology in the late 1800s and more recently the development of more advanced imaging (CT scans and magnetic resonance imaging) vastly improved the ability to diagnose injury and illness.

A third factor, urbanization, also played an important role in the centralization of medical facilities. Migration to the urban centers meant more one-person households and fewer extended-family living arrangements. People could no longer count on treatment at home. Home was an apartment building or boarding house, and likely inappropriate for convalescence. Without family nearby patients had no one to serve as caregiver anyway.

---

1 A more complete development of the history of the modern hospital can be found in Stevens (1989).

When hospitals were financed through taxation and philanthropy, patient fees were only of minor importance. As middle-class use of hospital services increased, changes in financing were inevitable. By 1900, patient fees comprised over one third of hospital income.

What has come to be known as the modern hospital began to emerge in the twentieth century. The important developments that led to today's acute care community hospital are summarized here:

- **1900 to 1915**: The distinguished Flexner Report (1910) served as a pointed condemnation of medical education. In its wake, bogus medical schools were closed, standards became more stringent, and the goal of "scientific medicine" was formulated. The general reform of medicine led to affiliations between medical schools and hospitals and ultimately the formation of the teaching hospital.

- **1920s**: Continued reforms were aimed at driving incompetent physicians out of the profession. Physician licensing became more structured and hospital admission privileges were restricted to members of certain medical societies.

  The decade also saw the role of nurses change dramatically. Prior to the 1928 reforms in nursing education, poorly trained volunteers or nurses in training did most of the in-hospital nursing. Trained nurses established community practices that directly competed with hospitals. After the reforms, nurses were no longer competitors with the hospitals.

- **1930s**: The reliance on patient fees caused severe financial problems for hospitals during the Great Depression. The introduction of private health insurance during the decade would later transform medical care financing. Modeled after a prepaid hospital plan for Dallas schoolteachers developed by Baylor University Hospital, the American Hospital Association (AHA) established the first Blue Cross plan and soon had a virtual monopoly in hospital insurance.

  The decade saw a revolution in pharmaceuticals. The most important advance was the development of sulfa drugs and penicillin. For the first time, physicians had the power to cure diseases based on infection.

- **1940s**: Wartime demands resulted in a sharp increase in the number of physicians and nurses in training. The war provided a unique opportunity to improve skills and also to develop new techniques. The federal government also became actively involved in providing hospital care. The passage of the Hill-Burton Act of 1946 dedicated the government to replacing an aging hospital infrastructure that had deteriorated during the Depression and war. With priority given to hospital construction in rural and poor parts of the country, Hill-Burton served to create a climate in the hospital sector making uncompensated care an expected element of the overall health care financing mechanism.

  Precluded from offering higher wages because of rigid price controls, companies were forced to compete for workers by offering better benefits packages, including group health insurance. A ruling by the National Labor Relations Board in 1948 made health insurance a permanent feature in labor negotiations by ruling that it was subject to **collective bargaining**. Tax-deductible for the employer and tax-exempt for the employee, group health plans now cover over one-half of all workers with private health insurance.

- **1950s**: Vaccines against polio and rubella marked the true beginning of high technology in medicine. These developments, combined with the widespread use of antibiotics, helped change the image of medicine. Physicians were no longer practitioners with limited knowledge able only

collective bargaining
The negotiation process whereby representatives of employers and employees agree upon the terms of a labor contract, including wages and benefits.

to ease suffering. We now expect to leave the doctor's office cured. The anticipated number of doctor and hospital visits during a person's lifetime increased significantly, along with the concern over how to pay for them. The result was an increased demand for private health insurance.

Advances in tools of medical research highlighted the decade. The light microscope with magnification of 2,000 times had been in use since the seventeenth century. The development of the electron microscope with magnification of one million times allowed the study of cell structure and metabolism. (Today, the scanning electron microscope can generate three-dimensional images.)

- **1960s:** Congress created Medicare and Medicaid, making the federal government the major purchaser of health care services. Physicians who opposed the program as "socialized medicine" and prophesied ruin under a government-run system soon learned to love it. No longer worried about the ability of elders and the indigent to pay their doctor bills, physicians' earnings rose rapidly. Today, over one half of physicians' income originates from government sources.

  The decade also witnessed the beginnings of the investor-owned, for-profit hospital system. Prior to the mid-1960s, for-profit hospitals were small, rare, and established to benefit clearly defined patient groups. Until the creation of Medicare and Medicaid, the general population with large numbers of elderly and uninsured was not a dependable source of revenue. Thus, Medicare and Medicaid, serving as a stable funding source, actually facilitated the development of the for-profit hospital sector.

- **1970s:** Explosive growth typified the medical care system: new hospitals and clinics, medical school admissions, foreign educated doctors, open-heart surgery, transplants, and helicopter ambulances. The total number of surgeries increased from 14.8 million in 1972 to 24.6 million in 1997. Much of the increase was likely necessary. Nonetheless, it was an ominous sign when the procedures most lucrative to physicians under the payment system in place escalated at the fastest rate.

  The intensity of medical interventions also increased dramatically. Intensive care units (ICUs) became widely used. Trauma centers were established in most areas. Although the trauma center is one of those expenses that may be worth the cost, the ICU in contrast has created a painful dilemma. Originally designed for temporary use following shock or surgery, its function has been extended to the terminally ill and the declining elderly—patients with little likelihood of recovery.

  All the developments of the past decade shared one thing in common. They are all expensive. Health care expenditures increased at an average annual rate of 13 percent during the 1970s. By the end of the decade, Medicare expenditures were growing at an annual rate of over 20 percent. Concerned by the spending growth, state rate setting legislation and certificate of need (CON) laws were used more frequently. CON laws required governmental approval for capital expansion projects in hospitals, including bed capacity and medical equipment. The avoidance of costly duplication of services and the reduction of excess capacity were used to justify such restrictions. In practice, CON laws served to reduce competition and actually limited the entry of HMOs and nursing homes in some markets (Mayo and McFarland, 1989).

- **1980s:** By 1982, health care expenditures exceeded 10 percent of gross domestic product for the first time. To slow the rate of growth in federal expenditures, Medicare initiated a new hospital reimbursement scheme based on the principal diagnosis rather than services performed.

Implemented in 1983, diagnosis-related groups (DRGs) have had profound effects on the hospital industry, moving a large percentage of the financing from retrospective to prospective payment.

- **1990s:** Managed care was the dominant factor affecting medical care delivery during the decade. Capitation and risk sharing have transformed the industry. Hospitals are no longer the revenue generators they once were; instead they have become cost centers. **Horizontal integration**, characterized by hospital mergers and consolidations, transformed an industry that was once highly fragmented with many stand-alone facilities into one where multihospital systems are common. A system characterized by underutilization and overstaffing now experiences a move toward integrated systems and a wave of not-for-profit to for-profit conversions. With administrators downsizing in the name of efficiency, many are concerned about the quality of care and the provision of indigent care.

> **horizontal integration**
> The merger of two or more firms that produce the same good or service.

The U.S. Institutional Setting

Hospitals are by far the most important institutional setting for the provision of medical services. In 2001, hospital expenditures totaled more than $451 billion, one third of national health care spending, and over four percent of GDP. In addition to high overall spending, the hospital is also the most expensive setting on a per-unit basis.

Hospital Classification

Hospitals are classified according to the length of stay, the major type of service delivered, and the type of ownership. Hospitals with average length of stay of less than 30 days are classified as short-term hospitals. Long-term hospitals are those with average length of stay of over 30 days.

Community Hospitals

Community hospitals are the most common hospital classified by types of services offered. Under the current classification scheme adopted in 1972, a community hospital is defined as a short-stay hospital, providing not only general services, but also specialty care, including obstetrics and gynecology; eye, ear, nose and throat; and rehabilitation and orthopedic services. Other hospitals are classified according to specialized services offered. These include hospitals that provide psychiatric services and hospitals that treat individuals with tuberculosis and other respiratory diseases.

Community hospitals are also classified according to control or ownership. The most prominent form of ownership is the private not-for-profit hospital, representing 61.1 percent of all hospitals in 2001. This figure understates somewhat the importance of this organizational form that tends to be on average larger than the other types, controlling 70.8 percent of all beds. For-profit hospitals represent 15.4 percent of all community hospitals and 13.2 percent of all beds. The remaining 23.5 percent of community hospitals and 16.0 percent of the beds are government owned, usually by the states. Community hospital figures do not include 243 federal hospitals, with over 51,000 beds.

Over 88 percent of all nonfederal hospitals are classified as community hospitals. Selected measures for the community hospital are shown in Table 9.1. The number of community hospitals in existence peaked in the early 1980s. Since that time the decline has been about one percent per year, until 2001 when the number stood at 4,908. Most of the decline has come from the small and rural hospitals, many of which had been government owned. The number of beds experienced a similar downward trend. In fact, until the mid-1980s, the number of beds was declining faster than the number of hospitals. The number of beds per 1,000 population stood at 4.38 in 1980. The steady decline since then left the United States with 2.90 beds per 1,000 in 2001. Despite the

The AHA news is a weekly online publication of the American Hospital Association. Access this site at **http://www.ahanews.com/**.

ISSUES IN MEDICAL CARE DELIVERY

FEDERAL HOSPITAL SUBSIDIES: EXPANSION IN THE FACE OF SURPLUS

Increasingly, hospitals are coming under pressure to expand their out-patient capabilities. The general trend in the inpatient market is down—admissions are down and the average length of stay continues to fall. At the same time the demand for outpatient procedures and places to perform them surges ahead. In 1980, less than one out of every six surgical procedures was done on an outpatient basis. Two decades later, over 60 percent were performed in an outpatient setting and the number continues to grow.

In the face of these trends and a general surplus of beds, hospitals in New York State continued to expand. The hospital pricing structure in the state created perverse economic incentives, making it profitable for hospitals to expand in spite of the surplus. The state's system of price controls enabled hospitals to base their prices on a combination of the interest paid on long-term debt and depreciation on their physical plant. Repayments on long-term debt generally include interest plus a small principal reduction, making it profitable for hospitals to borrow to expand.

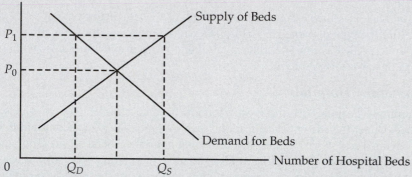

How does this situation result in a surplus? Using the graph above, we see that charging prices above the market equilibrium price (P_1) results in quantity supplied (Q_S) exceeding quantity demanded (Q_D). Some estimate that New York State has 40 percent more beds than patients.

For at least the first 15 years or so of a loan repayment, the depreciation expense tends to exceed the principal payments and the hospital is able to generate solid cash flows. As the hospital's physical plant ages, depreciation expense falls, so the regulated prices also fall. At about the same time, the principal repayment on the loan begins to climb. The only way out of the dilemma is to expand again, whether or not the market requires additional facilities.

Normally, the credit market regulates this tendency by making capital costly (if it is available at all). Relative to the national average, New York hospitals suffered from poor profit margins. As a result, many were cash poor. More than one fifth had such bad credit ratings that they were unable to raise money in the private capital markets.

Everyone needs a champion and New York hospitals found one in the Hospital Mortgage Insurance Program. Created in 1968, the program was originally intended to provide federal insurance on small loans (up to $5 million) to hospitals otherwise shut out of private capital markets. Since its inception, 300 hospitals in 40 states have used the guaranty program. The vast majority of the outstanding loans are to 64 of

New York's 221 hospitals. In contrast, only two Californian hospitals have federal loan guarantees, totaling a fraction of the New York total, and hospitals in 32 other states have none.

All good things must come to an end. The system of price controls was lifted on January 1, 1997. Harsh by some accounts and not subject to political manipulation, a market-driven transition to a deregulated system has not been easy. Staggered by a net loss of nearly $25 million, St. Luke's-Roosevelt Hospital in Manhattan merged with Beth Israel. Flushing Hospital in Queens filed for bankruptcy protection from its creditors. Even the elite New York Presbyterian Hospital did what was once considered unthinkable—it merged with for-profit Columbia.

Not all hospitals were losing money. In fact, 1997 was marked by an overall state hospital surplus of $739 million. But without the $1.3 billion in state subsidies for physician training and the provision of indigent care, the picture would not be as bright. Deregulation has cut deeply into hospital operating budgets, and life without subsidies began in 2001. Whether the system adjusts to market competition or collapses under its own bureaucratic weight will soon become clearer.

Source: Lucette Lagnado, "Hospitals' Building Sprees Subsidized by Government," *The Wall Street Journal*, November 22, 1996, A1; Lucette Lagnado, "New York Study Could Stoke Hospital Debate," *The Wall Street Journal*, January 25, 1999, B1, B4.

Key Concept 7
Competition

number of hospitals declining, the number of beds falling, and physicians admitting fewer patients, the average occupancy rates have also fallen dramatically. In 1980 on average over three fourths of all beds were occupied. By 1990 that fraction had fallen to barely two thirds and by 2001 it stood at 64.5 percent.

| Table 9.1 | Selected Characteristics of Non-Federal, Short-Stay Community Hospitals (various years 1970–2001) |

Measure	1970	1980	1985	1990	1995	1998	2000	2001
No. of hospitals	5,859	5,904	5,784	5,420	5,194	5,015	4,915	4,908
Beds (thousands)	848.2	992.0	1,003.1	929.4	872.7	840.0	823.6	826.0
Beds per 1,000 population	4.17	4.38	4.06	3.73	3.32	3.11	2.93	2.90
Admissions (thousands)	29,252	36,143	33,449	31,181	30,945	31,812	33,089	33,814
Admissions per 1,000 population	144.0	159.6	135.6	125.4	117.9	117.7	117.6	118.7
Resident U.S. Population	203.2	226.5	247.1	248.7	262.5	270.3	281.4	284.8
Average length of stay (days)	7.7	7.6	7.1	7.2	6.5	6.0	5.8	5.7
Percent occupancy	78.0	75.4	64.8	66.8	62.8	62.5	63.9	64.5
Outpatient visits (millions)	133.5	202.3	218.7	301.3	414.3	474.2	521.4	538.5
Outpatient visits per admission	4.57	5.60	6.54	9.66	13.39	14.91	15.76	15.93
Outpatient surgeries as a percent of total	—	16.3	34.6	50.5	58.1	61.6	62.7	63.0
Cost per day ($)	74	245	460	687	968	1,067	1,149	1,217
Cost per stay ($)	605	1,851	3,245	4,947	6,216	6,386	6,649	6,980

Source: *Statistical Abstracts of the United States*, various years; and National Center for Health Statistics (1996); and *Health, United States, 2003: With Chartbook on Trends in the Health of Americans*, Tables 95, 106, and 122, 2003.

The other major trends evident from the table have been driven by the goal of controlling costs. Since 1970, cost per day has increased over 16 times from $74 to $1,217. Cost per stay has increased 11 times from $605 to $6,980. To counter the rising costs, the focus has been on controlling inpatient hospital stays, the most expensive episode of care usually encountered. With admissions down, outpatient visits have increased substantially from 133.5 million in 1970 to 538.5 million in 2001. Almost 90 percent of all hospitals have outpatient departments performing 63 percent of all surgical operations. As a result, the average length of stay for inpatient services has fallen from 7.7 days to 5.7 days.

Even as the number of hospitals has decreased, the number of freestanding ambulatory care centers has increased dramatically, including surgical centers, physical therapy centers, and diagnostic imaging centers, many of which are owned and operated by physicians. Competing directly with hospitals, these facilities may have a competitive advantage since both rely on referrals from physicians for their patients. Government policy and professional ethics serve to reduce any conflict of interest by placing restrictions on self-referral to physician-owned facilities.

> **Policy Issue**
>
> For-profit clinics operate under a different set of requirements with respect to the provision of free care compared with not-for-profit hospitals.

The bigger issue may be the impact of these freestanding clinics on the ability of hospitals to provide free care for the indigent and uninsured. Many are for-profit and do not have a legal requirement to provide charity care. By taking only fully insured patients (called cream skimming), they reduce the operating base of hospitals and make cost shifting more difficult.

Teaching Hospitals

About 20 percent of all hospitals in the United States have an affiliation with one or more of the nation's 125 medical schools and sponsor at least one residency-training program. More than 400 hospitals are members in the Council of Teaching Hospitals of the Association of American Medical Colleges. To qualify for membership in this association, a hospital must participate in at least four approved residency programs. Nationwide, 80 of these teaching hospitals are university owned and 70 are operated by the Department of Veterans Affairs (AAMC, 1999).

> **Policy Issue**
>
> The nation's teaching hospitals shoulder a disproportionate share of the burden of providing free care to the indigent and uninsured.

Most of the teaching hospitals are located in major metropolitan areas with populations in excess of 1 million. On average they have more beds, longer patients stays, and higher occupancy rates than their nonteaching counterparts, with predictable results—higher costs. Not only are teaching and research expensive but also because of a significant presence in the inner city, these hospitals find their emergency rooms and outpatient clinics filled with uninsured patients seeking free care.

Recognizing the legitimacy of these higher costs of education and research, the federal government provides subsidies, both direct and indirect, to supplement hospital revenues. Direct subsidies include stipends for residents, salaries for teaching physicians, grants for research, and overhead payments for administrative expenses. Indirect subsidies are provided in the form of higher reimbursement rates for Medicare patients. With cutbacks in Medicare reimbursements, teaching hospitals are finding that they, too, must respond to the prospects of a more competitive marketplace.

Key Concept 7
Competition

Hospital Spending

The growth in the hospital sector can be seen more clearly upon examining the change in expenses (excluding new construction) for community hospitals and the total hospital sector. Hospital spending has increased from $9.3 billion in 1960 to over $451 billion in 2001. The average growth rates in spending were well over 10 percent per year through much of the 1980s. Since then spending has abated somewhat, increasing at less than 4 percent per year since 1995.

The moderation in spending growth may be in part attributable to the introduction of prospective payment in 1983. Hospital spending had increased to almost 40 percent of total health care expenditures by 1985. Since that time hospital spending has fallen to 32 percent of total health care expenditures.

Most hospital spending is by third-party payers. Government sources pay over 60 percent of all hospital spending with Medicare and Medicaid providing over three fourths of that amount. Private insurance pays about 30 percent. Patients pay 3.4 percent out-of-pocket and the remaining 5 percent is paid from other private funds, primarily charitable donations, and miscellaneous hospital revenues (gift shops, parking, and cafeterias). The patient share of hospital spending, three cents out of every $1, has fallen over the past 40 years from almost 21 cents in 1960.

With Medicare and Medicaid paying such a large percentage of the total hospital bill, government reimbursement rules play a big role in determining the financial stability of the hospital sector. Pressure from Congress to slow the rate of spending has contributed to a complicated system of subsidies and cross-subsidies among payers. Morrisey (1995) reported that Medicare paid 85 percent of the actual costs incurred by hospitals in 1992 and Medicaid paid 78 percent. In addition to these underpayments, hospitals provided billions of dollars in uncompensated care to the uninsured. To make up the shortfall, patients covered by private insurance were charged 138 percent of actual costs incurred in treating them, a practice called *cost shifting*.

Key Concept 5
Markets and Pricing

Structure of the Hospital Market

Economics predicts that competition in most markets improves economic welfare. This improvement in economic welfare comes about as a result of lower prices, improved efficiency, and higher quality. But does this prediction hold in the hospital sector? Before answering that question, maybe we should explore how competitive the hospital sector is in the first place.

Competition may be viewed from the perspective of how well a market fits the characteristics of the perfectly competitive model. Applying the discussion from Chapter 2, competition depends on the number of operating firms in the market, the nature of the product or services offered, the relative ease of entering the market with a competing firm, and the amount of information available to consumers.

Key Concept 7
Competition

Hospital markets may not fit the competitive model very well since so many of the structural characteristics of perfect competition are violated. Local markets, where most hospital services are purchased, typically have a limited number of hospitals.[2] Services are not standardized across hospitals. In fact, hospitals expend a considerable amount of resources to differentiate themselves from their rivals. Relatively uninformed consumers who, for the most part, leave the decision making to their physicians characterize the decision-making process. Third-party insurance pays for most of the care, leaving patients insensitive to price differences.

No theoretical basis is available for determining the minimum number of hospitals needed to sustain a competitive environment. How many providers are needed to promote competition? In many metropolitan areas numerous hospitals provide a complete range of medical services, conveniently located within a short distance of perhaps several hundred thousand residents. For example, the Dallas-Fort Worth metroplex, with a population of 4.86 million in 1998, had 70 hospitals, most located within a reasonable commute of one another. In fact, over 42 percent of the population of the United States lives in metropolitan areas with over 1.2 million inhabitants. Based on the number of hospitals per 1,000 inhabitants nationwide, a metropolitan area of this size would have approximately 23 hospitals. The other 58 percent of the population is distributed according to the data presented in Table 9.2. More than 70 percent of the population in 1990 lived in markets with more than 180,000 inhabitants, a minimum size necessary to provide a full range of acute care hospital services to the surrounding community. This size area could likely support three to four community hospitals.

http://

HCA Inc. owns and operates over 200 hospitals and 70 out-patient surgery centers in 24 states, England and Switzerland. A for-profit corporation, HCA's strategy is to build comprehensive networks of medical services in local markets and integrate various services to deliver patient care with maximum efficiency. Check it out at **http://www.hcahealthcare.com/.**

Key Concept 9
Market Failure

---

2 The markets for both primary and secondary care tend to be local in nature. The market for tertiary care, in contrast, is regional or even national in scope.

Back-of-the-Envelope

THE THEORY OF COST SHIFTING

How do hospitals provide free care to the uninsured? How can a hospital afford to provide care to Medicare patients at prices substantially below the price paid by those who have private insurance? The evidence seems to support the claim that hospitals merely shift the cost of care for the elderly and indigent to private pay patients (PPAC, 1995). According to Congressional reports, Medicare payment rates fell 11 percent below the cost of treating patients while private patients paid 29 percent more than cost. Are Medicare patients simply receiving a discount, or are private patients paying higher prices to subsidize care for the elderly?

Key Concept 6
Supply and Demand

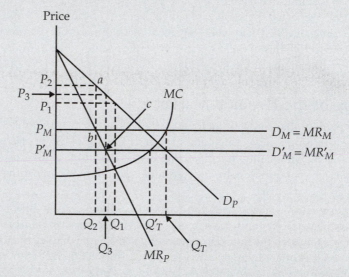

We can gain insights to these issues using a simple model of hospital behavior. In the diagram, a hospital treating only private patients will have a demand curve of D_P and marginal revenue curve of MR_P. Assuming profit (or surplus) maximization, the hospital will set $MR_P = MC$ and provide Q_1 services at P_1.

A hospital that accepts Medicare patients is obliged to accept Medicare prospective payment for the services provided. Typically, this means a lower price, P_M, represented by the demand curve D_M and marginal revenue curve MR_M. The hospital is faced with a new demand curve equal to D_P down to point *a*, dropping down to D_M thereafter. More importantly, the new marginal revenue curve is MR_P to point *b* and then becomes MR_M. Profit is maximized where $MR = MC$, providing Q_T services. The hospital sees Q_2 private patients and charges them a higher price P_2 ($> P_1$). The $(Q_T - Q_2)$ Medicare patients will be provided medical care at a price equal to P_M. (Note, at point *b* the hospital quits seeing private patients since beyond that point the marginal revenue from Medicare patients, MR_M, is greater than that from private patients, MR_P.)

Key Concept 3
Marginal Analysis

What happens when Medicare lowers the payment rates to hospitals (similar to what happened in the Balanced Budget Act of 1997)? In the diagram above, the Medicare price falls to P'_M and the Medicare demand and marginal revenue curves fall accordingly. The hospital's marginal revenue curve changes to MR_P down to point c and MR_M thereafter. Now more private patients are seen (Q_3) and the price they pay (P_3) is lower (but still greater than P_1). Likewise, fewer Medicare patients are served ($Q'_T - Q_3$).

This analysis seems to indicate that the government payment mechanism has a tremendous impact on the amount private patients pay for hospital services. In general, private-sector prices are higher due to Medicare. However, when Medicare lowers the rates paid to hospitals for treating the elderly, there is downward pressure on prices paid by everyone else.

Several extensions could be added to the analysis. Suppose that the hospital had constant marginal cost and significant excess capacity. In that case, the hospital would treat each payer group as separate markets and merely practice classic price discrimination. Under those conditions, changes in the payment structure for Medicare will have no impact on prices paid by the private sector. A second issue that could be examined deals with how low the Medicare price can fall before the elderly find themselves priced out of the market. If payment rates are set below the intersection of MR_p and MC, the hospital will find it unprofitable to treat Medicare patients period and will likely do everything possible (legally) to discourage their admission.

Source: Prospective Payment Assessment Commission (PPAC), *Medicare and the American Health Care System*, Report to Congress, June 1995; and Michael A. Morrisey, *Cost Shifting in Health Care: Separating Evidence from Rhetoric*, Washington, DC: AEI Press, 1995.

The fact that physicians make most of the important decisions regarding hospital care may be a problem if demand inducement can be shown to be extensive. As you may recall, most of the research has shown physicians tend to be responsible agents for their patients. Even though patients pay only a small percentage of their hospital bills, three percent on average, and may be unconcerned about prices, the third-party payers are concerned and expend a great deal of time and resources to cut costs.

Is the hospital market competitive? Several attempts have been made to examine the issue empirically. Held and Pauly (1983) found little evidence of price competition among hospitals. They do seem to compete, but competition is based on quality of care and other amenities, not price. Robinson et al. (1988) could find competition only on certain nonprice aspects of the hospital stay, in particular, longer stays in regions where there are more hospitals. Following this line of reasoning, research seems to indicate that as competition increases in the hospital sector, costs tend to increase (Luft et al., 1986; and Robinson and Luft, 1987).

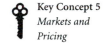 Key Concept 5
Markets and Pricing

Feldman and Dowd (1986) approached the question from a different perspective. They suggested that the answer to the question could be determined by estimating the price elasticity of demand for individual hospitals. Price elasticities close to infinity (or at least significantly greater than 1) would provide evidence for competitive markets. Using data from the early 1980s, they concluded that certain patient groups, especially Medicare patients, had no price sensitivity at all. Thus, hospital markets did not seem to be competitive.

Although early empirical evidence does not seem to support the hypothesis that hospital markets are competitive, the research was conducted prior to the recent expansion of managed care as a way of organizing and financing medical care delivery. As you may recall from Chapter 7, these changes have had a significant impact on

Table 9.2	Population Distribution United States, 1990

Metropolitan Area Size	Percent of Population
Fewer than 180,000	29
180,000 to 360,000	8
360,000–1.2 million	21
Greater than 1.2 million	42

Source: Kronick, et al. (1993).

ISSUES IN MEDICAL CARE DELIVERY

POPULATION REQUIRED TO SUPPORT A HOSPITAL

The gap in the availability of health care services between urban and rural areas has increased substantially with the recent changes in health care delivery, including improved transportation services, expanded use of outpatient services, and the increased use of medical technology. Access to health care services in a community is largely determined by the presence of a hospital. The empirical evidence seems to indicate that rural communities are underserved relative to their urban counterparts. Does it make more sense to bring medical services to rural communities or is it more efficient to bring rural residents to urban centers where medical services can be delivered more effectively?

Using 1996 cross-sectional data on hospital locations in Texas, Henderson and Taylor (2003) estimate the impact of patient demand and rural isolation on the availability of hospital services. Drawing from a large body of literature called central place theory, the authors estimate the minimum market size (or population threshold) needed to support any given number of hospitals. Their results suggest that the number of hospitals in a given geographic area depends on area demand patterns, usually measured by population size, population density, and per capita income, and factors affecting transportation costs, measured by rural isolation.

The empirical results suggest that the typical community in Texas, one that is 47 miles from the nearest metropolitan area with a per capita income of $18,000, must have a population of 35,675 to support a single community hospital and over 80,000 to support two. Results also identify a noticeable tradeoff between per capita income and population. Communities with higher per capita income require fewer residents to support a hospital. As per capita income approaches $30,000, the number of residents required to support a hospital falls below 20,000.

Many of the services available in the hospital setting are considered higher-ordered services, those services that are expensive to offer and require specialized resources to provide. Theory predicts that higher-ordered services will cluster in geographic areas that can support them, driving down the average cost of providing the service. As a result, the number of people required to support a hospital actually declines as a community becomes more urbanized due to these so-called agglomeration economies.

Source: James W. Henderson, and Beck A. Taylor, "Rural Isolation and the Availability of Hospital Services," *Journal of Rural Studies* 19, 2003, 363–372.

the nature of competition in medical care delivery. The use of diagnosis-related groups (DRGs) began to put pressure on hospitals in the mid-1980s to limit the use of non-price competitive strategies that had been so prevalent. The expanded use of prospective payment in managed care has resulted in more price competition. The relationship between payer and provider is changing dramatically, characterized by aggressive negotiations over prices. Some hospital markets may be more competitive than others, but all are experiencing increased competition.

Back to the original question, will increased competition in the hospital sector improve economic welfare? The answer to this question is rife with policy implications, particularly with respect to mergers, acquisitions, and collaborative decisions regarding services offered. There are two views on this issue. The first argues that increased competition leads to a "medical arms race" and the provision of services of questionable medical necessity. Two factors play an important role in the medical arms race. First,

Policy Issue

Will increased competition in the hospital sector improve economic welfare?

patients pay only a small percentage of their hospital costs and second, the prices paid for services are highly regulated with over one half of hospital services paid by Medicare and Medicaid. Because patient demand is price inelastic, hospitals do not practice price competition. Rather they compete for patients by providing more services and higher quality services than patients would demand under more normal conditions. Excessive quality is inefficient and does not unequivocally improve economic welfare. The alternative view argues that increased competition in the hospital sector yields the same benefits to economic welfare that it does in any other market, namely, lower prices, increased efficiency, and improved quality.

Key Concept 8
Efficiency

Early empirical research by Feldstein (1971) and Robinson and Luft (1985) provided support for the existence of a medical arms race in the hospital sector. Later research by Pauly (1987) and Dranove et al. (1992) supported the alternative view that competition in the hospital sector actually improved economic welfare by lowering prices and costs. This ambiguity has been cleared up to some extent by more recent empirical evidence. Dranove and White (1994) identified a trend beginning in the mid-1980s where increasing competition in the U.S. hospital sector lowered both price and cost. More recently, Gaynor and Haas-Wilson (1999) and Keeler, Melnick, and Zwanziger (1999) confirmed these results. Together, their research documented the price-reducing effects of competition in both the for-profit and the not-for-profit sectors. Kessler and McClellan (2000), correcting for certain empirical shortcomings of the previous research, found that increased competition in the hospital sector did increase prices and costs in the 1980s, lending support to the medical arms race explanation. At the same time, this quality-based competition resulted in improvements in medical outcomes for some patients, leaving unanswered the question of whether competition improved economic welfare. They went on, however, to find that competition in the 1990s not only increased quality in the hospital sector, but also lowered costs, unequivocally improving economic welfare. Testing the hypothesis that more efficient firms grow faster, Frech and Mobley (2000) confirmed that concentration in the hospital industry, via merger and consolidation, has improved efficiency in that industry.

The best evidence available at this time leads us to conclude that competition in the hospital sector during the 1980s did result in a medical arms race that improved the quality of care for some patients, but also drove up costs substantially. Furthermore, as competition continued to escalate in the 1990s quality continued to improve and costs began to fall, in spite of increased concentration, supporting the predictions of traditional economic analysis.

Hospital Pricing

The cost-plus pricing strategy practiced until the early 1980s was a product of a financing system where insurers, public and private, reimbursed on the basis of cost. The incentive to inflate costs to increase profit was pervasive. Improved facilities, better technology, and increased staffing led to increased cost and in turn increased profits. The move to prepayment established preadmission prices based on principal diagnosis.

Today's hospital pricing bears little association with costs. Medicare rules require hospitals to set uniform charges for all procedures as a prerequisite for participation in the program. In the early years of Medicare, charges were loosely correlated with hospital costs (plus the desired profit margin). Since the mid-1980s with the introduction of the DRG system, the link began to deteriorate. Powerful buyers—government, health plans, and large HMOs—began negotiating steep discounts from posted charges.

Nationwide, hospital charges bear little resemblance to hospital costs—varying from 28 percent above cost in Maryland to 178 percent above cost in California (Lagnado, 2003). Uninsured patients have no one looking after their interests. Medicare may pay as little as 15–20 percent of the official posted charges, whereas the uninsured are billed at posted prices. The people least able to afford the full price are the only ones required to pay it.

> ### Policy Issue
> Individuals without health insurance are often charged much higher prices for hospital services than those covered by Medicare or private insurance.

ISSUES IN MEDICAL CARE DELIVERY

FOR-PROFIT OR NOT-FOR-PROFIT: THAT'S A GOOD QUESTION

The practice of converting not-for-profit hospitals to investor-owned, for-profit hospitals has received a great deal of attention recently. State attorneys general have the oversight responsibilities in these cases since they involve the disbursement of charitable assets. Over one half the states and the U.S. Congress are considering legislation to regulate the conversion process. Public distrust for these for-profit conversions is evidenced by a Kaiser Family Foundation survey conducted in March 1997. By a margin of 42 percent to 20 percent, Americans responded that such conversions are bad for health care.

Between 1994 and 1996, over 100 not-for-profit community hospitals were taken over by for-profit hospital chains with Columbia/HCA leading the way with over 50 acquisitions. Along with these conversions has come the largest transfer of charitable assets in U.S. history—over $9 billion. The sale of Presbyterian/St. Luke's (P/SL) in Denver provides a good example of the magnitude of these conversions. When P/SL was sold in 1995, Colorado Trust was created with assets of $310 million, making it the largest single trust in Colorado. The purchase of Rose Medical Center by Columbia endowed the Rose Community Foundation with more than $175 million. The planned conversion of Blue Cross/Blue Shield into a for-profit entity may spin off over $300 million into a charitable foundation. Staggering as they may be, these numbers pale in comparison to the conversion of California Blue Cross, which created two new trusts with $3.2 billion in assets.

Critics have a number of legitimate concerns in the wake of these conversions.

- Are the charitable assets properly valued or are they being sold too cheaply?

- Will the transaction be subject to independent review?

- Is the community at risk of losing valuable health care services?

- Will the new entity continue to provide uncompensated care?

- Will the proceeds of the sale be used for appropriate charitable purposes? According to federal tax law, when a not-for-profit hospital is sold to a for-profit concern, the proceeds must be put into a charitable trust and used to promote the original not-for-profit mission.

- Will members of the not-for-profit board of directors or the for-profit purchaser benefit unfairly from the sale?

- Will the trust be independent of the hospital?

- Will hospital board members control the newly created charitable trust?

Proponents argue that these conversions are introducing an element of competition into markets characterized by complacency and inefficiency. Regardless of how you feel personally about these conversions, expect more as not-for-profit hospitals find that they must become part of larger, integrated systems to ensure their own survival as competition heats up for managed-care contracts.

Source: John Leifer, "Inside the Predator: Former Columbia Executive Tells How to Avoid Becoming the Giant's Next Victim," *Modern Healthcare*, April 14, 1997, 46; Tamar Lewin and Martin Gottlieb, "Health Care Dividend—A Special Report; In Hospital Sales, an Overlooked Side Effect," *The New York Times*, April 27, 1997, Section 1, page 1; and Stuart Steers, "Roll On, Columbia; The Nation's Largest For-Profit Hospital Chain is Out to Flatten its Denver Competition," *Denver Westword*, April 24, 1997.

The Role of the Not-for-Profit Organization in the Hospital Industry

Using the neoclassical model with profit-maximizing decision makers may seem inappropriate in an industry dominated by not-for-profit institutions. Physicians receive their training in not-for-profit medical schools. A large percentage of all hospitals are not-for-profit in nature, and for many years the regional not-for-profit carriers, Blue Cross and Blue Shield, dominated the health insurance industry.

At the beginning of the twentieth century, most hospitals were organized as not-for-profit institutions. Their main responsibility was the provision of free care for the poor and indigent. Hospitals were notorious institutions—avoided at all costs by any self-respecting person. Medical reform during the interwar period enhanced the quality and respectability of the industry. Paying customers provided the incentive for the development of the proprietary, for-profit institution. The financial challenges of the Great Depression and government policy favoring the not-for-profit structure led to the dominance of the private, not-for-profit hospital after the second World War. With their tax-exempt status, not-for-profit hospitals were able to accept tax-deductible, charitable contributions. Many also received construction subsidies from the federal government under the Hill-Burton Act. Some state legislatures even made the for-profit form illegal altogether. As a result, by 2000, over three-fourths of all community hospitals were either government owned or not-for-profit. Data presented in Table 9.3 show that the percentage of for-profit hospitals has been increasing steadily since 1980 when it stood at 12.5 percent of the total until 2001 when it stood at 15.4 percent. For-profit hospitals have increased their share of the total beds to 13.2 percent, at the expense of a shrinking share for government-owned hospitals.

The Not-for-Profit Organizational Form

Substantial differences can be seen in the institutional constraints facing for-profit and not-for-profit hospitals. For all practical purposes the differences can be summarized as differences in the right to transfer assets. A not-for-profit hospital does not have shareholders in the typical sense of the term. Thus, equity capital does not come from the sale of stock but from donations. Without shares of stock there are no dividends to be paid. Surplus funds are restricted and may not be used to provide *ex post* incentives to managers. In other words, hospital administrators may not receive dividends or other distributions of residual earnings at the end of the accounting period. Finally, in the event of liquidation or sale of assets, no individual owner receives the proceeds.

Only recently have economists begun to examine the incentive structure facing not-for-profit managers. Influential research by Alchian and Demsetz (1972) contrasted the incentives facing for-profit and the not-for-profit managers. Pauly (1987) extended the thinking by noting that all successful enterprises generate surplus income. Not-for-profit managers, unable to extract the surplus for themselves in the form of profit-sharing, will extract it in some nonpecuniary form.

Nature of Competition in the Not-for-Profit Sector

The popularity of the not-for-profit organizational form in the hospital industry may seem a bit odd given the dominance of the for-profit firm in the rest of the U.S. economy. Sloan (1988) addressed the conventional wisdom regarding the prevalence of not-for-profit hospitals. The first argument was based on asymmetric information in the hospital market. Because patients have a difficult time evaluating the quality of medical care, they prefer to purchase their medical care from providers who do not suffer from the profit motive. If this is true, however, there is no good explanation why virtually every other provider—physicians, optometrists, pharmacists, and dentists—works in the for-profit sector.

http://

The Shriners Hospitals for Crippled Children provides pediatric care to needy children at no charge. The organization operates 19 orthopedic units and three burn institutes. In addition, three of the hospitals specialize in treating spinal cord injuries. A guide to the Shriners hospitals is found at **http://www.shrinershq.org/Hospitals/index.html**.

Policy Issue

Is the provision of services through not-for-profit hospitals desired over provision through for-profits?

Key Concept 4
Self-Interest

Key Concept 7
Competition

Table 9.3	Number of Community Hospitals and Beds by Ownership Type, Various Years

Year	Number of Hospitals	For Profit		Non-government Non-Profit		Government	
		No.	%	No.	%	No.	%
1975	5,875	775	13.2	3,339	56.8	1,761	30.0
1980	5,830	730	12.5	3,322	57.0	1,778	30.5
1985	5,732	805	14.0	3,349	58.5	1,578	27.5
1990	5,384	749	13.9	3,191	59.3	1,444	26.8
1995	5,194	752	14.5	3,092	59.5	1,350	26.0
1997	5,057	797	15.8	3,000	59.3	1,260	24.9
1998	5,015	771	15.4	3,026	60.3	1,218	24.3
1999	4,956	747	15.1	3,012	60.8	1,197	24.1
2000	4,915	749	15.2	3,003	61.1	1,163	23.7
2001	4,908	754	15.4	2,998	61.1	1,156	23.6

Year	Number of Beds (thousands)	For Profit		Non-government Non-Profit		Government	
		No.	%	No.	%	No.	%
1975	941.8	73.5	7.8	658.2	69.9	210.2	22.3
1980	988.4	87.0	8.8	692.5	70.0	208.9	21.2
1985	1,000.7	103.9	10.4	707.5	70.7	189.3	18.9
1990	927.4	101.4	11.0	656.8	70.8	169.2	18.2
1995	872.7	105.7	12.1	609.7	69.9	157.3	18.0
1997	853.3	115.1	13.5	590.6	69.2	147.6	17.3
1998	840.0	113.0	13.4	587.7	70.0	139.4	16.6
1999	829.6	106.8	12.9	586.7	70.7	136.1	16.4
2000	823.6	109.9	13.3	583.0	70.8	130.7	15.9
2001	825.0	108.7	13.2	585.1	70.8	132.2	16.0

Source: *Health, United States, 2003: With Chartbook on the Health of Americans*, Table 106, 2003.

A second argument is based on the notion that profit-maximizing hospitals will not undertake any activity where the marginal revenue is less than the marginal cost. Activities such as biomedical research, medical education, and public health measures would not be provided at optimal levels. In addition, patients without insurance or other means of paying would be less likely to receive care. This line of reasoning, while relevant for teaching and large public hospitals, cannot explain why the rest of the not-for-profit sector engages in little research, undertakes few public health activities, and provides no more uncompensated care than hospitals in the for-profit sector (Sloan et al., 1986).

Based on arguments by Pauly and Redisch (1973) and Shalit (1977), hospitals are not-for-profit because this form of organization provides the most benefits for physicians. Patients do not purchase hospital services directly. Their physician-agents do it for them. Hospitals, rather than competing for patients actually compete for physicians, who admit the patients.[3] Physicians, interested in maximizing their own productivity, will have more control over decisions relating to input mix in the absence of the profit motive.

 Key Concept 4
Self-Interest

Many argue that even with the preponderance of not-for-profits in the industry, the profit-maximizing objective is a reasonable operating assumption. Operating margins (operating revenues less operating expenses) are positive for most hospitals, even the

---

3 Competition for physician referrals is more important than ever for hospital survival, particularly as system consolidations and for-profit conversions create integrated networks of medical care services.

not-for-profit ones. This operating surplus has many uses. It can be used to increase the incomes of staff physicians or other personnel or it can be used to promote desired activities such as teaching and research. To the extent that hospitals are run to further the interests of physicians, financial and otherwise, the use of the profit-maximizing model may be reasonable.

Thus, decision making in a not-for-profit hospital could resemble decision making in a for-profit hospital (Danzon, 1982). With free entry and free exit in the hospital sector, Newhouse (1970) notes that all hospitals, for-profit or not-for-profit, must produce efficiently to survive. The empirical evidence is far from unanimous on the issue. Zelder (1999) reviewed 24 studies comparing for-profit and not-for-profit performance in the hospital sector. One-half of the studies found no significant differences in operating behavior between the two organizational forms. The other 12 studies were split on the issue, with 7 favoring the for-profit form and 5 the not-for-profit form. Pauly (1987) best summarizes these results when he observed that holding size, quality, and teaching status constant, there is little difference in the provision of hospital care attributable to ownership status. The one exception is the operating performance of public not-for-profit hospitals. Zelder (1999) reviewed 15 studies comparing public and private hospital performance and found compelling evidence that private hospitals are more efficient than public hospitals.

Key Concept 8
Efficiency

Alternative Models of Hospital Behavior

Accepted alternatives to the profit-maximizing model share a common approach: utility maximization. In practice, profit maximization is simply a special case of utility maximization. The only practical difference between the two models is the way residual earnings are distributed. Because utility is unobservable, the challenge is to specify a model with an objective function that is observable.

Key Concept 4
Self-Interest

Utility Maximizing Models

According to these models, decision makers in a not-for-profit environment maximize utility subject to a break-even constraint. The objective of the decision makers may be their own utility. In this case, they will operate the hospital to maximize their own pecuniary and nonpecuniary benefits. Pecuniary benefits include salary and fringe benefits. Nonpecuniary benefits include the prestige and authority that go along with the position. Empirical research has explored many possible elements in the utility function for hospital administrators. The most popular include output and quality, or some combination of the two.

The utility-maximizing approach assumes that the hospital decision maker's objective is to be in charge of the largest or the highest quality hospital possible given the resources available. Studies by Newhouse (1970), Sloan (1980), and Danzon (1982) use this approach to modeling the behavior of not-for-profit hospital managers. Quality is typically measured by the level of technology, the type of facility and services, the quality of the staff, and the number of specialists. Running a hospital that ranks high in these quality measures provides a great deal of prestige to the manager. Recruiting quality staff is easier, as is generating charitable donations for further enhancements to quality.

In practice, the assumption of quality maximization is merely a variant of profit maximizing (and cost minimizing) behavior to support other objectives. Short-run profit maximizing behavior may be pursued in order to invest profit in quality. Adding quality in most cases serves to increase costs and shift demand. Quality enhancements are not free, and consumers have a demand for quality. Figure 9.1 provides an illustration of the hypothesized relationship between quality enhancements and the average cost and demand curves.

Suppose a not-for-profit hospital has average costs and demand depicted by AC_1 and D_1. The not-for-profit assumption implies that the hospital will operate where price

ISSUES IN MEDICAL CARE DELIVERY

REPORT ON THE TOP 100 U.S. HOSPITALS

"Looking good! How do I look? Do these pants make me look fat? That's the look I'm after." It's human nature to seek approval from others—whether it's how we look, how we behave, or, in the case of a hospital, how we're satisfying our patients. For the past several years two prominent health care consulting firms, HCIA, Inc., and William M. Mercer, Inc., have collaborated to compile an annual report card of the top 100 hospitals in the United States. The stated purpose of the report card is to recognize hospitals that provide "high-quality care, operate efficiently, and produce superior financial results" (*Top 100*). Although the report card is not intended as a tool for hospital choice decisions, recognition as one of America's top 100 hospitals is a public relations bonanza.

Ratings tend to encourage certain types of behavior. What does the Top 100 report card actually measure? The stated measures include financial management, operations, and clinical performance. Chen et al. (1999) use the hospital ratings to examine whether a top 100 rating makes any difference in the quality of care and patient outcomes. Using the diagnosis of acute myocardial infarction (AMI), their research compares the top 100 with nonrated hospitals in three areas: clinical outcomes, quality of care, and resource use.

Even though the top 100 hospitals had higher AMI volumes than nonrated hospitals, no difference was found in risk-adjusted mortality rates or readmission rates. If the quality of care is the same, where is the difference? The real difference between rated and nonrated hospitals is in the areas of resource use and financial performance. The average AMI stay in a top 100 hospital is 10 to 15 percent shorter and the cost of that stay is 5 to 13 percent lower. What does the report card actually measure? Rather than measuring clinical superiority, the report card as it is currently constructed seems to be measuring operating efficiency.

Source: *Top 100 Hospitals: Benchmarks for Success*, Baltimore, MD: HCIA, Inc., and New York: William M. Mercer, Inc., 1997; and Jersey Chen, Martha J. Radford, Yun Wang, Thomas A. Marciniak, and Harlan M. Krumholz, "Performance of the '100 Top Hospitals': What Does the Report Card Report?" *Health Affairs 18*(4), July/August 1999, 53–68.

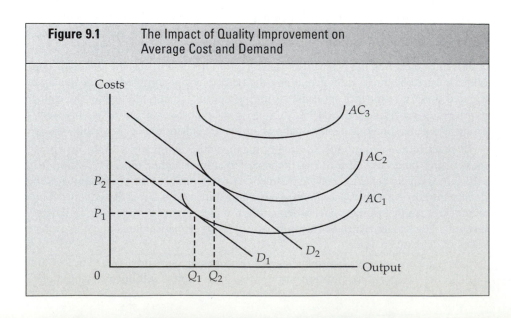

Figure 9.1   The Impact of Quality Improvement on Average Cost and Demand

and average cost are equal, indicating an output of Q_1 and price of P_1. An increase in quality moves the average costs up to AC_2. If the enhancement also increases demand, the demand curve shifts to D_2 and output and price increase to Q_2 and P_2. At some point, however, further increases in quality will increase costs only (to AC_3) without changing demand. At this point patients are unwilling to pay for quality improvements and hospital charges fall short of average costs. In other words, over-investing in certain quality improvements begins to produce a higher quality product than consumers are willing to buy. These models explain certain behavior, such as the investment in technology to increase prestige, but they shed little light on the important role that physicians play in the hospital setting.

Key Concept 2
Opportunity Cost

Physician-Control Models

If physicians are the relevant decision makers, they have a stake in what combination of inputs is used. Staff physicians may have a financial stake in maintaining an efficient operation. In contrast, private practice physicians with hospital-admitting privileges may be more concerned about their own productivity than hospital efficiency. Excess hospital capacity enables physicians to maximize their own incomes. Because the prices of other inputs are effectively zero to nonstaff physicians, they have little concern for the productivity or the actual prices of these inputs. Thus, any increase in demand is met by increases in hospital capacity rather than increases in physician staff. The excess capacity enables physicians to maximize the use of their own time.[4]

Key Concept 8
Efficiency

Physician control leads to technical inefficiency in production. Where the physician faces a zero price for other inputs, too many are used relative to physician inputs. This suggests that physicians are interested in the hospital's investing in additional services to increase hospital capacity, such as (1) interns and residents who provide services for which the physician can charge, (2) additional operating rooms and obstetric facilities, and (3) any other investment that will serve to economize on their own time.

The physician wants the hospital to price complementary services in order to increase demand for physicians' services. They also want the hospital to provide outpatient services and preventive care. The former reduces the risk of treating nonpaying patients. The latter is time intensive for the physician and is to be avoided.

Certain services provided by physicians and hospitals are somewhat substitutable for one another. As the number of physicians increases, more services will be provided in the physicians' offices than in the hospital. If payments for medical care are based on total price, the lower the hospital charges the greater the residual for the physician.

Payment for hospital services is separated from payment for physician services, making the physician neither financially responsible to the hospital nor accountable to the patient for the cost of the hospital portion of the care. Any attempt to control costs without the cooperation of physicians has little chance of success.

The Trend toward Multihospital Systems

One of the most important trends in the hospital market during the past two decades has been the increase in multihospital systems (see Ermann and Gabel, 1984; and Morrisey and Alexander, 1987). In 1975, one out of every four hospitals in the United States was part of a multihospital system.[5] Merger activity increased dramatically in the late 1980s. Over 1,300 separate hospital acquisitions took place between 1989 and 1993 (Danzon, 1994). By 1993, one out of every two hospitals was part of a multihospital system. Today, there are over 450 multihospital systems covering over 90 percent of all hospitals in the country (*Official National Hospital Blue Book*, 2000). Except for a few large

---

4 This phenomenon is unique to the American hospital system. In most countries a fairly distinct line of demarcation is drawn between hospital physicians and private-practice physicians. Mobility between the two categories is controlled, with few opportunities to practice in both simultaneously.

5 A multihospital system is defined as two or more hospitals that are owned, managed, or leased by a single entity.

systems such as Hospital Corporation of America (HCA), a nationwide chain of over 200 hospitals and 70 out-patient surgery centers, most consolidations in the industry have been among hospitals at the local level (Dranove et al., 1996).

The Theory of Consolidation

Mergers, acquisitions, and other forms of consolidation occur in the hospital industry for the same reasons they occur in any other industry. Horizontal integration allows businesses to (1) take advantage of economies of scale, (2) reduce administrative costs, and (3) improve customer access to information.[6]

Firms are said to experience economies of scale when long-run average costs fall as the size of the operation expands. The notion of scale economies can be seen more clearly in Figure 9.2. The figure depicts short-run average costs of producing a product with five different size plants, shown as AC_1 through AC_5. The average cost of production (LAC) falls as the scale or size of the operation increases up to a point. In this case, AC_3 represents the most efficient plant size, the one where economies of scale are exhausted and average cost minimized. Beyond that point, average costs increase as plant size increases, and the firm experiences diseconomies of scale.

If economies of scale are to result in improved efficiency, a number of technical advantages must be realized because of increased size. These advantages may include the ability to secure discounts through bulk purchasing and take advantage of specialization and division of labor, especially in the use of highly skilled personnel. Because case mix differs so dramatically from hospital to hospital, the relationship between cost and output is difficult to measure. Larger hospitals tend to treat more seriously ill patients and thus have higher average costs (Cowing, Holtman, and Powers, 1983; Vitaliano, 1987).

The relationship between cost and size may resemble more closely the average cost curves in Figure 9.3. Hospital A is on the higher long-run average cost curve (LAC_2) than either hospitals B or C because it provides more complicated services and treats sicker patients. Merely looking at the level of average cost would indicate that hospital C is more efficient than hospital A, which would be incorrect. With hospital B yet to fully capture all its economies and hospital C experiencing diseconomies of scale, hospital A is more efficient, relative to its service mix, than either of the other two hospitals.

The Empirical Evidence on Consolidation

Most of the empirical research on the growth of hospital systems and efficiency is based on data from a time period when cost-plus reimbursement was the standard practice.

Key Concept 8
Efficiency

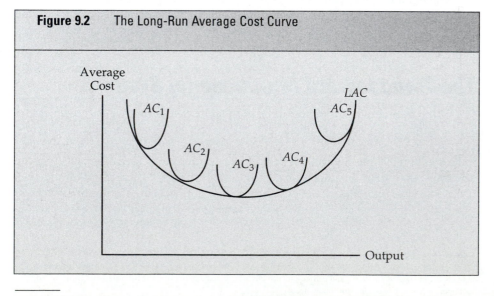

Figure 9.2   The Long-Run Average Cost Curve

Average Cost

AC_1 AC_2 AC_3 AC_4 AC_5 LAC

Output

---

6 Horizontal integration occurs when two or more firms that make the same product or provide the same service combine.

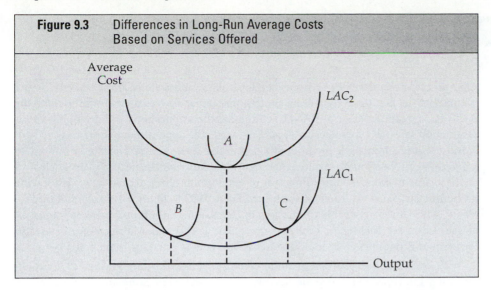

Figure 9.3 Differences in Long-Run Average Costs Based on Services Offered

Under these conditions hospitals had little incentive to lower costs (Renn et al., 1985; Santerre and Bennett, 1992).

As hospital reimbursement shifted from retrospective to prospective payment beginning in the mid-1980s, the efficiencies of the multihospital system have become more evident. Research by Dranove, Shandley, and Simon (1992) suggests that there may be substantial unexploited opportunities for economies of scale in the hospital industry, especially in smaller markets. Although antitrust policy has shown a tendency to reject the efficiency argument, these potential economies may serve as a justification for future hospital merger activity.

Dranove and Shanley (1995) focus on the marketing strategy used by hospital chains to promote brand-name identity. This strategy, similar to the one used by international franchises in the fast-food industry, has as its goal creating a perception of standardized quality in the minds of potential customers. Danzon (1994) argues that chains have a comparative advantage in providing information on product quality that customers value in their decision-making process. Given the uncertainties of the hospital market, customers seek out inexpensive information on quality and service. Identification with an established chain of respected hospitals improves customer access to information, in turn increasing demand and allowing higher margins over cost.

Mobley (1997) examines the differences in merger activity between for-profit and not-for-profit hospitals. Her findings indicate that for-profits and not-for-profits seem to have different motives for consolidating. For-profits apparently seek lucrative niche markets sheltered from competition. In contrast, the not-for-profit acquisitions are more focused on markets where managed care penetration is higher. By consolidating in markets with high managed-care penetration, they are better positioned to bargain with managed care plans. Also, hospitals can take advantage of the economies of scale without having to expand any one facility beyond its maximum level of efficiency. By satisfying the demand of the managed care plans for a full range of services, they are better able to compete in these market areas.

Consolidation activity presents an interesting challenge to antitrust policy. If consolidation leads to efficiency gains, then patients could benefit from higher quality care at lower prices. With the volume of consolidation activity that has taken place in the past decade, it is surprising how little consensus exists on the extent of scale economies in this industry.

Policy Issue

Will consolidation in the hospital industry benefit patients or providers?

Frank A. Sloan

After an undergraduate degree from Oberlin College and a Ph.D. from Harvard, Frank Sloan spent the first three years of his professional career as a research economist with the RAND Corporation. While at RAND, he explored the implications and extensions of his dissertation research on physicians' supply. An academic appointment at the University of Florida brought him back to the East Coast. After five years at Florida, he moved to Vanderbilt University in Nashville, Tennessee, where he spent the next 17 years as chair of the department and Centennial Professor of Economics. Three decades after first leaving his home state, Sloan returned to North Carolina in 1993 to become a member of the faculty at Duke University near his hometown of Greensboro. In addition to his appointment as the Alexander McMahon Professor of Health Policy and Management, he is also Professor of Economics and Senior Research Fellow at the Center for Demographic Studies.

With over 200 publications in some of the profession's most prestigious journals, including the *American Economic Review, Journal of Health Economics, Journal of the American Medical Association*, and *New England Journal of Medicine*, Sloan shows few signs of slowing down. If anything the pace of his scholarly activities has actually increased in the past few years. He is adding to the list of publications at a rate of five to six new journal articles per year and the flow of new ideas shows no signs of diminishing any time soon. Sloan typically has 10 to 15 articles being considered for publication at all times.

Sloan's early work focused on physicians and their workshops—the nation's hospitals. His article in the *Journal of the American Medical Association*, published in 1983, "More Doctors: What Will They Cost?" challenged the conventional wisdom that increasing physicians' supply would lower the cost of medical care. The paradox was striking. While economic theory suggested that more supply lowers costs, the physicians' service market did not seem to follow the same discipline as other markets. In the mid-1980s, his research interests began to shift. With separate articles on medical malpractice and medical care for the elderly, both published in 1985, a gradual change in research emphasis began. Today his scholarship interests lean heavily toward issues of tort liability and elder care.

His research exhibits a practical side as well. Over the years, Sloan has shown that economics is relevant to real world problems by lending his expertise as a private consultant to dozens of public and private organizations, including individual hospitals and hospital associations, pharmaceutical associations, physicians' associations, and federal agencies. He also provides litigation support for a number of law firms across the country, using his expertise as a forensic economist to testify in lawsuits requiring estimates of economic damages.

Over the years, Sloan has been the principal investigator on over 40 research grants, generating millions of dollars for his affiliated institutions. He is a member of the Institute of Medicine, National Academy of Science. Equally productive in the many roles he fills—teacher, writer, reviewer, consultant—his influence within health care circles knows no boundaries. He is currently studying long-term care issues in Germany and is working with the World Bank on a study of the health care system of Sri Lanka.

Source: Frank A. Sloan curriculum vitae and Duke University Web site.

Summary and Conclusions

Hospital care tends to be the most expensive aspect of medical care delivery. Dominated by the private not-for-profit hospital, the industry is responsible for approximately one third of all medical care spending. Of interest for policy purposes has been the recent increase in consolidations and mergers, particularly, the high-profile not-for-profit to for-profit conversions. Lessons to be learned from this chapter include:

- Efficiency is not rewarded in a cost-plus environment. Thus, finding little difference in efficiency between for-profit hospitals and not-for-profit hospitals is not surprising, or at least should not be. With the increasing popularity of managed care and prospective payment, only recently have hospitals been given an incentive to be efficient.

- The economic models predict that competition on the payment side will eventually eliminate the inefficiencies in the market. Inefficient hospitals become prime targets for acquisition by multihospital chains.

- As the inefficiencies are eliminated, so too is the ability to subsidize charity care for the uninsured and medical education. With increased pressure on hospitals to provide care to nonpaying patients, hospitals in turn will increase pressure on public policymakers to improve the social safety net for the more vulnerable population groups, including pregnant women, children, and the poor in general.

- Increased hospital competition in the 1980s promoted quality enhancement, not cost efficiency, leading to a medical arms race. Further competition in the 1990s continued to see quality improvements and at the same time cost efficiencies.

The changes that began in the 1980s pushed hospitals to become competitive and profit oriented. This corporate mentality has led to extensive local marketing, leveraging with debt, multihospital chains, and administrators earning salaries rivaling those of corporate executives. Will the industry become money oriented and self-serving or will the changes lead to one that is technologically innovative and caring?

Questions and Problems

1. What are the major criticisms of the for-profit hospital?

2. In theory, describe the different operating characteristics of the for-profit and the not-for-profit hospital.

3. The critical issue in the debate over the merits of the for-profit hospital structure is whether the profit motive has a negative impact on quality of care and access for the poor and uninsured. Is there a significant difference in quality and access between for-profit and not-for-profit hospitals? What is the empirical evidence? (Clearly distinguish between private not-for-profit hospitals and public hospitals.)

4. Does the not-for-profit structure in a hospital eliminate "for-profit behavior"? Explain.

5. What is cost-plus pricing? How does cost-plus pricing affect supplier behavior?

6. What is a horizontal merger? A vertical merger? Provide examples of each in the current hospital marketplace.

References

AAMC Council of Teaching Hospitals: Geographic Listing, Washington, D.C.: Association of American Medical Colleges, 1999.

Armen A. Alchian and Harold Demzetz, "Production, Information Costs, and Economic Organization," *American Economic Review* 62(5), December 1972, 777–795.

Thomas G. Cowing, Alphonse G. Holtmann, and Susan Powers, "Hospital Cost Analysis: A Survey and Evaluation of Recent Studies," in Richard M. Scheffler and Louis R. Rossiter, eds., *Advances in Health Economics and Health Services Research*, volume 4, Greenwich, CT: JAI Press, 1983, 257–303.

Patricia Danzon, "Hospital 'Profits': The Effects of Reimbursement Policies," *Journal of Health Economics* 1(1), May 1982, 29–52.

————, "Merger Mania," *Health Systems Review* 27(6), 1994, 18–28.

David Dranove, Amy Durkac, and Mark Shanley, "Are Multihospital Systems More Efficient?" *Health Affairs* 15(1), Spring 1996, 100–104.

David Dranove and Mark Shanley, "Cost Reductions or Reputation Enhancement as Motives for Mergers: The Logic of Multihospital Systems," *Strategic Management Journal* 16(1), January 1995, 55–74.

David Dranove, Mark Shanley, and Carol Simon, "Is Hospital Competition Wasteful?" *RAND Journal of Economics* 23(2), Summer 1992, 247–262.

David Dranove and William D. White, "Recent Theory and Evidence on Competition in Hospital Markets," *Journal of Economics and Management Strategy* 3(1), Spring 1994, 169–209.

Dan Ermann and Jon Gabel, "Multihospital Systems: Issues and Empirical Findings," *Health Affairs* 3(1), Spring 1984, 50–64.

Roger Feldman and Bryan Dowd, "Is There a Competitive Market for Hospital Services?" *Journal of Health Economics* 5(3), September 1986, 277–292.

Martin S. Feldstein, "Hospital Price Inflation: A Study of Nonprofit Price Dynamics," *American Economic Review* 61(5), December 1971, 853–872.

Abraham Flexner, *Medical Education in the United States and Canada*, Bulletin No. 4, The Carnegie Foundation for the Advancement of Teaching, Boston: D.B. Updike, 1910.

H. W. Frech III and Lee R. Mobley, "Efficiency, Growth, and Concentration: An Empirical Analysis of Hospital Markets," *Economic Inquiry* 38(3), July 2000, 369–384.

Martin Gaynor and Deborah Haas-Wilson, "Change, Consolidation, and Competition in Health Care Markets," *Journal of Economic Perspectives* 13(1), Winter 1999, 141–164.

Philip Held and Mark Pauly, "Competition and Efficiency in the End Stage Renal Disease Program," *Journal of Health Economics* 2(2), August 1983, 95–118.

Emmett B. Keeler, Glenn Melnick, and Jack Zwanziger, "The Changing Effects of Competition on Non-Profit and for-Profit Hospital Pricing Behavior," *Journal of Health Economics* 18(1), January 1999, 69–86.

Daniel P. Kessler and Mark B. McClellan, "Is Hospital Competition Socially Wasteful?" *Quarterly Journal of Economics* 115(2), May 2000, 577–615.

Richard Kronick, David C. Goodman, John Wennberg, and Edward Wagner, "The Marketplace in Health Care Reform: The Demographic Limitations of Managed Competition," *The New England Journal of Medicine* 328(2), January 14, 1993, 148–152.

Lucette Lagnado, "One Critical Appendectomy Later, Young Woman Has a $19,000 Debt," *The Wall Street Journal*, March 17, 2003, A1.

Harold S. Luft, James C. Robinson, Deborah Garnick, Susan C. Maerki, and Stephen J. McPhee, "The Role of Specialized Clinical Services in Competition among Hospitals," *Inquiry* 23(1), Spring 1986, 83–94.

John W. Mayo and Deborah A. McFarland, "Regulation, Market Structure, and Hospital Costs," *Southern Economic Journal* 55(3), January 1989, 559–569.

Lee R. Mobley, "Multihospital Chain Acquisitions and Competition in Local Healthcare Markets," *Review of Industrial Organization* 12(2), April 1997, 185–202.

Michael A. Morrisey, *Cost-Shifting in Health Care: Separating Evidence from Rhetoric* (Washington, DC: AEI Press, 1995).

Michael A. Morrisey and Jeffrey A. Alexander, "Hospital Participation in Multihospital Systems," in Richard M. Scheffler and Louis R. Rossiter, eds., *Advances in Health Economics and Health Services Research*, volume 7, Greenwich, CT: JAI Press, 1987, 59–82.

Joseph Newhouse, "Toward a Theory of Nonprofit Institutions: An Economic Model of a Hospital," *American Economic Review* 60(1), March 1970, 66–74.

Official National Hospital Blue Book, Atlanta, Georgia: Billian Publishing, Inc./Trans World Publishing, Inc., 2000.

Mark V. Pauly, "Nonprofit Firms in Medical Markets," *American Economic Review Proceedings* 77(2), May 1987, 257–262.

———— and Michael Redisch, "The Not-for-Profit Hospital as a Physicians' Cooperative," *American Economic Review* 63(1), March 1973, 87–99.

Steven C. Renn, Carl J. Schramm, J. Michael Watt, and Robert A. Derzon, "The Effects of Ownership and System Affiliation on the Economic Performance of Hospitals," *Inquiry* 22(3), Fall 1985, 219–236.

James C. Robinson and Harold S. Luft, "Competition and the Cost of Hospital Care, 1972 to 1982," *Journal of the American Medical Association* 257(23), June 19, 1987, 3241–3245.

————, "The Impact of Hospital Market Structure on Patient Volume, Average Length of Stay, and the Cost of Care," *Journal of Health Economics* 4(4), December 1985, 333–356.

————, Stephen J. McPhee, and Sandra S. Hunt, "Hospital Competition and Surgical Length of Stay," *Journal of the American Medical Association* 259(5), February 5, 1988, 696–700.

Rexford E. Santerre and Dana C. Bennett, "Hospital Market Structure and Cost Performance: A Case Study," *Eastern Economic Journal* 18(2), Spring 1992, 209–219.

Sol S. Shalit, " A Doctor-Hospital Cartel Theory," *Journal of Business* 50(1), January 1977, 1–20.

Frank A. Sloan, "Property Rights in the Hospital Industry," in *Health Care in America: The Political Economy of Hospitals and Health Insurance*, H.E. Frech III, ed., San Francisco: Pacific Research Institute for Public Policy, 1988, 103–141.

————, "The Internal Organization of Hospitals: A Descriptive Study," *Health Services Research* 15(3), Fall 1980, 203–230.

————, Joseph Valvona, and Ross Mullner, "Identifying the Issues: Statistical Profile," in Frank A. Sloan, James F. Blumstein, and James M. Perrin, eds., *Uncompensated Hospital Care: Rights and Responsibilities*, Baltimore, MD: Johns Hopkins University Press, 1986, 16–53.

Rosemary Stevens, *In Sickness and in Wealth: American Hospitals in the Twentieth Century*, New York: Basic Books Inc., 1989.

Donald F. Vitaliano, "On the Estimation of Hospital Cost Functions," *Journal of Health Economics* 6(4), December 1987, 305–318.

Marvin Zelder, "How Private Hospital Competition Can Improve Canadian Health Care," Online Public Policy Source Paper No. 35, Vancouver, B.C.: The Fraser Institute, 1999.

Chapter 10

Sociocultural Considerations

Americans spend more on medical care than anybody else in the world, whether measured in total dollars spent, per capita outlays, or as a share of total economic output. For all of our spending, it is not clear that we are any healthier than our foreign counterparts. In fact, critics of the system cite a never-ending litany of statistics primarily on life expectancy and infant mortality to bolster their argument. Their analyses are almost always followed by the conclusion that the U.S. health care delivery system is seriously flawed and in immediate need of radical overhaul. Is the U.S. medical care sector woefully negligent in providing the necessary care to improve health outcomes, or does something else explain high spending and outcomes that do not meet our high expectations? Is it appropriate to blame our medical care delivery system for the unfavorable international comparisons?

In this chapter, the first of four examining the confounding factors that contribute to high spending in the U.S. system, we will examine the state of American society as it affects the health and welfare of the population. A number of social problems and pathologies will be discussed—AIDS, drug abuse, poverty, violence, teenage pregnancies, illegitimacy, sexually transmitted diseases, alcohol abuse, cigarette smoking, and obesity. The goal of this chapter is to develop an understanding of how these social problems contribute to the cost of medical care and the health outcomes that we observe. These problems are not unique to the United States, but if we are to understand the challenges facing American health care, we must understand the extent of these societal problems and the confounding role they play in the delivery of medical care.

The Nature of Societal Problems

Two competing lines of thought address the nature of our society's problems: the liberal viewpoint and the conservative viewpoint.[1] From the liberal perspective, social problems have their origin in the economy's inability to provide sufficient income-earning opportunities, especially for many males in the lower socioeconomic class. This premise usually leads the commentator to call for more government involvement in social programs ranging from direct welfare payments to various training and retraining efforts, all requiring a substantial increase in federal budget outlays.

In contrast, the conservative perspective focuses on the breakdown of traditional family values as the primary cause of our social pathologies with the government as a significant contributor. Illegitimate births, single-parent families, and divorce lead to the phenomenon referred to as the "feminization of poverty." Children raised under these circumstances are more likely to drop out of school, abuse drugs, and participate

---

1 Although this dichotomous characterization serves as a handy way of describing ideological positions, problems arise in using ideological labels. Simultaneously, they can mean a great deal and nothing at all. Labels are used to stereotype individuals when in truth distinctions are often blurred depending on the issue. The generalizations that follow are meant to focus our discussion on the central differences in approach to social concerns that characterize the American political scene, recognizing that there are other ideologies of varying political importance that influence policymaking.

in illegal activities (Murray, 1993). This pattern of behavior is influenced by government involvement that creates incentives to reinforce these lifestyle choices. The purpose of this chapter is to examine these various social problems and pathologies and how they impact the delivery of medical care in the United States.

AIDS in America

acquired immunodeficiency syndrome (AIDS)
An infectious disease that results when the human immune system is so weakened by the human immunodeficiency virus (HIV) that the body can no longer fight off serious infections.

More than 42 million living people worldwide have been infected with the human immunodeficiency virus (HIV) that causes **acquired immunodeficiency syndrome (AIDS)** and more than 16 million have already died as a result of complications from the disease. By June 2001, over 767,000 U.S. cases were reported to the Centers for Disease Control (CDC) and over 400,000 Americans had died of the disease (CDC, 2002).

The Extent of AIDS in the United States

Acquired immunodeficiency syndrome, or AIDS, results when the human immune system is so weakened by HIV that the body can no longer fight off serious infections. A weakened immune system makes a person susceptible to other diseases: yeast infections of the mouth and throat, herpes infections, pneumonia, a form of cancer called Kaposi's sarcoma that produces purple blotches on the skin, and tuberculosis. Symptoms usually include fever, diarrhea, weight loss, fatigue, and enlarged lymph glands.

From 1981 (when AIDS was first discovered in clinical studies) until 2002, approximately 831,000 cases were reported in the United States (see Table 10.1). The fatality rate for those infected is quite high, over 56 percent for adults and children. About 40,000 new cases are now diagnosed annually in the United States.[2] Even though about half of the new cases are either homosexual or bisexual males or IV-drug users, transmission of the virus that causes AIDS has slowed dramatically in this segment of the population (see Table 10.2 for more details). Included in the 42,745 newly reported cases involving adults and adolescents in 2002 were 150 cases involving children less than 13 years of age, most infected during birth by their mothers who were also diagnosed with AIDS (CDC, 2002).[3]

Table 10.1	AIDS Cases by Year of Report			
Year	**Males, 13 Years and Older**	**Females, 13 Years and Older**	**Children < 13 Years Old**	**Total**
1985	7,504	524	131	8,159
1990	36,179	4,544	725	41,448
1995	56,689	12,978	745	70,412
1999	34,013	10,312	255	44,580
2000	30,135	9,958	189	40,282
2001	30,663	10,617	170	41,450
2002	31,644	10,951	150	42,745
All Years	676,609	145,696	8,807	831,112

Source: *Health, United States, 2003: With Chartbook on Trends in the Health of Americans*, 2003, Table 53.

---

2 In contrast, the American Cancer Society expected 212,600 new breast cancer diagnoses in 2003 and over 40,000 breast cancer deaths. For prostate cancer the numbers are 220,900 new cases and 28,900 deaths. In addition, 900,000 Americans die annually of cardiovascular diseases (including stroke) and 556,500 die of cancer (including breast and prostate cancer).
3 Worldwide the number of new AIDS cases is estimated at three million per year.

Table 10.2	AIDS Cases by Exposure Category
	U.S. Adults over age 13, Selected Years and Total to Date

Number, by Year of Report

Source	1990	1995	1998	1999	2000	2001[a]	Total To Date	Percent Distribution Total To Date
Total Cases	40,740	69,774	45,514	44,446	40,230	19,002	758,434	100.0
Homosexual/ bisexual males	23,658	30,944	16,878	15,632	13,648	6,241	357,583	47.1
IV drug users	9,270	18,802	10,691	9,878	8,099	3,169	184,247	24.3
Homosexual/ bisexual males and IV drug users	2,943	4,185	2,224	1,929	1,587	657	48,132	6.3
Heterosexual contact with IV drug user	1,484	2,794	1,894	1,769	1,490	611	28,368	3.7
Heterosexual contact; risk group unspecified	769	5,685	5,230	5,575	5,075	2,146	51,401	6.8
Hemophilia/ coagulation disorder	347	467	177	156	98	48	5,171	0.7
Blood transfusion recipient	770	572	277	268	297	96	8,698	1.1
Undetermined	1,499	6,325	8,143	9,239	9,939	6,043	74,834	9.9

Source: *Health, United States, 2002: With Chartbook on Trends in the Health of Americans,* 2002, Table 55.

a January through June.

At the end of 2001 an estimated 362,827 Americans were living with AIDS, and an estimated 800,000 to 900,000 were living with HIV (CDC, 2002). The evidence indicates that the rate of new cases has stabilized at approximately 40,000 new HIV infections per year and deaths have actually declined. Fortunately, the disease has not spread much beyond the traditional risk groups (which includes homosexual and bisexual males, IV drug users, and those who have sexual contact with them). These groups account for over 80 percent of the total infections. Heterosexual contact cases of AIDS have not grown as rapidly as initially predicted. Only about 80,000 have been reported to date (or about 10.5 percent of the total cases diagnosed) and of this number more than 28,000 had sexual partners who were members of the traditional risk groups.

CDC research (Holmberg, 1996) estimated that nearly one half of all new HIV infections occur in the drug-injecting population. Changing the behavior of the IV drug-using population represents the biggest challenge in the battle to control the spread of this disease. Unsafe practices, such as sharing needles and promiscuous sex, are the leading cause of infection.

Risk to the Population

In 1991 the sports world was shocked by the revelation that one of its superstars, Ervin "Magic" Johnson, tested positive for HIV. The lesson to the heterosexual community came in loud and clear: "We are all at risk . . . it can happen to anybody." It is true that AIDS shows no respect of race, gender, or socioeconomic status. In that sense, we are all at risk. But it is not true that we are all equally at risk of contracting the deadly virus.

The Centers for Disease Control provides health information and links to publications and statistics on disease prevention and control. Links are also available to *Mortality and Morbidity Weekly Report* and the journal *Emerging Infectious Diseases.* http://cdc.gov/

The transmission of the AIDS virus is primarily an inner-city problem that affects the minority community disproportionately and especially the intravenous drug-using segment of that community. By the end of 2000, almost two thirds of the new cases were among African-Americans, Latinos, and other minorities. The rate of cases per 100,000 population is seven times greater among blacks than among whites and two times the Hispanic rate.

The vast majority of AIDS cases are reported in the large urban centers: San Francisco, Los Angeles, Dallas, Houston, New Orleans, Chicago, Atlanta, Philadelphia, Newark, New York, Boston, Miami, and the District of Columbia. In fact, more than 60 percent of all cases originated in five states: New York, California, Florida, Texas, and New Jersey. Secondly, the incidence of AIDS is highest among minority groups, especially African-Americans and Puerto Rican Hispanics. Blacks constitute approximately 12 percent of the U.S. population and over 40 percent of the AIDS population. More than two thirds of all children under age 13 with AIDS are black; most were infected prenatally.

For the heterosexual community, the most important risk determinant is the identity of potential sexual partners. If an individual's sex partner has never been an IV drug user or the sex partner of an IV drug user and is not from one of the African or Caribbean countries where the disease is spread primarily through heterosexual contact, his or her chances of getting AIDS through heterosexual contact is 1 in 50,000. When the analysis is restricted to only the white population, the risk is reduced to one in 500,000.

Prostitutes and hemophiliacs are considered the primary sources of transmission of AIDS into the heterosexual community. But less than three percent of all reported cases in the United States are the result of someone not in a primary risk group acquiring AIDS from someone in such a group (this group is referred to as secondary cases).

Clearly, the lesson is "unprotected" sexual intercourse presents a risk of HIV transmission, but the greater risks involve homosexual contact and IV drug use. The transmission of HIV requires access to the bloodstream. Needle sharing provides the necessary access. Sexual transmission is a different issue. In the absence of genital bleeding and lesions, heterosexual sex provides minimal risk of transmission. These facts should not be interpreted to mean that we are to have a flippant attitude about the disease. Sexual behavior is still a primary determinant of risk. Abstinence until marriage and fidelity afterwards may be the only "safe sex" around, but a little common sense and knowledge of the facts can go a long way in providing a means of avoiding this disease. Prevention is the best protection.

Medical Care Issues

Hellinger's (1993) estimate for lifetime medical costs of treating an AIDS patient was $69,100, a downward revision from his 1992 estimate of $102,000.[4] The decrease was due to both shorter and less frequent hospital stays. Outpatient services have begun to substitute for costly hospital care. Hellinger also estimated that the cost of treating a person infected with HIV from the date of infection to the date of AIDS diagnosis at $50,174. Indications are that these costs will continue to rise.[5] First, the Food and Drug Administration (FDA) has approved the use of a class of drugs called "protease inhibitors" that deprive the AIDS virus of a critical enzyme it needs for reproduction. When combined with older drugs such as AZT and 3TC (sold under the brand name Epirir), this three-drug cocktail suppresses the AIDS virus to undetectable levels. Current scientific wisdom suggests that the drug regime begin early, even before AIDS symptoms develop. Treating more patients for longer periods of time could eventually increase lifetime costs over the recent estimates.

Now more people may benefit from drug therapy, currently priced at $12,000 to $16,000 per patient per year. Currently, AZT costs $3,500 per year, 3TC up to $2,800 per

---

4 The lifetime cost of treating AIDS is defined as the cost of treatment from the time of diagnosis until death.
5 Statement from Fred J. Hellinger, an economist with the HHS, as reported by Chase (1992).

year, and the protease inhibitor as high as $7,400 per year. The cost for patients in the advanced stages of the disease is substantially higher, at $20,000 to $27,000 per year. Treating all 500,000 reported HIV-positive and AIDS patients in the United States with the combination drug therapy would cost over $8 billion per year. Adding treatment for the additional 300,000 estimated unreported cases would drive up the cost of treatment another $3 billion, or $5 to $6 billion more than we are currently spending. These costs place treatment out of the reach of 90 percent of the world's AIDS sufferers, who live in Third World countries.

The proper paradigm for studying AIDS is cancer. Careful treatment can cause AIDS to go into remission, but currently available treatment does not represent a cure. In addition, there is clearly a downside to the treatment. Patients are placed on a strict regime of 15 pills per day. Missed doses can result in HIV levels rebounding in a drug-resistant mutant form. Researchers are skeptically hopeful that the results will be long lasting. Early evidence has indicated that if any of the virus is left in the bloodstream, it can rebound into a drug-resistant copy. For now at least, treatment with the standard three-drug cocktail can successfully extend the life expectancy of an AIDS patient by years. Clearly, longer lives mean more spending.

Although it is estimated that the majority of all AIDS care is financed by government sources, primarily Medicaid, the overall impact on the economy is relatively small. Total government spending on AIDS care and treatment approached $14 billion in 2001 (Foster et al., 2002). Spending on AIDS treatment is less than 1 percent of total health care spending, but its impact falls disproportionately on public hospitals, especially large teaching hospitals in urban areas.

> *Policy Issue*
> The cost of AIDS treatment falls disproportionately on large, public and teaching hospitals.

Possibly one of the most disturbing aspects of the AIDS problem is the rebirth of associated diseases once considered eradicated in the developed world, such as tuberculosis (TB). Less of a problem in the United States, worldwide TB is the cause of death of one third of the people with AIDS. The U.S. problem appears to be a new drug-resistant strain of TB appearing among the poor population. The likely cause is the failure of infected individuals to stick with a strict regime of antibiotics for the prescribed treatment period. In 1953, there were over 84,000 cases of TB reported in the United States. That number fell to 22,255 in 1984. By 1993, TB cases increased 14 percent to over 26,000, the largest single-year increase since 1953. Since 1993 new cases have fallen every year. By 2000, only 16,377 new cases were reported, down approximately one third over the decade.

The Worldwide Impact

AIDS has reached epidemic proportions in parts of the world. The fastest growing region for HIV infection is Southeast Asia where 2.5 million already have the disease. According to United Nations statistics, over 23 million sub-Saharan Africans have HIV or AIDS and over 13 million have already died from its complications (*Medical Industry Today*, 2000). In this part of the world, the primary transmission of the disease is through heterosexual contact and the male-to-female ratio of those affected stands at about one to one. Young adults are the main targets of the disease, and often husbands and wives infect each other. In some areas adult mortality (already high) is doubling and even tripling.

The impact has both social and economic components. The disease has left in its wake over 11 million orphaned children who have lost both parents to AIDS. Gaps are also being created in the workforce with prime-age workers being lost during their most productive years. Life expectancy after contracting AIDS is relatively short in developing countries, primarily due to the lack of funds allocated to caring for those affected. Daniel Tarantola of the Harvard School of Public Health reports that an African AIDS patient can expect to receive $400 in medical treatment during a single year. In contrast, an AIDS patient in the United States receives between $20,000 and $25,000 in AIDS-related medical care annually. More than 95 percent of all people

ISSUES IN MEDICAL CARE DELIVERY

IS ADDICTION RATIONAL?

When does a habit become an addiction? If you enjoy something and practice it regularly, are you addicted? People get addicted to all sorts of things, including cigarettes, alcohol, drugs, work, food, sex, music videos, and computer games. Like many other interesting questions concerning human behavior, economists have discovered that the theory of rational choice can tell us a great deal about addictive behavior itself and the optimal public policy to deal with it.

A paper by Becker and Murphy (1988) influenced the early economic literature on addiction. They show that consumers of addictive goods are rational, meaning that they consistently maximize utility over time, and that the potential for addiction increases if past consumption increases current consumption. Their model is also able to explain the observed instability of consumption that manifests itself in "cold turkey" withdrawal and binge consumption. They also show that people who discount the future more heavily are more likely to become addicts.

This model relies on the premise that individuals recognize the total cost of their addictive behavior, both in terms of the current monetary price of the addictive good and the cost in terms of the future. Within this framework, forward-looking behavior has one problem: It requires that individual behavior is time consistent—that future behavior is consistent with current desires regarding future behavior. Using the case of cigarette consumption, Gruber and Koszegi (2001) established that forward-looking behavior is not consistent over time. Incorporating time inconsistency into a model with forward-looking behavior, they show that the optimal government policy should take into consideration not only the externalities imposed on others, but also the "internalities" imposed on the addict.

As interest grows in regulating addictive behavior, we have seen increased taxation, increased regulation of public consumption, and a rash of litigation against the cigarette industry. Using standard values for average age and life expectancy, Gruber and Koszegi estimate that an extra year at the end of a worker's life is worth almost $100,000. Since the typical smoker dies 6.1 years prematurely, the cost of smoking a pack of cigarettes in terms of life-years lost is $30.45. Thus, the internal costs are over 100 times the external costs. Policy conclusions based on their research are a significant departure from those based on the earlier model. Even if the government considers only a small portion of the internal costs in establishing tax policy, a strong case could be made for a substantial increase in the current average excise tax of 65 cents per pack. Even if the external costs are also considered—second-hand smoke estimated at 19 to 70 cents per pack and the long-run costs of low birthweight due to maternal smoking estimated at 42 to 70 cents per pack—the internal costs still dwarf the calculation. This line of research has important implications for other forms of addictive behavior, in particular illegal drugs.

Source: Gary S. Becker and Kevin M. Murphy, "A Theory of Rational Addiction," *Journal of Political Economy 96*(4), August 1988, 675–700; and Jonathan Gruber and Botond Koszegi, "Is Addiction 'Rational'"? Theory and Evidence," *Quarterly Journal of Economics 116*(4), November 2001, 1261–1303.

with AIDS live or lived in the developing world, but only 6 percent of the money spent on treating the disease is spent in these countries (Chase, 1992).[6]

The long-term economic impact of AIDS will be determined by its impact on labor supply (Goldin as reported in Kelly, 1992). Fewer workers in the short run due

---

6 Part of the problem is the high cost of drug treatment. Responding to this issue, the U.S. government pledged to triple spending on combating AIDS in some of the world's poorest countries to $15 billion over the next five years, 2003 to 2008.

Back-of-the-Envelope

THE IMPACT OF SUPPLY SHOCKS ON WAGE RATES

Certain industries in the United States have already felt the impact of the rising AIDS-related death toll. Especially hard hit have been the apparel design and the arts and entertainment industries. How are these supply shocks transmitted to other sectors of the economy? A simple model of supply and demand can be used to show these effects.

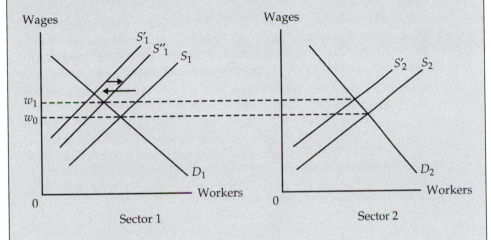

Consider two sectors of the economy employing similarly trained workers. Assuming competitive conditions, market adjustments will tend to equate wages across the two sectors at w_0. Suppose a significant supply shock reduces the number of available workers in Sector 1, shown by a leftward shift in supply from S_1 to S'_1. The wage increase in Sector 1 serves to draw Sector 2 workers to the now higher paying jobs. This causes the supply curve in Sector 2 to shift leftward from S_2 to S'_2, raising wages in that sector. The migration of workers causes downward pressure on Sector 1 wages due to the influx of new workers (supply curve shifts to S''_1). Falling wages in Sector 1 and rising wages in Sector 2 will eventually equilibrate at w_1, establishing a new equilibrium. The supply shock in Sector 1 serves to raise wages in both sectors.

Key Concept 5
Markets and Pricing

Key Concept 6
Supply and Demand

to AIDS-related mortality and fewer births due to the loss of child-bearing females means fewer workers in the long run.

Labor intensive industries worldwide will see their labor costs rise, increasing the incentives to mechanize or switch to less labor-intensive production. This is already happening in parts of Africa where farmers are switching from labor intensive crops like tobacco to root vegetables that require less labor. A shortage of labor in Africa not only means higher wages in Africa, but ultimately higher wages in the rest of the world. The irony of this epidemic is that even as total economic output may fall for countries that are the hardest hit by the disease, per capita output may actually increase due to a smaller population, meaning that individual living standards may actually rise.

Consequences of Drug Abuse[7]

Government sources (Kleiman et al., 1990) estimate that approximately one in one hundred Americans are regular users of cocaine. Our lack of knowledge on the addictive nature of prolonged use limits our ability to determine the long-term

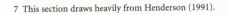

7 This section draws heavily from Henderson (1991).

consequences of regular use, but careful study of the phenomenon clearly shows that drug abuse takes a tremendous toll in terms of human suffering and economic costs to society.

The Nature and Extent of Drug Abuse

The good news: Overall drug use in the United States has fallen by 50 percent over the past 15 years. The bad news: Over half of current drug users are under 25 years of age. The latest National Household Survey on Drug Abuse (U.S. Department of Health and Human Services, 2002) shows:

- The percentage of Americans aged 12 and older who use drugs increased from 6.3 percent in 1999 to 7.1 percent in 2001.

- Drug use among those aged 12 to 17 increased to 10.8 percent in 2001, up from 9.7 percent in 2000. For those aged 18 to 25 usage is at its highest level since 1988, increasing to 15.6 percent of that age group.

- Marijuana use doubled from 1992 to 2001. Now 5.4 percent of the population aged 12 and older use the drug regularly.

- In 2001, an estimated 1.7 million Americans were current cocaine users and another 406,000 used crack.

- The monthly use of LSD and other hallucinogens almost tripled between 1992 and 1998. More than 86 percent of hallucinogen users and 76 percent of inhalant users were between the ages of 12 and 25.

- Among pregnant women aged 15 to 17, over 50 percent reported current drug use.

- The highest rate of illicit drug use in the United States is found among young adults between the ages of 18 and 20 years of age, with the rate of current users greater than 22 percent.

Despite the overall downward trend, drug use remains a significant American problem.

The Medical Consequences of Cocaine Use

The popularity of cocaine may be attributable to the widespread belief that it is nonaddictive and quite harmless when taken occasionally. Among the reasons given to justify its use are mild euphoria, increased alertness, decreased appetite, and enhanced energy. In reality, cocaine is one of the most dangerous drugs in use today. Evidence compiled from animal studies show cocaine to be a powerful reinforcing drug whose properties may lead to compulsive use (Bozarth and Wise, 1985; Dixon and Bejar, 1989). The administration of cocaine in recreational doses can result in sleep disorders, assaultive behavior, delirium, nausea, vomiting, chest pain, tremors, seizures, hypertension, hypothermia, respiratory paralysis, cardiac arrhythmias, and even death (Gawin, 1989; Pollin, 1985).

The medical community, only within the past decade, has begun to understand the serious coronary risk associated with cocaine use. Numerous studies have shown that the personal health risk associated with the occasional use of cocaine is significant. Anyone suffering from fixed coronary artery disease and even those who have no previous history of heart disease assume considerable risk by taking the drug.[8]

Cocaine causes increased heart rate, elevated systolic blood pressure, and a surge in myocardial oxygen demand. The evidence suggests that the cardiovascular effects of cocaine use include coronary thrombosis and spasm, life-threatening arrhythmias, and in certain cases, rupture of the ascending aorta.

The adverse effects of cocaine use do not end with acute coronary events. Cocaine use and cerebrovascular accidents are temporally related. Subarchanoid hemorrhaging,

---

8 Len Bias was an All-American basketball player at the University of Maryland. In 1986, he was the first-round draft choice of the Boston Celtics. On draft night, to celebrate his new-found wealth, friends talked him into taking cocaine. The 22-year-old died from an acute coronary less than 40 hours after the NBA draft.

stroke, convulsions, and seizures have followed intranasal administration (or snorting) of cocaine in recreational doses. These outcomes are all related to the sudden surge in blood pressure immediately following use of the drug.

The Drug Abuse Warning Network (DAWN) provides information on the effect of drug use on hospital emergency rooms across the country. In the twelve months ending June 2002, there were 657,500 drug-related emergency room episodes in the nation's hospitals. Of that number 188,000 were cocaine related, 91,500 heroin related, and 111,000 marijuana related. Most episodes were connected with a suicide attempt or dependence overdose (SAMHSA, 2002).

Cocaine Use in Pregnancy

Cocaine use has historically been a phenomenon primarily observed in middle-class males. Today, however, at least two million women use cocaine and crack. Most of these women are between the ages of 20 and 27 years of age, the prime childbearing ages. A recent study by the National Association for Perinatal Addiction Research and Education estimated that at least 8.25 percent and possibly as many as 10 percent of all pregnant women have used cocaine during their pregnancies. Chasnoff et al. (1985, 1989) have estimated that 11 percent of all births in the United States were to drug users and that 10 percent of the four million regular users (defined as those who take drugs more than 200 times per year) are pregnant women.

Evidence compiled by Culver et al. (1987) and Neerhof et al. (1989) indicate that this increased incidence of drug use has serious consequences for the infants exposed in utero. Cocaine, a known vasoconstrictor, can result in restricted blood flow to the fetus. It induces uterine contractions that can cause separation or rupture of the placenta. Depending on the specific gestational age of the fetus, this can result in spontaneous abortion or the onset of premature labor.

Cocaine has serious effects on birth outcome. Babies exposed to cocaine in utero have smaller than average birth weights and are more likely to suffer from congenital malformations. In particular, it has been shown that these infants are more likely to have serious gastrointestinal problems (complicated by a poor sucking reflex) and smaller than average head circumferences, resulting in higher than average rates of mental retardation. Cocaine-exposed infants are also at higher risk for stroke and sudden infant death syndrome.

Even after birth, infants can be exposed to cocaine through their mother's breast milk. The drug will remain in breast milk for up to 60 hours after administration. Thus, even occasional use by the mother can seriously affect the infant, causing hypertension, rapid heartbeat, sweating, excessive dilation of the pupils, and asphyxiation.

The Costs to Society

Substance abuse is the leading health cost problem in the United States today. Some estimates indicate that over 60 percent of our health care costs are devoted to the treatment of three categories of drugs: alcohol, nicotine, and illegal drugs. The health problems associated with these drugs include heart disease, emphysema, lung and other cancers, motor vehicle accidents, and birth defects.

Total cost to society of drug abuse runs into the billions of dollars. Drug abuse costs the American society approximately $110 billion per year in 1995 (Harwood, Fountain, and Livermore, 1998). Although this estimate includes the direct and indirect costs of medical care, lost productivity, and crime, it fails to adequately measure the emerging health costs of cocaine exposure to infants prior to birth, referred to as "cocaine babies."

The incidence of maternal drug use is difficult to detect. Drug screening is not a routine procedure in many hospital settings. In any event, recent cocaine use is not always obvious since it does not show up in urine tests until 48 hours after administration. The typical drug-exposed infant will spend 4 to 6 weeks in intensive care after birth at a cost of $61,500 (2002 dollars). It is not unusual for extremely low-birth-weight babies to have total hospital bills totaling in the hundreds of thousands of dollars. The reason is obvious: abnormally long hospital stays. Chasnoff et al. (1985) estimated that as many as 375,000 cocaine-exposed infants are born annually. At an average cost of $61,500, this results in an estimated total cost of $23 billion for intensive care alone.

The state of Florida estimates that it spent $700 million on the 17,500 cocaine-exposed infants born in 1987 to prepare them to enter kindergarten (U.S. Congress, 1987). In 2002 dollars that comes to over $1.1 billion, an average of $63,000 per child, or $12,500 per child per year. With 375,000 cocaine-exposed infants born each year nationwide, the annual preschool costs alone could reach $24 billion.

Estimates from California place the extra cost on the school system of educating a drug-exposed child at $14,000 per year (Trost, 1989). Spending at this level would mean an additional $100 billion in educational expenses annually (also 2002 dollars). Thus, the added costs to the economic system of drug-exposed children, including ICU charges, preschool expenses, and incremental educational expenses, could run as high as $147 billion annually.

Intervention Strategies

Strategies for intervening in the drug abuse problem are appropriately founded not on the magnitude of the economic costs but rather on the resources saved by additional spending (Sindelar, 1990). The magnitude of the economic costs alone is enough to stimulate our interest, but the question is, what should we do about it?

The first step in dealing with the drug problem is to establish realistic national goals. Is a drug-free America possible? Are we willing to spend the necessary resources to accomplish this ideal? Even if we are willing to spend the money, is it cost effective to do so? Would we be willing to tolerate the measures required to totally eliminate drugs? Or would the necessary measures be too oppressive to fit within our national concept of individual liberties?

At the other extreme, a great deal of attention has been focused on a competing alternative, namely legalize and tax. Such a strategy has one distinct advantage. It would lower the crime rate by removing an entire genre of criminal acts from the legal code. Opponents argue that in reality, the people who commit crimes to support their drug habits are not likely to become model citizens and productive employees if the possession and use of drugs is legalized.

Key Concept 3
Marginal Analysis

If economics is to contribute to this public policy discussion, we must begin to focus on the appropriate questions. Good policy is based on insights based on marginal analysis. From earlier discussions, we know this means the careful study of the cost effectiveness of alternative means of reducing drug use and abuse, whether they be interdiction, education, or treatment. Cost of illness studies are useful in focusing our attention on the sheer magnitude of the problem. But the answer to the complicated questions of optimal allocation of resources will require careful analysis of the effectiveness of individual programs in lowering costs and improving the quality of the lives affected by this national problem.

The Economic Impact of Tobacco and Alcohol Abuse

The health problems associated with alcohol and tobacco use place a serious burden on the U.S. medical sector. Estimating the cost to society requires that the consequences of this behavior be assigned certain economic values. The results of alcohol and tobacco consumption include not only the obvious health problems, such as heart disease, stroke, emphysema, cancer, and cirrhosis of the liver, but also include crime, auto fatalities, and lost productivity on the job.

Tobacco Use

CDC estimates show that the health-related economic costs associated with tobacco use averaged over $150 billion per year between 1995 and 1999 (CDC, 2002). More than 20

ISSUES IN MEDICAL CARE DELIVERY

WARNING LABELS FOUND ON ALCOHOL AND TOBACCO PRODUCTS

The warning label found on all alcoholic beverages sold in the United States (Title VIII of Public Law 100-690) states:

GOVERNMENT WARNING: (1) ACCORDING TO THE SURGEON GENERAL, WOMEN SHOULD NOT DRINK ALCOHOLIC BEVERAGES DURING PREGNANCY BECAUSE OF THE RISK OF BIRTH DEFECTS. (2) CONSUMPTION OF ALCOHOLIC BEVERAGES IMPAIRS YOUR ABILITY TO DRIVE A CAR OR OPERATE MACHINERY, AND MAY CAUSE HEALTH PROBLEMS.

In 1984, Congress enacted the Comprehensive Smoking Education Act requiring four specific warning label on cigarette packages:

"Cigarette Smoke Contains Carbon Monoxide"

"Quitting Smoking Now Greatly Reduces Serious Risks to Your Health"

"Smoking by Pregnant Women May Result in Fetal Injury, Premature Birth, and Low Birth Weight"

"Smoking Causes Lung Cancer, Heart Disease, Emphysema, and May Complicate Pregnancy"

As a result of an all-out assault on the cigarette industry by the federal government, the most recent warning label reads:

"Smoking Is Addictive"

On June 26, 2000, the Federal Trade Commission announced a settlement with the largest U.S. cigar manufacturers that included warning labels on cigar products. The five warnings will be placed on various types of advertising in a balanced manner. The warning labels include:

"Cigar Smoking Can Cause Cancers of the Mouth and Throat, Even If You Do Not Inhale"

"Cigars Are Not a Safe Alternative to Cigarettes"

"Tobacco Smoke Increases the Risk of Lung Cancer and Heart Disease, Even in Nonsmokers"

We truly have come a long way, baby.

Source: "Warning Label Fact Sheet," *Reducing Tobacco Use: A Report of the Surgeon General*, U.S. Department of Health and Human Services, 2000.

percent of all Medicaid spending was for smoking- and alcohol-related diseases (Rice et al., 1986). Even though the economic cost has been staggering, the toll in human suffering pales any dollar amounts that are reported. It is estimated that over 100,000 deaths are attributed to alcohol annually. When added to the estimated 400,000 deaths attributable to tobacco use, the total comes to a half million premature deaths each year from these two substances alone.

Peto et al. (1992) have estimated that over one fifth of the population of the developed world (over 250 million people) will die prematurely of tobacco-related diseases. Half of these deaths will come between the ages of 35 and 69, with the average tobacco user dying 23 years before the average nonuser of the same age category.

ISSUES IN MEDICAL CARE DELIVERY

IS CIGARETTE AND ALCOHOL CONSUMPTION SENSITIVE TO PRICE INCREASES?

Conventional wisdom would have us believe that individuals who smoke and drink will do so at any price. Several economic researchers have offered evidence that may force us to rethink this common belief (Becker, Grossman, and Murphy, 1993; Chaloupka, 1991; Chaloupka et al., 1993). Taking into consideration the powerful reinforcing properties of addictive substances (where increases in past consumption increase the marginal benefit of current consumption), this research finds evidence of rational addiction. In other words, consumers of addictive substances take into account the long-term harmful effects of their behavior when deciding how much of an addictive substance to consume.

As is the case with all goods, addictive and nonaddictive, long-run price elasticities are larger (in absolute value) than short-run elasticities. Consumers, when given enough time, have the ability to adjust to price changes by shifting to substitutes. The lesson from these studies is that in the long run addictive behavior is price sensitive; that is, raising cigarette and alcohol prices will reduce consumption over time.

Source: Gary S. Becker, Michael Grossman, and K. M. Murphy, "An Empirical Analysis of Cigarette Addiction," NBER Working Paper No. 3322, April 1990, revised March 1993; Frank J. Chaloupka, "Rational Addictive Behavior and Cigarette Smoking," *Journal of Political Economy* 99(4), August 1991, 722–742; and Frank J. Chaloupka, Michael Grossman, Gary S. Becker, and K. M. Murphy, "Alcohol Addiction: An Econometric Analysis," paper presented at the annual meeting of the American Economic Association, January 1993.

Key Concept 6
Supply and Demand

An overall decline in the prevalence of tobacco use in the United States has occurred among both males and females (see Table 10.3). Between 1965 and 2000, the average annual rate of decline was 1.5 percent for women and 2.4 percent for men. Young adults between the ages of 18 and 25 years report the highest prevalence of tobacco use. In 2001, 43.9 percent reported tobacco use of some kind—primarily cigarettes. Current cigarette use increases with age up to age 21—approximately 2 percent of 12 year olds

Table 10.3	Prevalence of Tobacco Use United States, 18 years of age and over		

		Percent Smokers	
Year		**Male**	**Female**
1965		51.2	33.7
1974		42.8	32.2
1979		37.0	30.1
1985		32.2	27.9
1990		28.0	22.9
1995		26.5	22.7
1997		27.1	22.2
1998		25.9	22.1
1999		25.2	21.6
2000		25.2	21.1

Source: *Health United States, 2002: With Chartbook on Trends in the Health of Americans,* 2002 Table 61.

Back-of-the-Envelope

ALCOHOL CONSUMPTION AND TRAFFIC DEATHS: THE CASE FOR HIGHER EXCISE TAXES

Motor vehicle accidents are the leading cause of death for persons under age 35. In over half of those fatal crashes, alcohol is a factor. A major dilemma for policymakers is how to reduce the number of alcohol-related traffic fatalities. In 1984 Congress passed the Federal Uniform Drinking Age Act, raising the legal drinking age to 21. States were forced to conform by the threat of losing federal highway funding.

Another suggested strategy to reduce fatalities is to raise the price of alcoholic beverages through the excise tax. Substantial evidence exists relating higher alcoholic beverage prices (and state excise tax rates on alcohol) to a lower incidence of youth alcohol consumption and, subsequently, to fewer deaths as a result of motor vehicle accidents (Chaloupka, Saffer, and Laizuthai; 1993). But raising excise taxes on alcohol to reduce consumption is a forgotten strategy. In 1991, the federal excise tax on beer and wine was raised for the first time since 1951, and the federal excise tax on distilled spirits for only the second time over that same 40-year period. How would an increase in excise taxes affect alcohol consumption?

In the diagrams the alcohol-dependent demand curve is drawn much steeper than that of the occasional drinker, indicating a more inelastic demand. An increase in the excise tax will shift the supply curve leftward (remember the vertical distance between S_1 and S_2 represents the amount of the excise tax increase). In both cases, the resulting price increase causes the quantity demanded to decrease. But in the case of the occasional drinker, quantity demanded falls considerably more than it does for the alcohol dependent.

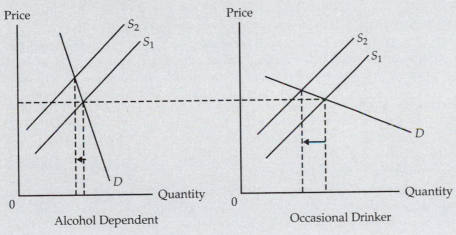

Due partly to lagging federal excise taxes, the real prices of alcoholic beverages have actually fallen in recent years. Between 1975 and 1990, the real price of beer fell 20 percent, the real price of wine 28 percent, and the real price of distilled spirits 32 percent. If real alcohol prices had actually remained constant, youth alcohol consumption would have been lower, along with fewer traffic fatalities. Chaloupka, Grossman, and Saffer (1993) estimate that if the federal excise tax on beer had been indexed to the rate of inflation since 1951 that approximately 5,000 fewer traffic fatalities would have occurred annually. In addition, a uniform minimum drinking age of 21 would have saved more than 650 lives per year prior to the Federal Uniform Drinking Age Act of 1984. This and other research (Manning et al., 1989) suggest that excise taxes on alcoholic beverages are probably below optimal levels.

Sources: Based on F. J. Chaloupka, H. Saffer, and A. Laizuthai, "Alcohol Price Policy and Youths: A Summary of Economic Research, *Journal of Research on Adolescence*, forthcoming; F. J. Chaloupka, Michael Grossman, and H. Saffer, "Alcohol Control Policies and Motor Vehicle Fatalities," *Journal of Legal Studies*, forthcoming; and Willard G. Manning, Emmett B. Keeler, Joseph P. Newhouse, Elizabeth M. Sloss, and Jeffrey Wasserman, "The Taxes of Sin: Do Smokers and Drinkers Pay Their Way?" *Journal of the American Medical Association* 261, March 17, 1989, 1604–1609.

report smoking cigarettes, increasing to 43.5 percent of 21 year olds. Among youth who smoked, one third were daily users. After age 21, the rates drop steadily, with only 18.3 percent of 60 to 64 year olds regularly using tobacco products. Males are more likely than females to use tobacco; however, almost 20 percent of pregnant women between the ages of 15 and 44 are regular smokers. Young adults aged 18 to 20 who are full-time college students are less likely to report current cigarette use than their non-college peers—32.9 percent versus 44.6 percent.

One of the reasons that women live longer in most societies is that they do not smoke with the same regularity as men. Even so, more than 500,000 women are dying worldwide every year of smoking-related illnesses. By the time today's young female population reaches middle age, more than one million females will be dying annually in the developed world alone. Richard Peto, head of the Oxford unit of the Imperial Cancer Research Fund, has said, "If women smoke like men, they will die like men" ("Ashes in Their Mouths," 1992).

Alcohol Use

Almost one-half of all Americans over the age of 12 report they currently use alcohol. The prevalence increases dramatically with age until early adulthood (ages 21 to 25) and then gradually declines. For Americans aged 21 to 25, the rate of current alcohol use is 64.3 percent. For those 60 to 64 years of age, it declines to 45.6 percent. The estimated cost of alcohol abuse was $166 billion in 1995 (Harwood, Fountain, and Livermore, 1998). The costs of alcohol abuse are significantly impacted by the loss of productivity of the estimated 100,000 Americans who die prematurely from the various illnesses and injuries related to the practice, including the 7,150 who lost their lives in automobile accidents where alcohol was a factor (NHTSA, 2002). The overall incidence of driving under the influence of alcohol (DUI) was up 11.1 percent in 2001 over the previous year. Among 18 to 25 year olds the incidence was up 22.8 percent.

Alcohol use is a two-edged sword. For some people even moderate alcohol consumption carries with it severe health risks. But for others there is substantial medical evidence that moderate consumption can actually be beneficial, the so-called "French Paradox."[9] The medical evidence is unclear. Recent research findings by Abramson et al. (2001) and Sacco et al. (1999) suggest that moderate daily consumption (one drink for women and two for men) offers some protection against the development of heart disease. Specifically, it raises HDL (the good cholesterol), lowers blood pressure, inhibits the formation of blood clots, and prevents arterial damage caused by LDL (the bad cholesterol).

Fetal exposure to large amounts of alcohol can be harmful, causing physical, mental, and behavioral damage to the child. Alcohol-related damage to a child include birth defects, alcohol-related neurodevelopmental disorders, and fetal alcohol syndrome (FAS). When a woman drinks large amounts of alcohol (four or more drinks per day) throughout pregnancy, there is a high likelihood that her baby will suffer one or more of these problems. Diagnosis of FAS is based on the incidence of certain unique facial features and mental deficiencies. Specific birth defects associated with fetal alcohol syndrome include serious growth retardation resulting in low birth weight and all the problems associated with it. Hearing loss, mental retardation, and physical abnormalities such as heart valve defects and cleft palate are also frequently observed.

Abel and Sokol (1987) estimate the incidence and cost of the disorder. Based on retrospective data, they report that incidence estimates average around 3 per 1,000 live births. Their review of 88,236 births placed the figure closer to 2 per 1,000. Using the lower estimate, the total number of children born annually suffering from FAS is over 8,000. Their estimate of the annual cost of the disorder is placed at $2.5 billion (2002 dollars).

---

9 The French Paradox refers to the observation that the French have less heart disease than Americans despite a high-fat diet. Red wine and olive oil are thought to be at least partially responsible.

Back-of-the-Envelope

THE QUESTION OF DRUG LEGALIZATION

Many proponents of drug legalization use economics to make their case. They argue that banned drugs are just that, banned. With no distinction among illegal substances, young people may get the impression that one is no worse than the other—PCP, crack cocaine, heroin, marijuana—they're all the same, aren't they? Consumers have no assurance regarding the quality of the drugs they buy and the government can generate no tax revenue from the sale and purchase of the banned substances. Public costs are high with a large percentage of the cost of police, courts, and prisons directly or indirectly attributable to the war on drugs. Despite all the spending to stop drug trafficking, only 10 to 15 percent of all drugs entering the country are seized. Proponents of legalization suggest that we control the sale of drugs, tax the profits, supervise production, and at the same time discourage their use.

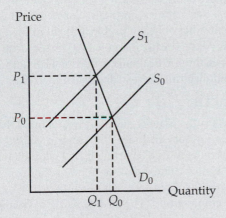

Citing the fact that increased spending for interdiction has little effect on the amount of drugs reaching the market, legalization proponents argue that the demand for drugs is likely to be inelastic. As depicted in the graph, when demand is relatively inelastic, increasing the cost to suppliers (and thus shifting the supply curve to the left) has little effect on the equilibrium quantity (reducing quantity from Q_0 to Q_1). The only thing the interdiction strategy accomplishes is to raise the price of drugs and increase the incentives for suppliers. In addition, those who use drugs are forced into lives of crime to support their expensive habit.

Opponents of legalization argue that prohibition may create crime by classifying certain activities as criminal, but it is not victimless crime. People under the influence of drugs are more likely to injure others, and the medical complications of drug use impose indirect costs on everybody. In any event, hard-core drug users were committing crimes long before they were using drugs. It is these hard-core users whose demand is price inelastic. For the millions who do not use drugs, demand is quite elastic. Any relaxation in standards will cause a substantial increase in use. The legal sanctions and the social stigma are enough to dissuade the curious. So the demand curve for these potential users is much flatter than the one shown above. Legalization will not only increase quantity demanded for this group, but will actually shift the demand curve to the right, further increasing consumption.

Organizations such as NORML (National Organization to Reform Marijuana Laws) argue that legalization of pot makes sense. They claim that it is nonaddictive, widely used, and no worse than alcohol. It is already the largest cash crop in the state of California. On the other hand, opponents ask the question: Do we need another

 Key Concept 5
Markets and Pricing

 Key Concept 6
Supply and Demand

social problem on the lines of tobacco and alcohol to add to the pathologies we already suffer? If we legalize, where do we draw the line? Do we stop at marijuana? Should PCP, crack, and LSD be added to the list? How soon before proponents begin calling on governing bodies in sports to sanction the use of anabolic steroids? Should we try to legislate the moral behavior of society? Or should we follow the libertarian (some would say, libertine) principles and tolerate such behavior? Expect disagreement when you bring up this topic at your next social gathering.

Source: James W. Henderson, "Economic Impact of Cocaine and Crack Abuse: Private and Social Issues," in Glen E. Lich, ed., *Doing Drugs and Dropping Out: Assessing the Costs to Society of Substance Abuse and Dropping Out of School.* A Report prepared for the Subcommittee on Economic Growth, Trade, and Taxes of the Joint Economic Committee, Congress of the United States, Washington, D.C.: U.S. Government Printing Office, August 1991.

Social Pathology

Many of the social problems we face in America find their way to the emergency rooms and trauma wards of our nation's hospitals. Substance abuse, violence, and sexual promiscuity lead to a number of health problems that our medical care sector must deal with on a daily basis. We've already discussed AIDS and drug abuse. In the following section, we will look at the medical effects of violence, both criminal and domestic, teenage pregnancy and illegitimacy, sexually transmitted diseases, and obesity.

Violence in America

Violent crimes in the United States totaled 1,436,611 in 2001, up slightly for the first time since 1992. This number includes 15,980 murders, 90,491 forcible rapes, and 907,219 aggravated assaults (U.S. Department of Justice, 2002). The male per capita homicide rate in the United States is 10 to 12 times those experienced in Britain and Germany and five times the rate in Canada (Schwartz, 1991). Death rates in America vary considerably by ethnic group. The leading cause of death for blacks between the ages of 15 and 24 is homicide. The homicide rate for black males in that age category is nine times the rate for white males. HIV is the leading cause of death for black males between ages 25 and 44. For whites in these two categories, accidents cause more deaths than any other cause. (Singh et al., 1996).

Virtually every homicide and forcible rape results in an emergency room visit. Moreover, U.S. hospital emergency rooms (ERs) report 100 assaults for every homicide visit. But of all the tragic consequences of criminal violence, possibly the most perplexing problem facing many poor, inner-city neighborhoods is domestic violence. Although it is not confined to the inner city or any particular ethnic group, this problem seems to manifest itself and grow in the culture and philosophy that thrives in the inner city.

Assault by a male partner is the leading cause of ER visits for women.[10] The relevant facts include (Browne, 1992):

- In an average 12-month period, two million American women are severely beaten by their male partners.

- A current or former male partner kills more than one half of the women murdered in the United States.

- Twenty percent of all adult women, 15 percent of all college women, and 12 percent of all adolescent girls will experience sexual abuse or assault during their lifetimes.

---

10 Even though "male partner" includes husbands and boyfriends, the latter are more likely to be abusive. Single, separated, and divorced women are more likely to be beaten by their boyfriends than wives by their husbands. McKibben et al. (1989) show a relationship between marital status and abuse, with single women being the victims of abusive behavior more often than married women. The setting of unmarried sex partners is the most violent domestic situation.

- More than one-third of all obstetric patients are abused while they are pregnant.

Whatever the causes of domestic violence, a greater acceptance of its use to settle disputes seems prevalent in our society. Whether it is traced to the decline in family values or whether it is the product of government neglect, domestic violence is an issue that is eating away at the moral fabric of our society. If we continue to experience this deterioration, no amount of spending on medical care will be able to reconstruct the broken lives and intense human suffering that it causes.

Teen Pregnancy

Critics of U.S. medical care often cite high infant mortality rates as evidence of a breakdown in the current delivery system. One can make a very compelling argument linking poverty and poor access to care with high mortality rates. According to data in Table 10.4, in 2001 the United States ranked twentieth in infant mortality among countries with populations greater than 2.5 million. At 6.9 deaths per 1,000 live births, the U.S. rate was twice that of Finland and Japan.[11]

Much of the evidence examining the cause of high infant mortality point to the high risk associated with low birthweight. Data indicate that the infant mortality rate for very low-birthweight babies (those born weighing less than 1,500 grams) was 252.8, over 90 times the rate of 2.7 for infants born weighing more than 2,500 grams. Even though these very low-birthweight babies comprise only about 1.4 percent of all births, they account for over 50 percent of all infant deaths (MacDorman and Atkinson, 1999).

Table 10.4	Infant Mortality, Selected Countries Death Rates per 1,000 Live Births, 1960–2001						
Country and 2001 Ranking	**1960**	**1970**	**1980**	**1990**	**1995**	**2000**	**2001**
1 Japan	30.7	13.1	7.5	4.6	4.3	3.2	3.1
2 Finland	21.0	13.2	7.6	5.6	4.0	3.8	3.2
3 Sweden	16.6	11.0	6.9	6.0	4.1	3.4	3.7
4 Norway	18.9	12.7	8.1	7.0	4.1	3.8	3.8
5 Spain	43.7	26.3	12.3	7.6	5.5	3.9	3.9
5 Italy	43.9	29.6	14.6	8.2	6.2	4.5	4.3
7 Austria	37.5	25.9	14.3	7.8	5.4	4.8	4.8
7 France	27.4	18.2	10.0	7.3	4.9	4.6	4.6
9 Germany	33.8	23.4	12.7	7.0	5.3	4.4	4.5
9 Switzerland	21.1	15.1	9.1	6.8	5.0	4.9	—
11 Denmark	21.5	14.2	8.4	7.5	5.0	5.3	4.9
12 Belgium	31.2	21.1	12.1	8.0	7.0	4.8	5.0
13 Australia	20.2	17.9	10.7	8.2	5.7	5.2	5.3
14 Netherlands	17.9	12.7	8.6	7.1	5.5	5.1	5.3
15 Canada	27.3	18.8	10.4	6.8	6.0	5.3	—
16 United Kingdom	22.5	18.5	12.1	7.9	6.0	5.6	5.5
17 Ireland	29.3	19.5	11.1	8.2	6.3	6.2	5.8
18 Greece	40.1	29.6	17.9	9.7	8.2	6.1	5.9
19 New Zealand	22.6	16.8	12.9	8.4	7.0	—	—
20 United States	26.0	20.0	12.6	9.2	8.0	6.9	—

Source: *OECD Health Data 2003*, Organization of Economic Cooperation and Development, 2003.

11 The U.S. infant mortality rate varies significantly across ethnic groups. The rate for blacks was 13.5, more than double the rate for whites at 5.7.

The incidence of low-weight births for seven advanced countries is shown in Table 10.5. The United States has the second highest rate of low-birthweight infants. Only Japan fares worse than the United States. Even though American babies have a higher median birth weight than the Swedish, the incidence of low birth weight is nearly twice as high in the United States as in Sweden.[12]

Are the high infant mortality statistics presenting an accurate picture of the U.S. health care delivery system? Studies based on data available from the International Collaborative Effort on Perinatal and Infant Mortality indicate that birthweight-specific perinatal mortality rates are actually higher in Japan and Norway than in the United States (Eberstadt, 1991; Hoffman, Bergsjol, and Denman, 1990).[13] True for both black and white infants, babies weighing less than 2,500 grams at birth have a better chance of survival in the United States than either of these two countries, despite the fact that both have considerably lower overall infant mortality rates. These findings suggest that the relatively poor infant mortality ranking of the United States is largely due to the higher proportion of very low birthweight infants. In addition, mothers have better chance of surviving childbirth in the United States than in Japan. The death rate for Japanese women during childbirth is four times higher than that of U.S. women (Singh, 1990). These facts suggest that medical care for infants and their mothers in the United States may be better than the infant mortality statistics would suggest.

Part of these differences in birthweights may be due to biological factors and the heterogeneous nature of the U.S. population. The median birthweight for white babies is higher than for black babies born in the United States. Even after adjusting for differences in mothers' age, education, and income, the proportion of low-birthweight babies is still twice as high for blacks as for whites, suggesting that at least part of the birthweight differential between blacks and whites may be due to physiological and behavioral differences among ethnic groups. In addition, the birthweight differential stays the same at all levels of prenatal care availability and use (Henderson, 1994).

An alternative explanation for the high incidence of low birthweight is the high rate of teen pregnancy and illegitimacy in this country. Both factors are strongly correlated with low birthweight and infant mortality. In fact, Eberstadt has stated that "if viewed as a medical condition, illegitimacy would be one of the leading killers of children in

Table 10.5	Percentage of Low-Weight Births Selected Countries, 2001
Country	**Less than 2,500 Grams**
United States	7.7
Canada	5.8[a]
Japan	8.8
France	6.5
United Kingdom	7.6
Germany	6.5[b]
Sweden	4.2

Source: OECD Health Data 2003, Organization of Economic Cooperation and Development, 2003.

a 2000
b 1999

_____

12 The incidence of low-birthweight babies continues to increase in the United States. In 2000, 7.5 percent of all infants born weighed less than 2,500 grams, 6.6 percent of white infants, 6.4 percent of Hispanic infants, and 13.0 percent of all black infants.

13 Perinatal mortality includes all fetal deaths that occur after a minimum of 28 weeks of gestation and all infant deaths that occur within one week of birth.

America" (Singh, 1990). Whether illegitimacy is a causal factor or merely associated with low birthweight is still a matter of serious debate among researchers.

Teen pregnancy and illegitimacy may actually serve as proxy variables for maternal behavior and attitude about the pregnancy.[14] Teen mothers are less likely to receive timely prenatal care and are more likely to smoke cigarettes, leading to inadequate weight gain, lower birthweights, and a higher incidence of preterm births (Ventura et al., 2000). The relationship between infant mortality rates and illegitimacy is striking. Eberstadt (1991) reports data from a pilot study by the National Center for Health Statistics indicating that unmarried college graduates (both black and white) have higher infant mortality rates than married women regardless of their educational attainment.

Table 10.6 compares the teen pregnancy rates in seven developed countries in 1996. The United States has a higher rate of teenage pregnancy than any of the others listed. At 64 per 1,000 females, it is two times the U.K. rate and 16 times the Japanese rate.[15]

In 1997, 32.4 percent of all U.S. births were to unmarried mothers, 25.8 percent of all white births, 40.9 percent of all Hispanic births, and 69.2 percent of all African-American births (MacDorman and Atkinson, 1999). In contrast, less than 1 percent of all Japanese mothers are teenagers or unmarried, due to the social stigma of such behavior. Interestingly, the same social customs and low infant mortality rates can be found among Japanese-American women (Wegman, 1993).

A bit of encouraging news about teenage and unmarried births in the United States is that the rates are falling in almost all categories. The teenage pregnancy rate fell 17.7 percent between 1991 and 1998. The black and Hispanic rates have fallen to 85.4 per 1,000 teenage females and 93.6 per 1,000 but are still approximately twice the white rate of 45.4. While the overall rate of teenage births has been declining since 1991, the proportion of births to unmarried teenagers rose to 78.9 percent in 1998. Even with this high rate of illegitimacy among teenage mothers, over 70 percent of the births to unmarried women are to mothers over the age of 20.

Limited access to prenatal care due to limited finances, while often cited as a factor in low birthweights, may not be the primary cause. In the District of Columbia, where

Table 10.6	Birth Rates for Teen-Age Mothers Selected Countries, 1996

Country	Births per 1,000 Females
United States	64
United Kingdom	33
Canada	27
Sweden	13
Italy	9
Netherlands	7
Japan	4

Source: Population Resource Center at **http://www.prcdc.org**

14 Research has shown that "mistimed or unwanted" babies were more likely to be born at low birthweights than those who were planned or "wanted" (Pamuk and Mosher, 1988).
15 The U.S. incidence was 11.8 percent in 2000 and has declined every year since 1991. Still, 10.6 percent of all white births, 16.2 percent of all Hispanic births, and 19.7 percent of all back births are to teenagers.

Policy Issue

Better access to prenatal care will improve birth outcomes. Is free care the answer?

prenatal care is provided free of charge at 11 of the city's 16 health clinics, the infant mortality rate is the nation's worst, 27 per 1,000 in 1989 (Singh, 1990). In other research, Murray and Bernfield (1988) studied over 31,000 births in California's Kaiser-Permanente hospitals where prenatal care and delivery were available on a prepaid basis. Adjusting for the mothers' age, education, and other characteristics related to risk, black mothers were more likely to forgo prenatal care completely, to begin prenatal care later than their white counterparts, and to have fewer prenatal physician visits when they do take advantage of their medical benefits. Black mothers in the study had twice the rate of low birthweight babies than whites.

Low birthweights lead to longer hospital stays, driving up the cost of newborn care. Normal-sized infants (weighing more than 2,500 grams) can expect to stay in the hospital around three days. Smaller infants, those weighing between 1,500 and 2,500 grams, have average stays of 24 days. Those born weighing less than 1,500 grams have average stays of 57 days and those weighing less than 1,000 grams, 89 days (McCormick, 1985). Low birthweight is a costly proposition; it is expensive and deadly.

Measurement problems and different ways of registering live births also contribute to the international differences in infant mortality rates (Liu et al., 1992). The World Health Organization (WHO) has a formal scheme to classify birth outcomes, but registration practices vary across countries. In deference to the WHO definition, an infant born in France that dies before its birth registration (anywhere from 24 to 48 hours after its birth) is counted as "false stillbirth." Japan's infant mortality rate may be artificially low as evidenced by an unusually high ratio of stillbirths to infant deaths.

Policy Issue

The infant mortality puzzle may be more complicated than high rates compared to other countries.

International comparisons are frequently made to stimulate policy discussions and therefore should be made cautiously. The infant mortality puzzle is an important health care issue. For a number of reasons, the U.S. ranking is relatively low. It is important that we understand these reasons if we are to further reduce infant mortality rates.

Sexually Transmitted Disease

Sexual promiscuity is undermining the public health of our nation. Unwise sexual practices such as first intercourse at an early age, a high frequency of intercourse, and multiple sex partners have led to an outright epidemic of sexually transmitted diseases (STDs). There are 25 diseases that are spread primarily through sexual activity, resulting in more than 15 million new STD infections each year, with two-thirds of those newly infected younger than 25 years of age. Cases of syphilis and gonorrhea are at all time lows, but others, such as herpes and chlamydia, continue to spread at alarming rates (CDC, 2000). Except for the common cold and the flu, STDs are the most common diseases in North America (CDC, 1993a and 1993b).

The Centers for Disease Control and Prevention (CDC) estimates that 65 million Americans have an incurable STD. Most are infected with genital herpes. A 1997 CDC study reported that 1.2 million adolescents, or 5.6 percent of the 12- to 19-year-old population, are infected with genital herpes. Additionally, the CDC estimates that 15 to 20 percent of all young people become infected with herpes by the time they reach adulthood. The CDC alone spends over $100 million annually for treatment and prevention of syphilis, gonorrhea, chlamydia, and herpes with little to show for it. Condom use is less effective in the prevention of herpes than for other STDs. Active herpes sores open up a pathway to the bloodstream, making those with open lesions more than 10 times more likely to acquire HIV than those without such lesions (Petersen, 1997).

The human papillomavirus (HPV) is the most common STD among young, sexually active populations. A recent study by Ho et al. (1998) found that approximately 14 percent of all women attending college are infected with HPV each year. Over 40 percent of the women in the study were infected with HPV during the three-year study period. HPV is particularly troublesome because most individuals who suffer from it are asymptomatic and HPV can lead to cervical, penile, and anal cancer.

Another growing problem is the number of reproductive age women suffering from chlamydia trachomatis. Over 40 percent of the 3 million chlamydia infections annually occur among 15- to 19-year-olds. In fact, the prevalence among teenage girls is ten percent. Asymptomatic in most infected women, if untreated it leads to pelvic inflammatory disease (PID). PID is an infection of the upper reproductive tract caused primarily by sexually transmitted organisms, affecting 10 to 15 percent of all reproductive-age women during their lifetimes. More than 250,000 women are hospitalized annually and more than 100,000 surgeries are performed due to PID. Approximately 20 percent of the women treated for PID will become infertile due to scarring of the fallopian tubes. Ten percent of the pregnancies in women with PID will be ectopic pregnancies. The cost of treating PID was approximately $10 billion in 2000.

Table 10.7 summarizes the cost of sexually transmitted diseases in the United States in 1994. The nine diseases listed had a combined cost of almost $19 billion with HIV, PID, HPV, and chlamydia ranked in the top four. In addition, STDs were responsible for 337,000 emergency room visits in 2000.

Obesity

Over the course of the past 25 years there has been an alarming increase in obesity in the United States. In the late 1970s, according to government survey data, fifteen percent of the adult population was obese. By 1988–1994 the rate of obesity had increased to 23 percent. Recent evidence from a 1999–2000 survey indicated that 30 percent of Americans fell into that category. Obesity is technically defined as a person with a body mass index (BMI) greater than 30.[16] Even though obesity is a problem affecting the entire developed world, no other country has the problem to the extent found in the United States.

An estimated 300,000 Americans die annually of causes related to obesity and a sedentary lifestyle (Mokdad et al., 2001). These deaths are caused by coronary artery disease, stroke, high blood pressure, cancer, and diabetes. Wolf and Colditz (1998) estimate that the direct costs of obesity amounted to $99.2 billion in 1995, or approximately 10 percent of total U.S. health care spending.

Research by Cutler, Glaeser, and Shapiro (2003) explains the increase as a result of higher calorie consumption. Women today consume 9 percent more than they did 20 years ago, and men consume 13 percent more. The reason for these increases: Food is cheaper, not only in terms of the hours required to earn the money to buy it, but in

Table 10.7	Estimated Cost of Selected STDs In Billions of Dollars, 1994

STD	Annual Cost
Sexually Transmitted HIV	$6.68
PID	4.15
HPV	3.83
Chlamydia	2.01
Gonorrhea	1.05
Cervical Cancer	0.74
Herpes Simplex	0.16
Syphilis	0.11
Chancroid	0.01

Source: Institute of Medicine, 1997.

---

16 $BMI = \dfrac{Weight \text{ (in kilograms)}}{Height \text{ (in meters)}^2}$ Optimal BMI is between 20 and 25. A person with a BMI between 25 and 30 is considered overweight.

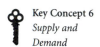

Key Concept 6
Supply and Demand

ISSUES IN MEDICAL CARE DELIVERY

IS "SAFE" SEX REALLY SAFE?

One of the costs of risky sexual practices is an increased likelihood of contracting a sexually transmitted disease, such as syphilis and gonorrhea or even AIDS. As with any activity involving human choice, the higher the perceived cost of engaging in risky sex, the less the demand for it. This suggests that by making sex "safer" through free condom distribution (by lowering the cost of risky behavior), public health officials may be increasing the incidence of the risky sexual behavior and actually increasing the incidence of sexually transmitted diseases.

The logic of this possibility is based on the fact that there is a demand curve for sex. It is difficult to know its exact shape, but most economists would agree that it is downward sloping. As the perceived cost of a sexual encounter (the risk of contracting a sexually transmitted disease) falls, the number of sexual encounters will increase. The size of the increase is determined by the "risk elasticity of demand for sex."

The risk elasticity of demand for sex is defined as the percentage change in number of sexual encounters divided by the percentage change in the risk of each encounter. If the risk elasticity is less than 1, then free condom distribution will reduce the incidence of disease. If it is greater than 1, however, the incidence of disease will increase.

Consider a closed community where condoms must be purchased and no one uses them. Based on research by Rosenberg et al. (1992), the risk of contracting a sexually transmitted disease (gonorrhea, trichomoniasis, and chlamydia) during unprotected sexual activity is 23.4 in 100. If the number of risky sexual encounters is 250 per week, there will be 58 new infections every week. Assume that condoms are now distributed free of charge and their use is widely encouraged through a sex education program. The use of condoms will result in a reduction in the incidence of STD to 18.8 per 100 risky sexual encounters (a 20 percent reduction).

If the demand for sex is inelastic and the risk elasticity of demand is –0.50, sexual intercourse will increase from 250 per week to 275 (a 10 percent increase). In that case, there will be only 52 new cases of STD every week, a 10 percent decrease. On the other hand, if the demand for sex is elastic and the risk elasticity of demand for sex is –1.5, sexual intercourse increases from 250 per week to 325 per week (a 30 percent increase). In that case, there will be 61 new cases of STD reported every week, a 5 percent increase.

Does the policy of making condoms available increase or decrease the number of cases of STD? While the value of risk elasticity of demand for sex is an empirical matter, there is some evidence that sexual activity is higher in those situations where condoms are widely available. According to Planned Parenthood, in schools with formal sex-ed programs and free condom distribution, the percentage of males engaging in sex increased from 60 to 84 percent and the use of condoms actually decreased (Family Planning Perspectives, 1994). Kasun's review (1994) of seven sex education programs with easy access to condoms revealed that six resulted in an increase in sexual activity.

Any attempt by policymakers to make sex "safer" could actually exacerbate the problems by encouraging sexual activity. Whether the incidence of STD infection increases or decreases depends on the value of the risk elasticity of demand for sex.

Sources: Dwight Lee, "Will Condoms Mean Less AIDS? It's a Question of Elasticity," *The Margin*, September/October 1989, 28; "As Adolescent Males Age, Risky Behavior Rises but Condom Use Decreases," *Family Planning Perspectives*, January/February 1994, 45–46; Jacqueline R. Kasun, "Condom Nation: Government Sex Education Programs Promote Teen Pregnancy," *Policy Review*, Spring 1994, 79; and Michael J. Rosenberg, Arthur Davidson, Jian-Hua Chen, Franklyn Judson, and John Douglas, "Barrier Contraceptives and Sexually Transmitted Diseases in Women: A Comparison of Female-Dependent Methods and Condoms," *American Journal of Public Health 82*(5), May 1992, 669–674.

terms of the time it takes to cook it. Remember, because demand curves slope downward, when something is cheaper, consumers demand more.

Not only is calorie consumption increasing, but much of what we buy to eat is processed before we get it—either in a restaurant or packaged and purchased in a grocery store. With more women working, less time is spent in food preparation. According to time use surveys, married women who work outside the home spent an average of 41 minutes a day in food chores in 1995 compared to 85 minutes a day 30 years earlier. For those women without jobs outside the home, the average was 69 minutes in 1995 compared to 138 minutes in 1965. The same trends were also true for single individuals (Wessel, 2003).

Consumers usually view decreases in price as a good thing. In the case of food, however, people may lack the self-control to limit their consumption to levels that are healthy. This may be one of the reasons that the European Union has taken such a strong stance against genetically altered food. The support of traditional agriculture may have health benefits for members of the developed world. The same may not be true for individuals living in less developed countries.

Summary and Conclusions

In this chapter we discussed a number of sociocultural concerns that affect the overall health of the population. Alcohol, tobacco, and drug use and their associated health problems increase the demand for medical care and are responsible for a large percentage of the overall health care spending in this country. The United States has a higher incidence of many of these confounding factors. For example, the rate of AIDS cases is three times higher in the United States than in Canada and six times higher than in Germany. In addition, the problem of drug-exposed infants is virtually nonexistent in Canada. Teen pregnancy, illegitimacy, domestic violence, the use and availability of handguns, STDs, and obesity are experienced at higher levels in the United States than in other developed countries around the world.

How does public policy impact these problems? Government's role is not limited to legislative options. The subsidy and tax options can also serve to encourage healthy behavior and discourage unhealthy behavior. The challenges are enormous and suggest that economics can play a role in this sensitive area of public policymaking.

Questions and Problems

1. How important is the deterioration of the social system in contributing to the health care spending crisis (assuming one exists)?

2. Is it important to characterize such social problems as alcoholism and drug abuse as diseases rather than behavior disorders? What are the implications of treating other social problems as diseases? What about anorexia? Obesity? Domestic violence? What are the implications for the medical care system of the proliferation of these new "diseases?"

3. What are the costs to society of cocaine use? Alcohol use? Tobacco use? Which of these presents the biggest problem? Explain.

4. "Drug use is a classic example of a victimless crime. Therefore it should not be prohibited." Comment.

5. "The best way to lower the incidence of sexually transmitted diseases is to make condoms widely available to teenagers and educate them in their proper use." Do you agree or disagree? Explain.

Key Concept 6
Supply and Demand

Key Concept 3
Opportunity Cost

http://

The American Public Health Association provides a multidisciplinary environment of professional exchange, study, and action for those interested in personal and environmental health issues.
http://www.apha.org/.

PROFILE

Jonathan Gruber

If the number of publications is a measure of the influence of a scholar, Jonathan Gruber may be the most influential health economist of the past decade. Since he received his Ph.D. in 1992, Gruber has published 56 articles in refereed journals, 31 book chapters, 4 edited volumes, and numerous essays. In addition, he has 8 working papers in the National Bureau of Economic Research (NBER) working paper series. Accomplishing this body of work in a lifetime is no minor feat; accomplishing it before your fortieth birthday is remarkable.

Born in New Jersey, Gruber received his undergraduate degree in economics from the Massachusetts Institute of Technology (MIT) in 1987 and moved to Harvard University where he studied under the direction of Lawrence Summers, that institution's current president. Introduced to the power of policy-oriented economics at an early age, Gruber spent two summers at the Brookings Institution in Washington, D.C. At Brookings he began applying his knowledge of economics to inform policymakers on issues of importance to ordinary Americans.

After graduating from Harvard, he returned to his undergraduate alma mater, a move that some view as dangerous for a scholarly career, especially for a first academic appointment. Whatever the possible pitfalls, Gruber's progression through the ranks is just short of remarkable—promoted to associate professor after three years and then full professor two years later. In addition to his position at MIT, he is a research associate at the NBER and director of their program on children. He is currently co-editor of the *Journal of Public Economics* and associate editor of the *Journal of Health Economics*. He has also served as Deputy Assistant Secretary for Economic Policy at the U.S. Treasury Department during the Clinton administration and is currently a member of the Congressional Budget Office Long-Term Modeling Advisory Group.

Trained in public finance and labor economics, Gruber's early work reflected that perspective, examining the impact of health insurance mandates on labor markets. His research interests turned quickly to more standard health economics issues. With articles published in some of the most prestigious journals in economics, Gruber is not relying on past accomplishments to guide public policy. His future research will focus on some of the most important issues in health policy, including the impact of public insurance programs (Medicaid and SCHIP) on health outcomes, the impact of reimbursement rates on the quality of nursing home care, and how religion and religiosity affect well-being.

Gruber has always had a penchant for looking at a well-discussed problem from a different perspective. Until his work on unemployment insurance, the focus in the literature was primarily on the labor market distortions of the program. Instead, Gruber studied the issue from the workers' perspective—looking at the impact on family consumption, savings, and labor supply decisions. His research on smoking and other addictive behavior has introduced a more realistic assumption of human behavior into the model (see "Is Addiction Rational?" in Issues in Medical Care Delivery earlier in this chapter). As a result of this improvement the normative implications for government policy options differ significantly from previous research.

Despite his scholarly success, Gruber's main avocation is his family—wife Andrea and three children. Whether it is spending time at the beach or just wrestling with his kids in the playroom, his goal is to strike a balance between a successful professional career and a fulfilling family life. Jonathan Gruber serves as an inspiration to all discouraged economists who think that what they do doesn't matter.

Source: Vita and personal correspondence.

References

E. L. Abel and R. J. Sokol, "Incidence of Fetal Alcohol Syndrome and Economic Impact of FAS-Related Anomalies," *Drug and Alcohol Dependence 19*, 1987, 51–70.

Jerome L. Abramson et al., "Moderate Alcohol Consumption and the Risk of Heart Failure Among Older Persons," *Journal of the American Medical Association 285*(15), April 18, 2001, 1971–1977.

"Ashes in their Mouths," *The Economist* 323, May 30, 1992, 86.

Michael A. Bozarth and Roy A. Wise, "Toxicity Associated with Long-Term Intravenous Heroin and Cocaine Self-Administration in the Rat," *Journal of the American Medical Association 254*(1), July 1, 1985, 81–83.

Angela Browne, "Violence Against Women: Relevance for Medical Practitioners," A Report by the Council on Scientific Affairs, *Journal of the American Medical Association 267*(23), June 17, 1992, 3184–3189.

Centers for Disease Control and Prevention (CDC), "Annual Smoking-Attributable Mortality, Years of Potential Life Lost, and Economic Costs—United States, 1995–1999," *Morbidity and Mortality Weekly Report Highlights 51*(14), April 12, 2002.

_____, *HIV/AIDS Surveillance Report 13*(2), 2002.

_____, Recommendations for the Prevention and Management of Chlamydia Trachomatis Infections, 1993, *Morbidity and Mortality Weekly Report,* Recommendations and Reports, 42, No. RR-12, August 6, 1993a.

_____, 1993 Sexually Transmitted Disease Treatment Guidelines, *Morbidity and Mortality Weekly Report,* Recommendations and Reports, 42, No. RR-14, September 24, 1993b.

_____, *Tracking the Hidden Epidemics: Trends in the STD Epidemics in the United States*, 2000.

_____, "Youth Tobacco Surveillance—United States, 1998–1999," *Morbidity and Mortality Weekly Report, Surveillance Summary 49*(SS10), October 13, 2000, 1–93.

Marilyn Chase, "Researcher Sees U.S. Cost of Treating AIDS Virus Rising Sharply by 1995," *The Wall Street Journal,* July 23, 1992, B8.

Ira J. Chasnoff, William J. Burns, Sidney H. Schnoll, and Kayreen A. Burns, "Cocaine Use in Pregnancy," *New England Journal of Medicine 313*(11), September 12, 1985, 666–669.

———, Dan R. Griffith, Scott MacGregor, Kathryn Dirkes, and Kayreen A. Burns, "Temporal Patterns of Cocaine Use in Pregnancy," *Journal of the American Medical Association 261*(12), March 15, 1989, 1741–1774.

Kenneth W. Culver, Arthur J. Ammann, J. Colin Partridge, Don F. Wong, Diane W. Wara, and Morton J. Cowan, "Lymphocyte Abnormalities in Infants Born to Drug-Abusing Mothers," *Journal of Pediatrics 111*(2), August 1987, 230–235.

David M. Cutler, Edward L. Glaeser, and Jesse M. Shapiro, "Why Have Americans Become More Obese?" NBER Working Paper No. 9446, Cambridge, MA: National Bureau of Economic Research, January 2003.

Suzanne Dixon and Raul Bejar, "Echoencephalographic Findings in Neonates Associated with Maternal Cocaine and Methanphetamine Use: Incidence and Clinical Correlates," *Journal of Pediatrics 115*(5), November 1989, 770–778.

Nicholas Eberstadt, "America's Infant-Mortality Puzzle," *The Public Interest* 105, Fall 1991, 30–47.

Scott Foster et al., *Federal HIV/AIDS Spending: A Budget Chartbook, Fiscal Year 2001*, Fourth Edition, The Henry J. Kaiser Family Foundation, June 2002.

Frank H. Gawin, "Cocaine Abuse and Addiction," *Journal of Family Practice 29*(2), August 1989, 193–197.

Henrick Harwood, Douglas Fountain, Gina Livermore, and the Lewin Group, "The Economic Costs of Alcohol and Drug Abuse in the United States, 1992," National Institute on Drug Abuse, National Institutes of Health, Publication Number 98-4327, September 1998.

Fred J. Hellinger, "The Lifetime Costs of Treating a Person with HIV," *Journal of the American Medical Association 270*(4), July 28, 1993, 474–478.

James W. Henderson, "Economic Impact of Cocaine and Crack Abuse: Private and Social Issues," in Glen E. Lich, ed., *Doing Drugs and Dropping Out: Assessing the Costs to Society of Substance Abuse and Dropping Out of School*. A Report prepared for the Subcommittee on Economic Growth, Trade, and Taxes of the Joint Economic Committee, Congress of the United States, Washington, DC: U.S. Government Printing Office, August 1991.

———, "The Cost Effectiveness of Prenatal Care," *Health Care Financing Review 15*(4), Summer 1994, 21–32.

Gloria Y. F. Ho, Robert Bierman, Leah Beardsley, Chee J. Chang, and Robert D. Burk, "Natural History of Cervicovaginal Papillomavirus Infection in Young Women," *New England Journal of Medicine 388*(7), February 12, 1998, 423–428.

H. J. Hoffman, P. Bergsjol, and D. W. Denman, "Trends in Birth Weight Specific Perinatal Mortality Rates: 1970–1983," *Proceedings of the International Collaborative Effort on Perinatal and Infant Mortality 2*, Hyattsville, MD: National Center for Health Statistics, March 1990.

Scott Holmberg, "The Estimated Prevalence and Incidence of HIV in 96 Large US Metropolitan Areas," *American Journal of Public Health 86*(5), May 1996, 642–654.

Cindy Kelly, "The Long-Term Effects of AIDS on the Economy," *The Margin*, Fall 1992, 38–39.

Mark A. R. Kleiman et al., *Hard-Core Cocaine Addicts: Measuring—and Fighting—the Epidemic*. A Staff Report prepared for the use of the Committee on the Judiciary, United States Senate. Washington, DC: U.S. Government Printing Office, 1990.

Korbin Liu, Marilyn Moon, Margaret Sulvetta, and Juhi Chawia, "International Infant Mortality Rankings: A Look Behind the Numbers," *Health Care Financing Review 13*(4), Summer 1992, 105–118.

Marian F. MacDorman and Jonnae O. Atkinson, "Infant Mortality Statistics from the 1997 Period Linked Birth/Infant Death Data Set," *National Vital Statistics Reports 47*(23), Hyattsville, Maryland: National Center for Health Statistics, 1999.

Marie C. McCormick, "The Contribution of Low Birthweight to Infant Mortality and Childhood Morbidity," *New England Journal of Medicine 312*(2), January 1985, 82–90.

Linda McKibben, Edward deVoss, and Eli H. Newberger, "Victimization of Mothers of Abused Children: A Controlled Study," *Pediatrics 84*(9), September 1989, 531–535.

Medical Industry Today, "Companies Agree to Cut Prices of HIV Drugs in Poor Nations," Medical Data International, Inc., MDI Online at **www.medicaldata.com**, May 12, 2000.

Ali H. Mokdad et al., "The Continuing Epidemics of Obesity and Diabetes in the United States," *Journal of the American Medical Association 286*(10), September 12, 2001, 1195–1200.

Charles Murray, "The Coming White Underclass," *The Wall Street Journal*, October 29, 1993, A12.

Jann L. Murray and Merton Bernfield, "The Differential Effect of Prenatal Care on the Incidence of Low Birth Weight Among Blacks and Whites in a Prepaid Health Care Plan," *New England Journal of Medicine 319*(21), November 24, 1988, 1385–1390.

National Highway Traffic Safety Administration (NHTSA), *The Economic Impact of Motor Vehicle Crashes, 2000*, U.S. Department of Transportation, HS809–446, May 2002.

Mark G. Neerhof, S. N. MacGregaor, S. S. Retzky, and T. P. Sullivan, "Cocaine Abuse During Pregnancy: Peripartum Prevalence and Perinatal Outcome," *American Journal of Obstetrics and Gynecology 161*(3), September 1989, 633–638.

E. R. Pamuk and W. D. Mosher, *Health Aspects of Pregnancy and Childbirth, United States, 1982*, Hyattsville, MD: National Center for Health Statistics, Series 23, No. 16, 1988, 52–53.

Andrea Petersen, "Overshadowed by AIDS, Herpes Spreads Alarmingly," *The Wall Street Journal*, December 10, 1997, B1, B12.

Richard Peto, Alan Lopez, Jillian Boreham, Michael Thun, and Clark Heath, Jr., "Mortality from Tobacco in Developed Countries: Indirect Estimation from National Vital Statistics," *The Lancet 339*(8804), May 1992, 1268–1278.

William Pollin, "The Danger of Cocaine," *Journal of the American Medical Association 254*(1), July 5, 1985, 98.

Dorothy P. Rice, T. A. Hodgson, P. Sinsheimer, W. Browner, and A. N. Kopstein, "The Economic Costs of the Health Effects of Smoking 1984," *Milbank Memorial Fund Quarterly, 64*(4), 1986, 489–547.

Ralph L. Sacco et al., "The Protective Effect of Moderate Alcohol Consumption on Ischemic Stroke," *Journal of the American Medical Association 281*(1), January 6, 1999, 53–60.

LeRoy Schwartz, "The Medical Costs of America's Social Ills," *The Wall Street Journal*, June 24, 1991, A12.

Jody L. Sindelar, "Economic Cost of Drug Studies: Critique and Research Agenda," Technical review paper sponsored by the National Institute on Drug Abuse, May 21–22, 1990.

Gopal K. Singh, Kenneth D. Kochanek, and Marian F. MacDorman, "Advance Report of Final Mortality Statistics, 1994," *Monthly Vital Statistics Report 45*(3) Supplement, Centers for Disease Control, September 30, 1996.

Harmeet K. D. Singh, "Stork Reality: Why America's Infants are Dying," *Policy Review*, Spring 1990, 56–63.

Substance Abuse and Mental Health Services Administration (SAMHSA), Reports and Tables from DAWN Emergency Department Component, 2002, [available at **http://www.samhsa.gov/oas/dawn.htm#Edcomp**].

Cathy Trost, "As Drug Babies Grow Older, Schools Strive to Meet Their Needs," *The Wall Street Journal*, December 27, 1989, A1, A3.

U.S. Congress, House of Representatives, *Cocaine Babies*, Hearing before the Select Committee on Narcotics Abuse and Control, 100th Congress, 1st Session, 1987.

U.S. Department of Health and Human Services, National Household Survey on Drug Abuse, 2002, Rockville, MD: National Institute on Drug Abuse, 2002.

U.S. Department of Justice, *Crime in the United States: Uniform Crime Reports*, 2002, Washington, DC: Federal Bureau of Investigation, 2002.

Stephanie J. Ventura, Sally C. Curtin, and T .J. Mathews, "Variations in Teenage Birth Rates, 1991–98: National and State Trends," *National Vital Statistics Reports 48*(6), Hyattsville, Maryland: National Center for Health Statistics, 2000.

Myron E. Wegman, "Annual Summary of Vital Statistics, 1992," *Pediatrics 92*(8), December 1993, 743–754.

David Wessel, "Americans are Getting Fatter, and Technology is to Blame," *The Wall Street Journal*, February 13, 2003, A2.

Anne Wolf and Graham Colditz, "Current Estimates of the Economics of Obesity in the United States," *Obesity Research 6*(2), March 1998, 97–106.

Chapter 11

The Aging of the Population

Economic theory often cites changing demographics as a major factor in determining the demand for goods and services. The popular notion that demand changes as an individual, family, or nation grows in size and matures is familiar to most students of economic theory. In fact, partly because of his pioneering research in life-cycle changes in savings, investment, and consumption, Franco Modigliani was awarded the Nobel Prize for Economic Science in 1985. When exploring the causes of high and rising medical care costs, the aging population makes everyone's top ten list.

In this chapter we will first examine the changing demographics of the population. As Americans live longer the changing age and gender structure will have a significant effect on medical care demand in the coming century. This chapter looks at overall spending on medical care by age category and spending on specific services—long-term care and end-of-life care. Elder care is often the focus of cost-control discussions, but just how big of a problem is it?

The Aging Population

Since 1950 the percentage of the U.S. population over the age of 65 has increased from 8.14 percent to almost 13 percent (see Table 11.1). Due primarily to low fertility rates, the percentage of the population less than 5 years of age has fallen from 10.78 percent to just under 8 percent. The "baby boom" population (those born between 1946 and 1964) may get a lot of attention regarding its demand for goods and services, but to date, they have had only a modest effect on demand for medical care services, largely fertility related. As this cohort begins to retire in 2010, the percentage of the population over the age of 65 will increase substantially, along with their medical costs.

The increase in the 65-plus population was relatively stable during much of the 1990s due to the relatively small birth cohort of the 1930s. The percentage of the population over the age of 65 will begin to rise from 13 percent in 2010 to over 20 percent in 2030. By that time almost 70 million Americans will be over age 65. The major concern for policymakers is that this rapidly growing aged population will not be matched by a growing working-age population—jeopardizing the solvency of the entire federal old-age entitlement apparatus, particularly Social Security and Medicare.

Up until now the age-sex composition of the population has contributed little to the growth in health expenditures. Studies by the Health Care Financing Administration examining the causes of the rise in medical care spending attribute less than 10 percent to the change in the age and sex composition of the population. Such factors as intensity of care and medical care price inflation have been much more important (Aaron, 1991; Gordon, 1992).

Key Concept 6
Supply and Demand

The American Association of Retired Persons (AARP) is dedicated to enriching the lives of older Americans. Issues papers, press releases, and other information relevant to the interests of elders is accessible at **http://www.aarp.org/**.

Policy Issue

How will federal entitlement programs remain solvent as the percentage of the population over age 65 continues to expand?

Table 11.1	Elderly Population in the United States Percentage of Total Resident Population, Various Years			
Year	**Over 65**	**65–74**	**75–84**	**Over 85**
1940	6.84	—	—	0.28
1950	8.09	5.53	2.18	0.38
1960	9.23	6.13	2.58	0.52
1970	9.87	6.12	3.01	0.74
1980	11.28	6.88	3.41	0.99
1990	12.49	7.26	4.03	1.21
1995	12.67	7.20	4.21	1.37
2000	12.63	6.72	4.50	1.57
2010	13.35	6.98	4.38	1.99
2020	16.37	9.48	4.75	2.14
2030	20.05	10.85	6.67	2.53
2040	20.73	9.14	7.86	3.73
2050	20.43	8.83	6.78	4.82

Source: *Economic Report of the President, 1994*, Table B-32, p. 305 and *Health, United States*, 2000, Table 1.

http://

The Administration on Aging provides access to statistical information on older persons, including profiles, projections, and trends. This site provides an excellent resource for topics on aging. Check it out at **http://www.aoa.dhhs.gov/.**

Life Expectancies

Life expectancies have risen dramatically during this century. Referring to Figure 11.1, the average American female was expected to live 48.3 years at birth in 1900. The average male was expected to live 46.3 years. For most of the century, life expectancies have risen steadily; males by 2.16 percent per year and females by 2.29 percent per year. By 2000, life expectancy at birth had risen to 74.1 years for men and 79.5 years for women. The most frequently cited Census Bureau projections predict that by the year 2020, the average life

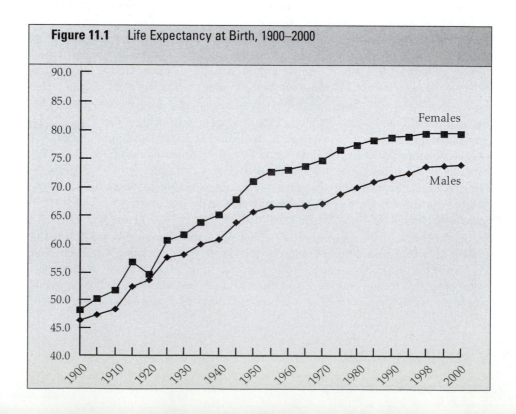

Figure 11.1   Life Expectancy at Birth, 1900–2000

Back-of-the-Envelope

WHY CASH PAYMENTS ARE PREFERRED TO IN-KIND TRANSFERS

Subsidies may be offered in the form of cash payments or in-kind transfers. Certain welfare benefits, such as Temporary Assistance for Needy Families (TANF), are distributed as actual cash payments to eligible enrollees. Others, such as Medicaid, come in the form of vouchers for specific goods and services, in this case medical care. Economists have long argued that recipients are better off in most cases, and no worse off, if the transfers are in the form of cash payments.

Envision an individual with preferences for medical services and other goods as depicted by the indifference curves U_1, U_2, and U_3. Given a money income constraint depicted by the budget line AC, the consumer reaches an optimum at B on indifference curve U_1. If this individual receives a voucher entitling him to free medical care in an amount equal to $CH = AF$, the new budget line becomes AFH. Under these conditions, the consumer finds a new optimum point at F with a new level of utility U_2.

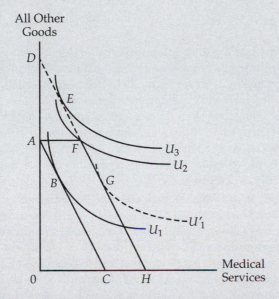

If, instead of a voucher, the individual had been given a cash subsidy in an amount large enough to purchase CH in medical services, the budget line would have been DH. The individual would be provided with additional consumption opportunities depicted by the dashed line DF. Under these circumstances, he would buy the optimum combination of medical services and other goods at E and enjoy a level of utility, U_3. If the individual has a relative preference for medical services, indifference curves U_2 and U_3 would be more steeply sloped and look more like $U'1$. Under these conditions, the individual would establish G as the optimum consumption point and be indifferent between a cash payment and an in-kind subsidy.

Vouchers are inefficient as long as the recipient's utility is the only consideration. Of course, in government welfare programs, taxpayers' preferences are also important. In the case of medical care, taxpayers may actually derive utility when welfare recipients consume specific quantities of medical services, or at least when the children of welfare recipients do so. Although a cash subsidy may leave a recipient better off, taxpayers may prefer in-kind subsidies to ensure that recipients receive a minimum level of medical services.

expectancy at birth will be 74.2 years for men and 82.0 years for women. By 2040, one-half of the men can expect to live 75.0 years and one-half of the women 83.1 years.[1]

The elimination of premature death, particularly infant mortality, maternal death, and death from acute illnesses, is a primary reason for this improvement. Improved living conditions, including clean water, sanitation, and other public health measures have also made significant contributions to longevity.

Mortality rates for the elderly are declining faster than any other age group. There is no overwhelming consensus on the reasons for this improvement. Some medical experts tend to think that the elderly are living longer because of healthier lifestyles, led by improved dietary habits, fewer smokers, and better exercise. Those more technologically inclined attribute the improved longevity to better medical care, especially better control of hypertension, special coronary care units, and open-heart surgery. In practice, the likely explanation includes elements of both perspectives.

More relevant to the issue of medical care spending is the number of years that a person is expected to live after reaching a certain age. In 2001, a male reaching age 65 could expect to live on average 16.4 more years; a female 19.4 more years. Once a person reached age 75, a male could expect to live an additional 10.2 years and a female 12.4 years (Fried et al., 2003).

Contrary to what many demographers believe, the elderly in the United States live longer than their counterparts in other developed nations. Manton and Vaupel (1995) compared life expectancies at older ages in the United States, Sweden, France, England, and Japan. Americans, male and female, fared better in terms of life expectancy and survival probabilities. Using data from the late 1980s, American men lived 7.0 years, on average, after their eightieth birthday and American women 9.1 years. An 80-year-old man would be expected to live 6.9 years in Japan, 6.5 in Sweden, 6.7 in France, and 6.2 in England. An 80-year-old woman would be expected to live 8.5 years in Japan, 8.3 in Sweden, 8.6 in France, and 8.1 in England.

A certain number of individuals in their 60s and 70s are frail and impaired, but most are healthy, active, and relatively well off. It is the rapid growth in the population over age 85 that presents a challenge to policymakers concerned with the rise in medical care spending. Individuals in the ninth and tenth decades of life begin to show their age. They are more prone to chronic conditions that lead to disability and the need for long-term care: Alzheimer's disease and other forms of dementia, Parkinson's disease, hypertension, diabetes, osteoarthritis, hip fractures, and peripheral vascular diseases. Today, an estimated 72,000 Americans are over 100 years old—the fastest growing age cohort in the country. By 2010, centenarians will number 129,000 and by 2050, one million (U.S. Census, 2002).

Medical Care Costs for the Elderly

The data on medical spending by age group is fragmentary. But the evidence suggests that as an individual ages, medical expenditures increase. Over one-half of lifetime medical costs are incurred after age 65. A look at Table 11.2 shows per capita spending on the elderly was $5,360 in 1987; about four times the $1,286 spent on the average nonelderly person, and seven times the $745 spent on each young person (those less than 19 years of age). Although the absolute levels of spending are obviously dated, the relative levels are reflective of the trends. In fact, relative spending levels across age groups changed little from 1977 to 1987 (Waldo et al., 1989). Even within the elderly population, the oldest old spend considerably more on medical care than the younger cohorts. In 1996, overall spending by those over 85 years of age is some 2.8 times that of the 65- to 69-year-old group ($16,465 versus $5,864). What is true for overall spending is also true for

---

1 All projections cited in this chapter are based on the Bureau of Census middle-mortality assumptions. The use of different mortality assumptions can change life expectancies by as much as four years in either direction and affect population projections similarly.

Table 11.2	Personal Medical Care Expenditures By Age and Type of Service, 1987				
Age Group	Personal Medical Care	Hospital Care	Physicians' Services	Nursing Home Services	Other
Less than 19	$ 745	$ 305	$ 181	$ 11	$248
19-64	1,535	695	373	46	421
65 and over	5,360	2,248	1,107	1,085	920
65-69	3,728	1,682	974	165	907
70-74	4,424	2,062	1,086	360	916
75-79	5,455	2,536	1,191	802	925
80-84	6,717	2,935	1,246	1,603	934
85 and over	9,178	3,231	1,262	3,738	947
All ages	1,776	773	408	161	433

Source: Daniel R. Waldo et al., "Health Expenditures by Age Group, 1977 and 1987," Health Care Financing Review 10(4), Summer 1989, Tables 3 and 4.

individual spending categories. Hospital care and physicians' services follow a pattern similar to overall spending. Per capita nursing home spending is more heavily weighted toward the oldest old. Those over the age of 85 spend $7,590 per capita on nursing home care or 20 times more than the 65–69-year-old age cohort (FIF, 2000).

The elderly comprise only 12 percent of the population, yet they consume over one-third of all medical resources. As the percentage of elderly in the population continues to increase, the percentage of medical care spending devoted to the elderly will rise proportionately.

Medical care spending depends on three factors: the quantity of care received, the intensity of that care, and the unit cost of care. The conventional wisdom attributes much of the medical cost explosion to the high cost of treating the elderly, particularly during the last year of life. Dying is expensive, but it still happens only once during a lifetime, regardless of age of death. Chronic problems do strike with increased frequency and severity as we age. The real issue is not the cost of dying, but the multiplicity of illnesses affecting us as we age and the increased use of services to treat those illnesses.

Policy Issue

The high cost of care associated with aging has more to do with the incidence of chronic illnesses than the cost of dying.

Quantity of Services

Empirical evidence suggests that it is the amount of services, rather than the kind of services, that distinguish high-use from low-use patients (Waldo et al., 1989). New technology has produced a general upward drift in costs, but the proliferation of procedures rather than the use of big-ticket items continues to fuel the increase in spending. Additionally, the growth in Medicare spending is due to an increase in service use across the entire eligible population—a larger percentage of enrollees receiving reimbursement and more services provided per enrollee.

Increased Intensity of Services

The use of most medical procedures increases as we age. Table 11.3 provides details of medical care utilization by age group for 2000. A greater proportion of the older cohorts are admitted to hospitals. Hospital admissions result in more days of hospital care and longer hospital stays for older individuals. As we get older we have more hospital outpatient visits, spend more time in the hospital, have more in-patient procedures, and visit our physicians more often. To be more precise, medical care usage increases until about age

Table 11.3	Utilization of Medical Care Resources Annually By Age Group, 2001				
Age Group	Out-Patient Visits per 100 Population	Days of Hospital Care per 100 Population	Inpatient Procedures per 100 Population (Males)	Inpatient Procedures per 100 Population (Females)	Physician Office Visits per 100 Population
Less than 18	29	31.2	4.0	3.7	233
18–44	25	34.9	5.0	19.5	222
45–64	34	61.6	16.2	15.2	373
65–74	40	123.9	37.6	33.0	625
Over 75	39	194.1	56.5	45.6	739
All persons	30	55.4	12.5	16.7	316

Source: Fried et al., *Health, United States*, 2003.

85 at which time it plateaus or even declines. The major exceptions to this rule-of-thumb are dental care and nursing home care. The use of dental care decreases while the use of nursing homes increases beyond age 85 (Arnett et al., 1986).

Some are inclined to blame the medical cost escalation on the aggressive use of heroic, life-sustaining treatment during the last stages of a person's life. To support their case, they usually cite anecdotal evidence such as the following (Clark, 1992). Before dying, one 90-year-old patient spent 41 days in the intensive care unit of a large metropolitan hospital. Suffering from severe pneumonia, a fractured hip, and gradual respiratory, kidney, and heart failure, his doctor never believed he would survive. Still, aggressive treatment, including a respirator, heart monitor, IV feeding tubes, antibiotics, X-rays, blood tests, and sedatives kept him alive. Upon admission he had a catheter inserted into his pulmonary artery to record cardiac output and an arterial line to monitor blood pressure. Before dying, he had 70 arterial blood gas analyses and 156 other blood tests, 38 X-rays, a cardiac ultrasound, and 13 blood transfusions. The bill to the taxpayers amounted to almost $100,000. In a nearby bed, a irreversibly brain-damaged patient received 50 blood tests, 16 X-rays, a CT-scan, two abdominal ultrasounds, numerous bacterial cultures, and five blood transfusions before dying after 18 days in the unit.

Stories such as these fuel the argument that our spending explosion is caused by the more intensive use of high technology medical care, especially care at the end of life. Suggesting that the medical care cost problem is due primarily to the intensive use of services at the end of life ignores the fact that the use of medical services is intensifying across the board. Overall evidence does suggest that one of the principal factors in the medical cost escalation is the increased use of new diagnostic and high technology services. Newhouse (1992) argues that the pace of new technology in medicine appears to be a primary determinant of increased medical care spending.

The Challenge of Treating Chronic Diseases

Medical progress has resulted in improved longevity and a change in the focus of medical research. The acute medical problems experienced at earlier ages no longer occupy our attention. Influenza, small pox, diphtheria, and polio, once feared, are no longer major concerns. Developments in medicine have exchanged these acute problems for chronic ones. Individuals once struck down by an acute illness early in life are surviving to experience chronic problems later in life. The trade-off is a low-cost early death with a more expensive later death.

ISSUES IN MEDICAL CARE DELIVERY

HAVE WE DISCOVERED THE MYTHICAL FOUNTAIN OF YOUTH?

The quest for immortality is fueled by our inherent fear of the unknown. Early explorers of the New World, led by Ponce de Leon, searched for the Fountain of Youth. Even the fictional archeological explorer Indiana Jones survived a crusade to see the restoration of life to those who drank from the Holy Grail used by Jesus to celebrate the Last Supper. Current exploration, somewhat more scientifically based, has taken the form of medical research into the gene that controls the aging process and the fierce debate that it fosters.

The current medical approach to the study of mortality is based on a model of disease. From this viewpoint, death results from disease. Except for trauma and violence, without disease there is no death. Actuarial data from the Social Security Administration predict that life expectancies will continue to climb throughout the next century. According to these estimates, white females born in 2080 will expect to live over 90 years.

Fries (1980) advocates a different viewpoint. From his perspective, the human life span is genetically determined. Organs that have substantial reserves to restore health after an illness at age 30 have very limited capacity at older ages. Thus, the elderly die, not from disease as much as the body's inability to restore health after an illness. Fries' perspective suggests a maximum life expectancy of 85 years.

Proponents of the theory of ever-increasing life expectancies must face the prospect that living longer does not necessarily mean living better. Aging still has its consequences. Currently, those consequences involve living a longer proportion of our lives affected by chronic disease. Unless we find a way to treat or minimize the effects of these chronic diseases, we will be faced with an increasing number of frail elderly in need of partial or total assistance for longer periods of time.

Proponents of a limited life expectancy see things differently. As life expectancies reach their upper limits, the period of diminished activity due to chronic illnesses diminishes, along with the need for costly medical care. Depending on which viewpoint is correct, the implications for future resource needs will be quite different.

Source: James F. Fries, "Aging, Natural Death, and the Compression of Morbidity," *New England Journal of Medicine 303*(3), July 17, 1980, 130–135; Edward L. Schneider and Jacob A. Brody, "Aging, Natural Death, and the Compression of Morbidity: Another View," *New England Journal of Medicine 309*(14), October 6, 1983, 854–856.

As Americans live longer the focus of attention shifts from responding to acute illnesses to treating chronic conditions such as hypertension, diabetes, heart disease, depression, and arthritis. In fact, these five chronic conditions were among the 15 most expensive conditions treated in 1997 (Cohen and Krauss, 2003). The combined cost of treating these five conditions was $141.4 billion, or 12.9 percent of total health care spending.

Hwang et al. (2001) estimate that over 125 million Americans suffered from one or more chronic conditions, a disability, or a functional limitation in 2000 (see Table 11.4). About 10.7 million of them have functional limitations in combination with one or more chronic conditions or a disability and need assistance to perform certain activities of daily living (ADL).[2] The cost of treating these individuals consumes approximately 75 percent of total health care spending. Health insurance generally provides better coverage for the treatment of acute care episodes than ongoing chronic care. As a result, services designed to slow the progression of chronic illnesses may not be covered or may have only limited coverage. And those needing assistance with ADL will find that most insurance plans do not pay for these services at all.

---

2 Activities of daily living are defined as the activities of basic self-care, including feeding, washing, and toileting.

ISSUES IN MEDICAL CARE DELIVERY

THE HIDDEN COSTS OF ELDER CARE

Discussions on the high cost of medical care for the elderly soon digresses to an examination of the billions spent on institutional care, particularly nursing home care. Although Medicaid pays for the long-term care needs of the indigent elderly population, most Americans have little protection against the rising costs of long-term care that averages over $55,000 per year. Some are purchasing long-term care insurance policies, but most find themselves exposed financially to the prospects of a large out-of-pocket outlay.

Understandably, the explicit costs of providing for the long-term needs of the elderly receive most of the headlines. A growing concern for individual families and the economic system in general is the hidden cost of caring for an aging relative. These hidden costs are measured in terms of lost productivity in the business sector. They are more significant today because of the high rates of labor force participation of females—the traditional caregivers for the elderly population.

Workers who care for elderly relatives have higher rates of absence, higher turnover, more stress, and frequent distractions. New research attempts to measure the effect of this misunderstood phenomenon. Estimates of the annual costs of elder care range from $2,500 to $3,142 per caregiver. These costs measure the lost productivity caused by absences, work interruptions, added administrative workload, and replacement costs for those who quit. Applying these estimates to the entire 123 million U.S. workforce places the productivity drain at nearly $8 billion per year.

Focusing on personal caregivers, these studies provide estimates that may represent only the tip of the iceberg. A more realistic estimate, including everyone else who provides elder care, would place the cost at substantially higher levels.

Over the course of the next 50 years, the ratio of elderly parents requiring assistance to caregivers (age 50 and over) will more than triple. Personal caregivers currently make up approximately 25 percent of the U.S. population. A 1997 study estimates the cost to the economy at between $11 and $29 billion in lost productivity (Met Life, 1997). The New Deal of the 1930s brought us Social Security. The New Frontier of the 1960s gave us Medicare and Medicaid. Don't be surprised if the next century produces the New Something-or-Other to address the critical issue of long-term care for the elderly.

Source: Sue Shellenbarger, "Study Tries to Lift Fog on Cost Employers Pay for Elder Care," *The Wall Street Journal*, July 1995, B1; Met Life & National Alliance for Caregiving, *The Met Life Study of Employer Costs for Working Caregivers*, Westport, CT: MetLife Mature Market Group and Bethesda, MD: National Alliance for Caregiving, 1997.

Key Concept 2
Opportunity Cost

Table 11.4	Americans with Chronic Conditions, Disabilities, and Functional Limitations

	Millions
Chronic condition only	87.8
Chronic condition and disability	21.5
Chronic condition, disability, and functional limitation	9.5
Chronic condition and functional limitation	1.2
Disability only	6.6
Total	126.6

Source: Hwang et al. (2001).

The Cost of Long-Term Care

The issue of long-term care is a growing concern in modern industrial societies. As societies develop and mature, they have more elderly and fewer children to provide elder care. Demographers concur that the primary cause of an aging population is not the increased longevity of the elderly, but the reduced fertility of the younger population. The result is fewer daughters and daughters-in-law, more of whom are working and have little time to take care of elderly parents. The only option available for many families is institutional care—sending the aging parent to a nursing home.

Those reaching the age of 85 today can expect to live longer, but their remaining years will be increasingly dominated by chronic health problems. As we age, episodes of illness increase in frequency and severity, along with the need for medical care for longer periods of time. The two major problems facing this age group are the various forms of dementia, including Alzheimer's disease, and hip fractures. The incidence of dementia doubles every five years after age 65. The median prevalence is 2.8 percent for those ages 65 to 74, increasing to 9 percent for those ages 74 to 84, and 28 percent for those over age 85 (Schneider and Guralnik, 1990).

Many view long-term care as the ticking medical care time bomb, especially as the baby boom generation begins to enter the oldest-old age category beginning in 2020. In 2000 over $100 billion was spent on nursing home care for the elderly—almost 7 percent of total health care spending. By 2040, we can expect to spend three to five times that amount in real terms. Federal and state government are the largest payers for long-term care, financing over 50 percent of the total spending primarily through Medicaid.

In 1999, more than 1.47 million elderly residents lived in nursing homes across America, 50 percent of whom were over age 85. The probability of residing in a nursing home increases with age. One percent of the population between the ages of 65 and 74 live in nursing homes. That figure increases to 4.7 percent of those between 75 and 84 and almost 18.3 percent of those over the age of 85. By 2040, the nursing home population may reach as high as 5.9 million, with at least 2 million of those over the age of 85. Over the next five decades, the 85-plus nursing home population will be almost twice as large as the total number of elderly currently residing in nursing homes (Fried et al., 2003).

Approximately 12 percent of those celebrating their sixty-fifth birthdays in 1950 lived to celebrate their ninetieth birthdays 25 years later. Today, almost 23 percent of all 65-year-olds will live to see that day. Because women are the prime beneficiaries of the advances in longevity, they tend to bear the burden of the problems of aging, relying on nursing home care to a much greater extent than men. Four of every five nursing home residents over the age of 85 are female. In 1991, for individuals between the ages of 65 and 74 there were 78 men for every 100 women. That same year, there were only 39 men for every 100 women over the age of 85. A majority of the women who live beyond age 75 have no husband. If two thirds of the men in the 65- to 74-year-old age bracket live with their wives, barely one half of the women in this age group will have husbands. It should come as no surprise that 75 percent of the nursing home residents are female—not because of higher morbidity but because they are more likely to be alone due to lower mortality.

The High Cost of Dying

The end-of-life medical episode tends to be expensive regardless of the age at death. The fact that three-fourths of all people who die each year are over age 65 makes this group the most intensive user of end-of-life care in the country. Further increases in life expectancy will increase the percentage of deaths that occur after age 65, shifting even more of this spending to the elderly population.

One out of every seven dollars spent on medical care every year is for treatment during the last six months of someone's life. Historically, government has been able to justify public spending as an investment that will enhance future productivity. To the extent that

ISSUES IN MEDICAL CARE DELIVERY

WHY DOESN'T GRANDMA HAVE LONG-TERM CARE INSURANCE?

Aging populations challenge modern societies to devise innovative alternatives to address the issue of long-term care for the elderly. Long-term care presents a relatively simple challenge—to provide personal care for aging individuals, many of whom have chronic conditions. The alternatives are straightforward—nursing homes, home health care, family, and friends.

Advocates for the elderly argue that the private sector is unresponsive to the long-term care needs of this group and that public programs are no more than a patchwork filled with gaps and holes. The high cost of long-term care is a major threat to the financial independence of the elderly. Coupled with relatively low rates of usage, this market seems well suited for the development of private insurance. In 2000, only 8.1 percent of the total cost of nursing home care was paid by private insurance. Is this another case of market failure? Why is the private insurance market so poorly developed?

The conventional wisdom suggests several answers. Individuals underestimate their need for long-term care. What would be a modest premium at an early age, say $1,700 per year at age 55, becomes prohibitive by age 80 when the need is recognized. In any case, many rely on the government safety net—Medicaid. All a person has to do is "spend down" his or her assets to become eligible for this federal program that pays for medical care for the indigent.

The purpose of private long-term-care insurance is to protect one's estate. Thus, failure to purchase insurance may not seem to be a rational choice for most of the elderly, especially members of the middle class who have modest levels of wealth to protect. Pauly (1990) argues that unless a person has a bequest motive, the rational individual would like to see all resources exhausted at the time of his or her death. Care and concern for a surviving spouse modifies Pauly's argument. But a surviving spouse has no such concerns. In fact, most individuals have no strong bequest motives as evidenced by their failure to purchase long-term-care insurance.

If prospective heirs are risk averse, they should be the ones buying long-term-care insurance for their aging parents. The incentive is twofold: to insure that the financial resources are available to pay for nursing home care and to protect a possible inheritance. Elderly parents discourage such purchases. Why? It distorts incentives. Insurance makes it easy to substitute institutional care for family care. An aging parent, reluctant to be placed in a nursing home, may desire to pay for institutional care out of the estate. That way the children recognize that putting Grandma into a nursing home reduces the prospective inheritance dollar for dollar. Having long-term-care insurance increases the likelihood that it will be used—a moral hazard that Grandma would like to avoid. The absence of a well-developed private market in long-term-care insurance may not be failure of the market. It may be a rational choice on the part of the elderly, improving their bargaining power if the need for personal care ever materializes.

Source: Mark V. Pauly, "The Rational Nonpurchase of Long-Term-Care Insurance," *Journal of Political Economy 98*(1), February 1990, 153–168.

Key Concept 4
Self-Interest

medical care enables a worker to get back on the job quicker and healthier, it generates an external benefit to the economy and merits subsidy. Education, economic infrastructure, and even national defense have payoffs that extend well into the future.

If medical care spending leads primarily to increasing the life expectancy of individuals who have already lived beyond retirement age, the productivity justification is undermined. The $100 billion spent on end-of-life care for the elderly has no such long-term payoff, making it a prime target of policymakers questioning the use of scarce resources. As we look for ways to trim spending, one of the most relevant issues becomes: Are the dollars put into end-of-life care the most cost-effective way to allocate our scarce medical care resources?

Many view critical care as a sinkhole for resources in the hospital industry. Average daily charges for the typical intensive care unit (ICU) range from $2,000 to $2,500 per day. It is not unusual for the majority of ICU beds to be occupied by people over age 65. In many hospitals the average age for patients in these units is between 85 and 90. The intensive care unit, originally intended for people with treatable illnesses with a reasonable chance of recovery, has become a repository for end-of-life care for terminally ill patients.

This problem is not unique to one hospital or a particular area of the country. A study by the Health Care Financing Administration estimated that 28 percent of the 1989 Medicare budget was spent on reimbursements to people over 65 in the last year of their lives, with most of that coming in the final 60 days (Clark, 1992). This high spending on individuals during the last year of life, amounting to about 1 percent of our GDP, is not a recent phenomenon. Data from 1967 (Piro and Lutins, 1967) show much the same situation with 22 percent of the spending on the 5 percent who died that year. Lubitz and Riley (1993) found that 27 to 30 percent of the Medicare disbursements took place during the last 12 months of life for the Medicare enrollees who died during the study period 1976 through 1988. Spending on those who died each year is over six times the spending on those who survived.

Taking all this into consideration, the evidence does not seem to support the claim that the cause of the increase in health care spending is the high cost of dying. For this to be true, it would have to be a new and growing phenomenon. In reality, there has been little change in the relative cost of treating dying patients. The percentage change in medical care spending for decedents and survivors has remained approximately constant over time.

Summary and Conclusions

The increasing number of the oldest old raises certain bioethical issues. There is already talk of rationing medical care to the oldest old (Callahan, 1987). Assisted suicide, euthanasia, and denial of treatment are all cutting-edge ethical issues. These issues are not unique to the United States. Throughout history every culture and every society has had to deal with how to allocate scarce resources. Whenever resources were marginalized, the elderly were the first to see their shares limited. The old Eskimo accepted his fate and willingly stepped onto the ice floe, never to be seen again.

Medical costs rise as we age. In part, our attitude toward death drives us to aggressively treat terminally ill patients, fueling the debate. Survey results by the Robert Wood Johnson Foundation show that Americans are not nearly so willing to accept this aspect of life as citizens of other countries. When asked what they would do if told by their personal physicians that they had an incurable and fatal disease, 90 percent of Americans over age 65 said they would seek a second opinion. One-third of Britons and one-half of Australians responded similarly ("The Immortal American," 1995).

As a result, Americans receive four times the number of bypass operations of the Japanese, Germans, and Britons. We have higher rates of use of all the major high-tech treatment and diagnostic services, including chemotherapy, kidney dialysis, and advanced imaging. The higher usage rates are due in part to the fact that the United States has very few supply restrictions, unlike the crude **triage** system used in Britain or the regionalized services in Canada.

Each year only about 1 percent of the U.S. population spends $30,000 or more per person on medical care. Of these high-cost users, over one half survive. It is easy to

http://

The U.S. Census Bureau is the official collector of demographic data on the people and economy of the United States. The site provides access to the official statistics primarily through its links to "Subjects A-Z." The Bureau's web address is **http://www.census.gov/**.

triage

A military screening technique adopted for use in a crowded emergency room to determine the order in which patients are treated. In battlefield hospitals three categories of patients are identified: those who will survive without care, those who will survive if they receive care, and those who will not survive regardless of the amount of care they receive.

Victor R. Fuchs

When asked to join the editorial board of the newly created *Journal of Health Economics* in 1980, Victor Fuchs expressed doubts about the wisdom of separating the study of health economics from the rest of economics. That his fears were not realized may be attributed largely to the example he set, insisting on rigor in the pursuit of relevance. Fuch's contributions have been so important that many consider him to be one of the founding fathers of health economics.

Fuchs' formal education was interrupted by military duty during World War II. After the war he attended New York University night school and worked as an international broker of animal furs in his father's business. He received a B.S. in business administration and then enrolled in Columbia University where he was awarded a Ph.D. in economics in 1955. As a member of the Columbia faculty, his early work on *The Economics of the Fur Industry* (1957) provided him with few opportunities for professional recognition. Denied tenure, he remained in New York, working at the Ford Foundation for two years before joining the staff at the National Bureau of Economic Research (NBER). After six years at the NBER he joined the faculty at City University of New York and then moved to Stanford University in 1974, where he is currently the Henry J. Kaiser, Jr. Professor of Economics.

Inspired by his earlier work measuring output and productivity in the service sector, Fuchs saw a research vacuum in the application of the economic perspective to issues relating to health and medical care. Equipped with a boundless curiosity and creative approach to thinking about social problems, Fuchs has garnered the reputation as one of the foremost empirical economists of our time.

One of his most important contributions to the study of health economics came in a 1967 paper published while he was still at the NBER.[3] In that paper he concluded a person's health status may be more dependent on lifestyle considerations than the level of medical care received. The theme that individual actions matter quickly became a part of the collective wisdom of epidemiologists and other health researchers.

His research in the early 1970s challenged the commonly held belief that the American Medical Association, through its limits on the number of physicians in training, was responsible for keeping medical care prices artificially high. Several studies testing the economic theory of physician-induced demand led him to conclude that more physicians would actually lead to higher levels of utilization and higher prices. These results were in sharp contrast to the conventional wisdom of the time and led many to question the relevance of the standard market model as applied to medical care. As a tribute to his research contribution, Harvard University Press anthologized 17 of his papers in 1986 under the title *The Health Economy*.

Since his move to Stanford, virtually all of his writing has been for general audiences or targeted at specialized groups (such as physicians) that have little or no formal training in economics. His work has been well received by noneconomists because of his straightforward empirical approach to questions that affect our daily lives—family, work, education, religion, and health.

Calling himself a "radical moderate," Fuchs strongly advocates a balanced approach to problem solving. While much of his work has policy relevance, his direct involvement in policy debates has been minimal. His approach to economic research may be characterized as positive rather than normative. He is more comfortable using data to explain factual observations than advancing specific policy measures.

Family and religion have played an important role in his life, proving that a world-class scholar can be a human being at the same time. Over the past decade he has

---

3 "The Basic Forces Influencing Costs of Medical Care," Report of the National Conference on Medical Costs, U.S. Department of Health, Education and Welfare. Washington, DC: U.S. Government Printing Office, 1967, 16–31.

increasingly ventured into research dealing with family matters. In his books dealing with family decision making (*How We Live*, 1983) and issues relating to women and children (*Women's Quest for Economic Equality*, 1988), he has shown no hesitancy in suggesting intervention strategies.

A sports enthusiast and part-time poet, he has also tried his hand at stand-up comedy. "As an academic and an economist I do not have to look far for material" (Fuchs, 1993).

Source: Joseph P. Newhouse, "Distinguished Fellow: In Honor of Victor Fuchs," *Journal of Economic Perspectives 6*(3), Summer 1992, 179–189; and Victor R. Fuchs, "Education and Its Consequences: My Philosophy of Life," *The American Economist 37*(2), Fall 1993, 17–24.

identify those who survive retrospectively. It is not nearly as easy to make that distinction prospectively. Given the uncertainty of medical diagnosis, it will be a sensitive task to devise a rationing scheme that could be used effectively.

For most middle-aged baby boomers the prospect of living longer and healthier is appealing. Bypass surgery may not lengthen my life, but if it enables me to enjoy tennis in my retirement years, who is to say it is not worth it? The policy issue is clear and will continue to grow in critical importance: Who should bear the costs of our desire for longer and happier lives?

> **Policy Issue**
>
> Who should bear the costs of our desire for longer and happier lives?

Many argue against the elderly paying more for medical services. They contend that a large number of the elderly are among the lowest earners in the country and can ill afford to spend an ever-increasing share of their incomes on medical care.[4] Others view this issue from the perspective of wealth instead of income and a very different picture emerges. In 1999 the median net worth of a household headed by a person between the ages of 65 and 69 was $190,000. In contrast, when the head of the household was a person between the ages of 45 and 54 (the age cohort with the highest median income), the median net worth was less than one-half of that amount, or $85,000 (FIF, 2000). From this perspective, the elderly are better off than most members of the middle class and can afford to pay more for the care they receive.

Researchers at the Cleveland Federal Reserve Bank provide a unique look at how the burden of paying for government spending on goods and services is distributed among current and future generations (Auerbach, Gokhale, and Kotlikoff, 1995). Using the 1993 benefit and tax structure, the typical 65-year-old American male could expect to receive transfers from Social Security, Medicare, and Medicaid, net of any taxes paid, in excess of $100,000 over his remaining lifetime. That same year the typical 65-year-old female could expect net transfers of almost $140,000 before her death. In fact, males over the age of 55 and females over the age of 50 could expect a positive net transfer over the remaining years of their lives. In contrast, younger Americans could expect a net tax payment. For example, a 25-year-old male had a prospective net tax burden (taxes over transfers) of $200,000 over his expected lifetime. Nowhere is fairness such an issue as it is when dealing with this generational imbalance.

If we examine the evidence thoughtfully and carefully, we must agree with Fuchs (1984) that "health care spending among the elderly is not so much a function of time since birth as it is a function of time to death" (p. 152). The apparent relationship between health care spending and the proximity to death is due primarily to the relationship between age and mortality. The end-of-life medical episode tends to be expensive. As we live longer, it is increasingly likely that this event will take place after age 65.

Is it cost effective to provide certain services to individuals once they reach a particular age—for example, kidney dialysis or organ transplants after age 65? The United States is still a long way from establishing a formal rationing scheme for medical care. It is a dangerous precedent, and we must be careful before

---

4 The evidence (Hurd, 1990) indicates that the real incomes of the elderly are on average 1.5 times that of the nonelderly.

ISSUES IN MEDICAL CARE DELIVERY

LIFE IS SHORT; MAKE IT COUNT

As for the days of our life, they contain seventy years,
Or if due to strength, eighty years,
Yet their pride is but labor and sorrow;
For soon it is gone and we fly away.

Psalms 90:10

Policy Issue

Should cost-effective care be the sole criterion for access to the medical care system?

embarking down that proverbial slippery slope. If cost-effective care were the sole criterion for access to the medical care system, we would end up with a society where euthanasia at retirement was the norm. What are the chances that we will one day initiate the end-of-life episode shown in the 1960s movie *Logan's Run*? In this futuristic society, everyone, at age 30, submitted himself or herself to the Carrousel for the final death spiral. Are the actions of Dr. Kevorkian the first step toward that future?

Questions and Problems

1. As individuals grow older, how does their demand for medical care change? How does aging affect the provision of medical services?

2. How will an aging population affect health policymakers in the twenty-first century?

3. In 1993, the Census Bureau estimated that elderly men were nearly twice as likely to be married and living with their spouses as elderly women (75 percent versus 41 percent). What are the economic and medical care implications of this phenomenon?

4. Since the passage of Medicare in 1965, what has happened to overall medical spending for the elderly? Per capita spending? Out-of-pocket spending? How does this compare with health care spending by the nonelderly?

5. The high cost of dying has been identified by some policymakers as a primary reason for increased medical spending by the elderly. What is the evidence?

References

Henry J. Aaron, *Serious and Unstable Condition: Financing America's Health Care*, Washington, DC: The Brookings Institute, 1991.

Ross H. Arnett, III, David R. McKusick, Sally T. Sonnefeld, and Carol S. Cowell, "Projections of Health Care Spending to 1990," *Health Care Financing Review 7*(3), Spring 1986, 1–36.

Alan J. Auerbach, Jagadeesh Gokhale, and Laurence J. Kotlikoff, "Restoring Generational Balance in U.S. Fiscal Policy: What Will It Take?" *Economic Review 31*(1), Quarter 1 1995, 2–12.

Daniel Callahan, *Setting Limits: Medical Goals in an Aging Society*, New York: Simon and Schuster, 1987.

Nicola Clark, "The High Cost of Dying," *The Wall Street Journal*, February 26, 1992, A22.

Joel W. Cohen and Nancy A. Krauss, "Spending and Service Use Among People With the Fifteen Most Costly Medical Conditions, 1977," *Health Affairs 22*(2), March/April 2003, 129–138.

Federal Interagency Forum on Aging-Related Statistics, *Older Americans 2000: Key Indicators of Well-Being*, National Center for Health Statistics, August 2000.

V. M. Fried et al., *Chartbook on Trends in the Health of Americans: Health, United States, 2003*, Hyattsville, MD: National Center for Health Statistics, 2003

Victor R. Fuchs, "'Though Much is Taken': Reflections on Aging, Health, and Medical Care," *Milbank Memorial Fund Quarterly 62*(2), Spring 1984, 143–166.

John Steele Gordon, "How America's Health Care Fell Ill," *American Heritage*, May/June 1992, 49–65.

Mike Hurd, "Research on the Elderly: Economic Status, Retirement, and Consumption and Saving," *Journal of Economic Literature 28*(2), June 1990, 565–637.

Wenke Hwang et al., "Out-of-Pocket Medical Spending for Care of Chronic Conditions," *Health Affairs* 20(6), November/December 2001, 267–278.

James Lubitz and Gerald Riley, "Trends in Medicare Payments in the Last Year of Life," *New England Journal of Medicine 328*(15), April 15, 1993, 1092–1096.

Kenneth G. Manton and James W. Vaupel, "Survival After the Age of 80 in the United States, Sweden, France, England, and Japan," *New England Journal of Medicine 333*(18), November 2, 1995, 1232–1235.

Joseph P. Newhouse," Medical Care Costs: How Much Welfare Loss?" *Journal of Economic Perspectives 6*(3), Summer 1992, 3–21.

P.A. Piro and T. Lutins, "Utilization and Reimbursement under Medicare for Persons Who Died in 1967 and 1968," Health Insurance Statistics, DHEW Pub. No. (SSA) 74–11702, Washington, DC: U.S. Government Printing Office, October 1967.

Edward L. Schneider and Jack M. Guralnik, "The Aging of America: Impact on Health Care Costs," *Journal of the American Medical Association 263*(17), May 2, 1990, 2335–2340.

"The Immortal American," *The Wall Street Journal*, May 31, 1995, A14.

U. S. Census, *National Population Projections: Summary Files,* **http://www.census.gov/population/www/projections/natsum-T3.html.2002.**

Daniel R. Waldo, Sally T. Sonnefeld, David R. McKusick, and Ross H. Arnett, III, "Health Expenditures by Age Group, 1977 and 1987," *Health Care Financing Review 10*(4), Summer 1989, 111–120.

Chapter 12

The Legal System and Medical Malpractice

Medical **malpractice** pits physicians against lawyers in a contentious debate with seemingly little common ground. Less than eight percent of all physicians were sued in 1996 (Kessler and McClellan, 2000a). The frequency was much greater in certain specialties—one out of every five surgeons and one out of every four OB/GYNs experienced malpractice actions against them. Lawsuits and the threat of lawsuits affect physicians' behavior in two ways. First, malpractice insurance premiums are a major practice expense for physicians. Since 1975, medical malpractice costs have increased at an annual rate of 11.6 percent, from $1.2 billion to $21.0 billion (Tillinghast-Towers Perrin, 2003). Depending on specialty and geographic location, annual premiums range from less than $10,000 to as high as $250,000. Many physicians are finding that large purchasers—managed care and government—do not allow them to pass on these costs to the patient in the form of

Policy Issue

Does the threat of lawsuits cause physicians to practice defensive medicine?

higher medical bills. Second, seeking to reduce their own risk of a lawsuit, physicians practice "defensive medicine," or the ordering of laboratory tests and procedures that otherwise have little or no medical benefit. Because of the high cost of medical malpractice premiums and the practice of defensive medicine, annual medical care spending is at least $60 billion and possibly as much as $100 billion higher (ACOG, 2003).

Are we experiencing a litigation explosion in medical care? Just how big of a problem is medical malpractice anyway? Is physician incompetence more widespread now

Policy Issue

Is there a litigation explosion in medical care? And if there is, what should we do about it?

than at any time in our history? Are medical injuries more frequent in the United States than in other advanced countries? Or is our system of compensating victims of medical injuries flawed?

Stories about surgeons amputating the wrong leg, operating on the wrong knee, or removing a toe without the consent of the patient seem to happen all too frequently. A woman mistakenly sterilized during a cesarean delivery or the wrong patient removed from a ventilator and dying can also shake our confidence in the quality of our medical care system.[1] Are these stories evidence of a decline in the quality of medical care in this country? Medical advances in recent decades and the growing demand to use these high-tech procedures have increased the risk of injury. It is no surprise that over half of all injury claims result from surgical procedures and related treatments where the use of sophisticated medical equipment is more frequent. Technological advances have created an environment in which procedures are risky and patients expect to be cured. Injuries associated with childbirth are among the most frequently litigated. Infants born with cerebral palsy provide a good case study.

With an incidence of two to three per 1,000 births, cerebral palsy is one of the most common physical disabilities in childhood. Children with cerebral palsy have little muscular control. Those who survive are typically wheelchair bound, incontinent, often mentally retarded, and in need of constant care. One-third of all lawsuits against

---

1 These incidents all occurred at the University Community Hospital in Tampa, Florida, in 1995.

obstetricians are for cerebral palsy, claiming physician error during childbirth as the cause. Results of a comprehensive survey of the medical literature led an international task force to conclude that cerebral palsy is usually caused before birth, because of genetic defects or antepartum infection (MacLennan, 1999). Despite the consensus medical opinion, juries regularly blame physicians and hand out large awards. No wonder the typical OB/GYN is sued 2.5 times over his or her career, and one-fourth receive their first suit during their residencies (ACOG, 2003).

These rising expectations, along with increased specialization in medical practice, have changed the nature of the physician-patient relationship. It is no longer the personalized experience it once was, but too often merely a market transaction, and an expensive one at that, between a masked physician and an anesthetized patient. Under these circumstances, we expect to get what we pay for. And we don't hesitate to seek satisfaction through the legal system if we're not happy with the outcome.

In this chapter we will explore the system of tort law in the United States, its English common-law basis, and its historical development. A discussion of the three functions of medical malpractice law and an examination of the frequency and severity of medical malpractice claims will follow. Finally, the case for tort reform will be examined. The appendix to this chapter is a discussion of the methodology currently used in valuing life in cases of wrongful death.

Tort Law in the United States

Medical malpractice law is a subset of tort law—a mechanism that governs the treatment of injuries to persons or property where crime and contracts are not involved. Tort law developed out of the system of English common law or case law. The distinctive feature of common law is that it is not codified like constitutional law or statutory law. It is a system based on a body of legal principles determined by judicial decision on a case-by-case basis. In other words, it is a flexible system that develops over time, adapting itself to the changing conditions of the sociolegal environment.

Decisions in common law follow the doctrine of **stare decisis**—that decisions of a higher court set legal precedents and are binding in all future cases. The most important feature of common law is its adherence to precedent. If no precedent exists, judges rule on the case on the basis of their concept of right and wrong.

stare decisis
The decisions of a higher court set legal precedents and are binding in all future cases.

The first reported medical malpractice case in the United States was *Cross v. Guthrey* (1794). The physician in this case, Dr. Guthrey, was found liable in the death of a woman following surgery. While it is commonly accepted that the basis for the American law of malpractice is the English common law, there were no English cases cited as precedents in this decision. Not until 1828 in the case of *Sumner v. Utley* did a U.S. case directly cite malpractice cases in England as precedents. From that time on, citing English cases became a common practice until the mid-nineteenth century.

The Function of Medical Malpractice Law

Modern medicine is inherently a dangerous undertaking. A medical care system that takes the responsibility for more ambitious interventions in the case of increasingly sicker patients will see the incidence of *iatrogenic disease* or injury increase, in turn increasing the number of tort cases. Medicine is continuously developing new techniques and more sophisticated medical technology and placing them in the hands of imperfect human agents. It is no wonder errors result, leading to harm to patients.

In most cases, the risks are obvious to the practitioner, if not the patient. The purpose of medical malpractice law is to force the physician to act as a responsible agent for the patient and expose the patient only to that level of risk that a fully informed patient would be willing to accept. In this context, medical malpractice law serves three functions: compensation, deterrence, and retribution.

Compensation

Tort law has evolved as a method of compensating individuals who are injured as a result of the negligent behavior of others. Compensatory damages are awarded to compensate the successful **plaintiff** for actual losses, both economic and noneconomic. Economic losses or specific damages include lost income and any tangible expenses, including all medical and rehabilitation expenses. Noneconomic losses or general damages include pain and suffering, disfigurement, shock, and loss of association.

The tort system compensates injured parties through the use of private **third-party liability** insurance. This is a mechanism of spreading the risk of loss among policyholders through the payment of insurance premiums. In the case of medical care, the losses are actually spread among patients who pay higher prices for medical care services. Thus, the cost of risk avoidance falls primarily on patients as providers pass through the cost of medical malpractice insurance to their customers in the form of higher fees.

Deterrence

It can be reasonably argued that the primary function of tort law is to deter specific behavior that causes injuries. In fact, if the tort system is evaluated according to a standard of economic efficiency, then its justification is based solely on its ability to deter injurious behavior. Compensation and the spreading of risk can actually be accomplished at a lower cost and more equitably through a mechanism of **first-party liability** where the patient buys health and disability insurance.

Injuries are costly. Likewise, steps taken to avoid injuries are also costly. The goal is not the avoidance of all accidents, but that only the optimal number of accidents will take place. Suppose that a $20,000 injury can be avoided by either the medical provider taking steps costing $1,000 or by the patient spending $10,000. In this case, it is in society's best interest for the provider to take the responsibility for accident prevention. Likewise, if prevention costs either provider or patient more than $20,000, then failure to take steps to prevent the injury should not be considered negligent behavior.[2]

The rules of tort will deter negligent behavior if the responsibility for compensating the victims of injurious behavior rests squarely on those who can prevent the losses at the lowest cost. Holding the low-cost avoider responsible for the costs of the injury should guarantee that efficient precautions will be taken to prevent such accidents in the future.

Retribution

A third function of the tort system is to exact retribution on those guilty of negligent behavior. Many legal scholars will argue that anyone responsible for an injury to another person should be punished for his or her actions. To the extent that the actions are intentional, only by assigning responsibility can we be sure that justice will be served.

The argument for **punitive damages** is based on the retribution function. Punitive damages serve the same purpose as criminal and civil penalties, such as jail sentences and fines, in the event that someone is guilty of particularly egregious or malicious behavior. In the case of large damage awards, punitive damages often make up a large percentage of the total compensation to the victim.[3]

plaintiff
The party to a lawsuit who brings charges against the other party, known as the defendant.

third-party liability
A situation in which the loss is paid for by the party causally responsible for the injury. Liability insurance is used to indemnify against loss in this case—for example, workers' compensation.

Key Concept 8
Economic Efficiency

first-party liability
Commonly referred to as *caveat emptor* (let the buyer beware). The person who suffers the loss pays for it. In most cases, the individual may buy first-party insurance to indemnify against the loss. This is the basis for fire and casualty insurance.

Key Concept 3
Marginal Analysis

punitive damages
The portion of a damage award designed to punish and deter deliberate and egregious wrongdoing.

---

2 The legal standard of negligence has been laid down by Judge Learned Hand, 159 Federal Reporter 2d 169 (1947), where he defines negligence as the failure to take precautions (measures to avoid injury) if the cost of taking precautions is less than the expected cost of damages averted. An economist would say, "if the marginal costs are less than the marginal benefits." According to this principle, negligence is defined as failure to take adequate precautions in a situation where $C < pD$; where C is the cost of taking precautions, p is the probability that damages will occur without intervention, and D is the amount of the damages.
3 Of course, if the defendant has insurance coverage that includes the payment of punitive damages, this function is not served efficiently.

The Growth in Medical Malpractice Claims

Physicians have been liable for negligent behavior since the late eighteenth century in this country (and much earlier in England), but medical malpractice lawsuits were rare until the 1960s. Several factors emerged during that decade to increase the risk of iatrogenic injury. The introduction of Medicare and Medicaid caused a significant increase in the utilization of medical services among the elderly and the indigent. Medical intervention was becoming increasingly complicated and invasive with, for example, open-heart surgery and organ transplantation becoming more common. Along with the increased complexity came the need for increased specialization among physicians. The result, some will conclude, is a breakdown in the physician-patient relationship, increasing the likelihood of a lawsuit.

Claims Frequency

Data from a 1956 survey of physicians conducted by the American Medical Association (AMA) implied an annual claims frequency of 1.54 per 100 physicians. A subsequent survey conducted in 1963 shows virtually no change in claims frequency. By the late 1960s, however, claims frequency had risen to 2.70 per 100 physicians. Records of the St. Paul Fire and Marine Insurance Company (the leading underwriter of medical malpractice insurance) indicated that between 1970 and 1975 claims frequency increased from 4.35 to 12.50 per 100 physicians. This led to a breakdown in the market for medical malpractice insurance in the mid-1970s. Malpractice premiums had failed to keep pace with the escalation in malpractice claims. As a result insurance premiums jumped as much as 300 percent in 1974–1975. In states where increases were denied by state regulators (especially in several New England states), many insurance carriers withdrew from the market entirely, causing a panic among many physicians' groups. Many physicians had to set up their own risk pools, bypassing the insurance industry completely.

 Key Concept 5
Markets and Pricing

Claims frequency leveled off and even dropped in many states during the last half of the 1970s. Rising gradually until the mid-1980s, claims frequency reached 10.2 per 100 physicians in 1985. Evidence presented in Table 12.1 shows that claims in 1996, while slightly lower than in 1985, remained at 9.0 per 100 physicians. Claims frequency differs significantly among specialties. General practitioners and internists have a much lower incidence of claims than surgeons, OB/GYNs, and radiologists. Since 1985, claims frequency has shown little change, but because of the decline in frequency in 1987, changes since that year have been statistically significant for internal medicine, surgery, and obstetrics and gynecology.[4]

Differences among specialties obviously reflect differences in the use of high-risk invasive and other surgical procedures. Technological advances may have contributed to the increased frequency of lawsuits against OB/GYN specialists—consistently one of the most frequently sued specialties in the United States. With an increased ability to save very low-birthweight and neurologically impaired infants, physicians are increasingly at risk of delivering imperfect babies. The uncertainty of the cause of the defect—whether it is due to genetic factors, prenatal infection, or poor medical care—increases the likelihood of a lawsuit. Also the longer **statute of limitations** for minors (up to ten years in many states) creates a backlog of potential claims to be resurrected as legal doctrines change or as medical breakthroughs improve the chances of a successful lawsuit. As a result, Zuckerman (1984) reported that 12 percent of the OB/GYN specialists have dropped obstetrics completely and another 23 percent have stopped performing certain high-risk procedures.

Policy Issue

What is the appropriate length of time for statutes of limitation in medical malpractice cases?

---

statute of limitations
The length of time that a plaintiff has to file a lawsuit after suffering an injury—usually 3-4 years for an adult and somewhat longer for children. In many states, the limitation runs from the date the injury is discovered or should have been discovered, not the actual date of the injury.

---

4 It should be noted that the medical malpractice process is a long and protracted process for both plaintiff and defendant. The median time from a medical injury to filing a claim is 25 months and the median from filing to resolution is 26 months. Even though the frequency of claims may seem high, the Harvard Medical Practice Study (1990) estimates that only one in eight negligently injured patients files a lawsuit. In addition, over 70 percent of all claims filed against physicians never result in payment to the patient. And of those that went to trial in 1996, over 69 percent were decided for the defendant.

Table 12.1	Claims Frequency per 100 Physicians By Specialty, 1985–1996					
Year	All Physicians	General/ Family Practice	Internal Medicine	Surgery	Obstetrics/ Gynecology	Radiology
1985	10.2	5.7	6.2	16.8	25.8	12.8
1986	9.2	7.6	5.5	15.8	13.0	11.5
1987	6.7	5.7	4.5	12.7	8.0	8.0
1988	6.4	6.2	4.3	10.2	15.1	5.2
1989	7.4	6.6	5.9	11.2	13.5	5.0
1990	7.7	5.9	6.2	11.5	11.9	8.7
1991	8.2	5.7	5.5	14.0	11.6	6.1
1992	9.1	6.9	7.3	15.5	15.6	11.5
1993	9.8	7.1	7.9	18.9	22.5	9.4
1994	9.5	6.7	5.7	16.9	19.2	10.5
1995	9.0	6.2	5.7	14.9	20.9	11.0
1996	9.0	6.7	5.3	14.9	13.1	16.8

Source: Martin L. Gonzalez, "Medical Professional Liability and Claims," *Socioeconomic Characteristics of Medical Practice*, Chicago: American Medical Association, various years.

Large differences in frequency of claims also occur across states. A survey of six states by the U.S. General Accounting Office (1986) indicated that in 1984, claims per 100 physicians ranged from 8.6 in Arkansas to 35.7 in New York. These differences may be due to differences in medical, demographic, and legal factors (see Danzon, 1986). States that have higher rates of surgical procedures per capita have higher claims frequency. Large urban populations are associated with high frequencies of lawsuits, due in part to a higher incidence of high-risk medical procedures in urban areas. After controlling for surgical procedures per capita and percentage of the population living in urban areas, per capita income and lawyers per capita do not have a significant, independent effect on claims frequency.[5]

Differences in common law doctrines and statutory laws across states are important determinants in explaining interstate differences in claims frequency. In particular, differences in statutes of limitation and the treatment of **collateral sources** of compensation result in differences in claims frequency across states. For every one-year reduction in the statute of limitations for adults, claims frequency falls by 8 percent, and states that enact collateral source offset rules have 14 percent fewer claims.

collateral sources
Compensation received from other sources; e.g., health insurance coverage for medical bills or disability payments. Current rules in most states prohibit the reduction in damages for collateral source payments.

Claims Severity

The severity of claims is typically measured in terms of the average damage award actually paid on all claims that resulted in a payment, regardless of whether the award was court ordered or an out-of-court settlement. Sandor (1957) reported that, up until that time, the largest court settlement in a medical malpractice case was $230,000 in 1955 (approximately $1.5 million in 2001 dollars). This may be contrasted with a May 2000 settlement in Cook County, Illinois, in the amount of $55 million.[6] Since 1955 the size of damage awards has steadily increased at a higher rate than the overall rate of price inflation. From 1971 to 1978, claims severity increased at a rate of 12.4 percent per year for physicians and surgeons and 18.9 percent per

5 This latter finding may come as a surprise to those who place the blame for the litigation explosion squarely on the number of lawyers practicing in the United States.
6 The case *Mederos v. Ravenswood Hospital* involved a 59-year-old female who began bleeding during a normal bronchoscopy but was not promptly intubated and suffered irreversible brain damage.

ISSUES IN MEDICAL CARE DELIVERY

PUNITIVE DAMAGES SEND A MESSAGE TO HEALTH PROVIDERS

Medical care reform is likely to result in an increase in the use of utilization management to control costs. The adoption of more formal requirements for the use of cost-effectiveness analysis is being slowed by our tort system. Unless the rules of tort allow for the gradual elimination of medical practices that provide only small marginal benefits, tort law may become an obstacle to more cost-effective patterns of medical care. Can the medical system make this transition within the structure of the current legal framework?

The following case points out the nature of the current debate. At the end of 1993, a California jury awarded more than $12 million in actual damages and $77 million in punitive damages to the estate of Nelene Fox, a woman who died earlier that year after having been denied a bone-marrow transplant to treat her breast cancer. The defendant, Health Net, a California-based health maintenance organization, refused to provide the treatment, claiming that it was still experimental in cases involving breast cancer. This case has had important consequences for HMOs and insurers who are struggling with the prospects of having to cover these and other controversial and expensive procedures. (Health Net paid the family of Christy deMeurers $1.02 million in 1995 following a similar charge.)

Recent evidence estimates the projected survival rates using the high-dose chemotherapy/transplant treatment to be somewhere between 30 and 32 percent after three years. In another study, the projected survival rates for patients with chemotherapy-responsive stage IV breast cancer using the high-dose chemotherapy/transplant treatment was 53 percent from five to more than nine years (Doctor's Guide, 1999).

Some doctors estimate that as many as one-third of the 180,000 women diagnosed with breast cancer are candidates for bone-marrow transplants at an average cost of $140,000. The potential cost of this procedure alone stands at over $8 billion per year, extending the lives of some 20,000 to 30,000 women.

Policymakers are looking to managed-care networks for relief from the growth in health care spending. At the same time Americans seem to be saying, "Reform the system, but don't take away any of my benefits." Will cost ever be a valid defense against a plaintiff's allegations that a medical practitioner failed to prescribe additional care, take additional precautions, or prolong hospitalization? Will the net benefit of a procedure ever be calculated ex ante, that is to say, in terms of the full social cost of the additional treatment relative to the expected benefits for that entire class of patients that find themselves in similar situations? Or will we continue to calculate the net benefit ex poste, based on a second guess of a treatment decision made on an individual patient? The implications of this decision are far-reaching.

Source: Michael Meyer and Andrew Murr, "Not My Health Care," *Newsweek*, January 10, 1994, 36–38; Erik Larson, "The Soul of an HMO," *Time*, January 22, 1996, 44–52; and Doctor's Guide Personal Edition, "High-Dose Chemo Plus Bone Marrow Transplant Effective For Advanced Breast Cancer," http://www.pslgroup.com/dg/101a2a.htm, May 1999.

year for hospitals. Coyte et al. (1991) report that the average claim grew from $51,000 to $109,200 between 1980 and 1986, or approximately 14 percent per year in real terms.

Moller (1996) studied verdicts reached in civil trials from 1985 to 1994. Based on evidence from 15 jurisdictions across the United States, trial rates seem to be flat or decreasing over this time period, reflecting an increased tendency to settle out of court rather than try the case. Of all civil cases, plaintiffs win medical malpractice cases least

ISSUES IN MEDICAL CARE DELIVERY

DO MORE LAWYERS MEAN MORE LAWSUITS?

Some analysts contend that the current proliferation of lawyers is a major factor in determining the number and severity of medical malpractice claims. The underlying economic theory supporting this argument is simple. Feldman (1979) and Sloan (1985) indicate that more lawyers mean lower salaries for lawyers and an incentive to accept malpractice cases with smaller expected awards (lower total losses and lower probability of winning). An alternative explanation provided by Danzon (1984) indicates that the relationship between the number of malpractice lawsuits and the number of lawyers is a statistical artifact caused by the attraction of urban areas and their high incidence of lawsuits. Is it possible to settle this dispute?

Evidence cited in Brennan et al. (1991) indicates that the number of negligent injuries in hospitals far exceeds the number of lawsuits brought against hospitals. Why aren't more of these claims pursued? Either the patient is not aware of the **negligence** or the expected award is less than the expected cost of bringing a lawsuit. If the expected cost of pursuing a claim is greater than the expected payout, there is no claim, regardless of its merit.

Whether a lawyer pursues a potential claimant depends on the lawyer's opportunity cost. A relatively high supply of lawyers in a particular geographic area will exert downward pressure on the price of legal services. Lawyers' opportunity costs will fall and lawyers will have an incentive to pursue alternative sources of income—including marginally profitable malpractice claims.

Southwick and Young (1992) have tested a simple model of supply and demand using county-level data of malpractice claims filed over a ten-year period in the state of Michigan. Their statistical test was carried out in two steps. First, they used a production function to estimate the number of lawyers required to provide full legal services in a region. Second, any surplus of lawyers would seek out lower valued opportunities, supporting the hypothesis that an excess supply of lawyers in a region will make lawyers less selective in the cases they accept. They conclude that the estimated surpluses at least partially explain the observation that more lawyers mean more lawsuits. Does this settle the argument? What do you think?

Sources: Lawrence Southwick, Jr. and Gary J. Young, "Lawyers and Medical Torts: Medical Malpractice Litigation as a Residual Option," *Applied Economics* 24(9), September 1992, 989–998.

---

negligence
When a patient is harmed as a result of substandard care and it is determined that the actions of a provider were responsible for the harm.

Key Concept 2
Opportunity Cost

Key Concept 6
Supply and Demand

---

often—33 percent of the time.[7] The median jury award was $300,000 in 1988. Median awards vary considerably across jurisdictions but are increasing in most. For example, from 1985 to 1989 the median jury award in a medical malpractice case in Los Angeles County was $220,000. By the 1990 to 1994 time period, it had increased to over $425,000 (in 1992 dollars). Nationwide the median award in medical malpractice cases was $500,000 in 1995, $700,000 in 1998, and $1 million in 2001. Awards differ according to the type of medical incident. The median award in childbirth cases is over $2 million, $750,000 in cases involving misdiagnosis, $668,000 in cases involving medication reactions, and $355,000 in surgical cases (Jury Verdict Research, 2003).

By the mid-1980s, over half of the total amount paid to plaintiffs in medical malpractice cases went to only 5 percent of the claimants. This skewness reflects the underlying distribution of the severity of injury. Most iatrogenic injuries are minor

---

7 According to a study by Jury Verdict Research (Felsenthal, 1994), of all the medical malpractice cases that went to court in 1987, patients won 42 percent of those brought against physicians and 59 percent of those brought against hospitals. By 1992, the percentages had dropped to 25 percent and 50 percent, respectively.

and receive relatively modest awards. Table 12.2 shows the distribution of injuries based on two studies: one by the California Medical Association (CMA) as reported in Danzon (1985) and the second the Harvard Medical Practice Study as reported in Brennan et al. (1991). The CMA study estimated roughly 1 in 120 hospital admissions resulted in an injury. Only 17 percent of the total injuries were due to negligence. The remainder can be properly classified as adverse outcomes that are to be expected as part of the normal risk of medical treatment. The Harvard Study estimated that 3.7 percent of all hospital admissions resulted in an adverse event, and 27.5 percent of these were due to negligence. Most injuries were relatively minor. A much larger percentage of the negligent injuries, however, resulted in permanent disability or death—true for both studies.[8]

Policy Issue

A significant number of negligent injuries that lead to minor disabilities are never litigated.

Some evidence points to a more rapid growth in large jury awards than in awards for more routine cases. In addition, compensation for pain and suffering seems to be a larger portion of these larger awards and increasing disproportionately relative to payments for economics damages (Danzon, 1990). Tillinghast-Towers Perrin (2003) report that noneconomic damages, including pain and suffering, amount to almost one-fourth of the total cost of the tort system, representing an amount greater than awards for economic damages.

International Differences

The legal system for dealing with medical malpractice claims in other countries is markedly different from that in the United States. These differences are, at least in part, responsible for the differences in the liability costs imposed on medical practitioners. Compared with the other advanced countries in the world, the United States spends two to five times more to settle tort disputes as a percentage of total economic output.[9] Even though the legal climate abroad is generally less favorable to potential

Table 12.2	Distribution of Injuries by Severity in Percentages of Total Injuries					
	CMA Study[a]			**Harvard Study**[b]		
Severity of Injury	**Negligent Injuries**	**Non-negligent Injuries**	**Total Injuries**	**Negligent Injuries**	**Non-negligent Injuries**	**Total Injuries**
Minor temporary disability	6.1	55.4	61.5	12.6	44.2	56.8
Major temporary disability	3.4	15.2	18.6	3.3	10.4	13.7
Minor permanent disability	1.6	5.0	6.6	0.8	2.0	2.8
Major permanent disability	1.3	1.8	3.1	0.9	3.0	3.9
Grave permanent disability	0.5	0.1	0.6	0.9	1.7	2.6
Death	4.1	5.5	9.6	7.0	6.6	13.6
Unknown	—	—	—	2.0	4.6	6.6
Total	17.0	83.0	100.00	27.6	72.4	100.0

a Patricia Danzon, *Medical Malpractice: Theory, Evidence, and Public Policy*, 1985.

b Troyen A. Brennan, et al., "Incidence of Adverse Events and Negligence in Hospitalized Patients: Results of the Harvard Medical Practice Study I," *New England Journal of Medicine 324*(6), February 7, 1991, Table 2.

8 These results have been corroborated by a study conducted by the Institute of Medicine (Kohn et al., 2000) estimating that somewhere between 2.9 and 3.7 percent of all hospital admissions result in injury to the patient. With over 33.6 million admissions in 1997, this translates into at least 44,000 and as many as 98,000 deaths in hospitals due to medical error.

9 Tillinghast-Towers Perrin's (1996) analysis tracks tort costs worldwide and has found that the U.S. system costs 250 percent of the average in the industrialized world. Tort costs amount to 0.5 percent of GDP in Japan, 0.8 percent in Canada, France, and the United Kingdom, 1.3 percent in Germany, and 2.2 percent in the United States. (By 2003 the percentage in the United States had edged up to 2.3 percent.)

plaintiffs, the upward trend in the frequency and severity of claims seems to be a worldwide phenomenon.

Data on malpractice claims in other countries tend to be less comprehensive than that available in the United States. The information in Table 12.3 indicates that the number and severity of malpractice claims is much higher in the United States than in either Canada or the United Kingdom. The number of claims per physician is roughly eight times higher in the United States than in Canada. Canada's average award of $77,200 in 1986 was less than three-fourths of the average malpractice award in the United States that same year.

Claims frequency in the United Kingdom, measured in terms of the population, varied across regions from 21 to 70 percent of the U.S. frequency. Severity of awards was also significantly lower. Based on data from the West Midlands region, the average award was less than one-fourth of the U.S. average.

Several important differences contribute to the differences in the size and frequency of claims. These include differences in legal rules, social values, and the costs of filing litigation. The differences are difficult to measure empirically, but their influence on the incentive structure affects the costs and benefits of filing lawsuits.

standard of care
The level of care established by the medical profession as the customary or accepted practice (the local custom) prevailing in the relevant specialty.

In theory, there is little difference in the negligence rule of liability across countries. Regardless of country, plaintiffs must show that negligent care from a medical provider caused an injury. More specifically, it must be shown that a duty of care existed, that the defendant failed to conform to the required **standard of care** (either by act or failure to act), that the plaintiff sustained damages, and that the breach of duty was the proximate cause of the injury.

Policy Issue

Why are claims frequency and severity so much higher in the United States than in other developed countries?

Some evidence indicates that differences in the rate of surgical procedures has some bearing on the frequency of malpractice lawsuits. But differences in the rate of lawsuits cannot be fully explained by differences in the rate of adverse surgical outcomes. Major differences in rules governing compensation determine the expected payoff from a lawsuit. Differences in punitive damages, caps on payments for pain and suffering, **contingency fees** for attorneys, and the U.S. rule on costs provide a greater incentive to sue.

contingency fees
Method of compensating the plaintiff's attorney whereby legal fees are calculated as a percentage of the total damage award and thus payable only if the plaintiff is successful. This practice is prohibited in most countries by the rules of legal ethics.

Punitive damages, often a substantial portion of large awards in the United States, are rare in other countries. Awards for pain and suffering are typically subject to judicial caps. The cap in Canada, set at $100,000 (Canadian) in 1978 and indexed to the rate of inflation, has reached around $200,000. The contingency fee system, used extensively in the United States, is used infrequently in Canada and is illegal in the United

Table 12.3	International Comparisons of Malpractice Awards Annual Claims Frequency and Severity		
	United States	**Canada**[a]	**United Kingdom**
Claims per 100 physicians	13.0[b]	1.67	na
Average claim awarded (in 1989 U.S. dollars)	$109,200[c]	$127,200	$24,000[b,d]
Claims per 100,000 population	29.4[e]	3.5–6.1	6.2–20.5[f,g]
Average malpractice insurance premium paid by physicians	$14,781[c]	$1,371[h]	$1,728[b]

Source: Patricia M. Danzon "The 'Crisis' in Medical Malpractice: A Comparison of Trends in the United States, Canada, the United Kingdom, and Australia," *Law, Medicine, and Health Care 18*(1–2), Spring–Summer 1990; and Peter C. Coyte et al., "Medical Malpractice—The Canadian Experience," *New England Journal of Medicine 324*(2), January 10, 1991, Table 1.

a 1989   e 1984

b 1988   f 1986–1987

c 1986   g Range across regions

d West Midlands region only   h 1987

Kingdom. The **English rule of costs**, where the loser pays court costs and all attorneys' fees, is the standard rule everywhere except the United States. The combined effect of these features lowers the expected return for a successful lawsuit and increases the expected cost of litigation for plaintiffs, which tends to discourage the initiation of lawsuits with little chance of success.

Most countries have uniform rules that govern tort claims nationwide. In contrast, the United States' system has fostered the development of a diverse standard of law in each of the 50 states. A judge alone, without the aid of a jury, decides almost all medical malpractice cases in Canada. Canadian judges tend to hand out more modest awards than American juries in similar situations.

With the frequency and severity of malpractice claims higher in the United States than either Canada or the United Kingdom, premiums for malpractice insurance are also higher. The average premium for U.S. physicians is roughly ten times higher than for practitioners in the other two. In addition, more than 90 percent of all Canadian physicians belong to the Canadian Medical Protective Association that provides universal, comprehensive, and unlimited coverage for its members in the event that they are sued.

Tort Reform

Some argue that since more patients suffer injuries resulting from negligence than actually file malpractice lawsuits, the real tort crisis consists of too few lawsuits, not too many. The major concern from an economic perspective is the system's efficiency in performing its three primary functions: compensation, deterrence, and retribution.

Cost of Malpractice

Malpractice insurance is expensive and, depending on the specialty, comprises an increasing portion of direct practice costs. Most physicians will purchase a malpractice insurance policy that provides basic coverage that includes $1 million per claim, up to a total of $3 million during a contract period. Typically, an excess coverage policy is also purchased, providing an extra $1 to 2 million in protection. The cost of premiums for all providers was $6.1 billion in 1995, up from less than $3 billion in 1982 but down from $8 billion in 1992.[10] From Table 12.4, malpractice premiums in 1998 represented around 4 to 6 percent of total practice costs for self-employed internists and general practitioners and 7 to 10 percent for specialists in obstetrics and gynecology, surgery, and anesthesiology. Premiums as a percentage of practice costs were down sharply from levels experienced in the late 1980s when they reached over 12 percent of practice costs for all physicians and over 30 percent of practice costs for anesthesiologists.

The average premium paid by the self-employed physician increased 8.8 percent per year between 1982 and 1997 from $5,800 to $14,200. Premiums varied considerably across specialty in 1997, ranging from $9,400 for the internal medicine to $33,000 for the OB/GYN. Inflation as measured by the consumer price index rose at an average rate of 3.8 percent over the decade. Practice revenues increased 7.5 percent per year over that same period causing premiums as a percentage of total practice revenues to increase slightly from 3.1 to 3.9.

Focusing on malpractice premiums underestimates the overall impact of medical malpractice on total health care expenditures. Other direct costs include time costs of medical practitioners, the mental strain of an actual litigation, and the disutility of the risk of a lawsuit. The direct costs may in fact be dwarfed by the indirect costs of the steps that practitioners take to avoid being sued. These steps include prevention and defensive medicine whose sole purpose is to reduce the risk of an injury or lawsuit. Low-benefit care

English rule of costs
Standard practice in most of the world where the loser of a lawsuit pays all court costs and attorneys' fees, including those of the winner.

Key Concept 3
Marginal Analysis

---

10 The added contribution of self-insured organizations, primarily hospitals, is estimated to be as high as $5.6 billion. When added to malpractice premiums, the total amounts to $11.7 billion, or 1.2 percent of health care expenditures in 1995, a figure that has remained relatively unchanged over the years.

Table 12.4	Malpractice Premiums as a Percentage of Professional Expenses Self-Employed Physicians by Specialty, 1982–1997				
Year	All Physicians	General/ Family Practice	Internal Medicine	Surgery	Obstetrics/ Gynecology	Anesthesiology
1982	7.4	4.6	4.9	9.5	10.0	20.4
1985	10.2	7.0	6.4	12.2	17.8	22.0
1986	10.8	6.1	6.4	14.3	19.6	21.2
1987	12.1	7.3	7.1	14.9	20.4	30.6
1988	11.3	7.7	6.6	14.1	18.6	24.7
1989	10.4	7.0	5.9	12.7	18.7	24.0
1990	9.7	5.8	6.6	11.3	16.1	23.4
1991	8.7	5.5	5.0	10.4	14.8	20.4
1992	7.6	5.2	4.9	8.6	14.3	17.5
1993	7.9	4.9	4.9	9.2	14.2	16.6
1994	8.2	5.4	4.6	8.9	19.0	17.3
1995	7.4	5.0	4.7	8.8	14.4	15.3
1996	6.5	4.0	4.6	7.1	13.2	10.3
1997	6.2	5.8	3.9	6.3	10.8	9.9
1998	6.4	4.1	6.4	7.0	9.5	—

Source: Martin L. Gonzalez, ed., *Socioeconomic Characteristics of Medical Practice*, Chicago: American Medical Association, various years.

provided because of the third-party payment mechanism may not be appropriately classified as defensive medicine. Defensive medicine is defined as services rendered that have little or no medical benefit; their provision is simply to reduce the risk of being sued.

Zuckerman (1984) surveyed physicians on changes in their practice patterns due to the threat of malpractice suits. He found that 41 percent of those who responded to his survey performed extra tests, 36 percent spent more time with their patients, 57 percent kept more detailed records, and 45 percent referred more cases to specialists. This does not represent prima facie evidence that these practices are necessarily wasteful. This may in fact be what the malpractice system is designed to do—to cause physicians to spend more time with patients, refer difficult cases to specialists, and just simply do a better job in treating the public.

Other research has attempted to differentiate between preventive practices and defensive steps that have little or no medical benefit. Reynolds et al. (1987) estimated that, in 1984, malpractice costs were responsible for an increase in the cost of physicians' services of between $12.1 and $13.7 billion. That same year, malpractice premiums totaled $3.0 billion and expenditures on physicians' services amounted to $75.4 billion. Combining the cost of defensive medicine and malpractice premiums totaled $15 to 18 billion, indicating that the total cost of medical malpractice may be 16 to 18 percent of the total spent on physicians' services. These estimates are substantially lower than earlier estimates by the American Medical Association (1983) that placed the annual cost of medical malpractice at up to $40 billion.

These facts do not tell the entire story for the individual physician. Economists argue that behavior is affected by marginal changes in the incentive structure as perceived by decision makers. In this case, the relevant marginal cost may be the increase in the average malpractice premiums relative to the average increase in practice revenues. In 1984, the additional malpractice premiums and changes in practice style averaged $5,900 per physician. This cost increase amounted to almost two-thirds of the $9,400 average increase in practice income. For the individual physician, malpractice premiums and the costs of avoidance are seen as absorbing most of the potential increase in real income.

Causes of Increased Litigation

What are the reasons for the increase in the frequency and severity of medical malpractice claims? Many legal and political commentators have offered their suggested answers. The alternative explanations run the entire ideological spectrum. Depending on which expert you ask, the blame might be placed on lawyers, medical practitioners, hospitals, patients, insurance companies, or society in general. The possibilities include:

1. *The increased supply of lawyers.* With over one million attorneys practicing nationwide, the pressure to find new clients and new sources of revenues is mounting. This provides the basis for the accusation that lawyers practice "ambulance chasing" (Southwick and Young, 1992).

2. *The increased litigiousness of U.S. society.* Medical expectations have changed in the past 50 years and Americans today are much more ready to question authority than was the case earlier in our history. We no longer expect only care from our medical providers, but cure. And if we don't get what we expect, we are much more likely to sue.

3. *The increase in medical costs and physicians' salaries.* American society has come to expect full warranties and money-back guarantees on everything purchased. As the perspective on medical care changed to one of a market transaction, medical care became more like any other commodity purchased. Consumers demand value for money spent. Anything as expensive as medical care, provided by highly paid practitioners, should be no different from any other consumer durable good purchased.

4. *The breakdown in the physician-patient relationship.* The rapport between physician and patient is the victim of medical technology. The increased complexity of medical care has had two major effects: first, it has increased the need for specialization among physicians and second, it has resulted in the use of more personnel in the actual treatment. Patients become isolated from their caregivers and are more likely to sue the person behind the mask. Levinson et al. (1997) provide evidence supporting the claim that poor communication between physician and patient increases the risk of a lawsuit.

5. *The pro-plaintiff trend in common-law doctrine.* The courts have gradually eroded the value of traditional defenses against malpractice and extended the scope of liability. The removal of immunity from lawsuit for nonprofit hospitals and the increased use of the legal doctrine of **respondeat superior** have increased the risk of lawsuit for hospitals. The plaintiff's costs in proving negligence are substantially lower, increasing the likelihood of filing a lawsuit.

6. *The size of damage awards.* Larger and more frequent payoffs place a floor under the amount that can be expected in an out-of-court settlement and increase the potential economic incentives for bringing suit.

7. *The number of surgical procedures.* As the number and complexity of surgeries has increased, so has the likelihood of adverse surgical outcomes. Surgical mishaps are much more visible and the consequences much more severe than the medical errors of omission, such as misdiagnosis or failure to treat.

In modeling a plaintiff's decision to file a malpractice suit, economists assume that the expected payoff from the lawsuit (probability of winning times the average award of a successful lawsuit) must be greater than the expected costs of filing (including legal expenses and the opportunity cost of time). Anything that increases the probability of winning, that increases the average size of a successful lawsuit, or that lowers the cost of filing a suit will increase the frequency of filing.

Suggestions for Reform

The current tort system is costly to operate. Currently, litigation costs and overhead expenses absorb up to 60 percent of the medical malpractice premiums paid by

Key Concept 3
Marginal Analysis

Key Concept 6
Supply and Demand

The Association of Trial Lawyers of America provides information about the American justice system, the courts, programs of public interest, and links to other legal sites. ATLA's monthly magazine is online.
http://www.atlanet.org/

respondeat superior
A principle that holds employers responsible for the actions of employees. In the case of medical malpractice, hospitals must exercise certain precautions to ensure that substandard care is not offered by its employees or physicians (whether salaried or not).

Key Concept 3
Marginal Analysis

strict liability
Legal principle where the
provider of care pays for any
harm whether negligent or not.

ISSUES IN MEDICAL CARE DELIVERY

IS NO-FAULT INSURANCE THE ANSWER TO THE TORT CRISIS?

Some legal scholars argue that tort reform requires a complete change in the liability doctrine from one of negligence to one of **strict liability**, or no-fault (Weiler, 1991). Although tort suits inflict considerable harm on medical practitioners, medical injuries inflict even more harm on patients. As few as one out of every ten patients injured actually files a malpractice claim. Only one out of every 25 who are injured as a result of negligence actually receives compensation. The problem with our tort system may in fact be too few lawsuits, not too many.

Can a no-fault system be created that will compensate victims of medical negligence and be cost-efficient at the same time? The shift to a no-fault system of liability would mean that any patient who suffers a medical injury that results in a loss would be eligible for compensation. This objective can be accomplished in several ways. The no-fault system could cover only economic losses or it could include noneconomic losses, including pain and suffering. It could be devised to compensate those who are not in the labor force and the retired by compensating for loss of household production, including cooking, cleaning, and childcare. Danzon (1985) estimates that the number of claims under such a system could increase by as many as fifty times its current level. Many small claims that are not litigated under the current system would be compensated, an improvement over the current system. But how would a no-fault system serve to deter negligence? Will immunity from a lawsuit serve as an incentive or disincentive to the provision of quality care. Under a no-fault system some other mechanism would have to serve the deterrence function, such as stronger professional sanctions against repeat offenders. Would a no-fault system improve efficiency? We still have a lot of work to do before we can answer that question fully.

Sources: Patricia M. Danzon, "The Medical Malpractice System: Facts and Reforms," in Mary Ann Baily and Warren I. Cikins, eds., *The Effects of Litigation on Health Care Costs*, Washington, DC: The Brookings Institute, 1985; and Paul C. Weiler, *Medical Malpractice on Trial*, Cambridge, MA: Howard University Press, 1991.

providers. In comparison, these costs amount to 40 percent of total premiums for work-related no-fault insurance and 20 percent of first-party insurance premiums. Based on evidence presented by Danzon (1985a), gross compensation in malpractice cases is on average twice the total economic loss and five times the out-of-pocket economic loss.[11]

One possible justification for continuing to pay the high cost of this system is deterrence. Critics of the system argue that in practice it provides little deterrence since most claims of malpractice are merely errors in judgment that cannot be avoided at any cost.

---

11 Danzon estimates that economic loss on average amounts to 75 percent of net compensation. In other words,

$$\text{Net compensation} = 1.33 \times \text{Economic loss}$$

Assuming that legal fees amount to one-third of gross compensation, then

$$\text{Net compensation} = 0.67 \times \text{gross compensation}$$

Substituting yields, Gross compensation = 2 × Economic loss. In addition, on average 60 percent of all economic loss is covered by other sources of public and private insurance. Thus,

$$\text{Out-of-pocket economic loss} = 0.40 \times \text{Economic loss}$$

After making appropriate substitutions, Gross compensation = 5 × Out-of-pocket economic loss.

ISSUES IN MEDICAL CARE DELIVERY

SILICONE BREAST IMPLANT LITIGATION: A CASE OF RENT-SEEKING BEHAVIOR

Economic rent is best understood as a payment to a resource that exceeds its true opportunity cost. Ann O. Krueger (1974) introduced the concept as a way of explaining the use of scarce resources to secure monopoly profits. It can best be understood by use of the following diagram.

In a competitive environment price, depicted by *PP*, reflects the underlying average cost of production. With demand *DD*, output would equal *Q*. Any distortion introduced into the market will raise price to *P′P′* and lower output to *Q′*. The dotted triangle depicts the social cost of the distortion measured by the lost consumer surplus. The shaded rectangle represents a transfer from consumers to producers, or economic rent.

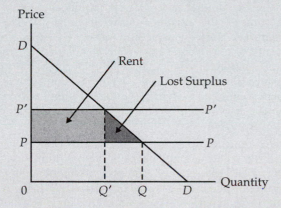

The case of the silicone gel breast implant provides a classic case of rent-seeking behavior. From 1962 to 1992 somewhere between 1.0 and 2.2 million women received breast implants in the United States and Canada. A large percentage of these implants were provided for reconstructive surgery following mastectomy, but most were strictly for cosmetic augmentation.

In the early 1990s a number of reports surfaced linking implants with a variety of illnesses, including lupus, scleroderma, joint swelling, and chronic fatigue. Public awareness was heightened with the December 10, 1990, broadcast of the CBS television show *Face-to-Face* entitled "Hazards of Silicone Breast Implants." The show presented a number of case reports claiming that implants were the cause of silicone poisoning in its recipients. Those women whose implants were not yet leaking or ruptured were said to be carrying around "ticking time bombs."

Where are the rents? As you might guess, the publicity sparked a firestorm of litigation. In addition to over 45 class action lawsuits, more than 19,000 individual product liability lawsuits were filed nationwide, most claiming unspecified economic damages. In suits where damages are specified, they range from $100,000 to $140 million. Although a number of these lawsuits were settled separately, a settlement in a national class action lawsuit provided a $4.25 billion settlement to members of the class of plaintiffs. Individual awards ranged from $105,000 to $1.4 million, based on the severity of the injury and age of the recipient.

Rents represent surplus transferred from customers of implant manufacturers to successful plaintiffs, their attorneys, and all the expert witnesses providing litigation

Economic rent
Payment for a good, service, or resource in excess of its opportunity cost. A situation that usually results because supply is inelastic.

support services in these cases. These "expert" witnesses include toxicologists, pathologists, and economists who make up to $500 per hour; many have received over $250,000 for their testimony. Attorneys paid by the contingency fee system receive up to 40 percent of the damage awards. According to *Forbes* magazine, one Houston firm had over 2,000 implant clients, and a partner in that firm reportedly made over $40 million in 1994 on implant litigation (Alster, 1999).

An interesting feature of this episode in tort history is how silicone implants were ever approved for human use in the first place. The product was never tested on human subjects. The product had already been in use for more than a decade when the FDA inherited jurisdiction with the passage of the Medical Devices Act in 1975. The product remained in use until 1992 pending the filing of safety data that were in fact never filed. The FDA, under intense pressure from the mounting case evidence concerning the product's safety, banned further use of the device in April 1992.

From a scientific viewpoint, case evidence is useful in formulating a theory, but inadequate for testing a hypothesis. In other words, the 300 plus medical case studies in the English literature, while compelling emotionally, are merely descriptive and prove nothing. The scientific issue is causation. The only way to prove causation is to compile scientific evidence showing that implants contribute to the diseases in question—an issue that has so far been avoided by the courts.

Several basic research studies have shown how silicone gel may influence the immune system. Three notable attempts studied the impact of silicone implants on the immune system. The Nurses' Health Study (Sanchez-Guerrero et al., 1994) and the Women's Health Study (Hennekens et al., 1996) used self-reporting data to examine the relationship. To date the only major epidemiological study on the issue was done at the Mayo Clinic (Gabriel et al., 1994). Based on these studies one would conclude that there is either no evidence of an "association between breast implants and connective-tissue disease" or no evidence of "large risks of connective-tissue diseases following breast implants."

These studies have their critics. Admittedly, they cannot be considered definitive. The original claim that silicone implants cause autoimmune diseases has become implants cause "atypical" disease. This claim presents a problem for science because atypical disease cannot be defined. If it can't be defined, it can't be studied systematically. It therefore presents an even bigger problem for defendants in the courts because the association between silicone implants and atypical disease cannot be disproved. To clear up the confusion, a federal judge appointed an independent panel of experts to examine the evidence and provide an opinion as to whether there is a connection between silicone implants and autoimmune diseases. Based on the panel's recommendation, the Institutes of Medicine declared that implants—saline or silicone—do not cause disease. Still, concerns about the safety of implants and their related side effects abound. Recent studies indicate that most women will have at least one rupture within 11 to 15 years. Despite the warnings, at least 130,000 women received implants in 1999.

And the saga is not over. In 2003 an FDA committee recommended that silicone implants be made available to women who want them. When rents are this large, participants manipulate evidence to ensure that they receive their fair share. Whether this rent-seeking behavior will leave women who desire reconstructive surgery with more or fewer options is yet to be determined.

Sources: Ann O. Krueger, "The Political Economy of the Rent-Seeking Society," *American Economic Review 64*(3), June 1974, 291–303; Jorge Sanchez-Guerrero, Graham A. Colditz, Elizabeth W. Karlson et al., "Silicone Breast Implants and the Risk of Connective-Tissue Diseases and Symptoms," *The New England Journal of Medicine 332*(25), June 22, 1995, 1666–1670; Charles H. Hennekens, Nancy R. Cook, Patricia R. Hebert et al., "Self-reported Breast Implants and Connective-Tissue Diseases in Female Health Professionals: A Retrospective Cohort Study," *Journal of the American Medical Association 275*(8), February 28, 1996, 616–621; and Sherine E. Gabriel, W. Michael O'Fallon, Leonard T. Kurland et al., "Risk of Connective-Tissue Diseases and Other Disorders After Breast Implantation," *The New England Journal of Medicine 330*(24), June 16, 1994, 1697–1702. Those interested in reading further on this topic may look at Marcia Angell, *Science on Trial: The Clash of Medical Evidence and the Law in the Breast Implant Case*, Norton, 1996; Norm Alster, "Getting the Middleman's Share," *Forbes 154*, July 4, 1999, 108–109.

But some studies conclude that improper performance is the most common claim in malpractice suits (Danzon, 1985b). Still virtually no empirical evidence supports the claim that the current tort system serves as an effective deterrent to negligent behavior. If compensation to victims is the primary function of the tort system, a more efficient way to accomplish this goal may exist.

Despite these problems, Danzon (1985a) has shown that the current system can be justified if it reduces negligent injuries by as little as ten percent. Based on empirical findings, she estimates that only one out of every 25 patients negligently injured receives compensation.[12] Litigation costs are worth incurring if one comparable injury is avoided for every one compensated, which would require only a four percent reduction in negligent injuries to justify the system. Adjusting the data for an increased incidence of compensation and other costs to the system increases the required reduction to ten percent.

Policy Issue

What is the best way to go about reforming how medical malpractice claims are litigated?

Empirical evidence suggests that modifications in the extent of damages will limit the severity of awards to successful plaintiffs. Danzon (1986) examined the impact of legislation passed in the 1970s on the severity of claims over the period 1975 to 1984. Her estimates indicate that a cap on the size of damages reduces the average award by 23 percent and the mandatory reduction of awards by the amount of collateral benefits reduces severity by 11 to 19 percent. Southwick et al. (1989) arrive at similar findings. They estimate reductions in severity of 23 percent for caps on noneconomic damages, 39 percent for caps on total damages, and 21 percent for mandatory collateral source offsets. Also of interest is their finding that limits on attorneys' fees have only a modest effect on either frequency or severity of claims.

Of the many suggestions for improving the tort system, the following recommendations are the most often cited:

1. *Caps on noneconomic damages.* Most advocates of reform recommend a limit on the damages awarded for pain and suffering. More than 20 states have enacted some form of limitation on noneconomic damages, a prevailing standard worldwide. California has placed a ceiling of $250,000 on pain and suffering awards; Canada has a $200,000 limit (with annual inflation adjustments). Danzon (1985b) points out that people, when given a choice, do not insure against pain and suffering. The tort system is designed to compensate victims for the cost of medical treatment, any rehabilitation expenses, lost earnings, and other monetary costs. Pain and suffering represents a real loss in the quality of life, but it is not a monetary loss. Because people do not voluntarily insure against pain and suffering, there is a real question whether the tort system should provide such insurance. Pain and suffering should be compensated in the event of permanent injuries. One alternative would set the amount of the award according to a schedule based on age of the victim and the severity of the injury, not arbitrarily on a case-by-case basis.

2. *Awards adjusted to reflect collateral sources.* Under this provision awards would be reduced by the amount of any past or future compensation the plaintiff may receive from insurance coverage or government sources. Fair collateral source rules would allow third-party payers the right to petition the courts for reimbursement for expenses they incur. Thus, the overall size of the award remains the same; only the distribution changes. This suggestion would reduce the likelihood that plaintiffs are overcompensated and ensure that those responsible for injuries pay the full costs of their negligence. More than 30 states mandate that the judge or jury consider collateral sources in determining the size of the award.

3. *Periodic payments for future losses.* Instead of a lump-sum payment up front, under this reform the award would be paid in installments. All past and present losses would be paid immediately and all future losses paid over the

---

12 Data from the Harvard Medical Practice Study (1990) place this figure at one out of every 16.

discounting
The process of translating future sums of money into their present values.

lifetime of the awardee. This would allow the defendant to purchase an annuity or set up a trust fund determined by the settlement. Opponents of this reform argue that the practice of **discounting** future losses already makes the desired adjustment in damages. If periodic payment is mandated, discounting future losses should be eliminated. Thirteen states have already made periodic payment mandatory for future damages.

4. *Limits on punitive damages.* Punitive damages are awarded to punish and deter intentional or reckless behavior or actions motivated by actual malice. Punitive damages do not include economic or noneconomic damages. They are not intended to compensate for any loss. Opponents of this reform argue that punitive damage awards against physicians are very rare but should be available without limit in cases where intentional or malicious conduct has caused patient injury. Danzon argues for the imposition of an uninsurable fine paid by those guilty of gross negligence. This fine would be paid to the government in lieu of punitive damages paid to the plaintiff. Such payments would help defer the public costs of the tort system.

joint-and-several liability
Allows successful plaintiffs to recover up to the full amount of a damage award from a single defendant if the other defendants are unable to pay.

discovery procedures
Rules that govern the ability of plaintiffs to compel the release of information that may be relevant to a case.

5. *Changes in certain legal rules.* Stricter rules on the statute of limitations, discovery, and **joint-and-several liability** would increase the cost to the plaintiff of filing a lawsuit and reduce their frequency. Some argue for limits on the statute of limitations. Long statutes of limitation expose practitioners to the retroactive application of standards of care that were not relevant when care was originally delivered. Still others would like to see reform in the **discovery procedures** to eliminate the tendency for many plaintiffs to sue first and verify later. Under 1995 legislation in Texas, a plaintiff has 90 days to file either a $5,000 bond for each defendant or a completed expert report analyzing the case. After 180 days if expert reports are not filed, the case may be dismissed and the bonds forfeited. The impact of the legislation has been dramatic. The number of new malpractice lawsuits has fallen by over one-third in the state's most populous jurisdiction, Harris County. Abolishing the legal principle of joint-and-several liability would eliminate the practice of including marginally responsible parties simply for their resource value. More than 30 states have modified their rules of joint-and-several liability.

alternative dispute resolution (ADR) mechanism
Means of settling lawsuits prior to a jury trial, including pretrial screenings and arbitration.

6. *Establishment of an **alternative dispute resolution (ADR) mechanism**.* Proponents of this reform see it as a low-cost way to handle many claims arising from medical practice. It might include setting up pretrial screenings and binding or nonbinding arbitration to settle most disputes. If individuals still desire a constitutionally guaranteed jury trial, the proceedings of the pretrial hearings could be admissible in court. Opponents argue that unless ADR is mandated it merely sets up an intermediate step in the judicial process that is unnecessary and costly. And a mandated ADR, no matter how it is constructed, serves to limit due process in the interest of making resolutions cheaper and quicker.

7. *Limits on contingency fees and the adoption of the English rule of costs.* Advocates of contingency fee reform argue for a sliding-scale fee structure, where attorneys would receive smaller percentages of the larger awards. This rule would provide attorneys with a greater incentive to accept cases where damages are smaller (since a larger percentage contingency fee is allowed). Approximately twenty states have already achieved some measure of contingency fee reform. The English rule of costs (where the loser pays all court costs and attorneys' fees) is a common practice worldwide. Proponents argue that these changes would provide full compensation to successful plaintiffs and full vindication to successful defendants. Kritzer (1995) expects a secondary insurance market to emerge to provide compensation for losers to cover court costs and fees. In theory, these changes would impose significant hardships on risk-averse plaintiffs and many valid claims (especially those with modest damages) would go unheard. In practice, the effectiveness of the secondary insurance market would determine the actual impact.

8. *Establishment of medical courts to hear all malpractice lawsuits.* Possibly the most radical solution to the medical malpractice dilemma is the creation of state medical courts. Judges with expertise in both law and medicine would head up these jury-less courts. Trained to evaluate scientific evidence, they would have the authority to determine liability and set award levels. Proponents argue that this change would lower administrative costs and result in faster and fairer settlements. Does it violate the constitutional guarantee of a trial by jury? Traffic court, family court, tax court, and disputes dealing with workers compensation cases function without the benefits of a jury. Great Britain, Japan, Germany, and France settle malpractice cases without a jury. A bill is working its way through Congress that would create a pilot program for up to nine states to experiment with medical courts.

Would any of these reforms work? One of the benefits of the 50 states having separate tort systems is the opportunity to examine differences in the frequency and severity of claims based on differences in the legal system. Many of the suggested reforms were enacted in California in 1975 with the passage of the Medical Injury Compensation Reform Act (MICRA). The California legislation is extremely controversial and has been described as the "premier legislation on tort reform in America" (Schwachman, 1992). The California reforms included the following:

1. A cap on noneconomic damages, including pain and suffering, of $250,000.

2. A sliding-scale contingency fee schedule for attorneys. The percentage fee decreases as the award increases.

3. A reasonable statute of limitations.

4. A system of periodic payments in cases where the award exceeds $50,000.

5. The disclosure of collateral payments available from other sources.

6. The implementation of a 90-day notice of intent to sue, providing a settlement period before the actual filing of a lawsuit.

7. The formation of an alternative dispute resolution panel to provide the option of presenting the case to voluntary binding arbitration.

8. Strengthening the authority of the medical profession to take disciplinary action, including probation, suspension, and revocation of license, for truly negligent behavior.

These actions have resulted in a significant moderation in the growth in medical malpractice premiums in California. Comparing premiums from other states is quite revealing. Table 12.5 compares the average malpractice premiums for three specialties in California and Florida. In 1979, the premiums were roughly the same for internal medicine, general surgery, and OB/GYN. By 1990, however, physicians practicing internal medicine in Florida paid over three times the premiums of their California counterparts. General surgeons in Florida paid premiums that were eight times higher and OB/GYNs paid premiums that were four times higher than those paid in California. Even with these differences, no evidence exists that would indicate that the quality of medical care differs substantially between the two states.

Policy Issue

Is MICRA the best model for U.S. malpractice reform?

| Table 12.5 | Comparison of Average Malpractice Premiums for Various Specialties |

Specialty	Florida		California	
	1979	1990	1979	1990
Internal Medicine	$ 2,488	$ 21,115	$ 3,507	$ 6,074
General Surgery	12,460	99,367	13,145	12,460
OB/GYN	20,715	185,486	15,471	45,414

Source: Schwachman, 1992.

PROFILE

Patricia M. Danzon

If the make-up of a Ph.D. dissertation committee can be used as an indicator of future success, then Patricia Danzon's climb to the pinnacle of her profession comes as no surprise. In addition to her supervising professor, Nobel Prize winner George Stigler, the other members of her committee included future Nobel laureates in economics Ronald Coase and Gary Becker.

Soon after she was born, her father moved the family from England to Pretoria, South Africa, where they lived until she was a teenager. Returning to England, Danzon graduated from Oxford University in 1968 with a B.A. in politics, philosophy, and economics. She decided to attend graduate school in the United States and applied to the six best graduate programs in economics. Only one, the University of Chicago, accepted her, and even provided a full fellowship to cover the cost of her studies.

Danzon received her Ph.D. in 1973 and began working for the RAND Corporation. She was able to turn her dissertation on exploring eminent domain into her first publication in the prestigious *Journal of Political Economy*. Her work with RAND initially dealt primarily with military manpower issues. Even though the issue was of growing importance with the end of the Viet Nam War and emergence of the all-volunteer army in the United States, Danzon was soon ready to tackle another challenge. At about this time, the first malpractice insurance crisis was gripping the medical community. Joseph Newhouse, then head of the health group at RAND, came to her suggesting that someone really ought to look into the problem from an economic perspective. Danzon saw this as an opportunity to combine three fields of study: health economics, insurance, and law and economics. She had to overcome one minor problem—her background was in law and economics, and she knew little about the other two. Undaunted by the limitation, she became self-taught in both health economics and insurance.

She was assigned as the staff person on professional liability at the California Commission on Tort Reform. There she teamed up with Dennis Smallwood to publish empirical research on the property/casualty industry in the 1980 *Bell Journal of Economics*, the first of over 40 books, journal articles, and book chapters on insurance and medical liability. Her work has been published in the most highly regarded journals in economics and health care, including the *American Economic Review*, the *Journal of Health Economics*, and *Health Affairs*. She may be best known for her book *Medical Malpractice: Theory, Evidence, and Public Policy* (Harvard University Press, 1985).

Danzon left RAND in 1980. After relatively short stays at Stanford's Hoover Institute and Duke University, she moved to the University of Pennsylvania in 1985 where she is the Celia Z. Moh Professor and Professor of Health Care Systems and Insurance and Risk Management at The Wharton School.

Over the past two decades, Danzon has emerged as an international expert on medical malpractice, but the exclusive focus on one issue left her desiring a little variety in her scholarly pursuits. So in 1991, funded by a grant from the University Research Council, Danzon ventured into a new field of study for her, the pharmaceutical industry. She has turned her interest in health care pharmaceutical pricing into consultancies with the World Bank, the Asian Development Bank, and the United States Agency for International Development, examining drug pricing in Europe and New Zealand.

Danzon has maintained a practical focus in her scholarly pursuits. The testing of economic theory with empirical evidence is a way of thinking she acquired during her graduate studies under Stigler and developed in the years since. Everyone interested in the study of health care, insurance, and legal liability is richer for her efforts.

Source: Curriculum vitae and personal correspondence.

Summary and Conclusions

In this chapter we examined the origins and purposes of tort law in the United States. Based on English common law, the system attempts to fulfill three functions: (1) to compensate victims of negligent actions for the losses they incur, (2) to deter negligent behavior, and (3) to punish those found guilty of particularly egregious or malicious behavior. To a degree the U.S. system fulfills these three functions, but at a very high price, upwards of 50 to 60 percent of the total awarded. For all the fanfare medical malpractice receives, at the national level it is probably not a major cost driver for health care spending. Malpractice insurance premiums as a percentage of total spending have remained at roughly the same level for the past several decades. The practice of defensive medicine (variously estimated) is important but not a growing issue. Does the threat of malpractice affect the medical practice decisions of the individual physician? In all likelihood it does, but that influence may not be a bad thing.

> ### Policy Issue
> Is the U.S. tort system accomplishing its intended goals fairly and efficiently?

Many have called for reforms to reduce claims frequency and size to provide more predictability. Others contend that the current system gives practitioners a free ride on the backs of American taxpayers who foot the bill for thousands of negligently injured patients who are shut out of the legal system. Are we really facing a medical malpractice explosion in this country? Are there too many lawsuits, or too few? Do the statistics indicate a need to improve medical practice? Or do they show a serious need for tort reform?

Despite the high cost, the tort system may still be worth the trouble if it serves to deter injurious behavior, but the tort system can only do so much to punish and deter. State medical boards, traditionally hesitant to discipline incompetent behavior, must take the lead in addressing this issue by expanding the use of sanctions including probation, suspension, and revocation of licenses. Until the public is certain that the medical profession is taking this issue seriously, we will continue to see juries used as inefficient instruments in addressing negligent behavior. No one has a bigger stake in the outcome of this debate than the patients who ultimately pay the bills. If meaningful reform is to happen, it will require our sincere efforts to ensure that the public interest is served instead of merely the special interest.

Questions and Problems

1. How serious is the issue of medical malpractice in the United States today?

2. What are the intended purposes of medical malpractice? Does the threat of a lawsuit accomplish these purposes?

3. "It is impossible to place a dollar value on life. In other words, life is priceless." How does this view create a dilemma for social decision making and effective resource allocation?

4. Environmentalists and economists often find themselves at odds with each other. The conflict between the Romantics and the rationalists surfaced again in the debate over air-quality standards set under the Clean Air Act of 1990. Under the law, the Environmental Protection Agency (EPA) must establish standards that promote public health. The EPA's cost-benefit analysis assigns a value for each life saved of $4.8 million. Is $4.8 million a reasonable value to place on each life saved? What questions would economists consider relevant in determining the value of a life? How would environmentalists react to the questions economists ask?

5. The term "iatroepidemic" describes a practice introduced into medicine without sound scientific evidence to establish its efficacy. Such practices result in systematic harm to large numbers of patients. Blood-letting during the fifteenth and sixteenth centuries, tonsillectomies in the 1950s, and the

practice of psychosurgery have been identified as practices with little thera-peutic value that actually harmed many patients. Can you think of several other examples of iatroepidemics? When systematic medical error imposes costs on individuals, who is to blame? Should individual physicians be liable for injuries under these situations?

References

American College of Obstetricians and Gynecologists, "Who Will Deliver My Baby? OB-GYNs, Patients Push U.S. Senate for Tort Reform," ACOG News Release, April 28, 2003.

American Medical Association, *Study of Professional Liability Costs*, Report of the Board of Trustees, 93–102, December 1983.

Troyen A. Brennan, Lucian L. Leape, Nan M. Larid, Liesi Hebert, A. Russell Localio, Ann G. Lawthers, Joseph P. Newhouse, Paul C. Weiler, and Howard H. Hiatt, "Incidence of Adverse Events and Negligence in Hospitalized Patients: Results of the Harvard Medical Practice Study I," *The New England Journal of Medicine 324*(6), February 7, 1991, 370–376.

Peter C. Coyte, Donald N. Dewees, and Michael J Trebilcock, "Medical Malpractice—The Canadian Experience," *The New England Journal of Medicine 324*(2), January 10, 1991, 89–93.

———, "The Frequency and Severity of Medical Malpractice Claims," *Journal of Law and Economics 27*(1), April 1984, 115–148.

———, "Liability and Liability Insurance for Medical Malpractice," *Journal of Health Economics 4*(4), December 1985, 309–331.

———, *Medical Malpractice: Theory, Evidence, and Public Policy*, Cambridge, MA: Harvard University Press, 1985a.

———, "The Medical Malpractice System: Facts and Reforms," in Mary Ann Baily and Warren I. Cikins, eds., *The Effects of Litigation on Health Care Costs*, Washington, DC: The Brookings Institute, 1985b.

———, "The Frequency and Severity of Medical Malpractice Claims: New Evidence," *Law and Contemporary Problems 49*(2), Spring 1986, 57.

———, "The 'Crisis' in Medical Malpractice: A Comparison of Trends in the United States, Canada, the United Kingdom, and Australia," *Law, Medicine, and Health Care 18*(1–2), Spring–Summer 1990, 48–58.

Roger Feldman, "The Determinants of Medical Malpractice Incidents: Theory of Contingency Fees and Empirical Evidence," *Atlantic Economic Journal 7*(4), December 1979, 59–65.

Edward Felsenthal, "Juries Display Less Sympathy in Injury Claims," *The Wall Street Journal*, March 21, 1994, B1, B7.

Martin L. Gonzalez, ed., *Socioeconomic Characteristics of Medical Practice 1994*, Center for Health Policy Research, American Medical Association, 1995.

Harvard Medical Practice Study, *Patient, Doctors, Lawyers: Medical Injury, Malpractice Litigation and Patient Compensation in New York*, Cambridge: Harvard University Press, 1990.

Institute of Medicine (2000)

Jury Verdict Research, "Current Award Trends in Personal Injury, 2002 Edition," *Personal Injury Valuation Handbook*. Jury Verdict Research® Series, Horsham, PA: LRP Publications, 2003.

Daniel P. Kessler and Mark B. McClellan, "How Liability Law Affects Medical Productivity," NBER Working Paper No. 7533, Cambridge, MA: National Bureau of Economic Research, February 2000a.

———, "Medical Liability, Managed Care, and Defensive Medicine," NBER Working Paper No. 7537, Cambridge, MA: National Bureau of Economic Research, February 2000b.

Linda T. Kohn, Janet M. Corrigan, and Molla S. Donaldson, eds., *To Err Is Human: Building a Safer Health System*, Washington, D.C.: National Academy Press, 2000.

Herbert M. Kritzer, The Reality of the English Rule: How It Works in England, What Difference It Makes, and What Might Happen Here, Testimony Prepared for the Subcommittee on Courts and Intellectual Property, U.S. House of Representatives, Committee on the Judiciary, February 6, 1995.

Wendy Levinson, Debra L. Roter, John P. Mullooly, Valerie T. Dull, and Richard M. Frankel, "The Relationship with Malpractice Claims Among Primary Care Physicians and Surgeons," *Journal of the American Medical Association 277*(7), February 19, 1997, 553–559.

Alastair MacLennan for the International Cerebral Palsy Task Force, "A Template for Defining a Causal Relation Between Acute Intrapartum Events and Cerebral Palsy: International Consensus Statement," *British Medical Journal* 319, October 16, 1999, 1054–1059.

Erik Moller, *Trends in Civil Jury Verdicts Since 1985*, Institute for Civil Justice, RAND Corporation, 1996.

Roger A. Reynolds, John A. Rizzo, and Martin L. Gonzalez, "The Cost of Medical Professional Liability," *Journal of the American Medical Association 257*(20), May 22/29, 1987, 2776–2781.

Andrew A. Sandor, "The History of Professional Liability Suits in the United States," *Journal of the American Medical Association 163*(6), February 9, 1957, 459–466.

B. Schwachman, "The Story of MICRA: Medical Injury Compensation Reform Act of California," *American Society of Anesthesiology Newsletter* 56, 1992, 16.

Frank A. Sloan, "State Responses to the Malpractice Insurance Crisis of the 1970s: An Empirical Assessment," *Journal of Health Politics, Policy and Law 9*(4), Winter 1985, 629–646.

Lawrence Southwick, Jr. and Gary J. Young, "Lawyers and Medical Torts: Medical Malpractice Litigation as a Residual Option," *Applied Economics 24*(9), September 1992, 989–998.

Tillinghast-Towers Perrin, "Tort Cost Trends: An International Perspective, 1995" (Stamford, CT: Tillinghast-Towers Perrin, 1996).

Tillinghast-Towers Perrin, "U.S. Tort Costs: 2002 Update" (Stamford, CT: Tillinghast-Towers Perrin, February 2003).

————, Paula M. Mergenhagen, and Randall R. Bovbjerg, "Effects of Tort Reforms on the Value of Closed Medical Malpractice Claims: A Microanalysis," *Journal of Health Politics, Policy, and Law 663*(14), Winter 1989, 663–689.

U. S. General Accounting Office, *Medical Malpractice Case Studies*, 1986.

Paul C. Weiler, *Medical Malpractice on Trial*, Cambridge, MA: Harvard University Press, 1991.

Stephen Zuckerman, "Medical Malpractice: Claims, Legal Costs, and the Practice of Defensive Medicine," *Health Affairs 3*(3), Fall 1984, 128–133.

Appendix 12A

Valuing Life in the Case of Wrongful Death

Years ago, placing a value on life was considered a meaningless exercise. Harry Monsen, a University of Illinois anatomy professor, calculated that the chemicals remaining in a cremated body were worth $7.28. Another anatomist, Howard Morowitz, figured that a live body was worth $6 million when the value of the hormones and DNA were included. On the other hand, Solomon S. Huebner began valuing lives using the time value of money beginning in 1905.

Methodological Considerations

Economists value human life in terms of the market's assessment of the value of the individual's productivity. Today's debate over value surrounds two major methodologies used for the calculation: the human capital method and the willingness-to-pay method.

Human capital (or lost economic output) is an approach where economic value is equal to the present value of lost future productivity, estimated by forgone earnings. The individual's value to society is measured by future production potential (using society's perspective). This can be written:

$$PV = \sum_{t=1}^{T} \frac{L_t}{(1+r)^t}$$

where PV is the present value of the lifetime labor income, L_t is the labor income in time period t, and r is the social rate of discount (the opportunity cost to society to invest in labor-saving programs).[1]

The human capital approach emphasizes the economic product and ignores other dimensions of illness and death as well as the value of relevant nonmarket activities, such as the value of pain and suffering, risk aversion, loss of leisure, and the loss of association.

The choice of discount rate greatly affects the outcome of the calculations with higher discount rates resulting in successively lower net present values. The

method is widely used, data are easily obtained, and the resulting values are objective and based on life expectancies, labor force participation rates, and projected earnings. Problems are incurred when valuing the life of a child or a homemaker for obvious reasons.

Willingness to pay (or hedonic approach to valuing life) criterion is a methodology that was proposed by Thomas Schelling of Harvard in 1968 and advanced by Kip Viscusi (1978). It purports that the value of life is reflected in payments the typical person would require to accept a small risk of death, or alternatively, the payment willingly made to reduce the risk. What are individuals "willing to pay" (or accept as compensation) for a change that will affect loss of life? What are you willing to pay ex ante to buy a small reduction in probability of death? Conceptually, everything contributing to individual well-being could be captured in a measure of the private valuation individuals place on small reductions in the risk of death.

Suppose a particular malady results in 1,000 deaths per million population. What if an intervention could reduce that number to 500? The question being asked is: What is the value of the 500 lives saved? Or alternatively: What is it worth to reduce the probability of death from 1 in 1,000 to 1 in 2,000? This question involves valuation. If it is worth x to avoid a p chance of dying, this implies that it is worth (x/p) to avoid certain death. Another way to look at this method would be to suppose that you belong to a group of 10,000 people, where one person will be chosen at random to be executed. How much would you willingly pay to be excluded from the group? The probability of being chosen is 1 in 10,000, or 0.0001. A person who pays $1,000 to avoid the lottery values his own life at $1,000/0.0001 or $10 million.

Several problems are inherent in using this technique on an individual basis:

1. The value of an outcome varies inversely with the probability of survival. A person who has an illness with a probability of survival of 5 percent may be willing to pay a great deal to increase that probability by 5 percentage points (thereby doubling the chance of survival). A relatively healthy

1 In practice, analysts often use the interest rate on risk-free investments as a measure of the discount rate. Frequently, the rate of long-term government bonds, say ten-year Treasuries, serves as a useful measure of the discount rate.

person with a 90 percent chance of survival is not as willing to make the same payment for the same 5 percentage point increment. In other words, healthy people are not likely to spend large sums to become healthier, but critically ill people are often willing to spend a great deal for even a relatively small chance of improvement. The paradox stems from the fact that people are unable to evaluate small relative changes in probabilities.

2. Time preference plays an important role in valuing outcomes. Interventions that yield benefits soon after costs are incurred tend to be valued more highly than interventions whose benefits materialize years later, other things being equal.

3. Uncertainty also plays a significant role in the calculation. Given that people seem to be risk-averse with respect to gains and risk-preferring with respect to losses, when offered a choice between a guaranteed gain of $500 and a 50 percent chance at $1,000, most people choose the sure thing. The role of medical research must be to accurately identify the benefits of a particular intervention.

Studies attempting to put this criterion into practice have taken various approaches, but the one most widely accepted by federal regulators (OSHA, EPA, etc.) is based on labor market studies examining interaction of job safety and pay (job hazard, injury rates, hazardous duty pay). The problems with these employment studies are numerous. Not only are labor markets imperfect but many people are not fully aware of the hazards they face on the job, or they enjoy dangerous work, or they simply may not be able to get less risky jobs.

A study by the National Bureau of Economic Research published in 1975 examined workers in high risk jobs and estimated the value of a life at around $1,050,000 (in 2001 dollars). Consensus opinion is that this is biased downward since people who elect to do high risk jobs cannot be thought of as typical in risk-reward tradeoff. When a more representative sample is chosen, the value of a life is estimated to be approximately $3 million.

Currently, federal agencies are allowed to do their own life valuations, and a good deal of variation exists. The Occupational Safety and Health Administration (OSHA) values life at $3.5 million in certain worker safety programs; the Environmental Protection Agency (EPA) uses values between $400,000 and $7.5 million; and the Federal Aviation Administration (FAA) estimates the value of life at $650,000 in cases of airline crashes.

One thing that the logic of "willingness to pay" emphasizes is that no single standard makes sense. We are dealing with different kinds of people, who have different priorities and different risk preferences. It is even true that the value of life varies for the same individual depending on circumstances. Calculations done when a person is facing almost certain death would show an extremely high value with the person willing to pay extraordinary sums for a small increase in probability of survival. The same person, under more normal circumstances, would not be willing to pay nearly as much for the same absolute increase in survival probability.

Valuation in Litigation

In the legal environment, the human capital approach dominates. There are two elements that the courts consider important—full economic loss and loss to survivors. Full economic loss is the sum of the discounted present value of the market economic loss (the individual's expected future earnings) and the nonmarket economic loss (expected future value of the goods and services produced in the home). The calculation involves determining current earnings, earnings growth, and a work-life discount (the amount of time the decedent would have worked in the future).

Loss to survivors includes two adjustments to full economic loss. The objective is to ensure that the family's economic situation is no better or no worse off than if the death had not occurred. First, the decedent's personal consumption is deducted (this would not have accrued to survivors anyway). Second, a tax adjustment is made. (Survivors would have benefited only from decedent's after-tax income and beneficiaries will have to pay taxes on interest earned from the compensation award.)

The calculation of full economic loss and loss to survivors includes seven elements: (1) base year earnings, (2) earnings growth, (3) work-life discount, (4) nonmarket loss, (5) personal consumption offset, (6) taxes, and (7) discount rates. It is a methodology that can be applied to a wide range of damage litigation situations, including wrongful death, personal injury, wrongful termination, and discrimination with only minor modifications.

To actually calculate the loss to survivors you must do the following (King and Smith, 1988):

1. Value the individual's contribution to the economy. This value is measured by determining how much the person was earning when the event (death, injury, termination) occurred. In other words, calculate base-year earnings.

2. Determine how much the person's income might have increased during the time he or she was not working, as measured by the rest of the expected work-life in the case of wrongful death or permanent disability. There are three separate components that normally affect salary growth: economy-wide growth in productivity, the normal life-cycle career wage progression (different for men and women), and individual productivity.

3. Estimate how much the person would have actually worked over the time not working. Determine the likely labor-force participation based on individual and group characteristics to arrive at the work-life discount.

4. Because individuals are involved in a number of household activities, estimate the number of hours the individual would have spent in these activities and place a value on each hour. The value of nonmarket activity is typically considered equal to the person's forgone market wage, which determines the value of non-market loss.

5. Reduce the total loss by the individual's proportion of family consumption (in the case of death). Money spent on personal consumption does not benefit the rest of the family. In the case of a disability, the increased costs for required medical care and rehabilitation should be added. This is the personal consumption offset.

6. The impact of taxes should be taken into consideration by counting only after-tax income and compensating for increased tax liabilities on investment income. This is the tax adjustment.

7. Because interest can be earned on compensation awards, if the award is equal to the loss dollar for dollar, the result will be overcompensation. Consequently, a discount rate must be used in calculating damages. This essential function expresses future losses in terms of their present value. The choice of discount rate is complicated by a number of issues that go far beyond the purpose of this appendix (see Henderson and Seward, 1999).

As you can tell by the discussion, determining the economic loss to survivors is no easy task. The process leaves enough latitude to ensure that attorneys and expert witnesses (often, economists) remain fully employed and always eager to try out new ideas and theories to test the limits of our tort system.

References

James W. Henderson and J. Allen Seward, "Risk Aversion and Overcompensation from the Risk-Free Discount Rate," *Journal of Legal Economics* 8(2), Fall 1998, 25–31.

Elizabeth M. King and James P. Smith, *Computing Economic Loss in Cases of Wrongful Death*, RAND: The Institute for Civil Justice, 1988.

Kip Viscusi, "Labor Market Valuation of Life and Limb: Empirical Evidence and Policy Implications," *Public Policy* 26(3), Summer 1978, 359–386.

Chapter 13

Technology in Medicine

Market forces are rapidly changing the health care industry. No aspect of industry has experienced more change than those associated with the development and marketing of medical technology. Medical innovations have improved the quality of life of countless individuals worldwide. Recent advances in pharmaceuticals, biotechnology, medical devices, and clinical procedures actually define medicine as we know it today. Even though society places a high value on technological innovation in medicine, it is one of the most misunderstood elements in the health care delivery system.

New technologies are praised for their live-saving benefits and criticized for their high price tags. Many analysts believe that advances in technology are responsible for much of the growth in medical expenditures (Evans, 1983; Newhouse, 1992). Improvements in the quality of care often have the simultaneous result of increasing the cost of care—in other words, as health status improves, financial status deteriorates. The basis of the technology dilemma is clear. On balance, new medical technology enhances health outcomes, but not every discovery results in an improvement in efficiency or quality of care. Given the nature of the research and development process, it is difficult to determine ex ante what innovations will be worth the added cost. The stakes are high. Worldwide expenditures on medical R&D are forecast to reach $260 billion by 2006. Market forces will dictate that innovations not only improve the quality of care, but also provide cost-effective treatments in a market increasingly dominated by cost-conscious payers.

In this chapter we will discuss the extreme cost pressures that advances in medical technology have placed on the medical care delivery systems in the United States and around the world. First, we will examine how **technological change** in medicine is diffused throughout the system. After a brief discussion of the economic theory of technological change, we will look into the cost implications in the health care industry and the role of insurance in creating incentives for research and development. Two case studies on the effect of technological change on the medical care industry will then be presented: advances in organ transplantation and research and development in the pharmaceutical industry. The final section will provide a summary and conclusions concerning the technology dilemma facing the medical care industry.

technological change
Any invention, innovation, or diffusion of knowledge that improves products or processes, typically measured in terms of increased productivity or economic growth.

The Diffusion of New Technology

Over the last 50 years, new technologies have changed the nature of medical practice. Physicians are no longer interested in, nor patients content with, a medical focus on caring for the sick and infirm. Medical practitioners are equipped to cure, and patients demand as much. The vast majority of the medical technology available in today's modern medical setting did not exist a half century ago. Current medical facilities would seem almost primitive without the technologically advanced diagnostic and surgical procedures now common in most of the developed world. Organ transplantation, open-heart surgery, diagnostic imaging, sophisticated cancer therapies, and in vitro fertilization are all part of the practitioner's arsenal to combat disease and other physical shortcomings. In the pharmaceutical industry alone, about 10 percent of the 200 top-selling drugs are new each year; and less than 25 percent of the drugs on that list 20 years ago are still there today.

The demand for new medical technology has created an increased demand for new ways to finance these improvements in medicine. Since the Second World War, the percentage of the U.S. population covered by some form of health insurance has risen from 10 percent to 85 percent. This growth in insurance coverage has extended the use of the new technologies to otherwise unreachable segments of the population, resulting in profit opportunities for their developers. As the potential for profits has increased, the expenditures on research and development in search of new technologies have also increased.

The Economics of Technological Change

Neoclassical economics loosely defines technological change as any invention, innovation, or diffusion of knowledge that improves products or processes. Technological change usually has cost or quality implications and is typically measured in terms of increased productivity or economic growth. In most cases, we think of technological change in terms of process innovation that lowers the cost of producing an existing product or service. Improvements in productivity are depicted by leftward shifts in the isoquant map as shown in left side of Figure 13.1. The isoquant Q_0 illustrates the alternative combinations of labor and capital that may be used to produce Q_0 units of output at a cost shown by the isocost curve I_0I_0. Cost-decreasing technological change allows the same output level to be produced with fewer inputs. The isoquant Q'_0 is drawn closer to the origin and tangent to a lower isocost curve I_1I_1.

Economists usually talk about technological change in terms of neutral or non-neutral change. Neutral change results in proportionate improvements in the marginal products of all inputs in the production process. Non-neutral change increases the

marginal products of some inputs more than others. Although interesting, neutral versus non-neutral technological change is not the most important issue facing health care policymakers. The really important issue is the impact of technological change on quality and cost. Often, technological improvements in medicine result in better outcomes for patients. Sophisticated technology often comes with a higher price tag.

Cost-increasing technological change is illustrated on the right side of Figure 13.1. Q_0 patients may be treated at a cost depicted by isocost curve I_0I_0. The higher isoquant Q'_0 and the higher isocost curve I_1I_1 show quality improvements that raise costs. But higher costs do not guarantee that all technological change improves outcomes. Therein lies the dilemma facing policymakers.

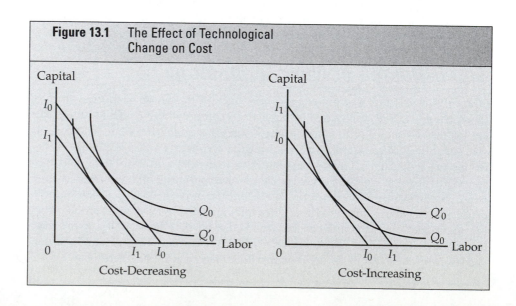

Figure 13.1   The Effect of Technological Change on Cost

Has innovation in medicine been cost-decreasing or cost-increasing? Research by Scitovsky (1985) seems to indicate that the question may have two answers. Advances in treating the common, everyday problems such as ear infections in children, simple fractures, and pulmonary infections seem to be cost-decreasing. In contrast, changes in the way more complicated problems are treated, such as heart attacks and breast cancer, tend to increase costs substantially.

How much of our increased spending is due to technological change? Newhouse (1992) argues that although it is difficult to determine, a large number of health experts view technological change as a primary cause of high health care spending.

The Levels of Technology

Progress in medicine may be categorized according to three levels of technology: **nontechnology**, **halfway technology**, and **high technology** (Thomas, 1975; Weisbrod, 1991). Nontechnology provides medical practitioners with the means of helping patients cope with illnesses that have no known cure. In the early 1980s, little was known about the treatment for AIDS. Given the nature of the disease, little could be done for patients beyond hospitalization and palliative care. No matter what was tried, the disease would run its course and the patient would die.

Halfway technology represents the next level of medical progress. At this level, medical practitioners treat patients who have a particular disease by trying to postpone its ill effects. Surgery, radiation treatment, and chemotherapy are halfway technologies directed at established cancer cells. Organ transplantation in the case of end-stage renal disease (ESRD) and the various drug combinations used in the treatment of AIDS are two treatments that fall into this category.

Recent advances in surgical techniques have shown positive results in terms of reduced pain, lower risk, shorter hospital stays, and faster recovery and rehabilitation. Whether this translates into an overall cost savings has yet to be determined systematically. Laparoscopic surgery is a less invasive alternative for many common surgeries. It is frequently used in ligament and cartilage repairs and for certain abdominal operations including gall bladder surgery, hernia repair, appendectomies, and hysterectomies. The principles are simple. A working space is established in the body cavity by inflating the peritoneal cavity with carbon dioxide. The laparoscope, a high-resolution video camera with 5–15 magnification, is inserted into the abdomen through an incision near the belly button. Instrumentation and lighting are introduced into the working space via a third incision. Unit costs are lower, even with longer surgical times at $1,200 per hour for operating room use, which presents a real dilemma for policymakers. Less invasive surgery is more patient friendly, meaning less pain and discomfort and shorter recovery periods. Patients interpret laparoscopic surgery as a higher quality alternative, prompting a greater demand for the procedure. For many surgeries, the higher volume offsets any unit cost savings and overall spending increases.

Finally, high technology becomes available when scientists understand the disease mechanisms and develop treatments that either prevent or cure the malady. High technology constitutes a shift in attention from the consequences of a disease to its causes. Immunizations for protecting individuals against contracting a disease and antibiotics for the treatment of bacterial infections are examples of high technology. The development of the small pox and polio vaccines took science to this level in the treatment of those two diseases. Tragically, at this stage in our medical knowledge, no high technology alternative has been established for the treatment of cancer, heart disease, or AIDS, contributing to the high cost of treatment in each case.

The process of technological change can be reasonably viewed as a series of events that lead us sequentially through these three stages of technology. The nature of the disease, the state of scientific knowledge, and the amount of resources devoted to research and development determine the length of time we remain at any one stage in this dynamic process. Though unverified empirically, it is theoretically plausible to assume that the

nontechnology
Medical intervention providing practitioners with the means of helping patients cope with illnesses that have no known cure.

halfway technology
The means of treating patients who have a particular disease by trying to postpone its ill effects. Surgery, radiation treatment, and chemotherapy are halfway technologies directed at established cancer cells.

high technology
Medical treatments that either prevent or cure a disease or malady.

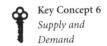
Key Concept 6
Supply and Demand

ISSUES IN MEDICAL CARE DELIVERY

THE HIGH COST OF "CABBAGES"

Nothing seems to attract the attention of the American public like the health of high-profile celebrities. Bob Dole and Rafael Palmeiro have become the spokespersons for Viagra. Katie Couric has joined the campaign against colon cancer and even went as far as televising her own colonoscopy. *Late Show* host David Letterman profiled the entire medical team who performed his much publicized quintuple heart bypass surgery. The one thing all these procedures have in common is their high cost. As recently as 1999, the average medical bill for a coronary artery bypass graft surgery (CABG, pronounced "cabbage") performed in the United States was around $30,000, including the surgeon's fee of around $5,000. This procedure, which requires a neck-to-naval incision in the patient's chest, sawing through the ribcage, and cracking open the chest, is available today only because of the advances in medical technology, including the cardiopulmonary bypass pump that serves to reoxygenate and circulate the patient's blood while the heart is stopped. The total expenditures for the 350,000 bypass surgeries performed every year is in excess of $10 billion.

The surgical alternative to the bypass operation is a procedure known as balloon angioplasty. In this procedure a cardiologist threads a tiny balloon into the clogged artery and inflates it to eliminate the blockage. Over 2 million are performed worldwide each year (almost 1 million in the United States alone), and the number is increasing at over 8 percent per year. Although less invasive, approximately 40 percent fail within the first six months (a process known as restenosis), requiring a repeat procedure or bypass surgery. (The failure rate has been reduced by 75 percent by introducing a small dose of radiation at the site of the blockage.)

Other less invasive surgical procedures for patients with less severe blockages are currently being tested. A "closed chest" technique developed by Intuitive Surgical, Inc. of Mountain View, California, uses a robotic device to perform endoscopic surgery on a beating heart. The surgeon performs the entire operation through three small incisions on the left side of the chest used to insert the surgical instruments and a video camera. The da Vinci system consists of a viewing and control console along with a robotic arm unit that positions the surgical instruments. The technique, used primarily in Germany at this time, is relatively expensive due to the high cost of the technology. Costs are expected to come down as more surgeries are performed and the system is shared with other disciplines. Smaller incisions mean less trauma to the patient, shorter hospital stays, and shorter recovery times. Proponents expect 1- to 2-day hospital stays with 1- to 2-week recovery periods compared with 4- to 7-day stays and up to a 3-month recovery period typical with traditional bypass surgery. The less-invasive alternatives to traditional open-heart surgery have as their goal similar outcomes at lower cost (Dodson, 2000).

Rival equipment makers competing for market share are fueling the excitement over the new techniques. On the buyers' side, insurance carriers that once paid the entire bill are routinely demanding and receiving huge discounts. As the price of a product or procedure continues to climb, purchasers begin seeking and demanding lower-cost alternatives.

Sources: Ron Winslow, "Surgeons Try New Ways to Fix the Heart," *The Wall Street Journal,* September 5, 1995, B1; "Hope and Hype Follow Heart-Surgery Method That's Easy on Patients," *The Wall Street Journal,* April 22, 1997, A1, A10; and Marcida Dodson, "Robot-Assisted Heart Bypass is Safe, Better for Patients, Researcher Says," *MDI Online,* http://www.medicaldata.com/members/mit/detail.asp?art=11160005&MITUID=204586, *Medical Industry Today,* November 16, 2000.

Key Concept 2
*Opportunity
Cost*

costs associated with any particular disease increase as treatment moves from nontechnology to halfway technology and then decrease as high technology is introduced.

There is no better example of this than the evolution of the treatment for polio. In the nontechnology state, victims of the disease died quickly of paralysis. There was little that medical science could do about the progression of the disease and costs were minimal. Science soon developed the halfway technology of the iron lung that prolonged life, but did nothing about the disease. Overall spending was much higher at this stage of technology. Finally, the introduction of the Salk and Sabin vaccines virtually eliminated polio from the United States and dramatically reduced the costs associated with the disease.

Growing evidence indicates that the dynamic process of technological change in medicine has been concentrated at the level of halfway technology.[1] The result is that technological change in health care has tended to be cost-increasing, especially with respect to many surgical and diagnostic procedures. Overall, expenditures increase as the technology improves and its use expands to include ever more complex cases.

The Role of Insurance in the Diffusion of Technology

To understand this link between technology and medical spending, one need only examine the incentive structure established by the medical care financing system. Most economists contend that the system of financing medical care has a profound effect on medical research and development (Weisbrod, 1991). Not only does medical technology expand the alternatives for treating certain diseases, it changes the very definition of disease. Conditions that were once considered outside the purview of the medical care system are now defined as illnesses.[2] An expanding definition of medical care places growing pressure on the financing mechanism to extend the availability of the new technology to an ever-growing segment of the patient population.

Until recently, medical care financing was dominated by a system of reimbursement that did not encourage cost savings. To the contrary, it encouraged the expansion of costly technology, even in cases where medical outcomes were only marginally improved. The increased availability of insurance has led to the widespread availability of medical technology and improved the prospects for additional profits to those developing even costlier treatments. Only recently has the incentive structure tilted away from encouraging cost-increasing halfway technology toward encouraging potentially cost-saving high technology.

http://

Infertility Resources is developed and maintained by Internet Health Resources Company and provides articles, services, and discussions of various infertility issues and treatments.
http://www.ihr.com/infertility/

Policy Issue

The availability of health insurance and the expanding definition of what constitutes health care have combined to create an environment where the expansion of costly technology is encouraged and rewarded.

The Case of Organ Transplantation

Organ transplantation provides a good illustration of the high cost of halfway technology. Successful organ transplantation is possibly the most remarkable advance in medical science in recent years. The ability to transplant body parts may have evoked horror in the minds of the readers of Mary Shelley's *Frankenstein* in the early nineteenth century. But today's audiences are less concerned with the prospect of science-run-amok and more conscious of the potential benefits of being able to improve the quality of life for thousands of individuals in need of functioning hearts, kidneys, livers, lungs, and other vital organs.

History of Organ Transplantation

The early history of organ transplantation was characterized by the inability of the scientific community to come up with a way to counter the human body's tendency to reject a foreign organ. Thus, the most consistently successful transplants were skin grafts from one part of a person's body to another and skin grafts between identical twins. The first cornea transplant from a cadaver donor took place in 1905, but because of the problem

---

1 The major exception to this statement is research and development in the biotechnology industry.
2 Success in the treatment of infertility with in vitro fertilization is a good example of the expanding definition of "illness."

ISSUES IN MEDICAL CARE DELIVERY

TREATING INFERTILITY

You meet Mr. or Miss right, fall in love, get married, have kids, and live happily ever after. It always happens that way in the storybooks, right? Many couples see their storybook romance short-circuited by the inability to conceive. In fact, over one million couples annually seek treatment for infertility. After all those years of trying not to get pregnant, now when it's finally time to start a family, suddenly you can't get pregnant. Faced with the prospect of childlessness, many seek aggressive treatment to deal with their reproductive deficiencies.

The standard treatment for infertility involves two common elements: induced ovulation and artificial insemination. Human menopausal gonadotropin is used to stimulate the ovaries causing them to produce a number of mature eggs simultaneously. The mature eggs are harvested mechanically and one of several mechanisms is used to combine eggs and sperm to produce human embryos.

The most widely publicized technique for treating infertility is in vitro fertilization (IVF). With IVF, sperm and eggs are combined in a petri dish and the fertilized eggs (usually 2 to 3) are transferred into the fallopian tubes. A number of variants on the IVF technique have been developed to improve the odds of a successful pregnancy. Intra-uterine insemination (IUI) involves the transfer of sperm into the uterus to coincide with the female's normal ovulation. Gamete intrafallopian transfer (GIFT) involves harvesting eggs and sperm and mechanically combining them in the fallopian tubes to more closely mimic the natural process.

The price of progress is high. The average cost of a single cycle of in vitro fertilization in 1992 was $8,000 (in 2001, the costs ranged from $8,000 to $15,000). The probability of delivering a live baby is between 10 and 15 percent on the first cycle, falling by about 1 percentage point per cycle thereafter. Given these odds, Neumann et al. (1994) estimated that the base cost per delivery with IVF was $66,667 for the first cycle (approximately $8,000/0.125) and $114,286 for the sixth cycle. For couples where the female is over age 40 or where there is male-factor infertility, the costs could range as high as $160,000 for a first cycle pregnancy to $800,000 for a sixth cycle pregnancy.

The higher costs do not end with the pregnancy. Assisted pregnancies have a much higher complication rate—more miscarriages, more premature births, lower birth weights, and higher rates of perinatal mortality—with the same result, higher costs. In addition, almost one-quarter of all IVF pregnancies result in multiple births, whereas they occur naturally in less than 1 percent of the total births. Higher-order births are more expensive. Callahan et al. (1994) estimated that the normal singleton birth costs $9,845, compared with $37,947 for twins and $109,765 for triplets.

These high costs highlight the dilemma facing policymakers. High costs increase pressure for insurance coverage to include infertility treatment. Should reproductive deficiencies be treated as a health care issue? The United States is not the only country struggling with this issue. The issue is far from settled in Canada, where Ontario is the only province where IVF is a covered benefit and only for women with bilateral tubal obstruction. As the costs climb and the number of couples seeking assistance increases, the pressures on insurance plans to include infertility treatment as a covered benefit will continue to mount.

Sources: Peter J. Neumann, Soheyla D. Gharib, and Milton C. Weinstein, "The Cost of a Successful Delivery with In Vitro Fertilization," *The New England Journal of Medicine 331(4)*, July 28, 1994, 239–243; Tamara L. Callahan, Janet E. Hall, Susan L. Ettner, Cindy L. Christiansen, Michael F. Greene, and William F. Crowley, Jr., "The Economic Impact of Multiple-Gestation Pregnancies and the Contribution of Assisted-Reproduction Techniques in Their Incidence," *The New England Journal of Medicine 331(4)*, July 28, 1994, 244–249; and John A. Collins, "Reproductive Technology—The Price of Progress," *The New England Journal of Medicine 331(4)*, July 28, 1994, 270–271.

Policy Issue

Should infertility be treated as a health care issue and should it be a covered benefit in the standard health insurance policy?

Key Concept 1
Scarcity and Choice

of tissue rejection, blood transfusions became the most promising avenue of transplantation research with the first successful transfusion performed in 1918.

Despite the problems, transplantation research continued, and in 1954 the first kidney transplant was performed. Although early outcomes were poor, results improved greatly after 1961 with the discovery of the immunosuppressive drug, azathioprine. Even with this advance, progress was slow. Early immunosuppressive therapy not only reduced the body's natural tendency to reject the transplanted organ, but also simultaneously destroyed the ability to fight off infections. The transplanted organs performed well, but patients were susceptible to common ailments and often died from complications unrelated to the transplant itself.

Encouraged by the prospects for even better immunosuppressive drugs, transplant research progressed cautiously. Further advances in medical technology enabled surgeons to perform the first successful heart transplant in 1967. Although survival rates were steadily improving, the inability to fight common infections was still the major problem facing transplant patients. For the next decade, the transplant community rode an emotional roller coaster, with hopes raised by one piece of promising immunosuppressive research only to be dashed by subsequent findings. Understandably, the accidental discovery of the immunosuppressive drug cyclosporine by a Swiss scientist in 1979 was greeted with a bit of healthy skepticism.

Clinical trials with cyclosporine began in the United States in 1980. Improved clinical results were experienced immediately—better graft survival, fewer episodes of tissue rejection, and shorter hospital stays. Professional skepticism abated as it became obvious that a new era in transplant surgery had begun. The medical community's new optimism led to the regular transplantation of the lung, heart/lung, and liver. Between 1981 and 1985, the frequency of these procedures increased 2,000 percent; from 31 transplant operations to 634 (see Table 13.1). Heart and kidney transplant recipients also benefited with heart transplants increasing from 62 to 719 per year and kidney transplants from 4,883 to 7,695.

As is the case with most medical procedures, increased success is followed by increased demand for the service. In addition, further advances in disciplines related to transplantation—immunology, histocompatability, organ preservation, and surgery— have contributed to an expansion in the population that can benefit from a transplant. In fact, growth in the use of the procedure would have been higher if the supply of donated organs were sufficient to meet the demands of the 109,160 Americans waiting for transplants as of March 2003. In fact, one-third of the patients waiting for a liver transplant and almost one-half of patients waiting for lung and intestine transplants died before suitable organs became available. In 2002, total reported deaths of those on all transplant waiting lists numbered 6,122. For all procedures, the number of people on waiting lists surpasses the number actually receiving transplants.

Key Concept 6
Supply and Demand

By 2002, almost 25,000 organ transplants were performed in the United States along with 10,000 bone marrow transplants.[3] One-year survival rates range from just over 60 percent for heart/lung recipients to over 97 percent for those receiving kidneys from living donors.

Current Organ Transplant Policy

The U.S. policy on organ transplantation has been shaped primarily by the National Organ Transplantation Act of 1984. The current concerns over transplant policy can be viewed on two levels. In the broader context, the problem is one of coping with the costs of catastrophic, life-threatening illnesses. Patients faced with the prospects of an organ transplant find themselves in double jeopardy. Not only is their illness life threatening but it also has the prospects of extreme financial disruption or even personal bankruptcy. The 2002 movie *John Q* is a gripping drama of the plight of John Archibald.

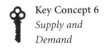

United Network for Organ Sharing (UNOS) Transplantation Information Site provides up-to-date statistics on transplant surgeries nationwide.
http://www.unos.org/

---

3 The average billed price of a bone marrow transplant was $167,200 in 1995.

Table 13.1	Number of U.S. Transplants Performed

Year	Kidney	Pancreas	Kidney/ Pancreas	Liver	Heart	Lung	Heart/Lung	Intestine
1990	9,285	66	452	2,655	2,078	203	52	5
1995	10,952	106	914	3,898	2,339	872	69	46
2000	13,361	435	904	4,920	2,184	957	48	80
2001	14,107	464	884	5,157	2,194	1,054	27	111
2002	14,722	546	903	5,327	2,153	1,042	33	107
Total to date	167,229	3,095	10,485	56,127	32,206	10,069	798	696
Candidates on Waiting List	80,399	1,408	2,420	16,963	3,787	3,804	196	183
1995 Average Billed Price[a]	$92,700	$66,600[b]	$150,000	$280,200	$222,700	$265,100	$264,400[b]	$132,285
Patient survival rate[c]	94.4–97.7							
1-year (%)[d]	89.4–94.9	94.9	na	85.3–88.2	85.1	76.6–72.2	65.7	na
3-year[e]		87.7	na	77.7–80.8	77.8	57.7–50.7	43.2	na

Source: Organ Procurement and Transplantation Network as of March 14, 2003 (**http://www.optn.org**).

a Includes hospital bill, physician fees, organ procurement, medication and all follow-up care for the first year after transplantation.

b 1993 cost (Millman & Robinson, Inc., HIAA, 1997, Table 5.24).

c Cadaveric donor and living donor for kidney, liver, and lung transplants.

d Based on 1999–2001 transplants.

e Based on 1996–1999 transplants.

Insured by a health plan that does not cover transplantation, the movie depicts the extreme actions that a father is willing to take to ensure that his dying son receives the treatment that he needs.

On a more specific level, organ transplantation policy is concerned with organ procurement. As patient survival rates have improved, demand for organs has increased dramatically. Nowhere is this more evident than in the case of kidney transplantation. With the one-year survival rates of 94 to 97 percent (depending on the source of the donor organ), those suffering from end-stage renal disease (ESRD) find a transplant to be a superior alternative to dialysis. Dialysis is time consuming, requiring 15 to 19 hours of treatment per week in two or three lengthy sessions. Transplant recipients are healthier and have fewer restrictions than dialysis patients. As a result, more than three times as many ESRD sufferers are on a waiting list for a transplant than the number who actually receive a transplant. In 2002, there were 14,722 kidneys transplanted in the United States and 80,399 on the waiting list at the end of the year.

Transplant Financing

The issue of funding for organ transplants is significant because of the relative expense of the surgical procedure and the annual cost of immunosuppressive therapy. Including the cost of harvesting the donor organ, the surgical cost of a kidney transplant averaged $92,700 in 1995; heart transplants average $222,700; and a liver transplant $265,100. Add to that the annual cost of antirejection drugs of $6,000 or more for as long as the recipient lives, and you have a very expensive proposition. Although most private insurance will cover the cost of transplants, there are a few exceptions. In

Policy Issue

Should organ transplantation be covered by private insurance? Why is kidney transplantation covered by Medicare's end-stage renal program?

some cases, liver transplants and bone marrow transplants are still considered experimental and are not covered.

The federal government began paying for organ transplants in the mid-1970s. The vast majority of the funding comes from three programs—Medicare, the Veterans Administration, and CHAMPUS (for active-duty military personnel and their dependents). The largest federal program for financing transplants is the ESRD program funded through Medicare. All individuals covered by Social Security suffering from ESRD are eligible for government funding for kidney transplantation and those who are Medicare eligible can get heart transplants.

Third-party payment has contributed to the shortage of available organs by increasing the demand for the procedure. Federal payment for kidney transplants became public policy after it was determined that a transplant was a cheaper treatment alternative to dialysis. Research by Eggers (1988) indicated that a kidney transplant was a more cost-effective treatment than dialysis, saving the ESRD program. Also, the National Health Service in Great Britain estimated that every successful kidney transplant saved the British National Health Service over £30,000 (approximately $45,000 in U.S. dollars) otherwise spent on chronic dialysis.

Extending payment for all categories of transplants may be sound public policy. It is easily categorized as a procedure typifying the **technological imperative**. Prospective recipients are real people with real lives. The technological capability to do something about their life-threatening conditions is available and ought to be used, regardless of ability to pay. The argument can also be made that it is possible to be generous because the additional financial exposure is modest in relative terms. Using data provided by the United Network for Organ Sharing (UNOS), the 1990 cost of meeting the excess demand for the six most common transplant procedures would have added an estimated $1.1 billion to total medical spending that year (see Table 13.2).[4]

technological imperative
The proposition that if a medical procedure is available to treat a problem, it should be utilized. If available for anyone, it should be available for everyone, regardless of ability to pay.

Organ Procurement

The major obstacle to increasing the number of transplants is not financing but the availability of **donable organs**. The majority of transplantable organs come from

donable organ
A human organ harvested from a cadaver or, in some cases, a living person, that is suitable for transplantation.

Table 13.2 | **Medical Costs of Organ Transplantation, 1990**

Organ	Number Transplanted	Estimated Cost[a] (millions)	Estimated Average Cost per Transplant	Number on Waiting List	Estimated Cost If Donor Organs were Available[b]	Total Estimated Cost (millions)
Kidney	9,433	$ 283.0	$ 30,000	17,689	$ 530.7	$ 813.7
Heart	1,998	219.8	110,000	1,761	193.7	413.5
Liver	2,534	582.8	230,000	1,082	248.9	831.7
Heart/Lung	52	10.4	200,000	254	50.8	61.2
Pancreas	529	21.2	40,000	432	17.3	38.5
Lung	187	41.8	218,000	264	59.0	100.8
Total	14,733	$1,159.0	—	21,464	$1,100.4	$2,259.4

Source: *Organ Transplants*, House Hearings, 1991.

a Number transplanted times average cost of the transplant procedure.

b Number on waiting list times average cost of the transplant procedure.

4 Many argue there are potential savings in the system that could be realized to cover these extra costs. For example, it is estimated that there are 10,000 patients in permanent vegetative states being kept alive at an average cost of $100,000. These costs alone amount to $1 billion annually.

brain-dead donors whose body functions are stabilized with the use of mechanical ventilators. Living donors frequently provide kidneys and bone marrow for transplantation. In some cases, portions of a lung or liver have been harvested from a living donor and transplanted into a close relative, usually a child of the donor.[5]

The organ procurement system in the United States is the largest in the world. Approximately 60 organ procurement organizations (OPOs) operate nationwide and are affiliated with over 4,500 community hospitals. These nonprofit organizations have been established to coordinate the efficient and equitable allocation of available organs. In theory, the availability of organs is based on several criteria: tissue match, length of time on the waiting list, and likelihood of success. In reality, there is no incentive for organs to be made available outside the hospital or region of origin. Pressure from Congress may change this tendency, but the overall problem of lack of availability has not yet been solved.

Between 1988 and 2002 the number of people waiting for transplants increased over four times as fast as the number of organ donors.[6] Over that same time period, almost 60,000 people died waiting for an organ transplant. The problem is twofold—a lack of donable organs and a failure of the organ procurement system.

Only about 6,000 to 10,000 people die annually under circumstances that would make them potential organ donors, usually suffering from head trauma. Of this number, approximately one-half actually become donors. Since there are so few potential donors relative to the demand for organs, every one counts.

The pressure to find new organ sources is intense. Medical criteria, such as age of donor and length of time that organs can be stored, are being relaxed to make more organs available. Transplant programs are accepting heart donors up to age 50, instead of the previous age limit of 35 for men and 40 to 45 for women. Preservation efforts have improved and kidneys, previously discarded after only 24 hours, are routinely kept up to 36 hours before transplantation, and in some cases up to 72 hours for particularly difficult tissue matches.

Another potential source of donor organs is the 2,000 to 3,000 anencephalic infants born every year. With most of the upper brain and skull missing, anencephalics will survive only a short period of time. The dilemma in using these infants as donors is that they usually have enough brain stem activity to breathe on their own and are not legally dead. For the organs to be useful, the baby must be placed on a respirator until brain function stops. Otherwise, the lack of oxygen will likely make the organs unusable.

In a desperate attempt to deal with the shortage of usable organs, some transplant centers are even experimenting with **xenografts**, the use of animal organs—specifically, baboon and chimpanzee hearts. Although most specialists do not consider this a long-term solution to the shortage of donable organs, it has kept some patients alive for as long as 20 days until a suitable organ became available.

xenografts
The use of animal organs for transplantation in humans.

Why Is There a Shortage of Donable Organs?

Some would argue that the shortage of organs is due to the reluctance of hospital personnel to bother the families of dying patients about using their organs for transplantation. According to Siminoff et al. (1995), almost 75 percent of the population say they would be willing to donate but only about 50 percent of those asked actually do. This discrepancy may contribute to the shortage. But ask an economist, especially one who is a true believer in the efficiency of markets, why there is an organ shortage and you will likely get a much different answer. From an economic perspective, everybody

---

5 At a press conference following the liver transplant operation of baseball great Mickey Mantle in the summer of 1995, the surgeon was asked if the donor of the liver was still alive. It was obvious to almost everyone in attendance that the question came from someone who knew a lot more about baseball than organ transplants.

6 There were 5,910 organ donors in 1988 with a waiting list at the end of the year standing at 16,026. In 2002, with a waiting list numbering over 80,000, organs were harvested from 12,793 different individuals. More than 6,600 of these were living, usually donating a kidney. (UNOS data as of March 14, 2003).

makes money off transplantation except the person supplying the organ, the most important element in the entire procedure. From a purely economic perspective, the reason for the organ shortage is simple—it is due to the poor assignment of property rights to human body parts. It would be relatively easy to solve the property rights issue if we could resolve the ethical issues that would accompany an open market for organs. Let's tackle the economic issues first. They tend to be the easiest in this case.

Structuring the assignment of property rights to organs can be done in several different ways. The current U.S. policy defining property rights to organs can be described as "required request." Congress institutionalized this structure in the 1986 Budget Reconciliation Act. In theory, this law requires that hospitals must inform transplant centers of all potential donors and hospital staff must discuss the prospects of donating with relatives of the dying patient. In addition, citizens must be given an opportunity to express their willingness to serve as donors when filling out tax forms and applying for drivers' licenses. In practice, doctors may be reluctant to approach grieving relatives, and relatives are reluctant to make organs available even when the loved one has signed a donor card.

In many cases, poor timing of the request is the reason for the family's refusal. Approximately two-thirds of the families of dying patients agree to donate organs when notification of impending death and the request for organs are two separate events. When the two are done simultaneously, the success rate is less than 20 percent.

Other approaches to organ donation are used across Europe. In Great Britain, the Human Tissue Act of 1961 establishes a policy that prospective donors must "contract in" the provision of their organs. In other words, unless a person is carrying a donor card, hospital personnel must presume the person is unwilling to serve as a donor. Most of the rest of Europe takes the opposite approach. "Presumed consent" governs the availability of prospective donors in Austria, the Czech Republic, Denmark, France, Poland, and Switzerland. All individuals are presumed to consent to the use of their organs unless specific instructions state the contrary.

> **Policy Issue**
>
> How should property rights to human organs be assigned?

No one method of organ donation has proved superior to any other and all countries share the same problem—a shortage of donable organs. The methods used throughout the world establish weak property rights in body parts. Individuals and families may give them away, but they may not sell them "for valuable consideration." Like any other market, when the price is held artificially below the equilibrium price, shortages will develop.

 Key Concept 5
Markets and Pricing

Supply and Demand for Donable Organs

Under the current organ procurement system utilized in the United States and most of the world, law limits the supply of donable organs to the number of organs that people are willing to donate without compensation. The economic result becomes quite clear when the system of securing donable kidneys is examined. In 2002, 14,722 kidneys were transplanted, all of which were made available with no payment to the person donating the organ. There were 80,399 people with ESRD on waiting lists to receive a transplant and more than 3,200 who died during the year while on the list. The situation is depicted in Figure 13.2. The demand for kidneys is depicted by the downward-sloping demand curve. The legal sanctions on compensating donors restricts the supply response to a single point on the quantity axis, point a.

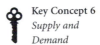 **Key Concept 6**
Supply and Demand

When kidneys are free to the recipient and donors receive no compensation, the quantity of kidneys demanded (95,121) exceeds the quantity supplied (14,722) by over 80,000. With only 14,722 kidneys transplanted, the estimated value (P_0) of a kidney is between \$25,000 and \$40,000.[7] In a free market for kidneys, however, donors would be

---

7 Some countries allow the sale of kidneys from live donors, notably India and Egypt. In these two situations, prices range from \$3,000 to \$5,000—roughly 5 to 10 times the 1991 per capita GDPs of these two countries. Five times U.S. per capita GDP that year would have been well over \$100,000 (Bailey, 1990). More recently, an FBI sting operation in New York City uncovered an attempt to broker organs of executed Chinese prisoners to U.S. transplant patients. Corneas were offered for \$5,000 per pair, livers for \$40,000, and kidneys for \$20,000 each (Gorman, 1998).

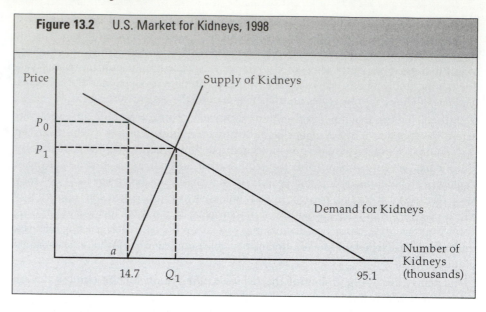

Figure 13.2   U.S. Market for Kidneys, 1998

responsive to changes in the going price of kidneys, and the supply curve would be upward sloping.

As the equilibrium price of a kidney rose from zero, the quantity supplied would increase and the quantity demanded would decrease—but by how much? Some experts estimate that if the price of a kidney (P_1) were $20,000, the number of donable organs would increase by 50 percent and Q_1 would be 22,050 (Simon, 1994).

Establishing Property Rights for Organs

For a market in donable organs to exist, living donors and families of dying patients must have the property rights to organs in order to sell them. Anyone proposing the establishment of strong property rights to human organs must be prepared to navigate an ethical minefield. Convincing the public to accept a market for organs harvested from cadavers is one thing, but allowing even fully informed living donors to sell body parts is not too popular. Donating a kidney to a sick relative is one thing (motivated by altruism), but selling one to the highest bidder smacks of greed or desperation. The trade in human organs would help meet the growing demand for transplantable body parts. It would also leave a certain segment of the population (those at the lower socioeconomic levels) vulnerable to economic manipulation. When faced with the death of a loved one, would they be too quick to "pull the plug" if faced with the prospect of receiving thousands of dollars for the harvested organs? How would a poor parent respond to the offer of $50,000 for an "unnecessary" kidney to be harvested from a son or daughter? What about the pressures on an unwed teenager, pregnant for the second or third time, asked to donate brain tissue and other organs from an aborted fetus for a price? Would we really be better off with a free market in human organs?

At this point in time, popular sentiment does not favor a free market in human organs. Those unwilling to support a strong market approach may be willing to experiment with a weaker version. Barney and Reynolds (1989) define a weak market approach as one in which tax incentives are used to encourage organ donation. This approach would also be compatible with providing subsidies to the donor's estate to cover funeral arrangements.

It is a fact that the current system of allocation, prohibiting all forms of compensation, is characterized by persistent and growing shortages. A market in human organs may solve the shortage problem, but it does not solve any of the ethical concerns shared

Policy Issue

Should a private market for organs be legal in order to increase the number of organs available for transplant?

by many. Do we really want a market where the organ goes to the highest bidder? Is it possible to come up with appropriate forms of compensation that meet with public approval and avoid some of the ethical booby traps? What do we gain? What do we lose?

The Pharmaceutical Industry

Economists began studying the pharmaceutical industry in response to questions that arose from the 1959 Congressional investigations of the Kefauver committee. The main issues that concerned the committee dealt with pricing, profitability, competition, product safety, and outlays for research and development.

Four decades have passed since the Kefauver investigation, but the issues remain the same. Fueled by concern over the high out-of-pocket spending by the elderly and rising government outlays through Medicare and Medicaid, many reformers today are targeting the pharmaceutical industry for more stringent drug-price regulation in an effort to curb overall health care spending.

Investment in the pharmaceutical industry can be characterized as high risk. Even so, rewards for success tend to be in line with other industries after adjusting for the level of risk. Between 1998 and 2002 the pharmaceutical industry consistently outperformed the Standard & Poor's 500. Average profit margins of biotech firms reached 24 percent in 2001, compared with 20 percent for branded pharmaceutical companies, and 16 percent for generic companies. Average profit margins in banking are around 13 percent and those in the real estate industry typically exceed 10 percent.

At the same time, the industry is praised and criticized for its performance; praised as a world leader in developing new chemical entities (NCE) and criticized for its financial success. But the odds of financial success for any one NCE are quite low. Grabowski and Vernon (1990) studied 100 new drugs introduced in the United States during the 1970s and found that only 30 had revenues that covered average expenditures on research and development.

For all the attention that the industry receives in the medical care reform debate, it is actually relatively small, only 9.9 percent of total health expenditures in 2001. Americans spend twice as much on computers and three times as much on automobiles as they do on prescription drugs. That figure is less than every European country except Sweden and Norway and far less than the Japanese, who spend 40 percent more per capita on drugs than Americans. The low percentage spent on pharmaceuticals in the United States is somewhat deceiving since working-aged adults with low hospitalization rates spend 20 to 25 percent of their individual health care dollars on pharmaceuticals. The Centers for Medicare and Medicaid Services (CMS) project national pharmaceutical spending to reach 14 percent of total health care spending by 2010, much closer to levels experienced in the 1950s and 1960s. The reasons for this increased spending are fairly obvious: increased utilization, an aging population, and the introduction of new therapeutic agents for the treatment of chronic conditions affecting the aging population.

Spending on prescription drugs has increased at double-digit rates for the last seven years. In fact, pharmaceutical spending is the fastest-growing component in the health care system, growing at twice the rate of all other health care services. Over one-half of the increase is attributable to eight categories of drugs—cholesterol reduction, arthritis, depression, high blood pressure, chronic pain, ulcer and stomach ailments, antiseizure, and diabetes—or more specifically, 23 individual drugs.

The Structure of the Industry

Traditionally, the United States has relied on private-sector initiative and market mechanisms to influence the direction of research and development in the overall economy. The pharmaceutical industry provides an interesting case study where government and academia have become intimately involved in the process of new product development. As in most cases, the U.S. government sponsors very little **applied research**, the purpose

http://

Pharmaceutical Research and Manufacturers of America (PhRMA) provides facts and figures on pharmaceutical research and drugs in development.
http://www.phrma.org/

http://

National Institutes of Health— one of the world's foremost biomedical research centers, and the Federal focal point for biomedical research in the United States.
http://www.nih.gov

applied research
Research whose purpose is typically the commercialization of a product.

basic research
Research whose purpose is to advance fundamental knowledge.

of which is usually the commercialization of a product. Through a network of nationally owned laboratories, such as the National Institutes of Health (NIH), and through grants to universities, government has taken a direct role in funding **basic research**, the purpose of which is to advance fundamental knowledge.

Basic research is essential. Denison (1985) argues that it is the primary source of the innovative technologies responsible for up to one-third of a nation's economic growth between 1929 and 1982. The U.S. leadership position in pharmaceuticals is due, at least in part, to a commitment to basic research, but ultimately the success of the pharmaceutical industry depends on its ability to discover, develop, and market new drugs.

International Issues

The U.S. supremacy in the development of new drugs is clear. Data from the Pharmaceutical Manufacturers Association reported by Weidenbaum (1993b) show that over 60 percent of the 1,265 new drugs introduced into the U.S. market between 1940 and 1990 were developed by U.S. firms (see Table 13.3). Switzerland was second with 89 new drug introductions, followed by the United Kingdom, Germany, and France. Mexico, with one-fourth the number of new drugs of France, still had twice as many discoveries as Canada. Furthermore, 45 percent of the 152 drugs introduced worldwide between 1975 and 1994 were developed in the United States. The United Kingdom was the country of origin in 14 percent of the cases, Switzerland in 9 percent, and Japan and Germany in 7 percent each (PhRMA, 2000). Europe's once thriving pharmaceutical industry is migrating to the United States. Since 1995, Pharmacia (Sweden), Novartis (Switzerland), Avantis (France/Germany), and GlaxoSmithKline (United Kingdom) have moved some aspect of their operations to the United States.

The Role of Research in the Age of Technology

The pharmaceutical industry relies heavily on research and development to discover new chemical compounds that increase longevity and improve the quality of life. Innovative research and the discovery of new compounds are becoming increasingly

Table 13.3	New Drugs Introduced into the U.S. Market 1940–1990	
Country of Origin	**Number of New Drugs**	**Percentage**
United States	764.0	60.4
Switzerland	89.0	7.0
United Kingdom	81.5	6.4
West Germany	73.0	5.8
France	39.5	3.1
Japan	26.5	2.1
Belgium	23.0	1.8
Sweden	18.5	1.5
Denmark	17.5	1.4
Holland	15.0	1.2
Italy	13.4	1.0
Mexico	10.0	0.8
Canada	5.0	0.4
Other Countries	14.0	1.1
Source not ascertained	75.0	6.0
Total	1,265	100.0

Source: Weidenbaum (1993b).

important in a world where government price controls are responsible for falling prices in many markets. Research and development (R&D) spending was $30.3 billion in 2001, up 16.6 percent over 2000 levels. Biotech firms spent an additional $15.6 billion that same year (CMS, 2003). With over 75 percent of the world's total R&D in pharmaceuticals concentrated in the United States, firms either innovate or they do not survive.

The introduction of new drugs has been shown to be a major determinant in profitability (Baily, 1972). The longer a drug is on the market, the lower its **return on sales**. Firms earn normal profits on older drugs and higher profits on newer drugs. The importance of discovering new chemical compounds leads pharmaceutical firms to spend a large percentage of their sales on research and development. Branded pharmaceutical companies spend an average of 13 percent on R&D, while biotech firms spend an average of 25 percent, a figure that is much higher than other technology-based industries. In comparison, the aerospace and defense industry spends 3.9 percent and the telecommunications industry spends 6.4 percent. The U.S. industry average, excluding drugs and medicine, is only 4.1 percent. In 1997, nine of the top twenty U.S. corporations ranked according to R&D spending were pharmaceutical companies.

The U.S. Food and Drug Administration (FDA) approved 89 new medicines in 2002, including 17 new molecular entities (NMEs), 9 new biologics, and 63 new medicines. In addition, 172 new indications for previously approved medicines were also approved. The 26 NMEs and biologics approved in 2002 target 18 different diseases affecting millions people worldwide. They include new treatments for hepatitis B and C, migraine headaches, schizophrenia, arthiritis, multiple sclerosis, and irritable bowel syndrome. The FDA has approved over 500 new drugs for use in the United States since 1980. Of that number only about 20 have been withdrawn for safety reasons.[8]

Prior to the mid-1970s, pharmaceutical research was mainly conducted on the basis of trial and error. Natural compounds would be extracted from dirt samples or plants and then injected into animals to see what would happen. As many as 60,000 compounds might be tried in order to develop a drug with annual sales of $100 million. Not until the late 1970s did scientists begin to understand the role of receptors in the body that block or trigger biochemical responses. It then became possible to fashion molecules to fit those receptors. One of the first chemical compounds to be developed this way was Tagamet, developed by SmithKline. This ulcer medication works by blocking a histamine receptor in the intestines that triggers the secretion of acid. It has proven far more effective than ordinary antacids, virtually eliminating the need for ulcer surgery. In 1986, less than 10 years after its introduction, Tagamet became the first billion-dollar-a-year drug in worldwide sales. By 1992 four drugs had reached this blockbuster status. In 1998 there were 29 and in 2000 there were 55. In 2001 the top selling drugs worldwide were Merck's Zocor with sales of $4.7 billion and Pfizer's Lipitor with sales of $4.4 billion.

The R&D Process

The profit potential for successful new drugs is exceptionally good. This is due, at least in part, to the patent protection that grants monopoly rights to the firm that discovers an NCE. This high-profit potential is offset to a large degree by the low probability that a chemical compound will find its way onto the shelves of the local pharmacy. The odds of getting a new drug approved by the Food and Drug Administration (FDA) are extremely low. For every 5,000 compounds evaluated, five enter human trials, and only one is approved for use. The odds of making a profit on an approved drug are even lower, with only 30 percent generating enough sales to cover average R&D expenditures.

The R&D process for a typical drug approval takes about 12 years, almost two times the 6.5 years it took in 1964. Testing progresses sequentially with the drug's status

return on sales
A financial measure of a firm's ability to generate after-tax profit out of its total sales. Calculated by dividing after-tax profit by total sales.

Activities of the U.S. Food and Drug Administration may be found at
http://www.fda.gov/.

Center for Genome Research at the Whitehead Institute for Biomedical Research in Cambridge, Massachusetts, contains information on the entire Genome project.
http://www.broad.mit.edu

---

8 Of these withdrawals, Bayer's $500 million cholesterol lowering drug Baycol was the most recent casualty, withdrawn because of complications associated with its use. Baycol use was linked to over 100 deaths and 1,700 suspected cases of rhabdomyolysis worldwide.

ISSUES IN MEDICAL CARE DELIVERY

ORPHAN DRUGS

Given the expense of developing new drugs, pharmaceutical firms seek to protect the rights to intellectual property through the use of **patent** law. Patents provide exclusive rights to the production of a product for a specified time period—usually 20 years. The long developmental period for the typical drug (12 to 15 years) means that the market benefit of the patent is usually only around 5 to 8 years.

The one important exception to this rule emerges when firms pursue "orphan drug" status for drugs used to treat rare diseases (defined by the FDA as those affecting fewer than 200,000 U.S. patients). Congress passed the Orphan Drug Act in 1983 to encourage the development of drugs that have limited commercial value. The status carries with it the exclusive marketing rights to the drug. As amended in 1984, the act makes it easier for firms to get orphan status for drugs that have market potential. For example, the drug Taxol (made from the bark of the Pacific yew tree) was approved for the treatment of ovarian cancer in 1992. With only 30,000 women affected by the cancer, orphan drug status seemed to make sense. Even before Taxol was designated an orphan drug, however, it was clear that its full market potential extended well beyond the treatment of ovarian cancer. The American Cancer Society has speculated that Taxol's commercial potential extends to other cancers—including malignant melanoma, breast cancer, and lung cancer—with over 300,000 potential beneficiaries. Taxol's 2001 U.S. sales were over $500 million.

Firms that receive orphan drug status for compounds that would have been developed without it stand to receive substantial economic rents—payments in excess of the minimum necessary to guarantee production. Granted, some drugs would never be developed without the provision of this status. But two of the top-selling biotech drugs—Epogen and Protropin—are orphan drugs. (Epogen's sales are approximately $2 billion per year, making it the most successful biotech drug on the market.)

Source: Suzanne Tregarthen, "Pharmaceutical Firms Seek Monopoly Protection from the U.S. Government," *The Margin*, Fall 1992, 50–51. *CMS Health Care Industry Market Update: Pharmaceuticals*, January 10, 2003, available at http://www.cms.hhs.gov/marketupdate.

reviewed periodically to determine whether the process will continue. Table 13.4 summarizes the steps in the pharmaceutical R&D process.

The preclinical phase of the R&D process includes a significant amount of discovery research undertaken to develop new concepts in treating diseases. This phase includes the

Table 13.4	Steps in the Pharmaceutical R&D Process

Testing Phase	Mean Phase Length (Years)
Preclinical	4.3
Phase I	1.0
Phase II	2.2
Phase III	2.8
FDA Review	1.5
Animal Testing	3.0*
Total Testing	11.8

Source: DiMasi et al. (2003).
*Conducted simultaneously with Phases I and II (DiMasi et al., 1991).

ISSUES IN MEDICAL CARE DELIVERY

BIOTECHNOLOGY: WHAT IS A FAIR PRICE?

The images that we have of gene splicing are, for the most part, the products of Hollywood movie magic. Cloning dinosaurs from DNA fragments in prehistoric mosquitoes makes good science fiction, but a more realistic assessment of the current state of biotechnological research reveals the potential for far more important commercial applications.

Biotechnology is an attempt to understand the basic function of the human body and disease. As an industry, biotechnology is relatively new. In the early 1970s scientists developed the capability of identifying specific genes and harnessing them to make the specific proteins the body uses to protect itself against disease. A 1980 Supreme Court ruling paved the way for the creation of biotechnology as an industry. The court ruled that scientists could patent the new life forms developed when genes were spliced into other organisms or cells.

Today over 1,300 biotech firms exist, employing over 100,000 nationwide. The industry has yet to turn a profit; however, investors are pouring billions in equity capital every year in search of the cures for such diseases as cancer, AIDS, and heart disease. The price of success is high. Amgen, Inc., sells a year's supply of EPO, a protein that counters anemia, for $4,000 to $6,000. The price of the human growth hormone sold by Genentech, Inc., can run as high as $18,000 per year.

No single product epitomizes the drug-pricing dilemma better than Ceredase, produced by Genzyme Corporation as a treatment for Gaucher's disease. Gaucher's disease is a rare genetic disorder in which the body fails to produce an essential enzyme to break down fat deposits in cells. If left untreated, body functions degenerate, vital organs enlarge, and joints deteriorate. Ceredase provides the enzyme, reversing any damage, but at an average cost of $150,000 per year (as high as $300,000 per year early in the treatment of the disease). Ceredase is expensive to produce. Extracted from human placentas, it takes 20,000 placentas or about 27 tons of afterbirth to produce a year's supply for one person. About 1,100 patients are currently being treated for the disorder, requiring 30,000 tons of placentas annually.

Given the high cost of production, Genzyme reached a break-even point on the drug in 1994, recovering its development costs. By the time the patent expired in 2002, the company was earning a 25 percent after-tax return on its investment. Is a 25 percent return too high, or is it needed to attract investors? Critics contend that the federal government's National Institutes of Health performed much of the scientific research and that Genzyme had what amounted to "a sure thing." In 1994, Genzyme developed a genetically engineered version of the drug, Cerezyme, that targeted the disease process itself. Both Ceredase and Cerezyme were developed as orphan drugs and are therefore very expensive.

Biotechnology as an industry is barely 20 years old. As new genetic discoveries are made, their economic implications are not always obvious. Discovery through basic research is one thing. Commercial application is a separate and oftentimes more complex issue. What is a fair price? Ask the sufferers of Gaucher's disease who are spared the costly surgeries to repair damage to vital organs and joints.

Sources: Elyse Tanouye, "What's Fair?" *The Wall Street Journal*, May 20, 1994, R11; Michael Waldholz, "An Industry in Adolescence," *The Wall Street Journal*, May 20, 1994, R4, and Genzyme's Web site **http://www.genzyme.com**.

Key Concept 5
Markets and Pricing

synthesis and extraction of a new chemical compound to determine whether it brings about the desired change in a biological system. After the new compound is synthesized it is screened for pharmacological activity and toxicity in the laboratory. For every 5,000 compounds synthesized, approximately five percent, or 250, are later tested in animals

(Weidenbaum, 1993b). When a promising compound is identified, firms will file an Investigational New Drug Application (IND) with the FDA. After 30 days, the firm will be allowed to begin three phases of clinical testing on humans.

The FDA approves approximately two percent, or only five of the 250 compounds tested in animals, for the three phases of human testing. Phase I testing is performed on a small number of healthy volunteers (usually 20 to 100) to determine the drug's safety profile—its toxicity to humans, absorption and distribution rates, safe dosage levels, metabolic effects, and other information needed to establish human tolerance to the compound. Phase II evaluation is the first of two controlled clinical trials conducted on a small number of volunteer patients the drug is intended to benefit (between 100 and 500). Efficacy and safety are the primary issues examined during this phase. The final development phase involves large-scale testing in hospital and outpatient settings and usually involves 1,000 to 5,000 patients. By using a large number of patients, Phase III testing gathers essential effectiveness and safety information by approximating the actual manner of usage in the event that marketing approval is eventually granted by the FDA.

Throughout the clinical testing period, additional long-term toxicology experiments on animals are performed. The purpose of these experiments is to determine the teratologic and carcinogenic effects of the compounds. At the same time, formulation work and process development are conducted to determine if the compound can be manufactured in quantities that are sufficient to satisfy potential demand for the drug. If the firm is satisfied with the evidence compiled from the clinical studies, it will submit a New Drug Application (NDA) to the FDA. The NDA typically runs over 100,000 pages and contains all the scientific information gathered during the clinical trials. By law the FDA is allowed six months to review each NDA. In practice the process takes over two and one-half years. The FDA ultimately approves for human use only one out of five compounds that reach the clinical trial stage.

The entire process is long and expensive. DiMasi et al. (2003) studied 538 investigational drugs first tested on humans between 1983 and 1994, out of which only 15 percent had been approved for marketing. They estimated the average out-of-pocket cost for a new approved drug was $403 million and the fully capitalized cost was $802 million in 2000. With costs growing at a compound rate of 7.4 percent, drug research initiated in 2001 will cost $970 million in out-of-pocket spending and $1.9 billion in fully capitalized costs over the 12-year period prior to FDA approval.

Drug Therapy: Price and Value

The cost of producing modern pharmaceutical drugs is high, but the relevant question is: Are they worth the high cost? If drug therapy reduces the need for more expensive treatments such as surgery, hospitalization, and long-term care, then it may be worth the price. The estimates in Table 13.5 show that for three disease categories—ulcers, heart disease, and gallstones—the cost of drug treatment ranges from less than one percent to 8.3 percent of the cost of surgery. More recent estimates by Lichtenberg (2001) indicate that more recently introduced drugs reduce all types of nondrug medical

Key Concept 2
Opportunity Cost

Table 13.5	The Cost of Drug Therapy vs. Surgery Three Disease Categories		
Disease Category	**Cost of Surgery**	**Cost of Drug Therapy**	**Drug Therapy as Percent of Surgery**
Ulcers	$28,900	$ 900	3.1
Heart Disease	43,370	300	0.7
Gallstones	12,000	1,000	8.3

Source: Murray Weidenbaum, "Are Drug Prices Too High?" *The Public Interest* 112, Summer 1993.

ISSUES IN MEDICAL CARE DELIVERY

GENE-BASED RESEARCH

Almost all of the new chemical entities discovered to date act on proteins, the chemicals that do the work in all living cells. But advances in basic research have pharmaceutical companies changing their focus to the development of drugs that act directly on human genes, not just the chemicals they produce.

A $3 billion international research effort called the Human Genome Project was undertaken to decode the estimated 100,000 genes that make up the human structure. As scientists discovered new genes, they were able to identify the molecular causes of certain inherited disorders and the way genes trigger common illnesses. In 1980, only 40 genes were known. In 2000, the project was declared complete. Recent discoveries include genes linked to lung cancer, osteoporosis, and Alzheimer's disease.

The basic notion behind gene research is that a defective gene—one that fails to produce a protein when it should or produces one when it should not—causes all illness. With the proper understanding of the genetic code, scientists hope to switch on genes to produce therapeutic proteins (gene therapy) and switch off genes so that they stop making harmful ones (gene blocking).

Despite the fact that over 1,500 disease-related genes have been isolated, there is no conclusive scientific evidence that gene therapy works. Still, the pharmaceutical industry is risking large sums of money betting that it will pay off in the future. While the cost-savings potential is enormous, we may be years away from a developed technology. The near-term market potential is highly speculative at this time; industry analysts estimate that sales could be upwards of tens of billions of dollars within the next two decades. Each gene produces its own protein, and each new protein is a potential new drug.

Sources: Clive Cookson, "Poised for the Big Switch-Off," *Financial Times*, April 22, 1993; and Laura Johannes, "Detailed Map of Genome is Now Ready," *The Wall Street Journal*, December 22, 1995, B1, B11.

---

spending by almost $4 for every $1 spent on the drug, 89 percent of which is due to a reduction in inpatient hospital expense.

The discovery of medicines to cure or significantly alter the progression of chronic and degenerative diseases represents the single best prescription for increasing profitability in the industry. Increased competition and government oversight have resulted in an environment where innovation is the key to survival. Finding a drug that deals effectively with diseases such as cancer, Alzheimer's disease, arthritis, and AIDS will not only save money, but will ensure healthy profit margins for the successful innovators.[9]

> **Policy Issue**
> Do pharmaceutical companies make too much money? Should government control drug prices?

Advertising and Promotion

Pharmaceutical companies have quickly learned the power of marketing. The industry spent $19.1 billion on marketing its products in 2001, up 22 percent over 2000 levels. For all the money spent on research and development, many pharmaceutical firms (especially those that specialize in copycat drugs) spend twice as much on administration and marketing. It is not uncommon for new drugs to sell at wholesale prices that are three to six times higher than their costs of production. These unusually high gross profit margins allow the drug companies to funnel large sums of money into advertising and promotion.

---

9 The Administration on Aging reports that almost $50 billion is spent annually on nursing home care for the elderly. In 1991, 13 drugs were under development to treat Alzheimer's disease alone. If one of these drugs would allow 10 percent of those affected to be treated at home, over $9 billion could be saved.

Policy Issue

Is it good policy to allow direct-to-consumer advertising for prescription drugs?

Key Concept 3
*Marginal
Analysis*

Most of the sales efforts are directed at providers—sending pharmaceutical representatives to see physicians, providing free samples, sponsoring seminars, and funding research—to educate them about the benefits of drugs.[10]

Although most pharmaceutical advertising is directed at physicians, the fastest growing segment is advertising directed at the end consumers. This so-called "direct to consumer" (DTC) advertising reached almost $600 million in 1996 and rose to $2.7 billion in 2001, approximately 14 percent of the total cost of promotion and advertising. This activity, essentially illegal prior to 1996, has been sparked by a new FDA policy that allows television advertising to provide information on the benefits of specific drugs by name without also listing all of the side effects and warnings that normally accompany print ads. Wording is still under consideration for the so-called "major statement" of risks similar to the disclosures used in ads for over-the-counter drugs. Television commercials are required to list a toll-free telephone number or Web-page address for viewers to contact to get the full disclosure information. Print advertising is unaffected by the new policy.

The new policy is extremely controversial. Pharmaceutical companies have always advertised in medical journals, read primarily by an audience that can understand the details of the disclosure statements. Some critics fear that the new advertising directed at consumers will simply motivate and not educate. The ads can urge consumers to read the fine print of the disclosure statements, call the toll-free number, access the Web site, or consult with a physician. Almost one-half of all physicians report an increase in specific drug requests, but less than 10 percent of patients ask for a specific drug. DTC provides vital information. Most physicians believe that DTC advertising informs and educates patients and the vast majority of patients say ads increase awareness of new drugs and improve communication with physicians about health issues (Moser, 2002).

The strategy has proved to be very effective. According to Jenkins (2000), the $1.8 billion spent in 1999 generated an extra $9 billion in sales. That may seem like a lot of advertising relative to sales, but these are marginal dollars. The advertising is aimed at unsatisfied demand from patients who otherwise would go undiagnosed and untreated. These revenues would not exist without the advertising. Since marginal production costs are a fraction of the selling price, the difference is all profit.

The next time you are watching television and one of these commercials comes on, don't reach for the remote—watch and learn. Notice the products that are being promoted. The pharmaceutical companies are not solely promoting the so-called lifestyle drugs in this manner (Viagra and Rogaine). They are promoting drugs for allergies, arthritis, depression, high cholesterol, asthma, obesity, and many more conditions that go largely untreated. The three most heavily advertised drugs in 2000 were Vioxx ($161 million), Prilosec ($108 million), and Claritin ($100 million). In fact, one-third of the DTC advertising in 2000 was for only ten drugs.[11]

Attracting the marginal patient makes economic sense. More sales will spread the overhead costs of R&D over more users, allowing the pharmaceutical companies to sell at lower prices.

The Role of Government

The FDA has been criticized for being too cautious in the regulatory process and thus causing substantial delays in the approval of new drugs. It is quite common for drugs discovered in U.S. research facilities or by U.S.-controlled firms to be introduced in Europe first and later in the United States. Kaitin et al. (1989) report that of the 155 new drugs introduced in both the United States and the United Kingdom between 1977 and 1987, three-fourths were available first in the United Kingdom. The average

10 Over one-half of all promotional spending is for sampling—providing free drug samples directly to physicians for distribution to their patients (CMS, 2003).

11 Those ten drugs were Vioxx, Prilosec, Claritin, Paxil, Zocor, Viagra, Celebrex, Flonase, Allegra, and Meridia.

Back-of-the-Envelope

PHARMACEUTICAL ADVERTISING: INFORMING OR MERELY PROMOTING?

What is the purpose of pharmaceutical advertising? Does it serve any useful purpose other than promoting a product? One argument subscribes to the notion that advertising provides patients, or their physician-agents, with information on the usefulness of the product. Whether the function is to provide information or merely to promote a consumer item, the economic impact is the same. Either way, it is clear that advertising is meant to change customer perception of the product and shift demand. The diagram shows that advertising expenditures shift the demand curve to the right from D_0 to D_1. As a result, the quantity demanded increases from Q_0 to Q_1.

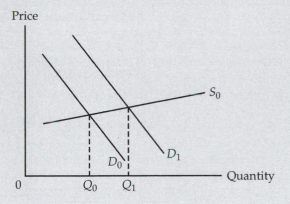

Whether advertising provides information or merely promotes the product, the intended result is more sales and higher prices.

Source: Mark A. Hurwitz and Richard E. Caves, "Persuasion or Information? Promotion and the Shares of Brand Name and Generic Pharmaceuticals," *Journal of Law and Economics* 31(2), October 1988, 299–320.

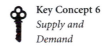

Key Concept 6
Supply and Demand

---

lag between availability in Britain and availability in the United States was five years for respiratory medicines, three years for cardiovascular medicines, and one year for endocrine medicines.

Grabowski and Vernon (1983) examined the trade-off from a statistical perspective. They explained FDA behavior as an attempt to minimize **Type I error**, or mistakenly allowing a harmful drug onto the market before it has been fully tested and determined to be harmful. The success in keeping the drug thalidomide out of the U.S. market in the 1960s is an excellent example of the benefits of minimizing Type I error.[12] The market functions to minimize **Type II error**, or delaying a beneficial drug from reaching the market until its safety and efficacy is fully understood. The cost of delaying a potentially beneficial drug from reaching the market is more difficult to determine. DiMasi et al. (1991) estimated that a one-year reduction in Phase I testing would save $13.5 million in R&D expenditures. That cost does not even begin to take into consideration the vast numbers of people who die prematurely because of FDA delays. Kazman (1990) estimated that 10,000 Americans died prematurely between 1967 and 1976 because of the FDA delay in approving beta blockers for reducing the risk of heart attacks.

A new commissioner at the FDA is attempting to reform the review process at the agency and shorten the average approval times. Appointed in 2002, Mark McClellan is

Type I error
Rejecting a hypothesis that is actually true.

Type II error
Accepting a hypothesis that is actually false.

> *Policy Issue*
> Is the FDA drug approval process too long and costly?

---

12 This tranquilizer, used widely in Europe to combat the symptoms of nausea in pregnant women, was responsible for thousands of serious birth defects where children were born without arms and legs.

Back-of-the-Envelope

GENERIC COMPETITION AND BRAND NAME PRICING

How does competition from a generic substitute affect the pricing of a name-brand drug? Many generics are based on the same chemical compound as their name-brand equivalents and therefore may be considered close substitutes. In theory the impact on pricing should work something line this: The brand-name drug sells for a high price, P_M in the left side of the diagram below. The generic substitute with its lower development costs is priced much lower at P_G.

Based on the theory we expect the introduction of low-price substitutes to cause the level of demand for the brand-name drug to fall, which is depicted by a leftward shift in the brand-name demand curve from D_0 to D_1, resulting in a lowering of its price to P'_M. Empirical research by Grabowski and Vernon (1992) supports this prediction—the more substitutes available, the lower the name-brand price.

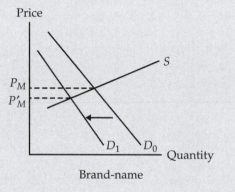

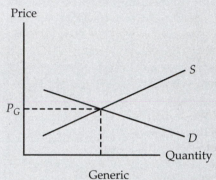

Source: Henry Grabowski and John Vernon, "Brand Loyalty, Entry, and Price Competition in Pharmaceuticals after the 1984 Drug Act," *Journal of Law and Economics 35*(2), October 1992, 331–350.

trained in both economics and medicine. This M.D./Ph.D. has made it clear that he wants to reduce product development costs by cutting average FDA review time from 18 months to 10 months for most drugs and 6 months for priority drugs. McClellan plans to give physicians a greater role in the approval process, a radical idea for any bureaucracy.

Future Directions for the Industry

The pharmaceutical industry has been widely criticized for high markups, high profit margins, and high and rising prices on its most popular products. Data on the 200 most frequently used drugs in 1993 show drug prices increasing at a rate of 3.1 percent. According to Wilkerson and Easton (1993), patient costs for the eight most widely used drugs increased at an average annual rate of 1.6 percent between 1985 and 1992. More recent data provided by IMS America estimate that brand-name drug prices increased 3.4 percent in 1995, compared to the rate of inflation for the economy as a whole that year estimated at 2.8 percent (CMS, 2003). At the same time generic drug prices fell by 12.8 percent. That same year, prices of the top 500 outpatient drugs increased by 4.6 percent.

Consumer advocates and certain members of Congress have long called for aggressive public policy to control the industry's ability to raise prices, thus limiting profitability. According to a U.S. Government Accounting Office (GAO) report (1992), price controls on prescription drugs in Canada have resulted in substantially lower prices there than in the United States. On average, the differential is reported to be 25 percent at the wholesale level. Price controls have had a choking effect on pharmaceutical research in Canada. Since price controls on prescription drugs were adopted in 1969, virtually no new pharmaceutical products have been developed in that country. In general, countries with the most stringent controls on pharmaceutical prices, for example, France and Austria, also do the least amount of research. Another GAO study (1994) compared prices of 77 leading branded pharmaceuticals in the United States and abroad and concluded that U.S. prices are substantially higher than those found in the United Kingdom and other European countries.

Research by Danzon (1994) probes the validity of this finding by examining the methodology on which it is based. Danzon concludes that GAO results are biased toward finding higher prices in the U.S. market. First, GAO research was based on an unrepresentative sample of drugs marketed in the United States. Only one of many possible dosage forms, strengths, and package sizes was included in the pricing survey. Second, it ignored the importance of generics that account for 47 percent of the dispensed prescriptions in the U.S. market in 2001, up from 18.6 percent at the end of 1984 (CMS, 2003). Generic competition in the United States has increased significantly in the last decade. Today, a generic competitor will receive approximately one-half of the new prescription volume in less than two months after its introduction. Generics were quick to enter the market when the two leading ulcer medications lost their patent protection. Tagamet's patent expired in 1994 and Zantac, the largest selling drug worldwide in 1993 with sales of $3.5 billion, began feeling generic competition in 1996 because of patent expiration.[13] Four of the five largest selling drugs in the world have already lost their patent protection. Branded drugs with combined 2001 sales of more than $30 billion lost their patent protection by 2004. Such industry giants as Merck's Vasotec and Pepcid and Lilly's Prozac are included on the list. Finally, the GAO study also ignored the practice of discounting and rebating that is a common practice, especially in managed care, Medicaid, and other government programs.

Danzon's 1996 study of drug prices in nine countries, taking these issues into consideration, reached far different conclusions. When unit prices (price per dose) were compared, Canada, Germany, Switzerland, and Sweden all had higher prices than the United States. Prices in the United Kingdom were 24 percent lower than in the United States (not 60 percent as in the GAO study), and prices in France were even lower.

Opponents of price controls (sometimes referred to as "**spending caps**" in policy discussions) claim that they have been uniformly disastrous, resulting in market distortions, shortages, poor quality, and black markets. In the case of the pharmaceutical industry, they argue that price controls will limit innovation, lower quality and availability, and result in reduced well-being of Americans. Price controls still receive widespread popular support. Proponents focus on the monopoly rents and the high markups, and they have a legitimate case. Who is right? Who is to blame? It is important to study the evidence, understand its implications, and make informed judgments.

spending cap
A limit on total spending for a given time period.

Summary and Conclusions

Much of the criticism of the medical care delivery system in the United States deals with the high levels of overall spending. Analysts agree that one of the primary reasons for increased spending is the third-party payment system. Individuals, patients, and providers fail to practice economizing behavior because there is very little direct benefit to the individual who economizes. The availability of insurance, public or private, and the social mandate of providing free care to those who cannot afford to purchase it themselves result in patients demanding and physicians supplying a level of care that, at the margin, provides little benefit for the resources expended.

Over the past 50 years insurance coverage has expanded to a larger segment of the population, providing a growing array of medical benefits. That expansion has also

---

13 Smith-Kline Beecham launched an aggressive counterattack on generics by releasing an over-the-counter version of its ulcer-treatment drug Tagamet before the expiration date of its patent.

Back-of-the-Envelope

THE ECONOMICS OF REGULATING DRUG PRICES

Advances in pharmaceuticals normally receive patent protection for a period of 20 years. The patent serves as an effective barrier to entry that insulates the firm from competitive pressures and grants monopoly power in the area of pricing practices. It does not mean that the pharmaceutical company can set any price it desires; price changes are still limited by demand. A profit-maximizing pricing strategy may include: establishing different prices in different markets (classic price discrimination), selling at prices that are many multiples of the actual cost of production (price is greater than marginal cost), and enjoying monopoly profits for the life of the patent.

Two additional features may help define the economics of drug pricing—the extremely high fixed costs of research and development and the extraordinarily long product development phase that extends through much of the patent protection period. The results may be shown in the accompanying diagram. The demand for a drug protected by a patent can be depicted by a relatively inelastic demand curve (D). Marginal revenue (MR), marginal cost (MC), average variable cost (AVC), and average total cost (ATC) are defined in the usual manner.

Key Concept 5
Markets and Pricing

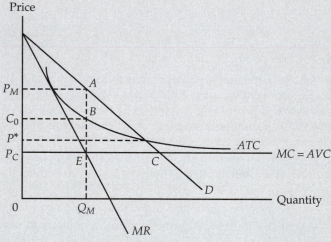

The monopolist first determines the level of output that will maximize profitability (at point E where $MR = MC$). In this case, the profit-maximizing quantity is Q_M. At this level of output, the pharmaceutical company will charge the maximum price that prospective customers are willing to pay (P_M in this example). The firm will earn monopoly profits (revenues in excess of fully allocated costs including the opportunity costs of invested capital) depicted by the rectangular area $P_M A B C_0$.

From society's perspective, this pricing strategy results in a dead-weight economic loss represented by the triangle ACE. This loss is caused by the voluntary quantity restrictions practiced by the supplier to ensure the profit-maximizing price P_M.

The government response to this situation is often price regulation. A price fixed at the competitive price (P_C) would satisfy the efficiency criterion ($P = MC$), but would result in a loss to the firm since the price would be less than the average total cost of production. This dilemma could be solved in one of two ways: set the price at P_C and subsidize the firm by the amount of the loss or set the price at P^* (where $P = ATC$ and the firm earns a normal profit) and sacrifice some efficiency.

Although this regulating strategy may seem simple in theory, it is actually quite complex in practice. Because the demand and cost curves are not known with certainty, regulators must rely on accounting data to make their "fair" pricing determination. Two issues dominate regulatory deliberations: defining the fair rate of return and determining what to include in average cost of production. The issues are complex and the stakes are high. Before venturing too far down the slippery slope of price regulation, it is important that we fully understand the implications of such policy changes.

ISSUES IN MEDICAL CARE DELIVERY

HERBAL CURES: COMPLEMENTARY MEDICINE OR QUACKERY?

Stop aging now. Miracle cure for your heart. The natural way. How can you be certain whether the so-called "alternative medicines" have the curative power their proponents claim, or whether the results represent merely a placebo effect? One thing is certain—a lot of Americans use herbal cures. One-third of the adult population or approximately 60 million say they frequently use herbal remedies. Eisenberg et al. (1997) estimated that Americans spent approximately $13.7 billion in 1990 on unconventional treatments, including herbal medicine.

Alternative therapies have not made their way into mainstream medicine in the United States. Pharmaceutical companies spend a lot of money promoting their patented "magic bullets" and have no vested interest in encouraging consumers to use natural substances instead. Most research on alternative treatments has been conducted in Europe and published in English-speaking journals such as *Lancet* and the *British Medical Journal*. In fact, most of the natural remedies available in the United States are produced in foreign countries, primarily Japan and Germany, and packaged for U.S. consumption.

The herbal remedies that Americans buy in health foods stores are widely used abroad to treat such common problems as depression, anxiety, migraine headaches, enlarged prostate, and dementia. Proponents of the herbal alternatives will recognize St. John's wort, valerian, feverfew, saw palmetto, and ginkgo as natural treatments for the listed ailments. Herbal remedies account for almost one-third of all over-the-counter medications sold in Germany, and over 80 percent of all German physicians prescribe them. With thousands of Americans harmed or killed each year from adverse drug reactions, it makes sense to study the effectiveness of these natural remedies.

Source: David M. Eisenberg, Ronald C. Kessler, Cindy Foster, Frances E. Norlock, David R. Calkins, and Thomas L. Delbanco, "Unconventional Medicine in the United States: Prevalence, Costs, and Patterns of Use," *New England Journal of Medicine* 328(4), January 28, 1997, 247–252.

created a powerful incentive for industry to develop new, and often more expensive, technologies to deal with maladies of modern society.

In this chapter, we have focused on the role that medical technology has played in exacerbating the health care spending problem in the United States. As new treatments are developed, the responsibility of paying for them falls squarely on the third-party insurance system. Because insurance makes treatment available to some, the pressure mounts to make the same level of treatment available to all, regardless of insurance coverage—thus, the technological imperative.

Medical research has accomplished countless miracles over the years, and especially in the lifetimes of most of those who are reading this book. The most important innovations include developments in the areas of diagnostic screening (MRI and CT scanning), the treatment of heart disease (ACE inhibitors, cardiac angioplasty, and CABG surgery), cataract removal and lens replacement, hip and knee replacement, ultrasound technology, laparoscopic surgery, and pharmaceuticals, including statins to treat high cholesterol and inhaled steroids to treat asthma (Fuchs and Sox, 2001). Is technological change worth the cost? Cutler and McClellan (2001) try to answer this question by examining five conditions—heart attacks, low-birthweight infants, depression, cataracts, and breast cancer. For each condition except breast cancer, the net benefits of the new treatment have been significantly positive due to substantial improvements in outcomes at reasonable costs.

Key Concept 3
*Marginal
Analysis*

Joseph P. Newhouse

After receiving his Ph.D. from Harvard in 1969, Joseph Newhouse spent the next 20 years of his professional career with the RAND Corporation. As senior staff economist and head of its economics department, he designed and directed the RAND Health Insurance Experiment, arguably the most important social experiment in health insurance policy in the United States. In that study, over 8,000 individuals in six different geographic areas were randomly assigned to insurance plans that differed in terms of premiums paid, copayments, and deductibles. Much of what we know today about the demand for medical care and health care financing may be traced to this pioneering research.

While at RAND, Newhouse also served on the faculties of the RAND Graduate School and the University of California at Los Angeles School of Medicine. Lured away by his alma mater in 1988, Newhouse joined the Harvard faculty where he is currently the John D. MacArthur Professor of Health Policy and Management and serves as the director of the Division of Health Policy Research and Education. In addition to his appointment in the Faculty of Arts and Sciences, he is a member of the faculties of Harvard's Medical School and School of Public Health, and the Kennedy School of Government. Under his direction in 1992, Harvard created an interdisciplinary Ph.D. program in health policy encompassing these four areas of study.

His curriculum vita lists almost 300 publications, including articles in the top journals in the fields of economics, statistics, and medicine. Early in his professional career his research focused on money and banking issues. Soon after joining RAND, his interests changed and his scholarship was redirected to hospital and physician issues. He has been listed in all three editions of *Who's Who in Economics* as being among the most cited economists from 1970 to 1992. He is the founding editor of the *Journal of Health Economics* and serves as member of the editorial board, associate editor, and referee for numerous others, including the *American Economic Review*, *Journal of Economic Perspectives*, and the *New England Journal of Medicine*.

As principal investigator in a number of research projects, he has generated over $100 million in grants and contracts from the Department of Health and Human Services, Health Care Financing Administration, the Robert Wood Johnson Foundation, and the Agency for Health Care Policy and Research. Over $80 million of that total stemmed from the RAND experiment that ran for almost two decades. Newhouse was recognized for his distinguished contribution to the field of public policy and management with the prestigious David N. Kershaw Award in 1983 for his distinguished contributions to the field of public policy analysis and management.

His current research interests include several natural experiments with the incentive structure of the federal Medicaid program and a project for the Bureau of Labor Statistics to improve the Consumer Price Index for medical care. He is also directing a major study of the managed care industry and is in the early stages of a project to study the organization and financing of medical care in the West Bank and Gaza. From his humble beginnings in Waterloo, Iowa, Joseph Newhouse has risen to become a central figure in health policy research and education in the United States.

Source: Harvard Faculty Research Book home page and Curriculum Vitae: Joseph Paul Newhouse.

It is important that we understand the close causality between the availability of medical technology and the ability to pay for it. In our desire to control expenditures, it is essential that we preserve the financial incentives that foster and promote scientific inquiry at its basic level and also reward the applied research that creates marketable products that enhance the quality of medical care for millions of Americans.

Using history as a guide, we might conclude that rapid technological change in medical care will lead to increased spending. If biotechnology provides for the effective treatment of genetic diseases, however, we could see a shift from cost-increasing halfway technology to cost-saving high technology. It is not just wishful thinking to expect advances in cell biology in the next few decades to lead to cures for certain types of cancers and even heart disease. It is equally important that the price mechanism not put these products out of the reach of those who stand to benefit from the discoveries.

Questions and Problems

1. What is the technological imperative? How does the changing medical environment (AIDS, drug-exposed infants, advances in organ transplantation) affect our ability to deal with the escalation of cost in medical care?

2. The ability of medical science to prolong life is growing rapidly. Such halfway technological advances are often costly and have a low probability of long-term success, but sometimes they work. Whose life should be saved? What allocation rule might be applied to ensure wise use of resources?

3. Suppose a cure for AIDS were discovered, but at a cost of $1.5 million per case to implement. How would you solve the resulting controversies over financing and selection of cases to be cured?

4. Discuss the overall effectiveness of the organ procurement system in the United States. What are its strengths and weaknesses?

5. What are the implications of an organ procurement system that allows individuals to sell organs in a market setting like any other commodity? What are the market alternatives to the current system as practiced in the United States and abroad?

6. Pharmaceutical spending is less than 8 percent of total health care spending in the United States. Why do you suppose the industry is the target of such severe criticism?

7. What are some of the important economic issues that help us understand availability and pricing in the pharmaceutical industry?

8. The supply of available organs for transplantation purposes is usually less than the demand. Some states require a two-year abstinence for an alcoholic to be eligible for a liver transplant. What is the economic rationale for such a requirement? Is it morally justified?

9. If individuals are allowed to sell their organs in the open market, should the proceeds from the sale be subject to taxation? If so, should a donated organ result in a tax-deductible charitable contribution? Should Americans be allowed to purchase organs abroad where the practice is legal? What are some other problems that will arise if a market for donable organs is allowed?

10. A person learns from a genetic test that she has a predisposition for a certain disease, say, Alzheimer's disease. Who should have access to that genetic information? Medical practitioners? Insurance companies? The person herself? Would you want to know? Why?

References

Ronald Bailey, "Should I Be Allowed to Buy Your Kidney?" *Forbes* 145(11), May 28, 1990, 365–372.

Martin N. Baily, "Research and Development Costs and Returns: The U.S. Pharmaceutical Industry," *Journal of Political Economy* 80(1), January/February 1972, 70–85.

L. Dwayne Barney and R. Larry Reynolds, "An Economic Analysis of Transplant Organs," *Atlantic Economic Journal* 17(3), September 1989, 12–20.

Centers for Medicare and Medicaid Services (CMS), *Health Care Industry Market Update: Pharmaceuticals*, January 10, 2003. Available at: **http://www.cms.hhs.gov/marketupdate.**

David M. Cutler and Mark McClellan, "Is Technological Change in Medicine Worth It?" *Health Affairs* 20(5), September/October 2001, 11–29.

Patricia M. Danzon, "Drug Price Controls, Wrong Prescription," *The Wall Street Journal*, February 4, 1994, A10.

Patricia M. Danzon, "International Drug Price Comparisons: Uses and Abuses," in Richard B. Helms, ed., *Competition Strategies in the Pharmaceutical Industry*, Washington, DC: The AEI Press, 1996.

Edward Denison, *Trends in American Economic Growth*, Washington, DC: Brookings Institution, 1985.

Joseph A. DiMasi, Ronald W. Hansen, and Henry G. Grabowski, "The Price of Innovation: New Estimates of Drug Development Costs," *Journal of Health Economics 22*, 2003, 151–185.

Joseph A. DiMasi, Ronald W. Hansen, Henry G. Grabowski, and Louis Lasagna, "Cost of Innovation in the Pharmaceutical Industry," *Journal of Health Economics 10*(2), July 1991, 107–142.

Paul W. Eggers, "Effect of Transplantation on Medicare End-Stage Renal Disease Program," *New England Journal of Medicine 318*(4), January 28, 1988, 223–229.

Roger W. Evans, "Health Care Technology and the Inevitability of Resource Allocation and Rationing Decisions, Part I," *Journal of the American Medical Association 249*(15), April 15, 1983, 2047–2053.

Victor R. Fuchs and Harold C. Sox, Jr., "Physicians' Views of the Relative Importance of Thirty Medical Innovations," *Health Affairs 20*(5), September/October 2001, 30–42.

Christine Gorman, "Body Parts for Sale," *Time 151*(9), March 9, 1998, 76.

Henry G. Grabowski and John Vernon, *The Regulation of Pharmaceuticals: Balancing the Benefits and Risks*, Washington, DC: American Enterprise Institute, 1983.

———, "A New Look at the Returns and Risks to Pharmaceutical R&D," *Management Science 36*(7), July 1990, 804–821.

———, "Brand Loyalty, Entry, and Price Competition in Pharmaceuticals after the 1984 Drug Act," *Journal of Law and Economics 35*(2), October 1992, 331–350.

Mark A. Hurwitz and Richard E. Caves, "Persuasion or Information? Promotion and the Shares of Brand Name and Generic Pharmaceuticals," *Journal of Law and Economics 31*(2), October 1988, 299–320.

Holman W. Jenkins Jr., "Lazy Insurers Hitch a Ride on the Drug Wars," *The Wall Street Journal*, August 9, 2000, A23.

Kenneth Kaitin, N. Mattison, F. K. Northington, and Louis Lasagna, "The Drug Lag: An Update of New Drug Introductions in the United States and in the United Kingdom, 1977 through 1987," *Clinical Pharmacology and Therapeutics*, August 1989, 121–138.

Sam Kazman, "Deadly Overcaution: FDA's Drug Approval Process," *Journal of Regulation and Social Costs*, September 1990.

Frank R. Lichtenberg, "Are the Benefits of Newer Drugs Worth Their Costs? Evidence from the 1996 MEPS," *Health Affairs 20*(5), September/October 2001, 241–251.

Joe Moser, "Direct-to-Consumer Advertising: Helpful of Costly? A Fact Sheet," Galen Institute, September 12, 2002. Available at http://www.galen.org/news/091202.html.

Joseph P. Newhouse, "Medical Care Costs: How Much Welfare Loss?" *Journal of Economic Perspectives 6*(3), Summer 1992, 3–21.

Organ Transplants: Choices and Criteria, Who Lives, Who Dies, Who Pays? Hearing Before the Select Committee on Aging, House of Representatives, 102d Congress, First Session, No. 102-806, April 26, 1991.

Pharmaceutical Research Manufacturers Association, *Pharmaceutical Industry Profile 2000*, Washington, D.C.: PhRMA, 2000.

Anne A. Scitovsky, "Changes in the Costs of Treatment of Selected Illnesses, 1971–1981," *Medical Care 23*(12), December 1985, 1345–1357.

Laura A. Siminoff, R. M. Arnold, A. L. Caplan, B. A. Virgnig, and D. L. Seltzer, "Public Policy Governing Organ and Tissue Procurement in the United States: Results from National Organ and Tissue Procurement," *Annals of Internal Medicine 123*(1), 1995, 10 ff.

Carol J. Simon, "Would You Sell Your Kidney?" *Economic Times 3*(1), Spring 1994, 14–16.

Lewis Thomas, *The Lives of a Cell*, New York: Bantam Books, 1975.

United Network of Organ Sharing Web site at http://www.unos.org/data,data for 2003.

U.S. General Accounting Office (GAO), *Prescription Drugs: Companies Typically Charge More in the United States Than in Canada*, Washington, DC: USGAO, 1992.

———, *Prescription Drugs: Spending Controls in Four European Countries*, Washington, DC: USGAO, 1994.

Murray Weidenbaum, "Are Drug Prices Too High?" *The Public Interest 112*, Summer 1993a, 84–89.

———, *Restraining Medicine Prices: Controls vs. Competition*, St. Louis, MO: Washington University Center for the Study of American Business, Policy Study No. 116, April 1993b.

Burton A. Weisbrod, "The Health Care Quadrilemma: An Essay on Technological Change, Insurance, Quality of Care, and Cost Containment," *Journal of Economic Literature 29*(2), June 1991, 523–552.

L. John Wilkerson and Robert Easton, ". . . But Don't Kill the Golden Goose," *The New York Times*, March 7, 1993, F13.

Chapter 14

Policies that Enhance Access

The federal government's role in funding medical care in the United States continues to be defined and revised. To date the major responsibility has been focused on vulnerable population groups—the poor, the elderly, military veterans, the disabled, and those with certain chronic diseases. Total government spending on health care, including federal, state, and local spending, was approximately $525 billion in 2001, including over $461 billion spent on Medicare and Medicaid. When expenditures on public health, research, construction, and administration are included, government's share of total health care spending approached 50 percent.

As Americans continue to debate the direction and shape of health care reform, the defining issue is the extent to which we are willing to embrace the principle of universal entitlement to medical care. The principle is already in place in the form of a legal framework that guarantees medical care to certain vulnerable segments of the population, namely, the elderly, those eligible for cash welfare assistance, and military veterans with service-related disabilities.

The development of government's role in the provision of medical care to these vulnerable populations is instructive as we examine public policy as it relates to health care reform. The government is instrumental in providing medical care to approximately 80 million people under the three major programs: Medicare, Medicaid, and Veterans' Affairs. Any major overhaul of the present medical care delivery system will have to carefully consider how these programs are affected.

Medicare: Medical Care for the Elderly

The elderly, defined as the adult population over the age of 65, are the fastest growing segment of the U.S. population. In 2001, they comprised 12.6 percent of the total population, but they accounted for over 19 percent of personal health care spending, 31 percent of the hospital spending, 20 percent of the physician spending, and the vast majority of spending for home health care, hospice services, renal dialysis, and nursing home care. Politically active, this group is comprised of over 35 million voters who are not afraid to let policymakers know how they feel about issues that affect their well-being.

Medicare was established in 1965 to guarantee elderly Americans access to quality health care regardless of their financial circumstances. When combined with Social Security, it represents the most important source of economic security for our nation's elderly. Serving 19.1 million in 1966, Medicare enrollment reached 40.6 million Americans in 2002, over 14 percent of the total population (see Table 14.1). This figure included 34.6 million senior citizens over age 65, approximately 5.8 million permanently disabled, and 320,000 suffering from end-stage kidney failure. Although 75 percent of the beneficiaries of Medicare are between the ages of 65 and 84, the disabled (comprising 14 percent of the total) and those over 85 (11 percent of the total) are the fastest growing segments. In 1966, the first complete year of the program, total Medicare spending was $1.6 billion. Medicare spending reached $265.7 billion in 2002 and is expected to grow to $309 billion by 2005 and $494.5 billion by 2012 (2003 Medicare Trustees Report).

Table 14.1	Actual and Projected Medicare Spending Calendar Years, 1966–2002, with Projections

Year	Total Number of Recipients (millions)	Total Spending (billions of current dollars)	Annual Rate of Change in Spending[a] (percent)
1966	19.1	$ 1.6	—
1970	20.1	7.5	45.6
1975	24.5	16.3	16.9
1980	28.0	36.8	17.7
1985	30.6	72.3	14.5
1990	33.7	111.0	9.0
1995	37.2	184.2	10.7
1996	37.7	200.3	8.7
1997	38.1	213.6	6.6
1998	38.5	213.4	0.0
1999	38.8	213.0	−0.2
2000	39.3	221.9	4.2
2001	39.6	244.8	10.3
2002	40.6	265.7	8.5
2005	42.3	309.1	5.2
2010	46.6	428.4	6.7
2012	49.2	494.5	7.5

Source: 2003 Annual Reports of the Board of Trustees of the HI and SMI Trust Funds, Tables 11.A2 and 11.A4.

a Average annual change from the previous entry.

Institutional Features

Administered by the Centers for Medicare and Medicaid Services (CMS), Medicare provides benefits through two programs: Part A and Part B. Part A is medical hospital insurance; Part B is supplemental medical insurance. Individuals (or their spouses) who have paid into the social security system for 10 years are automatically enrolled in Part A upon reaching their sixty-fifth birthday. Even though individuals may choose whether to enroll in Part B, more than 95 percent of all those who are eligible choose to enroll. Enrollees receive benefits in four categories of care: (1) inpatient hospital care, (2) medically necessary inpatient care in a skilled-nursing facility after an acute care hospital stay, (3) home health care, and (4) hospice care.

The basic idea underlying Part A payments is simple. The patient pays a deductible equal to the cost of the first day in the hospital; Medicare pays for days 2–60 with no coinsurance requirement; days 61–90 are covered but the patient must pay coinsurance equal to 25 percent of the deductible; and days 91–150 are covered if the lifetime reserve days are available with the patient paying coinsurance equal to 50 percent of the deductible amount. After 150 days in the hospital, Medicare pays nothing. This limitation is easily the most serious flaw in the current system because it provides enrollees with no protection against catastrophic losses.

The 2003 figures translate as follows. The first 60 days of inpatient hospital care during each benefit period is provided to patients with the only out-of-pocket expense being a deductible payment equal to $840.[1] The patient is responsible for a copayment

---

1 A benefit period is defined as the time period that begins on the first day the patient is admitted into the hospital and extends to 30 days after that patient is discharged.

of $210 per day for the next 30 days. After 90 days in the hospital during each benefit period, the patient is responsible for all costs unless reserve days are available.[2]

Additional benefits include 100 days in a skilled-nursing facility during each benefit period. This benefit is provided as a supplement to hospital care and is available only after a minimum three-day hospitalization. The first 20 days are provided at no charge to the patient; days 21–100 require a daily copayment of $105 (one-eighth of the hospital deductible). Beyond 100 days, the patient is responsible for the entire bill. Inpatient psychiatric care is available for up to a 190-day lifetime maximum. Home health benefits include up to four days of care per week with no limit and up to three full weeks of care per illness. Individuals with life expectancies of less than six months are eligible for 210 days of hospice care.

Participation in Part B is voluntary and pays for physicians' services and outpatient hospital services, including emergency room services, diagnostic testing, laboratory services, outpatient physical therapy, speech-pathology services, and durable medical equipment. Of interest to most participants is what Medicare does not cover. Routine physical examinations, most preventive care, and, most importantly, outpatient prescription drugs and custodial nursing home care are not included in the basic benefit package provided by Medicare.[3]

> **Policy Issue**
>
> The gaps in Medicare coverage include outpatient prescription drugs and long-term custodial care.

After the patient pays a $100 annual deductible, Part B pays 80 percent of the prescribed fee set by Medicare. The majority of physicians who accept Medicare **assignment** accept Medicare's reimbursement as payment in full for the covered services. By 1992, over half of the physicians were accepting Medicare assignment. **Participating physicians** who accept assignment bill over 90 percent of Part B's covered charges (Gillis, Lee, and Willke, 1992).

assignment
A Medicare policy providing physicians with a guaranteed payment of 80% of the allowable fee. By accepting assignment physicians agree to accept the allowable fee as full payment and forgo the practice of balance billing.

Who Pays?

Medicare funding comes from four major sources: payroll taxes, income taxes, trust fund interest, and enrollee premiums. Almost 90 percent of the funding comes directly and indirectly from individuals who are less than 65 years old. The remainder comes from those who are over 65 in the form of enrollee premiums. A payroll tax of 2.9 percent is levied on the gross income of all employees and is collected along with the Social Security tax. This tax is divided equally between employer and employee. Until 1994, tax law had included a cap on the income that was subject to the Medicare tax—$51,300 in 1990, $130,200 in 1992. Legislation passed in 1993 removed the income ceiling, subjecting all payroll income to the 2.9 percent Medicare levy.

participating physician
A physician who agrees to accept Medicare assignment.

This 2.9 percent payroll tax on all workers in the U.S. labor force (over $152 billion in 2002) is dedicated entirely to the trust fund to pay Part A benefits. In recent years, program receipts have exceeded benefit payments, accumulating a surplus in the Medicare trust fund amounting to $269 billion in 2002.[4] A major problem resurfaced in 1997 when spending outlays exceeded receipts by approximately $250 per enrollee. Congress acted in 1996 with the Balanced Budget Act, significantly reducing hospital spending. Coupled with higher than expected economic growth, the shortfall has turned into a surplus that is expected to run until 2013. According to the 2003 trustees' report, the trust fund is expected to remain solvent until 2026.[5]

Enrollees in Part B paid a monthly premium (usually deducted from the monthly Social Security check) equal to $58.70 in 2003, scheduled to rise to $105 by 2007. These

---

2 Each enrollee is provided 60 lifetime reserve days with a daily copayment of $380 that are used to pay hospital expenses beyond the 90 days of coverage during each benefit period. Once a patient uses these reserve days, Part A benefits stop after 90 days in the hospital during a benefit period.

3 This is true unless the participant is enrolled in an HMO; then many of these services are covered.

4 Many argue that because the "trust fund" is invested in interest-bearing U.S. Treasury securities, it is not really a trust fund at all. To use the fund, the federal government must liquidate the securities by reissuing debt, raising additional tax revenues, or printing money.

5 Changes were in fact implemented. See Issues in Medical Care Delivery "The Politics of Medicare."

Back-of-the-Envelope

THE IMPACT OF MEDICARE ASSIGNMENT ON MEDICAL PRACTICE

Physicians who provide care to Medicare patients must decide whether or not to accept the Medicare allowable fee as payment in full for the services provided. In other words, physicians must decide whether to take "assignment" on their Medicare patients. Physicians who take assignment bill Medicare and receive 80 percent of the allowable fee directly from the federal government. Those who do not take assignment bill their patients directly, but no more than 15 percent over the allowable fee. Medicare will pay 80 percent of the allowable fee to the patient, who in turn is responsible for paying the physician. The excess charges over the allowable fee is referred to as "**balance billing**." Physicians who take assignment are reasonably certain they will collect 80 percent of the allowable fee. Those who do not take assignment have no such assurances.

From the physician's perspective, the problem centers on the relationship between the fee usually charged for the service provided and the Medicare allowable fee, which is often much lower. The impact of assignment on the physicians' services market is addressed in the following diagram.

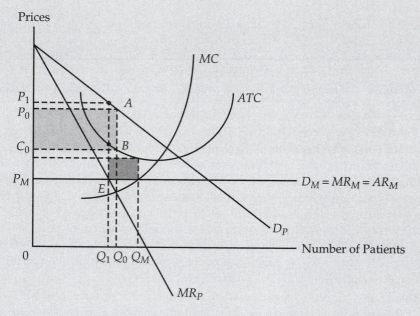

For those physicians who accept assignment, the market for a physician's services can be divided into two segments—private patients and Medicare. Private patient demand is given by the downward sloping demand curve labeled D_P. To maximize profits, the physician will set $MR_P = MC$ and provide Q_0 services at a price of P_0. Profits are depicted graphically by the shaded area bounded by the points P_0ABC_0.

Physicians who accept Medicare assignment agree to a fixed price P_M for their Medicare patients. As a price taker, the demand curve for this segment of the market becomes $D_M = MR_M = AR_M$. Now the physician is faced with a more complicated decision. The new marginal revenue curve has a floor established at P_M. The combined marginal revenue curve is now MR_P to point E (where MR_P and MR_M intersect) and MR_M thereafter. The physician will see a total of Q_M patients (Q_1 private patients and $Q_M - Q_1$ Medicare patients). Private patients now pay a higher price for services, P_1, sometimes labeled *cost shifting*.

Physicians complain that the Medicare allowable fee is below their average cost of providing medical services. In the diagram above, the shaded area between ATC and P_M shows this loss. Although providing care to the Medicare segment of the market

balance billing
Billing a patient for the difference between the physician's usual charge for a service and the maximum charge allowed by the patient's health plan.

may not cover fully allocated costs, each one of those transactions is reimbursed at a rate that covers the physician's opportunity cost; all relevant costs as measured by *MC*. Whether the physician is better off or worse off (determined by the change in profit) depends on whether the extra profits from private patients offsets the losses incurred in providing care to Medicare patients.

premiums finance approximately 25 percent of all Part B benefits. General tax revenues and interest on the assets of the Medicare trust fund cover the remainder.

Who Benefits?

Medicare's allocation pattern closely fits the usual experience of underwriting medical care spending for large groups. Underwriters often refer to this pattern as the 80–20 rule: 80 percent of the spending benefits 20 percent of the covered population. As illustrated in Table 14.2, about 30 million enrollees, or 80 percent of the eligible population, actually receive paid benefits every year. In 1999, with program outlays of $166.7 billion, approximately 75 percent purchased care for 11.3 percent of the beneficiaries whose per capita spending exceeded $10,000. Average spending for this high-cost group was $28,318. Approximately 85 percent of the outlays benefited the 6.9 million who spent more than $5,000 per capita, or 17.7 percent of the enrollees. The average spending for this group amounted to over $20,623. An additional 60.5 percent of the enrollees spent $24.4 billion or 14.6 percent of the total outlays. The other 24.7 percent received no paid benefits. Average spending per enrollee was $4,296; average spending for the 75.3 percent who actually received paid benefits was $5,706.

Medicare has proven to be a good financial investment for the individual enrollee. A couple retiring in 1994, who had paid the average Medicare tax since 1966, would have paid $20,000 in payroll taxes into the program (including the employer's share). Lifetime benefits, discounted to 1994, exceed the amount paid in premiums and taxes by an average of $117,200, or six times the amount paid into the system. Because Part B premiums account for only 25 percent of the outlays for medical benefits, an **actuarially fair premium** would have to be four times greater than the current $58.70, or $235 per month, to cover 100 percent of program spending.[6]

**actuarially fair
premium**
Insurance premium based on
the actuarial probability that an
event will occur.

Table 14.2	Medicare Payments Allocation, 1999

Payment Range	Number of Enrollees (millions)	Percent of Total	Spending (billions)	Percent of Total	Average per Enrollee
Over $20,000	2.3	5.9	$94.5	56.7	$41,087
$10,000–$19,999	2.1	5.4	30.1	18.1	14,333
$5,000–$9,999	2.5	6.4	17.7	10.6	7,103
$2,000–$4,999	4.2	10.8	13.5	8.1	3,210
$1,000–$1,999	4.1	10.6	5.8	3.5	1,431
$500–$999	4.3	11.0	3.1	1.9	723
Less than $500	9.7	25.0	2.0	1.2	206
Zero	9.6	24.7	0	0	0
Total	38.8	100.0	$166.7	100.0	$4,296

Source: *Health Care Financing Review: Medicare and Medicaid Statistical Supplement, 2001,* Table 16.

6 Private insurance coverage for comparable benefits under Parts A and B would cost the average 65-to 74-year-old between $6,400 and $8,500 per year ($500 to 700 per month).

Economic Consequences

Medicare's spending pattern highlights the fundamental flaw in Medicare coverage, the fact that it provides virtually no protection against low probability, catastrophic losses. For short hospital stays, Medicare pays virtually all the bill beyond the deductible. Longer hospital stays (in excess of 150 days) subject the individual to larger percentages of the total bill. This failure to cover infrequent, but very long hospital stays is the result of the original "spell-of-illness" concept originally considered beneficial to participants. Under this concept, if a patient is discharged from the hospital and then readmitted within seven days, the readmission is considered part of the same illness. As part of the same illness, the patient does not have to pay the deductible again. The intent is to save the patient from the financial burden of paying the deductible over and over and to guarantee that elders will seek care when it is needed. The unintended consequence of this provision is to increase the chance that a long hospital stay will expose the individual to the financial risk of a catastrophic illness—one where the patient is responsible for the entire bill after the 60 lifetime reserve days are exhausted.

Policy Issue

Medicare coverage provides little protection against catastrophic illnesses.

Key Concept 9
Market Failure

Overall, Medicare pays 87 percent of inpatient hospital charges and 67 percent of physician's services, but only 8.1 percent of outpatient prescription drugs and 0.5 percent of long-term care. Because of these gaps in coverage, an active supplementary insurance market has developed. In 1999, approximately 22.2 million of the elderly population had supplemental insurance benefits from Medicaid, private insurance companies, or their previous employers.[7] Only about one in ten had no supplemental insurance coverage. Many of the so-called "Medigap" policies have the same problem as Medicare itself—an "upside down" structure. In other words, they cover the up-front costs (deductibles and copayments) and provide for some noncovered expenses (such as outpatient prescription drugs), but they do not provide protection against catastrophic financial risk. In addition, they are costly, with annual premiums for the most popular plan at $1,065. However, most supplemental plans still do not offer outpatient prescription drug coverage. Plans that do are more expensive with average annual premiums of over $2,400 in 1998.

Key Concept 8
Efficiency

Medigap insurance
A supplemental insurance policy sold to Medicare-eligible individuals to pay the deductibles and coinsurance that are not covered by Medicare. These policies must conform to one of ten standardized benefit plans established by the federal government.

Federal law passed in the 1980s to regulate this growing insurance market failed to address this flaw completely. Congress created minimum standards for all **Medigap insurance** policies, but rather than provide true catastrophic coverage for the extremely rare, long hospital stay, the government has forced the private insurance market to provide Medigap policies that offer first-dollar coverage. This practice is not only inefficient, but it encourages participants to over-utilize medical resources and drives up the premium costs without providing genuine catastrophic insurance coverage. As a result, the typical senior pays approximately 31 percent of his or her own medical bills either out-of-pocket or through private insurance premiums (Vladeck and King, 1995; Dallek, 1996). In addition, Medicare does not cover most long-term care, mental illness treatment, or outpatient drug benefits, resulting in mounting political pressure on policymakers to act.

Since 1993 the elderly have begun leaving fee-for-service Medicare and enrolling in managed care plans, the basic Medicare+Choice program. By April 2002, almost 5.5 million elders, approximately 16 percent of the eligible population, were enrolled in 147 managed care plans, after peaking at 7 million enrollees in over 300 plans in 1999 (Hileman, 2002). Many HMOs are providing additional benefits, including prescription drugs and preventive care, not usually covered. Although more than one-half of the HMOs require an additional premium to enroll, joining allows the individual to drop the expensive Medigap policy, resulting in considerable savings.[8]

---

7 This number is down from 23.8 million covered by supplemental insurance in 1991. The decrease is offset by the increase in the number of elderly enrolled in Medicare managed care plans that all but eliminate the need for supplemental insurance.
8 The future of Medicare+Choice has been jeopardized by the low reimbursement rates enacted through the Balanced Budget Act of 1997. As many as one million of the 6.2 million elders enrolled in managed care in 2000 were displaced as many managed care companies dropped out of the Medicare+Choice program (Pallarito, 2000).

Key Concept 5
*Markets and
Pricing*

Back-of-the-Envelope

MEDICAL INFLATION AND MEDICARE

Many argue that medical care costs and spending were of little macroeconomic consequence until the mid 1960s when the government stepped up its involvement with the creation of Medicare and Medicaid. The theoretical underpinnings of this argument are fairly straightforward. In general, insurance coverage increases the demand for medical care. The elderly are no different.

In the diagram on the left, D_0 and D_1 represent the elderly demand before and after the passage of Medicare. This rightward shift in demand will result in increased utilization (Q_0 to Q_1), which is desirable, and increased prices (P_0 to P_1), which are not. Physicians who were treating their nonelderly patients and charging them the same price will find that the opportunity cost of their time has increased due to the higher prices paid by the elderly. Greater opportunity costs are shown by a leftward shift in the physicians' supply curve in the right side of the diagram, forcing prices paid by the nonelderly to rise accordingly. There are obviously other reasons for the rise in medical care spending, but as shown in the diagram Medicare's impact should not be ignored.

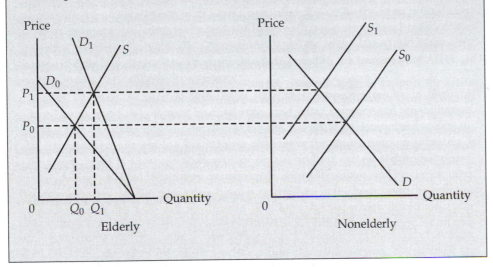

Medicaid: Medical Care for the Poor

Medicaid was passed in 1965 as part of the same legislative package with the federal Medicare program. The program served approximately 10 million low-income Americans in 1967, increasing to 40.2 million in 1999. Medicaid spending amounted to $1.66 billion in 1966 and grew to over $180 billion in 1999 and $216.2 billion in 2001 (see Table 14.3). Under current law, Medicaid is projected to continue growing at 9 percent per year over the next decade, reaching over $500 billion by 2012 (HCFA, 1999).

Institutional Features

Medicaid is a means-tested entitlement program, administered by the states and financed jointly with the federal government. The federal portion of Medicaid payments is based on each state's per capita income relative to national per capita income. The national average for federal matching rate was 57 percent in 2001, ranging from 50 to 76.8 percent.[9] The states have some flexibility in designing their own programs

---

9 The federal share, or federal medical assistance percentage (FMAP), is determined by the following formula:
$$FMAP = 1 - [(State\ per\ capita\ income)^2/(U.S.\ per\ capita\ income)^2] \times 0.45.$$

Table 14.3	Actual and Projected Medicaid Spending Select Years, 1966–2001

Year	Total Number of Recipients (millions)	Total Spending (billions of current dollars)[a]	Annual Rate of Change[b] (in percentages)
1966	10.0	$ 1.7	—
1970	—	4.9	30.3
1975	22.0	12.1	20.8
1980	21.6	24.0	13.8
1985	21.8	39.4	10.4
1990	25.3	69.8	11.8
1995	36.3	151.7	17.2
1996	36.1	154.4	1.8
1997	34.9	160.3	3.8
1998	40.1	168.9	5.4
1999	40.2	180.4	6.8
2000	—	195.5	8.4
2001	—	216.2	10.6

Source: *Health Care Financing Review: Medicare and Medicaid Statistical Supplement 2001*, Tables 85 and 88, April 2003; and State summaries available at **http://cms.hhs.gov/medicaid/mbes/sttotal.pdf**.

a Includes payments made to "disproportionate share hospitals."

b Average annual change from the previous entry.

as long as certain federal guidelines are met. These guidelines mandate that a basic medical benefits package must be provided to specific population groups, primarily low-income groups traditionally eligible for welfare. States also have some flexibility in determining the level of payment to providers. Beyond these requirements, states have the option of expanding benefits and covering additional groups. As a result, eligibility standards and benefits vary considerably, creating unequal coverage across the nation. Individuals who are eligible for benefits in one state would not be eligible under similar circumstances for benefits in another.

Mandated benefits cover a full range of services including both inpatient and outpatient hospital services, physicians' services, family planning services (not including abortion services), ambulatory care, diagnostic screenings, nursing home care, home health care, and nurse practitioners' services. Many states also include an optional benefits package covering outpatient prescription drugs, optometry and dental services, prosthetic devices, physical therapy, and intermediate care for the mentally retarded.

Eligibility

The original legislation provided coverage for recipients of public assistance, primarily single parent families, and the aged, blind, and disabled. Since its original enactment, 20 major legislative actions have expanded benefits to additional groups and covered additional services (Gruber, 2000b). These steps have resulted in the dramatic escalation in spending over the original projections. After moderating somewhat in the 1980s, spending increased over 25 percent per year in the early 1990s and has only recently settled down to single-digit annual increases.

Since the mid-1980s, the program has been marked by nearly continuous expansion of eligibility. Legislation during the 1984–1987 period weakened the link between eligibility for cash welfare assistance and Medicaid eligibility. These changes in eligibility standards foreshadowed later changes that have all but severed that link. The first major

ISSUES IN MEDICAL CARE DELIVERY

THE POLITICS OF MEDICARE

The 1965 legislation that created Medicare included aspects of the three major proposals that were popular at the time. Democrats favored a hospital trust fund that included mandatory participation and financing from a broad-based tax, which became Medicare, Part A. Republicans wanted traditional indemnity insurance with voluntary participation, funded by a premium paid by all participants, and subsidized out of general tax revenues, which became Medicare, Part B. Finally, the medical community, led by the American Medical Association, wanted medical insurance for the indigent paid out of general tax revenues, which became Medicaid.

Since the creation of the program, numerous changes have expanded the system's coverage and method of paying providers. Medical benefits for the disabled were added in 1975 and the end-stage renal program was created in 1980. Prospective payment to hospitals was put in place in 1983 and a relative value scale to pay physicians was started in 1994.

In addition to expanding benefits and controlling spending, Congress addressed the major weakness of the program in 1988, namely its inability to provide catastrophic financial protection, by passing the Medicare Catastrophic Coverage Act. Instead of a crowning achievement, this Act represents possibly one of the most embarrassing moments in Congressional history.

The intent of the legislation was to guard against the high cost of a prolonged or debilitating illness. The unique feature of the plan was that the entire cost of a social welfare program was borne by the intended beneficiaries. After considering its effect, the majority of the elderly population (or at least an extremely vocal minority) determined that the extra benefits provided by the program were not worth the added costs. Most Medicare beneficiaries already had supplemental coverage that they considered superior to the benefits provided by the new legislation. The failure of the act to provide additional benefits—especially long-term care benefits—led to its ultimate demise. Protests by the elderly and reversals in positions by advocates of the elderly, including the American Association of Retired People, led to the act's repeal in November 1989.

More recent legislation has attempted to address the expected shortfall in the hospital trust fund. According to the 1996 trustees' report, the trust fund was expected to run out of assets by 2001 if no changes to the system were adopted. Acting on this report, Congress included Medicare reform in the 1998 federal budget. Originally, the proposed reform package was designed to reduce Medicare spending growth by over $270 billion by reducing the fees paid to providers, increasing premiums and copayments to recipients, and extending the eligibility age to 67. Opposition quickly mobilized and successfully defeated the proposal, reinforcing the perception that Medicare is politically untouchable.

Congress was able to address the short-term insolvency by cutting provider payments by $115 billion over the 1998 to 2002 time period, extending the trust fund's solvency until the year 2029 at the time. Furthermore, the legislation encouraged enrollment in managed care plans and allowed the option of setting up medical savings accounts. But these changes were not enough to address the long-term structural deficiencies in the system that will become evident when the baby boom generation starts retiring in 2010. A bipartisan Congressional commission was formed in 1998 to study the problem and recommend alternative solutions for Congress to consider. The commission, headed by Democrat John Breaux, agreed on a reform package designed along the same lines as the Federal Employee Health

Benefit Plan that featured a choice of plans for all enrollees along with a prescription drug benefit. A threatened veto by President Clinton killed the bill in committee.

Since then President George W. Bush has voiced support for this plan as part of a promised overhaul of the Medicare system. Reform has proven to be elusive. Slim Republican majorities in the Congress may not allow the reform desired by the president. While the addition of a prescription drug benefit has been promised, no one seems in a hurry to get one passed.

Source: Thomas Rice, Katherine Desmond, and Jon Gabel, "The Medicare Catastrophic Coverage Act: A Post-Mortem," *Health Affairs, 9*(3), Fall 1990, 75–87.

change allowed states to cover children who met the financial standards but lived in two-parent households. By 1992, states were required to provide pregnancy-related benefits for pregnant women and children under age 6 who had family incomes that were less than 133 percent of the federal poverty level ($19,977 for a family of three in 2002).[10] Children aged 6 to 18 must also be covered if their family income is less than 100 percent of the poverty level ($15,020 for a family of three in 2002).

The second major change allowed states to extend coverage to the "medically needy" according to standards established by the state. Families who are not eligible for poverty-related coverage may be classified as "medically needy" if their income falls below an established level or if their medical expenses are very large. This category of coverage has become less important with the expansion of benefits to pregnant women and children. It remains, however, a significant source of benefits for the elderly and disabled.

Since 1987, most of the changes in the program have increased the income threshold for eligibility. Federal law required that all infants living in households with incomes at 75 percent of the poverty level be covered. Some states raised age eligibility to age 7 or 8 and others raised the threshold to as high as 185 percent of the poverty income level.

In the summer of 1996, Congress enacted a sweeping welfare reform bill that included changes to Medicaid. The main feature of the legislation was a new program called **Temporary Aid to Needy Families (TANF)**, replacing the old **Aid for Families with Dependent Children (AFDC)** program. Under TANF, each state receives a block grant (a fixed, lump-sum payment) to design its own welfare program, and more importantly, cash assistance is no longer a guaranteed entitlement to everyone who meets a state's eligibility requirements.

The Medicaid program was left virtually intact by this legislation, but several features of the new law affect Medicaid eligibility. One of the main paths to Medicaid eligibility had been through AFDC. Now that AFDC has been replaced by TANF, eligibility for TANF does not guarantee Medicaid benefits. In other words, the link between cash welfare assistance and Medicaid coverage has been severed. Possibly, the harshest aspect of the legislation deals with the treatment of legal immigrants. Under current law, legal immigrants arriving after August 22, 1996, are not eligible for Medicaid benefits until residing in the United States for five years. Even with the passage of TANF, states continue to base eligibility on the income thresholds used to determine eligibility for cash welfare assistance.

State Children's Health Insurance Program

Passage of the Balanced Budget Act of 1997 created the **State Children's Health Insurance Program (CHIP)** and provided nearly $40 billion in matching funds to states that provided health insurance to low-income children without insurance.[11] The

---

Temporary Aid to Needy Families (TANF)
Temporary Aid to Needy Families replaced the old AFDC program in 1996 as the main cash assistance program for the poor.

Aid for Families with Dependent Children (AFDC)
Aid for Families with Dependent Children, created in 1935, was the primary cash assistance program for the poor and needy in the U.S. welfare system until 1996, when it was replaced by a block-grant program.

State Children's Health Insurance Program (CHIP)
A state administered program, similar to Medicaid, targeted to provide affordable health insurance to low-income children who are otherwise ineligible for Medicaid benefits.

---

10 States are allowed to establish eligibility standards that extend benefits to families with incomes up to 185 percent of the poverty level.
11 Children in families with incomes exceeding the Medicare threshold but less than 200 percent of the federal poverty level are eligible.

amended Title XXI of the Social Security Act gave states the option of setting up separate insurance programs for children, expanding Medicaid to cover children, or a combination of the two. In 2002, over 5 million children were enrolled in CHIP, most in combined programs. CHIP programs must provide enrollees with the same benefits available under Medicaid. Patient out-of-pocket costs are allowed but are limited to five percent of family income.

Since its inception the program has expanded to cover other uninsured individuals in addition to eligible children. In 2001, four states (Minnesota, New Jersey, Rhode Island, and Wisconsin) received approval to cover parents of eligible children, expanding coverage to almost 350,000 adults. Premium assistance programs and family coverage waivers have also been passed in a number of states. Under these programs states are allowed to subsidize employers who offer insurance to otherwise eligible participants and in some cases purchase family coverage if it is proven to be cost effective.

Economic Consequences

Results of a study by the Kaiser Foundation (1995) conclude that most of the increase in Medicaid spending since 1988 has been due to three factors: (1) program expansions mandated by the federal government that have lead to dramatic increases in enrollment, (2) the overall increase in medical care costs, and (3) increases in reimbursement rates to hospitals and other providers.

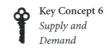

Key Concept 6
Supply and Demand

Congress moved to expand Medicaid eligibility as part of the Deficit Reduction Act of 1984. In an attempt to reduce infant mortality and improve access to child health services, the act was the first in a series of seven legislative steps that extended eligibility to all pregnant women and children under the age of 19.

At the same time, Congress also required the states to add new services to the mandatory benefits package. States must cover the services of nurse practitioners, care provided in community and migrant health centers, and any service needed to treat a condition discovered during a diagnostic screening, even if the treatment is considered an optional benefit.

In addition, Congress acted to improve reimbursement levels for providers. The 1980 Boren amendment allowed states to deviate from Medicare's cost-reimbursement system for hospitals and nursing homes but also required that reimbursement levels must be sufficient to allow for their efficient and economical operation. A decade later, hospitals and nursing homes began filing Boren lawsuits asking for federal review of the states' reimbursement systems, and within a year litigation was in progress in 29 states.

In order to increase physician participation and advance the goal of increasing health services for children and pregnant women, legislation was passed to improve payments to pediatricians and obstetricians. Hospitals that serve a **disproportionate share** of Medicaid patients receive supplemental payments as part of the Disproportionate Share Hospital Program, in part to make up for low initial reimbursement rates. According to the Kaiser Foundation study, "Dispro" payments accounted for over 16 percent of the increase in Medicaid spending between 1987 and 1992.

disproportionate share ("Dispro") payments
A payment adjustment under Medicare and Medicaid that pays hospitals that serve a large number of indigent patients.

Nationwide, approximately 60 percent of all Americans younger than age 65 living below the poverty level receive assistance through Medicaid. States set their own income threshold for eligibility so the percentages vary considerably from state to state. In 2002, the average income for an eligible family of three was $6,158, ranging from a low of $3,048 in Alabama to $40,224 in Minnesota. The average eligibility threshold for pregnant women with children has been established by federal law at a minimum of 133 percent of the poverty level, or $19,995, and ranges up to 185 percent of the poverty level, or $27,787. Since the early origins of federal involvement in medical care for the needy, spending has been concentrated in the states with the largest populations. In FY 1999 when spending was $153.5 billion (excluding disproportionate share payments to hospitals), almost half of that total was spent in the seven states with populations over 10 million (see Table 14.4). Nationwide, the average

Table 14.4	Medicaid Medical Vendor Payments, Fiscal Year 1999 Seven States with Populations over 10 million

State	Total Payments (in billions)	Payment per Beneficiary	Number of Beneficiaries (in millions)
California	$ 15.8	$2,307	6.85
Florida	6.4	2,712	2.36
Illinois	6.3	4,257	1.48
New York	25.4	8,301	3.06
Ohio	6.3	4,922	1.28
Pennsylvania	6.1	3,935	1.55
Texas	8.1	3,214	2.52
Seven-state total	74.4	3,895	19.10
Rest of the U.S.	79.1	3,752	21.08
Total U.S.	153.5	3,820	40.18

Source: *Health Care Financing Review: Medicare and Medicaid Statistical Supplement, 2001.*

payment per beneficiary was $3,820, compared to $3,895 for the seven large states and $3,752 for the remaining 43 states.

State differences in eligibility standards and average spending per beneficiary do not begin to tell the whole story of gaps in coverage across the country. Some Americans cannot qualify for Medicaid under any circumstances. Individuals with incomes over the eligibility standard or who do not fall within a certain category (notably blind, disabled, pregnant, or single-parent with dependent children) are, of course, ineligible. These requirements make it extremely difficult for males who are not blind or disabled and who are not living with children to establish eligibility for the program.

The Medicaid program was originally established to provide basic medical benefits, including hospital and physicians' services, for those who were receiving cash assistance through state welfare programs. Although medical payments for welfare recipients remain a key element of the program, nursing home care and home health care, primarily for the Medicare-eligible population, constitute over 70 percent of the total outlays. Table 14.5 summarizes the program spending by eligibility category. Over 70 percent of the program spending in FY 1999 went to the elderly and disabled. Per capita payments to these two groups were $11,268 and $9,832. Children and adults received approximately 26 percent of the total program outlays. Per capita payments for these two groups were $1,282 and $2,104.

Almost one-half of the poverty-level population is ineligible for Medicaid benefits of any kind and many of those who are eligible have a difficult time finding physicians who will treat them. Expansion of the program at the state level is unlikely since Medicaid is viewed as the one item in state budgets that is out of control. Mandated expansion of the eligible population resulted in a doubling of spending between 1989 and 1992. Not only has the number of beneficiaries increased, but diseases associated with lower socioeconomic groups have escalated, especially medical problems related to smoking, drug use, obesity, and AIDS. In fact, Medicaid has become the primary insurance carrier for many AIDS patients with the program paying for over 40 percent of all AIDS-related medical costs.

States have a limited range of responses to rising costs. Program cutbacks jeopardize federal funding, and tax increases jeopardize political careers. To date, only Oregon has moved to ration care by prioritizing services and restricting access to services that are not cost effective (more will be said about the Oregon plan in Chapter 17). Most states are turning to managed care to reduce Medicaid spending. In fact, almost 60 percent of

Table 14.5	Medicaid Spending by Eligibility Category Fiscal Year 1999				
Category	Number Payment per Capita	Percent of Eligible (in millions)	Total Total Eligible Population	Spending (in billions)	Percent of Total Spending
Aged	$11,268	3.8	9.4	$42.5	27.7
Disabled	9,832	6.7	16.7	65.9	42.9
Children	1,282	18.9	46.9	24.2	15.7
Adults	2,104	7.5	18.7	15.8	10.3
Other	1,545	3.3	8.4	5.1	3.3
Total	$3,818	40.2	100.0	$153.5	100.0

Source: *Health Care Financing Review: Medicare and Medicaid Statistical Supplement, 2001.*

the Medicaid population, or 23 million individuals were enrolled in managed care plans in 2002, making the Centers for Medicare and Medicaid Services, the agency that administers Medicare and Medicaid, the nation's largest purchaser of managed care.

Other Economic Issues

As with any other entitlement program, researchers are interested in its impact on the behavior and well being of its participants. Research has examined the economic impact of the Medicaid program to determine its effect on health outcomes, enrollment in private insurance, labor supply, family structure, and savings.

Health Outcomes

One of the stated goals of the Medicaid program is to improve the health of the eligible population. Although policymakers cannot legislate better health, they can improve access to providers in hopes that better access will result in better health outcomes. Expansions in eligibility since the mid-1980s have focused primarily on enrolling pregnant women and children. A number of studies have examined the connection between Medicaid eligibility and health outcomes for these two groups. Currie and Gruber (1996a) found evidence that Medicaid eligibility expansions among pregnant women improved prenatal care utilization and resulted in a reduction in the proportion of low-birthweight deliveries and an improvement in birth outcomes. They estimate that a 10 percent increase in Medicaid eligibility leads to a 2.8 percent decrease in infant mortality rates for the affected population. Currie and Gruber (1996b) also found that expansions in eligibility for children increased hospitalizations, but reduced avoidable hospitalizations. A 10 percent increase in eligibility resulted in a 3.4 percent decrease in child mortality rates, due to better access to primary and preventive care.

> **Policy Issue**
>
> To what extent does better access to medical care improve health outcomes?

Dubay et al. (2000) found that Medicaid expansions increased medical care utilization by pregnant women. However, their research showed no significant impact on the incidence of low birthweights. They conclude that their results are due to the fact that expansions in the early 1990s included mainly pregnant women with higher family incomes. Better birth outcomes are normally associated with higher family incomes in the first place. The lesson may be that further expansions to women with higher incomes will have even smaller marginal effects on birth outcomes.

Many policymakers are convinced that there is a shortage of physicians willing to serve the Medicaid population due to low reimbursement rates. Research has shown that higher fees increase physician participation in the program (Sloan, Mitchell, and Cromwell, 1978; Hadley, 1979; Mitchell,

> **Policy Issue**
>
> Does Medicare pay high enough fees to attract a sufficient number of physicians who are willing to treat its eligible participants?

1991), especially among physicians specializing in obstetrics and gynecology (Mitchell and Schurman, 1984; Adams, 1994). This research, however, does not make the connection between higher physician participation rates and better health outcomes.

Enrollment in Private Insurance

As the value of free, public insurance coverage increases, holders of costly, private insurance are likely to drop private coverage and enroll in Medicaid. Cutler and Gruber (1996) examine the economics of crowding out and conclude that hundreds of thousands of women have dropped private insurance as Medicaid expands eligibility. The decision to drop private insurance coverage is often encouraged by employers who decrease their own share of the private insurance premium creating an incentive to "voluntarily" drop private coverage.

Labor Supply

For individuals on public welfare assistance, Medicaid eligibility is a valuable benefit. Many hesitate to accept jobs fearing the loss of free, public health insurance. This so-called "welfare lock" has been documented by Yelowitz (1995) and Winkler (1991) and is especially profound in the case of women with small children. This literature is summarized in Gruber (2000a).

Family Structure

Another important aspect of Medicaid eligibility is its impact on family structure—the marriage decision and the decision to have children. Yelowitz (1998) showed that the Medicaid program as traditionally structured created a bias favoring single-parent families. Women with children remained single to qualify for the program because potential marriage partners may not have been able to provide health insurance for the families. Between 1987 and 1992 the fraction of women of childbearing age eligible for Medicaid doubled and the fraction of children eligible increased by 50 percent (Cutler and Gruber, 1996). Medicaid's pregnancy coverage lowers the cost of childbearing and its generous child coverage lowers the discounted present value of raising a child. These two factors resulted in a significant increase in fertility among eligible women (Joyce, Kaestner, and Kwan, 1998). In fact, Medicaid expansions were estimated to be responsible for up to a 10 percent increase in the birthrate for this group (Bitler and Zavodny, 2000).

Savings

Finally, Gruber and Yelowitz (1999) discuss the channels whereby Medicaid expansions have an impact on individual savings decisions. By reducing the financial risk associated with an illness, the need for precautionary savings is diminished. Research by Kotlikoff (1988) provides the empirical evidence supporting this claim. Most public assistance programs include an asset test whereby family wealth is a determining factor of eligibility.

> **Policy Issue**
>
> Easing Medicaid eligibility standards results in several important unintended consequences with their associated negative implications.

Hubbard, Skinner, and Zeldes (1995) show that the Medicaid asset test is empirically important, lowering the wealth holdings of Medicaid families by 16.3 percent. Another potentially important concern for policymakers is the possibility that the elderly will transfer assets to their children to qualify for Medicaid financing of nursing home care. While the evidence is mixed, there is some empirical support that at least a portion of the elderly engages in this activity (Norton, 2000; Cutler and Sheiner, 1994).[12]

Critics of Medicaid contend that eligibility standards create incentives and disincentives that lead to serious socioeconomic disruptions. Family breakups are promoted by basing eligibility standards on marital status. A disincentive for work arises when eligibility is predicated on income. Dependence is encouraged because disability is used for categorical eligibility. Illegitimate births are encouraged by tying eligibility to pregnancy and the presence of children in single-parent families. Possibly the single

---

12 In Germany, the incomes of the children of elderly parents are counted when calculating the resource base for government-provided nursing home care.

Key Concept 4
Self-Interest

greatest disruption is the minimum asset requirement for eligibility. This forces many elderly females into poverty in order to qualify for long-term care.

Those who defend the system contend that Medicaid provides coverage for millions of Americans who would otherwise have no health insurance. Those who are eligible for Medicaid are among the most vulnerable population subgroups in the country, including 18.9 million children, 8 million unwed mothers, almost 4 million seniors, and 6.7 million Americans who are either disabled or blind.

Other Government Programs

In addition to Medicare and Medicaid, the federal government administers several other major health care programs, serving approximately 30 million Americans and spending over $31 billion. Another 23 million military veterans who have private health insurance are eligible for benefits through the program administered by the Veterans' Administration.

Department of Defense

The U.S. Department of Defense (DOD) has established a medical care delivery system for military personnel and their dependents. Medical services are available for both active duty and retired members, including survivors of deceased personnel. The system is divided into two parts: (1) direct care and (2) Civilian Health and TriCare Standard, formerly called Civilian Health and Medical Program of the Uniformed Services (CHAMPUS). Uniformed Services Family Health Plan is an added option for military personnel and their dependents in seven geographic areas across the country.

The Department of Veterans Affairs has links to sites providing useful information of medical interest for military veterans and related statistics at
http://www.VA.gov.

The Armed Forces operate approximately 700 medical facilities, staffed with uniformed medical personnel. These facilities range from small clinics that provide limited services to large teaching hospitals. Most are located on military bases throughout the world. Most Americans have heard of Walter Reed Army Hospital and the Bethesda Naval Hospital in Washington, D.C., in connection with the medical care of members of Congress and the President. In 2001, the direct-care military system provided medical care to over 8 million beneficiaries, including 990,000 active duty personnel and their dependents, retirees and their dependents, and survivors of deceased military personnel.

DOD also administers TriCare, a health insurance plan originally created in 1966 as CHAMPUS to provide benefits similar to those available to civilian federal employees under the Federal Employees Health Benefit Plan (FEHBP). The benefits under TriCare are similar to any standard private insurance plan with deductibles and copayments. Hospital care must be provided at a military hospital if one is available. Otherwise, the plan is like any private insurance plan with recipients being able to purchase care from private providers.

Veterans' Administration Medical Care Program

The Department of Veterans' Affairs (VA) provides medical care to military veterans who meet established active-duty service requirements.[13] In addition, veterans with service-connected disabilities, low incomes, or other special status (such as prisoner of war or World War I veteran) are also eligible for benefits. As of 2003, single veterans without dependents with incomes of less than $24,644 were eligible for mandatory benefits. If married or single with one dependent, the income threshold rose to $29,576 and increased in increments of $1,653 for every dependent. To be exempt from copayments, the veteran's income plus net worth may not exceed $80,000. Veterans with incomes above these thresholds or nonservice-connected disabilities are placed in the discretionary-care category, where medical care is provided if space and resources are available.

The VA operates one of the largest health care delivery systems in the world. Approximately 203,000 employees provide medical services to about 17 percent of the 26

---

13 The active-duty service requirements vary depending on when the person entered the military.

ISSUES IN MEDICAL CARE DELIVERY

DEFINING SERVICE-CONNECTED DISABILITIES IN THE VA

A 1993 ruling by the Secretary of Veterans' Affairs significantly expanded the definition of "service-connected" disabilities. During the Viet Nam War, the U.S. military used the defoliant Agent Orange extensively. Now, decades later a large number of veterans are claiming that exposure to this substance is responsible for various medical problems. Under this ruling, Viet Nam veterans who suffer from certain types of respiratory problems are eligible for disability pensions and free medical care.

A similar scenario has emerged with the "Gulf War Syndrome," a mysterious medical problem afflicting about 100,000 veterans who fought in the Persian Gulf in 1990 and 1991. The most common complaints include chronic fatigue, headaches, skin rashes, muscle and joint pain, memory loss, sleep disorders, chronic diarrhea, and depression. At the request of Congress, an 18-member committee assembled by the Institutes of Medicine reviewed all the relevant research on the problem and issued its final report in late 1996 (Presidential Advisory Committee, 1996). Despite accusations of a cover-up of an incidental or accidental exposure to nerve agents, the committee found no scientific evidence to support a causal link between the symptoms and illnesses reported by Gulf War veterans and exposures while in the Gulf region to chemical or biological agents (Brown, 1996). Scientists from the Naval Research Center (2000) surveyed 1,500 veterans cataloging their symptoms and illnesses. They found veterans who had symptoms and veterans who were sick. They identified over 40 different conditions responsible for nearly 500 different diagnoses, but they did not find evidence of Gulf War-related illness.

Despite the lack of evidence, many still consider Gulf War Syndrome a serious long-term problem. Researchers from the Southwestern Medical Center of the University of Texas have found evidence that veterans who suffer from the symptoms may be at risk of developing neurological diseases, including Parkinson's. Still concerned about possible links, Congress has ordered a study to address a possible association between 33 specific chemical agents and the problems of Gulf War veterans (MIT, 2000). In April 2003 the DOD issued its final report on the subject, concluding that overexposure to certain pesticides may have contributed to the unexplained illnesses reported by some Gulf War veterans.

Sources: David Brown, "Scientists Say Evidence Lacking to Tie 'Syndrome' to 1991 Gulf War," *The Washington Post,* October 10, 1996, A06; *Presidential Advisory Committee on the Gulf War Veteran's Illnesses: Final Report,* Washington, DC: U.S. Government Printing Office, December 1996; Naval Research Center, "Factor Analysis of Self-Reported Symptoms: Does It Identify a Gulf War Syndrome?" *American Journal of Epidemiology,* August 2000; and Medical Industry Today, "Study Finds Link Between Gulf War Syndrome, Parkinson's," MDI Online, http://www.medtechinsight.com, September 21, 2000. Those interested in further information on the Gulf War Syndrome should visit GulfLINK at http://www.gulflink.osd.mil.

million living American veterans. In fiscal year 2003, the VA spent $25.9 billion on medical services. VA facilities are located in each of the 48 contiguous states, the District of Columbia, and Puerto Rico. The medical system is organized into 21 integrated networks for better resource allocation. In 2002 the VA operated 163 hospitals admitting over 567,000 patients, 850 ambulatory care and community-based outpatient clinics with 46.5 million patient visits annually, 137 nursing homes serving 50,000 patients, 43 domiciliaries serving 22,500 veterans, and 73 comprehensive home care programs. Long-term care is also provided in thousands of community nursing homes nationwide on a contractual basis and in over 70 state-run nursing homes on a per diem basis.

Over 6 million eligible veterans have enrolled to receive medical care that is generally free. Veterans who are placed in the discretionary-care category are required to contribute toward the cost of their care. Veterans are subject to four basic charges. For

PROFILE

John K. Iglehart

When listing individuals who have had a profound influence on intellectual thought in the area of health policy, the name of John K. Iglehart makes everyone's top ten. Born in Milwaukee, Mr. Iglehart received his B.S. in journalism at the University of Wisconsin in 1961. After four years with the *Milwaukee Sentinel,* he spent six years with the Associated Press in Chicago and eventually was promoted to night city editor. In 1969, he took a position with the *National Journal* in Washington, D.C., where he is still one of their contributing editors.

In addition to the numerous articles he has written in health and medical journals, Mr. Iglehart is the journalist in residence at the Harvard School of Public Health and national correspondent for the *New England Journal of Medicine.* In 1981, William B. Walsh, the founder of Project HOPE (Health Opportunities for People Everywhere), recruited him to guide the creation of a new health policy journal, *Health Affairs.* Under his direction, the journal's circulation has risen to over 10,000—the largest for a journal of its type. Dedicated to the goal of Project HOPE, *Health Affairs* has become a highly respected journal among academicians, policymakers, and journalists. Faculty all over the country are using the journal as a textbook in their health economics and policy classes. Policymakers have come to rely on it as a source of background information on the complexities of health care delivery and finance. Journalists quote its pages regularly, using it as a source of breaking news in health policy research.

Iglehart is widely known for his research on the medical care delivery systems of Canada, Germany, and Japan. His recent series in the *New England Journal of Medicine* on "The American Health Care System," with subtitles ranging from "Private Insurance" to "Medicare" to "Managed Care," provides an excellent introduction into the diverse viewpoints, proposals, and perspectives on the problems faced by the U.S. medical care delivery system today.

Source: Project HOPE Web site (**http://www.projecthope.org/**) and *Who's Who in America.*

hospital stays of fewer than 90 days, the required payment is equal to the Medicare hospital deductible plus $10 per day. For hospitalizations that extend beyond 90 days, there is an extra out-of-pocket charge equal to one-half of the Medicare hospital deductible plus $10 per day. Patients are charged $15 for outpatient primary care visits and $50 for specialty care visits. A $7 copayment is required for outpatient prescription drugs and charges for long-term care vary by type of service and ability to pay.

> *Policy Issue*
>
> How far does the federal government's responsibility extend in providing medical care to military veterans?

In addition to the 29,000 physicians employed by the VA, approximately 120,000 private-practice physicians treat veterans on a fee-for-service basis every year. In many ways these facts understate the VA's involvement with the medical care delivery system in the United States. The link between the VA and private sector medicine is evident in medical education. VA facilities are affiliated with 107 medical schools and 55 dental schools, training over 81,000 health professionals annually. Because of this link, approximately one-half of medical residents rotate through a VA medical facility every year.

The system is not without its critics. A U.S. Government Accounting Office study (1993) found extensive service delays that compromise the quality of care provided at even the best VA medical centers. More than 50 percent of the patients with routine medical care needs wait at least one hour to see a physician in the VA's emergency/screening clinics. One out of every eight patients suffering from an urgent medical problem had to wait at least one hour and some as much as three hours to see a physician. Those veterans requiring care at specialty clinics experienced long delays in scheduling appointments. The average waiting time for an appointment was 62 days, with over 60 percent waiting more than 30 days. Waits of over 120 days were not uncommon (one in ten experienced these lengthy delays).

The VA has experienced many significant accomplishments in its 65-year history. It has one of the best spinal-cord injury centers in the world and was instrumental in the development of the cardiac pacemaker and the CT scan. Researchers within the system are actively contributing to aging, women's health, AIDS, post-traumatic stress disorder, and other mental health issues. Funded research in 2001 was approximately $351 million. NIH grants and support from pharmaceutical companies contributed another $500 million, funding over 10,000 research projects. The VA medical system is experiencing many of the problems of a fixed-budget medical care system. When government attempts to micro-manage medical care delivery and provide "free" care to a well-organized constituency, shortages develop (the long waiting times) and the quality of specialized care deteriorates.

Key Concept 3
*Marginal
Analysis*

Summary and Conclusions

The history of American health care cannot be understood without careful consideration of the government's expanding role in providing medical care. Medicare and Medicaid were created in 1965 to provide access to medical care for the elderly and indigent, two of the nation's most vulnerable population groups. The programs proved to be a mixed blessing. Both have been successful in fulfilling their stated missions, providing care to over 62 million of the nation's poor, elderly, and disabled. The success has come at a tremendous cost, with the government spending over $500 billion on health care.[14]

Medicare and Medicaid reform will receive a great deal of attention in future Congressional sessions. Still, the electorate applies substantial pressure to maintain a balanced federal budget and a perception that spending in these two programs must be controlled for that to happen.

The introduction of prospective payment to hospitals (through the use of diagnosis-related groups) and physician payment reform (the relative value scale) represents major changes on the spending side.[15] About all that is left on the cost side of the ledger is the unpopular prospect of asking the elderly to accept a more moderate benefits package—something most policymakers are unwilling to do—or encourage seniors to enroll in health maintenance organizations, which is something that most seniors have been unwilling to do. The alternatives on the revenue side are equally problematic. The general population could be asked to pay more in taxes or the elderly could be asked to pay higher premiums and copayments.

The Balanced Budget Act of 1997, along with a booming economy, pushed back the expected date of Medicare's insolvency to the year 2026. The spending restrictions imposed by Congress have improved the short-term outlook for the system, and have changed the political debate considerably. In the short term, pressure to add an outpatient prescription drug benefit will continue to increase.[16] Adding a prescription drug benefit and restoring some of the cuts in hospital reimbursement will once again change the insolvency date and bring into focus the underlying problem facing the system. Policymakers have still not addressed the long-term demographic problem facing the system—the aging baby-boom generation—and the fact that Medicare is still insulated from the market forces that serve as a moderating influence on the rest of the health care sector. Like the rest of the health care sector, Medicare suffers from the same structural deficiencies brought on by a third-party payment system that insulates its recipients from any incentives to economize. If the system is to be put on a sound financial basis, its structural deficiencies must be addressed (Gokhale, 1997).

Key Concept 7
Competition

---

14 Considering only Medicare and Medicaid expenditures, every person in the United States pays an average of $1,400 in taxes to care for the poor and elderly.

15 These two cost-cutting measures are discussed in the next chapter.

16 In 2000, almost two-thirds of the elderly already had a prescription drug benefit through supplemental insurance or an HMO.

Questions and Problems

1. Comment on the following statement: "The proposal to increase Medicare cost sharing (increasing premiums, deductibles, and coinsurance) will deprive the elderly poor of needed medical services."

2. You have recently been hired as a research assistant to the Secretary of Health and Human Services. To keep the administration informed on health care issues, you have been asked to research options for changing the Medicare system. Current concerns stem from the fear that if Medicare remains an open-ended entitlement program, its share of the federal budget will continue to increase over time. Prepare a brief memo to the Secretary examining one or more of the following proposed changes. Use your best economic reasoning.

   a. A freeze in physicians' fees and a requirement of mandatory assignment.

   b. A plan to enroll everyone eligible for Medicare in managed care networks and pay a fixed capitated amount per enrollee equal to the current per capita Medicare spending level.

   c. Allowing all Medicare recipients to buy high-deductible insurance policies and use the premium savings to set up medical savings accounts.

3. One of the major problems in dealing with any welfare program is the tension between individual and social responsibility—Medicare is no different. Should adult children be responsible for the medical expenses of their parents? Where does individual (familial) responsibility end and social responsibility begin?

4. What is Medigap insurance? How does the existence of Medigap policies affect the cost of providing medical services to the elderly? Was Mark Pauly right in his observation that the provision of some insurance might be suboptimal ("The Economics of Moral Hazard: Comment," *American Economic Review 58*(2), June 1968, 531–538)?

5. Define the following terms.

   a. mandatory assignment

   b. balance billing

   c. capitation

   d. free choice of provider

   Describe the effect of each on the provision of medical care for the elderly.

References

E. Kathleen Adams, "The Effect of Increased Medicaid Fees on Physician Participation and Enrollee Service Utilization in Tennessee," *Inquiry 31*(2), Summer 1994, 173–189.

Marianne Bitler and Madeline Zavodny, "The Effect of Medicaid Eligibility Expansions on Births," Federal Reserve Bank of Atlanta, Working Paper 2000–4, March 2000.

Janet Currie and Jonathan Gruber, "Saving Babies: The Efficacy and Cost of Recent Changes in the Medicaid Eligibility of Pregnant Women," *Journal of Political Economy 104*(6), December 1996a, 1263–1296.

_____, "Health Insurance Eligibility, Utilization of Medical Care, and Child Health," *Quarterly Journal of Economics 111*(2), May 1996, 431–466.

David M. Cutler and Jonathan Gruber, "Does Public Insurance Crowd Out Private Insurance?" *Quarterly Journal of Economics 111*(2), May 1996, 391–430.

David M. Cutler and Louise Sheiner, "Policy Options for Long Term Care," in David Wise, ed., *Studies in the Economics of Aging*, Chicago: University of Chicago Press, 1994, 395–434.

Geraldine Dallek, "The Crushing Costs of Medicare Supplemental Policies," Washington: Families USA, No. 96–103, October 1996.

Lisa Dubay, Theodore Joyce, Robert Kaestner, and Genevieve Kenney, "Changes in Prenatal Care Timing and Low Birth Weight by Race and Socioeconomic Status: Implications for the Medicaid Expansions for Pregnant Women," *Health Services Research*, 2000.

Kurt D. Gillis, David W. Lee, and Richard J. Willke, "Physician-Based Measures of Medical Access," *Inquiry 29*(3), Fall 1992, 321–331.

Jagadeesh Gokhale, "Medicare: Usual and Customary Remedies Will No Longer Work," *Economic Commentary*, Federal Reserve Bank of Cleveland, April 1, 1997.

Jonathan Gruber, "Health Insurance and the Labor Market," in Joseph P. Newhouse and Anthony J. Culyer, eds., *Handbook of Health Economics,* Amsterdam: North Holland, 2000a.

_____, "Medicaid," National Bureau of Economic Research Working Paper 7829, August 2000b.

_____ and Aaron Yelowitz, "Public Health Insurance and Private Savings," *Journal of Political Economy 107*(6 Part 1), December 1999, 1249–1274.

Jack Hadley, "Physician Participation in Medicaid: Evidence from California," *Health Services Research 14,* 1979, 266–280.

Health Care Financing Administration, "National Health Expenditures Projections: 1998–2008," based on the 1999 Medicare Trustees' Reports, 1999.

Geoffrey R. Hileman et al., "Medicare+Choice Individual and Group Enrollment: 2001 and 2002," *Health Care Financing Review 24*(1), Fall 2002, 145–153.

R. Glenn Hubbard, Jonathan Skinner, and Stephen P. Zeldes, "Precautionary Saving and Social Insurance," *Journal of Political Economy 103*(2), April 1995, 360–399.

Theodore Joyce, Robert Kaestner, and Florence Kwan, "Is Medicaid Pronatalist: The Effect of Eligibility Expansion on Abortions and Births," *Family Planning Perspectives 30*(3), 1998, 108–113.

Kaiser Commission on the Future of Medicaid, Medicaid and Federal, State, and Local Budgets, Washington, DC: Kaiser Commission on the Future of Medicaid, May, 1995.

Laurence J. Kotlikoff, "Health Expenditures and Precautionary Saving," in Laurence J. Kotlikoff, ed., *What Determines Saving?* Cambridge: MIT Press, 1988, 141–162.

Janet B. Mitchell, "Physician Participation in Medicaid Revisited," *Medical Care 29,* 1991, 645–653.

_____ and Rachel Schurman, "Access to Private Obstetrics/Gynecological Services Under Medicaid," *Medical Care 22,* 1984, 1026–1037.

Edward C. Norton, "Long Term Care," in Anthony Culyer and Joseph Newhouse, eds., *Handbook of Health Economics,* Amsterdam: North Holland, 2000.

Karen Pallarito, "Study Raises Concerns about Future of Medicare HMO Program," *Reuters Medical News,* June 27, 2000.

Frank Sloan, Janet Mitchell, and Jerry Cromwell, "Physician Participation in State Medicaid Programs," *Journal of Human Resources 13*(Supplement) 1978, 211–245.

U.S. General Accounting Office (USGAO), "VA Health Care: Restructuring Ambulatory Care System Would Improve Services to Veterans," Report to the Chairman, Subcommittee on Oversight and Investigations, Committee on Veterans' Affairs, House of Representatives, October 1993.

Bruce C. Vladeck and Kathleen M. King, "Medicare at 30: Preparing for the Future," *Journal of the American Medical Association 274*(3), July 19, 1995, 259–262.

Anne E. Winkler, "The Incentive Effects of Medicaid on Women's Labor Supply," *Journal of Human Resources 26*(2), Spring 1991, 308–337.

Aaron Yelowitz, "The Medicaid Notch, Labor Supply, and Welfare Participation: Evidence from Eligibility Expansions," *Quarterly Journal of Economics 110*(4), November 1995, 909–939.

_____, "Will Extending Medicaid to Two-Parent Families Encourage Marriage?" *Journal of Human Resources 33*(4), Fall 1998, 833–865.

Appendix 14A

A Note on "Projections"

One of the intriguing questions that puzzles those with inquiring minds is "Just where do they come up with these numbers anyway?" Anyone who forecasts for a living knows that change is the order of the day. Seldom do things stay the same. Underlying economic conditions change and institutional characteristics change. About the only thing that stays the same is human nature, and that is sometimes the most unpredictable piece in the entire puzzle.

Forecasting, by its very nature, has an element of extrapolation associated with it. Examining trends and extending those trends into the future is a common technique used to project all sorts of economic variables. Currently, an estimated 4 million Americans are afflicted with Alzheimer's disease. With 1 percent of all 65-year-olds and 25 percent of all 85-year-olds diagnosed with the disease, as the number of elderly increase, especially the number who reach their eighty-fifth birthday, the number of people with Alzheimer's disease will skyrocket. It is expected that 15 million people will have the disorder by 2050, if an effective form of prevention and treatment is not found. Extrapolation plays a key role in this kind of prediction. There is nothing inherently wrong with making these predictions as long as we understand the qualifying statement, "if an effective form of prevention and treatment is not found."

Predictions of health care spending absorbing 25 to 40 percent of GDP by the year 2030 are political fodder in policymaking circles (Waldo et al., 1991). The spending scenarios necessary to bring about these results make little intuitive sense when examined closely. Centers for Medicare and Medicaid Services (CMS) projections shown in Table 14A.1 are based on actuarial models using trend analysis. According to CMS projections, personal health care spending will increase to approximately $2 trillion by 2012, representing 15.9 percent of GDP and $7,572 per capita. Actuarial projections reflect what would happen if nothing changed. The baseline projections assume a continuation of current policies and trends. In other words, current programs, regulations, and practices remain unchanged. In addition, economy-wide shocks, all technological innovation, and any reform of health care delivery and finance are ruled out.

In 1992, the Congressional Budget Office (CBO), known for its "fair" numbers, projected medical care spending at 18 percent of GDP by the year 2000 (Lemieux and Williams, 1992). The current conventional wisdom projects spending to reach 16 percent of GDP by the year 2010, a far cry from the 1992 CBO projections (Burner and Waldo, 1995).

Table 14A.1	National Health Care Expenditures 1980–1995 with Projections (2000, 2005, and 2008)					
Category	1980	1990	1995	2000	2005	2008
Personal Health Care (billions)	$217.0	$614.7	$879.3	$1,150.9	$1,586.4	$1,925.2
National Health Expenditures (billions)	247.3	697.4	993.7	1,316.2	1,799.5	2,176.6
Per Capita Personal Spending	923	2,364	3,220	4,031	5,343	6,341
Per Capita National Spending	1,052	2,689	3,638	4,611	6,061	7,170
National Spending as a Percent of GDP	8.9%	12.2%	13.7%	14.3%	15.6%	16.2%

Source: *1999 Annual Reports of the OASDI and Medicare Boards of Trustees to Congress* based on data from the Office of the Actuary, Health Care Financing Administration.

Policy based on these projections would call for immediate action, but for medical care spending to reach, say, 25 percent of GDP, substantially more than 25 percent of the annual changes in GDP must be spent in the health care sector. Except for recessionary periods, the change in health care spending relative to the change in GDP rarely reaches 0.15, placing an upper bound on the ratio of health care spending-to-GDP at 15 percent. In fact, over the period 1984 to 1990, the change in health care spending represented 15.5 percent of the total change in GDP and was never greater than 17 percent.

The key phrase in the above scenario is "except for recessionary periods." Over the past 35 years, only twice has the change in medical care spending exceeded 17 percent of the GDP change. The 1981–1982 recession and the 1990-1991 recession saw this figure rise to over 30 percent.

It is easy to criticize those who make predictions for a living. Meteorologists have difficulty forecasting what the weather will be like tomorrow morning. The economist always seems to have an explanation for why those interest rate predictions were incorrect. And when is the last time Sylvia Browne or even the Amazing Kreskin got it just right? Most projections are based on some variant of extrapolation, analyzing trends based on certain assumptions about the state of the world at some future date. The farther that date is into the future, the more careful we need to be about relying too heavily on those predictions. Remember what they say: "The only two things certain in this world are death and taxes."

References

Sally T. Burner and Daniel R. Waldo, "National Health Expenditure Projections, 1994–2005," *Health Care Financing Review 16*(4), Summer 1995, 221–242.

Jeffrey A. Lemieux and Christopher Williams, *Projections of National Health Expenditures,* Congress of the United States, Congressional Budget Office, October, 1992.

Daniel R. Waldo, Sally T. Sonnefeld, Jeffrey A. Lemieux, and David R. McKusick, "Health Spending Through 2000: Three Scenarios," *Health Affairs 10*(4), Winter 1991, 231–242.

Chapter 15

Policies to Contain Costs

As the cost of medical care rises, policymakers throughout the world have had to face difficult decisions concerning quality, access, and spending. The problems of medical care delivery affect the quality of life of millions of people, particularly the poor and uninsured. Concern for this segment of the population has resulted in the provision of universal coverage in most developed countries around the world (with the notable exception of the United States). With access guaranteed, spending has become the primary issue directing public debate.

This chapter examines the options available to policymakers in their quest to control rising costs and spending growth. Fee schedules, **global budgets**, and resource rationing are the topics of the first section. Next, the U.S. experience with these options is explored in a discussion of the Medicare payment mechanism. Prospective payments to hospitals with diagnosis-related groups and physicians' fee schedules using a relative value scale are examined here. Further analysis of cost containment through managed care and other market alternatives concludes the discussion.

> **global budget**
> A limit on the amount of money available to a health care system during a specified time period. All medically necessary care must be provided to all eligible patients within the limits placed on the provider by the fixed budget.

Policy Options

Systems that guarantee free access to medical care must eventually confront the issue of escalating costs. The way most health care delivery systems are organized, relying on the third-party payment system, no natural mechanisms control cost and spending. That task is left to policymakers who usually rely on a combination of three approaches to rein in spending growth: mandated fee schedules, global budgets, and resource rationing. Market economists classify all three under the same general heading of price controls and recognize the common element they share—interference with the market.

> **Policy Issue**
> How can a health care system that relies on third-party insurance control spending?

Policymakers soon realize that fee schedules by themselves cannot control spending. The two independent variables in the spending identity are price and quantity.[1] To control spending, one must control both price and quantity. Direct limits on the quantity of services available are too easily identified as rationing (the dreaded "R" word that all policymakers seek to avoid). Thus, the three cost-control measures go hand in hand. Once fee schedules are mandated, global budgeting soon follows. Inevitably, the unintended consequence of fee schedules and global budgeting is resource rationing. To paraphrase a wise saying: The road to rationing is paved with good intentions.

Key Concept 5
Markets and Pricing

Mandated Fee Schedules

Almost every government-run system has resorted to some form of price setting in an attempt to control spending. Whether referred to as a *price freeze* or a *price ceiling*, the price schedules are commonly negotiated between the government and representatives of the medical community. They may be interim, voluntary, or mandatory. Sometimes the prices are

> **Policy Issue**
> Are price ceilings and spending caps the way to control the problem of rising health care spending?

---

1 In other words, $TE = P \times Q$, where TE is total expenditures, P is price, and Q is quantity.

Back-of-the-Envelope

WHY A PRICE CEILING MAY NOT LOWER SPENDING

It is easy to understand why the casual observer could expect price controls to slow spending growth. Using the following diagram, the demand for medical care is depicted by the downward sloping demand curve, labeled D_0. For purposes of this discussion, assume that providers are accommodating to the wishes of the patient population and supply all the medical care desired at the prevailing price. If equilibrium is at point A, quantity Q_0 is demanded at price P_0. Total spending will be P_0 times Q_0, depicted by the area $0P_0AQ_0$. If a price ceiling is enacted at P_1, the new equilibrium will be at point B and quantity will be Q_1. Since demand for medical care is relatively price inelastic, the new level of spending, $0P_1BQ_1$, is less than before. (If the demand were relatively elastic, the new level of spending would be greater.)

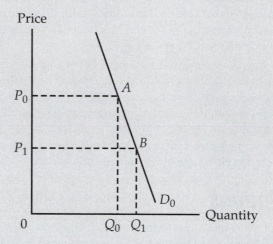

It would be great for policymakers if things worked out this way. Controlling the growth in medical care spending would be simple. Mandate lower prices in a market characterized by inelastic demand and spending levels will fall. Several problems are inherent in this approach. Providers will accommodate patient desires only up to a point. Drive the price down below cost and quantity supplied will go down. (That issue is discussed in the next Back-of-the-Envelope feature, "The Economics of Price Controls.") Even with accommodating providers, spending is likely to rise. The following diagram shows how.

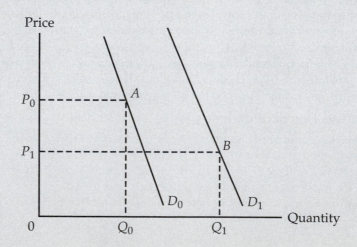

Key Concept 6
Supply and Demand

Begin with the same demand curve D_0, price P_0, quantity Q_0, and spending $0P_0AQ_0$. A price ceiling at P_1 creates an incentive for providers to increase service intensity and maybe even influence demand (remember the concept of supplier-induced demand). Expanding the size of the eligible population and incorporating advances in technology created for the uncontrolled segment of the market (three to four times larger than the controlled segment) work together to shift demand to the right to D_1. The resulting level of spending, $0P_1BQ_1$, is actually higher than before the drop in price.

loosely determined through a relative value schema that attempts to place a value on services according to some comparative scale. More often than not, this scale measures the political influence of the various specialties and not relative resource use.

Providers can still maintain their profit margins by lowering their own expenses. If there is waste in the system, price controls serve as a stimulus toward more efficient resource use. Thus, price controls can provide some short-term relief from the spiral of medical spending, but over time the short-term beneficial effects are exhausted. Providers often find that they can get around the controls (and the associated erosion in their incomes) by seeing more patients and treating them more intensively. Thus, physician-induced demand may actually shift the demand curve for services to the right, result in a higher level of spending, and an increase in the physician's income. This shift means less time spent with each patient, so more patients can be seen, and more follow-up visits scheduled. Another common practice to avoid the heavy hand of price controls is the unbundling of services. Unbundling refers to the practice of breaking down a service into its various component parts. Instead of billing for the service, the provider bills for each part of the treatment. The practice defies logic because the sum of the parts is greater than the whole. Standard care for treating a broken bone, when decomposed into its component parts with a separate bill for each, will cost more than the complete item. The amount that can be billed for an office visit, two X-rays, and a follow-up visit is often greater than the bill for the total package including the cast and its removal. A patient billed separately for the component parts of a wheelchair—wheels, armrests, cushions, and so on—will pay more than the cost of the complete item. A glucose monitoring kit will cost $12 at the local pharmacy, but as much as $250 when unbundled and each item sold separately.

Key Concept 7
Competition

Key Concept 8
Efficiency

Controlled prices seldom result in the desired level of spending. In almost every situation where price controls have been tried, the fee schedule is ultimately revised downward, either through some automatic mechanism or unilaterally by the government authority. A system of negotiated fee schedules eventually becomes one of regulated fee schedules with an elaborate government mechanism to ensure compliance.

Global Budgeting

Unable to control spending with fee schedules (and desiring to avoid the direct plunge into rationing), historically the next step has been to establish a global budget. Global budgets are nothing more than spending caps.[2] These caps may be established either as targeted or mandatory budgets. In politics, targeted caps serve merely as "backstop" measures. In other words, they are really not binding in the sense that they would force rationing. In reality, however, the targets soon become mandatory budgets and what was never intended becomes part of the apparatus of control.

Global budgets may be used in various ways. Canada and Germany set global budgets for hospitals, providing each institution with a set amount of money to be used to provide services to all comers. Should actual

Policy Issue

Will global budgeting for hospitals reduce spending in this sector?

---

2 Global budgets were referred to as "prospective budgets" in the U.S. health care reform terminology.

Back-of-the-Envelope

THE ECONOMICS OF PRICE CONTROLS

The impact of government-imposed price controls depends on the competitive nature of the market where they exist. In a competitive market, a binding price ceiling (one where the legal price is below the equilibrium price) will cause a shortage.

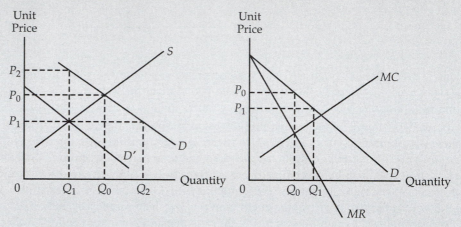

The left side of the diagram shows the demand curve (D) and supply curve (S) for a product sold in a competitive market. With no market interference, the equilibrium is established at the intersection of supply and demand, yielding the market-clearing price (P_0) and quantity (Q_0). If government uses its authority to set a binding price ceiling (P_1), producers will choose to produce at a lower level of output (Q_1). At the lower price, however, consumers will want more (Q_2). The resulting discrepancy between the quantity demanded and the quantity supplied ($Q_2 - Q_1$) is the shortage.

Ironically, the unintended consequence of this action to lower the price of the product has actually raised its effective price to consumers. How? In their quest to secure desired quantities of the product at the lower price, consumers will compete in other ways. If price does not serve to ration the product, another mechanism will emerge. Consumers will get up early, stay up late, become friends with producers, resort to bribes, and buy in large quantities when the product is available, all of which adds to the nonpecuniary cost of the product. Added to these costs is the anxiety brought about by the increased uncertainty of not knowing whether consumers will ever have as much of the product as they want.

Referring back to the diagram, the nonpecuniary costs grow until their combined effects shift the consumers' demand curve down to D'. At the new equilibrium, consumers are paying less in money terms (P_1) but more when the monetary costs and nonmonetary costs (P_2) are combined.

Price controls can be effective in a market controlled by a monopolist. The right side of the diagram shows a monopolist, as sole seller, facing the market demand curve and producing where marginal revenue (MR) equals marginal cost (MC). The equilibrium price and quantity are established at P_0 and Q_0. In this case, the government can set a price below P_0 and actually increase the quantity produced. A price ceiling set at P_1 will change the effective shape of the demand and marginal revenue curves. They both become a horizontal line at the ceiling price. Thus, marginal revenue (now P_1) equals marginal cost at the quantity Q_1.

Do price controls produce shortages, black markets, and reduced quality? It depends on the nature of the market, competitive or monopoly. How do price controls affect medical markets? It depends, once again, on which segment of the medical market being considered. The market for patented drugs probably fits the classical case of monopoly better than any other aspect of the medical market. A suitably chosen price could improve the efficiency in this market, assuming that regulators are clever enough to choose the right price. Failure to choose the right price will, however, lead to reduced research and development, fewer discoveries, and the loss of consumer welfare (read that "lost lives"). The markets for physicians' and hospital services are much closer to the competitive model and price controls are likely to have the undesirable effects.

At least one former government policy analyst seems to agree that price controls could lead to restrictions on the rate of technological development and ultimately the rationing of health care (Wagner, 1993). As director of the Congressional Budget Office (CBO), Robert Reischauer testified before the House Ways and Means health subcommittee on the possible effects of price controls on medical care. Research by the CBO (which conducts financial analysis for the Congress) concluded that price controls could severely limit the quality and quantity of medical care in the United States. Reischauer went on to argue that the only way to control medical care spending is by imposing global health care budgets at the national level. Thus, Reischauer exhibits the irony of government policymakers—arguing for and against price controls at the same time.

Source: Lynn Wagner, "CBO Head Warns Price Controls Could Severely Limit Quality, Quantity of Medical Care in the U.S.," *Modern Healthcare 23*(3), March 8, 1993, 22.

spending exceed budgeted spending, hospital providers are then faced with a dilemma. Providers handle this situation in a straightforward manner. Anything that can be delayed is delayed. Hospital wards are closed, operating rooms are unused, and personnel take unpaid vacations. All elective surgery is wait-listed until the next budget period. What resources remain available are used to treat only life-threatening conditions.

Resource Rationing

Frustrated with their inability to control medical spending with price controls even in a fixed-budget system, policymakers are left with their last alternative—resource rationing.[3] Policymakers rarely use the term *rationing*. But for all its various names, its results are the same—limiting access to the high-cost hospital and specialty sector.

The first step toward resource rationing begins with improving access to primary and preventive care by encouraging or possibly even mandating that more physicians practice primary and family medicine.[4] As the system evolves, primary care physicians are cast in the role of the "gatekeeper." Patients must first go through a gatekeeper before they are admitted to a hospital or are allowed to see a specialist.

To ensure cost containment, access to high-cost medical technology must be restricted. Designating certain facilities as technology centers usually accomplishes this task. Rationing takes the form of increased time cost of travel to distant facilities, especially for patients living in rural areas, and waiting lists.

In summary, price controls in medical care seem to benefit patients at the expense of providers, at least in the short term. Initially, this may seem desirable to many policymakers. The beneficial effects are immediate, but the harmful effects take longer to materialize and are difficult to understand. The lessons, however, are clear. After the initial cost efficiencies are realized, the lower prices associated with

---

3 A system where payment is based on capitation, including a significant portion of the managed care system in the United States, is a fixed-budget system.

4 Establishing quotas for residency programs or paying all providers according to the same fee schedule, creating strong incentives to specialize in primary care, may accomplish this step.

the fee schedules lead to fixed budgets and eventually limits on services. Targets become mandates and sooner or later, nonprice rationing becomes prevalent, resulting in an inefficient distribution of services among patients. Quality of care does not improve with controls; in fact it deteriorates. In the end, controls actually increase costs because the distortions created by controls stifle the innovative activities that would lower costs. So the root cause of increased spending, limited cost-conscious behavior on the part of buyers or sellers, is never addressed.

Cost-Containment Strategies in the United States

To date, providers in the United States have had limited experience with these popular rationing schemes.[5] Resource allocation is still primarily based on market mechanisms and not artificial controls. As medical prices continue to escalate, the pressure on policymakers to find a new approach has grown. Instead of developing policies that encourage market solutions, policymakers are more likely to propose government solutions that include price controls.

The U.S. government pays for almost one-half of the medical care provided in this country; therefore, government solutions have focused on controlling federal outlays, especially for Medicare and Medicaid. The temptation facing policymakers is the simplistic appeal of price controls to limit expenditures, which is much like trying to limit the spread of the flu by passing a law against running a temperature greater than 98.6 degrees Fahrenheit. You cannot legislate an illness out of existence. Likewise, you cannot legislate price increases out of existence. Price controls bring about unintended consequences that are potentially more difficult to deal with than the price increases they were designed to limit. Changes in Medicare reimbursement for hospitals and physicians over the past decade provide a good case study in the limitations of price controls in controlling medical spending.

Diagnosis Related Groups

Until 1983 Medicare reimbursed hospitals on a cost-plus basis for all inpatient services. The hospital provided services to an eligible recipient and billed Medicare for the cost of that care. Thus, payment was determined retrospectively, based on per-unit or per-service charges determined by what the hospital billed for the services provided. This payment mechanism, coupled with private third-party financing, was largely responsible for the increased volume and intensity of services observed in the hospital sector, and to varying degrees for the growing inefficiencies within the industry evidenced by overinvestment in capital equipment.

To counter the increased spending and the growing inefficiencies, federal strategy focused its cost-containment efforts on devising a prospective payment mechanism for the hospital sector. Introduced in 1983, prospective payment took the form of flat-rate reimbursement for hospitals based on principal diagnosis of the patient plus a number of adjustments.[6] In principle, prospective payment will provide economic incentives to conserve on the use of scarce medical resources and in turn hold down the growth in expenditures.

Diagnosis related groups (DRGs) have actually redefined the unit of measure used in determining Medicare payments. No longer are charges determined on a per-item or a

Key Concept 8
Efficiency

---

5 The notable exception has been state certificate-of-need (CON) legislation. The objective of CON laws was to limit the proliferation of capital expansion in the hospital industry. Most analysts would conclude the laws have experienced mixed results across the country.

6 The legislative history of prospective payment can be dated September 1982. It was then that the Tax Equity and Financial Responsibility Act became law, requiring the Secretary of Health and Human Services to report back to Congress with a prospective payment system by the end of 1982. The DRG system was created as an amendment to the Social Security Act and passed on April 20, 1983.

per-service basis. Now charges are determined in advance on a per-case basis. Payment is based on a point system and is determined by a reimbursement rate that is set for each case-weighted point. These relative weights are set nationally and adjusted for a rural or urban location, the number of residents and interns per bed for teaching facilities, and the number of low-income patients treated by the hospital. In 2000, the unadjusted reimbursement rate for hospitals in large urban areas was $3,951.03 per weighted point. Teaching hospitals received a percentage increment over that amount for every resident and intern. All hospitals receive a capital adjustment and certain hospitals that provide a substantial amount of free care are provided with a further adjustment.

Table 15.1 ranks the 25 most frequently used DRGs based on 2001 hospital discharge data for Medicare patients. Clearly, cases related to the heart, lung, and stomach dominate the list of hospital services provided to enrollees. Of all the 2001 Medicare hospital discharges, over 50 percent are represented in these 25 DRGs.

The Nature of DRGs

It is instructive to examine the organization of the DRG classification scheme. Medicare initially set up 467 DRG categories based on principal diagnosis, the age of the patient,

Table 15.1	Twenty-Five Most Frequent DRGs All Medicare Discharges, 2001	

Rank	Code	Description
1	127	Heart failure and shock
2	089	Simple pneumonia and pleurisy, age >17 with CC[a]
3	088	Chronic obstructive pulmonary disease
4	209	Major joint and limb reattachment procedures of lower extremity
5	116	Pacemaker implant or PTCA with coronary artery stent implant
6	014	Specific cerebrovascular disorders except transient ischemic attack
7	430	Psychoses
8	462	Rehabilitation
9	182	Esophagitis, gastroenteritis, and miscellaneous digestive disorders, age >17 with CC
10	296	Nutritional and miscellaneous metabolic disorders, age >17 with CC
11	143	Chest pain
12	174	Gastrointestinal hemorrhage with CC
13	138	Cardiac arrhythmia and conduction disorders with CC
14	320	Kidney and urinary tract infections, age >17 with CC
15	416	Septicemia, age >17
16	121	Circulatory disorders with acute myocardial infarction and cardiovascular complications, discharged alive
17	079	Respiratory infections and inflammations, age >17 with CC
18	132	Atherosclerosis with CC
19	015	Transient ischemic attack and precerebral occlusions
20	124	Circulatory disorders except acute myocardial infarction, with cardiac catheterization and complex diagnosis
21	148	Major small and large bowel procedures with CC
22	210	Hip and femur procedures except major joint, age >17 with CC
23	316	Renal failure
24	478	Other vascular procedures with CC
25	475	Respiratory system diagnosis with ventilator support

a Complication and/or comorbidity

Source: CMS, Medicare Rankings for all Short-Stay Hospitals, 2001.

the presence of comorbidity conditions, the use of surgical procedures, and the discharge status of the patient. There are currently 510 DRGs, each assigned a relative weight to approximate the resource usage of the average case within that diagnosis category.

Figure 15.1 provides details on the classification system and relative resource usage for a pregnant female who presents herself to the labor and delivery area of a hospital. Under these circumstances, the two possibilities are either the female is experiencing labor or she is not. A female in labor may or may not be experiencing complications and may end up delivering the baby in the normal manner (i.e., vaginal delivery) or may have a cesarean section. The normal delivery without complications or other procedures is DRG 373 with a resource-use weighting of 0.3973. The cesarean delivery with complications is DRG 370 and has a resource-use weighting of 0.9067, implying a little over two times the resource use of a DRG 373 delivery.

These eight related DRGs have relative resource weightings ranging from 0.2894 for false labor to 0.9067 for a cesarean delivery with complications. For a **monetary conversion factor** of $3,950 per weighting point, the hospital would be reimbursed $1,143 for

monetary conversion factor
A monetary value used to translate relative value units into dollar amounts to determine a fee schedule.

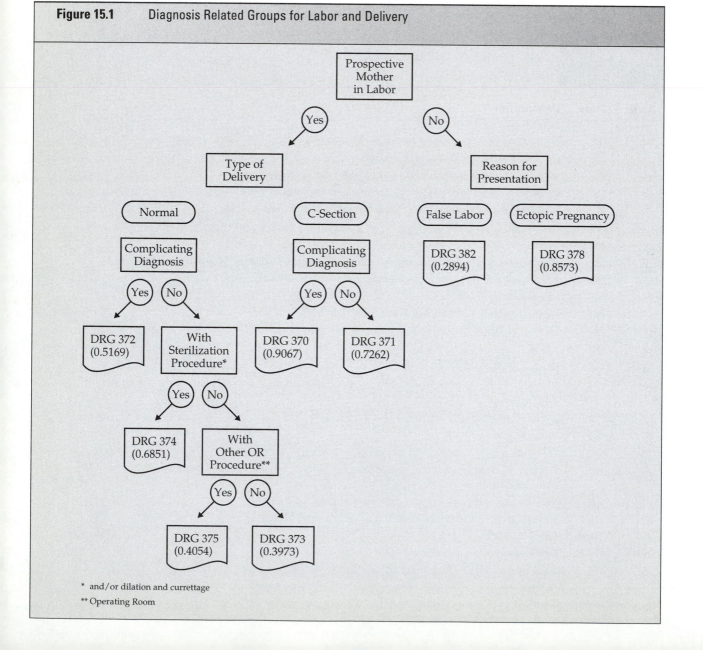

Figure 15.1   Diagnosis Related Groups for Labor and Delivery

* and/or dilation and currettage
** Operating Room

Back-of-the-Envelope

EXPLAINING THE SURGE IN OUTPATIENT VISITS

From 1988 to 1996, hospital admissions leveled off at 33 million per year while outpatient visits increased over 60 percent to 481 million per year. While inpatient expenses grew 55 percent, outpatient expenses grew 175 percent. Moderation in one segment of the market is being matched by unprecedented growth in the other. What's going on here? This shift may be understood, at least in part, by recognizing that the inpatient sector of the hospital market is regulated and the outpatient sector is not. The impact is depicted in the diagram.

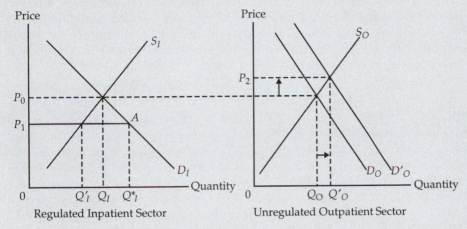

Equilibrium will take place in both sectors where their respective supply and demand curves intersect at price P_O. A price ceiling in the regulated inpatient sector changes the demand curve from D_I to $P_1 A D_I$ and the equilibrium quantity supplied falls from Q_I to Q'_I. With more people desiring inpatient services, Q^*_I, and fewer services provided, Q'_I patients are directed to the outpatient sector and resources are transferred to meet the higher level of demand. The result is easy to predict—higher service volume, higher prices, and greater spending.

the services provided a female experiencing false labor and $3,581 for a female with a complicating diagnosis receiving a cesarean section.[7]

Economic Impact of DRGs on Hospital Behavior

The stated goals of introducing prospective payment for hospitals were to control the growth in hospital spending under Medicare and promote cost efficiencies in the provision of hospital services. Evidence indicates that prospective payment has succeeded in reducing Medicare hospital expenditures (Russell and Manning, 1989). Using 1990 prices, the savings from prospective payment amounted to approximately $18 billion from what had earlier been projected for that year. Much of the savings can be attributed to decreases in the number of hospital admissions and the average length of a hospital stay. Between 1982 and 1985, the average length of stay for a Medicare patient fell 15 percent alone. In fact, the number of admissions and the average length of stay fell across the board in response to these changes in reimbursement, an indication of system-wide inefficiencies.

Policy Issue

How does the change to prospective payment affect medical care delivery in the hospital sector?

Key Concept 5
Markets and Pricing

7 There are further adjustments if the hospital is a teaching hospital, a rural hospital, or serves a disproportionate number of indigents.

In general, hospital reimbursement under Medicare is determined at the point of diagnosis.[8] If the cost of treatment is less than the DRG reimbursement rate, the hospital keeps the surplus.[9] If costs exceed reimbursement, the hospital absorbs the loss. In theory, hospitals that treat a large number of Medicare recipients in each diagnostic category should be able to cover costs with overall reimbursements. During the first few years after implementation of the program, hospitals experienced healthy operating margins on Medicare patients, ranging from 8 to 15 percent (Sheingold, 1989). These margins were due primarily to aggressive cost reductions and clever gaming of the DRG system.[10] In response, Congress legislated changes in reimbursement rates and by the late 1980s operating margins on Medicare patients were negative (Folland and Kleiman, 1990).

Evidence also indicates that the reduction in admissions was partially offset by an increase in outpatient services (Feinglass and Holloway, 1991). Thus, the principal question on whether Medicare prospective payment has reduced overall health care spending is somewhat ambiguous. In reality, whenever price controls are applied to one segment of the market, incentives encourage providers to transfer resources to the unregulated segment.

In 1997, the federal government faced what seemed at the time large and insurmountable budget deficits. Projections that year had the Medicare Hospital Insurance Trust Fund bankrupt by the year 2002 unless action was taken. Congress responded with the Balanced Budget Act of 1997 (BBA) that was supposed to reduce the growth of Medicare by $116 billion from 1998 to 2002. About one-half of these reductions were scheduled to come from reduced payments to hospitals. Subsequent projections estimate the five-year impact at over $200 billion, almost twice the intended result. The Lewin Group (1999) estimated that the BBA reductions would result in negative Medicare margins for the U.S. hospital industry, averaging a negative 4.4 percent by 2002. Forcing 70 percent of all hospitals to operate at negative margins was not the intention of Congress, so in 1999 the Balanced Budget Refinement Act was passed restoring an estimated $16 billion of the original reductions. Without further relief, Lewin (1999) estimated that 60 percent of all hospitals would still lose money on Medicare patients by the end of 2004.

Setting Physicians' Fees: Resource-Based Relative Value Scale (RBRVS)

Between 1975 and 1987 Medicare's spending per enrollee for physicians' services grew at a compound annual rate of 15.0 percent, or almost twice the compound rate of growth in per capita gross domestic product. Approximately half of this increase was due to an increase in prices and the other half was due to an increase in volume. Budgetary constraints in an era of deficit awareness highlighted two main concerns: (1) spending is not necessarily cost effective; and (2) previous payment schedules have inequitable rates between procedural services (i.e., surgery and invasive testing) and evaluation and management (E/M) services (i.e., office visits and consultations).

Key Concept 4
Self-Interest

An inequitable fee structure provides incentives to over-perform certain services and under-perform others. Medical school graduates can also be influenced by the distorted fee structure in their choice of specialty and the geographic location of their practice.

Fee-For-Service Payment Under Medicare

Under Medicare, the payment structure for physicians was based on the principle of "customary, prevailing, and reasonable" charges. Medicare payments were limited to the minimum of the customary, prevailing, and reasonable charges for a particular physician

---

8 Hospitals can petition for additional reimbursement in those cases where unusual circumstances drive the cost of treatment beyond expected levels.

9 The correct term is *surplus* in a not-for-profit hospital. In a for-profit hospital, the same concept is called *profit*.

10 In the late 1990s, Columbia/HCA was investigated for fraudulent practices in classifying patients and billing Medicare. In December 2000 they paid the U.S. government $850 million in criminal and civil penalties related to guilty pleas as the first stage in the settlement of the fraud actions against it.

ISSUES IN MEDICAL CARE DELIVERY

THE ROCHESTER MODEL

Presidential candidate Bill Clinton's 1992 visit to Rochester, New York, served to focus national attention on the city's medical care delivery system. Based on that visit, many felt it likely that as president, Mr. Clinton would use Rochester as a model for reform nationwide. Examination of the Rochester model provides insight into the importance of crafting local solutions to the health care delivery problem. During a period when only 85 percent of the U.S. population has some form of health insurance coverage, the Rochester plan provided insurance for over 93 percent of the residents of a six-county area.

Rochester's approach to medical care delivery has emerged over the past 40 years as a cooperative effort among medical care providers, local employers and their employees, and health insurance companies. A key reason for Rochester's success is the refusal of its seven area hospitals to participate in the so-called "medical arms race." Instead of competing for patients by investing in all the latest technologies, each hospital specializes in a different area—one offers neonatal intensive care, another cardiology, still another cancer therapy—thus, avoiding costly duplication of services. Physicians have given up some of their freedom by accepting a negotiated fee schedule that pays them approximately two-thirds of the fees charged elsewhere. Large corporations have played an important role by participating in the community insurance pool and rejecting the popular trend toward self-insurance.

Health insurance costs for local employers were $2,730 per employee in 1992, about 70 percent of the national average of $3,968. The source of these savings is the subject of intense debate. Proponents of the plan focus on the regional cooperation that holds down medical inflation. Officials from the Rochester Area Blue Cross attribute the savings to the expanded use of electronic claims processing, the high productivity of insurance industry employees, and the relatively low spending on advertising.

Critics of the plan argue that the cost savings are due to the large percentage of the population enrolled in managed care plans—over 55 percent of the 1.1 million residents. In addition, they point out that while medical costs are lower, they are escalating at the same rate in Rochester as they are in the rest of the country. They point out that hospitals must secure the approval of the area Hospital Corporation before expanding facilities or adding services. As a result, there have been no new hospital beds added in the community since the 1960s. Average occupancy rates are almost 90 percent as compared with barely 60 percent nationwide, which frequently results in overcrowding, canceled surgery, and regular closings of area emergency rooms because of the lack of available beds. The lesson to be learned from Rochester is simple. Whatever is decided nationally, it should not jeopardize a system created by a local community to solve community problems.

Sources: Sherry Jacobson, "Rochester's 'Model' Health Plan Suffers a Backlash from Clinton," *The Dallas Morning News*, June 12, 1994, 1A, 26A; and Milt Freudenheim, "Rochester: An American Success Story," in Erik Eckholm, *Solving America's Health Care Crisis*, New York: Times Books, 1993, 206–211.

practicing in a specific geographic area. The customary charge is defined as the median charge (50th percentile) of the physician's charges during the previous year. The prevailing charge is the charge at the 75th percentile of area physicians' charges for services during the previous year. The price the physician normally charged for the procedure was also factored into the process. If the actual charge was lower than the "customary, prevailing, and reasonable" charge, then it was the price allowed by Medicare.

Under the old fee-for-service system, physician payment had a built-in inflationary bias. Physicians had no incentive to compete on the basis of price. If a physician's actual charges were less than the customary charge in the area, the physician received the actual charge. The incentive was to raise fees to the customary charge. As fees escalated, physician and patient behavior was distorted. Physicians criticized the system as complex and unpredictable. Others argued that it was irrational, inequitable, and open to abuse.

Establishing a Relative Value Scale

In 1986 the Congress commissioned a study to determine the feasibility of developing a **resource-based relative value scale** (RBRVS) for physician payment. Hsiao et al. (1988) conducted a two-year study of physician compensation and developed resource-based relative values for physicians' services in 18 specialty areas.

A relative value scale is an index of the relative levels of resource use when physicians produce services or procedures. Although the relative value scale is denominated in nonmonetary units, the logical extension translates relative resource use into a fee schedule. To establish a fee schedule based on the RBRVS, relative values are multiplied by a monetary conversion factor (dollars per unit) to get dollar cost per service or procedure.

Relative value scales were first developed in the United States by individual state medical societies in response to the increased complexity of medical practice and the need to develop a means of determining the amount to charge for various services provided. In other countries, Japan for example, relative value scales are used in various forms to establish a technical basis for the established fee schedules. The relative value scale provides guidelines in establishing weights that reflect time to perform a procedure and its complexity. In theory, weighting should reflect changing technologies. As methods of treating various conditions change, so should the weighting.

Today, Medicare physician payment is based on the principle that differences in payments should reflect differences in work effort. Physicians incur three types of costs to produce medical services for their patients: (1) work effort measured by their own time, energy, and skill level; (2) the overhead cost of their practice; and (3) professional liability insurance premiums. The Medicare fee schedule calculates a total relative value unit for each service based on these costs.

Determining a Payment Schedule from Relative Values

A relative value scale does not automatically translate into a fee schedule. It is, however, simply a matter of applying a monetary conversion factor to the scale. Theoretically, once the conversion factor is set, the payment schedule is determined by applying it to the relative value units. Under the old Medicare method of payment, physicians were paid more for performing invasive medical procedures than for general medical services. RBRVS has tried to address these discrepancies. As a result, certain specialties experienced substantial increases in revenues as a result of the change, including family practice, internal medicine, and allergy and immunology. Other specialties, including thoracic and cardiovascular surgery, ophthalmology, pathology, radiology, dermatology, and general surgery saw decreases in revenue.

A fee system based on the relative value scale is designed to reduce the disparities between procedures and services. Such a system focuses on the time and effort involved in providing the medical procedure or service and rewards physicians accordingly. Allowable fees for invasive procedures fell while those for the general services rose. It is not surprising that specialists whose practices were primarily in the former group are vehemently opposed to the new system. General practice physicians whose practices fall predominantly in the latter group strongly supported the changes.

When the Medicare fee schedule was first implemented in 1992, the monetary conversion factor was $31 per relative value unit. A medical service with a relative weighting of 5 units would be paid $155 ($31 × 5). Congress adjusts the conversion factor annually. In

Key Concept 5
Markets and Pricing

resource-based relative value scale (RBRVS)
A classification system for physicians' services, using a weighting scheme that reflects the relative value of the various services performed. The RBRVS developed for Medicare by a group of Harvard researchers considers time, skill, and overhead cost required for each service. When used in conjunction with a monetary conversion factor, medical fees are determined.

ISSUES IN MEDICAL CARE DELIVERY

CAN PHYSICIANS COMPETE ON PRICE?

Competitive markets depend on the free flow of information if they are to perform their assigned task of efficiently allocating goods and services. Lack of information on the availability, quality, and/or price has been identified as a primary contributor to market failure in medical markets. Patients often find it difficult to acquire useful information on the pricing of physician services. Most have no idea what service or procedure to ask about and those who do have limited success in finding valid comparisons across types of physicians.

The American Medical Association (AMA) has proposed a new approach to make comparisons across individual physicians easier and more meaningful—the advance disclosure of service rates. Here's how it would work. With the Medicare fee scale (resource-based relative value scale) every procedure has an established point value. If every physician posted a single number, a multiplier or "cost-conversion factor," patients could quickly compare fee schedules by comparing this single number. For example, if the standard office visit for an established patient had a point value of 0.78, a physician with a multiplier of $40 would charge $31.20 for that office visit, and the physician with a multiplier of $55 would charge $42.90 for the same office visit. Patients would have a way of comparing prices quickly simply by knowing each physician's multiplier.

Fee-for-service medicine is under attack from managed care. As capitation becomes the standard payment mechanism, fewer and fewer patients will enjoy the flexibility of the fee-for-service option. It may be that the only way to guarantee the long-term availability of fee-for-service for the middle class is to provide more information to patients so they can make more informed and thus better decisions on how to spend their medical dollars. Instead of complaining about the resource-based relative value scale, the AMA has found a way for physicians to use it. What remains to be seen is whether physicians can enter into an environment where they have to compete on the prices they charge.

Source: George Anders, "AMA to Urge Doctors to Disclose Rates in Defending of Fee-for-Service Medicine," *The Wall Street Journal*, May 5, 1994, B12.

Key Concept 7
Competition

2001, it was $38.26. In order to hold down the growth in Medicare spending the factor was dropped to $36.20 in 2002.

The Economic Impact of a Fee Schedule for Physicians' Services

In theory, a resource-based relative value scale approximates the relative fee schedule that would emerge in perfectly competitive equilibrium. Hence, the RBRVS could provide a fair and equitable approach to compensating physicians for the services they provide. By removing the distortions in current fee structure, RBRVS would provide a neutral incentive structure for physicians in making medical decisions. By altering physician practice patterns, the rates of surgery, invasive diagnostic tests, and hospital use could be reduced significantly. Such an outcome would enhance the cost-effectiveness of medical care, leading to a reduction in the overall cost of health care.

In the long run, fee schedules based on RBRVS would even change the supply of physicians according to specialty. Changes in the relative rewards across specialties would alter the specialty choices of medical school graduates. It might even alter the geographic distribution of physicians, thus affecting the accessibility, cost, and quality of care in currently underserved areas.

Key Concept 8
Efficiency

Key Concept 5
Markets and Pricing

Physician response is easy to predict. Those who have a solid patient base in the private sector will begin to refuse new Medicare patients. The elderly will find it increasingly difficult to secure the services of a primary care physician. In 2001, almost 30 percent of U.S. physicians were not accepting new Medicare patients (Trude and Ginsberg, 2002). Hospital emergency rooms will become the best alternative source of care for a great number of the elderly population. Shortages of health services for the elderly will begin to develop as resources are shifted into the unregulated, private sector. Physicians will encounter the same forces with private patients insured by HMOs and PPOs. In either case, the lesson is clear: Those who do not ration via price will ration by queuing.

Managed Care Strategies

Medical care, whether in the United States or some other country around the world, has been traditionally provided on a fee-for-service basis. Because of spiraling expenditures, fee-for-service medical plans began taking on cost containment features during the 1980s. Frequently, these features include various aspects of the traditional managed care system: the use of a gatekeeper, required second surgical opinions, prior certification before hospital admission, utilization review, and preadmission hospital testing. These cost-control measures approach the issue from different perspectives. But their common goal is to ensure the provision of medically necessary services in the appropriate setting at the appropriate levels and costs.

The results of these strategies are to restrict access to certain kinds of medical care (such as hospital and specialty care), to redirect medical care delivery to less expensive locations (such as outpatient and ambulatory settings), and to monitor the use of medical products, supplies, and services (such as prescription drugs and prosthetic devices). Not only has fee-for-service adopted many of the cost-savings features of managed care, but managed care has increased its flexibility to better compete with fee-for-service. Instead of forcing recipients to use a closed panel of providers, more managed care systems offer open plans where recipients are allowed to use providers outside the panel, subject to a deductible and higher coinsurance rates. Thus, managed care and fee-for-service systems are looking for the right mix of cost control and flexibility to compete in a changing medical care environment.

Market Alternatives

Claiming government intervention as unnecessary and counterproductive, opponents of a government-run system argue that market alternatives are available. At least three are usually suggested: (1) capitation, (2) promotion of cost-reducing strategies in patient care systems and medical technology, and (3) increased competitiveness in health care delivery. Organizations are beginning to experiment with market forces and finding that significant cost savings are possible.

The growth of managed care has increased the use of capitation across the system. Under capitation, providers receive a fixed payment in advance to provide medically necessary care for a well-defined patient population. This arrangement shifts some of the financial risk to providers and encourages the incorporation of cost-reducing strategies into the delivery system. The market is not a magic pill; there are always trade-offs to consider. The danger is that providers will attempt to cut costs that will lead to quality deterioration. Remember: "There is no such thing as a free lunch."

Competitive bidding has also been a central factor in the market that has led to the cost savings. Firms have pooled resources to increase their purchasing power when dealing with medical providers, especially HMOs. In turn, the HMOs have increased bargaining power with providers because of overcapacity in hospitals and various specialty sectors.

Back-of-the-Envelope

THE ELEMENTS OF COST CONTROL IN MEDICAL CARE

Controlling medical care spending begins by controlling medical care costs. Cost control depends on the ability to control the major elements of costs: resource prices, resource productivity, and utilization of services. The derivation of the cost-control identity can be shown as follows. In a standard two-input production process, output (Q) is a function of inputs A and B.

$$Q = Q(A, B) \tag{1}$$

Production of Q using the most efficient combination of A and B results in total cost (C) equal to

$$C = P_A A + P_B B \tag{2}$$

where P_A is the price of input A and P_B is the price of input B. Average cost (AC) is defined as total cost divided by output or

$$AC = C/Q. \tag{3}$$

Substituting (2) into (3), we get

$$AC = \frac{P_A A}{Q} + \frac{P_B B}{Q}$$

$$AC = P_A\left(\frac{A}{Q}\right) + P_B\left(\frac{B}{Q}\right) \tag{4}$$

Note that (3) implies $C = AC \times Q$. Thus, when (4) is restated and generalizing to n inputs, we find that

$$C = \left[P_A\left(\frac{A}{Q}\right) + P_B\left(\frac{B}{Q}\right) + \ldots + P_N\left(\frac{N}{Q}\right) \right] Q \tag{5}$$

From (5), the first element in the cost-control identity is the level of input prices, P_A through P_N. If you want to reduce costs, you must control input prices. The second element is input productivity shown by the inverses of the technical efficiencies of the inputs, A/Q through N/Q. As input productivity increases, efficiency improves and costs fall. The final element is output, Q. Control the size of Q, limit utilization, and costs can be reduced.

The static world of cost identities may not provide much encouragement to would-be cost containers. Fuchs (1988), for one, argues against placing too much hope in our ability to moderate input prices, improve efficiency, or reduce utilization. Our ability to control cost may go back to equation (1), the production function for medical care itself. Cost-saving technological improvements and changes in the production mix from higher-priced to lower-priced inputs may provide some hope for continued moderation of medical costs.

Source: Victor R. Fuchs, "The Competition Revolution in Health Care," *Health Affairs* 7(3), Summer 1988, 5–24.

This excess supply creates a buyers' market and gives the HMOs more leverage when negotiating contracts with medical providers. These savings can then be passed on to group health plans in the form of lower premiums.

These competitive forces provide the catalyst for all sorts of innovative behavior on the part of providers to lower cost and improve quality. Examples of this include the industry's move to total quality management (TQM). Originated by the Japanese, TQM is an industrial-management technique aimed at analyzing every step in the service delivery process. When applied to medical care delivery, it identifies which steps add to cost without improving health outcomes, allowing providers to eliminate those steps that are identified as ineffective.

Mark B. McClellan

It took Republican president George W. Bush almost two years to find a commissioner for the Food and Drug Administration (FDA) that the Democrats in Congress would accept. The long wait ended in November 2002 when Mark B. McClellan was confirmed unanimously by the U.S. Senate. McClellan has a unique pedigree for the position, Ph.D. economist and board certified physician. He received his undergraduate education at the University of Texas at Austin and graduate degrees in public administration, medicine, and economics at Harvard and the Massachusetts Institute of Technology. He received his clinical training at Brigham and Women's Hospital in Boston and is board certified in internal medicine.

Upon finishing his residency he took a position as attending physician with Stanford Health Services and soon became the director of the Program on Health Outcomes Research at the Stanford Center for Health Policy. After a brief stint as Deputy Assistant Secretary for Economic Policy with the U.S. Department of Treasury, he was promoted to associate professor in the departments of economics and medicine at Stanford. He is associate editor of the *Journal of Health Economics* and visiting scholar with the American Enterprise Institute.

His publications include over 40 articles, books, and book chapters in some of the most prestigious journals in economics and health policy, including *American Economic Review*, *Journal of Health Economics*, *Health Affairs*, *RAND Journal of Economics*, and *Journal of Economic Perspectives*. In 1995, he received the *Review of Economic Studies* award for the outstanding dissertation in economics, and in 1997, the International Health Economics Association awarded him with the Kenneth Arrow Award for Best Paper in Health Economics. He also received Griliches Award for Best Empirical Paper in both the *Quarterly Journal of Economics* and *Journal of Political Economy* in 1999. His current research includes working papers on quality of care, health outcomes, medical productivity, managed care report cards, and end-of-life care.

Before his appointment as FDA chief, he served on the President's Council of Economic Advisers, and at the same time was senior policy director for health care and related economic issues for the White House. McClellan, who turned 40 in the summer of 2003, is no stranger to politics. His mother, Carole Keeton Strayhorn, is the Comptroller of Public Accounts for the state of Texas. His brother, Scott, is the White House Press Secretary for President George W. Bush. His grandfather, former dean of the University of Texas Law School, once told him: "If you haven't made anybody mad, you haven't done anything." If his grandfather's words ring true, there must be some pretty mad folks around the country right now.

Source: Personal vita and Department of Health and Human Services biography available at http://www.hhs.gov/about/bios/fda.html.

Summary and Conclusions

Health care systems around the world are struggling with the problem of increasing costs and growing expenditures. With the primary focus on the supply side of the exchange, government policy seems unable to stop the steady increase in spending. Options for the United States include many of the same strategies used by policymakers worldwide, including fee schedules, global budgeting, and resource rationing. Until recently, the U.S. experience with these measures has been limited primarily to state CON laws and Medicare price controls, including DRGs for hospitals and RBRVS for physicians. The success in slowing the growth in spending has been at least partially offset by a substantial increase in regulatory oversight. More recently the success of managed care in holding down the growth in spending makes the movement toward HMOs and PPOs more likely for enrollees in Medicare and Medicaid.

The growth in managed care presents the same concerns as the growth in any fixed-budget system—mandated fee schedules, global budgeting, and resource rationing. In fact, most managed care contracts with providers already incorporate the Medicare fee schedule into their reimbursement strategy. As a result the hospital DRG system and the relative value scale for physicians' services used by Medicare establishes a basis for virtually all provider payments in the private medical sector. The danger of managed care is its potential to transform the industry from its traditional medical mission to one more concerned with corporate issues, namely cost and returns. For better or for worse, profit incentives have invaded the not-for-profit sector. The positive changes associated with cost containment have resulted in an emphasis on the importance of lifestyle factors in determining health status, a concern for primary and preventive care, and a rethinking of the appropriateness, effectiveness, and efficiency of certain medical practices.

Questions and Problems

1. Compared to fee-for-service payment, what are the advantages and disadvantages of payment based on diagnosis-related groups?

2. What was the motivation for changing the way physicians are compensated in the Medicare system? What are the implications for physicians' behavior as the resource-based relative value scale is fully implemented?

3. In his testimony before the House Ways and Means health subcommittee, Robert Reischauer stated that Congressional Budget Office research concluded that price controls could severely limit the quality and quantity of medical care in the United States. He also argued that the only way to control medical care spending is by imposing global health care budgets at the national level. Explain how price controls can be bad and global budgets good.

4. Advocates of a market orientation argue that exclusive reliance on the visible hand of government will never bring spending under control. The missing component has been the invisible hand of the market pricing mechanism. Patients spending their own money have an incentive to control spending. Comment.

5. In 1994, 565 economists sent President Bill Clinton a letter warning against the economic consequences of price controls that played such a prominent role in his health care reform plan. The price controls included mandated fee schedules for fee-for-service medical plans, prospective budgets for regional health alliances, increases in health insurance premiums tied to the cost of living, and price ceilings on prescription drugs. Discuss the economics of price controls. Under what circumstances do they accomplish their intended purpose? When do they fail?

References

Joe Feinglass and James J. Holloway, "The Initial Impact of the Medicare Prospective Payment System on U.S. Health Care: A Review of the Literature," *Medical Care Review* 48(1), Spring 1991, 91–115.

Sherman T. Folland and Robert Kleiman, "The Effects of Prospective Payment under DRGs on the Market Value of Hospitals," *Quarterly Review of Economics and Business* 30(2), Summer 1990, 50–68.

William C. Hsiao, et al., A National Study of Resource-Based Relative Value Scales for Physician Services: Final Report to the Health Care Financing Administration, publication 17-C-98795/1–03, Boston: Harvard University School of Public Health, 1988.

The Lewin Group, "The Balanced Budget Act and Hospitals: The Dollars and Cents of Medicare Payment Cuts," American Hospital Association, May 1999.

Louise B. Russell and Carrie Lynn Manning, "The Effect of Prospective Payment on Medicare Expenditures," *New England Journal of Medicine* 320(7), February 16, 1989, 439–444.

Steven H. Sheingold, "The First Three Years of PPS: Impact on Medicare Costs," *Health Affairs* 8(3), Fall 1989, 191–204.

Sally Trude and Paul B. Ginsburg, "Growing Physician Access Problems Complicate Medicare Payment Debate," Issue Brief No. 55, Washington, DC: Center for Studying Health System Change, September 2002.

Lynn Wagner, "CBO Head Warns Price Controls Could Severely Limit Quality, Quantity of Medical Care in the U.S.," *Modern Healthcare* 23(3), March 8, 1993, 22.

Chapter 16

Medical Care Systems Worldwide

Anyone involved in the debate on health care reform in the United States will eventually get around to comparing the private insurance model used in the United States to the social insurance model used in the rest of the developed world. Comparisons across systems must be made carefully. Differences in population demographics, per capita income, disease incidences, and institutional features often make direct comparisons difficult to interpret.

In the following sections, we will discuss the health care delivery systems in the five major countries that are often compared to the U.S. system—Canada, France, Germany, Japan, and the United Kingdom. No attempt is made to glamorize or debase any system of health care delivery. Every one of these countries, including the United States, no matter how its medical care delivery is organized and financed, is struggling with a common problem—controlling the growth in medical care spending. These problems will be carefully documented, not for the purpose of rating the delivery mechanisms of those countries, but to show that reform in the United States must take on a structure that is uniquely American—one that will work within the U.S. institutional framework.

International Comparisons

Table 16.1, on page 386, provides a listing of several key statistics on population, economics, and health for the United States and the five countries discussed in this chapter: Canada, France, Germany, Japan, and the United Kingdom. In 2001, national populations ranged from 31.1 million in Canada to 284.8 million in the United States. The U.S. population is approximately four times the population of both France and the United Kingdom, three times that of Germany and twice Japan's. The United States has the largest economy as measured by gross domestic product (GDP), more than twice the size of the second largest, Japan. The widely used measure for relative standards of living, per capita GDP adjusted for purchasing power parity, is 22.1 percent higher in the United States than in Canada and 34.3 percent higher than in Germany.

Key Concept 2
Opportunity
Cost

Health care spending, whether measured in U.S. per capita dollars or as a percentage of GDP, is significantly higher in the United States than in any other country. Germany, Canada, and France are ranked second, third, and fourth according to the two measures. Per capita spending in the United Kingdom is barely one-third of that of the United States. Physicians per 1,000 population range from a low in Japan of 1.9 to a high in Germany and France of 3.3. The United States is ranked at the bottom of the list in terms of hospital beds per 1,000 at 2.9 beds and average length of hospital stay at 5.8 days. Japan tops the list in both categories with 16.5 beds per 1,000 and an average hospital stay of almost 41 days.[1]

---

1 Several cultural reasons explain why the Japanese average length of stay is so long—the sick are more pampered, more conditions are considered illnesses, and an emphasis on bed rest as a cure for most illnesses. For example, in contrast to the situation in the United States where Congress must legislate a mandatory two-day hospital stay after childbirth, the length of stay following childbirth in Japan approaches two weeks. In addition, long-term care for the elderly is provided primarily in the hospital setting, substantially increasing length-of-stay calculations.

ISSUES IN MEDICAL CARE DELIVERY

WHO HAS THE BEST HEALTH CARE SYSTEM?

In 2000 the World Health Organization (WHO) released a report ranking the health care systems of the world's 191 countries. The first attempt of its kind, the report attracted a great deal of media attention and surprised many health experts in its findings. The WHO rankings were based on five composite indicators: (1) the overall level of health of the population, (2) health inequality within the population, (3) health system responsiveness, (4) the distribution of responsiveness to measure, and (5) how fairly the financial burden is shared across different socioeconomic groups.

The health of the population was measured in terms of disability-adjusted life expectancy and disparities in that measure across groups. Health system responsiveness measured how well patients are served and the degree of service disparities among different groups. This composite index was compiled from surveys administered to 1,791 public health experts in 35 selected countries. The fairness of the financial burden was recorded as an index based on survey data measuring the percentage of household income beyond subsistence spent on health care. A weighting scheme was used to develop an index of overall performance, giving a 25 percent weight to each of categories 1, 2, and 5, and a 12.5 percent weight each to categories 3 and 4.

WHO Health Care System Performance, 1997

| | Health | | Responsiveness | | | | |
	Level	Distribution	Level	Distribution	Financial Fairness	Goal Attainment	Overall Performance
Canada	12	18	T7	T3	T17	7	30
France	3	12	T16	T3	T26	6	1
Germany	22	20	5	T3	T6	14	25
Japan	1	3	6	T3	T8	1	10
United Kingdom	14	2	T26	T3	T8	9	18
United States	24	32	1	T3	T54	15	37

Note: Tn indicates a tie for *n*th place.

Overall, the French health care system was rated number 1. The only other country examined in this chapter that made the top 10 was Japan, finishing at number 10. The top spots were filled by countries that usually don't come to mind in discussions of the world's best health care systems: Italy, Spain, Oman, and Austria. The next large developed country on the list was the United Kingdom at number 18. Germany finished 25th, Canada 30th, and the United States 37th.

Needless to say, the results were met with heavy criticism, mostly from those countries whose rankings did not meet expectations. Blendon, Kim, and Benson (2001) point out one methodological flaw in the WHO approach, namely that the rankings show little correlation between overall performance and the results of patient satisfaction surveys conducted in the countries. Italy, Portugal, and Greece ranked 2, 12, and 14 in the WHO study but consistently scored quite low on patient satisfaction surveys. And countries such as the Netherlands, Finland, and Denmark which ranked 17, 31, and 34, rated high in patient satisfaction.

Despite its flaws, despite the criticism, the WHO report was an attempt to do a thankless, but necessary task—developing a method to compare health care systems.

Sources: Robert J. Blendon, Minah Kim, and John M. Benson, "The Public Versus the World Health Organization on Health System Performance," *Health Affairs 20*(3), May/June 2001, 10–20; World Health Organization, "Health Systems: Improving Performance," *The World Health Report 2000*, Geneva: WHO, 2000.

Table 16.1	Key Statistics

2001	Canada	France	Germany	Japan	United Kingdom	United States
Population (millions)	31.1	59.2	82.4	127.1	58.8	284.8
GDP per capita[a]	28,811	26,879	26,199	26,652	26,315	35,182
Health Expenditures						
Health care spending per capita	2,792	2,561	2,808	1,984[c]	1,992	4,887
Health care spending (percent of GDP)	9.7	9.5	10.7	7.6[c]	7.6	13.9
Medical Services						
Number of physicians (per 1,000)	2.1	3.3	3.3	1.9[c]	2.0[c]	2.7[d]
Number of hospital beds (per 1,000)	3.2[c]	6.7[c]	6.3	16.5[e]	3.9	2.9
Average length of stay (days)	7.2[c]	8.5[c]	9.3	40.8[e]	7.0	5.8
Medical Technology[b]						
CT Scanners	9.5	9.6[c]	17.1[f]	84.4[d]	6.2[d]	13.1[c]
MRI Units	3.5	2.6[c]	6.2[f]	23.2[d]	4.6[d]	8.1[c]
Lithotripters	0.4	1.0[c]	1.7[f]	4.0[g]	—	2.9[c]
Patients undergoing dialysis	45.7[d]	—	64.0[c]	162.4[c]	27.0[d]	86.5[d]

a In U.S. purchasing power parity (PPP) dollars—the exchange rate where different currencies buy the same bundle of goods.

b Per 1 million population.

c 2000.

d 1999.

e 1998.

f 1997.

g 1993.

Source: *OECD Health Data 2003*, OECD, Paris, 2003.

Expenditures Across OECD Countries

Medical care spending in the United States is the highest in the world, both in per capita terms and as a percentage of gross domestic product. Although health care spending as a percentage of gross domestic product (health-to-GDP ratio) is the most widely used performance measure for the health care sector, it is important to remember that there are actually two components to this ratio. Comparisons at a given point in time tend to focus on the ratio alone. If countries are compared over time, however, it is important to examine both the change in health spending and the change in GDP. In other words, both the numerator and the denominator of the ratio are important.

Table 16.2 presents a comparison of the growth rates for health care sector components for the decades of the 1980s and 1990s. Annual growth rates in health care spending were considerably higher in the 1980s than in the 1990s. The average growth rate in nominal health care spending averaged 7.82 percent, ranging from 4.19 percent in Germany to 9.78 percent in the United States. Nominal spending growth slowed to an average of 5.16 percent in the 1990s, ranging from 3.82 percent in France to 6.80 percent in the United Kingdom. The highest growth rate in nominal spending per capita in the 1980s was 9.06 percent in France. During the 1990s the highest rate was 6.58 percent in

Table 16.2	Annual Compound Growth in Health Sector Components 1980s and 1990s, in percentages

Component	Canada 1980s	Canada 1990s	France 1980s	France 1990s	Germany 1980s	Germany 1990s	Japan 1980s	Japan 1990s	United Kingdom 1980s	United Kingdom 1990s	United States 1980s	United States 1990s
Nominal health care spending	9.64	3.89	9.64	3.82	4.19	6.87	4.73	3.83	8.91	6.80	9.78	5.76
Nominal per capita health care spending	8.47	2.89	9.06	3.48	4.11	4.12	4.19	3.57	8.78	6.58	8.90	4.59
Real health care spending[a]	3.76	2.23	4.61	2.38	1.24	6.21[c]	2.53	3.20[c]	2.04	2.61[c]	2.82	2.38
Real per capita health care spending[a]	2.65	1.25	4.08	2.04	1.16	2.10[c]	2.01	2.94[c]	1.89	2.42[c]	2.00	1.24
Real health care spending[b]	4.68	2.55	3.59	2.31	1.63	4.95	2.94	3.52	3.13	3.82	5.69	3.76
Real per capita health care spending[b]	3.57	1.57	2.72	1.97	1.54	2.24	2.42	3.26	2.97	3.61	4.84	2.61

Note: Measurements based on changes denominated in national currencies.

a Spending adjusted by the 1995 medical expenditures deflator.

b Spending adjusted by the 1995 GDP price deflator.

c 1990–1996.

Source: *OECD Health Data 2003*, OECD, Paris, 2003.

the United Kingdom. Germany and Japan consistently had the lowest rates of growth for both of these measures during the two decades.

Deflating health care expenditures by the medical care price index provides information on the change in the volume and intensity of service in this sector. Canada and France had the largest increase in volume and intensity of service during the 1980s, with real spending growing at rates of 3.76 percent and 4.61 percent per year when using total spending, and 2.65 percent and 4.08 percent when using per capita spending. During the 1990s the growth rates in real spending fell sharply, to as low as 2.23 percent for total spending in Canada, and 1.24 percent for per capita spending in the United States.

> **Policy Issue**
>
> Of all the major developed countries in the world, which one does the best job in controlling health care spending?

The same basic pattern emerges when using the GDP deflator. Using this index to adjust nominal spending into real terms actually expresses a measure of the opportunity cost of resources absorbed by the health care sector. The United States ranks at the top of the list during the 1980s and the United Kingdom gets that distinction during the 1990s, implying that Americans and Brits were giving up substantially more non-health-related spending to accommodate their health sectors during those decades.

Key Concept 2
Opportunity Cost

International Comparison of Medical Outcomes

Many argue that high spending in the United States might be tolerable if the resulting health outcomes were better. Using data in Table 16.3, when life expectancy at birth and infant mortality rates are used as the measure of health outcomes, the United States ranks at the bottom within the developed world. The rankings when using infant mortality rates are similar. The U.S. infant mortality rate of 6.9 per 1,000 live births is over two times the rate in Japan and 20 to 50 percent higher than the other comparison countries. Some of the factors that complicate the comparison of infant mortality rates

Table 16.3	Health Outcomes, 2000

| Country | Life Expectancy at Birth[a] | | Life Expectancy at Age 80[a] | | Infant Mortality Rate[b] |
	Males	Females	Males	Females	
Canada	76.7	82.0	7.8	9.7	5.3
France	75.2	83.0	7.4	9.3	4.6
Germany	74.7[c]	80.7[c]	6.8[c]	8.3[c]	4.4
Japan	77.7	84.6	8.0	10.6	3.2
United Kingdom	75.4	80.2	6.9	8.6	5.6
United States	74.1	79.5	7.6	9.1	6.9

a In years.

b Perinatal deaths per 1,000 live births.

c 1999.

Source: *OECD Health Data 2003*, Paris: Organization for Economic Cooperation and Development, 2003.

have already been discussed in Chapter 10, most notably the higher incidence of low birthweight babies born in the United States.[2]

Instead of life expectancy at birth, if life expectancy at age 80 is used, the rankings change substantially. Rankings for both male and female life expectancies in the United States improve to third and fourth. There are several explanations for this improvement as the individual ages. A large part of the difference in life expectancy at birth is due to differences in mortality factors at younger ages that have nothing to do with medical care delivery, such as the incidence of drug abuse, homicide, AIDS, and auto fatalities. The incidences of these factors tend to converge at older ages, and the differences in life expectancies may depict differences in the efficacy of health care delivery more accurately.

A third way to compare systems would examine differences in the effectiveness of treating various diseases. The World Health Organization (WHO) has published statistics on cancer incidence, mortality, and prevalence worldwide (Ferlay et al., 2001). Table 16.4 provides interesting insight into the effectiveness of treating cancer in the countries of

http://

The World Health Organization promotes health worldwide. Their web site provides important links for those interested in public health issues.
http://www.who.int

Table 16.4	Mortality Ratios for Cancer Selected Countries

| Country | Type of Cancer | | | | |
	Colon/Rectal	Breast	Cervical	Prostate	All Sites Except Skin
Canada	40.3	27.8	33.6	20.4	49.6
France	46.0	25.7	34.4	34.1	58.8
Germany	48.2	32.2	36.6	34.4	56.5
Japan	40.9	24.6	26.6	47.6	57.9
United Kingdom	53.0	35.8	41.9	46.0	65.7
United States	39.1	23.2	41.8	17.2	44.8
All Developed Countries	46.6	29.4	35.9	29.4	57.8

Source: J. Ferlay et al., *GLOBOCAN 2000: Cancer Incidence, Mortality, and Prevalence Worldwide*, Version 1.0, IARC Cancer Base No. 5, Lyon: IARC Press, 2001.

2 Low birthweight babies as a percentage of all births range from 5.8 percent in Canada to 8.1 percent in Japan. The percentage is 7.6 in the United States.

ISSUES IN MEDICAL CARE DELIVERY

MEDICAL CARE SPENDING AND INTERNATIONAL COMPETITIVENESS

General Motors spends $4.8 billion for worker health insurance, the equivalent of $1,200 for every car produced, or roughly the total public and private health budget for all 40 million South Africans. Is medical care spending making American business less competitive in the global marketplace? This popular notion has a great deal of intuitive appeal, especially when members of the business community make the arguments.

The micro argument examines the issue from the perspective of the individual firm. This argument assumes that the relevant price of labor is the cash wage paid to workers, and treats fringe benefits as an add-on cost. Under this scenario, the firm has only two options when faced with increasing fringe costs: (1) shift the costs forward to the firm's customers by raising product prices, or (2) shift the costs backward to the firm's owners by reducing the firm's profits. The former option makes the firm's products less competitive in the marketplace; the latter option makes the firm's stock less attractive in the equity capital market.

The macro argument examines the issue from the perspective of the entire economy. Much of our medical care spending represents pure consumption. By devoting a large fraction of gross domestic product to medical care, less is available for savings and capital formation. In addition, spending less on medical care would allow resources to be shifted to more productive activities that would enhance economic efficiency and international competitiveness.

Overall, the arguments that high medical care costs reduce competitiveness do not stand up under careful scrutiny. In particular, the micro argument ignores a third option available to firms faced with rising fringe costs, namely, to shift the costs of increased fringe benefits to the workers who receive them. This option may be accomplished by merely paying the workers lower cash wages. To understand this perspective realize that the relevant market-clearing wage is not solely the cash wage, but the value of the total compensation package, including cash wages, health benefits, retirement benefits, the firm's share of social security taxes, and other payroll taxes. It makes little sense to single out any one component of the total compensation package and blame it for the lack of competitiveness in the global marketplace. Instead, it is important to realize that workers who receive fewer fringe benefits will merely demand higher cash wages.

On the other hand, the macro argument is based on the assumption that consumer spending in every other economic sector is "more productive" than spending on medical care. Because of the dominance of third-party payment in the medical care sector, a large percentage of medical care spending may be wasteful. Patients who do not pay the true incremental costs of the procedures they receive demand services that provide little benefit. Suggesting that spending in one sector is "more productive" than spending in any other, however, begs an important consideration. Who decides what type of spending is more productive? Wouldn't we be better off if one-half of the lawyers left their chosen profession and got "more productive" jobs in other sectors? Why not get one-half of all college professors engaged in scholarly research to spend their time in activities that are "more productive," for example, undergraduate teaching?

The business sector's motivation to control medical care spending goes beyond the global competitiveness argument. Every dollar spent on medical care affects at least one of the firm's stakeholders: customers pay higher prices, workers accept

Key Concept 8
Efficiency

Policy Issue

Does the high cost of health insurance handicap U.S. business in the global market?

Key Concept 5
Markets and Pricing

Key Concept 2
Opportunity Cost

lower cash wages, and/or owners receive reduced profits. It is important that we use resources wisely, not just in the medical care sector, but also throughout the economy.

Source: Uwe E. Reinhardt, "Health Care Spending and American Competitiveness," *Health Affairs* 8(4), Winter 1989, 5–21.

Policy Issue

Is the United States getting its money's worth in terms of health outcomes for the money spend on health care?

interest. The mortality ratios listed in the table measure the estimated number of deaths that would occur as a result of the cancer relative to the number of estimated new cancer diagnoses. In other words, the mortality ratio is helpful in estimating the proportion of patients who will die from cancer in a given country. The calculation is actually the ratio of mortality to incidence.

Careful examination of the table shows that the United States has the lowest mortality ratio for colon/rectal, breast, and prostate cancer, and is below the average for all developed countries. In the summary measure, all sites except skin cancer, the U.S. does substantially better than the rest of the developed world. Only in cervical cancer is the U.S. performance significantly worse than the other countries listed. The important question that needs to be addressed is: Are differences in mortality between countries more related to the incidence of the disease or to differences in the quality of medical care received by those suffering from the disease? Mortality ratios may not provide the definitive answer to this question, but at the same time mortality rates and incidence rates are not good measures of the effectiveness of a health care system in treating various diseases.

Canadian National Health Insurance: Medicare

Canada is divided into ten provinces and two territories. Its total population is just over 31 million, most living within 100 miles of the United States border. These demographics create quite a challenge for health care delivery in the rest of the country where low population densities, long-distance travel requirements, and provider shortages are the norm. Only two provinces have populations exceeding one million and only four metropolitan areas have sufficient population to support integrated delivery systems. Canadian policymakers have responded to these challenges by creating a **national health insurance** system that has demonstrated the ability to deliver high-quality medical care to the entire population at slightly over one-half of the per capita cost of United States' health care.

The provisions of the 1984 Canada Health Act define the health care delivery system as it currently operates. Under the act, each provincial health plan is administered at the provincial level, provides universal access to comprehensive first-dollar coverage of all medically necessary services, and is portable across provinces. With minor exceptions, health coverage is available to all residents with no out-of-pocket charges. Most physicians are paid on a fee-for-service basis and enjoy a great deal of practice autonomy.[3]

The Canadian health care system began to take on its current form when the province of Saskatchewan set up a hospitalization plan immediately after the Second World War. In 1944, provincial voters elected a socialist-leaning government, the Cooperative Commonwealth Federation (now called the New Democratic Party). The province was plagued by the kind of medical problems that one might expect in a predominantly rural, low-income population—shortages of both hospital beds and medical practitioners. By 1947, two years after coming into power, the CCF delivered on its campaign promise to

national health insurance
A government-run health insurance system covering the entire population for a well-defined medical benefits package. Usually administered by a government or quasi-government agency and financed through some form of taxation.

http://

The Canadian Health Network provides links to over 30 health sites with information on Canadian medical care.
http://www.hc-sc.gc.ca/notice-avis/

---

3 About 90 percent of all primary care is provided by fee-for-service general practitioners. The rest is provided by salaried GPs working in local community health centers.

Back-of-the-Envelope

Negotiating Fee Schedules: Bilateral Monopoly in Canada

In practice, each province in Canada functions as a separate health care system. While the federal government helps finance the system using an income tax, most of the money is raised at the provincial level either through general tax revenues, payroll taxes, or premiums. Each provincial health ministry tightly controls hospital spending through global budgets. Hospitals are given a fixed operating budget at the beginning of each fiscal year. Spending on physicians' services is controlled in a number of different ways across the country. The basic tool for controlling spending on physicians' services is a mandatory fee schedule negotiated between the provincial health ministry representing the patients and the provincial medical society representing the physicians—a classic case of bilateral monopoly. Here is how it works.

Key Concept 3
Marginal Analysis

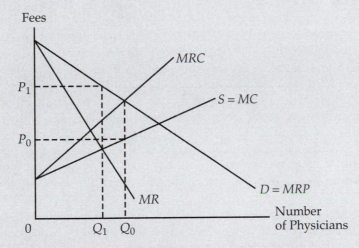

In the diagram, the demand curve for physicians' services is the marginal revenue product curve (MRP). This is the demand curve facing the medical association representing all the physicians in the province. The medical association functions in much the same way as a union, and behaves like a labor monopolist. The marginal revenue curve (MR) is derived from the demand curve. The supply curve (S) represents the opportunity cost, or marginal cost (MC) of making an additional physician member available to the market. If the medical association behaves like a profit (or economic rent) maximizer, it sets $MR = MC$ and offers Q_1 physicians at a fee schedule equivalent to P_1.

The health ministry, acting like a monopsonist, maximizes profit where $MRP = MRC$. From its perspective the optimal equilibrium will have Q_0 physicians available at a fee schedule equal to P_0. The final equilibrium will find fees somewhere between P_0 and P_1 and the number of physicians between Q_0 and Q_1.

In this situation negotiations will likely begin with the medical association offering to make Q_1 physicians available and the health ministry refusing to pay fees higher than P_0. If the health ministry wants more physicians, then higher fees must be paid. The trade-off will be made and a bargain will eventually be reached. In the Canadian case it is likely that the medical association is in a weaker position. If the demand curve in the above figure is more inelastic and the supply curve more elastic, then Q_0 is less than Q_1. The health ministry wants fewer physicians in practice than the medical association is willing to provide. No longer is a bargaining trade-off possible. In this case the provincial health ministries set utilization targets to control overall spending. If these targets are exceeded in one year, next year's fees are lowered accordingly, or physicians are forced to work for reduced fees until budgets are met, or income ceilings are established for individual physicians. The latter approach is taken in Quebec. Once physicians bill up to their quarterly limit, their fees are reduced by 75 percent for the remainder of the quarter. Many physicians who regularly reach their limit take time off at the end of each quarter. Many lease their office to colleagues in exchange for a percentage of those fees (Wolfe and Moran, 1993).

provide a system of socialized medicine and enacted the Saskatchewan Hospital Services Plan. The main feature of this plan was the creation of a regional system of hospitals: local hospitals for primary care, district hospitals for more complex cases, and base hospitals (in the two main cities) for the most difficult cases.

British Columbia, Saskatchewan's western neighbor, enacted its own hospital insurance plan in 1949, providing momentum for the creation of a national hospital insurance system. In 1956, the federal parliament enacted the Hospital and Diagnostic Services Act, laying the groundwork for a nationwide system of hospital insurance. By 1961, all ten provinces and the two territories had hospital insurance plans of their own with the federal government paying one-half of the costs.

Within a year, Saskatchewan moved to provide for the funding of physicians' services. The Saskatchewan Medical Care Insurance Act of 1962 was passed; its main provision was a binding fee schedule for physicians' services. As a result, physicians in the province orchestrated the first-ever physicians' strike in all of North America protesting the fixed fee schedule. To settle the dispute, the provincial government allowed the practice of "extra billing," which allowed physicians to charge fees in excess of those scheduled. Within two years the average medical incomes of physicians in Saskatchewan moved from last among the provinces to first, fueling the engine of reform.

The other provinces began to fall in line, but this time national legislation was enacted in half the time (four years instead of nine). By 1971, Canada had its national health insurance plan, providing coverage for both hospitalization and physicians' services. In order to receive matching funds from the federal government, each provincial plan had to meet certain national standards. This included universal eligibility, coverage of all medically necessary services (inpatient, outpatient, and physician), public administration, portability between provinces, and no financial barriers to service (meaning no hospital user charges and no extra billing by physicians).

The 50–50 cost sharing arrangement was abandoned by the federal government in 1977 and replaced with a per capita grant to the provinces. The result has been a steady erosion in the percentage of the costs covered by the federal government. The federal share has fallen from 30 percent in 1980 to 21.5 percent in 1996 (Naylor, 1999). With federal and provincial deficits considerably higher than U.S. per capita levels, the shifting financial burden has created a strong incentive to reduce spending and shift some of the expense onto the private sector. The public sector financed 75 percent of total health care spending in 1986. By 1996 that figure had dropped to 70 percent. The private sector covers 12.3 percent of hospital spending and 64.8 percent of pharmaceutical drug spending.

Many feel that it is inaccurate to characterize the Canadian system as "single-payer" since there is considerable variation among the provincial plans. In spite of the differences, it is fair to say that each provincial plan is a public-sector monopsony, serving as a single buyer of medical services within the province and holding medical care prices below market rates.

Theoretically, physician fee schedules are determined through bilateral negotiations at the provincial level between the Ministry of Health and the medical association. Practically, several provinces have reduced unilaterally the "binding" fee schedules. Five provinces (with 80 percent of the population) have mechanisms to control service

Key Concept 4
Self-Interest

Many of the provincial health ministries in Canada have their own web sites. The British Columbia Ministry of Health has its site at
http://www.gov.bc.ca/hlth/

volume by placing a limit on the quarterly gross billings allowed for the individual prac-titioner. Billings above the limit are reimbursed at one-fourth the prescribed fee sched-ule (Evans et al., 1989).[4] Several provinces have initiated an across-the-board reduction in fees of 25 percent for new physicians practicing in urban areas (for the purpose of reducing crowding in urban areas and scarcity in rural areas). To confront the fee prob-lem head-on, the Ministry of Health for British Columbia has begun setting fee sched-ules unilaterally. By U.S. standards, physicians' incomes are on average low. In 1995 the average income of self-employed physicians was $120,000, ranging from $104,000 for general practitioners to $144,000 for specialists (Grant and Oertel, 1997). The average physicians' income is about six times the average Canadian worker, but less than two-thirds that of the typical U.S. physician.

Private health insurance for covered services is illegal. But most Canadians have sup-plemental private insurance for uncovered services, such as prescription drugs and den-tal services. As a result, virtually all physicians are forced to participate and each health plan effectively serves all residents of the province.

If cost control is defined in terms of health care spending as a share of economic out-put, Canada has done far better in controlling health care costs than the United States. In 1970, Canada's health care spending as a share of GDP was 7.2 percent compared to the U.S. figure of 7.4 percent. Over the next two decades, the growth in spending of the health-to-GDP ratio was significantly slower in Canada than in the United States. In 1987, the health care sector represented 8.6 percent of GDP in Canada and 11.2 percent of GDP in the United States. Critics of the Canadian system argue that this is a statisti-cal phenomenon due, not to more effective cost control, but to faster economic growth. Between 1967 and 1987, real economic output in Canada increased 74 percent, while U.S. real output increased only 38 percent.

If cost control is measured in terms of growth in real per capita expenditures, the pic-ture looks somewhat different. Over the period 1967–1987, real per capita health care spending grew faster in Canada than in the United States. Over that time frame, Canada's compound annual growth rate in real health care spending was 4.58 percent compared to the 4.38 percent experienced in this country. Between 1981 and 2000 real per capita spending in Canada (adjusted by the medical expenditures price deflator) grew at a rate of 2.12 percent per year compared to 1.78 percent per year in the United States.

The key element in the Canadian strategy to control overall spending is the region-alization of high-tech services. Government regulators make resource allocation deci-sions. This control extends to capital investment in hospitals, specialty mix of medical practitioners, location of recent medical graduates, and the diffusion of high-tech diag-nostic and surgical equipment. In 1997 there were 53 magnetic resonance imagers in all of Canada, one for every 572,000 citizens. Contrast that to the 2,046 in the United States, one for every 130,800 Americans. Access to open-heart surgery and organ trans-plantation is also restricted. There were 14 lithotripters in Canada in 1997 compared to 627 in the United States. That same year there were 245 CT scanners in Canada, one for every 123,500 citizens. The United States had 3,667 CT scanners, one for every 73,000 Americans. A study by Harriman, McArthur, and Zelder (1999) compared the availabil-ity of medical technology in community hospitals in British Columbia with those in Washington and Oregon. They found Canadian deficits in several areas, including angioplasty, cardiac catheterization, and intensive care.

It can be argued that U.S. hospitals have excess capacity in these technology areas while, at the same time, Canada experiences a shortage. Waiting lists for certain surgi-cal and diagnostic procedures are common in Canada. In 2002 Canadians were waiting for over 1.1 million surgical procedures, an increase of 15 percent over 2001. Assuming one person per procedure, then 3.5 percent of the population is on a waiting list. Nationwide, the median wait from referral by a GP to treatment by a specialist was 16.5

---

4 Quebec has the strictest limitations with the billing threshold at $180,000 (U.S.).

weeks, ranging from 14.0 weeks in Ontario to 32.6 weeks in Saskatchewan. Median waiting times are longest for orthopedic surgery (32.0 weeks), plastic surgery (27.5 weeks), and ophthalmology treatment (26.6 weeks). General surgery and oncological services have waits ranging from 5.5 to 9.5 weeks. Comparisons between reasonable and actual waiting times were made for all 10 provinces and 13 specialties. The median waiting time is longer than Canadian physicians consider clinically reasonable in over 87 percent of the comparisons (Esmail and Walker, 2002b).[5]

Key Concept 6
Supply and Demand

The problem does not end there. If care requires diagnostic imaging, waiting times are even longer. In 2002 patients had to wait 5.2 weeks for a CT scan, 12.4 weeks for an MRI, and 3.2 weeks for an ultrasound. To avoid waits of 6 to 52 weeks, Canadians are paying up to $900 to have cataract surgery performed by private physicians. In Newfoundland, women must wait four months for first-time mammogram screenings. Thus, Canadians are sacrificing access to modern medical technology for first-dollar coverage for primary care. Treatment delays are causing problems for certain vulnerable segments of the Canadian population, particularly the elderly who cannot get reasonable access to the medical care they demand, including hip replacement, cataract surgery, and cardiovascular surgery.

Another cost-control measure is global budgeting. Hospitals are provided with annual budgets to cover their operating expenses. They are expected to serve every patient within the level of funding provided by this budget. The resource allocation decision falls squarely on hospital administrators across the country who must decide funding levels for the services offered.

Key Concept 2
Opportunity Cost

Several lessons can be learned from the Canadian experience. When government provides a product "free" to consumers, inevitably demand escalates and spending increases. Products provided at zero price are treated as if they have zero resource cost. Resource allocation decisions become more inefficient over time and government is forced either to raise more revenue or curb services. A number of the provincial health plans are moving to reduce spending by dropping services from the approved list of the "medically necessary." These include certain infertility treatments, routine newborn circumcisions, and tattoo removal, to name a few. A number of provinces have discontinued or changed the eligibility requirements for their dental plans for children (Leatt and Williams, 1997).

Key Concept 1
Scarcity and Choice

A second lesson is that everything has a cost. When care requires major diagnostic or surgical procedures, the "free" system must find some other mechanism to allocate scarce resources. The Canadian system delegates this authority to the government. Resource allocation is practiced, not through the price mechanism, but by setting limits on the investment in medical technology. Proponents will argue that using waiting lists as a rationing measure is reasonable and fair. Opponents find the lists unacceptable and an unwelcome encroachment on individual decision-making in the medical sector.

Proponents of the single-payer alternative must deal with the fact that Canadians face waiting lists for some medical services, especially for high-tech specialty care. To avoid delays in treatment, many Canadians travel south for more advanced treatment. The head of health insurance for the Ontario Ministry of Health views the availability of medical care in the United States as a safety valve for Canadians (Berss, 1993). Blendon et al. (1993) reported that nearly one-third of all Canadian physicians have referred patients to treatment facilities outside the country in the past five years. The comparable figure for German physicians was 19 percent and for U.S. physicians it was 7 percent.

Policy Issue

What are the economic and political consequences of changing the U.S. health care delivery system to a Canadian-style single-payer system?

These cross-border transactions reached record levels in the early 1990s. Until 1991 Canadians were reimbursed for 100 percent of all emergency care received abroad and 75 percent of the cost of all elective surgery. These generous benefits were lowered to a flat per diem of $400 (Canadian) for emergency services and $200 (Canadian) for elective surgery.

---

5 A clinically reasonable wait as defined by Canadian physicians is one-third to one-half longer than is considered reasonable by American physicians.

Since the change the number of Canadians seeking care in the United States has sharply declined. A rise has occurred in major orthopedic procedures, experimental cancer treatments, and TMJ treatments. Most of these procedures are covered by private travel health insurance purchased by more than 10 percent of the population (Katz et al., 1998).

Critics of the Canadian system must deal with the fact that most Canadians support their version of Medicare.[6] The single most important defense of medical care delivery in Canada is that it works relatively well. Regardless of the problems faced by the system, critics must face the reality that the medical care system provides Canadians with access to all "medically necessary hospital and physician services" at a fraction of the per capita cost of the U.S. system.

France: Equality, Liberty, Fraternity[7]

Even though France is often depicted as the birthplace of European democracy, the nation actually adopted a highly centralized system of government during the reign of Napoleon Bonaparte. Since that time, the French have tried to maintain a delicate balance between individual freedom and collective action. Economic and social policy is based, in varying degrees, on three principles that the French hold dear: (1) a national spirit of egalitarianism, (2) a respect for individual freedom, and (3) a commitment to minimal state intervention. In other words, the French attempt to strike a balance between solidarity, choice, and competition.

The potential for conflict among these principles is easy to recognize and nowhere is it more evident than in the nation's complex system of medical care delivery. The national spirit of egalitarianism is manifested in the preamble of the French Constitution: "The nation guarantees to all protection of health." The social security system serves not only to provide health insurance for everyone, but also as a mechanism to redistribute income and provide social solidarity. Respect for individual freedom is evident in the provision for patient choice and physician autonomy. Patients are free to choose their own physicians and may see a specialist without referral.

As economic theory would suggest, unconstrained pursuit of these two principles led to escalating costs. Again, patients who are provided with care at zero price use it as if it had zero resource cost. Providers who are free to treat with little consideration for cost effectiveness tend to over-prescribe. In 1960, the government intervened with regulatory reform, maintaining the principles of liberty and solidarity, but compromising the principle of **laissez faire**. In its place, state control over prices and budgets was substituted in an effort to moderate spending.

As in many other European countries, national health insurance in France grew out of a nineteenth-century system that provided certain industrial workers and miners with insurance through mutual aid societies, or **sickness funds**. Legislation passed in 1928 made membership compulsory for many low-wage occupations, but coverage was still far from universal. It was not until the post World War II period, when the economic and social infrastructure was being rebuilt, that everyone was brought into the system. The national health insurance system is administered through 16 regional and 133 local funds, each with a self-managing board. Seventeen other funds cover specific occupational groups, including agricultural workers, public employees, independent professionals, and full-time students. Deficits are also a common problem, and the system has consistently run a deficit since 1997. For example, the national insurance fund (covering 80 percent of the population) ran a combined $13 billion deficit in 2002–2003, creating strong dissatisfaction among patients and providers.[8]

Information about the Pasteur Institute's contributions, conferences, and publications may be found (much of it in English) at **http://www.pasteur.fr/ index-en.iphtml**

Key Concept 9
Market Failure

laissez faire
A French term meaning literally: "allow [them] to do." It depicts a situation where individuals and firms are allowed to pursue their own self-interests without government restraint.

sickness fund
Quasi-governmental groups that serve as insurance companies by collecting premiums and paying providers within the national health care system of France and Germany.

---

6 Canadian support for their health care system is slipping somewhat due primarily to their dissatisfaction with waiting lists. Almost one-half felt that recent changes had in fact hurt the system (Naylor, 1999).

7 This section is based on Henderson (1993).

8 Substantial financial reform is expected in the near future, with a transfer of some types of care to complementary insurance, including dental, optical, drugs, and hearing aids. Alternatively, some have suggested that national health insurance cover only a basic level of benefits with reimbursement based on strict guidelines, leaving complementary insurance to cover additional care depending on the preferences and willingness to pay of the individual (LePen, 2003).

Health policymakers have found it difficult to satisfy the goal of universal access and control cost at the same time. Financing is primarily from social insurance but with a significant private supplementary insurance component. The system was originally financed almost exclusively on a payroll tax. As of early 1994, the payroll tax had increased to 18.95 percent with employers paying two-thirds of the tax directly.[9] As of 2001, salary-based contributions accounted for only 60 percent of the total public financing with the remainder coming from a special income tax. Employers now pay 12.8 percent of an employee's salary into the health insurance fund and employees pay 0.75 percent. In addition, a tax on income and capital averages approximately 7.5 percent on income for those individuals who pay income tax. This reduced reliance on payroll taxes has taken some of the pressure off employers, but has not decreased the overall cost of coverage that now totals over 21 percent of the income of the typical worker.

All employees are covered by French social security legislation and must contribute to the national social security system. The system is divided into four branches: life and health insurance, occupational disability insurance, old-age pension, and family leave.

In addition to the premiums, patients must pay a substantial copayment for both ambulatory and hospital care. The typical arrangement is for the patient to pay the entire medical fee when services are received. After paying the physician, the patient may then apply for a reimbursement of 70 percent of the prescribed fee. The patient is responsible for any extra billing. Hospital patients must pay 20 percent for hospital services plus a daily room charge of approximately $12 (with a 30-day maximum that the patient must pay for). The hospital then bills the appropriate national health insurance fund for the balance. Patient copayments for laboratory tests and dental care are 30 percent. Patients must pay 35 to 65 percent of the cost of covered prescription drugs and 100 percent for noncovered prescription drugs.[10] To avoid copayments at the point of service and balance billings, the French have shown a preference for paying for complementary insurance. The role of private complementary insurance has expanded over the past 40 years, enabling the Franch to avoid most of the negative consequences associated with health care rationing. This coverage is available from mutual societies, not-for-profit insurance companies, and commercial for-profit insurance companies. In 2001, approximately 87 percent of the population purchased complementary coverage, up from 31 percent in 1960. Private insurance premiums vary depending on labor force status, but average 2.5 percent of wages (Pomey and Poullier, 1997).

As of 2001 there were approximately 195,000 physicians in active practice nationwide, 330 per 100,000 population.[11] About one-third of all physicians are in exclusively private practice and another one-third are fully salaried. The remainder have a mixed practice—they hold a salaried position with either a large public hospital or a municipality health center and, at the same time, have a part-time private practice. About one-half of the physicians are considered general practitioners. The other half consists of specialists, most with mixed practices.

Approximately 75 percent of medical practitioners are considered first-tier: 83 percent of all general practitioners and 62 percent of all specialists. First-tier physicians contract with the national health insurance agencies and are reimbursed on a fee-for-service basis according to a nationally negotiated fee schedule. The fee schedule combines a relative value scale (that assigns points to the various services and procedures) with a monetary conversion factor.[12]

---

9 This is somewhat high, even by European standards. By 1989, German employers were paying half of the health care premiums of their workers, which ranged from 8 to 16 percent of total payroll, with an average of 12.8 percent. U.S. employers were paying 7.81 percent of payroll in 1992.

10 Certain vital drugs required for individuals with serious or debilitating conditions are reimbursed 100 percent.

11 Lack of an official census of physicians makes the actual figure somewhat of a guess.

12 The French relative value scale assigns values for each service and procedure much like the Medicare RBRVS, but the relative weightings for procedures are not technical (i.e., they are not based on time, intensity, complexity, or training requirements as in the United States). They are based more on the political influence of the various specialties and consumer preferences. The crude nature of the RVS has created price distortions in the fee schedule that encourage inefficient medical practices (Rodwin, 1981).

Before 1980, physicians considered prestigious by a commission of their peers were allowed to charge fees that exceeded the legal ceiling. In 1980, pressure from physicians' organizations forced the government to allow any physician to apply for this second-tier status that carried with it the ability to balance bill at rates up to 50 percent over the approved fee schedule. By 1990, concern over high out-of-pocket costs for physicians' services led the government to suspend new entry into the second tier, effectively closing that means of resource allocation.[13] About 25 percent of all physicians are now second-tier.

Even with the pricing flexibility enjoyed by some physicians, fee schedules have had a significant effect on physicians' incomes. In 1997, the typical physician had an average income of about $60,160 (U.S. PPP dollars), ranging from $49,600 for general practitioners to $115,000 for surgeons (Pomey and Poullier, 1997). French physicians average less than one-third of what the typical American physician earned in 1997. Not only are French physicians' salaries low by U.S. standards, their relative position within the country has eroded over the course of the past two decades. In 1970, the average physician's salary was three times that of the average French wage and salary worker. By 1997, it was barely twice that.

Key Concept 2
Opportunity Cost

Most medical students study at one of 29 university-affiliated hospital centers located primarily in the regional capitals. Although first year admission at the 41 medical schools is open to all comers, entry into the second year is controlled by a quota, standing at 3,750 in 1995 (down from 8,588 in 1972). The stated goal of 250 physicians per 100,000 population has been exceeded somewhat and the geographic distribution of physicians is uneven, with shortages in the north and the rural areas. No policy has been enacted to limit physician autonomy.[14]

Hospital care is provided at one of three types of institutions—public hospitals, private nonprofit hospitals, and private for-profit clinics. In 1998, public-sector hospitals contained 72 percent of the total beds, private nonprofits had 6 percent, and private for-profit clinics 22 percent (Green and Irvine, 2001). The most prestigious functions are performed in the public institutions—teaching, basic research, and high-tech diagnostic and surgical procedures. Public hospitals account for 75 percent of the hospital expenses but less than 60 percent of the short-stay hospital days.

Reform in 1983 changed the nature of the hospital reimbursement mechanism. Public hospitals and the majority of the private nonprofit hospitals are covered by prospective global budgeting, with physicians receiving a salary. Patients cannot choose their physicians in a public hospital unless they have first seen the specialist during that physician's part-time private practice. Private for-profit clinics receive the national per diem payment, and physicians treating patients in those clinics receive the standard fee. Physicians in exclusively private practice cannot treat patients in public hospitals.[15]

Public hospitals are required by law to keep occupancy rates below 95 percent of capacity, they must remain open 24 hours per day, and they must maintain a fully equipped emergency room.[16] Private clinics usually focus on more profitable services—elective surgeries and maternity—and avoid the high-cost procedures. Not surprisingly, the average costs of public hospitals tend to be higher than private clinics. Over the years, clinics have been successful in maintaining profitability by "unbundling" their services and thus removing certain procedures from the standard per diem rates.

The introduction of advanced technology has caused policymakers some problems in controlling health care spending. In addition to the extra investment, modern medical equipment requires more technical expertise for those who operate the equipment. This

---

13 With about 25 percent of all physicians allowed to balance bill, private spending for physicians' services was 23.5 percent in 2001, covered by complementary insurance and out-of-pocket spending.

14 Policymakers continue to explore new ways to limit spending. Ministry of Health officials have considered the extension of utilization controls and prospective budgeting to individual physicians as a means of controlling expenditures on physicians' services (U.S. Government Accounting Office, November 1991).

15 A limited number can admit patients for outpatient services.

16 In order to promote uniform quality across the hospital system, air conditioning is not allowed. This restriction played a role in the high death toll, estimated at 15,000, resulting from the record heat wave experienced in central Europe in the summer of 2003.

requirement translates into advanced training for physicians, nurses, and technicians and greater rates of remuneration for this new expertise.

From 1980 to 1990, France experienced the largest increase in the volume and intensity of services among countries discussed in this chapter. This has increased the pressure to control the nominal increase in per capita health care spending. Recent increases in copayments are an attempt to dampen consumer demand and slow the rate of growth in spending.

Key Concept 9
Market Failure

Economic theory clearly indicates that strict budget controls will lead to lower investment in high-cost technology. Budget considerations require regulation of investment in medical equipment. The more stringent the controls, the harder it will be for hospitals to adequately maintain their facilities and invest in quality-enhancing medical equipment. Theoretically, equipment standards are set to meet physician recommendations, but in actual practice, investment in medical equipment is a fiscal decision made with the approval of the Ministry of Health. The evidence suggests that since the introduction of global budgeting in 1984, innovation has been adversely affected and quality of care has suffered. If French experience mirrors that of other countries that use global budgets for longer periods of time (e.g., Canada, Germany, and the United Kingdom), then we can expect spending controls to become more stringent and have an increasingly negative impact on quality (U.S. Government Accounting Office, November 1991).

> **Policy Issue**
>
> Is it possible to establish a tightly controlled national health care budget without creating shortages of medical technology?

The introduction and diffusion of new technology, especially that which requires costly equipment, has been much slower in France than in the United States. A look at Table 16.1 provides a summary of the adoption levels for four costly diagnostic and treatment services. The French have one lithotripter for every million residents (one per 350,000 in the United States), one MRI for every 380,000 (one per 123,500 in the United States), and one CT scanner for every 104,000 (one per 76,000 in the United States). France has 45.7 patients undergoing kidney dialysis per 100,000 people compared to 86.5 per 100,000 in the United States.

The national health insurance system in France covers virtually 100 percent of the country's population. In their quest for social solidarity and equality, however, the French have given up a lot. Practitioners have suffered an erosion in their real incomes relative to the rest of the population. The system imposes global budgets on public hospitals, limits the availability of medical technology, and requires high out-of-pocket spending in the name of cost control. Physician autonomy remains intact, at least in the private sector. Public support remains high, due at least in part to the system's ability to avoid the wait-list problems experienced in Canada and the United Kingdom. The French system is at a crossroads. Fundamental change is needed because of chronic operating deficits. But the change needed is a change in philosophy, something the French people are not prepared for (LePen, 2003).

Germany: Sickness Funds[17]

After World War II, Germany was divided into two separate entities by the Allies. The German Democratic Republic (East Germany) was under the influence of the former Soviet Union and adopted the socialist form of government. The Federal Republic of Germany (West Germany) maintained its connections with the West and continued to utilize the prewar economic system, including the health care delivery system. East and West Germany were unified by treaty in 1990, and since that time East Germany has been subjected to most West German laws, including legislation relating to the medical insurance system. With a combined population of 82.4 million, Germany is divided into 16 provinces or Laenders, each with a great deal of independence in determining matters related to health and education.

---

17 Thanks to Klaus Geldsetzer for his insightful comments on this section. Of course, any remaining errors and omissions are my responsibility.

The overall provision of health insurance, from organization to financing, is a provincial responsibility. Administrative control is the responsibility of approximately 420 sickness funds, financed by the social insurance scheme established by federal law.[18]

Germany's health care system has its origins in the "mutual aid societies" created in the early nineteenth century. The German system of social benefits is based on the concept of social insurance as embodied in three founding principles: social solidarity, subsidiarity, and corporatism. The principle of social solidarity means that government is obligated to provide access to a wide range of social benefits to all citizens, including medical care, old-age pensions, unemployment insurance, disability payments, maternity benefits, and other forms of social welfare, and that everybody contributes according to their ability to pay. Subsidiarity refers to a decentralized system where policy is implemented by the smallest administrative unit possible. Corporatism is manifested in the governing boards of sickness funds that have widespread participation from business, medical providers, and insurers.

By the time Otto von Bismarck became Germany's first chancellor in 1871, hundreds of sickness insurance funds were already in operation. Bismarck, a member of the Prussian aristocracy, saw the working class movement (represented by socialist-oriented political parties) as a threat. This concern led him to advocate the expansion of the existing sickness benefit societies to cover workers in all low-wage occupations. In 1883, the Sickness Insurance Act was passed, representing the first social insurance program organized on a national level.

Over the next 130 years, the system grew to the point where virtually all of the population is provided access to medical care. All individuals are required by law to have health insurance. Those earning less than €46,350 (about $55,600 in 2004) must join one of the sickness funds for their health care coverage. Those earning more than the threshold may choose private health insurance instead. Approximately 74 percent of the population are compelled to join a sickness fund. Another 14 percent are members voluntarily even though their income exceeds the statutory cut-off. The remaining 9 percent, about 7.5 million, have comprehensive private insurance. By 2001, approximately one of every ten Germans covered by sickness fund insurance also purchased private supplementary insurance to cover copayments and other amenities, including overseas treatment, greater privacy during treatment, and private-room supplements. Private insurance may be tailored to meet the needs of individual patients. Individuals may choose policies that offer full coverage with no deductibles or coinsurance requirements or they may instead choose policies with those features (Green and Irvine, 2001).

Individual health insurance premiums for workers enrolled in sickness funds are calculated on the basis of income and not age or the number of dependents. Premiums are collected through a payroll deduction that varies from 11.2 to 15.3 percent of a worker's gross salary.[19] The average contribution was 14.2 percent in 2003. An additional contribution for long-term care insurance of 1.7 percent of income has been required since 1996, bringing the average contribution for health insurance plus long-term care insurance to 15.9 percent of payroll. The average payroll tax has risen sharply over the past 40 years. It was 6.0 percent in 1950 and rose to 8.4 percent by 1960, 11.4 percent by 1980, and 13.4 percent in 1993. Employers pay half of the tax directly for their workers. The Federal Labor Administration or local welfare agencies pay the premiums of those who are unemployed.[20] Retirees pay a percentage of their pensions equal to the average contribution paid by workers. Private insurance premiums vary depending on the type of policy chosen and average 20 percent less than the average payroll tax. Private benefits are better, and per capita administrative costs are one-half those of the public system (Prewo, 1993).

---

18 Legislation passed in 1993 and 1997 encouraged competition among sickness funds and led to a decrease in their number from over 1,300 in 1993. The number is expected to fall even further as a result of mergers and acquisitions.

19 Premiums are capped by the income threshold. Workers earning more than €46,350 and choosing a public sickness fund pay a premium equal to 14 percent of the first €46,350, or €6,489. This premium also covers nonworking family members.

20 Low-income persons are also exempted from paying into the health insurance fund. The income limit for free care is approximately €500 per month in the east and €600 per month in the west.

Membership in a sickness fund entitles a person to a comprehensive package of medical and dental benefits. Germans can expect to receive high-quality care that includes hospital care, ambulatory care, prescription drugs, dental care, disability income benefits, and even visits to health spas. The system is weak in several areas. In particular, public health services and psychiatric services are minimal.

Copayments have risen recently but remain low by U.S. standards. The first office visit to a physician during a calendar quarter has a patient copay of $12. There are no copayments for preventitive care visits, including physicals, dental exams, and cancer screenings. Fees for prescription drugs are 10 percent of the drug's price, and range from $6 to $12. Hospital charges are about $12 per day for the first 28 days and inpatient preventive and rehabilitative care is about $13 per day. Copayments for dental services are another matter and many procedures have copayments as high as 50 to 100 percent of the cost. Children, low-income individuals, and the chronically ill are exempt from most copayments. A maximum copayment of two percent of annual taxable income applies to everyone.

The German health care system was experiencing the same problems as the rest of the developed world in controlling health care costs during the decades of the 1960s and 1970s. Economic recession in the mid-1970s forced government policymakers to address the issue of the growth in medical expenditures. In 1977, the first of over 40 health care acts was passed to control rising health care spending and avoid the financial collapse of the system. The stated goal was to limit the growth of health care expenditures to the growth of wages and salaries while maintaining open access to the system.

The results have been dramatic. Nominal per capita spending had increased at an annual rate of 12.2 percent during the 1970s. After initiation of the cost-control measures, the annual rate of growth in spending fell to 4.50 percent from 1980 to 1998. This record is second only to Japan among the major developed countries in the Organization of Economic Cooperation and Development (OECD).

Germany's success in controlling costs can be attributed to the institutional framework of the system itself. Physicians are divided into two categories: ambulatory care physicians and hospital physicians. Ambulatory care physicians are paid on a fee-for-service basis and, for the most part, are prohibited from treating patients in a hospital setting. Hospital physicians are paid a salary and are not allowed to treat patients on an outpatient basis. The fees that physicians are allowed to charge are determined through negotiations between the sickness funds and regional physicians' organizations.

Hospitals are paid under a dual financing scheme with operating expenses covered by the sickness funds and capital investments by the state. Diagnosis related groups (DRGs) have been introduced into the hospital sector. With over 2,000 hospitals subject to the growing list of DRGs, the health authorities hope to reduce the average length of stay, now among the highest in Europe, by 30 percent.[21]

More than 100,000 students attend one of the 29 medical schools run by the state. After completing the six-year curriculum, physicians must first practice in a hospital setting for six years before they are allowed to enter private practice. Approximately 9,500 graduate each year and enter hospital practice.

Key Concept 2
Opportunity
Cost

By linking medical expenditures to the income of sickness fund members, the success of the policy depends upon the continued growth in wages and salaries and the success of the negotiations between sickness funds and medical practitioners. The cost-containment measures have resulted in a dramatic decrease in the relative salaries of primary care physicians, which have fallen from 5.1 times the average for wage and salary workers in 1975 to 2.7 times that average in 1990. By U.S. standards, physicians salaries are relatively low. In 1998, the average German physician earned $96,000, with general practitioners receiving $80,000 on average and ENT specialists receiving $128,800 (Green and Irvine, 2001).

---

21 By 2004, the new compulsory system will contain between 600 and 800 DRGs.

In 1997, there were 2,040 general hospitals with 594,000 beds (41 percent publicly owned, 41 percent private not-for-profit, and 18 percent private for-profit). An additional 190,000 beds were available in 1,400 preventive care and rehabilitation facilities. Hospitals also have less high-technology diagnostic, therapeutic, and surgical equipment than is available in the typical urban hospital in the United States. Germany has 30 percent fewer MRI units per million compared to the United States, and 70 percent fewer lithotripters. The one area where Germany has more technology is CT scanners; they have 17.1 per million population compared to 13.1 per million in the United States.

Although the negotiated fee schedule controls the unit price of medical care, it does nothing to limit the volume of services provided. Individual physicians can increase their incomes by treating more patients, but if every physician tries this strategy, global budget limits reduce unit fees proportionately. Thus, physicians who treat sickness fund patients never know in advance exactly how much they will be paid for a certain procedure. Physicians who treat privately insured patients are allowed to charge fees that are up to 3.5 times higher than fees charged sickness fund patients. As a result, privately insured patients tend to get better service.

The German system suffers from several problems that bring into question its ability to contain costs over the long term. Real spending rose almost 50 percent between 1990 and 1996. Possibly the biggest problem with the system, shared with all systems discussed in this chapter, is its reliance on third-party payment, providing virtually no role for the cost-conscious consumer. Patients have little incentive to limit their demand. Medical providers have little incentive to limit their supply. The only competition is among medical practitioners to attract more patient volume. The ability of the system to control costs depends primarily on the relative bargaining power between sickness funds and medical providers. Because expenditures are determined by negotiations between these two groups, the recent success in controlling costs is the result of legislative reform that has shifted the relative bargaining strength to the sickness funds. Continued success depends on the willingness of physicians' organizations to accept the burden of the responsibility in controlling costs, which translates into falling relative incomes.

Key Concept 7
Competition

Recent reform has introduced a warning system, a budget-capping mechanism that directly challenges the independence of physicians. Those physicians whose per patient spending exceeds the average are subject to a medical practice review. Physicians who exceed the average spending by 5 to 15 percent must submit a letter of explanation. Those who exceed their budgets by 15 to 25 percent must convince a panel of physicians and sickness fund representatives that the spending was justified based on medical factors. Physicians exceeding their budgets by more than 25 percent are subject to fines in the form of reduced fees. About seven percent of German physicians receive notice of overspending each year and about half of those have their fees reduced. These fines amount to 100 percent of the amount in excess of 1.25 times their budgets.

The incentive structure created by the budget-capping mechanism has changed the way physicians relate to their patients. Anecdotal evidence indicates that physicians treat less-demanding patients less aggressively (which is cheaper) and that they use more expensive therapies and procedures that are not part of their budgets when less expensive means are available that are part of their budgets. Recent studies also indicate that private patients are up to four times more likely to receive the newest drugs than sickness fund patients (Green and Irvine, 2001).

Another problem with the system is its tendency to use resources inefficiently. Incentives promote the provision of invasive acute care procedures and discourage the provision of personal services. Based on the latest available OECD figures, Germans see their doctors more often, are provided more prescription drugs, have a higher hospital admission rate, and stay in the hospital longer than citizens of the major developed countries in the OECD. The average length of stay in the hospital is much longer in Germany than in the United States (9.3 days compared to 5.8 days). Significant excess capacity in the number of hospital beds relative to the population exists in Germany

where there are 6.3 beds per 1,000 population compared to 2.9 in the United States. Even with strict cost-containment measures for prescription drugs, average drug prices are higher in Germany than in any other member country of the European Community.

What lessons can be learned from the German system of medical care delivery? First and foremost, a system that provides comprehensive coverage and mandates universal participation is expensive. Germans paid an average of 15.9 percent of their gross income in premiums in 2003, and over 11 percent of total medical expenditures are unreimbursed out-of-pocket charges. Secondly, cost control in a government-run system is usually accomplished through a system of global budgets and caps on expenditures for physicians' services. Germany has managed to keep spending within targeted amounts by establishing an explicit trade-off between volume and price. In other words, when utilization is higher than anticipated, fees are lowered proportionately. Thirdly, spending caps instituted in 1985 as a temporary cost-containment measure have become permanent. Legislation adopted in 1993 and 1997, designed to increase competition among sickness funds, lowered pharmaceutical prices and physicians' fees, increased required copayments, and placed more regulations on hospital billing practices, all to reach desired spending targets. Even with all these changes, support for the system remains high, in part because wealthy Germans have a private insurance safety valve and with it the ability to buy more physician time and better services.

Policy Issue

How important is the private insurance safety valve in maintaining public support for a government-run health care system?

Japan: The Company Is People

One of the most notable accomplishments of Japanese postwar development has been the exceptionally good record of health and longevity of the population. Life expectancies at birth for both males and females ranks at the top of the industrialized countries (77.2 years for males and 84.0 years for females). Likewise, infant mortality rates are among the lowest of the countries charted by the OECD in 1998. Undoubtedly, the medical care system has contributed to this record, but the extent of the contribution is hard to define.[22]

The Japanese enjoy an environment that is relatively free of crime, pollution, and other social problems such as divorce, teen pregnancy, obesity, drug use, and HIV. When compared to the United States, the Japanese have a much lower incidence of alcohol consumption, AIDS, drug abuse, teen pregnancy, and motor vehicle accidents.[23] The Japanese diet is relatively low in fat, resulting, at least partially, in an extremely low rate of cardiovascular diseases (Murdo, 1993). Some Japanese health experts have stated that in comparison, the delivery of medical care in Japan is like treating only the middle class in California (Sterngold, 1992).

Japan is a country of 127.1 million living on four major islands and 3,900 smaller islands. With most of the land mass (about the size of California) covered by mountains, the vast majority of the population is crowded into the urban areas. The population density is over 12 times that of the United States, making it the third most densely populated nation in the world (behind only Bangladesh and South Korea). The country is divided into 47 prefectures with jurisdictional authority similar to that of states in the United States.

The medical care delivery system in Japan has evolved from the modernization efforts initiated during the Meiji Restoration dating from 1868. In the place of the primitive structure of the feudal system, the institutions and practices of the developed world were

---

22 If the health of a population is measured by disease incidence instead, then it is not nearly as evident whether the Japanese are healthier. Self-reported health status in surveys of Japanese citizens is among the lowest among OECD countries with less than one-half reporting their perceived health as good. That same figure is over 90 percent in the United States (OECD Health Data, 2003).

23 One major exception is the high percentage of the adult population that uses tobacco products.

ISSUES IN MEDICAL CARE DELIVERY

SWEDEN: THE WELFARE STATE

Sweden has long been considered the "model" Scandinavian country by its establishment of a middle ground between free market and government decision making. The centerpiece of the Social Democratic Party's welfare policy (in power for much of the postwar era) has been the national health insurance program. Here are the key statistics from 2001:

Key statistics Sweden, 2001

Population (millions)	8.9
GDP per capita	$26,052
Health care spending per capita	$ 2,270
Health care spending (percent of GDP)	8.7
Number of physicians (per 1,000)	3.0*
Number of hospital beds (per 1,000)	2.4*
Average length of stay (days)	5.0
CT Scanners	14.2**
MRI Units	7.9**

  * = 2000

** = 1999

Until 1955, health insurance was strictly voluntary. Even though its purchase was heavily subsidized, only about 70 percent of the population chose to be covered. A series of reforms over the next decade made health insurance mandatory and essentially guaranteed universal access for all Swedes. Legislation in the 1970s resulted in financing reform. Copayments were required for all ambulatory physician visits. Direct social insurance contributions from workers ended, replaced by a system fully funded by employer and taxpayer contributions.

The provision of health care is the responsibility of 20 county councils and one municipality under the central supervisory authority of the National Board of Welfare. More than 75 percent of the medical expenditures are financed through taxes: an 8.5 percent payroll tax paid by employers and a proportional tax levied by the county councils. This combined tax amounts to about 12 percent of income. The remainder of the funding comes from lump-sum payments from the national government and individual out-of-pocket payments (the latter amounting to about 15 percent of total spending in 2000).

The country is divided into six regions, each with at least one major regional hospital that provides complex care, including most high-tech diagnostic and surgical procedures. Each county is divided into districts, each with its own hospital facility to serve the local population. There are 89 acute-care hospitals and more than 950 health centers providing primary health care, creating a uniform regional medical care system.

The organizational pattern of the medical staffs in the hospitals and health centers had virtually eliminated private practitioners by 1980. Between 1980 and 1985 a growing number of physicians began practicing in the private market. It is estimated that by 1985 somewhere between one-third and one-half of the physician population was practicing in the private sector. Less than 6 percent were exclusively private-practice physicians with the remainder divided about evenly between part-time private practitioners and those moonlighting in addition to their salaried positions.

This growth in the private health care market underscored the nationwide challenge to the basic principles governing Swedish health care—equalitarianism, social solidarity, and cost effectiveness. While the principle of cost effectiveness is subordinated to the other two, it establishes a prioritization of care into four categories: (1) care for life-threatening acute diseases, serious chronic diseases, palliative care at the end of life, and care for those with reduced autonomy; (2) preventive and rehabilitative care with proven benefits; (3) care for less serious acute and chronic illnesses; and (4) other care.

Combined county and federal deficits have grown to alarming levels in recent years (reaching over 15 percent of GDP in 1995). This has resulted in a marked slowing in the growth in health care budgets and an increased emphasis on primary care and prevention at the expense of the more sophisticated technology. Top marginal tax rates of 85 percent (on incomes of $28,000 in U.S. equivalents) have prompted physicians' unions to bargain for leisure instead of income. As a result, the average work week of the public-sector physician has fallen to 28 hours. Average physicians' salaries were $63,150 in 2001, less than one-third of the U.S. average (Håkansson and Nordling, 1997). Low by U.S. standards, salaries have fallen from 3.6 times that of the average wage and salary in 1970 to 1.7 times in 1999. A large number of physicians moonlight in the private sector. Limited choice of physicians is a growing complaint among the population. There is also a growing demand for better service, shorter waiting times for appointments, and less use of waiting lists to ration scarce technology.

The waiting lists that plague every single-payer system in the world are also a problem in Sweden. Growing waiting lists presented both a medical and political problem in the 1980s. Median waiting times for hip replacement surgery were 1–3 years and those for cataract removal were one year. A series of reforms in the 1990s helped mitigate the problem. In 1992 maximum waiting time guarantees were implemented. The maximum wait from GP referral to specialist treatment is now 6 months.

Reforms in the latter half of the 1990s focused on cost control. Copayments are required on most medical services—about $15 for a GP visit, $30 to see a specialist in a hospital, and a hospital inpatient per diem of $10. Patients pay the full cost of pharmaceutical drugs up to $135 annually and are subject to copayments on spending up to a ceiling of $225 annually. Approximately 28 percent of pharmaceutical spending comes from these copayments. The introduction of a purchaser-provider split moved the system away from global budgeting for hospitals. Replaced by a DRG point system, introduced in the U.S. Medicare system two decades ago, the hospital payment mechanism creates incentives for more efficient delivery of medical care. Additionally, private providers are allowed to compete for contracts with public providers, encouraging efficiency throughout the system. Finally, reference pricing and the mandatory use of cost-effectiveness analysis in the introduction of new drugs and technology were also introduced.

By international standards, the Swedish health care system provides high-quality care at less than one-half of the per capita cost of U.S. health care. Policymakers have moved away from the pure single-payer model toward a blended private-public sector model. The shift away from the public-sector monopoly allows for a more consumer-driven health care system. Patients have relatively good access to high-technology services, such as CT scanners and MRIs. Even with a relatively uniform distribution of services, significant differences in medical outcomes persist across socioeconomic groups. But recent reforms have provided Swedes with improved options for private health care funded through private insurance. A small but significant private insurance market has developed that allows those who can afford it to bypass the waiting lists and receive treatment in the private sector. Approximately 115,000 Swedes, or one percent of the population, now have access to a better level of treatment, formalizing the two-tiered system that has existed for about 15 years. The introduction of this safety valve has resulted in lower costs and a more responsive health care delivery system.

Source: Rosenthal (1986), Lofgren (2002), Lofgren and Walker (2002), and Håkansson and Nordling (1997).

ISSUES IN MEDICAL CARE DELIVERY

IN SEARCH OF THE PERFECT BELLYBUTTON

Japanese women are increasingly taking action to correct one of those tiny flaws of nature—the misshapen bellybutton. Japanese culture is "bellybutton conscious." Japanese mothers save remnants of their baby's umbilical cords in a wooden box, much like American mothers save a lock of their newborn's hair. There, a "naval bent out of shape" means much the same as "your nose bent out of shape" in America. And in Japan "your mother has an outie" is a slang expression that would translate in America "yeah, right, give me a break."

Bare midriffs and body ornamentation require the fashion-conscious Japanese twenty-something woman to have the perfect bellybutton. And if nature did not provide one, then cosmetic surgery will. Plastic surgeons all across the country are charging up to $2,000 for this procedure that can turn an unattractive outie into a perfectly symmetrical fashion statement. Because it is not considered health care, the procedure is not covered by national health insurance.

Source: Norihiko Shirouzu, "Reconstruction Boom in Tokyo: Perfecting Imperfect Bellybuttons," *The Wall Street Journal*, October 5, 1995, B1.

adopted. Because Germany had what was considered the most advanced medical care system at that time, it was used as the model. The formation of "mutual aid associations" in the early 1900s served as the foundation for the medical care system. And like Germany, the development of these associations among workers had as much to do with controlling a disruptive socialist movement as with promoting social welfare. The promotion and improvement of public health is a national responsibility according to the constitution. Even so, universal coverage was not fully realized until 1961.

The Universal Health Insurance system is regulated by the Ministry of Health and Welfare. The entire population is organized into small, independently administered health insurance societies that serve as intermediaries for its members. Individuals and their dependents are assigned to one of these organizations according to profession, trade, or employer.

Prior to the Second World War, two national health insurance laws were enacted that serve as the basis for the modern-day system. The first act in 1922 created the Employee Health Insurance System (EHI) that now covers 64 percent of the population. Health coverage is provided by more than 5,000 independent plans providing government-managed health insurance for firms with 5 to 300 employees, society-managed health insurance for firms with more than 300 employees, seaman's insurance, public employees' insurance, and insurance for private school employees.

The second health insurance act passed in 1938 created the Citizens' Health Insurance System (CHI). The self-employed and pensioners comprising 36 percent of the population are covered under this plan. Since 1947, over 60 laws have been passed further defining the principles and policies of the national health care system. Because each plan was developed separately, they lack uniformity in terms of costs and cost-sharing arrangements.

Premiums are based on earnings, not health status or age. Employers are required by law to pay at least half of the monthly premium directly, which varies from 6.0 to 9.6 percent of monthly income, up to a maximum of $430 per household per month.[24]

---

24 The employer share ranges from 50 percent to 80 percent and averages 56 percent. The average payroll tax is 8.5 percent of income.

With few exceptions, each insurance plan sets its own premiums, which may vary as much as two times from plan to plan. Copayments in all plans were raised from 10 percent to 20 percent in 1997. Dependent copays are even higher for some types of services. CHI copayments are a uniform 30 percent, except for retirees who pay 20 percent.

Out-of-pocket expenditures are capped for each plan. EHI maximums are 63,000 yen per month (about $530) for most members. Certain low-wage recipients have a 30,000-yen maximum per person (about $260) per month. In 1983, the Health and Medical Services System for the Elderly was established. One of the expressed goals of the plan was to reduce the incidence of moral hazard by providing a modest cost-sharing arrangement. Individuals over age 70 and all those bedridden that are over age 65 must pay a modest user charge of 700 yen for every day in the hospital and 1,000 yen per month for outpatient care. All out-of-pocket copayment charges amount to 12 percent of total health care spending.

For 7.6 percent of GDP, the Japanese receive a comprehensive package of benefits for virtually every legal resident. Medical procedures that are not associated with the onset of a disease are not included in the basic insurance package. Virtually all preventive care, physical examinations, and procedures related to normal pregnancies are not covered by national health insurance. In fact, out-of-pocket spending for these services is not even counted as part of national health expenditures.[25]

Physicians fall into two categories: clinic-based and hospital-based. Clinic-based physicians operate out of more than 85,850 privately owned facilities. Over 22,000 of these clinics are actually short-term hospitals with fewer than 20 beds each. Statutory regulations requiring that patients be moved to hospitals after 48 hours are largely ignored and not enforced.

Medical services are provided on a fee-for-service basis using a fixed price, "point-fee" system. This negotiated schedule provides uniform pricing, regardless of specialty of physician and service setting, and thus offers few financial incentives to improve quality. Clinic-based physicians receive payments directly. Hospital-based physicians receive a salary, so hospitals receive payments for services performed there.

The number of clinic-based physicians has been falling for the past 30 years and thus their political influence is waning. In 1960, they comprised 45 percent of the total number of physicians. By 1988, this percentage had fallen to 30. There are several reasons for this decline: (1) the slowly increasing average age of clinic-based physicians, (2) land prices in urban areas have priced most newcomers out of the market, (3) the demand for high-tech diagnostic equipment that has allowed the large hospitals to siphon off much of this market share, and (4) a growing use of outpatient facilities has increased the use of large hospitals over clinics.

In 1994, physicians earned on average $53,000 adjusted for purchasing power parity, approximately two times the income of the average wage and salary worker in Japan and only one-third that of U.S. physicians (Nakahara, 1997). Clinic-based physicians earn on average about twice the income of hospital-based physicians. Physicians working in the nation's 9,286 hospitals are paid the same regardless of specialty. There are two things that keep hospitals adequately staffed: the prestige of a hospital appointment and the "expressions of gratitude" paid by patients to secure the services of a specialist. It is not uncommon for patients to provide gifts ranging from $1,000 to $3,000 to obtain the services of a prominent specialist. These hidden charges (some would call them bribes) are not documented and go largely untaxed.[26]

The typical Japanese citizen has an extreme aversion to invasive treatment. They prefer medication and bed rest to surgery. Thus, surgical rates are among the lowest in the

---

25 National expenditure data also excludes expenses for physical exams, vaccinations, prescription eyeglasses, prosthetic devices, and treatment by alternative providers such as acupuncturists. Items such as spending on public health and medical research are not classified as medical expenditures.

26 Interestingly enough, over half of the income of physicians is tax free in the first place. Until recently, 72 percent of a physician's income was free from income taxes. Changes in the tax code have reduced the preferential status so that only 52 to 72 percent escape taxation.

world (one-third the U.S. rates) and prescription drug use among the highest (over one-fourth of health care spending in 1997). In fact, the single most lucrative aspect of the clinic-based practice is the sale of prescription medicine. Not only are surgical rates low, but also organ transplantation is almost nonexistent. The Japanese failure to recognize death as the cessation of brain wave activity makes it extremely difficult to find suitable organ donors, placing an effective ban on transplants.

The point-fee system introduces a bias in the medical care delivery system favoring primary care. All physicians, regardless of specialty, practice like general practitioners, focusing on diagnostic and pharmaceutical services at the expense of technical and specialty care. Thus, no formal system of referral to specialists has emerged. Financial incentives encourage physicians to be protective of their patient volume. Secondly, expensive treatment areas tend to be ignored. Cancer treatment, neonatal pediatrics, and emergency/trauma medicine are specialties found only in the large public hospitals where there is little incentive to provide high-quality service.

Direct comparison between health care spending in Japan and the United States is difficult for reasons already mentioned. Maternity expenses, the direct cost of medical education and research, grants to public hospitals, and public health promotions, all included in the United States figure, are ignored by the Japanese. Including these alone would increase Japanese spending by 1.5 percent of GDP. In addition, private room charges add about $100 per day to a hospital stay that already averages over 40 days.[27]

Japanese physicians tend to overdiagnose and overmedicate. Patient volume tends to be high. It is not unusual for clinic-based physicians to see 30 to 35 patients per hour. Specialists tend to spend more time with each patient. By U.S. standards the total time spent with patients is still low. Ophthalmologists will see 15 patients per hour and OB/GYNs 15 to 20 per hour. Appointments are almost nonexistent. Patients are seen on a first-come-first-served basis. Long waits are common with queues for ambulatory visits and waiting lists for hospitalization.

Capital funding for hospital infrastructure must come from fee revenues. The Medical Care Law, amended in 1985 to "control the excessive increase in hospital beds," has restricted the establishment of private hospitals. The law placed a ceiling on the number of hospital beds per region and has made it virtually impossible to build new hospitals in urban areas (Yoshikawa, Shirouzu, and Holt, 1991). Even prestigious hospitals in urban areas, including Tokyo, are marked by poor infrastructure, small rooms, and few support staff.

The Japanese system of health care delivery is reflective of the basic approach business firms have toward their employees—"the company is people." Coverage is compulsory; participation is mandatory. The success of the system lies in its ability to control costs and to provide universal access. Criticism may be targeted at the issue of quality, which is to be expected. Service distortions almost always accompany fixed fee schedules. In this regard, Japan is not immune. But with its emphasis on equality and community, the health care system has served the Japanese well.

United Kingdom: National Health Service[28]

The British National Health Service (NHS) stands as a symbol of social equality and collective compassion. Under the Health Authorities Act of 1995, the 110 District Health Authorities and the 90 Family Health Service Organizations were merged and replaced by approximately 100 Unitary Health Authorities. Each serves the medical

Policy Issue

What role does culture play in the development of a national health care delivery system?

Key Concept 2
Opportunity Cost

The UK Department of Health with links to the NHS Executive home page can be found at **http://www.open.gov.uk/doh/dhhome.html.**

---

27 This figure includes both chronic and acute care hospital stays. It does not include stays in TB hospitals that average 207 days or stays in psychiatric hospitals that average 536 days.

28 Unless otherwise stated, institutional facts and figures are from "A Guide of the National Health Service," published by the NHS Executive, March 1995.

Back-of-the-Envelope

PROMOTING EQUALITY

The rationale behind the public provision of medical care is easy to explain. Market failure results in a level of care that is less than optimal. Two approaches have been used with varying degrees of success to promote a more equal sharing of scarce medical care resources—subsidize and ration. Subsidies for the poor increase the amount of care they receive and rationing reduces the amount of care provided to everyone else. Both policies promote a more equal distribution of medical care consumption. Why would a group of high-income consumers agree to limit their own access to care in the name of promoting equality? Lindsay (1969) provided a theoretical justification for the simultaneous use of rationing and subsidies to promote equality in medical care consumption.

In the diagram, D_1 and D_2 represent the respective demand curves for two different segments of the population. Group 1 has less income and a lower level of demand. Assuming a perfectly elastic supply, S, they will consume Q_1 units of medical care. Those with higher incomes have a higher level of demand, D_2, will consume Q_2 units of medical care. Countries, such as Great Britain and Canada, have chosen to address this inequality, $Q_2 - Q_1$, by providing universal coverage through taxation and subsidy, combined with placing limits on the availability of certain procedures.

The cost of these policies is shown in the right side of the diagram. The cost of producing equality via rationing is the consumer surplus forgone by the higher income group. The vertical distance between D_2 and S represents the forgone consumer surplus. Thus, the marginal cost of promoting equality through rationing, MC_R, has a slope equal to the absolute value of the slope of D_2. Every unit of care given up by group 2 creates a unit of equality at a marginal cost equal to the forgone consumer surplus of group 2.

To induce the poor to consume more than Q_1 requires a subsidy. This subsidy will never be greater than P_1, the cost of care. The subsidy must be at least equal to the difference between the value of care as perceived by members of the group, represented by D_1, and the price of care, P_1. The slope of MC_S will be less than the slope of MC_R since D_1 is more elastic than D_2. The marginal cost of promoting equality through a subsidy rises to point A and then becomes the horizontal line at P_1.

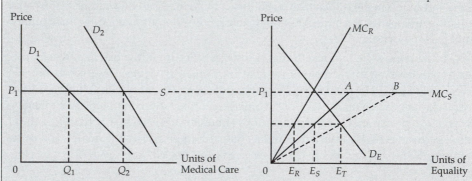

Using a combination of rationing and subsidies, more equality may be purchased at a lower overall cost. The combined marginal cost curve, $0B$, is the horizontal sum of MC_R and $0A$. Assuming D_E is the demand for equality in this case, a level of equality equal to E_T may be purchased using this combined strategy, E_R due to rationing and E_S due to the subsidy. Purchasing E_T equality using rationing or subsidies alone would require significantly higher spending. Countries that have a well-specified demand for equality can achieve desired levels at lower overall cost by using a combination of subsidies for the poor and limited availability of certain procedures to everyone.

Source: Cotton M. Lindsay, "Medical Care and the Economics of Sharing," *Economica*, November 1969, 351–362.

needs of about 500,000 people. With an overall budget of approximately £50 billion in 2000 and nearly one million employees, the NHS is the largest single employer in Europe.

The origins of the national health care system can be traced back to the early nineteenth century. As was the case throughout much of Europe, labor unions and other fraternal associations provided health insurance to their members. Employers encouraged their workers to join these mutual aid societies in order to reduce public demand for charity care.

In 1911, under the leadership of Prime Minister Lloyd George, the British Parliament passed the first National Health Insurance Act, strengthening the voluntary insurance program and providing a funding mechanism for indigent care. Although membership in a mutual aid society was not mandatory, most workers joined. Health benefits included the services of a general practitioner (GP) and prescription drugs. Specialty care and hospitalization were not covered under the law, but were provided through local government support and charity care.

The Second World War brought profound changes in the political and social attitudes toward health care in Britain. Before the end of the war, Winston Churchill appointed Sir William Beveridge to study the delivery of health care and make recommendations for change. The Beveridge Report of 1942 outlined a comprehensive national health insurance plan that would extend coverage to everyone, regardless of income level. The National Health Service Act was implemented in 1948. Its passage meant that the entire population was now covered under one plan, providing a comprehensive package of benefits, paid out of general tax revenues, and free to patients at the point of use.

The single-payer concept and limited supervision of providers kept the administrative costs of the system low, but from the beginning, the NHS was underfunded and dominated by the medical community. Budgetary constraints, especially during years of slow economic growth, politicized health care delivery and led to a series of crises (about one every three years) between government policymakers and medical practitioners.

The NHS inherited a geographic distribution of resources that favored the four metropolitan areas in and around London. One of the stated goals of the newly formed system was to eliminate the inequalities that existed. Targets were established to increase the availability of facilities in underserved regions and restrict the expansion of facilities in overserved regions. To accomplish this goal, it was necessary to implement "standstill budgets" in certain parts of the country, particularly the London area. Thus, the goal of equity has required policymakers to cut services in certain designated areas. The Black Report, released in 1980, found little evidence of change in resource availability. Even today, the per capita hospital spending among the health authorities differs as much as 40 percent. The number of private hospital beds in the Northeast Thames region is 8 times greater than in the Northern region. The rate of kidney dialysis and transplant procedures performed is almost 30 percent higher in metro London than in Yorkshire and 75 percent higher than in the Western Midlands.

Every citizen is registered with a general practitioner and receives all primary and preventive care in this setting. There are about 35,000 GPs in 9,000 practices, handling over 90 percent of all patients. The GP serves as "family doctor" for the patient and gatekeeper to the system of specialists or "consultants" and hospitals. Any patient that requires extensive testing or specialized treatment is referred to a consultant, that is a specialist, or is admitted directly into a hospital. Urgent cases are to be treated within a month, while those classified as nonurgent may have to wait up to a year.[29] Since the internal market reforms were initiated in 1992, the number of patients waiting for admission to NHS hospitals over 18 months has fallen to nearly zero.

---

29 According to Enthoven (1991, p. 64), patients in the queue system are told: "The doctor agrees you should have an operation; go home and we will call you to come into the hospital a week in advance in the next year or two."

Policy Issue

Are Americans willing to accept waiting lists for specialty care and certain surgical procedures as the price of universal coverage?

Largely because of the waiting lists for "elective" surgery, those who can afford private supplementary health insurance have purchased it. Over the past decade, the proportion of the population with private coverage has fallen to 11.5 percent due to increases in private premiums. Private insurance coverage is concentrated among those in the professional and managerial occupations, high-income earners, and those living in London and the southeast. Over two-thirds of those with private insurance have risk-rated group policies provided through their employers. Premiums must be paid out of pretax income and any benefit is taxable (subject to an income tax and a 5 percent premium tax). To a great extent, patients with private insurance still use the NHS for emergency and chronic care. The private system deals largely with "quality-of-life" issues such as hernia repair, gall-bladder disease, and hip replacements. About 20 percent of all nonemergency surgeries are paid for privately. Thus, the private system serves as a safety valve for wait-listed patients, much the same way the U.S. system serves as a safety valve for wait-listed Canadians. Critics of the private system argue that it has two main flaws: it takes the pressure off the national system, slowing improvements; and it creates a two-tiered system, undermining the perception of equality.

In the reformed NHS, general practitioners are independent contractors. They receive over half of their incomes from capitation payments and the rest from various incentives and allowances. For example, GPs receive additional pay for settling in underserved areas and bonuses for meeting immunization, screening, and vaccination targets. In 1992 the mean net earnings of British physicians was $120,000. In comparison, senior lawyers in private practice earned 2.5 times that amount. The pay scale for hospital-based physicians ranged from $63,500 to $81,900 in 1996 with 20 percent receiving bonuses beginning at $15,000 (Hatcher, 1997).

The NHS inherited nearly 3,000 hospitals at its inception. Today, fewer than half of them still exist. The number of hospital beds has also declined markedly from 480,000 in 1948 to less than 136,000 in 1999. The most recent OECD figures place hospital occupancy rates at over 80 percent for all hospitals, including acute-care beds (OECD, 2000). In early 2000, it was announced that the number of Britons waiting for hospital admission had reached 1.04 million, about two percent of the population. With fewer than 6 million hospital admissions in 1999, this means that there is one person on a list waiting for hospitalization for every six admissions. Much as the 40 million uninsured Americans symbolize the shortcomings of the U.S. system, the waiting list of over one million symbolizes the shortcomings of the British system.

Standard practice in Britain has been to place anyone requiring an "elective" procedure on a waiting list. Procedures such as cataract surgery, hip replacement surgery, coronary artery bypass surgery, and breast reconstruction following a mastectomy are defined as elective procedures. In other words, if it's not life threatening, it can wait. A good indicator of the realities of the waiting list in Britain can be found in the national standards from the Patient's Charter. First published in 1991, the charter guarantees the provision of inpatient hospital treatment within 18 months of referral, establishes a standard wait of 12 months for coronary artery bypass surgery, and provides a 26-week standard wait to see a hospital consultant after referral from a general practitioner. Patients are now able to log onto the NHS Web site and see the expected length of time they will have to wait for medical treatment in the hospital of their choosing.

The paternalistic tradition of the NHS is evident in this method of resource allocation. It is a system that is largely invisible and uniquely British. Not only are patients in the United Kingdom among the least informed in the developed world, the culture tends to leave medical decisions to the individual physician and seldom questions the medical authorities. Physicians are considered the sole authority on determining patient needs and have no real pressure to respond to patient desires. Thus, rationing may be disguised as a clinical decision.

British attitudes about waiting have changed since the end of World War II. As opportunities for productive enterprise have increased, acceptance for this method of rationing has decreased. As waiting lists grew, the problems were magnified and criticism abounded. Decision making was becoming more politicized, and overcentralization had led to managerial inefficiencies. The lack of economic incentives had completely stifled innovation. In response, the Thatcher government proposed major reforms that were implemented in 1991. *Working for Patients* (1989), a position paper on reform of the NHS, was an attempt to introduce competition and market incentives into the NHS in hopes of making it "more responsive to the needs of the patient."

Prior to the reform measures, each district was provided a fixed budget with no incentive for good performance. Greater efficiency and shorter waiting lists meant more referrals from other districts without an offsetting transfer of resources. Increased productivity added to workloads and not revenues. Under the reformed system, resources followed patients. Theoretically, each local health authority had the responsibility of buying medical care for the community it serves. Although each could contract with any provider throughout the nation, in practice, most contracting was still local.

The Thatcher reforms of 1993 created an internal market and GP fundholders, adding choice and competition to a system where little of either existed. But competition failed to bring about the desired results. Money did not follow patients due to weak incentives, particularly in the hospital sector. Without the ability to keep surpluses, hospital administrators sought bigger budgets. Since it was politically impossible to close a failed hospital, there was little incentive to provide services efficiently.

To be providers of health services, health organizations became NHS trusts, independent organizations competing for patients. At the same time, many GPs became fundholders with their own budgets. By 1995 all health care was being provided through NHS trusts, a significant cultural shift even for the British. GPs who did not become fundholders had their budgets centrally controlled by the NHS. Patients who received treatment from fundholders often received better treatment, a source of complaints among the rest of the patient population. A two-tiered system was quickly developing.

A new government came into power with a pledge to get rid of the internal market. As a result, the NHS was reorganized in 1997 for the fifth time in 25 years. The Blair reforms, based on a "third way" of running the NHS, changed GP fundholding by placing 30,000 general practitioners in one of 500 primary care trusts (PCTs). Each PCT is a fully-capitated budgetholder responsible for providing primary care, community health services, and virtually all other medical services for a geographically defined population of 50,000 to 250,000. The emphasis is no longer on a market model based on choice and competition, but on a government-run system based on collaboration and cooperation. Secondary care is provided through approximately 200 NHS hospital trusts, 400 small-scale community hospitals, and specialized tertiary care hospitals. In addition, PCTs are able to contract with approximately 230 private hospitals, most in one of five for-profit chains.

A major aspect of the new NHS is a 10-year plan promising more hospitals, more physicians, cleaner facilities, increased standards, and shorter waiting times. Recognizing that the biggest problem facing the NHS has always been underfunding, the NHS budget is scheduled to increase by one-half in nominal terms and over one-third in real terms between March 2000 and the end of 2005. This increase will require an average annual growth rate in NHS spending of 6.3 percent. For the goal to be met the maximum wait for an outpatient appointment will be three months and the maximum wait for an inpatient admission will be six months.

The most recent reforms have also created the National Institute for Clinical Excellence (NICE), a special health authority accountable to the Secretary of State for Health. NICE was established to determine the availability of treatments, technology, and services based on cost-effectiveness analysis. Under NICE guidelines, some treatments may be available to

Policy Issue

What is the appropriate role of cost effectiveness analysis in determining the availability of medical treatment?

ISSUES IN MEDICAL CARE DELIVERY

PHYSICIAN SUPPLY UNDER THE NATIONAL HEALTH SYSTEM

In labor markets where wages are determined by the market, employment levels are determined by the market-clearing wage in the short run and by expected life-time earnings in the long run. This situation exists in the U.S. health care industry today and existed in Britain before 1948 when the industry was nationalized.

Before National Health, British physicians were self-employed and earned over four times the income of manual workers. Today, they are employees of the government and earn barely two times that of manual workers. The resultant effect on physicians' supply has been remarkable. The aggregate physicians' supply curve fits that of the standard economic model—upward sloping. As the real wage spiraled downward, net emigration of trained British physicians increased, reaching 500 per year by the 1960s. The trend continued for the next decade and by the early 1970s, one-third of all NHS hospital staff was trained overseas (primarily in former Commonwealth countries). Without this infusion of foreign-trained physicians, there would be a serious shortage of trained medical practitioners in the NHS.

The lessons are clear for anyone interested in listening. The fees charged by physicians serve as market-clearing prices in the short run. Over time physician supply will adjust to those levels based on the expected lifetime earnings potential. When the government controls the price at comparatively low levels, physicians will seek better opportunities elsewhere. To fill the gaps left by the outflow of trained physicians, the system will attract alternatives to domestically trained physicians. The foreign-trained physicians who immigrate do so because they consider the employment opportunities offered in the controlled environment superior to those in their home countries.

Source: Cotton M. Lindsay, *National Health Issues: The British Experience*, Nutley, N.J.: Roche Laboratories, 1980.

Key Concept 2
Opportunity Cost

segments of the population with certain indicators and unavailable to others. For example, expensive drug treatment for Alzheimer's patients may be available for those who score over a cut-off level on cognitive tests and not available to those who score below the cut-off.

Health inequalities remain within the British system. Life expectancy is higher for professional and managerial groups than the unskilled. Limitations from long-standing illnesses are also substantially lower for those in the former group. Death rates from coronary heart disease are three times higher in blue-collar Manchester than white-collar Oxfordshire (*Independent Inquiry*, 1998). The system continues to have many strong supporters. Proponents point to a strong primary care system provided to everyone without regard to ability to pay. High-cost procedures that benefit only the few are rationed to ensure that the majority of the population receives basic care at a low cost.

Summary and Conclusions

As we have learned, private health insurance systems operate under three guiding principles: the insurance principle, whereby premiums are risk-rated; the equivalence principle, whereby the premium paid determines the level of coverage; and the principle of personal responsibility, whereby individuals are responsible for their own health and premiums reflect lifestyle choices. In contrast, social insurance systems operate under a different set of principles: the principle of self-administration, whereby payers and providers operate as independent entities with their rights and responsibilities determined

Back-of-the-Envelope

THE ECONOMICS OF A SAFETY-VALVE

The purpose of a safety valve is to relieve pressure. How is the notion of a safety valve relevant in analyzing medical care markets? Consider two medical care markets separated geographically, the primary market and the safety valve. Supply is restricted through limits on the number of operating rooms, imaging devices, and other procedures requiring sophisticated medical technology. To keep prices and spending down, the governing authorities place a price ceiling in the primary market as shown in the left side of the diagram below.

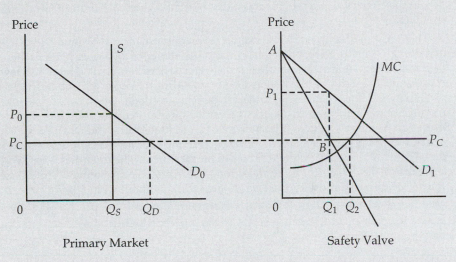

Primary Market   Safety Valve

The vertical supply curve, S, fixes the quantity supplied at Q_S. Instead of allowing the market price, P_0, to prevail, government sets a price ceiling at P_C and creates a shortage of $Q_D - Q_S$. The excess demand causes problems with waiting lists and angry patients. Given a certain degree of geographic mobility, patients in the primary market can travel to the unrestricted market, the safety valve, and receive treatment.

Suppose the payer in the primary market agrees to finance the care received in the safety valve at the controlled price, P_C. Providers in the unrestricted market face a marginal revenue curve with a downward-sloping segment, AB, and a horizontal segment, BP_0. Marginal cost crosses this combined marginal revenue curve at Q_2 output. If capacity in the unrestricted market is less than Q_1, all of the available capacity will be devoted to consumers in that market, since they willingly pay P_1. If providers in the unrestricted market have capacity beyond Q_1, those consumers shut out of the primary market can get care through the safety valve at price P_C. Providers in the unrestricted market practice price discrimination, charging P_1 to its original customers and P_C to the overflow from the primary market.

by law; the principle of social partnership, with costs shared by members of society (typically employers and employees); and the principle of social solidarity, whereby premiums are determined by the level of income.

As U.S. policymakers debate health care reform, it is important to recognize that no other country has actually solved the health-care spending problem. No patented solutions have been offered, only alternative approaches to the same problem. Proponents of the social insurance model will argue that countries like Canada, Germany, and France have better systems—delivering high-quality medical care to everyone with no financial barriers. Even though these systems meet the goal of universal access, they are not able to solve the overall spending problem.

ISSUES IN MEDICAL CARE DELIVERY

"A MATTER OF LIFE AND DEATH"

Baby boomers and their parents will remember the 1950s game show "Queen for a Day," where three women would tell their hard-luck stories to a studio audience. The one who received the most audience support would be chosen Queen-for-a-Day and receive a new washing machine or refrigerator or suite of furniture. The tears would flow as the crown was put into place and the royal robes draped over the new queen's shoulders.

That was America in the 1950s. A similar game show made its way onto Dutch television in the 1990s. Except this time it was not a matter of a new washing machine or a remodeled kitchen, it was often a matter of a new kidney or a bone marrow transplant. In a series partially sponsored by the Ministry of Health, viewers in the Netherlands witness real-life dramas of patients competing for scarce medical resources. Originally produced to focus attention on resource allocation in a government-run health care system, the show called "A Matter of Life and Death" pits two patients in need of life-saving procedures against one another. The one who receives the support of the studio audience receives the treatment. The loser dies. Every system must make decisions on the allocation of scarce medical resources. The Dutch system has chosen a most unusual way to pick winners and losers.

Source: "You Bet Your Life," *The Wall Street Journal*, October 29, 1993, A14.

National health insurance does not guarantee public satisfaction with the system. Results of several recent surveys by Blendon et al. (1990) and Donelan et al. (1999) are reported in Table 16.5. More than half of the citizens in six of the seven countries with nationalized systems responded that they felt that their systems needed fundamental changes or should be completely rebuilt, and fewer than half were happy with the way their systems worked. Citizens in Germany showed the greatest level of satisfaction with their system with 41 percent responding that they felt the system worked pretty well and only 48 percent seeing the need for fundamental or complete change. Discontent runs very high

Table 16.5	Public Opinion of Their Own Health Care Delivery System (in percentages)		
Country	Minor Changes Needed	Fundamental Changes Needed	Completely Rebuild System
Australia[b]	19	49	30
Canada[b]	20	56	23
France[a]	41	42	10
Germany[a]	41	35	13
Japan[a]	29	47	6
New Zealand[b]	9	57	32
United Kingdom[b]	25	58	14
United States[b]	17	46	33

Source: a Blendon, et al. (1990).

b Donelon et al. (1999).

Anthony J. Culyer

Desiring to "bring intellectual cohesion to the field," Tony Culyer has spent his professional career applying economic theory to the study of social problems, particularly those associated with health care. Born in Croydon, England, Culyer spent his early years in London during the Blitz. Moving frequently as a youth, his family finally settled in Worcester when he was a teenager. He attended Exeter University and graduated with a major in economics in 1964. After spending a year at the University of California at Los Angeles as a graduate student and teaching assistant, he returned to Exeter as a tutor and lecturer. He moved to the University of York in 1969 where he is now Director of Health Development and Professor and Head of the Department of Economics and Related Studies. Culyer is also vice chair of the newly formed National Institute for Clinical Excellence.

The year 1971 marked the beginning of a steady stream of contributions to the field of health economics. Nine journal articles that year, including "The Nature of the Commodity 'Health Care' and Its Efficient Location" published in *Oxford Economic Papers* and "Medical Care and the Economics of Giving" published in *Economica,* quickly established Culyer as a major figure in health economics, not only in England, but worldwide. Since that time, we can credit him with over 225 published articles, books, and monographs, in some of the leading medical and economics journals around the world. Since becoming involved in academic administration, his research output has slowed from its previous breakneck pace, but he remains productive.

In addition to a strong research agenda, Culyer has played an important public policy role, most recently in the redesign of the entire system of public funding of research and development in Britain's National Health System. As a consultant to the World Health Organization, the Office of Economic Cooperation and Development, and government agencies in Britain, Canada, and New Zealand, his influence in public policymaking is evidenced worldwide. As a teacher and mentor, Culyer has played a significant role in shaping the way a generation of British economists thinks about designing health care systems. Recognized for his work in the field of health economics, Culyer was awarded an honorary doctorate from the Stockholm School of Economics in 1999. That same year Queen Elizabeth II, in appreciation for his outstanding contribution to education in the United Kingdom, appointed him Commander of the British Empire.

Culyer considers church music his "private passion." His interest in the organ dates back to his teenage years at the King's School in Worcester. In addition to his position as organist in the rural Anglican parish church where he attends, Culyer also leads the choir and serves as the local chair of the Royal School of Church Music.

Keenly aware of the importance of sound analytical reasoning in the public policy arena, Culyer has spent his professional lifetime trying to expunge ad hoc reasoning and political ideology from social policymaking. His heavy involvement in government planning has provided him with a sound understanding of social systems and human nature. Lasting change does not come from a "top down" mechanism, but rather it is driven from the "bottom up."

Source: Anthony John Culyer, Curriculum Vitae, and personal correspondence.

in both Australia and New Zealand with 79 and 89 percent desiring fundamental or complete change in their respective systems. Canadians view their health care system similarly to the way Americans view theirs. In fact, Canadians had the biggest negative swing in their views over the decade of the 1990s. In the Blendon et al. (1990) survey, 56 percent of the respondents felt that only minor changes were needed in Canada's health care system and only 38 percent felt that fundamental changes or a completely rebuilt system was needed.

By the end of the decade only 20 percent of Canadians felt that minor changes were needed and 79 percent wanted fundamental or complete change.

One extremely interesting phenomenon emerges from this survey. Americans show a great deal of support for reforming the U.S. health care system: 89 percent see the need for fundamental changes or a complete restructuring of the system. At the same time, 83 percent of Americans are pleased with their own insurance coverage and the benefits provided (Jajich-Toth and Roper, 1990). Americans seem to be happy with the quality of the care they receive personally, but unhappy with the health care delivery system. More recent survey results by Blendon et al. (1995) show little change in consumer satisfaction since the earlier studies.

When health care is provided at zero cost, there is no incentive to limit demand. As cost pressure mounts, financing provisions change. The unintended consequences of trying to satisfy the competing goals of universal access and cost control can be seen in the emerging inequalities of a tiered system and the imposition of limits on access to costly technology. The lesson to be learned is that everything has a cost and what is promoted as free is really not free.

Key Concept 2
Opportunity Cost

A great deal of the public anxiety over the health care system has to do with cost, access, and gaps in coverage. Financial barriers to access can be eliminated but that does not guarantee that social disparities will disappear. National health insurance has done little to eliminate the inequalities across social classes in countries that use the social insurance model. Per capita consumption varies as much as 50 percent across income levels and 100 percent between occupational categories.

Proponents of the social insurance model argue that equal access will improve health outcomes, especially for the low-income, indigent population. Opponents point out that nationalized systems do not eliminate or even substantially reduce health differences among population subgroups. Infant mortality rates and life expectancies vary considerably across socioeconomic categories. For example, England's lowest socioeconomic group has infant mortality rates that are double those of the highest socioeconomic group, a difference that has persisted since the inception of the NHS.[30] It is no different in the United States where infant mortality rates for African Americans are roughly three to four times those of the white population.

Key Concept 1
Scarcity and Choice

Key Concept 6
Supply and Demand

If economics has anything to contribute to the health care reform debate it is this: If you do not allocate resources through the pricing mechanism, you do it through waiting lists and/or limiting the access to medical technology. Although the French and German health care systems have managed to avoid the queuing problem, other nationalized systems, including Canada and the United Kingdom, experience significant waits for certain procedures.

Policymakers have a growing awareness of their inability to control utilization and thus spending in the private sector where providers are paid on a fee-for-service basis with no spending caps. But cost control cannot be accomplished unless price controls and fixed budgets apply across the entire system. This inability to control expenditures for physicians' services and private hospitals leads to the extension of budget controls in these two areas. The results of this decision are easy to predict—just look at the queuing and technology rationing that takes place in the countries that use price controls, utilization controls, and fixed budgets system wide. The national insurance systems examined in this chapter all work reasonably well. But each has its safety valve: Canada has the United States, Britain and Germany have their private insurance sectors, Japan has its system of "gifts of appreciation" to ensure quality care, and France has, for now, maintained its commitment to the principle of "liberty" in the private sector. What would happen if these safety valves did not exist?

Policy Issue

What is the best way to ensure access to high-quality medical care while controlling cost at the same time? Or is it even possible to think in those terms?

---

30 Even in Scandinavia with its relatively homogeneous population, age-standardized mortality rates vary significantly across occupational categories. Certain low-income occupations, such as restaurant workers, have mortality rates that are twice as high as some high-income occupations, such as school teachers.

Questions and Problems

1. Suggest several reasons why health care spending is higher in the United States than in other countries.

2. "The fact that the United States spends more per capita on medical care than any other developed country is evidence of the failure of the U.S. system." Comment.

3. Some view health care systems of other developed countries as reasonable models for the reform of the U.S. health care system. Choose one of the systems discussed in this chapter and describe it in some detail. Provide reasons why you consider it workable or unworkable in the United States.

4. It takes a 13.4 percent payroll tax in Germany to finance a system that in 1993 consumed 10.6 percent of the nation's economic output. If the United States used this as a model, would you expect the average payroll tax charged to American workers to be larger or smaller than in Germany? Explain.

5. Ronald Coase in his classic October 1960 article "The Problem of Social Cost" in the *Journal of Law and Economics* 3(1), pp. 1–44, discussed collective ownership of resources. Collective ownership often means that no one takes care of resources, or at minimum that resources are not cared for as well as if they were privately owned. What are some of the problems with collective ownership in the health care industry? Can you think of some examples where collective ownership works? Where it does not work?

6. The Medicare system in the United States approximates the workings of a **single-payer system.** Using that program as evidence, critics say that expanding that program to cover all Americans "would give us all the compassion of the Internal Revenue Service and the efficiency of the postal service at Pentagon prices" (Constance Horner, HHS official under Bush, quoted in Stout, 1992). Proponents of a single-payer system point to our northern neighbors where the Canadian version of Medicare works reasonably well. Although the Canadian system is not perfect, most citizens are satisfied with their medical care, which is available regardless of social or economic status. What is the evidence?

7. In 1989 the Chrysler Corporation released figures showing that its employee health care costs were $5,970 per employee and $700 per vehicle produced. According to the report, its foreign competitors fared much better. Health care costs for automobile companies averaged $375 in France, $337 in Germany, and $246 in Japan, placing Chrysler at a competitive disadvantage. Is there anything wrong with this conclusion? What are the micro and macro arguments as they relate to this issue?

single-payer system
A system of financing medical care (usually associated with Canada) where payment comes from a single source, typically the government. The single payer has considerable influence over virtually every aspect of health care financing and delivery.

References

General

Henry J. Aaron, "Issues Every Plan to Reform Health Care Financing Must Confront," *Journal of Economic Perspectives* 8(3), Summer 1994, 31–43.

Robert J. Blendon and Humphrey Taylor, "Views on Health Care: Public Opinions in Three Nations," *Health Affairs* 8(1), Spring 1989, 149–157.

Cindy Jajich-Toth and Burns W. Roper, "Americans' Views on Health Care: A Study in Contradictions," *Health Affairs* 9(4), Winter 1990, 149–157.

———, Robert Leitman, Ian Morrison, and Karen Donelan, "Satisfaction with Health Systems in Ten Nations," *Health Affairs* 9(2), Summer 1990, 185–192.

———, Karen Donelan, Robert Leitman, Arnold Epstein, Joel C. Cantor, Alan B. Cohen, Ian Morrison, Thomas Moloney, Christian Koeck, and Samuel W. Levitt, "Physicians' Perspectives on Caring for Patients in the United States, Canada, and West Germany," *New England Journal of Medicine* 328(14), April 8, 1993, 1011–1016.

———, John Benson, Karen Donelan, Robert Leitman, Humphrey Taylor, Christian Koeck, and Daniel Gitterman, "Who Has the Best Health Care System? A Second Look," *Health Affairs* 14(4), Winter 1995, 220–230.

Karen Donelon, Robert J. Blendon, Cathy Schoen, Karen Davis, and Katherine Binns, "The Cost of Health System Change: Public Discontent in Five Nations," *Health Affairs* 18(3), May/June 1999, 206–216.

John C. Goodman and Gerald L. Musgrave, *Patient Power: Solving America's Health Care Crisis*, Washington, DC: Cato Institute, 1992.

David G. Green and Benedict Irvine, "Health Care in France and Germany: Lessons for the UK," London: Civitas, Institute for the Study of Civil Society, 2001.

Organization for Economic Cooperation and Development, *OECD Health Data, 2003*. A Comparative Analysis of 30 Countries, Paris: OECD, 2003.

Milton I. Roemer, *National Health Systems of the World, Volume One*, New York: Oxford University Press, 1991.

George J. Schieber and Jean-Pierre Poullier, "International Health Care Expenditure Trends: 1987," *Health Affairs* 8(3), Fall 1989, 167–177.

———, "International Health Spending: Issues and Trends," *Health Affairs* 10(1), Spring 1991, 106–116.

———, "Health Care Systems in Twenty-four Countries," *Health Affairs* 10(3), Fall 1991, 22–38.

———, and Leslie M. Greenwald, "U.S. Health Expenditure Performance: An International Comparison and Data Update," *Health Care Financing Review* 13(4), Summer 1992, 1–15.

Hilary Stout, "Health Care Choices: A Bigger Federal Role or a Market Approach?" *Wall Street Journal*, January 15, 1992, A1.

U.S. General Accounting Office, *Canadian Health Insurance: Lessons for the United States*, Washington, DC: United States General Accounting Office, June 1991.

———, *Health Care Spending and Control: The Experience of France, Germany, and Japan*, Washington, DC: United States General Accounting Office, November 1991.

Patrice R. Wolfe and Donald W. Moran, "Global Budgeting in the OECD Countries," *Health Care Financing Review* 14(3), Spring 1993, 55–71.

World Health Organization, "Health Systems: Improving Performance," *The World Health Report 2000*, Geneva: WHO, 2000.

Canada

Marcia Berss, "'Our System is Just Overwhelmed,'" *Forbes* 151(11), May 24, 1993, 40–41.

Nadeem Esmail and Michael Walker, "How Good is Canadian Health Care?" *Fraser Forum*, Vancouver: The Fraser Institute, August 2002a.

———, "Waiting Your Turn: Hospital Waiting Lists in Canada," 12th edition *Critical Issues Bulletin*, Vancouver: The Fraser Institute, September 2002b.

Robert G. Evans, Jonathan Lomas, Morris Barer, Roberta J. Labelle, Catherine Fooks, Gregory L. Stoddart, Geoffrey M. Anderson, David Feeny, Amiram Gafni, George W. Torrance, and William G. Tholl, "Controlling Health Expenditures—The Canadian Reality," *New England Journal of Medicine* 320(9), March 2, 1989, 571–577.

Hugh Grant and Ronald Oertel, "The Supply and Migration of Canadian Physicians, 1970–1995: Why We Should Learn to Love an Immigrant Doctor," *Canadian Journal of Regional Science* 21(2), Spring-Summer 1997, 157–168.

David Harriman, William McArthur, and Martin Zelder, "The Availability of Medical Technology in Canada: An International Comparative Study," *Public Policy Sources* No. 28, Vancouver, B.C.: The Fraser Institute, 1999.

Steven J. Katz, Diana Verrilli, and Morris L. Barer, "Canadians' Use of U.S. Medical Services," *Health Affairs* 17(1), January/February 1998, 225–235.

Peggy Leatt and A. Paul Williams, "The Health System of Canada," in Marshall W. Raffel ed., *Health Care and Reform in Industrialized Countries* (University Park, PA: The Pennsylvania University Press, 1997), 1–28.

C. David Naylor, "Health Care in Canada: Incrementalism Under Fiscal Duress," *Health Affairs* 18(3), May/June 1999, 9–26.

France

Jonathan E. Fielding and Pierre-Jean Lancry, "Lessons from France–'Vive la Difference': The French Health Care System and U.S. Health System Reform," *Journal of the American Medical Association* 270(6), August 11, 1993, 748–756.

James W. Henderson, "Equality, Liberty, Fraternity, and the Delivery of Health Care in France," *Journal of the Medical Association of Georgia* 82(12), December 1993, 657–660.

Jean-Francois Lacronique, "Health Services in France," in Marshall W. Raffel, ed., *Comparative Health Systems: Descriptive Analyses of Fourteen National Health Systems* (University Park: Pennsylvania State University, 1984), 258–285.

Claude LePen, "The French Health Care System: In Search of a New Model," Presentation at the European School of Health Economics, Health Economics of Pharmaceuticals and other Medical Interventions, Sophia Antipole, France, June 11, 2003.

Marie-Pascal Pomey and Jean-Pierre Poullier, "France's Health Policy Conundrum," in Marshall W. Raffel ed., *Health Care and Reform in Industrialized Countries* (University Park, PA: The Pennsylvania University Press, 1997), 49–75.

Jean-Pierre Poullier and Simone Sandier, "France," *Journal of Health Politics, Policy, and Law* 25(5), October 2000, 899–905.

Victor G. Rodwin, "The Marriage of National Health Insurance and La Medecine Liberale in France: A Costly Union," *Milbank Memorial Fund Quarterly* 59(1), 1981, 16–43.

Germany

Lawrence D. Brown and Volker E. Amelung, "'Manacled Competition': Market Reforms in German Health Care," *Health Affairs* 18(3), May/June 1999, 76–91.

Wolfgang Greiner and J.-Matthias Graf v.d. Schulenburg, "The Health System of Germany," in Marshall W. Raffel ed., *Health Care and Reform in Industrialized Countries* (University Park, PA: The Pennsylvania University Press, 1997), 76–104.

Jeremy W. Hurst, "Reform of Health Care in Germany," *Health Care Financing Review 12*(3), Spring 1991, 73–86.

———— and Jean-Pierre Poullier, "Paths to Health Reform," *OECD Observer 179*, December 1992/January 1993, 4–7.

John K. Iglehart, "Germany's Health Care System," in two parts, *New England Journal of Medicine 324*(7 and 24), February 14, 1991, 503–508; June 13, 1991, 1750–1756.

Martin Pfaff and Dietmar Wassener, "Germany," *Journal of Health Politics, Policy, and Law 25*(5), October 2000, 907–914.

Wilfried Prewo, "Germany Is Not a Model," *The Wall Street Journal*, February 1, 1993, A14.

Markus Schneider, "Health Care Cost Containment in the Federal Republic of Germany," *Health Care Financing Review 12*(3), Spring 1991, 87–101.

Japan

John K. Iglehart, "Japan's Medical Care System," in two parts, *New England Journal of Medicine 319*(12 and 17), September 22, 1988, 807–812; October 27, 1988, 1166–1172.

Naoki Ikegami, "Japanese Health Care: Low Cost Through Regulated Fees," *Health Affairs 10*(3), Fall 1991, 87–109.

————, "The Economics of Health Care in Japan," *Science 258*, October 23, 1992, 614–618.

———— and Creighton Campbell, "Health Care Reform in Japan: The Virtues of Muddling Through," *Health Affairs 18*(3), May/June 1999, 56–75.

Hyoung-Sun Jeong and Jeremy Hurst, "An Assessment of the Performance of the Japanese Health Care System," Labour Market and Social Policy—Occasional Papers No. 56, Paris: Organisation for Economic Co-operation and Development, December 2001.

Pat Murdo, "The Health Care Debate: What America is Considering, What Japan has Done," *JEI Report*, No. 8A, Japan Economic Institute, March 5, 1993.

Toshitaka Nakahara, "The Health System of Japan," in Marshall W. Raffel ed., *Health Care and Reform in Industrialized Countries* (University Park, PA: The Pennsylvania University Press, 1997), 105–133.

James Sterngold, "Japan's Health Care: Cradle, Grave and No Frills," *The New York Times*, December 28, 1992, A1, A8.

Aki Yoshikawa, Norihiko Shirouzu, and Matthew Holt, "How Does Japan Do It? Doctors and Hospitals in a Universal Health Care System," *Stanford Law & Policy Review 3*, Fall 1991, 111–137.

Sweden

Finn Diderichsen, "Sweden," *Journal of Health Politics, Policy, and Law 25*(5), October 2000, 931–935.

Stefan Håkansson and Sara Nordling, "The Health System of Sweden," in Marshall W. Raffel ed., *Health Care and Reform in Industrialized Countries* (University Park, PA: The Pennsylvania University Press, 1997), 191–225.

Ragnar Lofgren, "Health Care Waiting List Initiatives in Sweden," Public Policy Sources No. 62, Vancouver, Canada: The Fraser Institute, August 2002.

———— and Michael Walker, "The Swedish Health Care System: Recent Reforms, Problems, and Opportunities," Public Policy Sources No. 59, Vancouver, Canada: The Fraser Institute, July 2002.

Marilynn M. Rosenthal, "Beyond Equity: Swedish Health Policy and the Private Sector," *The Milbank Quarterly 64*(4), 1986, 592–621.

United Kingdom

Patricia Day and Rudolf Klein, "Britain's Health Care Experiment," *Health Affairs 10*(3), Fall 1991, 39–59.

Alain C. Enthoven, "Internal Market Reform of the British National Health Service," *Health Affairs 10*(3), Fall 1991, 60–70.

Max Gammon, "Among Britain's Ills, A Health Care Crisis," *The Wall Street Journal*, September 8, 1993, A12.

Peter R. Hatcher, "The Health System of the United Kingdom," in Marshall W. Raffel ed., *Health Care and Reform in Industrialized Countries* (University Park, PA: The Pennsylvania University Press, 1997), 227–261.

Independent Inquiry into Inequalities in Health (London: Her Majesty's Stationery Office, 1998).

Rudolph Klein, "Big Bang Health Care Reform—Does It Work? The Case of Britain's 1991 National Health Services Reforms," *The Milbank Quarterly 73*(3), 1995, 299–337.

————, "Why Britain's Conservatives Support a Socialist Health Care System," *Health Affairs 4*(1), Spring 1985, 41–58.

————, "Why Britain is Reorganizing Its National Health Service—Yet Again," *Health Affairs 17*(4) July/August 1998, 111–125.

Julian Le Grand, "Competition, Cooperation, or Control? Tales from the British National Health Service," *Health Affairs 18*(3), May/June 1999, 27–39.

David Mechanic, "The Americanization of the British National Health Service," *Health Affairs 14*(2), Summer 1995, 51–67.

Secretary of State for Health, *Working for Patients* (London: Her Majesty's Stationery Office, 1989).

Clive Smee, "United Kingdom," *Journal of Health Politics, Policy, and Law 25*(5), October 2000, 945–951.

Chapter 17

Medical Care Reform
in the United States

The new possibilities afforded by advances in medical science force us to deal with issues that previous generations never faced. As we live longer, the incidence of chronic conditions, such as Alzheimer's disease, arthritis, dementia, and stroke, increases dramatically. We can expect continued improvement of life-extending technologies, such as mechanical ventilation, artificial resuscitation, antibiotics, and artificial nutrition and hydration.

Using these technologies on ever-sicker categories of patients results in higher spending and spiraling costs. Quality and access are important, but cost issues including overall spending and affordability seem to be the overriding concern in the current environment. In this chapter, we will explore the nature of the medical care reform movement in the United States: the pressures behind the movement, the goals of reform, and the alternative strategies competing for acceptance.

The Push for Reform

Policy Issue
What kind of health care system does America want—government-run or market driven?

http://

Families USA is an advocacy group dedicated to the provision of health care to all Americans. The organization issues reports, works through the media, and strives to educate the general public, opinion leaders, and policymakers on issues relevant to the health-care marketplace. An extensive list of reports and other resources are available at **http://www.familiesusa.org**.

The temptation exists to turn the reform debate into a struggle among competing ideologies. We must be careful that the political battle does not become more important than its practical results. The issue being decided boils down to trust. Do we give the federal government the authority to decide the future of medical care? Should it be left in the hands of state government? Do we mandate coverage? Can a market really work in medical care delivery? Which presents the bigger problem, market failure or government failure?

The debate over reform of the medical sector is not new. Every Congressional session since 1916 has generated at least one piece of federal legislation proposing to modify the system in some way. The issues are still the same—quality, access, and affordability—but the debate has risen to a new intensity. Within the last two decades the upward cost spiral, exacerbated by a growing number of uninsured, has created an atmosphere of inevitability of reform in the arena of public opinion.

Recent polls show that roughly three-fourths of all Americans are personally satisfied with the medical care they receive, rating it excellent or good (Blendon et al., 1992, 1995; Donelan et al. 1999; and Robinson, 2000). In those same polls 80 percent of the respondents are convinced that the system needs fundamental changes to make it work better. These results may seem contradictory to some, but in reality they are not. Respondents are expressing a desire for both guaranteed access and lower costs. The policy dilemma is that these desires for guaranteed access and lower costs compete with each other and are not simultaneously achievable, so fully satisfying these competing desires is not entirely possible.

To understand the most recent push for reform, not just in the United States but worldwide, we must recognize the forces behind the reform movement (Musgrave, 1993). Some argue that concern for the poor and elderly has caused this most recent push for reform. Others focus on the millions of uninsured who have restricted access to the private medical care system. Admittedly, concern for these groups is a factor in the movement, but the real pressure for reform is coming from two main sources: the middle class and business. The middle class is demanding action because they are the group that feels the pressure. With limited resources, middle class workers see themselves as only a paycheck away from personal bankruptcy and charity care. Until recent changes in the insurance laws, many felt unable to change jobs for fear of being without health insurance during the typical waiting period before insurance coverage begins. Even though insurance plans are required to accept individuals transferring from other plans regardless of insurability, many workers must pay insurance premiums from their previous employment until their waiting period expires. Most workers feel the pinch of rising insurance premiums in the form of larger and larger payroll deductions. For this group, government involvement is perceived as shifting the financial burden to wealthy taxpayers or business.

And as far as most businesses are concerned, health insurance benefits are perceived as a big problem. With annual premiums rising from year to year, employee health benefits are often greater than the firm's profit margins. Although medical benefits represent only a small portion of the total cost of employing the typical worker, they represent a growing wedge between total compensation and salary income. As wages lag benefits, workers are becoming increasingly dissatisfied with the size of their take-home pay. A strong and growing sentiment in the business community desires to get rid of this problem by turning it over to the federal government. This case is one in which many policymakers are more than happy to accept the responsibility. Why? Because along with the responsibility comes control. Representing over 14 percent of total U.S. economic output, the medical industry is more than twice the size of the military industrial complex. The political stakes are enormous.

The Moral Issues—Is Medical Care a "Right"?[1]

It is essential that the issue of access to medical care be examined within a specific moral framework that clearly distinguishes between individual rights and social responsibility. The right to medical care has never been explicitly stated in this country. While the Declaration of Independence states a right to "life, liberty, and the pursuit of happiness," nowhere does it state that access to medical care is a necessary condition to those rights. If access to medical care is not a right, should it be? What is a right anyway?

> **Policy Issue**
>
> Do Americans consider access to medical care a right of citizenship?

A number of different ways can be used to define rights. Rights can be defined by a social contract. They may be stated explicitly as the right to health care in the French Constitution or implied as the right to an education in the United States. Legal rights may be defined by legislation. In the United States a person reaching the age of 65 has the legal right to have Medicare pay his or her medical bills. An alternative way to look at rights is through the notion of natural rights. The defining characteristic for a natural right is "Who provides it?" If you buy something with your own money, you have a right to it. If it is available to everyone through nature or God, it is a right. Things we receive through voluntary exchange or the generosity of others, we have a right to.[2] Taking something by force or stealing it does not give you a right to it.

In what sense is medical care a right? Consensus will be difficult to reach. But it is clear that in the United States we have created legal rights for the elderly and indigent based on the notion that we have a social responsibility to provide access to those who are unable to afford to purchase care on their own. Do we have a natural right to

---

1 The material in this section draws heavily from Henderson (1991).
2 If someone gives you something, you have a right to the gift, but no rights to future gifts.

medical care access? Most policymakers sidestep this discussion publicly and instead debate "access" to the health care system. One group argues for "universal coverage" through a system that requires mandatory participation, while the other supports "universal access" in a voluntary system where everyone can buy health insurance if they desire to do so. Parties on both sides, reluctant to address the rights issue, talk around each other about access.[3]

Common sense requires that we adopt a standard of medical care access that is politically acceptable, morally responsible, and economically affordable. To achieve these goals, we must come up with an acceptable definition of an appropriate level of medical care to determine the extent of our collective social responsibility of providing care to those who cannot afford to purchase it themselves. The economist's concept of appropriate is determined by the familiar marginalist's rule of thumb: The optimal level of care is defined as that amount of care where the benefit from the last unit received is just equal to its cost to society. Within this framework, the question of allocation is ultimately one of valuation of outcomes. What value do we place on life? What value do we place on reduced pain and suffering? How do these values change when those receiving medical care are ourselves? Relatives? Friends? Or total strangers?

Using the economic approach as a guide to public policy will require the placement of justifiable restrictions on the use of certain medical options in order to use resources wisely. The challenge will be to apply those restrictions uniformly across society without bias. Even so, it is difficult to imagine a society where the ability to pay becomes the primary determinate of life and death.

A national health care policy cannot provide every person with all the health care he or she may desire. Such an open-ended policy is not appropriate in an environment where health care is not the only objective. A national policy must be able to establish reasonable priorities and devise acceptable means to allocate resources sensibly.

Policy Issue

Are Americans ready to apply the principles of cost-effectiveness analysis to determine the appropriate level of care?

Key Concept 3
Marginal Analysis

The Goals of Reform

Key Concept 1
Scarcity and Choice

The challenge facing decision makers has always been one of attempting to satisfy the unlimited demands placed on the finite resources available to society. When dealing specifically with health policy, we must first recognize that health is not the only goal of society and may not be the most important goal. Individuals validate this claim daily in deciding to super-size their noontime fast food meals, smoke cigarettes, inject drugs, operate motor vehicles while under the influence of alcohol, and ride motorcycles without wearing helmets.

Medical care must be placed within the context of other goals considered important by society: national defense, education, economic competitiveness abroad, environmental protection, reduction in the incidence of poverty, and balancing the federal budget. To a large extent these are competing goals. The single-minded pursuit of one goal can lead to ever-larger expenditures in that area. In establishing spending priorities, health and medical care have a considerable advantage over other goals. The needs of this sector can be readily dramatized by citing individual cases where human welfare is involved and consequently spending priorities are easily shifted.

Three issues stand out as critical: who's covered, what's covered, and who pays. It is important to examine proposed reforms carefully, if not critically, and judge them by how well they satisfy these three criteria.

---

3 Politicians are not the only group uncomfortable with a "rights" discussion. Many economists view the purview of economics predominantly in terms of "positive analysis," designing an efficient system to accomplish a given goal. Goal determination is too close to "normative analysis" for comfort.

ISSUES IN MEDICAL CARE DELIVERY

THE TOP 10 MORAL IMPERATIVES FOR ESTABLISHING A NATIONAL HEALTH CARE POLICY

Crafting a national policy on medical care requires at least a consensus on a set of imperatives to serve as its moral-ethical base. The order in which the principles are presented is not meant to serve as a ranking, merely as a catalyst for discussion. As you read through the list, ask yourself the following questions. How do you feel about the ten principles presented? Which would you include on your Top 10 list? What other principles would you substitute for those you would leave off?

1. All human life has value.
2. Human nature, while not totally depraved, is subject to certain moral limitations.
3. Individuals, when given freedom of choice, should be responsible for their own actions.
4. Hard work is a virtue and should be rewarded.
5. Resources are scarce and, thus, should be used wisely.
6. We should show compassion for others, especially the poor and less fortunate.
7. Care for members of our own family is first an individual responsibility.
8. Poor health is often a random event—based on chance or genetics—and not necessarily a consequence of reckless or foolish behavior.
9. Life is short and death is inevitable.
10. Prevention is better than cure and often more cost effective.

Source: Based loosely on James W. Henderson, "Biblical Principles Applied to a National Health Policy," in Richard C. Chewning, ed., *Biblical Principles and Public Policy: The Practice* (Colorado Springs, CO: NavPress, 1991), 237–250.

Who's Covered?

Most participants in the reform debate will agree that one of the goals of the U.S. medical care system is universal coverage. Our concern over fairness has prompted a discussion over the transition from the current system to the new system (whatever its final form). It is easy to express support for universal coverage, but how do we get from where we are to where we want to be? Do we follow the familiar maxim, "Just do it," or do we follow a more prudent approach: "First, do no harm?"

Expanded access will require, at least initially, additional funding. Policymakers, by now sensitive to voter preferences, are wary of grandiose schemes that require substantial tax increases for their implementation. Concern over the cost of any change may necessitate the phasing in of access over a number of years, but any significant delay in coverage could be quickly labeled unfair to certain groups; the poor, the disabled, people of color, women (especially pregnant women), and children. Even with these concerns, the rallying cry for policymakers lately has become "incremental reform."

Policy Issue

Are Americans interested in a health care system that promotes universal coverage or universal access?

The task facing lawmakers is complicated by a general confusion over the wishes of the American public. Is the common perception of fairness based on the notion of equal access to the system or equal health outcomes or something else? Does equality mandate that everyone be required to participate or should participation be voluntary?

Improved access may be accomplished with a mandatory system featuring central control of the third-party payment mechanism. An example would be the single-payer system in the Canadian mold: defining a universal benefits package and limiting the choices available to those who can afford to pay for additional care by making private insurance illegal.

Alternatively, expanding coverage to groups at the margin represents a different approach to improving access. For example, expanding Medicaid eligibility to cover everyone with income below the federal poverty level would enhance the well being of this group and improve overall equity in the system. Providing coverage for immunizations and preventive care for all children and prenatal care for all pregnant women would not only satisfy some of the concerns of many reformers, but according to most estimates, save money in the long run. Private insurance reform could provide small business owners, their employees, and dependents access to group insurance at affordable rates.

Policy Issue

Are Americans willing to formally accept a multitiered health care system with more comprehensive coverage available to those who can afford it?

The incremental approach presents an interesting dilemma. Subsidized care for the poor, high-risk pools for the uninsurable, prenatal benefits for pregnant mothers living in poverty, and relaxing mandated benefits for small business insurance lead to a system where individuals have different levels of coverage based on their individual characteristics—health, income, employment status, and so on. In other words, reform geared to enhancing social welfare could easily lead to a medical care system that provides two-tiered, three-tiered, or n-tiered coverage. Are we willing to accept that outcome (or at minimum, formally admit that the system we have now is multitiered)?

What's Covered?

Policy Issue

What is the most politically acceptable way to ration medical care?

The next step is to define the basic benefits package. Reformers who suggest a basic benefits package that is less generous than those available in most private insurance plans are accused of promoting the rationing of services. What some critics call "rationing," economists call the "explicit allocation of scarce resources." In this context, defining a basic package of medical benefits is nothing more than an exercise in establishing priorities, determining how much money is to be spent, and allocating the funds to provide the services according to the rank ordering.

The decision-making process may be straightforward, but it is by no means easy. Competing interests will have different priorities. Opinions vary on how the rank-ordering should be applied. Certain groups will rely on medical guidelines. Others consider cost-effectiveness the determining factor. One group focuses on providing all essential care, the other on providing only necessary care.[4]

Even though we have to live with the ethical consequences of the medical care system, we must also pay for it. When a part of the system is collectively financed, it may be appropriate to consider a basic benefits package that is less generous than the standard insurance plan, even though a multitiered medical care system may not satisfy everyone's notion of the social ideal. Such a system, while not equal according to some definitions, is welfare enhancing. Those individuals who become eligible for the collectively provided plan are better off.

Who Pays and How Much?

In most cases, the efficient use of scarce resources requires cost-conscious consumers or at least decision makers that behave in a responsible manner. It means that individual consumers must pay for what they consume and benefit from any economizing behavior that they practice. In this regard, medical care is often considered different. Most health care systems—whether in the United States, Canada, or Europe—are collectively

---

Key Concept 1
Scarcity and Choice

The Moving Ideas page maintained by The Electronic Policy Network™ (**http://epn. org**) publishes the virtual magazine *The American Prospect* at **http://www.prospect.org**

---

4 Readers interested in learning more about the different approaches to defining "basic" care are encouraged to familiarize themselves with the debate over the Oregon Health Plan. Two studies that provide particularly good insight into this controversy are Eddy (1991) and Hadorn (1991).

ISSUES IN MEDICAL CARE DELIVERY

RATIONING IS ALREADY HERE

The debate over rising costs in health care has fueled a growing concern that many treatment decisions are based on financial pressures, not clinical evidence. The Society for Critical Care Medicine distributed the *SCCM Healthcare Resource Utilization Opinion Poll* to more than 5,000 of its members in 2002. One of the 11 questions asked was: "Have you rationed any of the following medications or procedures in the last 12 months?" In addition to high-cost drugs such as Activated Protein C (a high-powered antibiotic distributed by Eli Lilly under the brand name Xigris) and Paclitaxel (Bristol-Meyers Squibb's cancer drug Taxol), the list included MRI scans, PET scans, and coronary angiograms. Maybe even more interesting than what the respondents said they were rationing was the fact that less than one-third said that they never rationed.

Even though U.S. spending on medical care exceeds that of any other country using virtually any metric imaginable, there is not enough money or resources to provide everybody with all the medical care they desire. In a world characterized by scarcity, how do we determine who gets care and who does not? If we are unwilling to let the market price ration scarce resources, we must come up with another mechanism. The dilemma we face today stems from our unwillingness to establish a formal rationing mechanism. Other countries, particularly in Europe, have established formal guidelines that determine who receives a particular medication or treatment and under what circumstances they receive it. A drug treatment that is appropriate for a young and otherwise healthy patient may be considered inappropriate for an elderly patient with a history of heart disease or stroke. The younger patient would receive the treatment and probably recover while the older patient would be provided an alternative treatment and possibly die.

Is it ethical to withhold treatment from critically ill patients? Clearly most medical providers consider it unethical to withhold treatment if the primary reason is financial. However, most providers do not consider it unethical when patients and treatments are prioritized according to clinical based evidence. The problem most providers have with the current *ad hoc* system of rationing is that the decision is usually made under conditions of medical urgency. Providers desire formal guidelines, based on clear medical evidence. Most have no problem with interjecting a little cost-effectiveness analysis into the mix either. In fact, the bedside rationing that already takes place often takes costs and benefits into consideration. The problem with the current practice is that it is usually crafted in terms of the costs and benefits to the hospital and not the costs and benefits to the patient.

The U.S. health care system rations medical resources, a statement that is also true for every government-run system throughout the world. The difference is that most of our foreign neighbors are more open about the rationing mechanism they use and as a result it is one that has been subjected to national debate. At some point, we are going to be forced to admit that rationing occurs in the United States. Only then will we be able to move beyond the arbitrary guidelines of demand management and establish national norms based on medical evidence.

Source: A four-part series entitled "Who Gets Health Care? Rationing in an Age of Rising Costs," published on the front page of the *The Wall Street Journal* from September 12, 2003, through September 23, 2003. Geeta Anand, "The Big Secret in Health Care: Rationing is Here," September 12, 2003; Laurie McGinley, "Health Club: Behind Medicare's Decisions, An Invisible Web of Gatekeepers," September 16, 2003; Antonio Regalado, "To Sell Pricey Drug, Eli Lilly Fuels a Debate over Rationing," September 18, 2003; and Bernard Wysocki, Jr., "At One Hospital, A Stark Solution for Allocating Care," September 23, 2003.

Key Concept 6
*Supply and
Demand*

Key Concept 9
Market Failure

Key Concept 4
Self Interest

funded through some combination of taxes and insurance premiums. Thus, it is difficult to build into any system the individual discipline that is necessary to naturally ensure its efficient operation.

Every reform plan must eventually face the sobering issues of cost, affordability, and overall spending. Inevitably, expanding access and providing generous benefits will drive up costs and spending. How much are we willing to pay? Who is ultimately going to pay? Individuals spending their own money will answer these questions differently from those spending someone else's money. Normally, the burden of responsibility falls on the individual to provide for his or her own care, but under certain conditions, we deem it socially responsible to collectively provide for those who cannot provide for themselves.

The issue boils down to the distribution of the burden of the collectively provided portion of the medical care package. Is medical care primarily an individual or a collective responsibility? Should it be paid for by individuals, by employers, by taxpayers, or some combination of payers? How should the costs be distributed among the payer groups? The answers to these questions will not come easily, but they must be answered before any reform plan can be implemented.

Individual State Initiatives

As far as the national media is concerned, the reform debate is centered in Washington, D.C., but anyone following the issue closely understands that the real battle for reform is being fought at the state level. The stakes are high for the states. Health care costs are expanding rapidly, comprising over 25 percent of most state budgets. The federal legislative process works slowly, so state and local officials have no reason to sit around and wait for federal solutions. Many problems require federal involvement, mandating that employers provide their workers with health insurance, for example, but a lot can be done to improve medical care delivery without federal legislation. So while Congress debates the problem, legislators from Tallahassee to Austin to Olympia are passing legislation in their efforts to improve medical care delivery within their borders and provide incentives to control costs.

Universal Coverage in Hawaii

The state of Hawaii legislated a mandatory employer-based health insurance system almost 30 years ago. The principles behind the Prepaid Health Care Act of 1974 (PHCA) are simple. Employers are required to provide a generous benefit package for all employees working over 20 hours per week (dependent coverage is not mandated).

> **Policy Issue**
>
> Should the federal government allow additional states ERISA exemptions as they try to improve access to health care coverage?

The coverage, based on the 1974 law and subsequent amendments passed in 1976 and 1983, includes at least 120 days in the hospital annually and provisions for surgical, medical, and diagnostic procedures; outpatient services; emergency, maternity, and well-baby care; substance abuse and mental health programs; mammogram screening and even in-vitro fertilization. The employer must adopt one of two model plans or seek state approval of an alternative plan. One option is a standard fee-for-service insurance plan offered by the state's Blue Cross/Blue Shield organization. The other is a health maintenance organization plan offered by the Kaiser Foundation Health Plan, Inc.

In 1991, the State Health Insurance Program (SHIP) extended coverage to those still uninsured under PHCA. Technically, these two laws extend insurance coverage to the entire state population.[5] Employers are required to provide insurance to all employees who work over 20 hours per week. The outcome should come as no surprise. Many Hawaiians hold several part-time jobs with different employers. Working less than the legislated 20-hour minimum per week in each, over 11 percent of the state's nonelderly population is without insurance.

---

5 Prior to the legislation 90 percent of all Hawaiian workers had employment-based health insurance. Thus, the legislation added fewer than 50,000 individuals to the health insurance rolls.

Employers are required to pay at least one-half of the premiums, and the employee may not pay more than 1.5 percent of gross income directly toward premiums. In addition, employers do not have the option of increasing deductibles or coinsurance since this would result in coverage that falls below the minimum standards.

PHCA was successfully challenged in the courts as a violation of the Employee Retirement and Income Security Act of 1974 (ERISA), a decision upheld in 1981 by the U.S. Supreme Court.[6] The status of Hawaii's health care system was uncertain until 1983 when Ronald Reagan signed into law an ERISA exemption for PHCA, as long as no substantive changes are made in the 1974 act. Without this ERISA exemption, other states that try to copy the Hawaii plan will find health care reform much more expensive.

A major complaint of the Hawaii plan is its inflexibility. Firms wishing to offer an optional insurance package are not allowed to offer alternative benefits. In practice, all mandatory benefits must be provided, so "optional" only means "additional." The Hawaiian economy is dominated by small business with over 99 percent of its employers having fewer than 100 employees. Due to a relatively tight labor market, many employers have found it necessary to hire seniors who would prefer to have long-term care coverage rather than infertility benefits, but getting affordable options approved by state regulators has been difficult.

Hawaii's situation may be unique among the other states in the country. Its geographic isolation makes mobility, both business and individual, difficult. Proximity to the Asian market makes it attractive to business despite high costs including the high costs of mandated employee health insurance. Administrative costs are lower since 80 percent of all citizens are covered by one of the two main plans—either the Blue Cross/Blue Shield plan or the Kaiser plan.

Critics of the Hawaiian system point out that total health care spending has grown faster in Hawaii than in the United States as a whole. In the 1980s, the increase in nominal spending was 191 percent in Hawaii versus 163 percent in the rest of the country. Additionally, per capita spending is higher in Hawaii than in the rest of the country due primarily to higher Medicaid spending. Despite these complaints, insurance premiums in Hawaii are among the lowest in the country. Annual cost increases among the predominantly community-rated policies have slowed to less than 10 percent.

Responding to the growing costs, the state legislature passed Health QUEST in 1994. The legislation extends managed care to all public insurance beneficiaries and effectively combines SHIP and Medicaid recipients into one large purchasing pool.

The Oregon Health Plan

One of the most innovative approaches to health care reform attempted to date may be the Medicaid experiment in the state of Oregon. Controversial because of its deliberate rationing of services, surprisingly the Oregon Health Plan has relatively few opponents within the state. Its planners used input from every conceivable interest group—patients, providers, payers, suppliers—and provided numerous public forums for debate and discussion on the various aspects of the plan. After three years of work and one unsuccessful attempt to get the necessary federal waivers, the state was given permission to put the plan into effect in March 1993. Oregon, thus, became the first program to extend state-funded benefits to a larger number of recipients by limiting the services that are made available.

Key Concept 1
Scarcity and Choice

The original goal of the Oregon Health Plan was to provide health insurance coverage for all the state's citizens through either private health insurance or Medicaid. To maintain budgetary restraint, the plan set out to ration care by limiting the range of services covered under the basic benefits package. This aspect of the plan, placing limits on the types of

Policy Issue

Does the Oregon plan for rationing care serve as a politically acceptable model for the rest of the country?

---

6 ERISA does not require that employers establish or maintain specific benefit plans, but if a plan exists, it must conform to the provisions of the law, including minimum funding requirements and eligibility. The law precludes states from mandating that employers provide health insurance benefits. States regularly seek ERISA exemptions but few succeed.

ISSUES IN MEDICAL CARE DELIVERY

MINNESOTACARE: THE INCREMENTAL APPROACH TO REFORM

After years of study and numerous legislative setbacks, the Minnesota legislature passed a comprehensive medical care reform law in 1992. MinnesotaCare was a complex piece of legislation providing basic medical benefits for low-income families at subsidized rates and modifying insurance standards to lower the cost to small businesses. Begun as a modest plan to provide medical care to pregnant women and their young children, MinnesotaCare has evolved into a comprehensive system of statewide health care delivery.

The die was cast in 1987 when the Minnesota legislature passed a modest health care reform bill that provided basic care for pregnant women and children under age eight. Two years after the bill was enacted, the legislature voted to extend the age of eligibility for children to age 18. Soon the parents of those children were also covered. And middle-income residents earning up to $40,000 and temporarily out of work were also included.

MinnesotaCare provided insurance to approximately 144,000 residents in 2002. A program that was projected to cost $1.3 million annually actually cost $390 million. Minnesota taxpayers financed 55 percent of the cost, primarily from a 2 percent provider tax and a 1 percent premium tax. The remainder of the financing comes from enrollee premiums, copayments, and federal funding. In addition, the young and healthy have seen their premiums rise by as much as 93 percent since 1992. Their premiums have increased $600 million to provide access to the previously uninsured.

Starting in 1996 the state health commissioner was given the power to use price controls to hold costs down, and doctors and hospitals are forbidden to let per patient revenues rise by more than 5.3 percent annually. Practitioners are strongly encouraged to follow medical practice guidelines in treating their patients. Such a plan was not feasible in 1987 when the legislative process began, but a carefully orchestrated series of incremental reforms can get you where you want to go if you are patient enough. Once on the path toward universal coverage, it is difficult politically to turn back.

Sources: Barbara P. Yawn, William E. Jacott, and Roy A. Yawn, "MinnesotaCare (HealthRight): Myths and Miracles," *Journal of the American Medical Association 269*(4), January 27, 1993, 511–515, and Brigid McMenamin, "In Bed with the Devil," *Forbes, 156*(6), September 12, 1994, 200–210.

---

treatment available to patients, is the most controversial. Here is a clear case of politics versus economics. What's amazing about this situation is that the state's policymakers have been able to make the economic reality of choice politically acceptable.

The reform process began with the Oregon Health Services Commission placing over 10,000 diagnoses and treatments into roughly 700 diagnosis/treatment regimes. Using input from 50 town hall meetings across the state attended by over 1,000 citizens, the diagnosis/treatment categories were ranked according to community preferences, the effect of treatment on the patient's quality of life, and medical effectiveness. After the rank ordering was accomplished, the list was turned over to the actuaries from the Coopers & Lybrand accounting firm to determine the cost of providing care to the citizens of Oregon. Finally, the legislature determined how much money the state could afford to spend on the plan.

The legislature decided to provide a generous package of care equivalent to the typical group medical plan. Most preventive care, including physical exams, mammograms, Pap tests, and eye exams and fluoride treatments for children, was made part of the plan. Also included are dental care, noncosmetic surgical services, hospice care, prescription drugs, and psychiatric services. Specifically, it was determined that the first 585 services on the list would be funded. Services ranked below 585 would not be funded.[7] The Oregon legislature faced the reality of the economic trade-off and remained firm in its commitment. The result is a plan that clearly broadens the population receiving health care at the expense of limiting the services covered. This sort of pragmatism is unusual given the political pressures on elected officials.

The first stage of the Oregon Health Plan extended Medicaid eligibility to all citizens who have income below the federal poverty level. The second stage, slated to go into effect in 1995, would have required all employers to provide comparable benefits to all their employees, including dependent coverage. Enactment of the second stage required the action of the U.S. Congress, specifically a waiver of certain provisions of ERISA, but Congress did not provide the necessary waivers, so the only expansion in coverage was the addition of 126,000 to the Medicaid rolls.

Critics of the approach from across the ideological spectrum argue that the process was flawed from the beginning, claiming that the diagnosis/treatment rankings were based on political considerations, bowing to pressures from disease constituencies and other special interest groups, including the elderly and provider groups instead of the stated criteria. Others argue that the plan's provisions determine who lives and who dies, who suffers and how much—valuing one person's life over another in a somewhat arbitrary fashion. Early results were not encouraging. Medicaid spending rose faster under the new plan compared with previous coverage. To pay for the expanded coverage the legislature had to levy a 2 percent tax on the gross receipts of health care providers, shifting the costs of the plan to private insurance consumers. Attempts at further reforms were soundly defeated in 2002 when the electorate voted 4–1 against a state-level single payer plan.

Oregon may not serve as the prototypical state for national health care reform because of its homogeneous population, but the state has made a serious effort to expand services to a larger segment of the indigent population. Oregon has approached the problem by systematizing the process. Rather than the haphazard rationing scheme that we have accepted nationally, the state has embraced an open approach. How it survives the test of time will play an important role in determining the direction of national reform.

Other State Reforms

Most of the other attempts to reform medical care delivery at the state level have not been as extensive as Hawaii and Oregon. Two-thirds of the states have enacted legislation to authorize small-business purchasing pools. These insurance pools will provide small companies with leverage to negotiate more favorable premiums.

Several states, including Maryland, Montana, Vermont, and Washington, have taken steps to control expenditures on medical care by enacting limits on overall spending and limiting fees charged by practitioners. Legislation passed in Maryland requires all insurers to provide a standard benefits package, with premiums based on community ratings, for firms of 2 to 50 employees. A commission has also been established to develop and implement a uniform payment system for all providers.

Clearly states have taken the initiative in reform of the medical care delivery system in this country. Many of the efforts are piecemeal in nature and focused primarily on improving access to the traditional health insurance system. Given the lack of a national consensus on the direction of reform, the states are beginning to view themselves as laboratories to test the various reform alternatives. For all practical purposes,

Key Concept 1
Scarcity and Choice

---

7 The plan covers diagnosis for all conditions, but not all treatment. In general, the conditions that are not covered include those where treatment is considered (1) less effective than treatments ranked higher on the list, (2) ineffective and the condition will run a natural course regardless, (3) cosmetic in nature, or (4) futile. A complete list of the treatments not covered can be found in Mahar (1993).

this constitutes a series of real-world experiments to determine what works and what does not work. Insights can then be drawn on what should be incorporated into a national plan and what should be avoided.

Health Insurance Mandates

As concerns over access and quality continue to mount, both the federal and state governments have intervened to correct the perceived deficiencies in the health insurance market. Government policymakers have generally responded by introducing additional regulation. Since 1983, state governments alone have passed over 800 health insurance mandates, taking the forms of mandated benefits, providers, and processes, bringing the cumulative number of mandates to over 1,100. The federal government has passed a series of laws creating federal mandates ensuring portability of insurance, mental health parity, minimum hospital stays after childbirth, and minimum hospital stays following mastectomy surgery.

Mandates are legislative requirements that some health insurance purchasers be given access, for example, to certain services or service providers. Typical legislation requires that health insurers provide or at least offer certain benefits, covers procedures when provided by alternative providers, or establishes processes that insurers must follow. Benefit mandates are requirements for specific treatments, services, or procedures that health insurance policies must cover. Examples of benefit mandates include alcohol and drug treatment, contraceptives, mammography screening, prostate cancer screening, and well-child care. Provider mandates require that insurance policies cover the services of specific providers such as chiropractors, acupuncturists, nurse practitioners, and psychologists. Process mandates impose requirements on how health plans must operate internally as they seek to balance treatment quality and cost containment. They include **guaranteed issue**, guaranteed renewability, restrictions on the exclusions of preexisting conditions, and the imposition of community rated premiums.

guaranteed issue
A feature of an insurance policy that requires the insurer to accept all applicants and guarantee renewal as long as premiums are paid, regardless of the health status of the applicant.

The Economics of Mandates

Mandates are not free. They impose significant economic and social costs on their intended beneficiaries. The propensity of legislative policymakers to add more mandates, especially process mandates, will have long-term consequences on the ability of the health care system to provide access to quality care at affordable prices.

From a public interest perspective, mandates are designed to correct deficiencies in the health insurance market. Insurers and purchasers may unknowingly undervalue the benefits of certain types of care, such as substance abuse treatment and mental health treatment, resulting in a demand for treatment that is too low from a societal perspective. Without mandates, adverse selection is a significant problem with high-risk individuals choosing to enroll in plans offering more extensive coverage and low-risk individuals choosing low-benefit plans.

Some policymakers view the addition of mandates as a way of improving insurance coverage without the costs that usually accompany the improvements. But mandates are not free. They impose economic and social costs on the same people they intend to benefit. These costs can include higher premiums, lower wages, higher unemployment, and an increase in the number of uninsured.

In general, research indicates that mandates increase the costs of health care systems (USGAO, 1996; USGAO, 1997; Sing et. al. 1998; Mitchell, 1990; Longley, 1994; Gabel and Jensen, 1989; Jensen and Morrisey, 1999). The cost of mandates is often estimated by calculating the share of claims associated with the different categories of spending associated with those mandates, called the current expenditures approach. Using the current expenditures approach, mandated benefits are responsible for anywhere from 5 percent to 22 percent of total claims. Alternatively, estimates based on actuarial projections are used to

ISSUES IN MEDICAL CARE DELIVERY

HOW TO GET A HEALTH CARE REFORM BILL THROUGH CONGRESS

Passing a health care reform bill will be no easy accomplishment. In addition to satisfying all the special interest groups on the plan itself, 1990 legislation prohibits any entitlement or tax-law change from adding to the overall budget deficit. If health care reform is to become law, it must be paid for by specific taxes or identified budget savings.

Five Congressional committees have jurisdiction over health care issues—three in the House of Representatives and two in the Senate. On the House side the Ways and Means Committee is the most influential, having jurisdiction over all matters dealing with taxes and appropriations. Other House committees with jurisdiction are Energy and Commerce and Education and Labor. On the Senate side the two key committees are the Finance Committee and the Labor and Human Resources Committee.

Any bill reported out of the three House committees must be sent to the Rules Committee where the rules governing the floor debate are determined. These rules include whether amendments will be considered, how much time will be allotted to debate, and how long each speaker will be allowed to talk. If more than one bill is received, the differences must be reconciled before a bill is submitted to the entire House.

If two separate bills emerge on the Senate side, they both could be sent to the floor for debate. Under no circumstances will more than one bill emerge from either chamber of Congress. If bills pass both chambers, the two versions must then go to a joint House/Senate Conference Committee where a single bill will emerge. That bill must pass both houses and be signed by the president before it becomes law.

The ideological differences between Democrats and Republicans have been enormous in the health care reform debate. It was, however, the division between moderate and liberal Democrats that kept them from uniting behind a single health care reform bill in 1994. As the opposition party the Republicans were united in their dislike for certain provisions of the Clinton plan, especially the employer mandate. In their new role as majority party Republicans likewise have been unable to build a consensus and pass a substantive health care reform bill. Congress is currently stalled in its attempt to add a prescription drug benefit to Medicare even though everyone seems to want one. As is the case with most important economic issues, politics plays a big role.

Source: Sherry Jacobson, "Road to Health Care Reform Gets Jammed," *Dallas Morning News*, April 11, 1994, 1A, 8A.

estimate the increase in premiums due to specific mandates. Using the actuarial approach, the added costs of the various mental health mandates have been estimated to range from 2 percent to 21 percent. Process mandates have also been evaluated with the cost of ranging up to 19 percent. Acs et al. (1992) estimated the impact of mandates on premium costs using a national cross-section of firm-level data, and found premiums to be 4 percent to 13 percent higher as a direct result of state-level mandates.

A third approach, called the hedonic pricing approach, provides a way to estimate the marginal impact of different insurance options on the overall price of a standard policy sold in different geographic regions of the country. Researchers using the hedonic pricing approach, including Gabel and Jensen (1989), Jensen and Morrisey (1990), and Henderson, Seward, and Taylor (2003), have found that while many mandated benefits raise premiums, some actually lower them. Mandates requiring plans to cover bone-mass measurement, drug abuse treatment, infertility services, and off-label drug use tend to raise premiums. But mandating that policies cover alcoholism treatment, contraceptives, diabetic supplies, emergency services, and treatment provided by nurse practitioners and psychiatric nurses actually lower premiums.

The evidence from the studies on the cost of mandates creates an interesting problem for policymakers. Mandates are popular among certain well-defined constituencies: providers of clinical services, patient advocacy groups, and other political interest groups. Faced with pressure from the various special interest groups and the uncertainty of the true cost of mandates, legislation passes easily. In 1998, almost 100 bills passed state legislatures mandating new health care benefits. Mandated benefits attempt to make marginal improvements in the insurance benefits of those with insurance but often at a price.

The economics of mandates are clear. If firms already offer the mandated benefit, there is no tangible effect on the availability of insurance or premium costs. However, firms that do not voluntarily offer the mandated coverage will be required to add it to their employees' benefit package, which will increase the cost of health insurance for those firms. Advocates of additional mandates argue that the new coverage benefits recipients. But recipients end up paying for the new coverage. Evidence presented by Jensen and Morrisey (1999) indicates that workers pay for mandated benefits in three ways: lower wages, fewer benefits, and higher premiums. Given ERISA exemptions, larger firms avoid mandates by self-insuring. Because owners of small businesses do not have the option of self-insuring, they are disproportionately affected by mandates (Jensen, Cotter, and Morrisey, 1995). Additionally, one in four uninsured Americans is without health insurance because of mandates.

One reason that a large percentage of our working poor remains uninsured is that state mandates make private insurance unaffordable for many, especially true for small business owners, their employees, and families who represent the majority of the employed uninsured in this country.

The States' Approach to Mandates

The average number of mandates per state in 1998 was 22, ranging from a low of 10 in Idaho to a high of 47 in Maryland. Mandated coverage for providers was the most common. Most states require that insurance pay for medical services when they are provided by psychologists, chiropractors, optometrists, dentists, podiatrists, and nurse midwives. In addition, some states require coverage for acupuncturists, oral surgeons, speech therapists, and naturopaths. Mandates requiring coverage for mammography screening, alcoholism treatment, off-label drug use, well-child care, and drug abuse treatment are also common. A few states require coverage for ambulance transportation, in vitro fertilization, long-term care, and prescription drugs. Many of the mandates are considered by some to be little more than income protection for certain provider groups.

Many larger firms avoid the mandates by self-insuring, paying for medical care costs as they arise. This tendency does not imply that all mandates should be eliminated. Many argue that the best approach would be for the federal government to preempt state mandates and set national standards. Such standards might include an annual catastrophic limit on the out-of-pocket spending for an individual family, continuity of coverage for job losers and changers, automatic newborn coverage, and a prohibition on waiting periods and on exclusions for preexisting conditions. Reducing the number of mandates seems to be an integral part of any plan serious about increasing the availability of health insurance to those who are currently uninsured. Many argue for a basic-benefits package free of most mandates to enable insurance firms to market plans to small businesses at significantly lower premiums.

Mandated benefits and a mandatory system are quite different concepts. There is nothing inconsistent about requiring everyone to have insurance coverage and, at the

Back-of-the-Envelope

THE ECONOMICS OF EMPLOYER MANDATES

Proponents of a universal system recognize that mandatory participation must be part of the system. Mandatory participation may take the form of government provision or some type of mandate, employer or individual. As a tool of social policy, mandates occupy the middle ground between the status quo and government provision. Conservatives prefer mandates to government provision and liberals prefer mandates to the status quo. The employer mandate has occupied the compromise position in U.S. public policy debates as far back as the Nixon administration.

The case for mandating the employer provision of benefits is clear. The argument goes something like this: As with all merit goods, individuals underestimate the value of health insurance by underestimating the probability of a catastrophic loss due to illness. Because of the difficulty in making these kinds of intertemporal calculations, participation in a health insurance program should be mandatory. In the case of medical care, society may value equal consumption more highly than in the case of other goods and thus mandate that a certain level of benefits be available to everyone. Finally, the externalities associated with medical care may be quite large. Even though the prevention of the spread of contagious disease is one aspect of this argument, the inability to pay for medical care creates pressures on society to pay the bills. This unwillingness to deny medical care to those in need is evidenced by the fact that 40 million uninsured Americans receive free care amounting to approximately one-half of the medical care received by the privately insured.

Those who argue against the employer mandate point out that it helps only those 60 percent who have some labor force attachment. The mandate places a wedge between the marginal cost of hiring an additional worker and the wage that can be offered. In other words, as benefit costs increase actual wages decrease. Unable to adjust the wages of workers earning close to the minimum wage, employers are forced to eliminate some jobs, thereby creating unemployment in some sectors. Low-wage industries such as retail, construction, restaurants, agriculture, and personal and household services would be affected more than the rest of the economy.

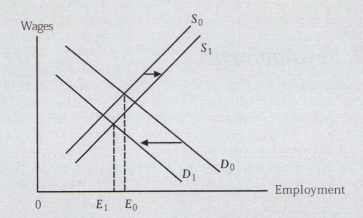

Economists tend to view mandated benefits as a disguised tax. Even though the viewpoint is true to a certain extent, it is not quite that simple. In the diagram, consider the original equilibrium of D_0 and S_0 with employment of E_0. A mandatory benefit that costs $\$_x$ per hour shifts the employer's demand for workers down by that amount. If the worker values the mandated benefit at $\$_x$ per hour, then the supply curve shifts out by the same amount and wages fall by $\$_x$ per hour and employment remains at E_0. However, workers are notorious in underestimating the value of health insurance, so the supply curve shifts by less than $\$_x$. Wages fall by some fraction of $\$_x$ per hour, but employment also falls from E_0 to E_1.

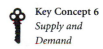

Key Concept 6
Supply and Demand

> It is an issue without an easy policy stance. Because of the externalities associated with health insurance and the tendency of workers to underestimate its value, some argue that it is appropriate for government to intervene and mandate coverage. Others focus on the potential job losses and the associated dislocations that they will cause. As the debate rages on, we are no closer to a solution to the problem of the uninsured. The lesson may be there are no solutions, only competing alternatives with their own individual drawbacks. This is an issue that cannot be ignored. It will not go away on its own.
>
> **Source**: Lawrence H. Summers, "Some Simple Economics of Mandated Benefits," *American Economic Review 79*, May 1989, 177–183; and Carlos Bonilla, "The Price of a Health Care Mandate," *The Wall Street Journal*, August 20, 1993.

same time, reducing the number of mandated benefits. A system that provides for universal coverage will eliminate the need for insurance companies to individually rate employee groups according to risk categories. The common insurance practice of experience rating, where premiums are based on the actual claims made by the group, makes underwriting the risk of small groups problematic. With over one-half of all U.S. workers either employed in groups of fewer than 100 or self-employed, the ability of group insurance to spread risk is compromised. Thus, a system where everyone must have insurance coverage opens the possibility of community rating, where underwriting risk is spread over the entire population. With the exception of Hawaii, states cannot require employers to provide health insurance to their employees because federal law, specifically ERISA, preempts state law on all issues dealing with employee benefits.

Policy Issue

Is comprehensive reform possible in the United States, or must we settle for the incremental approach?

The individual states have recognized the limitations they face in changing health care delivery within their borders. The more comprehensive proposals, the ambitious plans with far-reaching provisions mandating employer provision of insurance, capping health insurance premiums, and requiring plans to follow managed care guidelines, have all failed to pass. The reform plans that have passed may be viewed as sequential in nature. They do not try to fix everything at once. The more comprehensive plans tend to get carved up by the special interests. The only approach that seems to work is based on gradualism, an important lesson for would-be reformers.

U.S. Policy Alternatives

A growing sentiment among Americans favors changing the way health care is delivered and financed, but little consensus has emerged on how to do it. Three alternative strategies routinely compete for acceptance: (1) the all-government, single-payer option, (2) mandated insurance coverage secured through place of employment, and (3) expanded use of market incentives to encourage and enable individuals to purchase insurance. Americans are split almost equally into thirds when asked which of the three options they prefer. These three alternatives will be discussed in turn. We will then examine the compromise alternative, **managed competition**, that served as the basis of the Clinton health care reform plan in 1994.

Single-Payer National Health Insurance

The all-government, single-payer option attracts its support primarily from the proponents of universal insurance coverage. Under this system, everyone would participate in a single health plan, administered and financed by the government or a quasi-governmental agency. A basic benefits package, defined to cover all medically necessary services, would be available to the entire population. Private insurance that duplicates covered services is viewed as a way for the wealthy to create for themselves a higher level of care. Following the Canadian model strictly requires the ban on certain types of private insurance to unite everyone into one equal plan. The elimination of financial barriers to the highest

http://

The U.S. House of Representatives and the U.S. Senate have home pages that provide access to information about the legislative process, individual members, and the various committees. Links are also provided to review schedules of activities and access information available from Congress. Check them out at **http://www.house.gov/** and **http://www.senate.gov/**.

managed competition
A health care reform plan first popularized by economist Alain Enthoven, whereby individuals are given a choice among competing health plans. A standard feature is the formation of health insurance alliances to increase the bargaining power of insurance purchasers.

Back-of-the-Envelope

EMPLOYMENT RESPONSE TO INCREASES IN LABOR COSTS

The question of how much mandated labor costs will reduce employment opportunities has raged in policy circles for decades. Every time the debate turns to whether the minimum wage should be raised, both sides cite evidence from their research on what to expect. The direction of the change is not open to serious dispute. Even the strongest supporters of increases in minimum wages agree that employment opportunities will be reduced. The major controversy is the size of the employment effect. The answer is simple. It all depends on the size of the price elasticity of demand for labor.

A mandated benefit will have much the same effect on demand for labor as an increase in the minimum wage. As part of the total compensation package, each adds to the cost of hiring a worker. The employment effects are shown in the following diagrams.

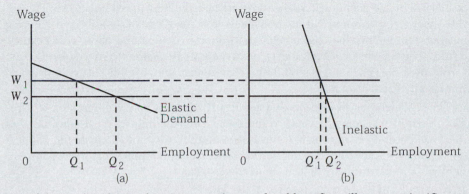

(a)   (b)

If demand is elastic, then increases in mandated benefits will cause a significant decline in employment, from Q_2 to Q_1 in Panel A. On the other hand, if demand is inelastic as in Panel B, then the decline in employment opportunities will be minimal, Q_2' to Q_1' in this case.

Key Concept 5
Markets and Pricing

standards of care prohibits any form of deductible or copayment. In contrast, the Swedish model allows private insurance and requires a modest copayment from patients when they receive medical services.

Physicians would not bill patients directly. Instead, they would bill the single payer according to a fee schedule determined through negotiations between representatives of the medical profession and the single payer. Hospitals' reimbursement strategies vary considerably. Paid either on a fee-for-service or per-diem basis, hospitals merely bill the appropriate government agency for reimbursement. If, however, hospitals are provided with global budgets, the traditional bill no longer exists. They become unnecessary since hospitals receive a periodic appropriation. The single payer establishes global budgets annually. Hospitals are required to treat all patients who seek care. Spending is capped at the level established by the global operating budget. All capital acquisitions, including all diagnostic and high-tech surgical equipment, must be approved by the single payer and are typically paid out of a separate capital budget, controlling overall investment in medical technology.

The theoretical model that applies to the single-payer approach is referred to as *monopsony*. Under a monopsonistic health care system, the government is the only health care buyer. This is not socialized medicine in its pure form. Health care delivery is still based in the private sector, but it requires deep involvement by the government in setting global budgets for hospitals and nursing homes, establishing a ceiling on overall spending, and setting allowable fees for providers. Many proponents of this plan even recommend that growth in health care spending be limited to the growth in the economy, usually measured by the annual percentage change in gross domestic product.

The main advantage of a single-payer system is its administrative simplicity. Only one paper trail is created in a single-payer system—provider to payer. The U.S. system with its labyrinth of private insurance carriers is administratively complex and the source of much of the "unnecessary" spending. Another important advantage is that everyone is covered regardless of employment status or financial circumstances. Furthermore, because it requires little or no out-of-pocket spending, financing is not a barrier to access in any way. Proponents will argue that the single-payer system is the most equitable and efficient way to strike a balance between cost, access, and quality.

On the other hand, critics will argue that within the so-called strengths of the single-payer system lay its weaknesses. It may not be socialized medicine, but it increases government involvement in a system that already has too much. A single-payer system results in a higher tax burden. Higher taxes are netted out by the elimination of the private insurance premium, but as individuals lose the direct responsibility of paying insurance premiums, they also lose the motivation to do anything about rising expenditures. The benefits of wellness programs and aggressive action to reduce spending are spread over the entire population. Individual savings are insignificant in a system of community-rated insurance.

Key Concept 3
Marginal
Analysis

The argument for a single-payer system usually focuses on the duplication of services caused by a system populated by multiple insurers. Eliminate the duplication and costs will naturally come down. If this is the solution, why not eliminate the duplication in other markets? Because duplication is beneficial. It ensures that if one source of supply is cut off, another will be there to take its place.

Employer-Based Health Insurance

More than 90 percent of the privately insured nonelderly population receives health insurance coverage through the workplace (EBRI, 2000). In keeping with this tradition, many reformers rely on a strategy that builds on the employer-based system. The popularity of employer-sponsored health insurance (ESI) is due to three important factors. First, administering insurance in a large group setting leads to economies of scale. Second, the workplace is an ideal setting to pool risk since workers are on average healthier than nonworkers and they form groups to work, not to buy health insurance. Finally, the U.S. tax code provides favorable tax treatment for health insurance benefits. This favorable treatment can be traced back to the wage-and-price controls in place during World War II. Considered different from all other forms of compensation, employers began providing health coverage as a substitute for increased pay. Not only were health benefits outside wage-and-price guidelines, but the Internal Revenue Service (IRS) also excluded them from taxable income, a benefit worth over $100 billion today. This IRS decision, subsequently upheld in a 1954 Supreme Court decision, has had a tremendous impact on the structure of the health insurance industry. Anyone doubting the power of tax incentives in shaping behavior need only study this example to gain an appreciation for their importance.

Employer-Mandated Insurance

The concept of forcing employers to provide health care coverage for their workers originated from the belief that employers are better equipped to manage and finance health care delivery. The proponents of employer mandates have used this market-based principle to support their plan to provide universal insurance coverage to all working Americans and their dependents.

Employer mandates are commonly used across the world as a means of financing health care access. One way of implementing an employer mandate is through the so-called

play-or-pay approach. Under play-or-pay, employers would be required to purchase a basic health care package for their employees as defined by lawmakers. Employers would also have a second option. Instead of providing the basic benefits package, they could pay for a government-sponsored health plan through a new tax (most likely a payroll tax based on a certain percentage of total payroll).

Even strong proponents of play-or-pay recognize that the mechanism makes no provisions for the unemployed. And play-or-pay would likely increase considerably the number of uninsured. A study by the Joint Economic Committee of Congress estimated that play-or-pay with a 7 percent payroll tax option would increase unemployment by some 700,000 workers, with over half of firms affected employing fewer than 20 workers. In a study prepared for the Employment Policies Institute, June and David O'Neill estimate that such a mandate would lead to a loss of 3.1 million jobs (Bonilla, 1993). This mandated increase in labor costs would impact disproportionately on seven low-wage industries, including restaurants, retail trade, construction, personal services, and agriculture.

Most firms in the United States already spend 10 to 12 percent of payroll on medical costs. If the tax rate for participation in the government-sponsored plan is set at a lower level, many firms would be motivated to move to the public system. The Congressional Budget Office estimated that one-half of the U.S. population would ultimately move to the government plan. With those numbers we would soon have a system of health care delivery largely dominated by the federal government.

Individual Mandates

Some notable health experts have suggested that the way to minimize the free-rider problem is to require individuals to provide their own insurance coverage (Reinhardt, 1992). Instead of an employer mandate, they prefer an **individual mandate**. This approach to mandated coverage is similar to the way automobile liability insurance is required for all registered vehicles.

By taking the employer out of the business of providing health benefits, individuals would be more aware of the actual costs of their health insurance (Pauly, 1994). Current arrangements perpetuate the myth that employers pay health insurance premiums. Business and labor have fostered this myth, creating the impression that employers are providing health benefits at no cost to the employee. Even the reference to a premium split between employer and employee is a veiled attempt to promote the idea that the employer pays. Business firms do not pay for health benefits. Treated as a cost of doing business, this expense is passed on to customers in the form of higher prices, absorbed by owners in the form of lower profits, or forced on employees in the form of lower wages and higher unemployment. In competitive industries where prices are market driven and profits modest, employers shift most of their health insurance costs onto workers. The shift is subtle and often unnoticed, but real nevertheless. Actual wages are lower and nonmedical benefits are less generous (Jensen and Morrisey, 1999).

Implementation of an individual mandate would require that employees who currently have health benefits receive the "employer-paid" portion of the premium as gross income. To purchase insurance coverage the individual would then use these funds. An individual mandate would expose the myth of employer-paid insurance by making the employee more aware of the cost of medical coverage.

Market-Based Alternatives[8]

At the heart of the debate between advocates of market-based alternatives and those who would give the government a bigger role in the delivery and financing of medical care is a basic ideological struggle. Can the market for medical care work like the market for other commodities? Or is medical care different, an exception to the basic laws

---

8 Three market-oriented think tanks in Washington best typify the market approach to health care reform debate: the American Enterprise Institute, the Heritage Foundation, and the Cato Institute. The National Center for Policy Analysis is an active think tank located outside "the Beltway."

---

play or pay
A health care reform feature whereby employers would either "play" by providing health care coverage to their employees or "pay" a payroll tax to fund government-provided insurance.

http://

The Office of Management and Budget helps in formulating the President's spending plans, evaluating the effectiveness of agency programs, policies, and procedures, assessing competing funding demands among agencies, and setting funding priorities. The site provides information on the role and organization of OMB and links to important budgetary documents. See http://www.whitehouse.gov/omb.

individual mandate
A legal requirement that individuals carry their own insurance protection.

http://

The Congressional Budget Office (CBO) provides the Congress with economic and budgetary information. The CBO develops forecasts and projections that serve as a baseline for measuring the effects of proposed changes in taxing and spending laws. The site with links to reports and publications and other information sources is found at http://cbo.gov/.

http://

The Cato Institute is a nonpartisan public policy research foundation with libertarian leanings. Their Web page spotlights research papers and books examining the role of government. The site provides numerous links to policy-related papers.
http://www.cato.org/

ISSUES IN MEDICAL CARE DELIVERY

DOES LACK OF PORTABILITY RESULT IN JOB-LOCK?

Are employees who have health problems locked into their jobs because health insurance policies fail to provide benefits for preexisting conditions? A great deal of anecdotal evidence seems to support the link between job mobility and health insurance. In a CBS/*New York Times* poll, for example, 30 percent of the individuals questioned stated that they or a member of their household stayed in a job they wanted to leave primarily because of health insurance. Such polls, while informative, do not provide a sound empirical basis for the existence of insurance-related **job-lock**.

To answer the question of whether job-lock exists, it is important to understand what it is. Job-lock may be defined as a situation where an employee decides to keep a job that he or she would rather leave for fear of losing health insurance coverage due to a preexisting medical problem. Job-lock is an important economy-wide concern if workers are precluded from moving to jobs where they are more productive. To the extent that this occurs, overall economic output is reduced.

Using data from the 1987 National Medical Expenditure Survey, Madrian (1994) was able to identify several tendencies. Individuals with high medical bills are less likely to leave a job that offers health insurance. The larger the family, the less likely a worker will leave a job that offers health insurance. Husbands with pregnant wives are less likely to leave a job that offers health insurance. In the study sample, job-lock reduced voluntary turnover of those employees with health insurance from 16 percent to 12 percent, a 25 percent reduction in the voluntary turnover rate.

The 1985 COBRA (Consolidated Omnibus Budget Reconciliation Act) provided in principle some relief from job-lock by offering an option whereby workers who changed jobs could continue coverage for up to 18 months by paying 102 percent of the premium cost. In practice, employees found that a monthly premium of $400 to $500 was a significant impediment to mobility. The Health Insurance Portability and Accountability Act passed by Congress in 1996 was intended to provide the legislative muscle to force insurance companies to expand portability and end the problem of job-lock. Whether its practical implementation will live up to legislative intent is an issue that is yet to be decided.

Source: Brigitte C. Madrian, "Employment-Based Health Insurance and Job Mobility: Is There Evidence of Job-Lock?" *The Quarterly Journal of Economics, 109*(1), February 1994, 27–54.

---

job-lock
The inability of individual employees to change jobs because preexisting medical conditions make them or one of their dependents ineligible for health insurance benefits under a new plan.

Policy Issue
Can market incentives be effectively used in the financing and provision of medical care in a way that also promotes fairness?

---

of economics and unsuited for market delivery? Will a medical care market work like one in automobiles or personal computers? Or should it be insulated from the market like defense and the interstate highway system?

Nearly every other developed country in the world has virtually given up on the market as a primary means of delivering health care. Only the United States and the Republic of South Africa rely on market mechanisms to any extent to address the important issues of cost and access.

Critics of market-based medical care argue from the unchallenged premise that private markets cannot be expected to address such a fundamentally important issue as the delivery of medical care. Highly respected health economist Uwe Reinhardt has noted that "no one can distribute Gucci loafers better than the market, but a pure market cannot distribute health care" (quoted in Stout, 1992).

This ideological debate allows no room for compromise. In many ways the middle ground is the most difficult to defend. An example is the recent experience with President Clinton's 1994 health care reform proposal. Defenders of the market attacked the plan as a government takeover and those who wanted a government-run system attacked it as a half-measure, not fully addressing the real problems.

Policy Issue

Is meaningful health care reform possible considering the ideological divide among the American electorate?

The Market Approach

The failures of the current system are evident everywhere in limited access for the uninsured and high costs for everyone, but advocates of a market approach do not see these as market failures. In fact, the shortcomings are viewed as the government's failure to promote competitive markets as a means of addressing the problems of access and cost.

The market approach to health care reform is most commonly associated with the use of the tax code to make people more sensitive to the cost of medical care and health insurance reform to improve access for the uninsured and uninsurable. Tax credits or vouchers are suggested as one way to encourage low-income families to buy their own health insurance. This option would be limited to families with incomes less than some modest percentage of the poverty income level, usually 150 to 200 percent. At the heart of the debate is whether a $500 credit or voucher (or any amount less than the full insurance premium) would be sufficient for a family with a $20,000 annual income to purchase its own insurance. Critics argue that this is nothing more than a symbolic gesture and would have little real impact on the number of uninsured. Proponents do not expect miracles from this proposal but do feel that a credit or voucher system would increase access for many low-income Americans. The goal of market proponents is to improve access, not by creating a vast system of government mandates, prospective budgets, price controls, and bureaucratic alliances, but by establishing a mechanism that provides incentives at the margin to encourage some to take responsibility for their own care.[9]

Many market advocates believe the major distortion in the health insurance market is the tax treatment of employer-sponsored health insurance. Because employer-sponsored health benefits are not treated as taxable income, employees have become desensitized to the actual cost of health insurance. Those reformers with the courage of their convictions have recommended a change in the tax exemption. A complete elimination of the tax exemption or at least a limit on the current subsidy would represent a big step in promoting cost-conscious behavior on the part of the consuming public. In addition, this change could result in as much as a $100 billion increase in income tax revenues that could be used to finance other parts of the reform plan, lower taxes, or reduce the federal budget deficit.

Proponents of the market approach see insurance reform as an essential element in improving access to the medical care system. A common complaint addressed by recent reform dealt with certain insurance practices that denied insurance coverage to certain vulnerable groups—job losers, job changers, and those with chronic medical conditions. The Health Insurance Portability and Accountability Act (HIPAA) of 1997 addressed the portability issue, effectively guaranteeing group-to-group portability for job changers who have at least 18 months of continuous coverage under their old plans. HIPAA also requires that companies selling insurance in the small group market (groups of less than 50 employees) guarantee issue of all insurance options regardless of the health status of individual members of the group. Finally, all coverage in the individual market must be guaranteed renewable. Despite these extensions, there is still limited access for the uninsured who have preexisting medical conditions, and insurance does not have to be affordable. States still make their own decisions on regulating premiums.

Another problem that limits insurance availability is that individuals and small businesses are forced into small risk pools for underwriting purposes. Unable to spread risk over an appropriately large group, premiums are significantly higher because of the

http://

The Heritage Foundation is a think tank whose mission is to formulate and promote conservative public policies based on the principles of free enterprise, limited government, individual freedom, traditional American values, and a strong national defense. The site includes a library, resource bank, and links to government and other public policy organizations.
http://www.heritage.org/

 Key Concept 3
Marginal Analysis

http://

The National Center for Policy Analysis attempts to develop and promote private alternatives to government regulation and control, solving problems by relying on the strengths of the competitive, entrepreneurial private sector. The site provides links to policy briefings, the organization's cybrary, and their publication *Executive Alert.*
http://www.public-policy.org/ web.public-policy.org/index.php

---

9 Many market proponents seriously consider tax credits or vouchers as a possible replacement for Medicare and Medicaid.

high costs of administering small risk pools, and are subject to large increases in the event of a single catastrophic loss.

A market solution to this problem must include measures to make it easier to form large risk pools. Concentrating purchasing power and spreading risk lower costs. Specifically, antitrust laws that inhibit or prevent cooperative arrangements must be repealed or amended. Such changes would expedite the creation of health insurance purchasing cooperatives (or HIPCs, referred to as "Hipics") to enhance access and lower the cost of insurance for individuals and small groups.

In another important cost-control measure, proponents of the market alternative recommend incentives for people to enroll in managed care plans. Over the past decade the private sector has experienced an unprecedented growth in managed care enrollments. At the same time, public sector programs, especially Medicare, have not followed the same trends (less than 20 percent of Medicare enrollees who have a choice are in managed care plans).

<table>
<tr><td>

Policy Issue

Do individual consumers have the ability to make their own decisions about matters concerning their own medical care?

</td><td>

The market alternative is built around the core idea that individual decisions are better than collective decisions. The market plan would provide more power to the individual, whereas, the main alternatives would give more power to the government. The real debate is between those who believe that individuals can make their own decisions in matters involving medical care and those who think that medical care is too complex to rely on individual initiative.

</td></tr>
</table>

 Key Concept 4
Self-Interest

Medical Savings Accounts[10]

For many who believe that free enterprise works and that the market is the best way to organize the delivery of goods and services, medical care delivery presents a conundrum. Many are content to argue market failure and recommend reliance on a government-run plan, but government action has proven susceptible to many of the same failings of the market, plus others that are more difficult to correct. Most policy experts agree that the primary reason for the suboptimal results of the market in medical care delivery is the dominance of the third-party payment mechanism.

<table>
<tr><td>

Policy Issue

Is it possible to make medical consumers cost conscious and at the same time create a system that treats the sick and poor fairly?

</td><td>

Defenders of the market believe that if the market is to work in medical care, individuals must spend their own money at the point of service. Even though holders of a private insurance policy spend their own money on premiums (or their employer spends it for them), once paid, they represent a sunk cost and are irrelevant in the decision-making process. Faced with zero (or low) marginal cost of care, individuals tend to overconsume—that is, demand care that adds little to prospective outcomes. For the consumption decision to be optimal (in the economic

</td></tr>
</table>

 Key Concept 3
Marginal Analysis

sense), individuals must take into consideration the alternative uses of the resources. If individuals are to economize on the use of resources, they must realize a direct benefit from their own economizing behavior.

For the market to work in medical care, consumers must spend their own money for routine (meaning high frequency, low cost) medical services. In turn, to protect against

<table>
<tr><td>

Policy Issue

If you spend $2,500 on your annual health insurance premium and don't receive $2,500 worth of medical care, are you getting your money's worth?

</td><td>

catastrophic (meaning low frequency, high cost) expenses, individuals would purchase a high-deductible indemnity insurance policy. Insurers use deductibles and coinsurance to get policyholders to spend their money more wisely, but often even small deductibles and low coinsurance rates create problems. For a single mother with three children, even a trip to the doctor to treat an earache can mean a financial hardship. Without money to pay the deductible, the earache often goes untreated, resulting in higher spending for an emergency room visit at a later date,

</td></tr>
</table>

---

10 Congress enacted a limited demonstration project in 1996, due to sunset at the end of 2003. A number of restrictions limit its appeal. For example, only the self-employed and those who work for small firms (with fewer than 50 employees) can receive the tax benefits envisioned originally.

and possibly long-term hearing loss for the child. The main drawback of large deductibles is handled with the medical savings account (MSA).

How Medical Savings Accounts Work. The basic idea is simple. Instead of buying a traditional indemnity insurance policy, individuals would purchase a high deductible insurance policy, say $3,000, that would cover only medical expenses above that amount. Each year, approximately 90 percent of all claims and 70 percent of all medical spending are for amounts totaling less than $3,000. Annual deductibles in this range would result in significant savings on insurance premiums.[11] Individuals would bank these premium savings in their medical savings account to cover the first $3,000 spent on medical care.

The individual would have the medical savings account to pay for the first $3,000 in expenses. The catastrophic insurance policy would cover all expenses in excess of $3,000. If medical expenses were less, the money would remain in the savings account. Accumulations in these accounts would be available to pay future health insurance premiums or other medical expenses, such as long-term care where current insurance coverage is especially weak. The important aspect of the plan is that the savings account belongs to the individual. It would grow through annual deposits and earn interest.

Advantages of Medical Savings Accounts. The major advantage of the medical savings account is that it puts the individual in control of his or her own medical spending. Proponents of MSAs assert that the main reason medical markets fail is there is no incentive to practice economizing behavior—either for the provider or the patient. With medical savings accounts, patients are spending their own money (at least, for the first $3,000) and have an incentive to economize. Rather than being indifferent to the prices they pay, consumers will benefit from shopping around. Such an environment is representative of consumer sovereignty, in the real sense of the classical economic concept.

Policy Issue

Is it possible to change the way Americans view health insurance? Or will they always treat it as pre-paid medical care?

Key Concept 7
Competition

Individual self-interest would take over. With patients benefiting from their own economizing behavior, savings balances would grow as spending moderated. Estimates of reduced spending are based primarily on the experience of individual employers. Over 1,000 private employers provide MSA-type plans to their workers and are enjoying significant cost reductions. For example, the Golden Rule Insurance Company began offering its employees a medical savings account plan in 1993. In the first year of the plan, over 80 percent of its employees participated in the program, spending an average of $1,250 of their MSA deposits and receiving an average reimbursement at the end of the year in excess of $600. By 1995, the plan had over 90 percent participation with the average refund approaching $1,000.

Key Concept 4
Self-Interest

Arguments against Medical Savings Accounts. Many do not believe that the MSA concept can work on a nationwide scale, dismissing the MSA idea because it allows too much individual discretion in choosing medical care. Critics think that most people are incapable of making informed decisions about the quality and quantity of health care they need. Anything short of universally mandated free care does not provide the proper incentives for individuals to seek the correct mix of primary and preventive care. They fear that individuals with medical savings accounts would be tempted to save their money rather than spend it when they or their children are sick (U.S. House of Representatives, 1993).

Many are hesitant to back the concept of the medical savings account for fear that what may work for a small segment of the community may not work for the whole population. Medical savings accounts may work well for those who are healthy, but what about the small percentage of the

Policy Issue

Can medical savings accounts work effectively for the sick and poor?

---

11 Golden Rule Insurance Company surveyed four insurance underwriters (Washington National, Pyramid Life, Time, and Union Bankers) in ten U.S. cities (Cincinnati, Dallas, Denver, Des Moines, Indianapolis, Omaha, Peoria, Portland, Richmond, and Scranton) on the price of a $2,500 deductible policy for a two-parent family with children. The survey results listed a median health insurance premium of $1,650. This amount represents a significant savings over the cost of a traditional indemnity insurance policy.

Key Concept 7
Competition

population that gets sick? How would those unfortunate enough to have large medical bills be protected at a reasonable cost? Others worry that individual MSA holders would be no match for the more powerful provider networks. Group buying may be the best way to combat the concentration on the sellers' side of the market.

Managed Competition

Can choice and competition, principles that have served us well in other sectors of the economy, be made to work in the medical care sector? To work, choice must mean more than whatever your employer chooses for you. Competition must be encouraged at the point where the consumer purchase decision is made, and that is either at the time when the type of health insurance coverage is determined or at the point of buying the care. The model of managed competition was first introduced by Alain Enthoven under the title "Consumer Choice Health Plan" (Enthoven, 1978). Revised and clarified extensively since its early beginnings, managed competition emerged as a central element of President Clinton's 1994 reform package.[12] Proponents of managed competition see it as a way to increase competition in the market for health insurance. In most employer-provided plans, the employee has little choice. As members of the same group, all employees get the plan provided by the employer—fee-for-service or managed care—and rarely have the option of choosing between the two.

Under managed competition employers would be required to make competing health plans available to all full-time employees. Employees, in turn, would choose among the competing plans, including fee-for-service, health maintenance organizations, preferred provider organizations, and point-of-service plans. Under most circumstances, employees would have a choice of a minimum of three plans. The employer would contribute a fixed sum toward the purchase of the health plan—the key element in managed competition.

Insurers would set premiums based on the basic benefit package specified by the legislation. The average premium of all eligible plans is called the "average employment-based plan cost" (referred to as APC in the following discussion). The employer would pay at least 80 percent of the APC, regardless of the cost of the actual plan chosen. The employee would pay the balance. The 80 percent employer share would be treated as a tax-free benefit. Any employer contribution in excess of 80 percent of APC would be considered taxable income. The employee share would be paid out of after-tax income.

For example, suppose three basic plans are available. Plan 1 costs $1,600, Plan 2 costs $2,000, and Plan 3 costs $2,400. The APC of the these three plans is $2,000. The employer is required to pay 80 percent of the APC, or $1,600. Employees choosing Plan 1 would pay nothing extra. Those choosing Plan 3 would pay $800 extra. If the employer pays more than $1,600, the additional benefit is treated the same as ordinary income and taxed at the employee's highest marginal rate.

Proponents of managed competition see it as a way of making employees more price conscious and encouraging insurers to hold down costs in order to make plans more attractive. Policymakers who consider themselves moderates consider managed competition a workable middle ground between those advocating a government-run system and those wanting the market to play a bigger role. They see it solving the social problems of a growing class of uninsured and at the same time capturing many of the cost-saving benefits of competition.

Those opposed to managed competition feel that the emphasis is on management and not competition (Goodman, 1993). Government management requires that a standard benefit package be defined by law. The political battle becomes one of what is included in the basic plan and what is not. Special interest lobbies are bound to put pressure on lawmakers to include additional benefits in the basic plan.[13]

Project HOPE (Health Opportunities for People Everywhere) provides health education, health policy research, and humanitarian assistance in over 70 countries, including the United States. Community projects in Texas and West Virginia are featured at
http://www.projecthope.org/.

---

12 After details of Clinton's plan began to surface, Enthoven penned a harsh criticism of the President's version of "managed competition" (Enthoven, 1993).

13 Take, for example, the expanded benefits package suggested in the Clinton Health Care Plan that had some 40 pages of benefits and their explanations listed in Subtitle B of the proposed act.

ISSUES IN MEDICAL CARE DELIVERY

MANAGED COMPETITION IN PRACTICE: THE FEDERAL EMPLOYEES HEALTH BENEFIT PLAN

The Federal Employees Health Benefit Plan (FEHBP) was enacted in 1959 to cover all civilian employees of the federal government, including Congress, the executive branch, the judicial branch, civilian employees of the Pentagon, and federal retirees. Currently, FEHBP insures over 9 million civilians (one out of every 25 Americans), making it the largest employer-sponsored health insurance program in the country.

The distinguishing feature of the plan is that recipients are allowed to choose their own health benefits package from among nearly 400 private health insurance plans. Depending on geographic location, each individual has at least 21 and in some cases as many as 37 plans from which to choose. The plans range from traditional Blue Cross/Blue Shield health insurance plans to one of over 300 managed care plans (HMOs). Premium costs vary depending on the type of coverage desired with the federal government paying around 70 percent of the average premium.

Each November brings with it an "open season" where federal employees have several weeks to decide which type of coverage to choose for the upcoming year. Plans are marketed by health insurance companies, HMOs, local hospitals, and employee associations. Many consider the FEHBP a model for nationwide reform, but before nationwide implementation of this system is possible, fully informed consumers must be the norm, not the exception. Federal employees get plenty of information to assist them in making their decisions. Their options are clearly spelled out in advertising, associational newsletters, and independently published consumer guides. When consumers perceive that they will benefit from additional information, they will demand information, and it will be provided.

In recent years, the growth rate in the average FEHBP premium has been significantly below rates experienced among private sector plans. After a 3 percent increase in premiums in 1994, they actually fell by 3.4 percent in 1995. Average premiums in 1996 increased 0.4 percent with one-fourth of the plans actually experiencing reductions in premiums. With all the plans available, two-thirds of the enrollees use one of six fee-for-service plans, and only three of the 400 plus HMOs have over 25,000 participants.

Given the number of choices available, enrollees tend to select health plans based on their own expected usage. In other words, enrollees self-select according to their likelihood of using medical care. To the extent that this market segmentation takes place, it actually defeats the purpose of insurance—the spreading of risk. Fine-tuning the system might include actually limiting the number of choices available to reduce this tendency. Though the system is by no means perfect, it works reasonably well for a large number of enrollees and is even considered by some analysts as a model for reform of the Medicare system.

Source: Robert E. Moffit, "FEHBP Controls Costs Again: More Lessons for Medicare Reformers," *The Heritage Foundation F.Y.I. No. 64*, September 25, 1995.

Key Concept 3
Marginal Analysis

Managed competition places a strong emphasis on managed care as a way of controlling costs. Uniform billing procedures, including standardized forms and electronic billing, are suggested as ways of reducing administrative costs. The stipulation of guaranteed issue on the part of the insurer would be balanced by mandatory participation on the part of the public. Otherwise, the rational decision for the low-risk population (the healthy) would be to forgo insurance until they became sick.

For a market to work in medical care, cost-conscious behavior must become the rule rather than the exception. The two points of purchase in the medical marketplace are when the individual makes the decision of what type of medical plan to purchase and when the individual actually receives the service. Advocates of managed competition feel that, based on equity considerations, a system based on competition at the point of purchasing health insurance offers the best alternative for bringing competitive forces to bear in this market. Advocates of medical savings accounts disagree, viewing competition at the point of purchasing medical care as the appropriate choice.

Market Response to Uncertainty[14]

As was stated earlier, employer-sponsored insurance has been the dominant feature of the private-sector health insurance market in the United States for the past 60 years. In all likelihood, most Americans will continue to receive health insurance coverage through their place of employment as long as public policy does not deviate substantially from the current state of affairs. This fact does not mitigate employer concerns over the ramifications of a changing public policy. Eliminating or even modifying the tax-exempt status of the health benefit would have a significant impact on the number of workers who are offered health insurance and the nature of the benefit package they would receive. Gruber (2001) estimates that each one-percentage point increase in the after-tax price of health insurance would decrease the likelihood that workers would be offered insurance by 0.74 percentage points. Using this estimate, eliminating the tax exemption for ESI would lead to a 22-percentage point decrease in the probability of receiving health insurance for a person in the 30 percent marginal tax bracket.

Another concern for many employers who offer health benefits is the prospect that Congress will impose new federal oversight on health care delivery in the name of patients' rights. A Patients' Bill of Rights would likely impose hundreds of new federal regulations on private-sector health plans, adding new rules and standards governing the delivery of care and increasing the employer's liability for decisions regarding the type of plan offered. Employers are concerned that if the new rules expand the patient's rights to sue health plans for denial of care, both plans and employers will be subject to litigation. This expanded threat of liability may cause employers to reexamine and modify their role in choosing health plans.

Many firms are not waiting around for the federal government to extend its oversight and are already making changes in the way the health care benefit is administered (Martin et al., 2002). Instead of following the current model for ESI, where a single comprehensive plan is offered, many employers are adopting a consumer-driven model that gives employees more plan options that vary in terms of coverage and price— something that looks suspiciously like Enthoven's managed competition. Under these circumstances, it is the employee who chooses the plan. Consequently, the employer's responsibility becomes principally financial, providing an allowance or voucher to the employee for the express purpose of purchasing health insurance.

The movement to limit employer involvement and increase employee choice—it may be too early to call it a trend—has led to the introduction of the *defined contribution plan*. Even though it is not a new concept in employee benefits, the defined contribution as applied to health insurance has not extended much beyond the administration of the Federal Employee Health Benefit Plan discussed earlier. A shift to the defined contribution model will shift the primary responsibility of plan choice from the employer to the employee. Depending on how much responsibility they are willing to give up, employers can contract with a single insurance carrier or multiple carriers who can offer a few options or a wide range of options. The choice depends on the size of the group and the ability of the underwriter to maintain the integrity of the individual risk pools.

---

14 This section relies on a previously published paper by Henderson and Taylor (2002).

The shift to the defined contribution model raises a number of policy concerns, namely the tax-exempt status of the employer contribution and the segmentation of employee risk pools. Under current practices, the tax-exemption for the employer contribution remains intact as long as it may be used solely for the purchase of health insurance. If all or part of the contribution may be used for anything else, the tax-exemption may be questioned. Refundable tax credits may solve the dilemma by allowing the employee to decide how much of the voucher to spend on health insurance. The part spent on health insurance would be tax exempt while the part spent on anything else would be taxable income.

As their popularity expands and plan options increase, defined contribution plans will contribute to the segmentation of risk pools. Employees with health problems will continue to purchase comprehensive plans with high premiums. Employees without health problems, unwilling to pay the high premiums, will choose catastrophic plans with high deductibles and lower premiums. The cost of comprehensive plans will increase as healthy employees leave them and risk pooling will jeopardize the very existence of comprehensive plans. As premiums rise, individuals with chronic conditions may not be able to afford health insurance. Employers would then be faced with the prospects of having a segmented workforce, those who are healthy having health coverage, and those with chronic health conditions not having it. The challenge for policymakers is obvious. Market solutions to problems are not always pleasant. It becomes the responsibility of government to shape public policy to make sure these types of market failures do not adversely affect those population groups who are most vulnerable—namely, the sick and poor.

Summary and Conclusions

A good starting point in establishing a health care policy is to set realistic goals and establish reasonable priorities. In other words, we are forced to make difficult choices. This is the purview of economics and one of the reasons that economics has been referred to as the "dismal science." In establishing a realistic medical care policy, we as a society recognize a moral responsibility to provide an adequate level of health care for those who through no fault of their own cannot afford it. And we as individual beneficiaries of the health care system must recognize a personal responsibility to share (to the extent we are able) in providing the resources to make health care available to everyone.

Health care reform is a daunting challenge for U.S. policymakers. The public wants change, but there is little consensus on how to achieve it. Government action seems inevitable, but the extent of that action is likely to fall far short of what anyone could have imagined shortly after the Clinton Plan was first introduced in 1993. It does not mean, however, that we have lost the opportunity to improve the system. This historic "window" is not likely to close anytime soon; at least, not as long as the public's desire for change remains strong.

But it is unlikely that any comprehensive plan for a government takeover of health care delivery will ever happen. Instead, we will probably witness a series of incremental steps to add coverage and access to groups at the margin. For example, in 1997 Congress enacted the State Children's Health Insurance Program (CHIP), providing matching funds to states that provided health insurance to low-income children without insurance. Estimated to cover over 2 million children nationwide, CHIP represents the largest expansion of health insurance coverage for children since enactment of Medicaid in 1965.

With so many Americans satisfied with their personal medical care arrangements, the call for reform seems motivated either out of concern for those without health insurance coverage or because of the perceived risk of joining the ranks of the uninsured. The proper diagnosis is essential if medical treatment is to be effective. Likewise, it is imperative that system reform is based on a correct diagnosis of the problem. Many suggestions for reform focus on symptoms, but the real problem is that we spend other

ISSUES IN MEDICAL CARE DELIVERY

CLINTONCARE: ITS DEVELOPMENT AND DOWNFALL

Bill Clinton took the oath of office in January 1993 to become the forty-second president of the United States. With both houses of Congress controlled by the Democratic Party, most followers of politics expected that reform of the health care system, Clinton's top domestic priority, would soon become the law of the land. The Clinton team adopted the same "War Room" strategy that successfully catapulted him into the presidency. Setting an ambitious 100-day deadline, Clinton and his advisers began the process of drafting what many considered the most important piece of social legislation since the New Deal.

The two most visible players on the Clinton team were his wife, Hillary Rodham Clinton, and long-time friend and fellow Rhodes scholar, Ira Magaziner. As head of the health care reform task force, Ms. Clinton's primary responsibility was to sell the plan. Magaziner, Clinton's senior policy adviser and "health czar," supervised the day-to-day activities of the task force and became the primary drafter of the final plan presented to Congress in October 1993.

The development of the plan may be traced back to late 1991 when candidate Clinton made health care reform a major plank in his presidential platform. His early plan "National Health Insurance Reform to Cut Costs and Cover Everybody" may be described as a government-run play-or-pay system. After receiving his party's nomination in August 1992, it became clear that the electorate supported a more market-oriented approach. In the final months of the presidential campaign, Clinton's approach shifted from play-or-pay to managed competition.

The idea for a health care task force emerged from the early policy discussions as a way to buy time, work out the details of the proposal, and build support for managed competition. After announcing the plan in his State of the Union address in February 1993, Clinton and his advisers went about the task of organizing the 511-member task force. Magaziner served as overseer of the operation, presiding over the major meetings, or "tollgates," as they are known in management theory. Some called it "policy-wonk heaven"; others said it was more like the Spanish Inquisition. These tollgate sessions lasted as long as 16 hours and served to inform Magaziner on the progress and direction of the committee meetings. Magaziner soon became the choke point in the flow of information. Little was committed to paper; everything was in his head. Although the task force missed the 100-day deadline, the plan was almost complete by June, except for one troubling detail—how to finance it.

The broader tasks of running the country began taking up precious administration time and using up political goodwill. The better part of summer 1993 was spent in a particularly nasty budget battle that the president finally won by a 51–50 vote in the Senate with Vice President Al Gore casting the tie-breaking vote. Foreign policy issues such as the military intervention in Somalia also took up valuable time and energy.

Finally, on September 22, 1993, before a joint session of Congress, President Clinton announced his reform plan. Called by Ms. Clinton "the most anticipated document since Moses came down off Mount Sinai with the ten commandments," the legislative proposal filled 1,342 pages, and was accompanied by an 800-page explanation and a paperback summary available in most local bookstores. The main principles of the plan as outlined in his speech were easy to support—security, simplicity, savings, choice, quality, and responsibility. The ensuing debate focused on the details.

The plan was a remarkable document in scope and premise. It called for universal coverage as an entitlement, community rating of health insurance premiums, employer mandates, baseline (global) budgeting, uniform fee schedules, and the creation of 250 quasi-governmental agencies called **health alliances**. These health alliances would be under the supervision of a National Health Board created to issue regulations, establish

health alliances
Called by various names, including health insurance purchasing cooperative (HIPC), it provides a way for small employers to act collectively to purchase health insurance. Typically geographically based and not-for-profit, the alliance contracts with insurers and/or providers for medical coverage for its members.

requirements for state health plans, monitor compliance, and enforce budgets. The plan bowed to the interests of some groups and ignored those of others. The VA system would remain intact and even receive additional funding. The AMA wanted limits on awards for pain and suffering in medical malpractice cases, but the influence of the Trial Lawyers of America kept these limits out of the plan.

According to the president, everything in the plan was negotiable except universal coverage. In a classic good cop/bad cop routine, however, one administration spokesperson would talk about compromise while another would criticize those who openly opposed aspects of the plan. Clinton found himself sidetracked again, spending the better part of the fall in the debate over the North American Free Trade Agreement (NAFTA). Instead of focusing on health care, Clinton had to fight a traditional ally, the AFL-CIO, over free trade. Ms. Clinton had early success on Capital Hill in committee hearings discussing the plan. Opponents were effectively muted in their criticism by her command over the details and her personal style.

Nevertheless, criticism came from all sides. Even members of the president's Cabinet and key economic advisers had doubts about aspects of the plan, especially its financing assumptions. Opposition from several important special interest groups had to be addressed. The Health Insurance Association of America, fighting for its very existence, was quite vocal in opposing the plan. The association spent over $14 million on a series of "Harry and Louise" television advertisements featuring a young professional couple questioning various provisions in the plan and calling for "a better way" to fix health care. Small business, represented by the Chamber of Commerce, the National Association of Manufacturers, and the National Federation of Independent Business, was critical of the employer mandate.

At the same time a number of alternative plans were being considered in Congress. Senator Paul Wellstone of Minnesota headed the single-payer group that occupied the left-of-center position. Representative Jim Cooper of Tennessee led the market-reform legislators with the main right-of-center alternative. As Congress debated through the summer of 1994, Republicans became convinced they could defeat the president and his bill. Public support for the president's version of health care reform had waned from 57 percent approval when it was first introduced to 37 percent. As the legislative session drew to a close in the early fall, it was difficult to find a member of Congress who would vote for any health care reform bill, even one he or she had personally sponsored.

Legislation that looked so promising in 1993 failed miserably in 1994. What went wrong? Many different perspectives offer reasons for the plan's failure: The process was too secretive, the framers were politically naïve, they wasted too much time on details, and the plan was too complicated. Each of these perspectives may contain an element of the truth, but a separate line of reasoning may come closer to explaining the demise of the plan—trust. Who do you trust to organize health care delivery? Americans in general are a bit cynical about government's ability to run anything efficiently. In the end, the administration apparently failed to convince the public that health care was any different. The process seemed to breed suspicion rather than communicate ideas. By the fall of 1994, fewer than one in six Americans felt they clearly understood the plan, down from one in five just after its introduction. Proponents tried to sell the middle class on the basis of security—"health care that's always there." Opponents focused on cost, and in the end Americans were not willing to pay the price for a program they did not understand fully.

Whitewater and other personal scandals touching the president himself eroded the trust factor with many Americans. In the end, the Democratic majority in Congress was never able to bring health care legislation to a vote. Mid-term elections in 1994 swept the Republican Party to its first majority in both houses of Congress in over 40 years, and changed the dynamics of health care legislation for some time to come. It is true that these events took place in the past, but their importance remains. Those who ignore past events are doomed to repeat past mistakes.

Policy Issue
Do Americans trust government enough to support the implementation of a government-run health care system?

Sources: Robert J. Blendon, Mollyann Brodie, and John Benson, "What Happened to Americans' Support for the Clinton Health Plan?" *Health Affairs 14*(1), Spring 1995, 24–26; Daniel Yankelovich, "The Debate that Wasn't: The Public and the Clinton Plan," *Health Affairs 14*(1), Spring 1995, 7–23; and Walter Zelman and Larry D. Brown, "Looking Back on Health Care Reform: 'No Easy Choices,'" *Health Affairs 17*(6), November/December 1998, 61–68.

ISSUES IN MEDICAL CARE DELIVERY

IS THE MEDIA BIASED?

As the health care reform debate heated up in Washington, lobbyists and journalists lined up to shape public opinion on key issues and important features of the respective health care plans. Even while the "Harry and Louise" spots, sponsored by the Health Insurance Association of America, were being denounced as unethical and incorrect, the disinformation from the other side of the debate was largely ignored.

The media focus was not on the substantive issues of whether we have a right to health care, how to translate that right (if it exists) into a means of financing, and how a particular plan would affect the macroeconomy. The issues that the media chose to cover dealt with the politics of reform.

MediaNomics, published by the Media Research Center, analyzed the contents of the four major networks' evening news shows, including ABC, CBS, CNN, and NBC. During the month from June 15 through July 15, 1994, only 12 of the 68 reports on health care reform examined policy issues. The other 56 covered the political aspects of the reform debate. Of the 12 policy stories, nine were on the economic aspects of the various plans under consideration (primarily the Clinton plan) and the other three were about individuals who were faced with financial problems due to poor insurance coverage.

These reports contained interviews of 208 people. Given the emphasis of the reports, it is no surprise that 141 of the interviewees were politicians. What may come as a surprise is that 102 were Democrats speaking in support of the President's plan. Only 16 business representatives were interviewed and six of these favored the President's call for employer mandates. Nine insurance executives made it on screen with NBC interviewing seven of these. ABC and CNN each interviewed one and CBS did not see fit to talk to a single representative of the insurance industry. Physicians were among the least interviewed during the debate. Seven were interviewed by NBC and one by CBS. The other two networks could not find a physician who had anything of merit to add to the debate.

ABC's *World News Tonight* had 18 stories during the time period, all on politics. Economic considerations do not carry the same audience appeal. Although it may be difficult to summarize complex issues into 10-second sound bites, Democrats seem to monopolize even those brief moments on stage. Of the 55 politicians contributing to the program, 40 were Democrats.

Is the media biased in its presentation of the issues surrounding health care reform? Without answering the question directly, at minimum we can say that the television coverage of the debate demonstrated an interesting pattern. Early stories may have helped create a crisis atmosphere, but the focus soon shifted to politics. As this side of the story gained momentum, virtually all other aspects of the debate were ignored.

Sources: L. Brent Bozell III, "TV Viewers Await Universal Coverage," *The Wall Street Journal*, August 23, 1994, A12; and James W. Henderson, "The Politics of Health Care Reform," *Journal of the Medical Association of Georgia* 84(1), January 1995, 35–37.

people's money. Reliance on the third-party payment mechanism desensitizes buyers to the true cost of the care they receive. The only way to ensure predictable access at reasonable prices is for individuals to exercise personal responsibility by spending their own money.

Differences in health care delivery systems worldwide reflect differences in the availability of resources and differences in the respective cultures. The attitude of the

Alain Enthoven

Without question, Alain Enthoven is a leading figure in the health care reform movement worldwide. His ideas have helped shape recent reforms in England and the Netherlands. It was also Enthoven who served as the intellectual backbone of the now-famous "Jackson Hole Group" that has regularly studied and discussed health care reform since the mid-1970s. A respected Stanford economist, Enthoven is a strong proponent of managed competition, having developed the idea in collaboration with his long-time friend Dr. Paul Ellwood.

After completing his undergraduate work at Stanford, he won a Rhodes scholarship to study at Oxford. In 1956, he completed his Ph.D. in economics from MIT and went to work for the RAND Corporation in Santa Monica, California. His early work was on defense issues, and he soon became knowledgeable in the ways of the federal government. He became well known in government circles and went to work in the Pentagon in 1961. During his years in Washington, he became a director of Georgetown University. While on the board, he was chairman of the committee that built a major medical center at the school and created the university's group-practice HMO.

In 1973, he began consulting with the Kaiser-Permanente Group in California, where he developed most of his ideas for reforming medical care. That same year Enthoven joined the Stanford faculty where he is now the Marriner S. Eccles Professor of Public and Private Management, Emeritus, in the Graduate School of Business.

Conservative Democrats looking for an alternative to the Canadian-style single-payer approach have turned to Enthoven's plan of managed competition. Like many plans created by economists, when the politicians get through with them, they are barely recognizable. The major change that Enthoven found distasteful was the addition of budget caps (or price controls). Given his work developing the theory of managed competition, it is somewhat surprising that Enthoven was left off President Clinton's 1993 national task force on health care reform. Enthoven, nevertheless, is confident that policymakers will ultimately turn to managed competition as the only reform plan that can work within the American system.

Enthoven (1988) argued that "reform should start with cost-conscious choices made by the educated middle class. In this way, the organizational cultures of the health plans are created in an environment in which they serve intelligent, relatively informed people who have choices."

Sources: John Huber, "The Abandoned Father of Health-Care Reform," *The New York Times Magazine*, July 18, 1993, 24–26, 36–37; and Alain Enthoven, *Theory and Practice of Managed Competition in Health Care Finance*, Professor Dr. F. DeVries Lectures in Economics: Theory, Institutions, Policy, Volume 9, Amsterdam: North-Holland, 1988.

typical purchaser of medical care in the United States is to exhaust every possible course of treatment with little regard to its cost. Everything must be done to cure any disease or illness. Cost is not a consideration when you're talking about a human life. In contrast, attitudes in other countries are very different. For example, British and Japanese societies are more ready to accept the inevitability of illness and are better prepared to deal with its consequences.

Instead of envying health care systems abroad, policymakers in the United States ought to envision reform that is compatible with the social and ideological characteristics that make America unique. Only then can we successfully implement a change that will work for all Americans. The real issue in the debate over medical care reform is political choice. The degree of government involvement is determined by political feasibility. The issue is whether the electorate desires a predominantly public or a private solution to health care delivery and financing. The inherent danger in our desire to reform the system is that we politicize an issue that should be apolitical. Our experience has taught us that whenever resource allocation is brought into the realm of political control, it becomes politicized, whether we like it or not.

Questions and Problems

1. What are the respective roles of the federal government and the state governments in providing health services?

2. Nationwide hundreds of state mandates require the provision of certain benefits or the coverage of certain providers for firms that make private health insurance available for their employees. Do these mandates address specific failures in the private insurance market or do they reflect the political strength of certain provider groups, such as chiropractors and faith healers?

3. Describe a piece of health care legislation that is currently being discussed or one that has recently been passed into law either at the state or federal level. What problem is the legislation trying to address? How much is it expected to cost? How will the extra spending be financed? What are the major objections to the legislation?

4. The United States health care delivery system has been criticized for its structural defects: high costs, large numbers of uninsured, and a failure to promote high quality health in the population. What possible approaches to health care reform do you think are morally acceptable, economically effective, and politically feasible? Elaborate on the key features of your own national health care policy proposal.

5. Altman and Rodwin ("Halfway Competitive Markets and Ineffective Regulation," *Journal of Health Policy, Politics, and Law 13*(2), Summer 1988, 323–339) argue that the medical care system in the United States exhibits neither effective competition nor effective government regulation. Would we be better off if we decisively adopted one approach or the other? Explain.

6. Is death an enemy that is to be fought off at all costs or is it a condition of life that is to be accepted? How does the way we answer this question affect the kind of health care system we might embrace?

7. Should we shy away from specifying a collectively provided benefits package that is less generous than the standard package available to those who can afford to pay for it? Is that fair? Not everyone can afford to drive a Lexus either. Is that fair?

8. In what sense do Americans have a right to medical care? In what sense is access to medical care not a right? How have the reforms in Oregon and Hawaii helped define the nature of the right to medical care in this country?

References

Gregory Acs, Colin Winterbottom, and Sheila Zedlewski, "Employers' Payroll and Insurance Costs: Implications for Play or Pay Employer Mandates," in *Health Benefits and the Workforce*, Washington, D.C.: U.S. Department of Labor, 1992.

Robert J. Blendon, Jennifer N. Edwards, and Andrew L. Hyams, "Making the Critical Choices," *Journal of the American Medical Association 267*(18), May 13, 1992, 2509–2520.

———, John Benson, Karen Donelan, Robert Leitman, Humphrey Taylor, Christian Koeck, and David Gitterman, "Who Has the Best Health Care System? A Second Look," *Health Affairs 14*(4), Winter 1995, 220–230.

Carlos Bonilla, "The Price of a Health Care Mandate," *The Wall Street Journal*, August 20, 1993, A10.

Karen Donelon, Robert J. Blendon, Cathy Schoen, Karen Davis, and Katherine Binns, "The Cost of Health System Change: Public Discontent in Five Nations," *Health Affairs 18*(3), May/June 1999, 206–216.

David M. Eddy, "What Care is 'Essential'? What Services are 'Basic'?" *Journal of the American Medical Association 265*(6), February 13, 1991, 782, 786–788.

Employee Benefit Research Institute, "Sources of Health Insurance and Characteristics of the Uninsured: Analysis of the March 1999 Current Population Survey," Washington, DC: EBRI, 2000.

Alain C. Enthoven, "Consumer Choice Health Plan," *New England Journal of Medicine 298*(12 and 13), March 23 and March 30, 1978, 650–658 and 709–720.

———, *Theory and Practice of Managed Competition in Health Care Finance*, Professor Dr. F. DeVries Lectures in Economics: Theory, Institutions, Policy, Volume 9, Amsterdam: North-Holland, 1988b.

————, "A Good Health Care Idea Gone Bad," *Wall Street Journal*, October 7, 1993, A18.

Jon R. Gabel and Gail A. Jensen, "The Price of State Mandated Benefits," *Inquiry 26*, Winter 1989, 419–431.

John C. Goodman, "Managed Competition: Too Little Competition," *Wall Street Journal*, January 7, 1993, A14.

Jonathan Gruber, "The Impact of the Tax System on Health Insurance Coverage," *International Journal of Health Care Finance and Economics 1*(3/4) December 2001, 293–304.

David C. Hadorn, "Setting Health Care Priorities in Oregon: Cost-Effectiveness Meets the Rule of Reason," *Journal of the American Medical Association 265*(17), May 1, 1991, 2218–2225.

James W. Henderson, "Biblical Principles Applied to a National Health Policy," in Richard C. Chewning, ed., *Biblical Principles and Public Policy: The Practice* (Colorado Springs, CO: NavPress, 1991), 237–250.

————, "The Politics of Health Care Reform," *Journal of the Medical Association of Georgia 84*(1), January 1995, 35–37.

————, J. Allen Seward, and Beck A. Taylor, "The Economic Costs of State Level Health Insurance Mandates," Baylor University Economics Department Working Paper, 2003.

———— and Beck A. Taylor, "Employer-Sponsored Health Insurance: Past, Present, and Future," *Journal of Forensic Economics 15*(2), 2002, 181–194.

Gail A. Jensen, Kevin D. Cotter, and Michael A. Morrisey, "State Insurance Regulation and Employers' Decisions to Self-Insure," The Journal of Risk and Insurance 62, June 1995, 185–213.

Gail A. Jensen and Michael A. Morrisey, *Mandated Benefit Laws and Employer-Sponsored Health Insurance* (Washington, D.C.: Health Insurance Association of America, 1999).

Dianne Longley, "Mandated Health Insurance Benefits: Report on Insurance Company Claims and Premium Costs 1992–1993," prepared for the Mandated Health Insurance Review Panel, Texas Department of Insurance. November 1994.

Maggie Mahar, "Memo to Hillary: Here's How to Cure What Ails Our Health-Care System," *Barron's*, March 1, 1993, 8–11 ff.

Katherine E. Martin et al., *Shifting Responsibilities: Models of Defined Contribution* (Washington, D.C.: Academy for Health Services Research and Health Policy, February 2002).

Olivia S. Mitchell, "The Effects of Mandating Benefits Packages," *Research in Labor Economics*, Volume 11, JAI Press Inc., 1990, 297–320.

Robert E. Moffit, "FEHBP Controls Costs Again: More Lessons for Medicare Reformers," *The Heritage Foundation* F.Y.I. No. 64, September 25, 1995.

Gerald L. Musgrave, "Emotions, Politics and Economics: An Introduction to Health Care," *Business Economics 28*, April 1993, 7–10.

Mark V. Pauly, "Making a Case for Employer-Enforced Individual Mandates," *Health Affairs 13*(2), Spring (II) 1994, 21–33.

Uwe Reinhardt, "You Pay When Business Bankrolls Health Care," *The Wall Street Journal*, December 2, 1992, A10.

Ray Robinson, "Managed Care in the United States: A Dilemma for Evidence-Based Policy?" *Health Economics 9*(1), January 2000, 1–7.

Merrile Sing, Steven Hill, Suzanne Smolkin, and Nancy Heiser, "The Cost and Effects of Parity for Mental Health and Substance Abuse Insurance Benefits," U.S. Department of Health and Human Services, Public Health Service, Substance Abuse and Mental Health Services Administration, Rockville, MD, 1998.

Hilary Stout, "Health Care Choices: A Bigger Federal Role of a Market Approach?" *The Wall Street Journal*, January 15, 1992, A1.

United States General Accounting Office, *Employment-Based Health Insurance: Costs Increase and Family Coverage Decreases*, Report to the Ranking Minority Member, Subcommittee on Children and Families, Committee on Labor and Human Resources, United States Senate, February 1997.

United States General Accounting Office, *Health Insurance Regulation: Varying State Requirements Affect Cost of Insurance*, Report to the Honorable James M. Jeffords, U.S. Senate, GAO/HEHS-96-161, Washington, D.C., August 1996.

United States General Accounting Office, *Private Health Insurance: Continued Erosion of Coverage Linked to Cost Pressures*, Report to the Chairman, Committee on Labor and Human Resources, United States Senate, July 1997.

United States House of Representatives, *The President's Health Care Reform Proposal,* Hearings before the Committee on Ways and Means, House of Representatives, 103rd Congress, 1st Session, Washington, DC: U.S. Government Printing Office, 1993.

Barbara P. Yawn, William E. Jacott, and Roy A. Yawn, "MinnesotaCare (Health Right): Myths and Miracles," *Journal of the American Medical Association 269*(4), January 27, 1993, 511–515.

Chapter 18

Lessons for Public Policy

Throughout the book we have attempted to use the ten key economic concepts as guiding principles to organize our approach to the study of health economics. Some of the lessons are obvious, some not quite so obvious. Many of the following propositions are likely to prompt some disagreement because they are not all based on positive analysis. By the very nature of public policy discussions some are laced with normative implications. By now though, you are armed with many of the economic tools that will help you analyze the issues more carefully. Bracket numbers represent the chapters where the principle is discussed more fully.

Scarcity and Choice

Economics recognizes the problem of limited resources and unlimited wants and desires. Without enough resources to satisfy all the desires of all the people, we are faced with the challenge of allocating those resources among competing objectives.

- We must face the fact that resources used in the delivery of medical care have alternative uses that are also beneficial. To strike a balance between scarce resources and unlimited wants involves making choices. We cannot have everything we want. In the world where most of us live, trade-offs are inevitable [2].

Opportunity Cost

Everything and everyone has alternatives. Time and resources used to satisfy one set of desires cannot be used to satisfy another set. The cost of any decision or action is measured in terms of the value placed on the opportunity forgone.

- Medical care decisions involve costs as well as benefits. For many clinicians, allowing cost considerations into treatment decisions is morally repugnant. To counter this feeling, it is essential that practitioners have knowledge of the fundamentals of economics to provide a foundation for understanding the issues that affect medical care delivery and policy [2].

Marginal Analysis

The economic way of thinking about the optimal resource allocation may be classified as marginal decision making. Choices are seldom made on an all-or-nothing basis—they are made "at the margin." Decision makers weigh the trade-offs, considering the incremental benefits and incremental costs of decisions they are about to make. This principle manifests itself in medical markets in the following ways.

- When the marginal cost to the consumer is held at artificially low levels, resources are treated as if they have little or no value—a prescription for overconsumption [2].

- Balancing incremental benefits and incremental costs is essential for optimal resource allocation. Most choices in medical care involve determining the level of an activity, not its very existence. Decision making is seldom an all-or-nothing proposition. It usually involves a trade-off. If we are to spend a little more on one thing, we must spend a little less on something else [2].

- In an economy where productivity is growing in most sectors and declining in none, consumers can have more of everything. True of many service industries, including education, the arts, and medical care, the benefits of economy-wide productivity gains may be transferred to enable consumers to consume more of these superior goods [3].

- The relevant issues deal with marginal changes in utilization and spending, not overall utilization and spending [5].

- Medical care spending is not the only way to improve the health status of an individual or population. Other factors, including lifestyle choices and genetics, play important roles [5].

- Risk-averse individuals will insure against low-probability, high-loss events, such as hospitalizations. Insurance covering routine care, such as primary and preventive care, physical examinations, and teeth cleaning, is not as common [6].

- People often engage in opportunistic behavior after they enter into an insurance contract because their behavior cannot be monitored. The fact that a person has insurance coverage increases expected medical care spending. Having insurance (1) increases the likelihood of purchasing medical services and (2) induces higher spending in the event of an illness. In other words, lowering the cost of medical care to the individual through the availability of insurance increases usage [6].

- The apparent relationship between health care spending and the proximity to death is due primarily to the relationship between age and mortality [11].

Self-Interest

Economic decision makers are motivated to pursue their own self-interest. People respond to incentives and practice economizing behavior only when they individually benefit from such behavior. According to Adam Smith, this pursuit of self-interest leads each individual to a course of action that promotes the general welfare of everyone in society.

- Decision making is dominated by the pursuit of self-interest [1].

- Human behavior is responsive to incentives and constraints. If you want people to practice economizing behavior, each must benefit individually from his or her own economizing. People spending other people's money show little concern for how it is spent. People spending their own money tend to spend it more wisely [2].

- When consumers perceive that acquiring and using information best serve their own interests, they demand that information [3].

- Decisions must be made by well-informed, cost-conscious consumers. Motivated by self-interest and adequately informed about treatment alternatives, cost-conscious consumers will economize because they will personally benefit from their own economizing behavior [3].

- The patient/buyer must be an active participant in the decision-making process if cost containment is to be achieved without artificial controls—mandatory fee schedules, fixed budgets, and resource rationing [3].

- Good health is not always the primary goal in life for most people. Individual behavior proves this daily. Motorists fail to buckle their seat belts, cyclists refuse to wear helmets, millions engage in risky sexual practices, and others use drugs, smoke cigarettes, and consume unhealthy quantities of alcohol [5].

- If we ignore the demand side of the market, we may be forgoing one of the most powerful forces available for cost control: individual self-interest [5].

- Economic incentives matter in determining the demand for medical care [5].

- The differences between the for-profit and the not-for-profit organizational form may be classified as differences in property rights. The differences affect the incentive structure facing decision makers [9].

- Patients and providers fail to practice economizing behavior because there is very little direct benefit to the individual who economizes [13].

- When consumers perceive that they will benefit from additional information, they will demand information, and it will be provided [17].

Markets and Pricing

The market has proven to be the most efficient way to allocate scarce resources. The market accomplishes its tasks through a system of prices, Adam Smith's "invisible hand." Resources can be allocated by the market because everyone and everything has a price. The price mechanism becomes a way to bring a firm's output decisions into balance with consumer desires—something that we refer to as equilibrium.

- Providing all necessary care for a fixed fee changes the nature of the physician-patient relationship [1].

- With Medicare and Medicaid paying such a large percentage of the total hospital bill, government reimbursement rules play a big role in determining the financial stability of the hospital sector [9].

- As the inefficiencies in the hospital system are eliminated, so too is the ability to subsidize charity care for the uninsured and medical education, increasing the pressure on public policymakers to improve the social safety net for the more vulnerable population groups, including pregnant women, children, and the poor in general [9].

Supply and Demand

Pricing and output decisions are based on the underlying forces of supply and demand. Goods and services are allocated among competing uses by equating the consumers' willingness to pay and the suppliers' willingness to provide—rationing via prices.

- The amount of medical care demanded increases as the cost to the individual declines [1].

- The favorable tax treatment for employer-based health insurance distorts the composition of the typical employee compensation package [6].

- Information costs are a central factor in economic decision making [6].

- Managed care can control utilization when patient choice is restricted and physician practice controlled [7].

- The problems inherent in any system emphasize cost containment over quality and access. Patient desires for expensive treatments will be sacrificed to the demand to control costs and spending [7].

- Where the physician faces a zero price for other medical inputs, too many are used relative to physician inputs, resulting in inefficiencies [9].

- When the price is held artificially below the equilibrium price, shortages will develop [13].

- When government attempts to micromanage medical care delivery and provide "free" care to a well-organized constituency, shortages develop (long waiting times) and the quality of specialized care deteriorates [14].

- After the initial cost efficiencies are realized, the lower prices associated with the mandatory fee schedules lead to fixed budgets and eventually limits on services [15].

Competition

Competition forces the resource owners to use their resources to promote the highest possible satisfaction of society: consumers, producers, and investors. If resource owners do this well, they are rewarded. If they are inept or inefficient, they are penalized. Competition takes production out of the hands of the less competent and into the hands of the more efficient—constantly promoting more efficient methods of production.

- Competition among providers is essential for well-functioning markets. Competition guards against undue concentration because substitutes are readily available. Consumer demand becomes more sensitive to price changes [3].

- Competition forces providers to charge prices reflecting their costs. Consolidations leading to the concentration of market power will allow providers to act more like monopolists and price their services above costs [8].

- Competition on the demand side of the market serves to reduce inefficiencies. Inefficient hospitals become prime targets for acquisition by multihospital chains [9].

- The nature of competition in a market dominated by nonprofit providers does not promote cost efficiency but instead quality enhancement. Providers have little incentive to increase productivity. Consumers have no incentive to limit their demand and providers have no incentive to limit their supply. This is a prescription for increased spending [9].

Efficiency

Economic efficiency measures how well resources are being used to promote social welfare. Inefficient outcomes waste resources, while the efficient use of scarce resources enhances social welfare.

- Specialization leads to cost savings through a more efficient allocation of resources [7].

- Given the wide range of managed care arrangements, we must be cautious about forming conclusions on the overall effectiveness of the new forms in controlling costs [7].

- Efficiency is not rewarded in a cost-plus environment. Thus, finding little difference in efficiency between for-profit hospitals and not-for-profit hospitals is not surprising, or at least should not be. With the increasing use of managed care and prospective payment, only recently have hospitals been given an incentive to be efficient [9].

Market Failure

Free markets sometimes fail to promote the efficient use of resources by either producing more or less than the optimal level of output. Sources of market failure include natural monopoly, externalities in production and consumption, and public goods. Other market imperfections such as incomplete information and immobile resources also contribute to this problem.

- Policymaking based on sound economics is better than policymaking in an economic vacuum [2].

- Various imperfections in medical markets make the dual task of delivering a product equitably and efficiently more difficult [3].

- Market power insulates a firm from the competitive forces that insure optimal resource allocation, resulting in a loss to society [3].

- The purpose of insurance is to share risk, not wealth. Policymakers, even those not increased in wealth redistribution, have used market failure to justify the provision of social insurance as a safety net [6].

- Because the private insurance market cannot provide adequate insurance for those with preexisting conditions, this becomes a collective responsibility if this group is to have access to medical care [6].

- Cream skimming is the result of regulation in the insurance industry, not competition [6].

- The market has found it increasingly difficult to subsidize care for the elderly, the indigent, and the uninsured, providing justification for collective action through government to ensure access for these groups [6].

- Hospital markets may not fit the competitive model very well since so many of the structural characteristics of perfect competition are violated [9].

Comparative Advantage

Markets promote economic efficiency and ensure that all mutually beneficial transactions occur when individuals are free to engage in exchange based on opportunity cost. Every transaction that will benefit both a consumer and a provider takes place. The market system is grounded in the concept of consumer sovereignty: what is produced is determined by what people want and are able to buy. No one individual or group dictates what must be produced or purchased. No one limits the range of choice. Everyone specializes in the activity they do best; the one with the lowest opportunity cost.

- Transferring decision making from the private sector to the public sector substitutes bureaucratic discipline for economic discipline [3].

- Cost-conscious decisions are possible only if consumers who desire to enter the market have money to spend. Often phrased in terms of equity, the real issue is economic self-sufficiency. For medical care markets, this requires either universal insurance coverage or universal access to insurance. The choice depends on whether the majority of the populace is concerned with equal outcomes or equal opportunities. Satisfying this condition ensures that the system is morally acceptable to a majority of the people [3].

Final Reflections

By now you should be aware of the issues that can make the study of health economics both fascinating and frustrating. Those of you with little background in economics are likely fascinated with the wide range of issues where economics has relevance. If you were expecting answers to many of the questions that confront policymakers, you are likely frustrated. Economics does not promise answers, only a systematic way to study the alternatives we face.

Whether this ends your formal training in health economics or is merely the first of many courses you will take, let this be the beginning of a lifetime of inquiry into health care issues using the tools of analysis introduced in this text. Remember, taking one course or reading one book cannot possibly teach you everything about health economics. Fortunately, the field is rich with opportunities for further research and study. Visit my Web site occasionally and share your insights with our news group: **http://business. baylor.edu/Jim_Henderson/**

Glossary

acquired immunodeficiency syndrome (AIDS) An infectious disease that results when the human immune system is so weakened by the human immunodeficiency virus (HIV) that the body can no longer fight off serious infections.

actuarially fair premium Insurance premium based on the actuarial probability that an event will occur.

Aid for Families with Dependent Children (AFDC) Aid for Families with Dependent Children, created in 1935, was the primary cash assistance program for the poor and needy in the U.S. welfare system until 1996, when it was replaced by a block-grant program.

allocative efficiency The situation in which producers make the goods and services that consumers desire. For every item the marginal cost of production is less than or equal to the marginal benefit received by consumers.

alternative disputeresolution (ADR) mechanism Means of settling lawsuits prior to a jury trial, including pretrial screenings and arbitration.

any willing provider A situation in which a managed care organization allows any medical provider to become part of the network of providers for the covered group. Often, state law will require this practice.

applied research Research whose purpose is typically the commercialization of a product.

arbitrage The practice of simultaneously buying a commodity at one price and selling it at a higher price.

assignment A Medicare policy providing physicians with a guaranteed payment of 80% of the allowable fee. By accepting assignment physicians agree to accept the allowable fee as full payment and forgo the practice of balance billing.

asymmetric information A situation in which information is unequally distributed between the individuals in a transaction. The person with more information will have an unfair advantage in determining the terms of any agreement.

balance billing Billing a patient for the difference between the physician's usual charge for a service and the maximum charge allowed by the patient's health plan.

basic research Research whose purpose is to advance fundamental knowledge.

bilateral monopoly A situation with monopoly on the seller's side of the market and monopsony on the buyer's side.

capitation A payment method providing a fixed, per capita payment to providers for a specified medical benefits package. Providers are required to treat a well-defined population for a fixed sum of money paid in advance without regard to the number or nature of the services provided to each person. This payment method is a characteristic of health maintenance organizations and many preferred provider organizations.

case management A method of coordinating the provision of medical care for patients with specific high-cost diagnoses such as cancer and heart disease.

Centers for Disease Control Established in 1946, this agency of the U.S. Department of Health and Human Services is charged with promoting the public health of Americans around the world.

certificate of need Regulations that attempt to avoid the costly duplication of services in the hospital industry. Providers are required to secure a certificate of need before undertaking a major expansion of facilities or services.

closed panel A designated network of providers that serve the recipients of a health care plan. Patients are not allowed to choose a provider outside the network.

coinsurance A standard feature of health insurance policies that requires the insured person to pay a certain percentage of a medical bill, usually 10 to 30 percent, physician visit or hospital stay.

collateral sources Compensation received from other sources; e.g., health insurance coverage for medical bills or disability payments. Current rules in most states prohibit the reduction in damages for collateral source payments.

collective bargaining The negotiation process whereby representatives of employers and employees agree upon the terms of a labor contract, including wages and benefits.

community rating Basing health insurance premiums on the health care utilization experience of the entire population of a specific geographic area. Premiums are the same for all individuals regardless of age, sex, risk, or prior use of health care services.

contingency fees Method of compensating the plaintiff's attorney whereby legal fees are calculated as a percentage of the total damage award and thus payable only if the plaintiff is successful. This practice is prohibited in most countries by the rules of legal ethics.

copayment A standard feature of many managed care plans that require the insured person to pay a fixed sum for each office visit, hospital stay, or prescription drug.

cost containment Strategies used to control the total spending on health care services.

cost shifting The practice of charging higher prices to one group of patients, usually those with health insurance, in order to provide free care to the uninsured or discounted care to those served by Medicare and Medicaid.

cost-plus pricing A pricing scheme in which a percentage profit is added to average cost.

cream skimming A practice of pricing insurance policies so that healthy (low-risk) individuals will purchase coverage and those with a history of costly medical problems (high-risk) will not.

cross-price elasticity The sensitivity of consumer demand for good A as the price of good B changes.

deadweight loss The combined loss in consumer and producer surplus resulting from price variations above the competitive equilibrium price due to monopoly or government action.

deductible The amount of money that an insured person must pay before a health plan begins paying for all or part of the covered expenses.

defensive medicine Medical services provided that have little or no medical benefit; their provision is simply to reduce the risk of being sued.

diagnosis-related group A patient classification scheme based on certain demographic, diagnostic, and therapeutic characteristics developed by Medicare and used to compensate hospitals.

direct contract model HMO A managed care organization that establishes contractual relationships with individual physicians to provide care for a specific group of patients.

discounting The process of translating future sums of money into their present values.

discovery procedures Rules that govern the ability of plaintiffs to compel the release of information that may be relevant to a case.

disproportionate share ("Dispro") payments A payment adjustment under Medicare and Medicaid that pays hospitals that serve a large number of indigent patients.

donable organ A human organ harvested from a cadaver or, in some cases, a living person, that is suitable for transplantation.

economic efficiency Producing at a point where average product is maximized and average variable cost is minimized.

economic rent Payment for a good, service, or resource in excess of its opportunity cost. A situation that usually results because supply is inelastic.

economizing behavior When individuals choose to limit their demand for goods and services voluntarily to save money.

Employee Retirement Income Security Act (ERISA) Federal legislation passed in 1974 that sets minimum standards on employee benefit plans, such as pension, health insurance, and disability. The statute protects the interests of employees in matters concerning eligibility for benefits. The law also protects employers from certain state regulations. For example, states are not allowed to regulate self-insured plans and cannot mandate that employers provide health insurance to their employees.

employer mandate A feature of certain health care reform proposals requiring employers to provide health insurance for their employees.

English rule of costs Standard practice in most of the world where the loser of a lawsuit pays all court costs and attorneys' fees, including those of the winner.

entitlement program Government assistance programs where eligibility is determined by a specified criteria, such as age, health status, and level of income. These programs include Social Security, Medicare, Medicaid, TANF, and many more.

equilibrium The market-clearing price where every consumer wanting to purchase the good finds a willing seller.

expected value of an outcome The weighted average of all possible outcomes, with the probabilities of those outcomes used as weights. In other words, $E(x) = S\ x_i p_i$, where $E(x)$ is the expected value, x_i is the ith outcome, and p_i is its associated probability. The expected value is summed over all possible outcomes.

experience rating Basing health insurance premiums on the utilization experience of a specific insured group. Premiums may vary by age, sex, or other risk factors and are often taken into consideration prior to use of medical services.

externality A cost or benefit that spills over to parties not directly involved in the actual transaction and thus is ignored by the buyer and seller.

fee-for-service The traditional payment method for medical care where a provider bills for each episode of care.

financial risk The risk associated with contractual obligations that require fixed monetary outlays.

first-party liability Commonly referred to as caveat emptor (let the buyer beware). The person who suffers the loss pays for it. In most cases, the individual may buy first-party insurance to indemnify against the loss. This is the basis for fire and casualty insurance.

Flexner Report A 1910 report published as part of a critical review of medical education in the United States. The response of the medical establishment led to significant changes in the accreditation procedures of medical schools and an improvement in the quality of medical care.

Food and Drug Administration (FDA) A public health agency charged with protecting American consumers by enforcing federal public health laws. Food, medicine, medical devices, and cosmetics are under the jurisdiction of the FDA.

formulary A list of approved pharmaceutical drugs that will be covered under a health plan. Other drugs are typically unavailable to members of the plan.

free rider An individual who does not buy insurance knowing that in the event of a serious illness medical care will be provided free of charge.

gatekeeper A primary care physician who directs health care delivery and determines whether patients are allowed access to specialty care.

global budget A limit on the amount of money available to a health care system during a specified time period. All medically necessary care must be provided to all eligible patients within the limits placed on the provider by the fixed budget.

gross domestic product (GDP) The monetary value of the goods and services produced in a country during a given time period, usually a year.

group insurance A plan whereby an entire group receives insurance under a single policy. The insurance is actually issued to the plan holder, usually an employer or association.

group-model HMO A group of physicians, often a large multispecialty group practice, that agrees to provide medical care to a defined patient group (usually the employees of the corporation) in return for a fixed per capita fee or for discounted fees. The physicians often provide medical care to several different groups concurrently.

guaranteed issue A feature of an insurance policy that requires the insurer to accept all applicants and guarantee renewal as long as premiums are paid, regardless of the health status of the applicant.

halfway technology The means of treating patients who have a particular disease by trying to postpone its ill effects. Surgery, radiation treatment, and chemotherapy are halfway technologies directed at established cancer cells.

health alliances Called by various names, including health insurance purchasing cooperative (HIPC), it provides a way for small employers to act collectively to purchase health insurance. Typically geographically based and not-for-profit, the alliance contracts with insurers and/or providers for medical coverage for its members.

health maintenance organization (HMO) An insurer and provider of medical care.

high technology Medical treatments that either prevent or cure a disease or malady.

horizontal integration The merger of two or more firms that produce the same good or service.

iatrogenic disease An injury or illness resulting from medical treatment.

income elasticity of demand The sensitivity of demand to changes in consumer income, determined by the percentage change in quantity demanded relative to the percentage change in consumer income.

indemnity insurance Insurance based on the principle that someone suffering an economic loss receives a payment approximately equal to the size of the loss. An insured person who suffers a loss merely makes a claim and receives compensation equal to the loss.

Independent Practice Association (IPA) An organized group of health care providers that offers medical services to a specified group of enrollees of a health plan. Providers typically maintain their private practices and at the same time agree to the practice guidelines established by the health plan.

individual mandate A legal requirement that individuals carry their own insurance protection.

in-kind transfer Welfare subsidies provided in the form of vouchers for specific goods and services, such as food stamps and Medicaid.

job-lock The inability of individual employees to change jobs because preexisting medical conditions make them or one of their dependents ineligible for health insurance benefits under a new plan.

joint-and-several liability Allows successful plaintiffs to recover up to the full amount of a damage award from a single defendant if the other defendants are unable to pay.

laissez faire A French term meaning literally: "allow [them] to do." It depicts a situation where individuals and firms are allowed to pursue their own self-interests without government restraint.

luxury or superior good Goods are considered superior if an increase in consumer income causes the percentage of the consumer's income spent on the good to increase, and vice versa.

major medical Health insurance to provide coverage for major illnesses requiring large financial outlays, characterized by payment for all expenses above a specified maximum out-of-pocket amount paid by the insured (often $1,000 to $5,000).

managed care A medical care delivery system that integrates the financing and provision of health care into one organization.

managed competition A health care reform plan first popularized by economist Alain Enthoven, whereby individuals are given a choice among competing health plans. A standard feature is the formation of health insurance alliances to increase the bargaining power of insurance purchasers.

marginal benefit The change in total benefits resulting from a one-unit change in the level of output.

marginal cost The change in total cost resulting from a one-unit change in the level of output.

marginal revenue product The change in total revenue resulting from the sale of the output produced by an additional unit of a resource.

market failure A situation in which a market fails to produce the socially optimal level of output.

Medicaid Health insurance for the poor financed jointly by the federal government and the states.

medical savings account A tax-exempt savings account used in conjunction with high-deductible health insurance. Individuals pay their own medical expenses using funds from the savings account up to the amount of the deductible. Once the deductible is met, the insurance policy pays all or most of the covered expenses.

Medicare Health insurance for the elderly provided under an amendment to the Social Security Act, divided into two parts, mandatory hospital insurance and voluntary physicians insurance.

Medigap insurance A supplemental insurance policy sold to Medicare-eligible individuals to pay the deductibles and coinsurance that are not covered by Medicare. These policies must conform to one of ten standardized benefit plans established by the federal government.

merit good A good whose benefits are not fully appreciated by the average consumer, and thus should be provided collectively.

microeconomics The study of individual decision making, pricing behavior, and market organization.

monetary conversion factor A monetary value used to translate relative value units into dollar amounts to determine a fee schedule.

moral hazard Insurance coverage increases both the likelihood of making a claim and the actual size of the claim. Insurance reduces the net out-of-pocket price of medical services and thus increases the quantity demanded.

morbidity The incidence and probability of illness or disability.

mortality The probability of death at different ages, usually expressed as the number of deaths for a given population, either 1,000 or 100,000, or the expected number of years of life remaining at a given age.

national health insurance A government-run health insurance system covering the entire population for a well-defined medical benefits package. Usually administered by a government or quasi-government agency and financed through some form of taxation.

natural monopoly A firm becomes a natural monopoly based on its ability to provide a good or service at a lower cost than anyone else and to satisfy consumer demand completely.

necessity A good or service with an income elasticity between 0 and 1.

negligence When a patient is harmed as a result of substandard care and it is determined that the actions of a provider were responsible for the harm.

neoclassical economics A branch of economic thought using microeconomic principles to defend the efficacy of perfectly competitive markets in resource allocation.

net loading costs The difference between the actual premium and the minimum cost of the insurance based on actuarial principles.

network-model HMO A managed care organization that contracts with several different providers, including physicians' practices and hospitals, in order to make a full range of medical services available to its enrollees.

no-fault A method of compensating for injury where no attempt is made to determine fault. The magnitude of injury becomes the basis of the compensation and is the only issue in the legal proceedings.

nonexcludable goods A situation in which it is difficult to limit access to a good or service to a specific group of consumers. If the item is available to anyone, it becomes available to everyone.

nonrival goods A situation in which the consumption of a good or service by one individual does not limit the amount available to anyone else.

nontechnology Medical intervention providing practitioners with the means of helping patients cope with illnesses that have no known cure.

normative analysis An economic statement based on opinion or ideology.

opportunity cost The cost of a decision based on the value of the foregone opportunity.

optimal output levels A market equilibrium where the marginal benefit received from every unit of output is greater or equal to the marginal cost of producing each unit. The social optimum is that output level where the marginal benefit of the last unit produced is equal to its marginal cost.

optimizing behavior (or optimization) A technique used to determine the best or most favorable outcome in a particular situation.

participating physician A physician who agrees to accept Medicare assignment.

patent An exclusive right to supply a good for a specific time period, usually 20 years. It serves as a barrier to entry, virtually eliminating all competition for the life of the patent.

physician-induced demand A situation in which providers take advantage of uninformed consumers to purchase services that are largely unnecessary.

plaintiff The party to a lawsuit who brings charges against the other party, known as the defendant.

point-of-service plan (POS) A hybrid managed care plan that combines the features of a prepaid plan and a fee-for-service plan. Enrollees use network physicians with minimal out-of-pocket expense and may choose to go out of the network by paying a higher coinsurance rate.

portability A feature of an insurance policy that allows the individual to maintain coverage in the event of a job change.

positive analysis A factually based statement whose validity can be tested empirically.

practice guideline A specific statement about the appropriate course of treatment that should be taken for patients with given medical conditions.

preexisting condition A medical condition caused by an injury or disease that exists prior to the application for health insurance. Policies often exclude them from individual coverage or at minimum include them only after a waiting period (usually 6–12 months).

preferred provider organization (PPO) An agreement between a group of medical providers and an insurance company or employer to provide health care services to a well-defined group according to a well-defined fee schedule. By accepting discount fees, providers are included on the list of preferred providers.

premium A periodic payment required to purchase an insurance policy.

prepaid group practice An arrangement through which a group contracts with a number of providers who agree to provide medical services to members of the group for a fixed, capitated payment.

price ceiling The maximum price that can be charged for a good or service, set by law.

price discrimination The practice of selling the same good or service to two different consumers for different prices. The price differential is not based on differences in cost.

price floor The minimum price that can be charged for a good or service, set by law.

primary and preventive care Basic medical services that focus on prevention and treatment. Traditionally, primary care physicians have been family practitioners, gynecologists, and pediatricians.

principal-agent relationship A relationship in which one person (the principal) gives another person (the agent) authority to make decisions on his or her behalf.

probability The likelihood or chance that the event will occur. Probability is measured as a ratio that ranges in value from 0 to 1. A probability of 1 means that an event is certain to happen—it happens every time. A probability of 0.25 means that the event happens one-fourth of the time.

prospective payment Payment determined prior to the provision of services. A feature of many managed care organizations that base payment on capitation.

public good A good that is nonrival in distribution and nonexclusive in consumption.

public health Collective action undertaken by government agencies to ensure the health of the community. These efforts include the prevention of disease, identification of health problems, and the assurance of sanitary conditions, especially in the areas of water treatment and waste disposal.

punitive damages The portion of a damage award designed to punish and deter deliberate and egregious wrongdoing.

rate of return The amount earned on an investment translated into an annual interest rate.

rational behavior A key behavioral assumption in neoclassical economics that decision makers act in a purposeful manner. In other words, their actions are directed toward achieving an objective.

rational ignorance A situation where consumers stop seeking information on a prospective purchase because the expected cost of the additional search exceeds the expected benefits.

reinsurance Stop-loss insurance purchased by a health plan to protect itself against losses that exceed a specific dollar amount per claim, per individual, or per year.

relative value scale An index that assigns weights to various medical services used to determine the relative fees assigned to them.

resource-based relative value scale (RBRVS) A classification system for physicians' services, using a weighting scheme that reflects the relative value of the various services performed. The RBRVS developed for Medicare by a group of Harvard researchers considers time, skill, and overhead cost required for each service. When used in conjunction with a monetary conversion factor, medical fees are determined.

respondeat superior A principle that holds employers responsible for the actions of employees. In the case of medical malpractice, hospitals must exercise certain precautions to ensure that substandard care is not offered by its employees or physicians (whether salaried or not).

retrospective payment Payment determined after delivery of the good or service. Traditional fee-for-service medicine determines payment retrospectively.

return on sales A financial measure of a firm's ability to generate after-tax profit out of its total sales. Calculated by dividing after-tax profit by total sales.

risk A state in which multiple outcomes are possible and the likelihood of each possible outcome is known or can be estimated.

scarcity A situation that exists when the amount of a good or service demanded in the aggregate exceeds the amount available at a zero price.

self-insurance A group practice of not buying health insurance, but setting aside funds in the amount of the combined premiums to cover any losses incurred by members of the group.

self-interest A behavioral assumption of neoclassical economics that individuals are motivated to promote their own interests.

sickness fund Quasi-governmental groups that serve as insurance companies by collecting premiums and paying providers within the national health care system of France and Germany.

single-payer system A system of financing medical care (usually associated with Canada) where payment comes from a single source, typically the government. The single payer has considerable influence over virtually every aspect of health care financing and delivery.

social insurance Serves as the basis of all government redistribution programs. An insurance plan supported by tax revenues and available to everyone regardless of age, health status, and ability to pay.

spending cap A limit on total spending for a given time period.

staff-model HMO An HMO in which physicians are employees of the HMO. Their incomes are usually paid in the form of a fixed salary, but may include supplemental payments based on some measure of performance.

standard of care The level of care established by the medical profession as the customary or accepted practice (the local custom) prevailing in the relevant specialty.

stare decisis The decisions of a higher court set legal precedents and are binding in all future cases.

State Children's Health Insurance Program (CHIP) A state administered program, similar to Medicaid, targeted to provide affordable health insurance to low-income children who are otherwise ineligible for Medicaid benefits.

statute of limitations The length of time that a plaintiff has to file a lawsuit after suffering an injury—usually 3-4 years for an adult and somewhat longer for children. In many states, the limitation runs from the date the injury is discovered or should have been discovered, not the actual date of the injury.

strict liability Legal principle where the provider of care pays for any harm whether negligent or not.

technical efficiency Efficiency in production, or cost efficiency.

technological change Any invention, innovation, or diffusion of knowledge that improves products or processes, typically measured in terms of increased productivity or economic growth.

technological imperative The proposition that if a medical procedure is available to treat a problem, it should be utilized. If available for anyone, it should be available for everyone, regardless of ability to pay.

Temporary Aid to Needy Families (TANF) Temporary Aid to Needy Families replaced the old AFDC program in 1996 as the main cash assistance program for the poor.

third-party liability A situation in which the loss is paid for by the party causally responsible for the injury. Liability insurance is used to indemnify against loss in this case—for example, workers' compensation.

third-party payers A health insurance arrangement where the individual (or agent of the individual) pays a set premium to a third party (an insurance company, managed care organization, or the government), which in turn pays for health care services.

triage A military screening technique adopted for use in a crowded emergency room to determine the order in which patients are treated. In battlefield hospitals three categories of patients are identified: those who will survive without care, those who will survive if they receive care, and those who will not survive regardless of the amount of care they receive.

Type I error Rejecting a hypothesis that is actually true.

Type II error Accepting a hypothesis that is actually false.

unbundling Separating a number of related procedures and treating them as individual services for payment purposes.

uncertainty A state in which multiple outcomes are possible but the likelihood of any one outcome is not known.

uncertainty A state in which multiple outcomes are possible but the likelihood of any one outcome is not known.

underwriting The insurance practice of determining whether or not an application for insurance will be accepted. In the process, premiums are also determined. Factors considered may include age, sex, health status, and prior use of health care services.

universal access A guarantee that all citizens who desire health insurance will have access to health insurance regardless of income or health status. Those who cannot afford insurance are usually subsidized and participation is voluntary.

universal coverage A guarantee that all citizens will have health insurance coverage regardless of income or health status. Coverage usually includes a well-defined benefits package and mandatory participation

usual, customary, and reasonable charges A price ceiling set to limit fees to the minimum of the billed charge, the price customarily charged by the provider, and the prevailing charge in the geographic region.

utilization review Evaluating the appropriateness and efficiency of prescribed medical services and procedures, including hospital admissions, lengths of stay, and discharge procedures. Utilization review may be conducted concurrently or retrospectively.

workers' compensation Insurance to protect employees against financial loss caused by work-related injury or illness.

xenografts The use of animal organs for transplantation in humans.

Index